CRITICAL SOCIAL ISSUES IN AMERICAN EDUCATION

Democracy and Meaning in a Globalizing World

Third Edition

Sociocultural, Political, and Historical Studies in Education
Joel Spring, Editor

For a complete list of titles in LEA's Sociocultural, Political, and Historical Studies in Education Series, please contact Lawrence Erlbaum Associates, Publishers at www.erlbaum.com

CRITICAL SOCIAL ISSUES IN AMERICAN EDUCATION

Democracy and Meaning in a Globalizing World

Third Edition

Edited by

H. Svi Shapiro
David E. Purpel
University of North Carolina, Greensboro

LEA LAWRENCE ERLBAUM ASSOCIATES, PUBLISHERS
2005   Mahwah, New Jersey   London

Lawrence Erlbaum Associates, Inc., Publishers
10 Industrial Avenue
Mahwah, New Jersey 07430

Cover design by Kathryn Houghtaling Lacey

Library of Congress Cataloging-in-Publication Data

Critical social issues in American education : democracy and meaning in a globalizing
    world / edited by H. Svi Shapiro and David E. Purpel. — 3rd ed.
        p.   cm. — (Sociocultural, political, and historical studies in education)
    Includes bibliographical references and index.
    ISBN 0-8058-4452-X (pbk. : alk. paper)
        1. Critical pedagogy—United States.   2. Education—Social aspects—United States.
    3. Education—Political aspects—United States.   I. Shapiro, H. Svi.
    II. Purpel, David E..   III. Series.

LC196.5.U6C75   2004
370.11'5—dc22   2004046923
                                                                                        CIP

Books published by Lawrence Erlbaum Associates are printed on acid-free paper,
and their bindings are chosen for strength and durability.

Printed in the United States of America

Contents

Preface

This volume, like the editions that preceded it, is predicated on the following assumption: Educators must see their work as inextricably linked to conflicts, stresses, and crises of the social world—whether these appear in forms that might be cultural, moral, political, economic, ecological, or spiritual. It is impossible to make sense of what is happening educationally if what is occurring is not placed in the context of the strains, struggles, and contradictions in both our national and global communities. Issues such as the growing administrative control over teachers' lives, allegations about the mediocrity of American schools, the crisis of funding, concern about what is called educational *excellence*, the impoverishment of increasing numbers of children and adolescents, the influence of the media on young lives, fears about moral degeneration, school violence, bitter contention over the nature of the curriculum and of school knowledge, and widening disparities in educational achievement among ethnic and racial groups all must be seen, at the same time, as both critical issues in American education and as metaphors for the larger human and societal situation. It is this connection that is central to the selection of articles in this book. What happens in school, or as part of the educational experience, reflects, expresses, and mediates profound questions about the direction and nature of the society we inhabit.

We attempted to organize the readings in this book in a thematically meaningful structure. The five sections offer a useful way to make sense of the problems and concerns that confront us. Each section is preceded by a brief essay that introduces the readings. Still the organization must be viewed as only a heuristic measure. In the real world, issues do not come neatly and conveniently packaged or compartmentalized. One problem or crisis flows out of and into another, forming interrelated aspects of a social totality. Whether one aspect of this totality should be seen as fundamental (as in some way determining all others) is the subject of much intellectual controversy. Those who assert that the key is found in global capitalism, patriarchy, modernity, or elsewhere dispute where the lion's share of the blame must go. Reflections of this debate can be found in the pages of this book.

The volume broadly follows the lines of our earlier editions, although many of the readings are new. We have also addressed issues that have more recently emerged as especially significant (such as the concern with the implications of globalization, commercialism, and violence as well as the ever-increasing influence of high-stakes testing). However, the overarching concerns that shaped the previous editions—the influence of capitalism, social justice, marginality and difference, the meaning of democracy and citizenship, and the political and moral nature of curriculum—continue to shape the work.

The readings in this collection represent important, sometimes seminal, statements on critical social and educational issues. They offer a perspective on both the long-range and more immediate problems and issues we face as a national and global community, and they provide a consideration of these concerns at both applied and theoretical levels. We hope the reader experiences the disjunction between readings that deal explicitly with education and those whose concerns are broader, not as something jarring, but as moments of a connected dialectic—a vehicle for moving between the distinct, but very related, aspects of a single social world. Most of all, however, we hope readers feel they have gained something by giving up a limited, narrow discourse that dominates so much of current professional education for one that is broader in its sweep—even if this broader vision is also sometimes a dispiriting one. It is hard to dispute that the pages of this volume are filled with a terrible commentary on the human condition. Yet as we have often found, attempting to connect the field of education to the most serious and pressing concerns of humankind, however overwhelming this sometimes feels, ultimately elevates the significance that educators attach to their work. We hope this conviction is borne out by those who make use of this text.

We wish to acknowledge the importance of our students in the cultural studies program. Their passion for a critical understanding of our world and their courage to venture along often difficult personal and professional paths in pursuit of transforming our culture continue to inspire us as to the possibilities of real social and educational change in often bleak circumstances.

—Svi Shapiro
Greensboro, NC

Introduction

In this volume, our goal is to provide a focus for thinking about education in the context of a society that now, in this first decade of a new millennium, is faced with a range of critical, sometimes catastrophic, issues and problems, such as poverty and growing social injustice; AIDS; racism, sexism, and homophobic forms of exclusion; depersonalization of social and political life; the moral and spiritual consequences of the commercialization of culture; an unaccountable global economy; and the ecological deterioration of the planet. Our concern is not only for American society, but also for the larger global community.

We start from the conviction that as both citizens and educators we dare not ignore these issues and problems. Educational discourse in both professional and public circles has become narrow and often trivial in its emphasis. This volume is offered as part of our continuing efforts to resist and transform the assumptions and concerns of such discourse. For education to become a humanly vital, ethically responsible endeavor, infused with a serious commitment to democratic values, we must understand its connection to the urgent and pressing issues laid out in this text. These issues represent what we believe to be the most critical issues that we and our children face as we move into the 21st century.

This volume is intended to work on two levels. First, we are concerned with developing an awareness concerning how education is connected to the wider structures of social, cultural, political, and economic life. Any attempt to apprehend the nature and purpose of education in the United States requires us to grasp the interrelatedness between schooling and the larger culture. The readings were selected to heighten understanding of these links. For example, some of the chapters examine how educational reform has been a response to a corporate or right-wing political agenda. Others explore how changes in education are connected to the restructuring of American labor during an era of global management. Further readings discuss ways in which the process of schooling legitimizes the hierarchies of social class, race, and gender and transmits the dominant ideology of economic competition and individualism.

It is important to add here that we have come to appreciate the debilitating and demoralizing effects on students of critical analyses that only criticize. Empowering human beings for the purpose of social change requires, we believe, not merely brilliantly insightful criticism, but also the vision of alternatives that can be positively embraced and ultimately worked for. Such description helps us to re-image the future and make, in Maxine Greene's words, "the strange familiar." Thus, on a second level, our goal in this volume is to encourage not only a critical examination of our present social reality, but also a serious discussion of alternatives—of what a transformed society and educational process might look like—through what Henry Giroux called a "language of possibility." This volume provides elements of what might be termed a *new paradigm* for conceiving of our social, cultural, economic, political, and moral worlds, as well as how we think of education.

The major theme of this text—that education is intimately connected to the major social concerns and issues of our time—challenges the conventional, frequently shallow terms of educational discourse. What is perhaps unusual about the collection is that we have included not only chapters specifically about education, but also those that provide a broader social perspective. In this way, we hope to maintain dialectic between the issues and problems of education and those of the larger society.

The collection is also intended to focus on issues we believe to be crucial aspects of a growing world crisis. In this context, a word is in order about what this volume is not. The readings are not offered as a contribution to the preparation of impartial social scientists nor are they intended for detached voyeurs of a catastrophic global condition filled, as it is, with human suffering of enormous proportions. What we intend, in presenting these readings, is to increasingly challenge educators to define education as a political and ethical activity explicitly connected to the making of a world in which such suffering is significantly reduced. Indeed the fact that professional and theoretical discourse about education is not centered on the immense problems confronting humanity indicates the degree to which it has been trivialized and rendered impotent in addressing the dangerous issues confronting humankind today.

As educators and future educators, we must understand what is happening around us (as well as to us) because it is this that we must actively address in our work. In a world in which 40,000 children die each day from malnutrition and 600 million children barely survive on a dollar a day, any other kind of education represents a failure of our deepest human responsibilities.

Many of the students we teach find disturbing, even shocking, our efforts to deliberately connect the work of teachers to an ethically committed, politically charged pedagogy. This link flies in the face of many teachers' best instincts about the moral neutrality of what is taught and the impartial role of teachers. Our primary response to those teachers is to point to the substantial literature about schools that clearly demonstrates education is a human practice that is inextricably also a moral and political practice. We believe that education is always (and everywhere) about the business of legitimizing and reproducing existing social relations, values, and ways of life—or about working to oppose them. Shaull (1988) expressed it clearly: "There is no such thing as a *neutral* educational process. Education either functions as an instrument which is used to facilitate the integration of the younger generation into the logic of the present system and bring about conformity to it, or it becomes 'the practice of freedom,' the means by which men and women deal critically and creatively with reality and discover how to participate in the transformation of their world" (p. 15).

Our volume is specifically organized to raise awareness of what is at stake in this country and in the world as we move into the 21st century. More than this, however, we hope that it cries out for the need for us to act as citizens and educators to address the pain, conflicts, and crises that pervade our national life and the life of the planet. Through consideration of the issues addressed in this volume, we hope to contribute to increased awareness and greater human commitment. We are not suggesting that simple, easy answers are always available, nor are we arguing that policy choices can be merely read off from ethical commitments. Yet this is not to say that there are no responses or solutions to the problems and crises discussed in this text. We believe there are. The most honest stance we can take—one that is neither simplistically hopeful nor bleakly hopeless—is to alert our readers to the often contradictory demands and pulls of the modern (or perhaps more accurately postmodern) condition. Thus, one consideration guiding the selection of the readings in this volume is what we perceive to be some of the most difficult dilemmas of our time: the free-market economy versus democratic and egalitarian values; the assertion of cultural differences versus community; social justice and responsibility versus individual freedom; moral commitment versus the uncertainty of truth or knowledge; full employment versus the end of the work-oriented culture; and a culture predicated on endless consumption versus the responsibility of limiting our use of global resources.

The issues raised in this volume have shaped and will shape the present and future condition of all our lives—our hopes, fears, anxieties, and dreams. Addressing these issues is not simply a matter of referring and deferring to the experts because we all know a great deal about them (even if, as Michael Polanyi noted, we frequently know "more than we can say"). Antonio Gramsci, the Italian Marxist philosopher, taught us to recognize that in the often-maligned (especially in academic circles) common sense of people, there are penetrating insights into the nature and workings of our social reality. Gramsci and those influenced by him tell us that, in dealing with our lived world, we are all unavoidably philosophers and interpreters of the culture. This world in crisis is the world in which all of us struggle to survive, produce meaning, and derive joy. In our post 9-11 world, we have been forced to recognize that the problems we are concerned with are not just faraway events depicted on the TV news programs, but ones that affect our everyday lives. They shape our sense of security, physical and emotional well-being, degree of freedom, and how we think about neighbors and others in our society. It must be added, however, that although we all know about and have something to say about these matters, in the classroom students are often unable to speak. Many voices are never heard. Such silence, as those who have studied the lives of the disempowered have made abundantly clear, is also an important dimension of the crisis. It is the consequence of schools that systematically devalue and exclude the voices of many students. It reflects, too, the choice of many schools to close off those areas of concern that may reveal dispute, contention, or passionate conviction.

Of course taking seriously the voices of students certainly undermines the teacher's possibility of covering the curriculum. Yet this is a problem that does not worry us too much because covering a prescribed number of text pages or topics or sequencing the topics in the right order are problems more relevant to bureaucrats than to teachers. Our concern for the readers of this book is of a different type. Through these chapters, we hope that students confront the truly critical issues that face us as individual human beings, as citizens of U.S. society, and as members of a global community—and consider what are or should be the consequences of these issues for education. We have tried to assemble here more than just another reader in the social foundations of education. Our goal is to offer a set of readings that demands a critical encounter between the reader and education's social, moral, spiritual, and political dimensions at this important historical moment.

This volume developed out of our work as teachers in the social foundations of education. Specifically, it reflects themes and concerns that formed an important focus of the work in a course for graduate students entitled "Critical Social Issues in American Education." Although students come to the class for a variety of reasons and with diverse emotions, by the end most admit that it represented a significant and influential departure in the way they learned to think about and approach their work in the field of education. Quite apart from the idiosyncratic qualities of the course and the teacher, it is clear that the changes students experience point to important issues in the nature and discourse of educational studies—issues that, in turn, raise fundamental questions about the relevance or adequacy of these studies to the extraordinary conditions that we and our children face today as members of both national and global communities.

The language of educational studies with its emphasis on skills, methods, and techniques is more and more devoid of any serious or sustained engagement with the concept of society. Such studies are a stunning example of what Jacoby so aptly termed "social amnesia." In this view of the educational process, students, teachers, administrators, and policymakers are abstracted from their positions within a historically constituted culture—individuals magically stripped of the results of their life-long immersion in the social world. The amnesia that Jacoby referred to is a *forgetting* that we come to be who we are through a process in which our very subjectivity is shaped in the institutions of our social world. Through this process we are gendered, come to speak a language, are situated as members of a social class and race, and assume the characteristics of a national, religious, or other type of community. None of these aspects can be separated from the relational or social nature of human existence. Indeed the very predilection to see our individuality apart from its social context is an important manifestation of our social consciousness. It reflects an ideology that mystifies and distorts the nature of human identity, indeed in which consciousness denies its own social origins. It is the consequence of a national culture that has historically demanded personal self-sufficiency, promoted an aggressive individualism, and celebrated those who, in search of better things, could appear to ignore or deny their historic ties and communal dependencies. From this point of view, human beings appear as somehow entirely freed from social determination.

Our apparently asocial consciousness, however, is not merely intellectually bogus. More important, it is politically crippling. It denies us full awareness of the way in which all of our lives are embedded in social relationships structured through and around conditions of power. From the bedroom and kitchen to the classroom, office, or factory, social relationships imply political relationships. It should be added, in our particular world, that these relationships are almost always hierarchical, implying the systematic control of some human beings by others.

What kind of an educational discourse ignores, denies, or forgets the social and political nature of human existence? It is, in fact, one to which most students in the United States are exposed. It is one that puts overwhelming emphasis on methodological and psychological perspectives (e.g., in the study of learning theories, human development, instructional methodologies, or curriculum planning). The theoretical discourse most likely acknowledges a sphere of influence on the student that includes the family and the school as an institution, but little is said about the wider circles of influence that shape human lives, constitute the very conditions and meanings of educational practice, and form our understanding of what school is meant to accomplish in this culture at this particular moment in history. The circumscribed, nonsociological perspective of most educational theorizing reifies our school world. It teaches us to accept as a given most of what appears in this world. Notions of childhood and adolescence, the roles of student and teacher, the kinds of knowledge considered valid and valuable, and the very purpose of schools—all the areas that constitute the educational world—become taken-for-granted assumptions or facts, not social practices that can be challenged or even transformed.

Not to locate schooling in the larger culture or society is to attempt to grapple with educational issues with one arm tied behind one's back. It is a fraudulent intellectual endeavor that disables those whose business is education and who study education so that they might in some way apprehend the real universe in which they work. Semester after semester, we are confronted by individuals whose often considerable time spent as students in a university School of Education has made them social amnesiacs—individuals whose studies in education have excluded any substantial intellectual encounter with their society or culture. Such students are seriously disabled by a professional discourse that disconnects them from any critical interrogation of the culture that shapes their existence as well as the social circumstance of the young people they will teach. Any expectation that educators truly address their human and ethical responsibilities requires an understanding of the unprecedented, indeed cataclysmic, social forces transforming our world. It requires, at a minimum, some development of what C. Wright Mills called a "sociological imagination." Painfully, we are only too aware of how little opportunity is usually offered to students in professional educational training to acquire this. Nonetheless, the stakes in human lives are too great to abandon the attempt. However limited or blocked the opportunities, our children's future and the fate of the earth are in question. We are convinced that only if educators become educated to the cultural conditions that surround and shape our work is change toward a more just, democratic, and compassionate world remotely possible.

REFERENCE

Shaull, R. (1988). Introduction. In P. Freire (Ed.), *Pedagogy of the oppressed* (p. 15). New York: Continuum.

SOCIAL JUSTICE AND DEMOCRACY: UNMET PROMISES

One of the most enduring dimensions of the American experience is the story of people continuing to press for a greater measure of justice in their lives. It is a story chronicled in struggles around community, work, school, and home life as individuals have constantly looked for ways to resist the processes of dehumanization, subordination, and exploitation. In a variety of ways, people have fought and continue to fight for more dignity, more control over their lives, and the resources to be able to live with decency. They do so as workers, consumers, students, migrants, members of minority groups, women, oppressed sexual groups, and people marginalized by virtue of age, disability, illness, and more. As the slogan of the women's movement, "the personal is political," has taken hold, the struggle for more equality involves increasing dimensions of the self, moving into areas of life hitherto unimaginable.

Despite the ebb and flow of these struggles, their essential continuity should come as no surprise. Our egalitarian faith is, after all, an inescapable component of the republican discourse of the nation. It is a much proclaimed virtue, deeply rooted in both naturalistic social philosophy and the Judeo-Christian values that structure the culture's official language. Perhaps what should be considered more surprising is not the impulse toward greater equality, but the way in which this impulse is tempered, cooled out, or accommodated to existing inequalities and hierarchical social relations. It is this fact that is an important dimension of the readings in this part of the book. In contrast to important elements of conventional educational discourse that emphasize the way schooling facilitates upward social mobility, our concern is with the way the vision of a just society is reconciled with the massive inequities of our social, economic, and political lives. What must be faced and understood is the coexistence of powerful movements of the disadvantaged demanding redress for the unmet promises of the society, with the continued—indeed intensifying—injustices produced through the divisions of class, race, gender, and other social distinctions. As our authors make clear, these unmet promises are more than moral or philosophical abstractions. The United States is moving with alarming speed toward an era marked by grotesque disparities of income and conditions of life. It becomes increasingly difficult to escape an awareness of the millions of our fellow citizens (including an unprecedented number of children) who are without adequate shelter, food, or other basic provisions of life such as medical insurance. The fact that this continued during the period of the 1990s, in what was said to be the longest peace-time economic recovery, indicates that the massive poverty is no aberration, but a deeply structured, enduring aspect of our social reality.

Beyond presenting the harsh reality of social injustice in contemporary America, we wish to pursue two related questions. The first is concerned with how this situation has come to be; what are the social, economic, and political dynamics of inequality in this country? In addressing this issue, we look at the policies and conditions that have produced startling levels of inequality in income and opportunities among our citizens. Second, we are concerned with the nature of the ideology that manages to reconcile quite spectacular levels of inequality with the values of democracy. Those who think about democracy have always recognized the ways in which inequalities of wealth and power threaten democracy. It is clear, for example, that poverty is a critical form of disenfranchisement; the poor are much less likely to vote, and they regard the political process as providing them with little in the way of support or meaning. It is also painfully obvious today that the extraordinary concentrations of individual wealth and corporate power vitiate the capacity of ordinary people to control the everyday world. It is now impossible to ignore the corruption of politics in America (and, as we show in the section on *Globalization*, elsewhere in the world), where powerful interest groups and lobbies shape the political process, organize elections, and set the social, economic, and cultural agendas.

Beyond the question of control is the crisis of the very meaning of *democracy*. As Stuart Ewan pointed out, the *democracy of expression* is being replaced by a *democracy of images*. In other words, the very notion of citizenship, which in a democracy carries the meaning of public discourse, critical debate, and civic thoughtfulness, is giving way to the idea of democracy as all about consumer choice and buying goods. Choosing in this brave new world of consumer capitalism centers not on educated decision making bearing on the policies and people that affect our economic and social lives, but on our ability to choose between competing brands of toothpaste, cereal, or fashions. There is, in short, a trivialization of democracy as the role of citizen is replaced by that of consumer. Not surprisingly this process is accompanied by the disappearance of those public spaces where a rich and vibrant civic culture can flourish (we are reminded occasionally of what this means when we are able to witness the kind of social change, with all of its mass involvement, that has occurred in places like South Africa or Eastern Europe). In their place is the Disney-like world of the shopping mall, which (despite the nostalgia of names like "Town Square") really exist only for the purpose of one's private shopping expeditions. The much celebrated book, *Bowling Alone*, made clear that the active civic culture and community life on which democracy depends is, in the United States, in decline.

Of course as our readings here and elsewhere in this volume make clear, the twin crises of growing social inequality and democracy are both reflected in and mediated by schools. Schools continue to reflect the salience of class and race to the very question of who is educationally successful. Despite the rhetoric of meritocracy, schools continue to strongly mirror the gross disparities of wealth and cultural capital in their selection of who is able to realize their full potentialities as human beings. Where democracy has always spoken to the vision of a society in which all citizens might have the opportunity to develop as fully as possible, the reality of our deeply unequal social structure has mocked such pretensions. Despite that, public education remains an important terrain of struggle in the effort of disadvantaged groups to win more opportunities and the chance of a better life for their children.

The classroom too remains a site of struggle by those teachers who envisage education as being more than vocational preparation or *test prep*. For them school may still be a place where young minds learn to think critically, sensitivities are deepened, and human beings engage and explore questions of serious human, social, and moral consequence. In short there is here the hope that schools might be places for democratic renewal.

Finally, against the heavy hand of hierarchical and bureaucratic control, schools might, in the minds of some educators, parents, and interested citizens, offer spaces where a participatory democratic culture flourishes. Such a culture would model the ethos of care, social responsibility, and shared decision making that would be the hallmarks of a genuine democratic community in the 21st century.

The readings in this section certainly take up and expand these issues and themes. We have retained from our previous edition the piece by Christine Sleeter and Carl Grant (chap. 5, this volume). They argue that, although society is committed to the notion of education as a primary tool for reducing inequality, educational practices continue to perpetuate and validate inequality. They see a school system that maintains grouping and hierarchical policies and practices that work against women, the poor, people of color, and the disabled. This thesis is supported in other readings. For example, there is an examination by Sue Books (chap. 2, this volume) of the way school funding and court decisions conspire to produce gross disparities in funding for public schools across the nation—a result that has especially detrimental results for poor students and students of color. In another piece, Linda McNeil (chap. 4, this volume) considers how high-stakes, state-mandated testing, which is now a ubiquitous dimension of the educational landscape, despite its democratic pretensions, perpetuates inequities for minority students.

Much of this is put into broader historical perspective by John Rury (chap. 3, this volume), who explores the relationship between democracy and the comprehensive high school in the post-World War II era. Especially important in this piece is the vastly different experience of education in inner-city and suburban communities, and the way that democratic aspirations for education have foundered on the rock of a society that continues to be fragmented by race and ethnicity, social class, and economic opportunity. This theme receives extraordinary amplification in the piece by Paul Krugman (chap. 1, this volume), who demonstrates that America is now a society in which wealth is more unequally distributed than at any time since the 1920s. The new concentrations of wealth, says the author, are a direct threat to our democracy. He notes:

> It's all too easy to see how we may become a country in which the big rewards are reserved for people with the right connections; in which ordinary people see little hope of advancement; in which political involvement seems pointless, because in the end the interests of the elite always get served.

Finally, Stanley Aronowitz (chap. 6, this volume) considers the plight of public higher education in the present era—one in which the socioeconomic environment is inimical to any goals that go beyond credentialing and acquiring job skills. In this sense, many public colleges and universities have abdicated any meaningful commitment to the development of citizens able to "participate in key decisions affecting the polity." This role, he says, has been consigned to one of the distribution requirements of the first 2 years of a baccalaureate degree. Business imperatives, both within and without the institution, are antithetical to the kind of imagination, critical thought, and ethical concerns that are integral to democratic education.

The readings selected here reflect a critical account of the purpose of schooling in the United States. The authors in this part insist that the real nature and purposes of education can only be grasped if we view schools as cultural and political sites that give legitimacy to the way social relations and cultural values are patterned in this society. From this perspective, all our talk about education's connection to the full realization of human potential, the creation of a socially just community, and preparation for life in a democratic society is a denial or avoidance of the arguably real work of schools. Such talk fails to grasp the way powerful social and ideological interests seek to integrate schools into the system of hierarchy, social differentiation, and commodified human relationships.

1

▼▼▼▼▼▼▼

For Richer*

Paul Krugman

THE DISAPPEARING MIDDLE

When I was a teenager growing up on Long Island, one of my favorite excursions was a trip to see the great Gilded Age mansions of the North Shore. Those mansions weren't just pieces of architectural history. They were monuments to a bygone social era, one in which the rich could afford the armies of servants needed to maintain a house the size of a European palace. By the time I saw them, of course, that era was long past. Almost none of the Long Island mansions were still private residences. Those that hadn't been turned into museums were occupied by nursing homes or private schools.

For the America I grew up in—the America of the 1950's and 1960's—was a middle-class society, both in reality and in feel. The vast income and wealth inequalities of the Gilded Age had disappeared. Yes, of course, there was the poverty of the underclass—but the conventional wisdom of the time viewed that as a social rather than an economic problem. Yes, of course, some wealthy businessmen and heirs to large fortunes lived far better than the average American. But they weren't rich the way the robber barons who built the mansions had been rich, and there weren't that many of them. The days when plutocrats were a force to be reckoned with in American society, economically or politically, seemed long past.

Daily experience confirmed the sense of a fairly equal society. The economic disparities you were conscious of were quite muted. Highly educated

---

professionals—middle managers, college teachers, even lawyers—often claimed that they earned less than unionized blue-collar workers. Those considered very well off lived in split-levels, had a housecleaner come in once a week and took summer vacations in Europe. But they sent their kids to public schools and drove themselves to work, just like everyone else.

But that was long ago. The middle-class America of my youth was another country.

We are now living in a new Gilded Age, as extravagant as the original. Mansions have made a comeback. Back in 1999 this magazine profiled Thierr Despont, the "eminence of excess," an architect who specializes in designing houses for the superrich. His creations typically range from 20,000 to 60,000 square feet; houses at the upper end of his range are not much smaller than the White House. Needless to say, the armies of servants are back, too. So are the yachts. Still, even J.P. Morgan didn't have a Gulfstream.

As the story about Despont suggests, it's not fair to say that the fact of widening inequality in America has gone unreported. Yet glimpses of the lifestyles of the rich and tasteless don't necessarily add up in people's minds to a clear picture of the tectonic shifts that have taken place in the distribution of income and wealth in this country. My sense is that few people are aware of just how much the gap between the very rich and the rest has widened over a relatively short period of time. In fact, even bringing up the subject exposes you to charges of "class warfare," the "politics of envy" and so on. And very few people indeed are willing to talk about the profound effects—economic, social and political—of that widening gap.

Yet you can't understand what's happening in America today without understanding the extent, causes and consequences of the vast increase in inequality that has taken place over the last three decades, and in particular the astonishing concentration of income and wealth in just a few hands. To make sense of the current wave of corporate scandal, you need to understand how the man in the gray flannel suit has been replaced by the imperial C.E.O. The concentration of income at the top is a key reason that the United States, for all its economic achievements, has more poverty and lower life expectancy than any other major advanced nation. Above all, the growing concentration of wealth has reshaped our political system: it is at the root both of a general shift to the right and of an extreme polarization of our politics.

But before we get to all that, let's take a look at who gets what.

THE NEW GILDED AGE

The Securities and Exchange Commission hath no fury like a woman scorned. The messy divorce proceedings of Jack Welch, the legendary former C.E.O. of General Electric, have had one unintended benefit: they have given us a peek at the perks of the corporate elite, which are normally hidden from public view. For it turns out that when Welch retired, he was granted for life the use of a Manhattan apartment (including food, wine and laundry), access to corporate jets and a variety of other in-kind benefits, worth at least $2 million a year. The perks were revealing: they illustrated the extent to which corporate leaders now expect to be treated like *ancien régime* royalty. In monetary terms, however, the perks must have meant little to Welch. In 2000, his last full year running G.E., Welch was paid $123 million, mainly in stock and stock options.

Is it news that C.E.O.s of large American corporations make a lot of money? Actually, it is. They were always well paid compared with the average worker, but there is simply no comparison between what executives got a generation ago and what they are paid today.

Over the past 30 years most people have seen only modest salary increases: the average annual salary in America, expressed in 1998 dollars (that is, adjusted for inflation), rose from $32,522 in 1970 to $35,864 in 1999. That's about a 10 percent increase over 29 years—progress, but not much. Over the same period, however, according to Fortune magazine, the average real annual compensation of the top 100 C.E.O.s went from $1.3 million—39 times the pay of an average worker—to $37.5 million, more than 1,000 times the pay of ordinary workers.

The explosion in C.E.O. pay over the past 30 years is an amazing story in its own right, and an important one. But it is only the most spectacular indicator of a broader story, the reconcentration of income and wealth in the U.S. The rich have always been different from you and me, but they are far more different now than they were not long ago—indeed, they are as different now as they were when F. Scott Fitzgerald made his famous remark.

That's a controversial statement, though it shouldn't be. For at least the past 15 years it has been hard to deny the evidence for growing inequality in the United States. Census data clearly show a rising share of income going to the top 20 percent of families, and within that top 20 percent to the top 5 percent, with a declining share going to families in the middle. Nonetheless, denial of that evidence is a sizable, well-financed industry. Conservative think tanks have produced scores of studies that try to discredit the data, the methodology and, not least, the motives of those who report the obvious. Studies that appear to refute claims of increasing inequality receive prominent endorsements on editorial pages and are eagerly cited by right-leaning government officials. Four years ago Alan Greenspan (why did anyone ever think that he was nonpartisan?) gave a keynote speech at the Federal Reserve's annual Jackson Hole conference that amounted to an attempt to deny that there has been any real increase in inequality in America.

The concerted effort to deny that inequality is increasing is itself a symptom of the growing influence of our emerging plutocracy (more on this later).

So is the fierce defense of the backup position, that inequality doesn't matter—or maybe even that, to use Martha Stewart's signature phrase, it's a good thing. Meanwhile, politically motivated smoke screens aside, the reality of increasing inequality is not in doubt. In fact, the census data understate the case, because for technical reasons those data tend to undercount very high incomes—for example, it's unlikely that they reflect the explosion in C.E.O. compensation. And other evidence makes it clear not only that inequality is increasing but that the action gets bigger the closer you get to the top. That is, it's not simply that the top 20 percent of families have had bigger percentage gains than families near the middle: the top 5 percent have done better than the next 15, the top 1 percent better than the next 4, and so on up to Bill Gates.

Studies that try to do a better job of tracking high incomes have found startling results. For example, a recent study by the nonpartisan Congressional Budget Office used income tax data and other sources to improve on the census estimates. The C.B.O. study found that between 1979 and 1997, the after-tax incomes of the top 1 percent of families rose 157 percent, compared with only a 10 percent gain for families near the middle of the income distribution. Even more startling results come from a new study by Thomas Piketty, at the French research institute Cepremap, and Emmanuel Saez, who is now at the University of California at Berkeley. Using income tax data, Piketty and Saez have produced estimates of the incomes of the well-to-do, the rich and the very rich back to 1913.

The first point you learn from these new estimates is that the middle-class America of my youth is best thought of not as the normal state of our society, but as an interregnum between Gilded Ages. America before 1930 was a society in which a small number of very rich people controlled a large share of the nation's wealth. We became a middle-class society only after the concentration of income at the top dropped sharply during the New Deal, and especially during World War II. The economic historians Claudia Goldin and Robert Margo have dubbed the narrowing of income gaps during those years the Great Compression. Incomes then stayed fairly equally distributed until the 1970s: the rapid rise in incomes during the first postwar generation was very evenly spread across the population.

Since the 1970s, however, income gaps have been rapidly widening. Piketty and Saez confirm what I suspected: by most measures we are, in fact, back to the days of "The Great Gatsby." After 30 years in which the income shares of the top 10 percent of taxpayers, the top 1 percent and so on were far below their levels in the 1920s, all are very nearly back where they were.

And the big winners are the very, very rich. One ploy often used to play down growing inequality is to rely on rather coarse statistical breakdowns—dividing the population into five "quintiles," each containing 20 percent of families, or at most 10 "deciles." Indeed, Greenspan's speech at Jackson Hole relied mainly on decile data. From there it's a short step to denying that we're really talking about the rich at all. For example, a conservative commentator might concede, grudgingly, that there has been some increase in the share of national income going to the top 10 percent of taxpayers, but then point out that anyone with an income over $81,000 in that top 10 percent. So we're just talking about shifts within the middle class, right?

Wrong: the top 10 percent contains a lot of people whom we would still consider middle class, but they weren't the big winners. Most of the gains in the share of the top 10 percent of taxpayers over the past 30 years were actually gains to the top 1 percent, rather than the next 9 percent. In 1998 the top 1 percent started at $230,000. In turn, 60 percent of the gains of that top 1 percent went to the top 0.1 percent, those with incomes of more than $790,000. And almost half of those gains went to a mere 13,000 taxpayers, the top 0.01 percent, who had an income of at least $3.6 million and an average income of $17 million.

A stickler for detail might point out that the Piketty-Saez estimates end in 1998 and that the C.B.O. numbers end a year earlier. Have the trends shown in the data reversed? Almost surely not. In fact, all indications are that the explosion of incomes at the top continued through 2000. Since then the plunge in stock prices must have put some crimp in high incomes—but census data show inequality continuing to increase in 2001, mainly because of the severe effects of the recession on the working poor and near poor. When the recession ends, we can be sure that we will find ourselves a society in which income inequality is even higher than it was in the late 1990s.

So claims that we've entered a second Gilded Age aren't exaggerated. In America's middle-class era, the mansion-building, yacht-owning classes had pretty much disappeared. According to Piketty and Saez, in 1970 the top 0.01 percent of taxpayers had 0.7 percent of total income—that is, they earned "only" 70 times as much as the average, not enough to buy or maintain a mega-residence. But in 1998 the top 0.01 percent received more than 3 percent of all income. That meant that the 13,000 richest families in America had almost as much income as the 20 million poorest households; those 13,000 families had incomes 300 times that of average families.

And let me repeat: this transformation has happened very quickly, and it is still going on. You might think that 1987, the year Tom Wolfe published his novel "The Bonfire of the Vanities" and Oliver Stone released his movie "Wall Street," marked the high tide of America's new money culture. But in 1987 the top 0.01 percent earned only about 40 percent of what they do today, and top executives less than a fifth as much. The America of "Wall Street" and "The Bonfire of the Vanities" was positively egalitarian compared with the country we live in today.

UNDOING THE NEW DEAL

In the middle of the 1980s, as economists became aware that something important was happening to the distribution of income in America, they formulated three main hypotheses about its causes.

The "globalization" hypothesis tied America's changing income distribution to the growth of world trade, and especially the growing imports of manufactured goods from the third world. Its basic message was that blue-collar workers—the sort of people who in my youth often made as much money as college-educated middle managers—were losing ground in the face of competition from low-wage workers in Asia. A result was stagnation or decline in the wages of ordinary people, with a growing share of national income going to the highly educated.

A second hypothesis, "skill-biased technological change," situated the cause of growing inequality not in foreign trade but in domestic innovation. The torrid pace of progress in information technology, so the story went, had increased the demand for the highly skilled and educated. And so the income distribution increasingly favored brains rather than brawn.

Finally, the "superstar" hypothesis—named by the Chicago economist Sherwin Rosen—offered a variant on the technological story. It argued that modern technologies of communication often turn competition into a tournament in which the winner is richly rewarded, while the runners-up get far less. The classic example—which gives the theory its new name—is the entertainment business. As Rosen pointed out, in bygone days there were hundreds of comedians making a modest living at live shows in the borscht belt and other places. Now they are mostly gone; what is left is a handful of superstar TV comedians.

The debates among these hypotheses—particularly the debate between those who attributed growing inequality to globalization and those who attributed it to technology—were many and bitter. I was a participant in those debates myself. But I won't dwell on them, because in the last few years there has been a growing sense among economists that none of these hypotheses works.

I don't mean to say that there was nothing to these stories. Yet as more evidence has accumulated, each of the hypotheses has seemed increasingly inadequate. Globalization can explain part of the relative decline in blue-collar wages, but it can't explain the 2,500 percent rise in C.E.O. incomes. Technology may explain why the salary premium associated with a college education has risen, but it's hard to match up with the huge increase in inequality among the college-educated, with little progress for many but gigantic gains at the top. The superstar theory works for Jay Leno, but not for the thousands of people who have become awesomely rich without going on TV.

The Great Compression—the substantial reduction in inequality during the New Deal and the Second World War—also seems hard to understand in terms of the usual theories. During World War II Franklin Roosevelt used government control over wages to compress wage gaps. But if the middle-class society that emerged from the war was an artificial creation, why did it persist for another 30 years?

Some—by no means all—economists trying to understand growing inequality have begun to take seriously a hypothesis that would have been considered irredeemably fuzzy-minded not long ago. This view stresses the role of social norms in setting limits to inequality. According to this view, the New Deal had a more profound impact on American society than even its most ardent admirers have suggested: it imposed norms of relative equality in pay that persisted for more than 30 years, creating the broadly middle-class society we came to take for granted. But those norms began to unravel in the 1970s and have done so at an accelerating pace.

Exhibit A for this view is the story of executive compensation. In the 1960s, America's great corporations behaved more like socialist republics than like cutthroat capitalist enterprises, and top executives behaved more like public-spirited bureaucrats than like captains of industry. I'm not exaggerating. Consider the description of executive behavior offered by John Kenneth Galbraith in his 1967 book, "The New Industrial State": "Management does not go out ruthlessly to reward itself—a sound management is expected to exercise restraint." Managerial self-dealing was a thing of the past: "With the power of decision goes opportunity for making money. . . . Were everyone to seek to do so . . . the corporation would be a chaos of competitive avarice. But these are not the sort of thing that a good company man does; a remarkably effective code bans such behavior. Group decision-making insures, moreover, that almost everyone's actions and even thoughts are known to others. This acts to enforce the code and, more than incidentally, a high standard of personal honesty as well."

Thirty-five years on, a cover article in Fortune is titled "You Bought, They Sold." "All over corporate America," reads the blurb, "top execs were cashing in stocks even as their companies were tanking. Who was left holding the bag? You." As I said, we've become a different country.

Let's leave actual malfeasance on one side for a moment, and ask how the relatively modest salaries of top executives 30 years ago became the gigantic pay packages of today. There are two main stories, both of which emphasize changing norms rather than pure economics. The more optimistic story draws an analogy between the explosion of C.E.O. pay and the explosion of baseball salaries with the introduction of free agency. According to this story, highly paid C.E.O.s really are worth it, because having the right man in that job makes a huge difference. The more pessimistic view—which I find more plausible—is that competition for talent is a minor factor. Yes, a great executive can make a big difference—but those huge pay packages have been going as often as not to executives whose performance is mediocre at best. The key reason executives are paid so much now is that they appoint the members of the corporate board that determines their compensation and control many of the perks that board members count on. So it's not the invisible hand of the market that leads to those monumental executive incomes; it's the invisible handshake in the boardroom.

But then why weren't executives paid lavishly 30 years ago? Again, it's a matter of corporate culture. For a generation after World War II, fear of outrage kept executive salaries in check. Now the outrage is gone. That is, the explosion of executive pay represents a social change rather than the purely economic forces of supply and demand. We should think of it not as a market trend like the rising value of waterfront property, but as something more like the sexual revolution of the 1960s—a relaxation of old strictures, a new permissiveness, but in this case the permissiveness is financial rather than sexual. Sure enough, John Kenneth Galbraith described the honest executive of 1967 as being one who "eschews the lovely, available and even naked woman by whom he is intimately surrounded." By the end of the 1990s, the executive motto might as well have been "If it feels good, do it."

How did this change in corporate culture happen? Economists and management theorists are only beginning to explore that question, but it's easy to suggest a few factors. One was the changing structure of financial markets. In his new book, "Searching for a Corporate Savior," Rakesh Khurana of Harvard Business School suggests that during the 1980s and 1990s, "managerial capitalism"—the world of the man in the gray flannel suit—was replaced by "investor capitalism." Institutional investors weren't willing to let a C.E.O. choose his own successor from inside the corporation; they wanted heroic leaders, often outsiders, and were willing to pay immense sums to get them. The subtitle of Khurana's book, by the way, is "The Irrational Quest for Charismatic C.E.O.'s."

But fashionable management theorists didn't think it was irrational. Since the 1980s there has been ever more emphasis on the importance of "leadership"—meaning personal, charismatic leadership. When Lee Iacocca of Chrysler became a business celebrity in the early 1980s, he was practically alone: Khurana reports that in 1980 only one issue of Business Week featured a C.E.O. on its cover. By 1999 the number was up to 19. And once it was considered normal, even necessary, for a C.E.O. to be famous, it also became easier to make him rich.

Economists also did their bit to legitimize previously unthinkable levels of executive pay. During the 1980s and 1990s a torrent of academic papers—popularized in business magazines and incorporated into consultants' recommendations—argued that Gordon Gekko was right: greed is good; greed works. In order to get the best performance out of executives, these papers argued, it was necessary to align their interests with those of stockholders. And the way to do that was with large grants of stock or stock options.

It's hard to escape the suspicion that these new intellectual justifications for soaring executive pay were as much effect as cause. I'm not suggesting that management theorists and economists were personally corrupt. It would have been a subtle, unconscious process: the ideas that were taken up by business schools, that led to nice speaking and consulting fees, tended to be the ones that ratified an existing trend, and thereby gave it legitimacy.

What economists like Piketty and Saez are now suggesting is that the story of executive compensation is representative of a broader story. Much more than economists and free-market advocates like to imagine, wages—particularly at the top—are determined by social norms. What happened during the 1930s and 1940s was that new norms of equality were established, largely through the political process. What happened in the 1980s and 1990s was that those norms unraveled, replaced by an ethos of "anything goes." And a result was an explosion of income at the top of the scale.

THE PRICE OF INEQUALITY

It was one of those revealing moments. Responding to an e-mail message from a Canadian viewer, Robert Novak of "Crossfire" delivered a little speech: "Marg, like most Canadians, you're ill informed and wrong. The U.S. has the longest standard of living—longest life expectancy of any country in the world, including Canada. That's the truth."

But it was Novak who had his facts wrong. Canadians can expect to live about two years longer than Americans. In fact, life expectancy in the U.S. is well below that in Canada, Japan and every major nation in Western Europe. On average, we can expect lives a bit shorter than those of Greeks, a bit longer than those of Portuguese. Male life expectancy is lower in the U.S. than it is in Costa Rica.

Still, you can understand why Novak assumed that we were No. 1. After all, we really are the richest major nation, with real G.D.P. per capita about 20 percent higher than Canada's. And it has been an article of faith in this country that a rising tide lifts all boats. Doesn't our high and rising national wealth translate into a high standard of living—including good medical care—for all Americans?

Well, no. Although America has higher per capita income than other advanced countries, it turns out that that's mainly because our rich are much richer. And here's a radical thought: if the rich get more, that leaves less for everyone else.

That statement—which is simply a matter of arithmetic—is guaranteed to bring accusations of "class warfare." If the accuser gets more specific, he'll probably offer two reasons that it's foolish to make a fuss over the high incomes of a few people at the top of the income distribution. First, he'll tell you that what the elite get may look like a lot of money, but it's still a small share of the total—that is, when all is said and done the rich aren't getting that big a piece of the pie. Second, he'll tell you that trying to do anything to reduce incomes at the top will hurt, not help, people further down the distribution, because attempts to redistribute income damage incentives.

These arguments for lack of concern are plausible. And they were entirely correct, once upon a time—namely, back when we had a middle-class society. But there's a lot less truth to them now.

First, the share of the rich in total income is no longer trivial. These days 1 percent of families receive about 16 percent of total pretax income, and have about 14 percent of after-tax income. That share has roughly doubled over the past 30 years, and is now about as large as the share of the bottom 40 percent of the population. That's a big shift of income to the top; as a matter of pure arithmetic, it must mean that the incomes of less well off families grew considerably more slowly than average income. And they did. Adjusting for inflation, average family income—total income divided by the number of families—grew 28 percent from 1979 to 1997. But median family income— the income of a family in the middle of the distribution, a better indicator of how typical American families are doing—grew only 10 percent. And the incomes of the bottom fifth of families actually fell slightly.

Let me belabor this point for a bit. We pride ourselves, with considerable justification, on our record of economic growth. But over the last few decades it's remarkable how little of that growth has trickled down to ordinary families. Median family income has risen only about 0.5 percent per year—and as far as we can tell from somewhat unreliable data, just about all of that increase was due to wives working longer hours, with little or no gain in real wages. Furthermore, numbers about income don't reflect the growing riskiness of life for ordinary workers. In the days when General Motors was known in-house as Generous Motors, many workers felt that they had considerable job security—the company wouldn't fire them except in extremis. Many had contracts that guaranteed health insurance, even if they were laid off; they had pension benefits that did not depend on the stock market. Now mass firings from long-established companies are commonplace; losing your job means losing your insurance; and as millions of people have been learning, a 401(k) plan is no guarantee of a comfortable retirement.

Still, many people will say that while the U.S. economic system may generate a lot of inequality, it also generates much higher incomes than any alternative, so that everyone is better off. That was the moral Business Week tried to convey in its recent special issue with "25 Ideas for a Changing World." One of those ideas was "the rich get richer, and that's O.K." High incomes at the top, the conventional wisdom declares, are the result of a free-market system that provides huge incentives for performance. And the system delivers that performance, which means that wealth at the top doesn't come at the expense of the rest of us.

A skeptic might point out that the explosion in executive compensation seems at best loosely related to actual performance. Jack Welch was one of the 10 highest-paid executives in the United States in 2000, and you could argue that he earned it. But did Dennis Kozlowski of Tyco, or Gerald Levin of Time Warner, who were also in the top 10? A skeptic might also point out that even during the economic boom of the late 1990s, U.S. productivity growth was no better than it was during the great postwar expansion, which corresponds to the era when America was truly middle class and C.E.O.s were modestly paid technocrats.

But can we produce any direct evidence about the effects of inequality? We can't rerun our own history and ask what would have happened if the social norms of middle-class America had continued to limit incomes at the top, and if government policy had leaned against rising inequality instead of reinforcing it, which is what actually happened. But we can compare ourselves with other advanced countries. And the results are somewhat surprising.

Many Americans assume that because we are the richest country in the world, with real G.D.P. per capita higher than that of other major advanced countries, Americans must be better off across the board—that it's not just our rich who are richer than their counterparts abroad, but that the typical American family is much better off than the typical family elsewhere, and that even our poor are well off by foreign standards.

But it's not true. Let me use the example of Sweden, that great conservative *bête noire*.

A few months ago the conservative cyberpundit Glenn Reynolds made a splash when he pointed out that Sweden's G.D.P. per capita is roughly comparable with that of Mississippi—see, those foolish believers in the welfare state have impoverished themselves! Presumably he assumed that this means that the typical Swede is as poor as the typical resident of Mississippi, and therefore much worse off than the typical American.

But life expectancy in Sweden is about three years higher than that in the U.S. Infant mortality is half the U.S. level, and less than a third the rate in Mississippi. Functional illiteracy is much less common than in the U.S.

How is this possible? One answer is that G.D.P. per capita is in some ways a misleading measure. Swedes take longer vacations than Americans, so they work fewer hours per year. That's a choice, not a failure of economic performance. Real G.D.P. per hour worked is 16 percent lower than in the United States, which makes Swedish productivity about the same as Canada's.

But the main point is that though Sweden may have lower average income than the United States, that's mainly because our rich are so much richer. The median Swedish family has a standard of living roughly comparable with that of the median U.S. family: wages are if anything higher in Sweden, and a higher tax burden is offset by public provision of health care and generally better public services. And as you move further down the income distribution, Swedish living standards are way ahead of those in the U.S. Swedish families with children that are at the 10th percentile—poorer than 90 percent of the population—have incomes 60 percent higher than their U.S. counterparts. And very few people in Sweden experience the deep poverty that is all too common in the United States. One measure: in 1994 only 6 percent of Swedes lived on less than $11 per day, compared with 14 percent in the U.S.

The moral of this comparison is that even if you think that America's high levels of inequality are the price of our high level of national income, it's not at all clear that this price is worth paying. The reason conservatives engage in bouts of Sweden-bashing is that they want to convince us that there is no tradeoff between economic efficiency and equity—that if you try to take from the rich and give to the poor, you actually make everyone worse off. But the comparison between the U.S. and other advanced countries doesn't support this conclusion at all. Yes, we are the richest major nation. But because so much of our national income is concentrated in relatively few hands, large numbers of Americans are worse off economically than their counterparts in other advanced countries.

And we might even offer a challenge from the other side: inequality in the United States has arguably reached levels where it is counterproductive. That is, you can make a case that our society would be richer if its richest members didn't get quite so much.

I could make this argument on historical grounds. The most impressive economic growth in U.S. history coincided with the middle-class interregnum, the post-World War II generation, when incomes were most evenly distributed. But let's focus on a specific case, the extraordinary pay packages of today's top executives. Are these good for the economy?

Until recently it was almost unchallenged conventional wisdom that, whatever else you might say, the new imperial C.E.O.s had delivered results that dwarfed the expense of their compensation. But now that the stock bubble has burst, it has become increasingly clear that there was a price to those big pay packages, after all. In fact, the price paid by shareholders and society at large may have been many times larger than the amount actually paid to the executives.

It's easy to get boggled by the details of corporate scandal—insider loans, stock options, special-purpose entities, mark-to-market, round-tripping. But there's a simple reason that the details are so complicated. All of these schemes were designed to benefit corporate insiders—to inflate the pay of the C.E.O. and his inner circle. That is, they were all about the "chaos of competitive avarice" that, according to John Kenneth Galbraith, had been ruled out in the corporation of the 1960s. But while all restraint has vanished within the

American corporation, the outside world—including stockholders—is still prudish, and open looting by executives is still not acceptable. So the looting has to be camouflaged, taking place through complicated schemes that can be rationalized to outsiders as clever corporate strategies.

Economists who study crime tell us that crime is inefficient—that is, the costs of crime to the economy are much larger than the amount stolen. Crime, and the fear of crime, divert resources away from productive uses: criminals spend their time stealing rather than producing, and potential victims spend time and money trying to protect their property. Also, the things people do to avoid becoming victims—like avoiding dangerous districts—have a cost even if they succeed in averting an actual crime.

The same holds true of corporate malfeasance, whether or not it actually involves breaking the law. Executives who devote their time to creating innovative ways to divert shareholder money into their own pockets probably aren't running the real business very well (think Enron, WorldCom, Tyco, Global Crossing, Adelphia . . .). Investments chosen because they create the illusion of profitability while insiders cash in their stock options are a waste of scarce resources. And if the supply of funds from lenders and shareholders dries up because of a lack of trust, the economy as a whole suffers. Just ask Indonesia.

The argument for a system in which some people get very rich has always been that the lure of wealth provides powerful incentives. But the question is, incentives to do what? As we learn more about what has actually been going on in corporate America, it's becoming less and less clear whether those incentives have actually made executives work on behalf of the rest of us.

INEQUALITY AND POLITICS

In September the Senate debated a proposed measure that would impose a one-time capital gains tax on Americans who renounce their citizenship in order to avoid paying U.S. taxes. Senator Phil Gramm was not pleased, declaring that the proposal was "right out of Nazi Germany." Pretty strong language, but no stronger than the metaphor Daniel Mitchell of the Heritage Foundation used, in an op-ed article in The Washington Times, to describe a bill designed to prevent corporations from rechartering abroad for tax purposes: Mitchell described this legislation as the "Dred Scott tax bill," referring to the infamous 1857 Supreme Court ruling that required free states to return escaped slaves.

Twenty years ago, would a prominent senator have likened those who want wealthy people to pay taxes to Nazis? Would a member of a think tank with close ties to the administration have drawn a parallel between corporate taxation and slavery? I don't think so. The remarks by Gramm and Mitchell, while stronger than usual, were indicators of two huge changes in American politics. One is the growing polarization of our politics—our politicians are less and less inclined to offer even the appearance of moderation. The other is the growing tendency of policy and policy makers to cater to the interests of the wealthy. And I mean the wealthy, not the merely well-off: only someone with a net worth of at least several million dollars is likely to find it worthwhile to become a tax exile.

You don't need a political scientist to tell you that modern American politics is bitterly polarized. But wasn't it always thus? No, it wasn't. From World War II until the 1970s—the same era during which income inequality was historically low—political partisanship was much more muted than it is today. That's not just a subjective assessment. My Princeton political science colleagues Nolan McCarty and Howard Rosenthal, together with Keith Poole at the University of Houston, have done a statistical analysis showing that the voting behavior of a congressman is much better predicted by his party affiliation today than it was 25 years ago. In fact, the division between the parties is sharper now than it has been since the 1920s.

What are the parties divided about? The answer is simple: economics. McCarty, Rosenthal and Poole write that "voting in Congress is highly ideological—one-dimensional left/right, liberal versus conservative." It may sound simplistic to describe Democrats as the party that wants to tax the rich and help the poor, and Republicans as the party that wants to keep taxes and social spending as low as possible. And during the era of middle-class America that would indeed have been simplistic: politics wasn't defined by economic issues. But that was a different country; as McCarty, Rosenthal and Poole put it, "If income and wealth are distributed in a fairly equitable way, little is to be gained for politicians to organize politics around nonexistent conflicts." Now the conflicts are real, and our politics is organized around them. In other words, the growing inequality of our incomes probably lies behind the growing divisiveness of our politics.

But the politics of rich and poor hasn't played out the way you might think. Since the incomes of America's wealthy have soared while ordinary families have seen at best small gains, you might have expected politicians to seek votes by proposing to soak the rich. In fact, however, the polarization of politics has occurred because the Republicans have moved to the right, not because the Democrats have moved to the left. And actual economic policy has moved steadily in favor of the wealthy. The major tax cuts of the past 25 years, the Reagan cuts in the 1980s and the recent Bush cuts, were both heavily tilted toward the very well off. (Despite obfuscations, it remains true that more than half the Bush tax cut will eventually go to the top 1 percent of families.) The major tax increase over that period, the increase in payroll taxes in the 1980s, fell most heavily on working-class families.

The most remarkable example of how politics has shifted in favor of the wealthy—an example that helps us understand why economic policy has reinforced, not countered, the movement toward greater inequality—is the drive to repeal the estate tax. The estate tax is, overwhelmingly, a tax on the wealthy. In 1999, only the top 2 percent of estates paid any tax at all, and half the estate tax was paid by only 3,300 estates, 0.16 percent of the total, with a minimum value of $5 million and an average value of $17 million. A quarter of the tax was paid by just 467 estates worth more than $20 million. Tales of family farms and businesses broken up to pay the estate tax are basically rural legends; hardly any real examples have been found, despite diligent searching.

You might have thought that a tax that falls on so few people yet yields a significant amount of revenue would be politically popular; you certainly wouldn't expect widespread opposition. Moreover, there has long been an argument that the estate tax promotes democratic values, precisely because it limits the ability of the wealthy to form dynasties. So why has there been a powerful political drive to repeal the estate tax, and why was such a repeal a centerpiece of the Bush tax cut?

There is an economic argument for repealing the estate tax, but it's hard to believe that many people take it seriously. More significant for members of Congress, surely, is the question of who would benefit from repeal: while those who will actually benefit from estate tax repeal are few in number, they have a lot of money and control, even more (corporate C.E.O.s can now count on leaving taxable estates behind). That is, they are the sort of people who command the attention of politicians in search of campaign funds.

But it's not just about campaign contributions: much of the general public has been convinced that the estate tax is a bad thing. If you try talking about the tax to a group of moderately prosperous retirees, you get some interesting reactions. They refer to it as the "death tax"; many of them believe that their estates will face punitive taxation, even though most of them will pay little or nothing; they are convinced that small businesses and family farms bear the brunt of the tax.

These misconceptions don't arise by accident. They have, instead, been deliberately promoted. For example, a Heritage Foundation document titled "Time to Repeal Federal Death Taxes: The Nightmare of the American Dream" emphasizes stories that rarely, if ever, happen in real life: "Small-business owners, particularly minority owners, suffer anxious moments wondering whether the businesses they hope to hand down to their children will be destroyed by the death tax bill, . . . Women whose children are grown struggle to find ways to re-enter the work force without upsetting the family's estate tax avoidance plan." And who finances the Heritage Foundation? Why, foundations created by wealthy families, of course.

The point is that it is no accident that strongly conservative views, views that militate against taxes on the rich, have spread even as the rich get richer compared with the rest of us: in addition to directly buying influence, money can be used to shape public perceptions. The liberal group People for the American Way's report on how conservative foundations have deployed vast sums to support think tanks, friendly media and other institutions that promote right-wing causes is titled "Buying a Movement."

Not to put too fine a point on it: as the rich get richer, they can buy a lot of things besides goods and services. Money buys political influence; used cleverly, it also buys intellectual influence. A result is that growing income disparities in the United States, far from leading to demands to soak the rich, have been accompanied by a growing movement to let them keep more of their earnings and to pass their wealth on to their children.

This obviously raises the possibility of a self-reinforcing process. As the gap between the rich and the rest of the population grows, economic policy increasingly caters to the interests of the elite, while public services for the population at large—above all, public education—are starved of resources. As policy increasingly favors the interests of the rich and neglects the interests of the general population, income disparities grow even wider.

PLUTOCRACY?

In 1924, the mansions of Long Island's North Shore were still in their full glory, as was the political power of the class that owned them. When Gov. Al Smith of New York proposed building a system of parks on Long Island, the mansion owners were bitterly opposed. One baron—Horace Havemeyer, the "sultan of sugar"—warned that North Shore towns would be "overrun with rabble from the city." "Rabble?" Smith said. "That's me you're talking about." In the end New Yorkers got their parks, but it was close: the interests of a few hundred wealthy families nearly prevailed over those of New York City's middle class.

America in the 1920s wasn't a feudal society. But it was a nation in which vast privilege—often inherited privilege—stood in contrast to vast misery. It was also a nation in which the government, more often than not, served the interests of the privileged and ignored the aspirations of ordinary people.

Those days are past—or are they? Income inequality in America has now returned to the levels of the 1920s. Inherited wealth doesn't yet play a big part in our society, but given time—and the repeal of the estate tax—we will grow ourselves a hereditary elite just as set apart from the concerns of ordinary Americans as old Horace Havemeyer. And the new elite, like the old, will have enormous political power.

Kevin Phillips concludes his book "Wealth and Democracy" with a grim warning: "Either democracy must be renewed, with politics brought back to life, or wealth is likely to cement a new and less democratic regime—plutocracy by some other name." It's a pretty extreme line, but we live in extreme times. Even if the forms of democracy remain, they may become meaningless. It's all too easy to see how we may become a country in which the big rewards are reserved for people with the right connections; in which ordinary people see little hope of advancement; in which political involvement seems pointless, because in the end the interests of the elite always get served.

Am I being too pessimistic? Even my liberal friends tell me not to worry, that our system has great resilience, that the center will hold. I hope they're right, but they may be looking in the rearview mirror. Our optimism about America, our belief that in the end our nation always finds its way, comes from the past—a past in which we were a middle-class society. But that was another country.

2

▼▼▼▼▼▼▼

Funding Accountability:
States, Courts, and Public Responsibility*

Sue Books

> *In all our stringent calls for "accountability," do we ever consider that maybe we as members of a society ought to hold ourselves more accountable for all of our children?*
>
> —Sarah Ryan, public school teacher in Manhattan

In a speech he gave in 1965 Vaclav Havel (1991) critiques "a way of thinking that turns away from the core of the matter to something else" (15). In the speech, later published as an essay, "On Evasive Thinking," the former president of Czechoslovakia offers as an example some commentary published after a woman in Prague was killed when a stone window ledge came loose and fell on her. The commentator argued that, of course, window ledges ought not fall, but also praised the fact that public criticism of such events was then possible and spoke about the enormous progress Czechoslovakia had made as a country.

> To illustrate this he mentioned that whereas before young girls used to wear duffel coats, today they dress in the latest Parisian fashions. This rather graphic example of the achievement of our time ultimately led him to ask whether there wasn't, after all, just a little too much criticism, and he appealed to us not to limit ourselves to what he called local matters, but to focus on themes that were

---

more worthy of the dignity of the human mission and more appropriate to the humanistic notion of man. (Havel 1991, 10–11)

Such "false contextualization," Havel (1991) argues, enables people to evade responsibility:

> It holds the world back: it prevents whoever has it in his power to solve the problem of the Prague facades from understanding that he bears responsibility for something and that he can't lie his way out of that responsibility, either by conducting a victorious war against duffel coats, or by abstract talk about the prospects of mankind. (24)

I recall Havel's discussion of evasive thinking at a time when practices of high-stakes testing have swept the nation as a way to rectify a presumed lack of "accountability" in public schooling and when the federal No Child Left Behind Act of 2001 promises to leave plenty of children behind as schools that fail to make "adequate yearly progress," defined in terms of student pass rates on state tests, lose federal funding. These policies and practices, touted as a way to drive educational reform, have been institutionalized despite evidence that tests that make or break promotion or graduation are educationally counterproductive (Amrein & Berliner 2002a, 2002b; Heubert & Hauser 1999), despite continuing and significant disparities in school funding (The Education Trust 2002; *Quality Counts 2003*; Verstegen 2002), despite state budget crises nationwide that threaten to exacerbate these disparities, and despite the fact that almost every state constitution includes language that gives the state, and not individual school districts, final responsibility for public education.[1]

The public discourse on accountability, reflected in state and federal policies and practices, evades this broader context of state obligation. Instead, the discourse construes accountability as school-based—and, beyond this, as child-, family-, and community-based. In fact, 49 of 50 states have education clauses in their constitutions that require some level of public schooling (Reed 2001). This tension between a school-based notion of accountability reflected in state and federal policies and practices, on one hand, and constitutional language focused on state responsibility for public schooling, on the other, surfaces in court battles over school funding and conditions. These cases confront courts with the need to reconcile competing notions of accountability: state responsibility for public schooling versus a school-based notion of accountability.

From one perspective, competing notions of accountability provide an opportunity for states to reconsider school funding policies and practices in light of heightened expectations (or demands) with respect to student achievement. Publicizing the results of standardized tests, as the No Child Left Behind Act requires, highlights the plight of the poorest districts (Koch 1999). As Hugh Price, president of the National Urban League, argues,

"States have unwittingly backed themselves into an interesting position" by establishing standards all students are required to meet, as they now have "a moral and financial and legal obligation" to make sure all students do in fact have the opportunity to meet the standards (quoted in Koch 1999). Recent decisions in school funding cases are not encouraging in this regard, however, as courts are not necessarily affirming this broad conception of state obligation. Rather, in many cases courts are reigning in state responsibility without regard for the short- and long-term consequences for young people.

The discussion that follows looks more specifically at how courts in three states have reasoned about state obligation in light of concerns with accountability. I look at decisions in high-profile school funding cases in New York and Ohio as well as a decision in Illinois that illustrates the ease with which courts can simply opt out and abdicate responsibility. A review of the status of school funding with respect to equity provides a context for consideration of these cases, followed by discussion of the question of accountability, the role of the courts, and the responsibility of the broader public.

Savage Inequalities: Then and Now

Jonathan Kozol's *Savage Inequalities: Children in America's Schools*, published in 1991, documented gross disparities in funding for public schools across the nation. These disparities were not random, but rather patterned, predictable, and consequential. Children in wealthier and mostly white school districts tended to get much more than children in poorer districts serving largely children of color—more of almost everything money can buy for schools: nice buildings, good teachers, up-to-date textbooks, extracurricular activities, and so on. This meant that most children in wealthy districts such as Winnetka in Illinois, Cherry Hill in New Jersey, or Great Neck in New York enjoyed safe, sanitary, state-of-the-art school buildings; well qualified and adequately compensated teachers dedicated to their students' intellectual development; and plenty of opportunities to participate in art, music, and sports programs. Many children in poor districts, however, faced years of schooling in unsanitary, dangerous buildings; teachers lacking full credentials or a series of substitutes; outdated books that were often rationed because there weren't enough to go around; and few extracurricular activities at all. Consequently, some children learned they are special, deserving, and full of potential while others learned "they are not wanted" and don't really matter (Kozol 1991, 35).

What has happened since Kozol's powerful cry of outrage? According to the National Center for Education Statistics, average state spending per pupil in 2002 ranged from a high of $11,009 in the District of Columbia to a low of $4,769 in Utah (Park, 2003)—a gap of $6,240. For a class of 25 students, the difference is $156,000. For a school of 500, $3.12 million, and over 12 years of schooling, the disparity grows to $37.4 million.

Disparities in spending within states are also alarming. The Education Trust (2002) found that in 30 of 47 states studied, school districts with the highest child-poverty rates have substantially less state and local money to spend per student than districts with the lowest child-poverty rates. In New York, the gap in state and local revenues between the 25% of districts educating the highest percentages of poor children and the 25% educating the lowest percentages is $2,152 per student. Between two elementary schools of 400 students each, "this gap translates into a difference of $860,800 . . . enough to compete with elite suburban schools for the most qualified teachers and to provide the kinds of additional instructional time and other resources that research and data show can make a difference" (Education Trust, 2002, 2). Right behind New York is Illinois, with a per-student spending gap of $2,060; Montana, with a gap of $1,535; and Michigan, with a gap of $1,248. It is not necessary to show a direct correlation between funding and achievement to recognize the truth of Thurgood Marshall's assertion, written in dissent in a landmark school funding case decided in 1973: "It is an inescapable fact that if one district has more funds available per pupil than another district, the former will have greater choice in educational planning than will the latter" (*San Antonio v. Rodriguez* 1973).

Funding disparities show up, among other places, in the condition of school buildings. A 1996 report by the U.S. General Accounting Office (GAO) documented the need for an investment of at least $112 billion in the nation's school buildings for repairs and upgrades alone. At that time, about one-third of all school buildings needed "extensive repair or replacement" and about half needed some repair, with most of the problems in central-city schools (GAO 1996, 1, 18). Since then, the problem has worsened. In its 2001 report card on the nation's infrastructure, the American Society of Civil Engineers (ASCE) reported that the facilities problem had become a $127 billion deficit, gave a D-minus for the overall condition of the nation's schools, and noted: "School facility problems vary by location (urban versus suburban) and community characteristics (poor versus wealthy). Generally speaking, the largest portion of schools reporting deficient conditions are in central cities serving 50% minority students and 70% poor students. Schools in rural areas also tend to be inadequate."

Averages and sum totals provide an overview, but do not tell the whole story. Many students attend schools in good repair with more than adequate funding. The students in decaying and inadequately funded schools in disproportionate numbers are students living in poor neighborhoods, students of color, and students with greater-than-average needs (Anyon 1997, The Education Trust 2002, GAO 1996). The Education Trust (2002) review found that in 31 of 47 states, districts with the highest proportions of students of color had substantially less state and local dollars to spend per student than districts with low percentages of students of color. Again, the gap in New York State was the largest: $2,033 per student between the quarter of districts with the lowest and the quarter with the highest enrollments of students of color.

"Despite a great deal of rhetoric about the general failure of the public school system, the problem of inadequate schooling is more often not a state-wide, but a local, overwhelmingly urban problem" (McUsic 1999, 128). The problem continues in part because "no state has yet been willing to fund poor urban schools at a level that would (after discounting costs for special needs) finance a straightforward education curriculum at the same level enjoyed by the average suburban schools" (McUsic 1999, 130). About 70% of the students in the nation's 55 largest city school systems are African American or Hispanic, almost all of these systems (92%) have poverty rates above the state average, and 85% have disproportionately high percentages of English language learners (Council of Great City Schools 2001). Fewer than one-third of the students graduate from many of these schools (Taylor 2000).

This state of affairs persists despite the fact that as of 2003, plaintiffs had prevailed in school funding cases in 25 states (Advocacy Center for Children's Educational Success with Standards 2003). Conditions in many schools around the nation are now so bad that advocates are suing for neither equitable nor necessarily even adequate funding, but simply for some assurance that children will be provided with the barest semblance of schooling—books, qualified teachers, safe and sanitary buildings, and working toilets accessible to students. Consider, for example, the situation in California. A class-action lawsuit filed in California State Superior Court in 2000, *Williams v. State*, documents conditions at 18 "substandard schools" serving approximately 23,600 students, overwhelmingly poor children, children learning English, and children of color.[2] Luther Burbank Middle School in San Francisco is representative of the schools described in the original complaint:

> Some math, science, and other core classes, do not have even enough textbooks for all the students in a single class to use during the school day. . . . The social studies textbook . . . is so old it does not reflect the breakup of the former Soviet Union. . . . [The school] is infested with vermin and roaches. . . . One dead rodent has remained, decomposing, in a corner in the gymnasium since the beginning of the school year. . . . The school library is rarely open [and] has no librarian. . . . Two of the three bathrooms . . . are locked all day, every day. The third bathroom is locked during lunch and other periods . . . so there are times during school when no bathroom at all is available for students to use. Students have urinated or defecated on themselves at school because they could not get into an unlocked bathroom. . . . The school has no air conditioning. On hot days classroom temperatures climb into the 90s. . . . In winter, children often wear coats, hats, and gloves during class to keep warm. (*Williams v. State* 2000, 19–21)

Since originally filed, the suit has grown to include more students. Also, the state governor has counter-sued, with the argument that local districts and not the state are responsible for school conditions. "We cannot have the governor out in our local school districts making sure there is toilet paper in all the bathrooms," said Secretary of Education Kerry Mazzoni (quoted in Gewertz 2001). Proceedings on the cross-claims have been stayed. However, the verdict was still out in the summer of 2003 for students at Luther Burbank and many other schools in similarly awful conditions. Let me turn therefore to some recent cases in which courts have made determinations of state obligation with respect to school funding and school conditions.

School Funding in New York:
Campaign for Fiscal Equity v. State

In June 2003, the New York Court of Appeals, the state's highest court, overturned a lower-level ruling, reinstated a trial-court finding that New York must provide an opportunity for a "meaningful high school education" to all students, and ordered the state, by the end of July 2004, to implement funding and accountability reforms to ensure that this happens for students in the New York City public schools. "Tens of thousands of students are placed in overcrowded classrooms, taught by unqualified teachers, and provided with inadequate facilities and equipment. The number of children in these straits is large enough to represent a systemic failure," Chief Judge Judith Kaye wrote in the majority opinion (*Campaign for Fiscal Equity v. State* 2003, 22). At issue in the case was the adequacy and equity of the funding specifically of New York City schools, which for the six years prior to the trial-court ruling consistently were shortchanged in state-aid allocations and for more than a decade spent less per pupil than the state average, taking student need into account (*Campaign for Fiscal Equity v. State of New York* 2001, 166).[3] Documents submitted in the case showed New York City public schools educate 73% of all students of color in the state, and 84% of all students in the city schools are students of color.

The original trial judge, Leland DeGrasse, considered the broad context: What resources have been provided to the state's public schools? How equitably have these resources been distributed, and with what consequences for students? The 190-page decision documents inequities and inadequacies with respect to teacher quality, curricula, building conditions, and books and other supplies. It cites statistics for 1997–1998 that show almost 14% of New York City public school teachers were not certified in any subject they taught and describes school buildings in the city in a "parlous physical state" after a "history of neglect" (*Campaign for Fiscal Equity v. State* 2001, 62).

DeGrasse affirmed a "causal link" between resource-based "input" and "output" measures, such as graduation and dropout rates and standardized test scores; stressed the consequences of funding inequities and inadequacies for students in the city schools, a majority of whom "leave high school unprepared for more than low-paying work, unprepared for college, and unprepared for the duties placed upon them by a democratic society"; and declared, "The schools have broken a covenant with students, and with society" (*Campaign for Fiscal Equity v. State* 2001, 109–110). DeGrasse noted that fewer than 12% of all ninth-graders in the city schools historically have received a Regents diploma, which requires passing scores on a series of standardized exams and which, with a few exceptions, is now the only diploma available.[4] Also, only half of all New York City public school students who started ninth grade in 1996 and stayed in school made it to the 12th grade in four years. Of the city's public school graduates entering the City University of New York, approximately four-fifths needed remediation—evidence, DeGrasse said, of "a public school system that is foundering" (*Campaign for Fiscal Equity v. State* 2001, 101).

Based on an interpretation of language in the state constitution, New York must provide a "sound basic education" statewide. DeGrasse dismissed the state's contention that this amounts essentially to an eighth- or ninth-grade level of competency in reading and a sixth-grade level in math. He also rejected plaintiffs' argument that a "sound basic education" ought to be substantively defined in terms of the Regents Learning Standards, which he characterized as "state of the art." Instead, DeGrasse took what he called a middle-ground position and argued that "a sound basic education consists of the foundational skills that students need to become productive citizens capable of civic engagement and sustaining competitive employment" (*Campaign for Fiscal Equity v. State* 2001, 26). In other words, high school graduates ought not be relegated to the ranks of the working poor. DeGrasse suggested that although preparation for future employment ought not be the sole rationale for public education, graduates' realistic job prospects should be considered in determining the quality of schooling the state must provide. "While the greatest expansion in the local labor market might be composed of low level service jobs, such jobs frequently do not pay a living wage," he wrote. "A sound basic education would give New York City's high school graduates the opportunity to move beyond such work" (*Campaign for Fiscal Equity v. State* 2001, 23).

New York's governor, George Pataki, immediately appealed the trial-court ruling. "Courts may not find a denial of an opportunity for a sound basic education unless the program provided by a school has deficiencies so debilitating that it is tantamount to no education at all," the state argued and insisted this is not the case in New York City.[5] A panel of the Appellate Division of the Supreme Court reversed the trial court in 2002. Justice Alfred Lerner, writing for the majority, said DeGrasse had set the standard for a sound basic education too high, and that plaintiffs had shown neither a causal link between educational quality and state funding policy nor that the education provided in city schools falls below the constitutional standard. The appellate court argued that a sound basic education need not prepare graduates for "competitive employment," but rather should enable them "to get a job, and support [themselves], and thereby not be a charge on the public fisc"—and added as explanation: "Society needs workers in all levels of jobs, the majority of which may very well be low level" (*Campaign for Fiscal Equity v. State* 2002, 13). The court suggested that students can learn to read well enough to land a job by the eighth or ninth grade, and that this level of education is being provided, even in New York City.

The Court of Appeals rejected this standard of state obligation, but opted not to tie the practical definition of a "meaningful high school education" to the state's Regent Learning Standards. High school students now must pass a series of tests pegged to these standards to graduate. The court also warned other distressed districts not to regard its ruling as a green light: "New York City schools have the *most* student need in the State and the *highest* local costs yet receive some of the *lowest* per-student funding and have some of the *worst* results. Plaintiffs in other districts who cannot demonstrate a similar combination may find tougher going in the court" (*Campaign for Fiscal Equity v. State* 2003, 54). The court directed the state to ascertain the actual cost of providing a "sound basic education" in New York City and to devise a system that ensures every school has the resources it needs to do this.

School Funding in Ohio: *DeRolph v. State*

In May 2003, the Ohio Supreme Court said what it had said four times before: the state's system of school funding is unconstitutional. The court also made clear that responsibility for fixing the problem lies with the legislature, not the court, which leaves plaintiffs with no legal recourse if legislators opt not to change the state's school funding system. "It's like the court said, 'You are guilty but you are free,' " said William Phillis, executive director of the Ohio Coalition for Equity and Adequacy of School Funding, which filed the lawsuit, *DeRolph v. State of Ohio*, in 1991 (quoted in Zehr 2003, 15). At issue has been an "over-reliance on property taxes" leading to disparities in resources so significant that the court repeatedly found the state in violation of its constitutional requirement to provide a "thorough and efficient system of common schools." Education Week's *Quality Counts 2003* review of public education gives Ohio a D-minus in resource equity for 2002.

In 2001 the court found the state's school funding system would be constitutional if the state increased its aid to public schools. That decision represented what a 4–3 majority characterized as a compromise it could live with in the interest of bringing the then 10-year-old matter to a close. "No one is served by continued uncertainty and fractious debate," Chief Justice Thomas

Moyer wrote. "In that spirit, we have created the consensus that should terminate the role of this court in the dispute" (*DeRolph III* 2001, 3).

Gov. Bob Taft and legislators in Ohio subsequently asked the court to reconsider its ruling in light of the economic fallout of the September 11, 2001, attack on the United States, which they said would make it difficult to find the additional $1.2 billion the court had asked them to invest in public schools (Richard 2001). The court agreed and issued a final decision weeks before a new term began, when two newly elected justices would change its makeup. "The consensus arrived at in *DeRolph III* was in many ways the result of impatience," Justice Pfeifer wrote in the 2002 decision. "Upon being asked to reconsider that decision, we have changed our collective mind" (*DeRolph V* 2002, 2–3). Accordingly, the court once again found the state's school funding system unconstitutional and directed the General Assembly to enact a school-funding scheme that is "thorough and efficient," but provided no deadline or enforcement mechanism.

The case began in 1991 when a group of very poor small rural and large urban districts filed a complaint that painted a horror-story picture:

> The Nelsonville York Elementary School . . . is sliding down a hill at a rate of an inch a month. . . . At Eastern Brown High School, the learning-disabled classroom is a converted storage room with no windows for ventilation. . . . In the Dawson-Bryant school system, where a coal heating system is used, students are . . . breathing coal dust which . . . covers the students' desks after accumulating overnight. Band members . . . use a former coal bin for practice sessions where there is no ventilation whatsoever. The Northern Local School District has . . . been plagued with . . . outdated sewage systems which have actually caused raw sewage to flow into the baseball field . . . and . . . arsenic in the drinking water. (quoted in Petronicolos & New 1999, 406)

At the time, approximately $3,000 a year was being spent on students in Ohio's poorest districts, compared with $11,000 per year on students in much wealthier districts (Drummond 2000).

Ohio in the last few years has increased the number of credits required for high school graduation, has instituted a fourth-grade reading test on which promotion hinges, and has started requiring annual performance reviews for school districts, accompanied by report cards. "We agree that accountability is an important component of a system that provides funds," Justice Alice Robie Resnick wrote in the 2000 majority opinion. "What is problematic, however, is a system that increases academic requirements and accountability, yet fails to provide adequate funding." Characterizing the new "standards of accountability" as "unfunded mandates," the court urged that they "be accompanied by . . . a commitment to provide extra resources and support to students and schools who start out furthest from the goal line" and continued the case for another year (*DeRolph II* 2000).

In their dissenting opinions in 2001, Justices Resnick and Francis Sweeney continued to frame state obligation in terms of heightened responsibility to ensure adequate funding in light of statewide expectations for student achievement and to eliminate disparities that shortchange poor children:

> With statewide standards and statewide testing, we should recognize that we have a state system of common schools. The state bears the ultimate responsibility to solve problems (in partnership with the local districts) that have been formerly viewed as local. (Resnick in *DeRolph III* 2001, 93)

> At the end of the day, can we truly say that we have been victorious? . . . Can we say that the children in poor, rural, or urban areas have been given the same opportunities as their peers who happen to be blessed with the good fortune of living in wealthy districts with a high property tax base? . . . The hallmark of a thorough and efficient form of public education is that it works as well for the least advantaged as it does for the most advantaged. The funding system advocated by the majority sadly misses the mark. (Sweeney in *DeRolph III* 2001, 100–101)

For the moment, these voices have prevailed in the legal arena only. After a standoff with the state legislature, Gov. Bob Taft cut $90 million in state aid to public schools as part of a plan to close a $720 million state budget gap (Reid, 2003).

School Conditions in Illinois: *Lewis E. v. Spagnolo*

In 1995 a group of parents and guardians in Illinois sued the state and local school boards over the appalling conditions of the public schools in critically impoverished East St. Louis. The class-action lawsuit challenged not funding per se, but rather basic conditions. Plaintiffs cited dangerous buildings and schools without such fundamentals as teachers and books as evidence that state and local school district officials were violating the state constitution, which requires Illinois to provide "an efficient system of high quality public educational institutions and services." At the time, every student in the district was African American and almost all were living in poverty (Jerald 1998). Seven years later in 2002 the student population was 99% African American, 1% Hispanic, and 92% of the students were from low-income families.

Among the original plaintiffs was Anita Hicks, mother of twin boys in the first grade at Jackson Math and Science Academy.

> Hicks' disillusionment with her children's school began with the discovery that there was no teacher posted to the twins' first-grade room. Every time she asked why, the explanations changed. . . . "They were bringing in people off the street to baby-sit with the students," Hicks said. "There'd be days when no adult was

in the room. A teacher would pop in from next door just to check on them." . . .
When teachers were absent, classes were marched down to the gym to sit idle all
day, parents charged. One group of 3rd graders had had, as their substitute, a
sixth-grade student. (Grossman 1997, 1)

After a series of lower court rulings, the case landed in the Illinois Supreme
Court, which ruled in 1999 that although the constitution requires the state to
provide an "efficient" and "high quality" public school system, "quality" is a
political question for the legislature, not a legal one for the court (*Lewis E. v.
Spagnolo* 1999). The court did not suggest that East St. Louis students were
receiving a minimally adequate education, but rather that the problem was
not its to fix.

In a sharp dissent from the majority, Chief Justice Freeman condemned
the "intolerable and illegal conditions" in what, he said, had become "one of
the worst [school] systems in the nation."

Strangers wander in and out of junior high schools. Fire alarms malfunction,
and firefighters find emergency exits chained shut as they rescue children from
burning schools. Classrooms are sealed to protect students from asbestos and
dangerous structural flaws. In dark corridors, light bulbs go unreplaced and
rain seeps through leaky roofs. In heavy rains backed-up sewers flood school
kitchens, boilers, and electrical systems, resulting in student evacuations and
cancelled classes. Bathrooms are unsanitary and water fountains are dry or
spew brown water. In winter, students sit through classes wearing heavy coats
because broken windows and faulty boilers go unrepaired. They struggle to
learn using meager instructional equipment and tattered, dated textbooks.
School libraries are locked or destroyed by fire. Children never know whether
they will have a teacher. (*Lewis E. v. Spagnolo* 1999)

To the majority contention that the question before the court was an inap-
propriate one of politics, Freeman countered that plaintiffs were not asking
the court "to enter the arena of Illinois public school policy," but simply "to
do its job and interpret the Illinois Constitution" (*Lewis E. v. Spagnolo* 1999).
He also pointed out that the majority did not dispute the horrendous conditions of the East St. Louis schools, but nevertheless did not "adequately relate the effect that these abhorrent physical conditions have on schoolchildren" (*Lewis E. v. Spagnolo* 1999). Indeed, the majority opinion failed to
address the consequences of the squalid school conditions for young people
at all.

Not surprisingly, educational achievement in the district has been and still
is low. Most of the students fail to meet the state's minimum learning goals,
only about half graduate high school, "and many who manage to graduate
are ill-prepared for skilled jobs, college, or meaningful participation in a democratic society," Freeman wrote (*Lewis E. v. Spagnolo* 1999). The 2002 dis-

trict report card showed only 14.6% of the graduating class of 2002 had passing scores on the American College Test (ACT) Assessment.

An oversight panel created by the state reported in 2001 that although the East St. Louis district had been "saved from financial 'insolvency,' " it continued "to be academically troubled and one of the lowest performing school districts in the state." The panel attributed problems to local governance and to a "minority population . . . among the highest in any large urban district [that] requires many special services and unique approaches to the teaching program," and concluded that current funding is adequate (Financial Oversight Panel for East St. Louis School District 2001). An Education Funding Advisory Board (2002) created by the Illinois General Assembly issued a report in 2002 that called for minor changes in the distribution of state aid to public schools that, it said, should create a "leveling up effect" (17).

Accountability, State Obligation, and Public Responsibility

Recent studies suggest test-driven accountability policies not only are failing to foster student learning, but often are educationally counterproductive (Amrein & Berliner 2002a, 2002b; Heubert & Hauser 1999). Amrein and Berliner (2002b) assessed academic achievement in 27 states with high-stakes testing policies for grades 1 through 8 and in 18 states with make-or-break high school graduation exams, and concluded:

> After the implementation of high-stakes tests, nothing much happens. That is, no consistent effects across states were noted, scores seem to go up or down in a random pattern, after high-stakes tests are introduced. . . . [Also] after the implementation of high school graduation exams, academic achievement apparently decreases. . . . On balance, these analyses suggest that high-stakes tests and high school graduation exams may tend to inhibit the academic achievement of students, not foster their academic growth. (57–58)

Using National Assessment of Educational Progress scores as a measure of student learning, Amrein and Berliner (2002b) found that after high stakes were attached to tests, eighth-grade math achievement increased slightly, but fourth-grade math achievement decreased, and fourth-grade reading achievement stayed about the same overall. After states implemented high school graduation exams, scores on the ACT, the Scholastic Aptitude Test, and Advanced Placement exams declined overall.

Sadly, poor students and students of color seem to be suffering the most from these ill-conceived policies and practices. These students are failing make-or-break exams in disproportionate numbers, undoubtedly because they are being tested on material they have not been taught or been taught well

(Amrein & Berliner 2002a). Many, it seems, are opting to drop out of school rather than face tests they suspect they cannot pass (Amrein & Berliner 2002a), often with the encouragement of administrators seeking to exclude potentially low scores from their schools' tallies (McNeil 2000, Orel 2003).

What happens to these students? Certainly they face the bleakest of job prospects. In 1999, during a celebrated economic boom, only 54% of young people 16 to 24 years old who lacked a high school diploma or a General Equivalency Diploma (GED) certificate (and also were not in school) had jobs, compared to 75% of high school graduates and almost 89% of four-year-college graduates. For young African-Americans, the prospects were even worse. Less than a quarter of those 16 to 24 years old who were not in school and lacked a diploma or GED had full-time work (Herbert 2001).

Of course, not everyone views statistics like these with alarm. From one perspective, the fact that some students are not graduating and consequently are not faring well in a competitive (and, as I write, shrinking) job market proves the strength of the standards. If everyone could reach them, how high would they be? The judge in the high-profile court case focused on high-stakes testing in Texas spoke for many when he argued that "receipt of an education that does not meet some minimal standards is an adverse impact just as surely as failure to receive a diploma" (*GI Forum v. TEA* 2000, 13). From this perspective, the failures prove the success of the policy: standards have been established and upheld.

Yet, the means to this end of upholding standards is production of failure, using young people as instruments. In a study of newly legislated policies in Georgia designed to end "social promotion," Livingston and Livingston (2002) predict that 35% to 50% of all fourth, sixth, and eighth graders in economically declining rural counties, a quarter of which "fall into the 'all-Black' school system category," will be denied promotion to the next grade. This practice almost certainly will increase future dropout rates, albeit at a significant cost saving to the state. Livingston and Livingston (2002) raise the question pointedly:

> Is this legislation really intended to improve education or is it a strategy to reduce the State's financial obligation to the rural poor? It is clear that failing masses of poor children will not improve pedagogy because punishing children with retention does not change teaching. What we do know is that the association between retention and dropping out is noted consistently throughout educational research. . . . Because these 39 counties are very poor, and the tax base available for public schools is small, the State of Georgia compensates for this revenue deficiency by making exceptionally large contributions to these counties. Thus, while not stated as policy, it cannot be ignored that the CRCT [Criterion Referenced Competency Test Results] will most likely save the State a considerable amount of money by reducing the number of students in school in these counties.

A similar question, of course, could be raised about many other states' willingness to pay for the schooling of poor children, especially in times like ours when states across the nation are struggling to cope with a weak economy and with the consequences of years of tax cuts primarily benefiting the wealthiest. "The dirty little secret of the nation is that we do not wish to spend our money on other people's children—and the poor are the other people" (Proefriedt 2002, 8). To Proefriedt's assertion I would add that in the absence of a broad public commitment to public education, courts cannot be counted on to step forward in any clear or reliable way to force political leaders to look out for poor children. Legal interpretations of state obligation matter tremendously, but go only so far. Indeed, "Law books are filled with wonderful paper victories which have never been implemented" (Karp 1995, 25) in the absence of the requisite political will.

As the employment statistics just cited suggest, schooling has become almost the only path to a job that pays a living wage, and such jobs in turn have become almost the only path to social respect and any measure of economic security. Most of the young people who do not graduate high school "lack basic job skills as well as solid literacy and numbers proficiencies, and they are neither working nor looking for jobs. They are not in vocational training. They are not in manufacturing. They are not part of the information age. They are not included in the American conversation" (Jack Wuest, quoted in Herbert 2001). Given these social stakes, state accountability to students—versus school accountability to taxpayers—becomes critical.

Kozol (1991) concluded his outcry against "savage inequalities" in the funding and school conditions he documented across the country with an appeal to a consciousness of fairness and relationship:

> Surely there is enough for everyone within this country. It is a tragedy that these good things are not more widely shared. All our children ought to be allowed a stake in the enormous richness of America. Whether they were born to poor white Appalachians or to wealthy Texans, to poor black people in the Bronx or to rich people in Manhasset, they are all quite wonderful and innocent when they are small. We soil them needlessly. (233)

Words of outrage evoking a similar consciousness of fairness and relationship can be found in the legal discourse on accountability today. DeGrasse spoke of a "covenant broken" in New York (*Campaign for Fiscal Equity v. State* 2001, 110). Freeman protested that the majority in Illinois had "nail[ed] the door shut" to plaintiffs seeking some modicum of educational opportunity, without considering the effect "abhorrent physical conditions have on schoolchildren" (*Lewis E. v. Spagnolo* 1999). In Ohio, Sweeney asked rhetorically, "Can we say that the children in poor, rural, or urban areas have been given the same opportunities as their peers who happen to be blessed with the good fortune of living in wealthy districts with a high property tax base?" (*DeRolph III* 2001, 100). In other words, is our collective conscience clean?

These sentiments have not been turned into law, however. The significance of the ruling in New York is not yet clear. Although the court-ordered remedy is limited to New York City, the court ruling sends the message that the state cannot shirk its constitutional responsibility simply because it is expensive. At the same time, as the Ohio case makes clear, a court order does not guarantee a political response. Poor children in Ohio arguably remain the pawns in an ongoing tug-of-war between the State Supreme Court, the state legislature, and the governor, and poor children in Illinois seemingly have been thrown a small bone, or perhaps only an empty promise thereof.

Let me conclude with two related thoughts. First, the fundamental moral issues involved in the battle against an alleged lack of accountability ought not be evaded with a vague discourse of upholding standards, likely no more than a cover for a far more concrete agenda of reigning in state obligation to the poor in the interest of directing state resources elsewhere. In the decade since Kozol (1991) made his impassioned plea for a heightened consciousness of intergenerational responsibility, states across the nation have made promotion and graduation more difficult. At the same time, viable employment in jobs paying a living wage has been all but closed to people without a high school diploma. As Price (quoted in Koch 1999) suggests and as many of those sitting on our state courts also realize, with these higher stakes comes a greater responsibility for funding meaningful educational opportunity— funding in the broadest sense of the word, of supporting and making something possible. Although more money surely does not guarantee better schooling, demanding more of young people (and their teachers) without providing real opportunity is grossly unfair.

Secondly, even if meaningful educational opportunity was funded in all its complexity, even if courts nationwide required states to do this, what of those young people who still could not or would not jump through the hoops of accountability? In his critique of the assumptions underlying the public debate on standards, testing, and accountability, William Proefriedt (2001) tells this story, from a biography of Lyndon Johnson:

> When he was a very young boy living on a farm with his parents, his closest playmate was a Mexican-American boy named Huisso. Young Lyndon wanted to race on horseback with Huisso. But Huisso's horse was thin and weak. Johnson took feed from his own bins and doubled the intake of Huisso's horse in an effort to make him stronger for the race. Twice they raced, and Johnson's horse won easily. "So we tried one more time, and Huisso pushed his horse hard as he had ever pushed anything. This time the horse seemed to be moving much faster, but in the middle of the race it simply slipped out from under him. It had collapsed. It was dead. It was too much, I guess, too much running, too much food, too much care. It just didn't seem fair after all we had done."

Proefriedt shares his own feelings about the narrative:

> It's an un-American story. It breaks with the whole sense of future possibility that is so much a part of the American dream. . . . It's a dangerous story because it might be used by those who would turn back the clock on whatever efforts the nation is presently making for the educational opportunity of our poorest children. It is a troubling story, to me, because however much I want to believe in the infinite possibilities for every American child, I keep seeing that image of Huisso's dead horse.

I too am haunted by this prophetic image. Forced to compete in contests not made for them, many young people are suffering and will continue to suffer sometimes terrible consequences.

The public as well as legal discourse on accountability need to be broadened or enriched to include consideration of this reality of socially constructed failure and of the older generation's responsibility to young people who cannot or will not—in any case, do not—follow a standardized academic path. Does the older generation simply wash its hands, having done its job of certifying who does and does not deserve access to the world of viable employment? Young people pay the price for the widespread but rarely spoken beliefs about human potential and deserving that run just below the surface in the public discourse on accountability and the policies, practices, and court decisions it has spawned. Our systems of school accountability gain moral legitimacy from the belief that anyone can make it, if he or she simply tries. The corollary, of course, is that anyone who doesn't lacks the requisite will power or strength of character. Such a belief comes at a cost: "Our sense of solidarity with our fellow citizens is lost by the wayside. We set our standards, assume some moral deficiency in those who cannot meet them, and consign them to a well-deserved poverty" (Proefriedt 2001).

The public discourse on accountability does not reckon with such fundamental moral questions as the relationship between those who set the standards of accountability and those who fail to meet them. Instead, it focuses narrowly on the relationship between schools and taxpayers and all too often takes as the measure of accountability the mere act of reporting out the test scores of schools and students. In a sharp critique of the decision in the high-stakes testing case in Texas, Rachel Moran (2000) warns of the costs of such evasion: "High-stakes tests cannot work miracles in failing systems. The examinations are a yardstick and, yes, even a stick, but they are not a magic wand. And, unlike a television game show, America cannot conveniently arrange for those who fail the tests to disappear, nor can its responsibilities to these children be promptly forgotten." A consciousness of separation, of disconnection, of us and them, evades the fundamental responsibility one generation has to the next—to those who are younger, less experienced, and more vulnerable in a society that demands we prove our worth.

Courts clearly have a role to play in the ongoing struggle for equal educational opportunity. However, there is no guarantee that courts will hold a state legislature's feet to the fire, and plenty of evidence that they often do not. Ultimately, the public must affirm or create the intergenerational bonds of care and connection that could and should give rise to a meaningful concept of accountability in matters of schooling. The stakes have been raised for students across the board, but supports for learning remain tied to highly inequitable and in many places wholly inadequate systems of funding. Fixing this problem will require more than hoping for the best from the courts, which all too often turn "away from the core of the matter" (Havel 1991, 15). At a minimum, responding to the problems of gross shortcomings in the provision of educational opportunity and of socially constructed failure will require a broad public consciousness of responsibility to young people, including and especially those harmed by systems of "accountability."

ACKNOWLEDGEMENT

I would like to thank Paul Edlund and two anonymous reviewers for their insights and very helpful comments on an earlier draft of this article.

NOTES

1. The language in these education clauses is generally vague and varies considerably, "from simple declarations that create a system of schools to broad assertions about the fundamental importance of education within the state" (Reed 2001, 12). State constitutions require Maryland, New Jersey, Ohio, Pennsylvania, and West Virginia to provide students with a "thorough and efficient" education whereas Indiana, Minnesota, North Carolina, Oregon, and South Dakota are to provide a "general and uniform" education throughout the state.

2. The suit charges that California has reneged on its constitutional obligation to oversee a statewide school system that provides even the rock-bottom necessities. Plaintiffs are neither asking the state to determine the cost of an adequate education nor seeking to eliminate disparities in per-pupil spending. Rather, "This suit returns to the oldest state function, which is to provide a minimal floor of educational provisions below which no school should drop. In the early 1900s, the state's major role was to ensure that all schools met a minimum floor. They inspected facilities, looked at toilets, and worried about teacher credentials" (Michael Kirst, quoted in Sandham 2000).

3. In 1997–1998, New York City spent $1,247 less per pupil, in state and local funds combined, than any other major school district in the state. From 1994 to 2000 New York City received only 34% to 35.7% of the total state aid, although 37% of all public school students in the state were enrolled in its schools (*Campaign for Fiscal Equity v. State* 2001).

4. Students in New York previously have been able to graduate either with a local diploma or with a Regents diploma, which requires a more rigorous program of study. Starting in spring 2003, students, with few exceptions, must pass five Regents exams to graduate.

5. The Appeals Brief Submitted by the State of New York can be retrieved from the Campaign for Fiscal Equity web site: http://www.cfequity.org/stateappeal8-13-01.html

REFERENCES

Advocacy Center for Children's Success with Standards. 2003, June 27. State by state. Retrieved from http://www.accessednetowrk.org

American Society of Civil Engineers. 2001. *Full Report Card for 2001*. Retrieved from http://www.asce.org/reportcard/index.cfm

Amrein, Audrey L., and Berliner, David C. 2002a. "High-Stakes Testing, Uncertainty, and Student Learning." *Education Policy Analysis Archives, 10*(18). Retrieved from http://epaa.asu.edu/epaa./v10n18/

Amrein, Audrey L., and Berliner, David C. 2002b. *The Impact of High-Stakes Tests on Student Academic Performance: An Analysis of NAEP Results in States with High-Stakes Tests and ACT, SAT, and AP Test Results in States with High School Graduation Exams*. Report No. EPSL-0211-126. Tempe, AZ: Arizona State University, Education Policy Research Unit. Retrieved from http://www.greatlakescenter.org/pub/H-S%20Impact%20final.pdf

Anyon, Jean. 1997. *Ghetto Schooling: A Political Economy of Urban Educational Reform*. New York Teachers College Press.

Campaign for Fiscal Equity v. State of New York, 719 N.Y.S. 2d. 475. 2001. Retrieved from http://www.cfequity.org/decision/html

Campaign for Fiscal Equity v. State of New York, 2002. Retrieved from http://www.cfequity.org/decision/html

Campaign for Fiscal Equity v. State of New York, 2003. Retrieved from http://www.cfequity.org/decision/html

Council of Great City Schools. 2001. *Beating the Odds: A City-By-City Analysis of the Student Performance and Achievement Gaps on State Assessments*. Washington, DC: Author.

DeRolph v. State, 97 Ohio St.3d. 2002. (*DeRolph V*)

DeRolph v. State, 93 Ohio St.3d. 2001. (*DeRolph III*)

DeRolph v. State, 88 Ohio St.3d. 2000. (*DeRolph II*). Retrieved from http://www.bricker.com/attserv/practice/education/schoolfund/briefs/990570.htm

Drummond, Suzanne E. 2000. "Déjà vu: The State of School Funding in Ohio After *DeRolph II*." *University of Cincinnati Law Review, 68*: 435–461.

Education Funding Advisory Board. 2002, October. *Recommendations for systemic reform of funding for elementary and secondary education in Illinois*. Report prepared by Author.

The Education Trust. 2002, August 8. "The Funding Gap: Low-Income and Minority Students Receive Fewer Dollars." *Education Trust Data Bulletin*. Retrieved from http://www.edtrust.org/main/documents/investment.pdf

Financial Oversight Panel for East St. Louis School District No. 189. 2002, September. *Annual Report to the State Superintendent*.

Gewertz, Catherine. 2001, Jan. 10. "California Governor Blames Districts for Poor Conditions." *Education Week, 20*(16), p. 23.

GI Forum v. Texas Education Agency, 87 F. Sup 2d 667 (W.D. Tex. 2000).

Grossman, Ron. 1997. "The East St. Louis Challenge: Whose Job is Education?" *Chicago Tribune*, pp. 1, 15.

Havel, Vaclav. 1991. "On Evasive Thinking." In Paul Wilson (Ed.), *Open Letters: Selected Writings 1965–1990* (pp. 10–24). New York: Knopf.

Herbert, Bob. 2001, Sept. 3. "In America; On the Way to Nowhere." *The New York Times*.

Heubert, Jay P., and Hauser, Robert M. (Eds.). 1999. *High Stakes: Testing for Tracking, Promotion, and Graduation*. National Research Council, Committee on Appropriate Test Use. Washington, DC: National Academy Press.

Jerald, Craig D. 1998, Jan. 8. "By the Numbers: The Urban Picture." In *Quality Counts 1998* [special report]. *Education Week*. Can be retrieved from http://www.edweek/org/sreports/qc98

Karp, Stan. 1995. "Money, Schools, & Courts: State by State Battles against Inequality." *Z Magazine* (December): 25–29.

Koch, Kathy. 1999, December 10. "Reforming School Funding." *CQ Researcher, 9*(46).

Kozol, Jonathan. 1991. *Savage Inequalities: Children in America's Schools*. New York: Crown.

Lewis E. v. Spagnolo, 83382 (Ill. S. Ct. 1999). Retrieved from http://www.state.il.us/court/Opinions/SupremeCourt/1999/April/Opinions/HTML/83382.htm

Livingston, Donald R., and Livingston, Sharon M. 2002. Failing Georgia: The case against the ban on social promotion. *Education Policy Analysis Archives, 10*(49). Retrieved from http://epaa.asu.edu/epaa/v10n49/

McNeil, Linda M. 2000. *Contradictions of School Reform: Educational Costs of Standardized Testing*. New York: Routledge.

McUsic, Molly S. 1999. "The Law's Role in the Distribution of Education: The Promises and Pitfalls of School Finance Legislation." In Jay P. Heubert (Ed.), *Law and School Reform: Six Strategies of Promoting Educational Equity* (pp. 88–159). New Haven: Yale University Press.

Moran, Rachel. 2000. "Sorting and Reforming: High-Stakes Testing in the Public Schools." *Akron Law Review, 34*(1): 107–135.

Orel, Steve. 2003. Left behind in Birmingham: 522 pushed-out students. In R. Cossett Lent & G. Pipkin (Eds.), *Silent no more: Voice of courage in Americans schools* (pp. 1–14). Portsmouth, NH: Heinemann.

Park, Jennifer. 2003, March 19. Hot topics: School finance. Retrieved from http://www.edweek.com

Petronicolos, Loucas, and New, William S. 1999. "Anti-Immigrant Legislation, Social Justice, and the Right to Equal Educational Opportunity." *American Educational Research Journal, 36*(3): 373–408.

Proefriedt, William A. 2002, December 2. "Opening doors." *America, 187*(18): 6–9.

Proefriedt, William A. 2001, July 11. "Dead Horses, Buried Assumptions." *Education Week, 20*(42), pp. 48, 50–51.

Quality Counts 2002: Building Blocks for Success. 2002. "Resources: Equity." *Education Week*.

Quality Counts 2003. 2003. "Resources: Equity." *Education Week*.

Reed, Douglas S. 2001. *On Equal Terms: The Constitutional Politics of Educational Opportunity*. Princeton: Princeton University Press.

Reid, Karla S. 2003, March 19. "School aid is casualty of Ohio's budget war." *Education Week, 22*(16), p. 13.

Richard, Alan. 2001, Nov. 14. "Ohio Justices Set to Revisit Funding Case." *Education Week, 21*(4), p. 24.

Richard, Alan. 2002, March 27. "News in Brief: A State Capitals Roundup. Ohio School Finance Case." *Education Week, 21*(28), p. 21.

Sandham, Jessica L. 2000, May 24. "California Schools Lack Basics, Suit Alleges." *Education Week, 19*(37), pp. 1, 29.

San Antonio Independent School District v. Rodriguez, 411 U.S. 1. 1973.

Taylor, William L. 2000, Nov. 15. "Standards, Tests, and Civil Rights." *Education Week, 20*(11), pp. 40–41, 56.

U.S. General Accounting Office. 1996, June. *School Facilities: America's Schools Report Differing Conditions*. GAO/HEHS-96-103.

Verstegen, Deborah A. 2002. "Financing the New Adequacy: Towards New Models of State Finance Systems That Support Standards Based Reforms." *Journal of Education Finance, 27*(3): 749–781.

Williams et al. v. State of California. Complaint retrieved from http://www.aclunc.org/students/ca-school-complaint.html

Zehr, Mary. 2003, May 28. "Ohio Court Declares End to DeRolph School Funding Case." *Education Week, 22*(38): 15.

3

▼▼▼▼▼▼▼

Democracy's High School?
Social Change and American Secondary
Education in the Post-Conant Era*

John L. Rury

James Bryant Conant issued his famous report *The American High School Today* in 1959, giving voice to a clear and influential reaffirmation of the comprehensive secondary school. Just two years later he published another study, perhaps somewhat less influential, in *Slums and Suburbs* (1961), and five years after that he completed his final report on secondary education, *The Comprehensive High School* (1967). Two of these books were about the nation as a whole, but especially about the small and mid-sized communities that most Americans considered a cultural norm; *Slums and Suburbs* focused on the country's major metropolitan areas—big cities and the communities around them. A scientist who served as president of Harvard for twenty years, followed by tours as U.S. High Commissioner and ambassador to West Germany, Conant was among the period's most visible intellectual figures, and he dedicated the closing years of his public life to educational reform. His vision in these works makes an interesting point of departure for consideration of the forces that have shaped the American high school in the latter half of the twentieth century.[1] The question such a treatment raises is whether the comprehensive high school, and the democratic ideal that it represented at the time of Conant's reports, is possible in a society as divided by race, social class, and culture as the United States is today. This is particularly true when one examines secondary education in metropolitan America, where about 80 percent of American youth live and learn at the start of the twenty-first century (Fox, 1985; Goldsmith and Blakely, 1992).

The comprehensive high school, as defined by the Cardinal Principles Report of 1918, was premised on the idea of the common school (Hampel, 1986; Krug, 1972). This was a point that impressed Conant and that he emphasized in each of these books. In *The American High School Today* he wrote that the comprehensive high school was "characteristic of our society" and represented the nation's "devotion to ideals of equality of opportunity and equality of status" (p. 8). Taking the point even further two years later, he declared that "in small independent cities and consolidated rural districts the widely comprehensive high school functions as an effective instrument of democracy." Even if they were tracked into different courses of study, the students would be bound together in a common core of subject areas and in the social and cultural life of the high school as an institution. Moreover, he specified that all students should take a special "Problems of Democracy" course, featuring a cross-section of the student body, with ample opportunity for discussion and debate (Conant, 1959, 1967). The popularity of Conant's books suggested that this was an image of the high school that resonated deeply with many Americans. As historians have noted, the comprehensive high school became a model for school districts across the country, including those in large cities (Cremin, 1961; Herbst, 1996; Angus and Mirel, 1999). It was a break with the past and with prevailing practices in other countries, which had been characterized by specialization in secondary education. The egalitarian and democratic ethos of the public high school, at least through much of the twentieth century, was a peculiarly American cultural artifact (Krug, 1972; Goldin, 2001).

Amy Gutmann's *Democratic Education* (1999), a widely cited examination of educational principles and practices, argues that democracy is the product of deliberative practices that must be carefully taught and nurtured if they are to be sustained. She identified the development of democratic character as a fundamentally moral enterprise and a process that is as inherently difficult to effect as it is critical to endeavor. Within schools, democracy cannot be reduced to a topic in the academic curriculum or an object of extracurricular activities. Gutmann suggests that it must permeate the institution, infusing relations between teachers and students, affecting the students themselves, and extending outward to the larger community. Democracy demands diversity and requires deliberation and discussion to flourish. It also enjoins authority, particularly in schools. Democracy is not license, and it entails a responsibility to community and to humanity. These principles, articulated at considerable length by Gutmann and a wide range of other scholars, are deeply rooted in American culture and have a long pedigree in educational thought. They are typically identified with John Dewey and progressive education but extend back to Horace Mann, the common school, and the educational writings of the early republic (Pratte, 1988; Kaestle, 1983). Conant's vision of the comprehensive high school reflected this tradition, particularly his concern with ensuring diversity in the student body and requiring a course that allowed students an opportunity for deliberation about the problems of society. But in the years following his articulation of these principles, they seemingly became ever more difficult to sustain. This trend troubled Conant profoundly, and it helps explain why he devoted so much time and energy to attempting to reform secondary education.

As indicated earlier, of course, the comprehensive high school also was rooted in a principle of curricular differentiation. At the same time that it represented the ideals of equality and democracy, it acknowledged the fact that individuals were destined to play a variety of roles in the larger society. This too was appealing to Conant and to other devotees of all-inclusive secondary education. It represented a practical solution to the problem of varying interests and abilities in a large and diverse society, and linked the institution to the labor market. At the same time that the high school prepared the most academically gifted students, it would also provide vocational training for those destined to menial careers. Conant favored ability grouping within subjects over forming explicit "tracks" to distinguish these groups of students, and he argued that some subjects—such as civics—ought to be taught in common. But there could be little doubt that the comprehensive high school was supposed to separate students along curricular lines, in accordance with what educational leaders expected to be their eventual occupational roles in society (Conant, 1959). This practice might be described, in historical terms, as a legacy of social efficiency, of the Progressive Era impulse to use the schools to assign students to various social strata (Kliebard, 1995). By the time Conant wrote his books the practice was well-established in American secondary education and so familiar that it occasioned little commentary.

A final theme in Conant's vision of the comprehensive ideal in secondary education, functionally linked to the first two, was school size. This too was considered a practical matter. Conant did not believe that small high schools could produce high academic standards or that they could enroll enough students to provide differentiated curricular options. As a consequence, he was an enthusiastic proponent of school consolidation, particularly in rural areas where small schools were most commonplace. He felt that large high schools, with as many as a thousand or more students, provided the diversity necessary for academic specialization and for building the inclusive democratic ethos of the comprehensive high school ideal (Conant, 1959). For Conant and his supporters, there was never any doubt that bigger was better, at least within certain limits.

These were the principal features of the comprehensive high school, as offered by Conant and adopted by school districts across the country. The question today is just how these ideas have been treated by history and how the comprehensive vision has changed—at least in practice—in the four decades since Conant published *Slums and Suburbs*. The discussion that follows features an examination of historical contingencies that have affected the democratic vision of secondary education articulated by Conant and elaborated by Amy Gutmann and other commentators.[2] In particular, I focus on the question of race and its impact on the schools, the development of a pervasive youth culture that accompanied the rise of the high school, and changes in the U.S. economy over the past several decades. Each of these developments posed a challenge to Conant's idea of a democratic high school. I also consider the major reports and commentaries on the high school published since Conant's own reports. The methodology employed in this article is that of historical exposition and critical analysis, identifying points of discontinuity with certain principles and practices in the wake of social change on a national scale. In this way it is possible to see the road that American high schools have traveled in the past forty years, at least as regards the question of democratic education. Conant's vision of a uniquely American form of secondary school has grown inherently problematic since the middle of the twentieth century. Examining the historical record is indispensable to understanding why.

RACE AND THE COMPREHENSIVE HIGH SCHOOL

Conant's 1959 report, which reaffirmed the ideal of the comprehensive high school, did not address the question of race, but in the years following its publication racial inequity became the overriding issue in the nation's principal urban school districts. Racism came to affect the spatial organization of cities in ways that other facets of social organization had not. Blacks were highly segregated from Whites, a feature of urban life that was enforced with violence as well as with legal and quasi-legal action (Massey and Denton, 1993). Educational resources, of course, were also spatially distributed, a point that Conant recognized in writing *Slums and Suburbs*. Such inequality, as he acknowledged, posed perhaps the greatest challenge to the comprehensive high school as a fundamental institution of American civilization.

Much of this history is well known, of course. World War II had barely ended when a grand migration to suburbia began in most of the nation's largest cities. Pressured by severe housing shortages in the central cities and encouraged by public policies that stimulated road building and guaranteed cheap private transportation, Americans began flocking to newly opened developments on the fringes of the urban core areas. Between 1940 and 1960, the country's suburban population grew by some 27 million, or more than twice the numerical increase in the population of central cities during the same period. As a result, the share of metropolitan area population living in central cities dropped from nearly 63 percent in 1940 to 51 percent in 1960. The decline continued thereafter, and by 1980 only 40 percent of the country's metropolitan area population lived in central cities, with the rest in surrounding suburbs (Fox, 1985; Jackson, 1985; Teaford, 1990).

Migrants from central cities were disproportionately young, middle class, and upwardly mobile. The availability of Veterans Administration and Federal Housing Authority loans in the decades immediately following World War II, along with housing shortages in central cities, made the suburbs especially attractive to new families. The expanding economy provided a stable source of employment, particularly in downtown office complexes but also in rapidly developing suburban retail and manufacturing centers. A postwar marriage boom added more than ten million new households within a decade. And the baby boom made relatively cheap homes in suburban subdivisions difficult to resist (Palen, 1992; Fox, 1985).

Suburban migrants were also overwhelmingly White. By 1960, when the suburban population roughly equaled that of the central cities, less than 5 percent of suburbanites were African American (Goldsmith and Blakely, 1992). Thirty years later they were fewer than 10 percent and were largely segregated in separate suburban communities. This was partly because of subtle but effective practices of discrimination that discouraged Blacks from buying homes in these areas. As a group, Whites were allowed to move into these new burgeoning, affluent communities on the edge of the expanding metropolitan areas. And as they moved to suburbia, the populations of the country's central cities became older, poorer, and darker in complexion (Massey and Denton, 1993; Teaford, 1990; Jackson, 1985).

The proportion of central city population that is White has diminished each decade since 1950, falling from more than 80 percent to about a third in the 1990s. While the Black population increased rapidly in the 1950s and 1960s, leveling off at about a third of central city residents, the number of Hispanics has increased significantly since the 1970s. As William Julius Wilson has noted, poverty levels increased significantly among all groups of city residents in the closing decades of the twentieth century, but particularly among Blacks. Whereas some 11 percent of central city residents were poor in the mid-1970s and 18 percent of central city Blacks, by 1990 the figures had jumped to almost 20 percent and 34 percent, respectively (Wilson, 1987; Goldsmith and Blakely, 1992).

It was the early stages of this process of change that Conant confronted at the end of the 1950s. The decades following World War II witnessed a profound transformation of American metropolitan areas, creating a new cultural geography defined by race and income. This had a dramatic effect on many aspects of life in the nation's major metropolitan areas. For large numbers of urban and suburban residents there were few shared public spaces and social experiences. Stereotypical images fostered by the development of mass media created an atmosphere of mistrust and fear (Fox, 1985). And one area where this process had an almost immediate impact was public education.

Beginning in the 1950s, questions of equity in Black and White schooling became major policy issues facing urban school districts (Rury, 1999; Kantor and Brenzel, 1993). In the nation's urban high schools, the question of race came to be a source of great dissension, a point of differentiation that defined the institution in new ways. The 1954 Brown decision helped to put schools at the very center of the emerging national civil rights movement. In large metropolitan areas this led to conflict over desegregation and equality, initially in the South but eventually in other regions also (Hochschild, 1985). In the major urban areas, the impact of these issues was decisive.

In the following decade the conflicts escalated as the Black population of urban school districts approached a majority, particularly in large northern cities. Despite protests, schools remained highly segregated, closely mirroring patterns of residential exclusion in urban areas (Orfield et al., 1996; Rury, 1999). This was clearly evident in secondary education. As early as 1963, for instance, high schools in Chicago were highly segregated by race, largely because of residential segregation (Havighurst, 1964). In all but four schools, the student body was nearly 90 percent or more Black or White, despite the fact that the district's population was almost evenly divided between the two groups. The vast majority of predominantly Black schools, moreover, reported low achievement scores and high dropout rates. This pattern was evident in other large cities in this period (Harrison, 1972). The movement of Blacks into northern urban school districts was marked by high levels of segregation—or racial isolation—and big Black-White differences in educational outcomes (Mirel, 1993; Stolee, 1993; Wells and Crain, 1997). The situation did not bode well for Conant's vision of the comprehensive high school.

This, of course, is what led Conant to write *Slums and Suburbs*. Given his inherently conservative disposition, he was hardly a proponent of wholesale desegregation, and when he visited Chicago to collect data for *The American High School Today* he chose not to publish school-level statistics to avoid the question of racial inequities (Hampel, 1986). The differences that Conant observed in writing *Slums and Suburbs*, however, gave him pause in advocating the comprehensive high school as a model for big city school districts. Yet he had no answer to the dilemma posed by the disparities in educational and social resources on either side of the urban-suburban divide. And the differences would grow more stark in the years to come (Wells and Crain, 1997; Kozol, 1991). In Chicago, non-Hispanic Whites were less than 20 percent of the student body by 1980, and in 1990 they were barely 10 percent. Numbers such as these made meaningful integration a virtual impossibility, particularly in the system's sixty large high schools (Kleppner, 1984; Chicago Tribune, 1999; Chicago Assembly, 1998). The ideal of the comprehensive high school functioning as a microcosm of American society was inconceivable in these circumstances.

The story elsewhere was similar. By the time the 1971 Keyes decision opened the door to federally mandated desegregation in northern and western urban school districts, the term "white flight" had already become a part of the national vocabulary. The Millikan I decision just two years later foreclosed the possibility of legally mandated desegregation plans across urban-suburban district lines. And as a result, the racial profile of schools on either side of the big city district lines became increasingly stark. By the 1980s a small minority of urban public school students were White, and an even smaller—though growing—portion of suburban students were Black (Orfield et al., 1996). In the meantime, the portion of the nation's population living outside metropolitan areas continued to decline (Goldsmith and Blakely, 1992). If Conant had hoped that schools in nonmetropolitan communities would provide the model for others to follow, this became less tenable with time.

These changes had a particularly big impact on the culture of American high schools. As secondary education in major metropolitan areas became characterized by a sharp pattern of racial segregation, it was closely associated in the public mind with perceptions about the quality of education (Wells and Crain, 1997). This was evident in the early 1960s in large northern cities and became ever more pronounced as the desegregation struggles in public education reached a peak in the 1970s (Orfield, 1978; Hochschild, 1985). Of course, Conant had examined extant patterns of segregation in *Slums and Suburbs*, but the differences between urban and suburban high schools grew more striking in the decades that followed. By the end of the 1980s there were relatively few public high schools in large cities with a significant number of White students, and few schools that could be classified as academically excellent (Bettis, 1996; Mora, 1997; Sexton and Nickel, 1992). In short, urban and suburban school districts became ever more dissimilar in the years following the protracted struggle over desegregation (Stone, 1998).

In the four decades since Conant wrote *The American High School Today*, the common school experience in secondary education appears to have become disconcertingly elusive. Gutmann (1999) has asserted that the distribution of schooling is a critical dimension of democracy in education. Even more, she has argued that racial segregation represents a profound challenge to the realization of democratic principles. "If children continue to be distributed among schools according to neighborhoods," she wrote, "the education of Black students will continue to be limited in ways that violate the democratic standard of nonexclusion" (p. 162). Residential segregation, which has changed relatively little with the growth of large minority populations in American cities, has made it difficult to realize a level of heterogeneity in many high schools student bodies that would meet Gutmann's standard

(Orfield et al., 1996; Rumberger and Willms, 1992). Even when secondary schools have managed to achieve greater diversity, moreover, race and ethnicity have proved to be profoundly divisive issues, making it difficult to sustain the deliberative processes so essential to democratic education (Cusick, 1983; Grant, 1988; Peshkin, 1991). As metropolitan areas have grown in size and complexity, these patterns of differentiation have maintained their salience; in fact, the divisions are most stark in the largest and most complex urban areas (Orfield et al., 1996). If the comprehensive high school was supposed to bring students from different backgrounds together, it certainly has not succeeded in accomplishing this in the nation's major metropolitan regions, at least as concerns race and social class (Mora, 1997; Wells and Crain, 1997). In this respect, and in these settings, Conant's vision certainly has not been fulfilled.

The Rise of a Youth Culture

As the high school became more popular it inevitably reached a wider range of Americans, including larger numbers of working-class youth. This was a part of Conant's vision of a school that brought youth from various social classes and groups together. He believed that the high school should be a universal American institution, even if he did not feel everyone should study the same subjects. Statistical evidence points to the success of his arguments. High school enrollments climbed dramatically, from less than six million in 1950 to more than thirteen million in 1970 (National Center for Educational Statistics, 1995). Such growth was a consequence both of the baby boom and improved rates of high school attendance (West, 1996). By the end of the 1950s, more than 80 percent of American teenagers attended high school, making it virtually a universal experience for the first time in American history (Angus and Mirel, 1999). This had a number of important consequences.

One was the fact that adolescents as a social group were segregated from the rest of society for a significant amount of time each week, through most of the year, in institutions where they constituted the vast majority of the population. Because of age grading and the differentiated structure of most high schools, they did not even have systematic contact with youth in different age groups, such as young adults over 18 or 19. This social exclusion contributed to the development of what James S. Coleman described as the "adolescent society" in this period, based largely in the American high school (Coleman, 1961, 1965). And it was an important component of what many observers of American life at the time referred to as the "youth culture" (Cohen, 1997).

High schools were a critical component of the development of this phenomenon. An astute early observer of American youth, Coleman argued that the social world of high school adolescence was defined by status groups associated with different sorts of school activities. In general, he found that athletics played an especially important role in the social life of high school students, especially for boys. Academic performance was less important, although it may have gained significance as students progressed through school (Coleman, 1961). Following Coleman's lead, other studies examined the influence of the larger youth culture, which was commercially directed by record companies, the radio, television and print media, and a host of other enterprises. Adolescents had preferred distinctive forms of music for several decades, and dancing had been popular with the rise of dating as a distinctive teenage activity in the 1920s and 1930s (Palladino, 1996; Modell, 1989). But the rise of the youth culture in the 1950s was even more pervasive and telling in its impact on the larger society. In part, its influence was due to the development of universal high school enrollment, something virtually all youth came to have in common.

In the 1950s new forms of teenage entertainment came into being, with the rapid rise of rock'n'roll music as a popular idiom. New dances came into play also, and youth culture became associated with a variety of new forms of consumption. Fast cars, cigarette smoking, alcohol, and the hint of sexual promiscuity came to represent the new youth culture and to distinguish it from the clean-cut images of youth from earlier decades. Despite attempts at censorship, these images were spread through the media, including radio, the movies, and increasingly ubiquitous television. It is doubtful that any more than a minority of youth actually engaged in such activities routinely; but even for those who did not, the idea of rebellion against adult mores exerted a powerful appeal (Gilbert, 1986; Hawes and Hiner, 1985). And it was an impulse that would exert even greater influence in the decades to follow.

It was not long before yet other forms of self-expression became evident among adolescents, and a struggle ensued over control of the cultural atmosphere in public high schools. If music and movies were important features of youth culture, clothing may have been even more momentous; it represented one of the first fields of conflict about student autonomy. High school students in earlier decades had dressed like miniature adults, boys wearing coats and ties and girls dresses or skirts, behavior often governed by codes of varying degrees of formality. As the number of students in school increased, these standards of dress began to be challenged. One study in Milwaukee found that by the latter 1950s high school students had shed coats, ties, and dresses in favor of slacks, shirts, and sweaters (Haubrich, 1993). In the 1960s these tendencies were extended even further, as ever more casual and provocative styles became fashionable. At the same time, trends in fashion came to reflect racially and ethnically linked tastes, further aggravating those divisions (Grant, 1988). There was resistance to these trends from faculty and administrators, but high school dress codes eventually became a subject of student protest and were eliminated in schools across the country (Sparks, 1983). By the 1970s jeans and t-shirts were the norm in many schools, and adolescent tastes were becoming a major force in the world of adult fashion (Davis, 1992; Palladino, 1996).

At about the same time there was a dramatic shift in sexual mores, with a corresponding change in teenage behavior. Rates of nonmarital sex among teenagers increased significantly in the early 1970s, jumping from less than 20 percent to more than a third. Sexuality became a prominent feature of popular culture and a central aspect of the rapidly evolving high school-based adolescent society. By the latter 1970s there was a movement to make sex education a major element of the secondary curriculum (Chilman, 1978; Esman, 1990; Palladino, 1996). At the same time teenage pregnancy had become a major issue in national politics, and widespread perceptions of moral decline in American youth contributed to the success of neoconservative politicians (Vinovskis, 1988).

These developments were abetted by a general movement to expand students' rights in high schools across the country. In 1969 the U.S. Supreme Court handed down its decision in the case *Tinker v. Des Moines Independent School District*, wherein it ruled that a suspension of two students for wearing black armbands to protest the Vietnam War represented a violation of their First Amendment rights (Zirkel, 1999). *Tinker* set off a wave of litigation that soon broadened the definition of self-expression to include everything from dress to hairstyles, to displays of affection on school premises. While not all such challenges to the conventional authority of schools were successful, educators found themselves on the defensive, forced to justify traditional policies and practices that had existed for generations (National Commission on the Reform of Secondary Education, 1973). The new legal standard became one of requiring an educational rationale for policies governing the behavior of students, and many school districts chose to minimize such measures rather than risk additional protests and potential litigation (Olson, 1972). These events helped to usher in a new era of permissiveness in the nation's high schools. As Gerald Grant argued in his poignant case study of a suburban high school, adult authority, once arguably the principal characteristic of these institutions, was at a historically low ebb (Grant, 1988).

All of these trends in the lives of youth coincided with the movement to consolidate and expand high schools across the country, which Conant had endorsed so enthusiastically. Published federal statistics indicate that the average size of public high schools more than doubled between 1950 and 1970, from about two hundred to nearly five hundred students. These figures probably understate the size of most schools, however, because of the large number of small rural districts included. Ernest Boyer, writing in the early 1980s, put the number of high schools at only about 16,000, far fewer than the government's count of 24,362, which would have made the average enrollment nearly 900 (Boyer, 1983). *High School and Beyond* data collected in the 1970s and 1980s corroborate this estimate, indicating that the typical public high school at that time had some 875 students and more than 40 percent had more than 900 (Bryk, Lee, and Holland, 1993). It was the larger schools, of course, that enrolled the majority of the nation's high school students and continue to do so today. These big institutions historically have been concentrated in urban areas, but many suburban districts also established large secondary schools as their teenage populations expanded in the postwar years. For most metropolitan youth, in that case, the institutional norm became a large, differentiated public high school. On the question of school size, Conant's arguments appear to have won the day.

Ironically, the development of larger high schools, with greater numbers of students and psychological distance between adolescents and adults, may have hastened the development of a school-based youth culture and the movement to expand student rights. In their analysis of high school size in the 1960s, Barker and Gump (1964) found that greater numbers of students were excluded from school activities in larger schools, a condition that contributed to more widespread alienation from the institution. More recent research has associated a loss of adult control in larger schools and a reduction in the degree of personalism in contact between students and adults. A number of research articles have argued that greater school size inhibits student learning, especially when it makes it difficult for adolescents and adults to communicate meaningfully (Haller, 1992; Sizer, 1996). This point was made emphatically by scholars comparing private—particularly Catholic—and public high schools. These authors reported that school size was a significant factor in accounting for the superior academic performance and school climate of private institutions (Bryk, Lee, and Holland, 1993; Coleman, Hoffer, and Kilgore, 1982). What is more, the moral authority of adults in these smaller schools was perceived to be much greater than in larger public institutions. Of course, the Catholic schools were largely sheltered from the litigation initiated with *Tinker*, but they did have to contend with developments in the larger youth culture. By and large, recent research suggests that they appear to have managed this task better than many of their counterparts in the public sector. Bigger, it turned out, was not always better, at least as regards the role of adult authority in the lives of high schools.

As Gutmann notes in *Democratic Education* (1999), adults play a potentially critical role in fostering and modeling the participatory and deliberative processes that are so vital to sustaining democratic principles in an educational setting. Democracy requires discipline in addition to individual or group expression and a willingness to abide by rules or conventions that are collectively determined. Gutmann points out that even the most democratic schools do not permit students to determine the curriculum or the basic structure of the school day. The very premise of schooling, after all, is that children have something to learn from adults, and it is the task of adults in such circumstances to serve as leaders and exemplars for the students. She quotes John Dewey in establishing a need for "control" and "habits of mind which secure social changes without introducing disorder" (p. 94). Democracy is not a license for unfettered self-expression, which often appeared to be the goal of the students' rights movement in the high schools (Grant, 1988). The appearance of the student movement in the 1960s may have provided an opportunity for enhancing democratic consideration, but the size and bureaucratic orientation of most public secondary schools made such a prospect remote. Once the issues had been defined in terms of litigation, the possibility of a deliberative process leading to a democratic resolution of the issue became even more distant.

The growing size of schools affected more than just adult authority; it also made it difficult for students to identify with the institution as a coherent community of interests. This seems to have been especially true in big cities, in schools with large minority student populations (Meier, 1996; Lee and Smith, 1997), but it was also evident in suburban institutions. The effects of such disaffection are evident in many recent studies. Pamela Bettis (1996) has described the lack of efficacy experienced by urban youth in large schools; Signithia Fordham (1996) has suggested that large all-Black high schools engender a student culture of resistance to academic achievement. In her perceptive analysis of student cultures in a suburban setting, *Jocks and Burnouts*, Penelope Eckert (1989) found a high level of disengagement among working-class youth, for whom the school had come to represent a point of negative reference. The development of overt student cultures of "resistance" in such settings was observed to have been assisted by the very size of the schools. Indeed, Eckert has reported that opposition appeared to decline as the size of the school decreased (p. 98). There is considerable evidence, on the other hand, that smaller schools—again, especially Catholic schools that foster a clear sense of community—have greater success with urban students (Greeley, 1982). Conant's insistence on the need for larger schools, in that case, may have contributed to some of the most difficult problems faced by American secondary education in recent years.

As Coleman and other observers have noted, youth culture often took the immediate community and its values as a point of departure. This accounted for the heavy value placed on athletics and other school activities valued by adults (Coleman, 1961). But with the social and economic differentiation of the metropolitan landscape, this emphasis on community values has resulted in a variegated adolescent culture, or, alternatively, a set of youth subcultures (Coleman, 1965). This also meant, of course, that school-based peer societies were defined by culturally distinct groups of youth. Even within the same school, questions of race and social class became important points of distinction, creating lines of differentiation that further compromised the democratic ideal of the institution (Peshkin, 1991). In this respect, the youth culture was hardly a force for democracy or egalitarian principles.

These issues represented a side of secondary education that many observers appear to have overlooked. They posed problems that Conant clearly had not anticipated; even Amy Gutmann has not addressed this dimension of democratic schooling. But everyone has responsibility in sustaining democracy, even students and their advocates. In the wake of the conflicts over student rights, adults and students alike resigned themselves to simply performing their socially assigned tasks, whether teaching and learning a given subject, fulfilling an administrative function, or becoming a better athlete. The idea of belonging to a coherent community of interests where important decisions are made through democratic deliberation was often abandoned altogether, even in schools where democratic traditions appear to have been quite strong (Grant, 1988). In the place of common deliberation emerged a peculiar contest of competing of coexisting interest groups, each pursuing its own goals in a setting defined by legal rights and obligations but with little sense of unity in purpose or underlying values (Boyer, 1983; Powell, Farrar, and Cohen, 1985). As Callan (1997) has noted, however, pluralism demands attention to common obligations to foster democratic values. This purpose too often was lost in the American high school that emerged from the period of the rising youth culture and student rights. Paradoxically, it was an institution that featured unprecedented levels of personal freedom, but a diminished comprehension of democratic education and its practice.

High Schools, Youth, and the Changing Urban Economy

Another important facet of urban life that changed in the postwar period was the economy and its relationship to the educational system. In the immediate postwar period, industrial jobs were plentiful, and it was the prospect of employment in the booming factories of the great northern cities that drew African Americans out of the South in the 1950s. Despite periodic downturns, the urban-industrial economy was flush during the 1950s but already showed signs of change in the following decade (Teaford, 1990). By the mid-1960s some observers already were warning that the demand for unskilled labor would be limited in the future, although their projections underestimated the rate of long-term change (Havighurst, 1966; Harrison, 1972). No one, however, anticipated the shifting relationship of education and employment that characterized the closing decades of the century.

The very idea of the comprehensive high school, of course, was premised on the principle of differentiation: the notion that high school youth are destined to enter a variety of occupational fields upon graduation. As noted earlier, this was in large part a legacy of the Progressive Era and of the social efficiency rationale for the vocational education movement. The cardinal principle of that rationale was that the high school should be preparation for life, and vocational education advocates maintained that there were many different roads that students could take in their working careers. Such arguments certainly rang true in the 1920s, when a fraction of the high school-aged population attended school, even in the cities (Krug, 1972). And they continued to make sense in the immediate postwar period. Industrial employment remained quite robust, and even if many high school graduates did not take jobs as manual laborers, the rationale for vocational training was still rather clear (Coleman, 1965). As the urban economy changed, however, the relevance of vocational training weakened. And vocational education was supplanted by a variety of other curricular options, particularly by the "general course" (Angus and Mirel, 1999).

Even if the sectoral distribution of employment did not change in the short term, the economy was evolving in new ways and demanding new skills of entry-level workers. Literacy requirements in the workplace were rising, especially in the 1960s and 1970s, at the same time that the academic quality of urban high schools began to falter (Levine and Zipp, 1993; Ginzberg, 1975). This disparity was a major element of the crisis of urban education that emerged in the 1970s and 1980s. And it was linked to the rising national interest in education reflected in the publication of *A Nation at Risk* in the early 1980s (National Commission on Excellence in Education, 1983). In many cities employers expressed concern about the poor quality of inner-city high schools and the difficulties employers faced in finding capable workers. Such concerns became more commonplace in the latter 1980s as employment opportunities in downtown offices expanded rapidly in banking, financial services, and insurance (Levine and Trachtman, 1988). It was the dawn of a new era.

These changes were tied to a set of larger shifts in the American economy that have received much attention in recent years. When Conant wrote *The American High School Today* more than a quarter of all U.S. workers were employed in manufacturing. When employees in industry were added to other sectors of the economy requiring similar skills, more than 40 percent of the labor force could be classified as "blue collar," both skilled and unskilled. Another 35 percent were clerical workers, most of them employed in urban offices. By contrast, managerial and professional employment accounted for less than a quarter of the nation's overall employment (Long, 1958; Levy, 1987). Thus it appeared quite reasonable for Conant and others to surmise that the majority of American youth would not require education beyond the secondary level. For those students, vocational or commercial training would be most appropriate. Only a minority of the "brightest" youth need be prepared for post-secondary education (Conant, 1959, 1961).

The basic occupational structure of the American labor force changed slowly through the 1960s, with a gradual shift away from employment in manufacturing and greater numbers of workers in the "service sector." In 1970 more than a quarter of the nation's workers were employed in manufacturing, and the number of positions requiring higher education had changed relatively little. But the years that followed witnessed a dramatic transformation that continues to unfold today. Beginning in the 1970s and accelerating in the decades that followed, the number of manufacturing jobs began to plummet (Levy, 1987). Nationwide, the proportion of the labor force employed in manufacturing fell from about a quarter to 18 percent between 1970 and 1990 (Murphy and Welch, 1993). The impact was evident first in the cities, as noted above, but it eventually affected all areas of the country. Economists speculate that it was due both to technological change and to the movement of jobs to other countries (Abramovitz and David, 1996). This set of changes came to have important implications for schools. The number of jobs for which relatively little formal education was necessary had begun to contract.

Jobs in manufacturing were replaced by positions in offices and by growth in managerial, technical, and professional employment. This change was slow to develop, but beginning in the 1980s a shift toward jobs requiring progressively higher levels of education had become evident (Murphy and Welch, 1989; Cohn and Hughes, 1994). It was reflected in wage rates for workers with different levels of education. At the start of the 1970s the hourly earnings for employees with less than a high school education and for college graduates were about seven dollars apart, and high school graduates earned only about $1.50 more per hour than nongraduates. Because of the large cohort of college graduates produced in the 1960s and 1970s, the advantage of a college degree actually shrank appreciably in the 1970s, and in 1979 only about six dollars separated the hourly wages of high school dropouts and college graduates. But after that, the gap began to widen, and by the mid-1990s college graduates earned nearly ten dollars more per hour than high school dropouts, and more than seven dollars per hour than high school graduates (Datazone, 1999). In other words, the labor market began to pay even bigger returns to students who went to college.

These changes occurred because of two trends, both of which spurred higher college enrollments. First, dollar returns to college education increased slightly across the 1980s and into the 1990s by roughly 7 percent. At the same time, however, the wages of high school dropouts fell by more than a quarter, and those of high school graduates declined by about 8 percent (Stern, 1989; Murphy and Welch, 1993). Because of these developments, especially the dramatic decline for high school dropouts, the earnings premium for attending college became greater than at any time in the postwar period. This, not surprisingly, helped to spur a corresponding jump in college enrollments. In the early 1980s less than half of high school seniors continued on to college; by the latter 1990s the figure approached 70 percent (Dougherty, 1997; Kelinson, 1998). These, of course, were rational decisions, given the decline of employment opportunities for students without higher education and the growing wage differentials. By 1990 it was calculated that a college degree was, on average, worth half a million dollars more than a high school diploma in lifetime earnings. Figures such as these helped to make the idea of attending college attractive to a much broader range of American youth than it had been just two decades earlier (Hunt, 1995).

A dramatic rise in the female labor force in the 1970s and 1980s also contributed to this general trend. Among the most rapidly growing areas of female employment were the professions and other jobs requiring some measure of higher education. Consequently, female enrollments in college climbed sharply, particularly in the 1980s and 1990s. This growth occurred despite a lower responsiveness in female enrollments to wage dividends for college (Averett and Burton, 1996). By the 1980s, women outnumbered men among undergraduates for the first time in American history, with more than half enrolling in college within a year of high school graduation (National Center for Educational Statistics, 1995). This development contributed to the rapid rise in the number of students continuing on to college in the 1990s; indeed, the rate of college entry among women was then about 10 percent greater than among men.

Across the country educational expectations rose in the latter twentieth century. In an analysis of White high school graduates in 1960 and 1980, Marlis Buchmann found that students' expectations of the highest degree they would earn changed significantly between these two cohorts. Altogether, the number expecting simply to end their education at high school fell from more than a quarter to just 18 percent, almost a 30 percent drop. At the same time, those expecting to earn graduate or advanced professional degrees increased from about 12 to more than 21 percent (Buchmann, 1989). These trends would only accelerate in the years to follow.

Such changes in students' educational plans can be interpreted as a rational response to the changing job market. As Buchmann and a number of other observers have noted, the earning power of high school diplomas faded in the 1980s, at the same time that the economic returns of a college education began to increase significantly. This decline was partly due to shifts in the occupational structure, with the decline in manufacturing employment. But it was also due to the growing preference of employers to hire workers—especially beginning employees—with higher levels of education (Carnevale and Desrochers, 1997). In a thoughtful analysis of BLS data, Kevin Murphy and Finis Welch have argued that employment of workers with college education increased in all industrial sectors in the 1980s, contributing to a broad rising demand for higher levels of educational attainment. These changes helped to fuel a continuing expansion of the higher education sector, despite smaller numbers of high school graduates, through the latter 1980s and early 1990s (Murphy and Welch, 1993). By the middle of the 1990s, a majority of high school graduates across the country were continuing on to some form or another of higher education (Kelinson, 1998).

With these dramatic changes in the national economy, the stakes of educational decisions made by teenagers became ever higher. Christopher Jencks and other social scientists recently have found that future earnings were tied to skill levels measured by tests for cohorts born in the 1960s and 1970s, just when urban schools appear to have failed in large measure to effectively transmit the requisite skills. For students who did not develop their academic skills in high school, and who chose not to continue on to some form of higher education, real wages declined in the decades following 1979. Given this, it is little wonder that enrollments in academic courses increased in this period. It was a reasoned response to the development of a new economic reality in metropolitan America (Jencks, 1998).

The changing economy helped to underscore the importance of educational differences between inner-city and suburban communities. Although the latter generally kept pace with the new expectations of the economy, the former fell farther behind (Harrison, 1972; Sexton and Nickel, 1992). In particular, big city schools were poorly served by traditional vocational programs. Economist John Bishop (1989) has argued that occupational education is least effective when it is not carefully matched to existing jobs. As the number of central city manufacturing jobs fell in the 1970s and 1980s, they were replaced by service positions, many of which required a broad range of academic skills rather than specific job training. And as the technical requirements of office jobs increased, many employers in the cities began to look for even higher educational credentials. One estimate suggests that as many as 52 percent of future jobs in metropolitan areas will require at least some college preparation (Dougherty, 1997). These developments pose a challenge to urban high schools.

The emphasis today, as never before in recent history, is on academic skills, and this is evident in the behavior of educators and employers alike (Stern, 1989; Sexton and Nickel, 1992; Wilson, 1995). Meanwhile, interest in schools as a forum for democratic education appears to have faded. Conant and other advocates of the comprehensive high school believed that the allocation of students to various types of curricula would correspond to the demand for various skills in the labor market. The historical development of the economy and recent changes in high school enrollments have proved this view to be correct in certain respects. The picture that has emerged in the past fifteen years, however, is quite different from Conant's view in the latter 1950s. In response to the controversies of the early 1980s, and particularly the publication of *A Nation at Risk*, education has come to be seen increasingly in economic terms, reflecting a growing belief that there is a connection between academic achievement and economic success. As a result, academic requirements for graduation have been raised for the majority of high school students, and vocational curricula serve a shrinking minority. Studies of Catholic high schools have argued that their success has been partly due to their generally undifferentiated academic curriculum (Bryk, Lee, and Holland, 1993). Critics of the high school today argue that all students should be provided with a rigorous academic curriculum if they are to succeed in the economy of the future (Angus and Mirel, 1999). But few, if any, of these commentators seem to be concerned with the question of democracy.

In a striking analysis of recent developments, David Labaree (1997) has suggested that American education is increasingly preoccupied with providing credentials for individual advancement and less with preparing effective citizens or promoting national economic welfare. Along with a number of other observers, he has noted a decline in public concern with citizenship and civic-mindedness. Like Gutmann, he acknowledges that simply having academically strong schools is not enough to sustain a healthy democratic polity into the future. As Benjamin Barber (1996) has pointed out, the new academic preoccupation of American high schools, in that case, does not always appear to represent a return to common purposes that may presage a renewed democratic impulse in secondary education. Rather, it often seems to be a determined attempt to realize higher economic rewards, with relatively little concern for collective welfare or deliberative processes. Instead of allocating students to different careers by way of a varied curriculum, the new academic high schools assume positions in a highly structured status hierarchy dictated by their average test scores, with only the barest pretense of equivalency.

In the new academically oriented economy, the role of secondary education increasingly seems to be helping identify winners and losers. Indeed, as Linda McNeil has shown in a study of Texas schools, standardized tests can serve to exclude other legitimate purposes of education, a process she declares inimical to democratic ends in education (McNeil, 2000, p. 264). Gutmann (1990) and Barber (1996) note that the pursuit of individual goals at the expense of civic virtue is hardly conducive to the cultivation of democratic values. If such a narrow conception of schooling is achieved, it is a legitimate question whether the comprehensive high school envisioned by Conant would become an anachronism. If the high school is to become little more than a preparatory school, and post-secondary institutions are the means to allocating individuals to their occupational destinations, in what sense does the high school retain its democratic and egalitarian purposes? Can it still be described as the institution that brings the disparate elements of society together? Or do academic distinctions acquire even greater significance in the new precollegiate ethos of the institution? These are questions, it appears, that secondary educators will have to confront in the twenty-first century.

A Retreat from Democracy?

In his extensive history of the comprehensive high school, William Wraga (1994) has argued that the past several decades have represented a "disintegration" of this peculiarly American form of secondary education. If one examines evidence from the various commissions appointed to examine the high school in this period, as Wraga has done, it is hard to disagree with this assessment. What is more, secondary schools seem to have turned decisively away from the idea that democratic principles ought to reside at the very center of the enterprise. Buffeted by the forces of social change described above, America's high schools appear largely to have abandoned the quest for commonality, and democracy became a term rarely invoked in connection with secondary education.

Signs of change were evident as early as 1970, just three years after Conant's second report. That year saw publication of a volume titled *High School 1980: The Shape of the Future in American Secondary Education*, compiled by Alvin C. Eurich under the auspices of the Academy for Educational Development (a nonprofit planning agency) (Eurich, 1970). It featured an essay by Conant, an impassioned plea for the comprehensive high school as a solution to the problems facing public education, but also included chapters on alternative high schools, "schools without walls," and curricular reform in a number of subject areas. All of the authors recognized that the changing social and economic configuration of the country's metropolitan regions posed a significant challenge to the schools. For his part, Conant asserted that the comprehensive high school represented "the best way out of the present segregated situation," and that a goal should be "the creation of high schools which shall be widely comprehensive not only as regards the economic backgrounds and vocational desires of the students, but in terms of the color of the skins of those who are attending" (p. 72). But the other authors presented quite a different vision. They offered other options that they believed would better address the problems at hand. Kenneth Clark called for a new system of schools to compete with failed inner-city public institutions, a source of competition and improved opportunities for minority youth. Others stressed even more exotic possibilities, such as learning from life itself. Such suggestions were a sign of the times; it was, after all, a period of innovation and change, and Conant was virtually alone in his commitment to bringing the various elements of society together within the walls of a single institution. "I am an advocate of the comprehensive high school," he wrote somewhat somberly, "but I must admit that the future of this type of institution is far from certain in the United States" (p. 73). Subsequent reports from his fellow educators would bear this observation out.

Just three years later, the National Commission on the Reform of Secondary Education, formed at the behest of the Kettering Foundation, issued *The*

Reform of Secondary Education: A Report to the Public and the Profession
(1973). Assembled by a 21-member panel of educators and experts, this report featured input from more than two hundred other educators on a variety
of topics; it was intended to be both encyclopedic and representative of the
best thinking in the field. The very fact of its existence, of course, suggested
that many people thought a fundamental change was needed in the nation's
secondary schools. Predicting a drop in high school enrollments due to the
declining birthrate, the commission predicted that "as little as 40 percent of
the student population may be graduated from conventional comprehensive
high schools" in the following decade, and that the others would use "bypass
mechanisms" or "select from a wide variety of alternatives" to get their diplomas. In its recommendations, the commission advocated public support for
"non-formal sources of learning" and credit by examination for knowledge
and skills acquired through life experience. It also recommended the GED as
an alternative to the traditional high school diploma, along with college level
tests in specific subjects. All of these measures were intended to provide
greater freedom and flexibility to students, to allow them to achieve their
goals through a variety of means.

What was absent in the commission's report was any sense of commonality, shared experience, or deliberative process of the sort featured in
Gutmann's discussion of democratic education. In its treatment of national
goals for secondary education the term democracy is not used. Instead, there
is mention of cultivating an "appreciation for others," an "ability to adjust to
change," a "respect for law and order," the "clarification of values," and "appreciation of the achievement of man" (pp. 33–34). While these indeed may
well be features or outcomes of a deliberative process of the sort envisioned
by Conant and described more completely by Gutmann, they are hardly
equivalent to it. For her part, Gutmann is sharply critical of values clarification, which she argues "encourages children in the false subjectivism that 'I
have my opinion and you have yours and who's to say who's right?' " She describes it as a weak morality, one that "does not take the demands of democratic justice seriously" (p. 56). It was, however, symptomatic of a new era in
secondary education in the early 1970s. The ethos represented by the commission's report was one of individual choice and fulfillment, not collective contemplation and responsible decision making. It reflected the fragmentation of
the larger society and a time when no one wanted to be accused of representing a repressive mainstream tradition in American civilization. Democratic
values may have been represented in a willingness to let all voices be heard,
but there was no effort to ensure that anyone had to listen. As Callan (1997)
has argued, pluralism without the discipline of a deliberative commonality is
hardly conducive to democracy. In this regard the report represented a step
backward from the demands of democratic education.

Ten years after the commission published its report, yet another public discussion of the high school was initiated by the appearance of Ernest Boyer's *High School: A Report on Secondary Education in America* (1983). Sponsored by the Carnegie Foundation for the Advancement of Teaching, Boyer's report was issued in response to a widely perceived sense of malaise in the nation's secondary schools. Boyer aimed to find ways to revitalize these institutions and focused on four essential goals. These included teaching students to think critically and preparing them for the job market, but they also entailed helping students to learn about the world around them and enabling them to "fulfill their social and civic obligations through school and community service." Written in an engaging and informative style, Boyer's report discussed the myriad dimensions of making high schools better places to learn, and improving the quality of teaching and learning across the curriculum. Unlike the earlier document, it did not dwell on organizational forms, alternatives to the comprehensive high school, or values clarification. Instead, Boyer attempted to focus on core principles, emphasizing the responsibility of all schools to provide the best basic education possible, regardless of the backgrounds or individual goals of their students.

Boyer addressed the question of democracy in his discussion of civic education, stressing the need for all students to understand the functions and operating principles of government. He tipped his hat toward the principles of democracy by suggesting that students read works by classical political thinkers and that they become involved in small-scale civic action projects outside the classroom. But in neither case did he make democratic education an explicit goal of these exercises, instead simply declaring that "civics is an important part of the core of common learning" and "ignorance about government and how it functions is not an acceptable alternative" (pp. 105–106). It is also clear that he intended democratic values to flow from service learning, a feature of his recommendations that he considered a major innovation, but this too was not an explicitly stated objective of the experience. At the end of his discussion of service he quoted Dewey on the need for common purposes in a school, suggesting that the goal of service learning is values education. But the values he identified were morally vague: "to help all students understand that to be fully human one must serve" (p. 215). Although certainly democratic in spirit, this too fell short of the explicitly deliberative and dialogical process of democratic education that Conant had endorsed. As Richard Pratte (1988) has noted, service learning often was democratic only in a weak sense, like values clarification, allowing opportunities for individual expression of commitment to others, but without focusing on the need for collective discussion and making hard choices.[3]

The years immediately following the appearance of Boyer's report were filled with yet other critiques of secondary education. The most influential of these were the books cosponsored by the National Association of Secondary School Principals and the Commission on Educational Issues of the National Association of Independent Schools. Collectively titled "A Study of High Schools," the best known of these volumes was *Horace's Compromise*, written by Theodore Sizer (1984). In many respects, Sizer's complaints about the nation's secondary schools echoed Boyer's critique. The schools were hobbled by a mind-numbing lack of purpose, they had lost their academic vitality, the faculty was overburdened, and the students were uninterested. Sizer focused his attention on the most basic elements of education, the relationship between teachers and students, the curriculum, and the fundamental purposes of the school: academic instruction. He did not dwell on the larger social functions of education, and democratic education was not an important topic in his book. The same was true of the other volumes in the series, with the exception of Robert Hampel's (1985) historical account of the high school since 1940. Arthur Powell, Eleanor Farrar, and David Cohen (1985) decried the lack of coherence in large, comprehensive public high schools, comparing them to shopping malls, but did not address the question of democracy or democratic education. Their critique, along with Sizer's, focused on the size and impersonality of the institution and its failure to demand high levels of academic performance from either teachers or students. Implicit in these accounts was a plea for smaller, simpler institutions, where scholastic objectives could be pursued with rigor, and without compromise or distraction. Taken together, these studies represented a powerful vision of reform but one that said relatively little about democracy in education.

The books by Boyer, Sizer, Powell et al., and other critics of the secondary schools were published immediately after the appearance of *A Nation at Risk*. Their collective concern with academic standards was well suited to the growing national interest in improving the scholastic performance of all public schools. Sizer's work was instrumental in establishing the Coalition of Essential Schools, an important network of innovative high schools. These works also contributed to the sense that all high schools ought to be judged on the basis of academic achievement, an idea that was linked to the economic reasoning spelled out in *A Nation at Risk* and other national reform documents of the 1980s and 1990s. Eventually, this notion became expressed in a national movement for systemic reform, wherein school performance is largely determined by standardized tests scores of one type or another. This impulse of course has produced a potent incentive for schools to improve their record of academic attainment, but it has hardly provided an atmosphere conducive to the cultivation of democratic values. As noted earlier, democratic education appears to have been overlooked as the nation's secondary schools have become ever more concerned with boosting scholastic achievement. If the history of professional commentary about secondary schooling over the past thirty years has been any guide, it is an issue that has been neglected for quite some time.

CONCLUSION

There is a chilling moment in Jonathan Kozol's book *Savage Inequalities* (1991) when he describes meeting with a group of affluent students from a suburban high school. In a discussion of the prospects for closing the funding gaps that contribute to enormous inequities between their own school and those in the nearby city, one student responds, "I don't see why we should do it. How could it be of benefit to us?" (p. 126). This sentiment is a graphic reminder of the potential consequences of making education integral to economic success in life and points to the dire importance of democratic education in a society as fragmented by race and ethnicity, social class and economic opportunity as the United States is at the beginning of the twenty-first century. Unfortunately, as the foregoing has demonstrated, democracy is a topic that has largely been ignored or overlooked in the nation's high schools, in spite of the ardent efforts of James Conant throughout the closing years of his life. As Conant recognized, the very historical processes that have made democratic education so difficult to achieve in secondary schools are the factors that make it so critically important. Yet it is an issue that has received scant attention from policymakers in the past several decades.

A number of historical developments converged in the decades following World War II to make James Conant's vision of the high school problematic, at least in the nation's large metropolitan areas. Racial segregation and the movement of southern Blacks to northern cities divided urban and suburban school districts, creating sharp disparities in educational resource allocation and curricular orientation. Where Conant had imagined the comprehensive high school as an instrument of democratic socialization, by the 1970s it had evolved into an agency of racial isolation and alienation. This process was rooted in patterns of residential segregation, of course, but was abetted by the emergence of a youth culture that served to challenge adult authority in the schools and also became fragmented along racial lines with time. Conant's insistence on the importance of large schools may have helped to compromise adult control in the face of the growing influence of the youth culture. The relaxation of rules and changing standards of conduct, spurred by students rights litigation, helped to make the schools into centers of an elaborate social world for adolescents, diverting energy and enthusiasm away from academic interests. Even if Conant was not a proponent of many of the reforms in student life, his campaign for larger schools helped to set the stage for other developments in the development of a school-based "adolescent society" in the postwar period. As it turns out, this was hardly conducive to the cultivation of democratic values.

Finally, changes in the economy altered the very premise of a comprehensive high school. Conant already had noted the heavily academic orientation of suburban high schools in the 1960s. In the 1980s this tendency became even more pronounced, as ever-larger numbers of high school graduates entered colleges of one sort or another. The rationale for vocational education became weaker as the manufacturing sector of the economy stagnated or even disappeared, as it had in many larger cities by the 1980s. By the last decade of the century, high schools across the country were offering stronger academic programs to all students. In the face of significant change in the economy and the rapidly rising value of academic skills, the academic curriculum was not suitable for only the most gifted students. The old comprehensive high school has been acquiring an increasingly academic demeanor, but this did not mean that secondary education had assumed the purposes of a common school. Instead, the new achievement focus contributed to an atmosphere of competition and recrimination, in institutions where self-worth came to be judged on criteria increasingly determined by standardized tests.

The growing fragmentation of metropolitan society, the impact of the youth culture, and the changing economy appear to have exerted a telling influence on would-be educational reformers in the past several decades. Responding to shifting social conditions, they have been quick to advocate abandonment of old approaches to secondary education and to embrace reforms intended to bring the institution into line with new realities. This certainly appeared to be true of the 1973 report of the National Commission on the Reform of Secondary Education. It may have been somewhat less the case with Boyer or the reports that made up "A Study of High School," but they too were ready to critique existing practices and suggest new directions. As the old comprehensive model of secondary education is jettisoned, certain elements of the traditional conception of the high school appear to have been forgotten. This is what seems to have happened with regard to democratic education, particularly the ideals of civic exchange, moral reasoning, and collective deliberation advocated by its most thoughtful proponents.

In a recently published collection of essays titled *The New American High School* (1999), David Marsh and Judy Codding declare that "it is time to abolish the comprehensive high school" (p. xiii). The focus of their book is improvement of instruction and insuring that all students reach a high level of academic achievement. But like other commentaries on secondary education published in the past several decades, they are silent on the issue of democratic education. At the start of a new century, few observers discuss the high school as an instrument for bringing students from different backgrounds together. Smaller schools are being urged to give adults greater authority and to diminish the influence of the youth culture in all of its varied manifestations; and the differentiated curriculum is giving way to a greater interest in academic preparation, driven in large part by changes in the economy and in public perceptions about the importance of education, especially at the post-secondary level. Thus it may indeed be the case that the age of the comprehensive high school is drawing to a close.

But the issue of democracy raised by Conant still needs resolution. As Amy Gutmann notes in the conclusion to *Democratic Education*, practices and policies that improve the academic performance of students sometimes prove inimical to their moral development. She questions whether choosing to emphasize the academic performance of students while ignoring their "political education" in the principles and practices of democracy is morally defensible. In the end, she suggests that it is not that "the cultivation of the virtues, knowledge, and skills necessary for political participation has moral primacy over other purposes of public education in a democratic society" (p. 286). Thus, whereas it is fine to urge greater scholastic accomplishment, it should not come at the expense of education in the principles and practices of democracy.[4]

Observations such as these leave a number of questions unanswered regarding the comprehensive high school and Conant's vision of an institution representing the ideals of the common school. Given the recent critiques of the large, complex institutions that have served American adolescents in the past, what is the best institutional arrangement for the great variety of youth to be educated in the coming century? Is it enough simply to say that everyone will study the same curriculum, and is such a policy fundamentally democratic? Surely there will be a need for some occupational training, even if secondary education becomes more uniformly academic in orientation. There is also the question of the high school's overt role in contributing to the democratic ethos of American society, what Gutmann describes as "political education." As noted earlier, at the same time that the institution's role in curricular differentiation seems to have diminished somewhat, its role in augmenting social and cultural distinctions in society appears to have grown larger. Segregation and inequity still distort the distribution of educational resources and stymie the prospect of meaningful deliberation between different groups of budding young citizens. And the youth culture saps and diverts the energies of millions of students at the same time that it represents a vast reservoir of enthusiasm and insight that could be harnessed for the purposes of democratic training. If James Conant were alive today, he almost certainly would find these developments most troubling. It is difficult to see how anyone who is concerned with the long-term well-being of American civilization could disagree.

NOTES

The preparation of this paper was supported by the Spencer Foundation. Earlier versions were presented at New York University, the University of Georgia, and Washington University in St. Louis. Parts of it also served as the basis for a vice presidential address to Division F of the American Educational Research Association at its annual meeting in Montreal in 1999. Audience members in each of these venues offered helpful suggestions for improvement; in particular I would like to thank Floyd Hammack and the members of his seminar on the future of the comprehensive high school, who inspired me to begin research on this project, along with Jeffrey Mirel, Mary Ann Dzuback, and William Wraga. Linda McNeil and several anonymous reviewers also provided useful ideas for revision.

1. It is important to note that Conant was representing a deeply rooted tradition in American education at the time that his first statement on the comprehensive high school was published. As William Wraga (1994) has pointed out, the comprehensive ideal and a commitment to democratic principles in education had been clearly articulated in the *Cardinal Principles of Education* and were well established by the middle of the twentieth century. "During the 1930s and 1940s," Wraga writes, "greater emphasis was placed upon the social function of the public schools." As a result, "the comprehensive high school model garnered unprecedented and virtually unmatched support" (p. 59). It was the "heyday" of democratic public secondary education. This was the heritage of the ideas that Conant gave expression to in the latter 1950s, 1960s, and early 1970s. Unfortunately, little is known about the actual practice of democratic education in American high schools in the period preceding Conant's reports. David Angus and Jeffrey Mirel (1999) have suggested that Conant's stature as a scientist, Ivy League president, and cold warrior served to give his statements about secondary education special importance. They maintain that his 1959 report helped to deflect a number of attacks on the comprehensive high school, preserving it as the predominant form of public secondary education in the postwar period.

2. Gutmann is hardly the only scholar who has considered the question of democratic education in recent years. For example, Richard Pratte dealt with it in his book *The Civic Imperative* (1988), in which he maintained that the preparation of citizens cannot be narrowly conceived and that public education should be construed fundamentally as a moral enterprise intended to make good people, who then will become good citizens. Similarly, Butts (1988) and Beyer (1989) have argued that democratic education must go well beyond requiring various forms of participation in civic life. More recently, Benjamin Barber (1996) has suggested that democratic values must permeate public education if it is to provide a "literacy to live in a civil society" and competence to participate in democratic life. Callan (1997) has called for a renewed commitment to common schooling to forge the trust, goodwill, and loyalty necessary to underpin democracy in a pluralistic society. Gutmann's treatment of these questions, however, is unusually comprehensive, and it is widely recognized. For these reasons her book provides a useful point of reference interpreting the historical developments outlined in this paper.

3. For a thoughtful discussion of service learning, and its limitations as a vehicle for democratic education, see Lisman (1998). Like Pratte, Barber, and Callan, Lisman suggests that civic education is a morally complex undertaking, one that demands the continuous attention of students and teachers alike, and a deliberate engagement with the larger social context. The body of critical scholarship represented by these works can be considered an extension of the historically grounded arguments that Conant gave expression to some four decades earlier. Unfortunately, these perspectives rarely seem to penetrate the contemporary policy discourse concerning education in the United States.

4. There is, of course, the sticky question of school choice to consider as well, an issue that has permeated policy debates about all levels of public education for more than a decade. It is a question with profound implications for democratic education, as Gutmann (1999) and a

number of other commentators have noted, but it is not specifically a question linked to *secondary* education. For this reason I have decided not to make it a focal point in this essay. On the general question of school choice and its impact on democratic forms of education, see Kozol (1992).

REFERENCES

Abramovitz, Moses, and Paul A. David. (1996). "Technological Change and the Rise of Intangible Investments: The U.S. Economy's Growth-Path in the Twentieth Century." In OECD Documents, *Employment and Growth in the Knowledge-based Economy*, 35–60. Paris: Organization for Economic Cooperation and Development.

Angus, David, and Jeffrey Mirel. (1999). *The Failed Promise of the American High School, 1890–1895*. New York: Teachers College Press.

Averett, Susan L., and Mark I. Burton. (1996). "College Attendance and the College Wage Premium. Differences by Gender." *Economics of Education Review* 15 (February): 37–49.

Barber, Benjamin R. (1996). *An Aristocracy of Everyone: The Politics of Education and the Future of America*. New York: Oxford University Press.

Barker, R. G., and P. V. Gump. (1964). *Big School, Small School*. Stanford, CA: Stanford University Press.

Bettis, Pamela J. (1996). "Urban Students, Liminality, and the Postindustrial Context." *Sociology of Education* 69 (April): 105–25.

Beyer, Landon E. (1989). "The Social and Educational Conditions for Democracy: Perspectives and Imperatives." *Journal of Curriculum and Supervision* 4 (2): 178–186.

Bishop, John. (1989). "Occupational Training in High School: When Does It Pay Off?" *Economics of Education Review* 8 (1): 1–15.

Boyer, Ernest L. (1983). *High School: A Report on Secondary Education in America*. New York: Harper & Row.

Bryk, Anthony, Valarie E. Lee, and Peter B. Holland. (1993). *Catholic Schools and the Common Good*. Cambridge, Mass.: Harvard University Press.

Buchmann, Marlis. (1989). *The Script of Life in Modern Society: Entry into Adulthood in a Changing World*. Chicago: University of Chicago Press.

Butts, R. Freeman. (1988). "The Moral Imperative for American Schools: 'Inflame the Civic Temper.' " *American Journal of Education* 96 (2): 162–194.

Callan, Eamon. (1997). *Creating Citizens: Political Education and Liberal Democracy*. Oxford, New York: Oxford University Press.

Carnevale, Anthony P., and Donna M. Desrochers. (1997). "The Role of the Community College in the New Economy: Spotlight on Education." *Community College Journal* 67 (April–May): 26–33.

The Chicago Assembly. (1998). *Educational Reform for the Twenty-first Century*. Chicago: Harris Graduate School of Public Policy.

The Chicago Tribune. (1999). "Chicago, a Work in Progress: For Schools, It's Only a Start." February 12, 1, 13.

Chilman, Catherine S. (1978). *Adolescent Sexuality in a Changing American Society: Social and Psychological Perspectives*. Washington, D.C.: Government Printing Office.

Cohen, Ronald. (1997). "The Delinquents: Censorship and Youth Culture in Recent U.S. History," *History of Education Quarterly* 37 (Fall): 251–270.

Cohn, Elchanan, and Woodrow W. Hughes. (1994). "A Benefit-Cost Analysis of Investment in College Education in the United States, 1969–1985." *Economics of Education Review* 13 (April): 109–23.

Coleman, James. (1961). *The Adolescent Society: The Social Life of the Teenager and Its Impact on Education*. New York: Basic Books.

Coleman, James. (1965). *Adolescents and the Schools*. New York: Basic Books.

Coleman, James, T. Hoffer, and S. Kilgore. (1982). *High School Achievement: Public, Catholic and Private Schools Compared*. New York: Basic Books.

Conant, James B. (1959). *The American High School Today: A First Report to Interested Citizens*. New York: McGraw Hill.

Conant, James B. (1961). *Slums and Suburbs: A Commentary on Schools in Metropolitan Areas*. New York: McGraw Hill.

Conant, James B. (1967). *The Comprehensive High School: A Second Report to Interested Citizens*. New York: McGraw Hill.

Cremin, Lawrence A. (1961). *Transformation of the School: Progressivism in American Education, 1876–1957*. New York: Alfred Knopf.

Cusick, Philip A. (1983). *The Egalitarian Ideal and the American High School: Studies of Three Schools*. New York: Longman.

Davis, Fred. (1992). *Fashion, Culture and Identity*. Chicago: University of Chicago Press.

Dougherty, Kevin J. (1997). "Mass Higher Education: What Is Its Impetus? What Is Its Impact?" *Teachers College Record*, 99 (Fall): 66–72.

Eckert, Penelope. (1989). *Jocks and Burnouts: Social Categories and Identity in the High School*. New York: Teachers College Press.

Economic Policy Institute. (1999). "Average Real Hourly Wages of All Workers by Education, 1973–1997." Retrieved in January 1999 from The Datazone (http://epinet.org/datazone/wagebyed_all.html).

Esman, Aaron H. (1990). *Adolescence and Culture*. New York: Columbia University Press.

Eurich, Alvin C., ed. (1970). *High School 1980: The Shape of the Future in American Secondary Education*. New York: Pittman Publishing.

Fordham, Signithia. (1996). *Blacked Out: Dilemmas of Race, Identity and Success at Capitol High*. Chicago: University of Chicago Press.

Fox, Kenneth. (1985). *Metropolitan America: Urban Life and Urban Policy in the United States, 1940–1980*. New Brunswick, N.J.: Rutgers University Press.

Gilbert, James B. (1986). *A Cycle of Outrage: America's Response to the Juvenile Delinquent of the 1950s*. New York: Oxford University Press.

Ginzberg, Eli. (1975). *The Manpower Connection: Education and Work*. Cambridge, Mass.: Harvard University Press.

Goldin, Claudia. (2001). "The Human Capital Century and American Leadership: Virtues of the Past." *Journal of Economic History* 61 (June): 263–92.

Goldsmith, William W., and Edward J. Blakely. (1992). *Separate Societies: Poverty and Inequality in U.S. Cities*. Philadelphia: Temple University Press.

Grant, Gerald. (1988). *The World We Created at Hamilton High*. Cambridge, Mass.: Harvard University Press.

Greeley, Andrew. (1982). *Catholic Schools and Minority Students*. New Brunswick, N.J.: Transaction Books.

Gutmann, Amy. (1990). "Democratic Education in Difficult Times." *Teachers College Record* 92 (1): 7–20.

Gutmann, Amy. (1999). *Democratic Education*. Princeton, N.J.: Princeton University Press.

Haller, Emil J. (1992). "High School Size and Student Indiscipline: Another Aspect of the School Consolidation Issue?" *Educational Evaluation and Policy Analysis* 14 (Summer): 145–56.

Hampel, Robert L. (1986). *The Last Little Citadel: American High Schools since 1940*. Boston: Houghton Mifflin.

Harrison, Bennett. (1972). *Education, Training and the Urban Ghetto*. Baltimore: Johns Hopkins University Press.

Haubrich, Paul. (1993). "Student Life in Milwaukee High Schools, 1920–1985." In J. L. Rury and F. A. Cassell, eds., *Seeds of Crisis, Public Schooling in Milwaukee since 1920*. Madison: University of Wisconsin Press.

Havighurst, Robert. (1964). *The Public Schools of Chicago: A Survey for the Board of Education of the City of Chicago*. Chicago: Board of Education of the City of Chicago.

Havighurst, Robert. (1966). *Education in Metropolitan Areas*. Boston: Allyn and Bacon.

Hawes, Joseph M., and N. Ray Hiner. (1985). *American Childhood: A Research Guide and Handbook*. Westport, Conn.: Greenwood Press.

Herbst, Jurgen. (1996). *The Once and Future School: Three Hundred and Fifty Years of American Secondary Education*. New York: Routledge.

Hochschild, Jennifer. (1985). *The New American Dilemma: Liberal Democracy and School Desegregation*. New Haven, Conn.: Yale University Press.

Hunt, Earl. (1995). *Will We Be Smart Enough? A Cognitive Analysis of the Coming Workforce*. New York: Russell Sage Foundation.

Jackson, Kenneth. (1985). *The Crabgrass Frontier: The Suburbanization of the United States*. New York: Oxford University Press.

Jencks, Christophe. (1998). "The Black-White Test Score Gap. An Introduction." In C. Jencks and M. Phillips, eds., *The Black-White Test Score Gap*. Washington, D.C.: Brookings Institution Press.

Kaestle, Carl F. (1983). *Pillars of the Republic: Common Schools and American Society, 1790–1860*. New York: Hill and Wang.

Kantor, Harvey, and Barbara Brenzel. (1993). "Urban Education and the 'Truly Disadvantaged': The Historical Roots of the Contemporary Crisis, 1945–1990." In M. B. Katz, ed., *The Underclass Debate: Views from History*. Princeton, N.J.: Princeton University Press. 366–401.

Kelinson, Jonathan W. (1998). "Trends in College Degrees." *Occupational Outlook Quarterly* 42 (2): 22–27.

Kleppner, Paul. (1984). *Chicago Divided: The Making of a Black Mayor*. DeKalb: Northern Illinois University Press.

Kliebard, Herbert. (1995). *The Struggle for the American Curriculum, 1893–1958* (2d ed.). New York: Routledge.

Kozol, Jonathan. (1991). *Savage Inequalities: Children in America's Schools*. New York: Crown Publishers.

Kozol, Jonathan. (1992). "I Dislike the Idea of Choice, and I Want to Tell You Why." *Educational Leadership* 50 (3): 90–92.

Krug, Edward A. (1972). *The American High School, 1920–1940*. Madison: University of Wisconsin Press.

Labaree, David. (1997). *How to Succeed in School without Really Learning: The Credentials Race in American Education*. New Haven, Conn.: Yale University Press.

Lee, Valerie, and Julia Smith. (1997). "High School Size: Which Works Best and for Whom?" *Educational Evaluation and Policy Analysis,* 19 (3): 205–27.

Levine, Marc, and John F. Zipp. (1993). "A City at Risk: The Changing Social and Economic Context of Public Schooling in Milwaukee." In J. L. Rury and F. A. Cassell, eds., *Seeds of Crisis: Public Schooling in Milwaukee since 1920*. Madison: University of Wisconsin Press, 42–73.

Levine, M., and R. Trachtman. (1988). *American Business and the Public Schools: Case Studies of Corporate Involvement in Public Education*. New York: Teachers College Press.

Levy, Frank. (1987). *Dollars and Dreams: The Changing American Income Distribution*. New York: Russell Sage Foundation.

Lisman, C. David. (1998). *Toward a Civil Society: Civic Literacy and Service Learning*. Westport, Conn.: Bergin & Garvey.

Long, Clarence D. (1958). *The Labor Force under Changing Income and Employment*. Princeton, N.J.: Princeton University Press.

Marsh, David D., and Judy Codding, eds. (1999). *The New American High School*. Thousand Oaks, CA: Corwin Press.

Massey, Douglas, and Nancy Denton. (1993). *American Apartheid: Segregation and the Making of the Underclass*. Cambridge, Mass.: Harvard University Press.

McNeil, Linda M. (2000). *Contradictions of School Reform: Educational Costs of Standardized Testing*. New York: Routledge.

Meier, Deborah. (1996). "Supposing That . . ." *Phi Delta Kappan* 78 (4): 271–76.

Mirel, Jeffrey. (1993). *The Rise and Fall of an Urban School System: Detroit, 1907–1981*. Ann Arbor: University of Michigan Press.

Modell, John. (1989). *Into One's Own: From Youth to Adulthood in the United States, 1920–1975*. Berkeley: University of California Press.

Mora, Marie T. (1997). "Attendance, Schooling Quality, and the Demand for Education of Mexican Americans, African Americans, and Non-Hispanic Whites." *Economics of Education Review* 16 (4): 407–18.

Murphy, Kevin M., and Finis Welch. (1989). "Wage Premiums for College Graduates: Recent Growth and Possible Explanations." *Educational Researcher* 18 (4): 17–26.

Murphy, Kevin M., and Finis Welch. (1993). "Industrial Change and the Importance of Skill." In S. Danziger and P. Gottschalk, eds., *Uneven Tides: Rising Inequality in America*, 101–132. New York: Russell Sage Foundation.

National Center for Educational Statistics. (1995). *Digest of Educational Statistics 1995*. Washington, D.C.: U.S. Department of Education, Office of Educational Research and Improvement.

National Commission on Excellence in Education. (1983). *A Nation at Risk: The Imperative for Educational Reform*. Washington, D.C.: Government Printing Office.

National Commission on the Reform of Secondary Education. (1973). *The Reform of Secondary Education: A Report to the Public and the Profession*. New York: McGraw-Hill.

Olson, Ronald K. (1972). "Tinker and the Administrator." *School & Society* 100 (February): 86–9.

Orfield, Gary. (1978). *Must We Bus? Segregated Schools and National Policy*. Washington, D.C.: Brookings Institution Press.

Orfield, Gary, Susan Eaton, and the Harvard Project on School Desegregation. (1996). *Dismantling Desegregation: The Quiet Reversal of Brown v. Board of Education*. New York: New Press.

Palen, J. John. (1992). *The Urban World* (4th ed.). New York: McGraw Hill.

Palladino, Grace. (1996). *Teenagers: An American History*. New York: Basic Books.

Peshkin, Alan. (1991). *The Color of Strangers, the Color of Friends*. Chicago: University of Chicago Press.

Powell, Arthur G., Eleanor Farrar, and David K. Cohen. (1985). *The Shopping Mall High School: Winners and Losers in the Educational Marketplace*. Boston: Houghton Mifflin.

Pratte, Richard. (1988). *The Civic Imperative: Examining the Need for Civic Education*. New York: Teachers College Press.

Rumberger, Russell, and J. Douglas Willms. (1992). "The Impact of Racial and Ethnic Segregation on the Achievement Gap in California High Schools." *Educational Evaluation and Policy Analysis* 14 (4): 377–96.

Rury, John. (1999). "Race, Space and the Politics of Chicago's Public Schools: Benjamin Willis and the Tragedy of Urban Education." *History of Education Quarterly* 39 (2): 117–42.

Sexton, Edwin, and Janet F. Nickel. (1992). "The Effects of School Location on the Earnings of Black and White Youths." *Economics of Education Review* 11 (January): 11–18.

Sizer, Theodore. (1996). "New Hope for High Schools." *American School Board Journal* 183 (September): 37–40.

Sparks, Richard K. (1983). "Before You Bring Back School Dress Codes, Recognize that the Courts Frown upon Attempts to 'Restrict' Students' Rights." *American School Board Journal* 170 (7): 24–25.

Stern, David. (1989). "Labor Market Experience of Teenagers with and without High School Diplomas." *Economics of Education Review* 8 (3): 233–46.

Stolee, Michael. (1993). "The Milwaukee Desegregation Case." In J. L. Rury and F. A. Cassell, eds., *Seeds of Crisis: Public Schooling in Milwaukee since 1920*. Madison: University of Wisconsin Press.

Stone, Clarence N. (1998). Introduction. In C. Stone, ed., *Changing Urban Education*. Lawrence: University Press of Kansas.

Teaford, Jon C. (1990). *Rough Road to Renaissance: Urban Revitalization in America, 1940–1985*. Baltimore: Johns Hopkins University Press.

Vinovskis, Maris A. (1988). *An "Epidemic" of Adolescent Pregnancy? Some Historical and Policy Considerations*. New York: Oxford University Press.

Wells, Amy Stuart, and Robert L. Crain. (1997). *Stepping over the Color Line: African American Students in White Suburban Schools*. New Haven, Conn.: Yale University Press.

West, Elliot. (1996). *Growing Up in Twentieth-Century America: A History and Reference Guide*. Westport, Conn.: Greenwood Press.

Wilson, William J. (1987). *The Truly Disadvantaged: The Inner City, the Underclass, and Public Policy*. Chicago: University of Chicago Press.

Wilson, William J. (1995). *When Work Disappears: The World of the New Urban Poor*. New York: Alfred A. Knopf.

Wong, Kenneth, Robert Breeben, L. Lynn, and Gail Sunderman. (1997). *Integrated Governance as a School Reform Strategy in the Chicago Public Schools*. Chicago: Department of Education and Harris Graduate School of Public Policy Studies, University of Chicago.

Wraga, William. (1994). *Democracy's High School: The Comprehensive High School and Educational Reform in the United States*. Lanham, Md.: University Press of America.

Zirkel, Perry A. (1999). "The 30th Anniversary of 'Tinker.' " *Phi Delta Kappan* 81 (September): 34–40, 58.

4

▼▼▼▼▼▼▼

Creating New Inequalities:
Contradictions of Reform*

Linda M. McNeil

The enduring legacy of Ross Perot's school reforms in Texas is not merely the strengthening of bureaucratic controls at the expense of teaching and learning. It is also the legitimating of a language of accountability as the governing principle in public schools. Incipient in the Perot reforms was the shifting of control over public schooling away from "the public" and away from the profession—and toward business-controlled management accountability systems. These systems use children's scores on standardized tests to measure the quality of the performance of teachers and principals, and they even use a school's aggregate student scores as data for the comparative "ratings" of schools.

There have been several iterations of state testing and test-driven curricula implemented since the reforms first began under the Perot legislation in Texas in the mid-1980s. The current Texas Assessment of Academic Skills (TAAS) is rarely referred to by its full name. It is known by its advocates in the state government and among the state's business leaders as "the Texas Accountability System," the reform that has "shaped up" schools. It is touted as the system that holds "teachers and principals accountable." In many schools, tenure for principals has been replaced by "performance contracts," with "performance" measured by a single indicator—the aggregation of student TAAS scores in the school. Publicity about the "Texas Accountability

System," centered on rising test scores, has generated copycat legislation in a number of states, where standardized testing of students is increasingly being used as the central mechanism for decisions about student learning, teacher and administrator practice, and even whole-school quality.[1]

Teachers know well that most reforms have a short life and that "this too shall pass." The specific rules and prescriptions enacted under the Perot reforms did, indeed, pass. But the institutionalizing of a shift in the locus of control over curriculum, teaching, and assessment, which began with the legislated reforms of the 1980s, has more than persisted.

As a result, a very narrow set of numerical indicators (student scores on statewide tests) has become the *only* language of currency in education policy in the state. Principals report that there can be little discussion of children's development, of cultural relevance, of children's contributions to classroom knowledge and interactions, or of those engaging sidebar experiences at the margins of the official curriculum where children often do their best learning. According to urban principals, many have supervisors who tell them quite pointedly, "Don't talk to me about anything else until the TAAS scores start to go up."

Teachers also report that the margins—those spaces where even in highly prescriptive school settings they have always been able to "really teach"—are shrinking as the accountability system becomes increasingly stringent, with teacher and principal pay tied to student scores. Under the Perot reforms, teachers were still sometimes able to juggle the official, prescribed, and tested curriculum with what they wanted their students to learn.[2] Even if they had to teach two contradictory lessons in order to ensure that students encountered the "real" information (as well as the test-based facts), many teachers managed to do so in order that their students did not lose out on a chance for a real education. Under TAAS, there are fewer and fewer opportunities for authentic teaching.

A continued legacy, then, of the Perot reforms is that the testing of students increasingly drives curriculum and compromises both teaching and the role of students in learning. This prescriptive teaching creates a new form of discrimination as teaching to the fragmented and narrow information on the test comes to substitute for a substantive curriculum in the schools of poor and minority youths. Disaggregating school-level scores by children's race appears to be an attempt to promote equity, but the high stakes attached to the scores have made many schools replace the regular curriculum in minority students' classrooms with test-prep materials that have virtually no value beyond practicing for the tests. The scores go up in these classrooms, but academic quality goes down. The result is a growing inequality between the content and quality of education provided to white, middle-class children and that provided to those in poor and minority schools.

MANDATING A NONCURRICULUM

In minority schools, in the urban school district where I conducted case studies, and in many schools across Texas, substantial class time is spent practicing bubbling in answers and learning to recognize "distractor" (obviously wrong) answers. Students are drilled on such strategies as the pep rally cheer "Three in a row? No, No, No!" (If you have answered "b" three times in a row, you know that at least one of those answers is likely to be wrong, because the maker of a test would not be likely to construct three questions in a row with the same answer indicator.) The basis for such advice comes from the publishers of test-prep materials, many of whom send consultants into schools—for a substantial price—to help plan pep rallies and to "train" teachers to use the TAAS-prep kits.

Under the Perot-era system of test-driven curricula, the observed teachers retained some discretion over how to "teach" to the test-based curriculum. They could teach the numbered curricular content items (as the district directed them to do). They could ignore the official, numbered curriculum and hope that their students would do well on the tests by virtue of having learned from the lessons the teacher had developed. Or they could try to juggle the two—an important option when they saw that the test-based curriculum format so trivialized and fragmented course content that the "knowledge" represented was too far removed from the curriculum the teachers wanted their students to learn. The testing, by having students select among provided responses, negated the teachers' desires that their students construct meaning, that they come to understandings, or that they connect course content with their prior knowledge.

Teachers, even those who know their subjects and their students well, have much less latitude when their principals purchase TAAS-prep materials to be used in lieu of the regular curriculum. The decision to use such materials forces teachers to set aside their own best knowledge of their subject in order to drill their students on information whose primary (often sole) usefulness is its likely inclusion on the test. A particular example reveals not only how test prep diminishes the role of the teacher, but also how it distances course content from the cultures of the students.

One teacher, a graduate of an Ivy League university with a master's degree from a second selective college, had spent considerable time and personal money assembling a rich collection of historical and literary works of importance in Latino culture. Her building of this classroom resource collection for her high school students was extremely important given the school's lack of a library. Her students responded to her initiative with a real enthusiasm to study and learn. Upon returning from lunch one day, she was dismayed to see that the books for her week's lessons had been set aside. In the center of her desk was a stack of test-prep booklets with a note saying, "Use these instead of your regular curriculum until after the TAAS." The TAAS test date was three months away. (The prep materials were covered with military camouflage designs, calling for "war against the TAAS." The company's consultants came to the school in camouflage gear to do a TAAS pep rally for the students and faculty.)

This teacher reported that her principal, a person dedicated to these students and to their need to pass the TAAS in order to graduate, had used almost the entire year's instructional budget to purchase these expensive materials. The cost was merely one problem. Inside the practice booklets for the "reading" test were single-page activities, with brief nonsense paragraphs, followed by TAAS-type multiple-choice questions. This teacher's student who had been analyzing the poetry of Ga Soto and exploring the initiation theme *Bless Me, Ultima*, had to set aside this intellectual work to spend more than half of every class period working through the TAAS-prep booklet. This is not an isolated horror story. It is a case all too representative of the displacement of curriculum in the name of raising building-level test scores in minority schools.

The imposition throughout the entire school of TAAS-prep as a substitute curriculum recast the role of teachers, making them into people who need outside consultants to tell them ways to raise test scores (and to "pep them up"). That these commercial materials were imposed precluded resistance on the teachers' part. It also made it difficult for teachers to make accommodations at the margins, to try to hold onto the more substantive curriculum and cultural connections essential to real learning.

When their students' learning is represented by the narrow indicators of a test like the TAAS, teachers lose the capacity to bring into the discussion of the school program their knowledge of what children are learning. Test scores generated by centralized testing systems like the TAAS—and by test-prep materials aimed at producing better scores—are not reliable indicators of learning. It is here where the effects on low-performing students, particularly minority students, begin to skew the possibilities for their access to a richer education.

At the school whose principal had purchased the high-priced test-prep materials and at other Latino schools where TAAS-prep is replacing the curriculum, teachers report that, even though many more students are passing TAAS "reading" tests, few of their students are actual readers. Few of them can use reading for assignments in other classes; few choose to read or to share books with their friends. In schools where TAAS reading scores are going up, by whatever means, there is little or no will to address this gap. First, so much publicity surrounds the rising scores—and the principals' job security and superintendents' bonuses are contingent on that rise—that the problem of nonreaders is swept under the rug. Second, with the problem hidden, there can be no leverage to add the necessary resources, change the teaching, or invite discussions about the sources of the problem. In fact, the opposite occurs: the rise in scores is used to justify even more TAAS-prep, even more pep rallies, even more substituting of test-based programs for a serious curriculum.

Advocates of TAAS sometimes argue that being able to pass the reading skills section of TAAS is better than not being able to read at all. However, teachers are reporting that the kind of test prep frequently done to raise test scores may actually hamper students' ability to learn to read for meaning. In fact, high school students report that in the test-prep drills and on the TAAS reading section, they frequently mark answers without reading the sample of text: they merely match key words in the answer choice with key words in the text. And elementary teachers note that so many months of "reading" the practice samples and answering multiple-choice questions on them undermines their students' ability to read sustained passages of several pages. The reading samples are material the students are *meant to forget* the minute they mark their answers; at all grade levels this read-and-forget activity is using up the school year with a noncurriculum.

That this is happening chiefly in African American and Latino schools means that the gap between what these children learn and what the children in non-test-prep—usually middle-class and white—schools learn is widening even more dramatically. The subjects not yet tested (science, arts, social studies) are also affected as teachers in historically low-performing schools (minority, poor) are increasingly required to stop teaching those subjects in order to use class time to drill for TAAS math or reading—not to teach reading, but to drill for reading or grammar sections of the TAAS. As Angela Valenzuela has noted, under this system there is a growing, cumulative deficit separating minority students from the education being provided their more privileged peers.[3]

What is happening to and with students under the test-prep system—and what is happening to their access to curriculum content—is completely absent from consideration under an accounting system that uses only one set of indicators on which to base administrative, economic, and instructional decisions in schools.

Equally serious in its consequences is the legacy of institutionalizing the externalized authority over schools. During the years of desegregation, there were public discussions of the purposes of education, the role of the school in the community, and the issue of who should be educated and who should govern access to and provision for education. There were even debates over what constituted a public language with which to discuss public education— the languages of equity, of academic quality, and of community values all intersected and mutually informed the highly contested decisions regarding means to break the power of segregation. When education is governed by an "accountability system," these public languages are displaced by an expert technical language. When educational practice and policy are subsumed under a narrow set of indicators, then the only vocabulary for discussing those practices and policies and their effects on various groups of students is the vocabulary of the indicators—in this case, scores on a single set of tests.

Behind the test scores and the technical policy debates, however, is the growing reality that the Texas system of educational accountability is harming children, teaching, and the content of public schooling. Even more significant for the long run, this system of testing is restratifying education by race and class.

THE NEW DISCRIMINATION

The educational losses that a centralized, standardized system of testing creates for minority students are many. What such youngsters are taught, how they are taught, how their learning is assessed and represented in school records, what is omitted from their education—all these factors are hidden in the system of testing and in the accounting system that reports its results. The narrowing of the curriculum in test-prep schools is creating a new kind of discrimination—one based not on a blatant stratification of access to knowledge through tracking, but one that uses the appearance of sameness to mask persistent inequalities.

This masking shows up first in the words of well-meaning people who restratify expectations by a focus on "basics." The myth that standardization produces sameness—and therefore equity—is based on the notion that standardization "brings up the bottom." The idea is that everyone should get the fundamentals. First, students have to "get the basics" before they can get to the "creative" or "interesting" part of the curriculum. According to this myth, any good teacher or good school will "go beyond the basics" to provide a creative, interesting education.

There is increasing evidence that this focus on "basics" is being applied to minority children, who are viewed as "other people's children."[4] If "those children" are somehow different from "our children" (who are getting the regular curriculum), then they should be grateful for an education that provides them for the first time with the basics. But evidence from classrooms points out several flaws in the constructing of curriculum around the needs of "those students" for the basics.

First, students learn the "basics" when they undertake purposeful instructional activities, when they have models of thinking to emulate, and when they can see how new skills can be applied at the next level. The teachers in the schools in which I conducted case studies (heirs to Dewey and others) engaged students' minds so that they could learn both the "basics" and the ideas and knowledge that cannot be sequenced in a linear fashion because they are part of an organic whole. Yet officials' pride in the TAAS system stems largely from the notion that, "for the first time, those students are getting the same education that *our* students have been getting." The sameness is false, because the resources provided to the schools of minority children and to the academic tracks in which they are frequently placed are dramatically inferior to those provided to the schools and tracks of white, middle-class children. The apparent "sameness" of the test masks these persistent disparities in the conditions of learning that the children face.

That the political climate is becoming more accepting of this patronizing characterization of minority children was made graphically clear at an event in which Latino students would be demonstrating their learning. A white corporate executive had sponsored the implementation of several packaged curricula in Latino schools in a poor neighborhood. Each of the programs was expensive, including classroom materials, consultants to train the teachers to use the materials, tests to evaluate the students' mastery of the content, and so on. The curricular programs, in math and reading, were aimed at the "basics."

The Latino children, dressed in their Sunday best, filed in by grade level to demonstrate their skills in basic math operations. The children's parents and teachers were seated in the large hall. Between the performances by groups of children, the corporate executive would talk about the program. After one group of children had exhibited their skills in adding, he looked over the heads of the Latino parents to the white corporate and community leaders standing around the room and said, "Isn't this great? Now, this may not be the math you would want for *your* children, but for *these* children—isn't this just great?" His remarks were met with smiles and nods.

The pervasiveness of TAAS-prep as a substitute for the curriculum in poor and minority schools is legitimized by the tacit (and mistaken) understanding that for such children repetitive practice in test-drill workbooks may be better than what they had before and is useful in raising their test scores.

Data are beginning to emerge that document the exact opposite. In a compelling study to be released this year, Walter Haney has analyzed graduation rates of cohorts of high school students from 1978 to the present. Using official data from the Texas Education Agency, Haney tracked ninth-grade cohorts to graduation. In 1978, more than 60% of black students and almost 60% of Latinos graduated—15% below the average graduation rate for whites. By 1990, after four years of the Perot-era standardization reforms, graduation rates for blacks, Latinos, and whites had all dropped. By 1990, according to Haney, *fewer than 50% of all black and Latino* ninth-graders made it to graduation. (The graduation rate for whites was more than 70%.) The gap between minorities and whites was widening. By 1999, Haney's data show that the white graduation rate had regained its 1978 level (around 75%). The graduation rate for Latinos and blacks, however, remained below 50%.[5]

Standardization may, through intensive test-practice drills, "raise scores." But standardization has not enhanced children's learning. To those who would say that the graduation rate is dropping because the TAAS is "raising the bar," one must answer that to increase cut-off scores and make no investment in equalizing educational resources is no reform. It is a creative new form of discrimination.

MASKING INEQUITIES

The TAAS system of testing restratifies access to knowledge in schools. It further harms the education of poor and minority youths by masking historical and persistent inequities. When the precursor to TAAS was implemented in the 1980s, two rationales were given. First, it would provide an "objective measurement" of the curriculum. Second, according to a central office administrator, it would ensure that "Algebra I at [a poor, minority high school] is the same as Algebra I at [a suburban, middle- to upper-middle-class, mostly white high school]." The imposition of the test-based curriculum, however, carried with it no new resources for the historically under-resourced schools. Sameness, without massive investments at the under-resourced schools, is achieved by "leveling down" from the top, if at all. It is a poor proxy for equity.

The TAAS system of test-driven accountability masks the inequities that have for decades built unequal structures of schooling in Texas. The investments in expensive systems of testing, test design, test contracts and subcontracts, training of teachers and administrators to implement the tests, test security, realignment of curricula with tests, and the production of test-prep materials serve a political function in centralizing control over education and linking public education to private commerce.[6] But these expenditures do nothing to reverse the serious inequities that have widened over time across the state. In fact, investments in the "accountability system" are cynically seen to obviate the need for new investments in the schools. Even more cynical is the inverting of investments related to accountability *not* to equalize resources but to reward those whose scores go up: the investment comes as a reward for compliance, not as a means to ensure educational improvement.

Meanwhile, scarce resources at the school and district levels are being invested in those materials and activities that will raise scores, not in curricula of lasting intellectual or practical value to students. Experience over the past five years—the period in which principals have traded tenure for TAAS-based performance contracts—shows that it is the historically under-resourced schools, those serving the greatest numbers of poor and minority students, that have shifted their already scarce resources into the purchase of test-prep materials.

Jean Anyon writes compellingly in *Ghetto Schooling* about the pauperization of central city Newark—the dwindling of neighborhood resources in all areas of funding and public goods—as whites left those parts of the city.[7] The poverty of the people and the institutions that remained was a result of this pauperization by alliances of more powerful political and economic interests. In much the same way, the stratifying of academic resources in the name of compliance with an accountability system is pauperizing many urban schools, which only serves to compound their academic insufficiencies, since they are already academically weak and there is little public will to address their lack of resources.

ACCOUNTABLE TO WHOM?

Accountability implies responsibility to a higher authority: being held to account for or being obligated to account to. Within the urban district I have studied and in the state of Texas, during the Perot reforms and at present, accountability has been invoked to locate the problems of schooling at the level of the lowest employees, the teachers. The use of the word itself distracts from the historical inequities in funding, staff allocation, investment in materials, and social support from the broader community. By implying a hierarchy and a culpability at the bottom of the system, such calls for accountability empower those who use the term. The presumption is that those who are calling for accountability feel that they are in control and that others (located beneath them) must answer to them. A common feint is to claim that "the public demands accountability"—though, when the public has tried to demand accountability in education, it has traditionally tried to make the top of the education structure responsive to its particular school and community.

The current accountability system bases assessment of schools and school personnel on children's test scores. A system of education that reduces student learning to scores on a single state test—and uses those scores for such high-stakes decisions as grade promotion and high school graduation—rules out the possibility of discussing student learning in terms of cognitive and intellectual development, in terms of growth, in terms of social awareness and social conscience, in terms of social and emotional development. It is as if the "whole child" has become a stick figure. Upper-level administrators who tell principals not to speak about their students on their programs except in terms of TAAS scores are participating in the de-legitimating of students as young human beings.

Furthermore, the reduction of students to test scores has two contradictory but equally depersonalizing effects. First, the individual scores ignore the social and collaborative aspects of learning. Second, in the reporting of scores, children are subsumed into depersonalized, often meaningless, aggregates. A 75% passing rate at a school this year may appear to be an improvement over a 66% passing rate at the same school last year, but in an urban setting there is no assurance that even half of the children are the same in two successive years.

The accountability system likewise depersonalizes teachers, flattening any representation of their particular practice into the aggregate pass rates for their schools. The role of principal has been severely limited; principals now have greater authority to allocate resources for activities aimed at raising test scores but less discretionary power to undertake other kinds of work in their schools or to have that work recognized.

The use of a language of accountability also takes the discussion of public schooling away from the normal language of families and communities. Parents feel that they have to master a jargon to understand how their children are doing; teachers feel mystified by the mathematical formulas that can turn known weak schools into "exemplary" ones. Parents report feeling confused by their children's TAAS report sheets.

Finally, "accountability" is a closed system that allows no critique. The only questions about the system that generate a response are those having to do with technical aspects: At what point should children whose first language is not English have to take the reading portion of TAAS in English? Are the test questions valid? Are they culturally biased? Is the cut-off score for graduation set too high or too low? Questions about technical tinkering are tolerated. And to all such questions, there is one basic answer: more controls. If there is lax security, the test materials must be more tightly controlled. If scores are going up, then test prep must be working. If scores are slipping, then more test prep must be needed. There is no acknowledgment among district or state officials that the real problem is not cheating by altering answer sheets. Instead, the real problem inherent in such an accountability system is that it severely undermines teaching and learning, while masking problems within the school.

The educational costs of standardization, then, include not only the direct impact on teaching and learning, but also the high costs of compliance when compliance silences professional expertise and marginalizes parental and public discourse.

If the language of accountability comes to dominate public school policy, it will eliminate the means by which the public—parents and teachers and other citizens of a community—can challenge the system of accountability. We have already seen the harmful effects of such a system on curriculum and teaching. We have seen its tendencies to create new forms of discrimination as its control mechanisms reward those administrators who shift resources into the means of compliance rather than toward improving the quality of education—a pervasive pattern in minority schools with a history of low scores on standardized tests.

More than two decades ago in *Legislated Learning*, Arthur Wise warned that attempts to legislate learning and to legislate teaching frequently have "perverse effects."[8] He was speaking of the kinds of effects that have been documented in the poor and minority schools described here in their responses to the TAAS. And the effects within schools and school systems may not be nearly so "perverse" as the effects within our system of democracy, because these attempts to legislate and control learning reduce the public's possibilities for retaining democratic governance of schools once the controls are in place. One reason for this—mentioned above—is that an accountability-based control system, because it is a closed system, structures out possibilities for external criticism.

Throughout the history of public schooling in America, maintaining our democracy has been cited as the fundamental justification for public support of schools. Education is essential for effective citizenship, for playing an active role in the economic, cultural, and political life of the nation. Democracy has been both the real reason for extending an education to all children and—at times—the cover story that masked our failure to provide such an education equitably. Even when the education we provided was inequitable, it carried such democratic slogans as "separate but equal." Given our democratic heritage, the ways in which the language of accountability is displacing democratic discourse need to be carefully examined.

The current accountability system has been implemented slowly and in stages. First came state tests that held almost no consequence for students; then came state tests that held moderate consequences for students (scores were recorded in their records but not used for high-stakes decisions). Now the system uses students' scores for the evaluation of teachers, principals, schools, and even districts. Students who have been in school only during the past 10 years (the life span of the TAAS) know nothing different. Teachers who have taught for fewer than 10 years and who have not come in from another state assume outcomes testing to be a sad but "inevitable" feature of schooling. The incremental normalizing of an accountability system and the casual use of its language in conversations about education can silence criticism and stifle the potential to pose counter models and to envision alternative possibilities. That is the insidious power of the language of accountability: to sound just enough like common sense not to be recognized as a language meant to reinforce unequal power relations.

It is only by understanding the differential effects of accountability systems on varied groups of students, on teachers, on parents, and on communities that we can know whether they serve our children and our goals for public education well. And it is only by going inside schools and inside classrooms that we can begin to build that understanding at a deeply informed level.

These highly rationalized and technical systems of schooling are being touted as very beneficial for their states and districts—after all, test scores are rising. When we examine such systems more closely, however, we may find that these benefits prove to be short-lived and as artificial and inflated as the test scores produced by months of test preparation. And we may also find that the costs of these systems are being borne by the weakest participants in our education systems—the children. The slogans of "reform" can be truly seductive. As researchers and as citizens we need to look behind those slogans and see what effects our fancy systems are having on the children.

NOTES

1. Jay Heubert and Robert Hauser, eds., *High Stakes: Testing for Tracking, Promotion, and Graduation* (Washington, D.C.: National Research Council, 1998).
2. Linda M. McNeil, *Contradictions of School Reform: Educational Costs of Standardized Testing* (New York: Routledge, 2000), chap. 6.
3. Linda M. McNeil and Angela Valenzuela, "Harmful Effects of the TAAS System of Testing in Texas: Beneath the Accountability Rhetoric," in Mindy Kornhaber, Gary Orfield, and Michal Kurlaendar, eds., *Raising Standards or Raising Barriers? Inequality and High-Stakes Testing in Public Education* (New York: Century Foundation, forthcoming).
4. Lisa Delpit, *Other People's Children: Cultural Conflict in the Classroom* (New York: New Press, 1995).
5. Walter Haney, "Study of Texas Education Agency Statistics on Cohorts of Texas High School Students, 1978–1998," unpublished paper, Center for the Study of Testing, Evaluation, and Educational Policy, Boston College, 1999.
6. Walter Haney, George Madaus, and Robert Lyons, *The Fractured Marketplace of Standardized Testing* (Boston: Kluwer Academic Publishers, 1993).
7. Jean Anyon, *Ghetto Schooling: A Political Economy of Urban Educational Reform* (New York: Teachers College Press, 1997).
8. Arthur Wise, *Legislated Learning: The Bureaucratization of the American Classroom* (Berkeley: University of California Press, 1979).

5

▼▼▼▼▼▼▼

Illusions of Progress:
Business as Usual*

Christine E. Sleeter and Carl Grant

Before we discuss approaches that teachers can take to deal constructively with race, class, gender, and disability, it is important to describe what often occurs in many classrooms and schools. School, it has been observed, reflects society. Just as a few improvements in society may give an incomplete or inaccurate view of progress in reducing racism, sexism, class bias, and bias against disabilities, a few improvements in our schools are similarly misleading. In many schools, one can readily observe students of color and White students socializing; girls in classes such as wood shop and auto shop, once considered the exclusive domain of the boys; boys in home economics classes, once considered no-man's-land; Spanish spoken in mathematics classes; and students in wheelchairs attending proms and participating in many other school events. Also, in some schools the cheering squad, band, and sports teams often reflect the diversity of the student body. Moreover, it is not unusual in integrated schools for a person of color to be the president of the student council, a class officer, or a member of the queen's court.

Furthermore, most teachers and school administrators support equal opportunity and access to all courses and activities for all students enrolled in the school: They support events that recognize the contributions of people of color and women; many welcome mainstreamed special education students into their classes; most will not tolerate sexist behavior in the classroom; and virtually all support having students from different socioeconomic status attend the same school. Also, many teachers examine their curriculum materials for bias, are willing to attend workshops dealing with multicultural education, and try to avoid using any instructional materials that are obviously biased.

These examples suggest that success for all students is the order of business in classrooms and schools. However, to the discerning observer, much has been left out. Like the society we described earlier, schools are beset with problems related to race, class, gender, and disability.

Our description of "business as usual" is based on several studies published during the 1980s and 1990s in which researchers observed what actually takes place in the schools. We will describe the main patterns that emerge. We acknowledge that schools and classrooms vary, although those that vary significantly are usually few and far between. We invite you to compare this description with schools with which you may be familiar. We have organized this description into five categories: how teachers teach, what teachers teach, how students are grouped, other patterns, and student culture.

How Teachers Teach

Many studies have found strong similarities in how teachers teach (Bigler & Lockard, 1992; Cuban, 1984; Everhart, 1983; Goodlad, 1984; Grant & Sleeter, 1986; Page, 1991; Sleeter, 1992; Trueba, Jacobs, & Kirton, 1990). Cuban (1984) summarizes these well, drawing on his own research. He separates the elementary and secondary levels, acknowledging a greater diversity among elementary teachers than among secondary teachers. Cuban reports that in elementary classrooms he came to expect a number of regularities. Almost half of the teachers (43 percent) put up a daily schedule on the blackboard. If it was time for reading, the teachers would work with one group and assign the same seatwork or varied tasks to the rest of the class. If it was time for math, social studies, science, or language arts, generally the teachers would work from a text with the entire class answering questions from the text, ditto sheets, or workbooks (p. 220).

Both Cuban, in his study of 6 school districts, and Goodlad (1984), in his study of 13 elementary–middle–high school feeder systems, found that many elementary teachers deviate from this pattern by individualizing instruction, using learning centers, and using small groups. However, the majority favored teacher-centered, large-group instruction in which all students work on the same tasks and in which much of the work depends on the textbook, ditto sheets, or workbooks.

At the secondary level, there is much more uniformity. Cuban describes the main pattern as "rows of tablet-arm chairs facing a teacher who is talking, asking, listening to student answers, and supervising the entire class for most of the period—a time that is occasionally punctuated by a student report, a panel, or a film" (p. 222). Cuban found labs in science classes to offer the main variation from this pattern in academic courses: Goodlad added that vocational, physical education, and art classes involve more varied activities and much more hands-on learning. Page's (1991) study of eight lower-track classrooms in two middle-class high schools revealed that the teachers arrange the classrooms so that students can proceed in simple, step-by-step routines to learn practical skills. She posits that the teachers dominate classroom talk without being domineering, and they "teach by remote control, without calling attention to themselves as teachers" (p. 147).

These patterns have several implications for student diversity. One implication is that students whose learning style diverges from predominant teaching styles are at a disadvantage. For example, Shade (1989) argues that African American students suffer academically in schools because their learning style tends to be oriented toward cooperation, content about people, discussion and hands-on work, and whole-to-part learning, which conflicts with the independent, task-oriented, reading-oriented, part-to-whole style that most teachers employ with most students. As another example, Deyhle (1985) found that young Navajo students interpret tests as games, in contrast to White students who view tests as serious business, a result of different home socialization. Whereas White children learn early to display knowledge publicly for evaluation, Navajo children learn at a young age that serious learning is private and therefore do not exert their best effort when tested. Furthermore, Goodlad notes that the activities used in nonacademic areas, such as industrial arts, attract students who prefer active involvement in learning. This approach may help lure lower-class and minority students, more than middle-class White students, into these areas and away from academics.

A second implication is that students whose skills deviate from those of the majority present a problem for the classroom teacher, because most teachers individualize very little. The main solution schools have used has been to place such students in remedial or special education classes or to track them. This has created additional problems.

Clearly, this uniformity in teaching procedures conflicts with the mainstreaming movement. In a study of one junior high school, we found that regular education teachers modified their procedures only minimally for mainstreamed students, and they expected everybody else to learn at the same rate, through the same instruction procedures and materials (Grant & Sleeter, 1986). It seems that regular and special educators often find themselves in conflict over the intent of PL 94–142: Many regular educators view special education as a place to put students whose skills deviate significantly from the majority, while special education teachers are trying to move students from special education back into the mainstream and wish to see regular education teachers become more flexible in how they teach.

Similarly, many bilingual education teachers find themselves in conflict with "regular" classroom teachers over the specific needs of limited English proficiency (LEP) students. Although sent to other classrooms for reading, mathematics, or other instruction, LEP students are often "mainstreamed" in art, music, and physical education. Unfortunately, some teachers refuse to alter their standard approaches to meet the needs of these students. Instead, the students' language and cultural background is sometimes perceived as a handicap, and they are then "diagnosed" and treated as learning disabled (Trueba et al., 1990).

A third implication is that much instruction given in classrooms is uninteresting and alienating for many students. In our study of a junior high school, the word students used most often to describe instruction was *boring*. Goodlad (1984) describes classrooms as emotionally flat. Students who do not readily identify with schooling, with their teachers, or with the content being taught tend to become turned off and disengaged. This seems particularly true when the content is unrelated to the students' experiential background. Everhart (1983) describes an incident in a junior high classroom in which students were filling in a worksheet after reading about Switzerland in their textbooks. Not having been to Switzerland, and not having been provided experiences to develop visual, aural, or tactile imagery about Switzerland, the students discussed the weekend football game while completing an assignment that to them was merely verbal gymnastics.

Of course, there are some excellent and dynamic teachers. Unfortunately, much of the usual classroom instruction discourages some students, turns off others, and fails to engage the minds of many. Further, those who tend to become turned off, disengaged, or frustrated are disproportionately lower-class students and students of color. (Students mainstreamed from special education may also become frustrated and disengaged, but they usually have the support and help of a special education teacher.)

There is another instructional problem that occurs in some classrooms. Research has found that many teachers interact with, call on, praise, and intellectually challenge students who are White, male, and middle class more than other students in the same classroom and that they reprimand Black male students the most (Jackson & Cosca, 1974; Sadker & Sadker, 1982). For example, Table 5.1 illustrates the average proportion of questions and praise that girls and boys received in several classrooms at three different times during the year. In the first and third observations, boys received proportionately more questions and praise than girls. During the second observation, teachers were monitoring their behavior because results of the first observation had been shared with them, but by the third observation they had returned to their earlier pattern. Further, as the year progressed, boys initiated an increasingly larger proportion of student-initiated questions (Sleeter, 1992). Teachers are usually unaware that they are showing favorit-

TABLE 5.1
Teacher-Student Interaction: Gender Patterns

Average Classroom Composition:
Females   46%
Males   54%

	OBS. #1 (24 classrooms)	OBS. #2 (14 classrooms)	OBS. #3 (16 classrooms)
Who Gets Called On:	%	%	%
Females	39	47	38
Males	61	53	62
Who Gets Praised:			
Females	32	51	43
Males	68	49	57
Which Students Initiate Questions:			
Females	35	22	19
Males	55	78	81

SOURCE: C. E. Sleeter (1992), *Keepers of the American dream*, London: The Falmer Press, p. 127.

ism, but such bias can benefit members of advantaged social groups when it occurs.

Bigler and Lockard (1992) observed that the teachers they interviewed reported that the reason students tell parents they did "nothing" in school is "not due to the lack of talented teachers or their desire to teach, but as a direct result of too much to do, insufficient time to do it and increasing intrusion on teaching time" (pp. 63–64). Bigler and Lockard's observation would generate very little debate among researchers who study classroom life. Nevertheless, overtaxation of teachers, lack of teaching and planning time, and classroom interruptions most directly impact students who are marginalized and can least afford it.

What Teachers Teach

Goodlad's (1984) study of 38 schools nationwide provides a comprehensive view of what teachers today are teaching. We will not provide extensive description, but rather we will note salient findings. The main finding was school-to-school uniformity, especially at the secondary level. Goodlad summarized two subject areas as follows: "Overall, the impression that emerged from the analysis of English and language arts was one of great curricular similarity from school to school. This impression comes through even more strongly for mathematics" (p. 208). He found that teachers in both subject areas emphasized the acquisition of skills, often apart from context or real-life use. Social studies and science at the elementary level varied considerably from classroom to classroom, often being grounded in students' experiential background. For example, primary-grade social studies usually revolved around the family and neighborhood. At the secondary level, however, social studies content became increasingly alike from one classroom to another and increasingly removed from student experience. More variation was found in what was taught in the arts and vocational areas. Goodlad also found heavy emphasis on rote learning: Although teachers often said they were developing higher-level thinking skills, their tests overwhelmingly emphasized the regurgitation of memorized material.

Curricula emphasize the White wealthy male experience, although less so today than 25 years ago. In 1990, we analyzed 47 textbooks that were in use in grades 1 through 8, with copyright dates between 1980 and 1988. The analysis included social studies, reading and language arts, science, and mathematics textbooks. The results supported the following conclusion:

> Whites consistently dominate textbooks, although their margin of dominance varies widely. Whites receive the most attention, are shown in the widest variety of roles, and dominate the story line and lists of accomplishments. Blacks are the next most included racial group. However, the books show Blacks in a more limited range of roles than Whites and give only a sketchy account of Black history and little sense of contemporary Black life. Asian Americans and Hispanic Americans appear mainly as figures on the landscape with virtually no history or contemporary ethnic experience. . . . Native Americans appear mainly as historical figures. . . . Males predominate in most books; but even in books in which females have a major presence, females of color are shown very little. One gains little sense of the history or culture of women, and learns very little about sexism or current issues involving gender. . . . Social class is not treated in the books much at all. . . . The image that books in all subject areas convey is that the United States is not stratified on the basis of social class, that almost everyone is middle-class, that there is no poverty and no great wealth. . . . Disability is ignored as well. (Sleeter & Grant, 1991, pp. 97–98)

Furthermore, there seems to be more cultural diversity in curricular materials than in the actual content teachers teach. It is important for us to point out that, although an increasing number of teachers do use culturally pluralistic and nonsexist materials, most of these teachers do not refer very often to people of color or women when talking or lecturing (Grant & Sleeter, 1986). Thus, what teachers teach when doing "business as usual" includes people of color somewhat, and in a supplementary way, but Whites still predominate; it includes White females, but males still dominate; it includes disabled people sporadically; and it virtually excludes the experience of those living below the middle class.

The curriculum responds most actively to diversity when there are non-English-speaking students. Since the Supreme Court decision in *Lau v. Nichols* (1974), schools have been required to provide help in learning English as well as instruction in the child's language while the child is learning English. Under business as usual, this seems to mean providing bilingual or English as a Second Language (ESL) instruction for as short a time as possible until minimal English proficiency is achieved. For example, Guthrie (1985) studied a Chinese-English bilingual program in California. She found that the Chinese community wanted its children to learn the Chinese language and culture, whereas the school system expected bilingual education to work toward as rapid a transition to English as possible. Debates at the federal level during the 1980s and into the 1990s support the school system's expectation: Debates revolve around how to teach English most effectively, not how to promote bilingualism. (Interestingly, however, business as usual does encourage college-bound English-speaking students to acquire minimal competence in a second, usually Western European, language.)

So far, our description suggests that all students of a given grade level are taught much the same thing, regardless of geographic region, student interest, or cultural background, except in the case of non-English-speaking students. This characterization is only partially correct. There does appear to be a standard curriculum that most teachers use as a guide. It is not codified in a national curriculum guide; rather, it is codified in standardized achievement tests and text materials, which are more alike than different for any given subject area. Teachers tend to use the content of text materials and standardized tests as the basis for what they teach. They then modify this material to fit the average skill level of a class and, to a much lesser degree, student interest and experiential background. For example, consider the teachers in the junior high school studied by Grant and Sleeter (1986). When asked how they decided what to teach, most teachers reported starting with an idea of what students at that grade level should know in that subject area, then adjusting forward or backward to most students' current level of mastery. In this case, students were behind grade level in most areas, so teachers either retreated to earlier material or watered down grade-level material to make it simpler. Student interest rarely affected what these teachers taught.

Goodlad's (1984) study of 38 schools supports this finding. The main variation he found in content was between tracks or ability groups. Teachers beefed up or watered down content in response to student skill level. Student interest played at most a minor role in determining the curriculum. Geographic locale played no role. Student cultural background played a minor role. Because track or ability group plays the main role in determining how teachers vary both instruction and content, we turn next to how students are grouped.

How Students Are Grouped

Within school districts, students are grouped in various ways: by school, by ability group or track, by special education need, and by interest (in the form of electives). We will discuss aspects of grouping under business as usual as they relate to race, social class, gender, and handicap.

First, although schools are supposed to be racially desegregated, they do not need to be desegregated on the basis of social class. It is quite common for schools to serve primarily or solely upper-class, middle-class, working-class, or lower-class students; and schools serving different social classes are not alike. They differ somewhat in the availability of resources, such as computers (Campbell, 1984) and in the salaries they are able to offer. They differ strikingly in curriculum and instruction. For example, based on observations in five schools, Anyon (1981) reported differences that are virtually the same as those we will describe between tracks.

Racial desegregation is also less a reality than many of us would like to believe, particularly for language-minority students. Although the segregation of African American students has decreased, the segregation of Hispanic students has increased (Orfield, 1986). The majority of Hispanic students attend schools that serve predominantly minority populations. This increased segregation of Hispanic students interferes with their acquisition of English-language competence (Garcia, 1986) and is related to higher high school dropout rates. In addition, the schools that Hispanic students attend are largely inferior, reporting the highest dropout rates, lowest achievement rates, and greatest problems with teacher turnover, overcrowding, and gangs (Kyle, Lane, Sween, & Triana, 1986). As Orum and Vincent (1984) put it, "Hispanics now have the dubious distinction of being not only the most undereducated group of American children, but also the most highly segregated" (p. 26).

A second important kind of grouping is ability grouping, extensively found in elementary schools, and tracking, a pervasive feature of high schools in the major academic areas. The pros and cons of ability grouping are a continuous focus of debate among teachers, as demonstrated on the "Speak Out" page of the American Federation of Teachers' publication *On Campus* (Lucas, 1992; Mitchell, 1992). Here, two teachers argued their positions on ability grouping, one basically arguing that ability grouping can create a label that lasts a lifetime and the other arguing that talented students must not be ignored. Based on a review of research on the effects of tracking, Oakes (1985) reports that although many people assume that ability grouping and tracking are best for most students, the evidence points clearly to the conclusion that "no group of students has been found to benefit consistently from being in a homogeneous group," and those in the middle and lower groups are often affected negatively (p. 7). Her own investigation of 25 secondary schools across the country in the late 1970s found considerable tracking being used. In multiracial schools, upper-track classes were disproportionately White, whereas lower-track classes were disproportionately minority and lower-class. Upper-track students tended to receive the following: at least

80% of class time spent on instruction, considerable homework, more varied teaching activities, clear instruction, emphasis on higher-level thinking skills, and exposure to content that would gain them access to college. Lower-track students, on the other hand, received about 67% of class time spent on instruction, half (or less) the homework of upper-track students, varied materials but very routinized instructional activities, less clarity in instruction, emphasis on rote memory, and content oriented around everyday-life skills (which may seem practical but also may block access to college). Most upper-track students reported enthusiasm for school and feelings of personal competence, whereas lower-track students were often turned off to school and felt academically incompetent. These are the same sorts of differences Anyon (1981) found between upper-class and working-class schools.

These studies clearly show that students are being grouped partly on the basis of race and social class and then are taught differently. Upper-track and upper-class students are offered more instructional time, more challenge, interesting and effective instruction, opportunities to think, and preparation for college. Lower-track and lower-class students tend to receive routine and dull instruction, less challenge, memory work, and little or no preparation for college. Middle groups receive something in between. Although people often say that these groupings meet students' instructional needs and provide opportunity for advancement, lower groups for the most part are being turned off to school and are not being pushed to catch up, causing them to grow increasingly different from other groups as they proceed through school. For this reason, schools have been very accurately described as a sorting machine, slotting the young for a stratified labor market (Spring, 1976).

A third problem is the proportionately small numbers of female students in upper-level mathematics and science courses and in computer courses. It appears that although girls may take almost as many mathematics and science courses as boys, they often avoid the more difficult courses, which greatly hinders access to mathematics and science majors in college (Fennema, 1984).

A fourth aspect of grouping is special education, which in many ways fits into the tracking system, although less so for the physically, visually, and hearing impaired than for other categories. Gifted classes are still disproportionately White, whereas classes for the mentally retarded and emotionally disturbed are disproportionately African American (Table 5.2). In some schools, Hispanic students are overrepresented in special education; in some, they are placed in bilingual education whether this is appropriate or not. Learning disability classes appear to be shifting from protective areas for White, middle-class, failing children to remedial classes for students previously classified as retarded or slow (Sleeter, 1986). The nature of content and, to some extent, instruction parallels distinctions between upper and lower tracks. However, special education teachers often do a better job than most

TABLE 5.2
Percentage of Students in Disability Categories by Race

	Enrollment by Race (%)				
	American Indian	Asian	Hispanic	Black	White
Total Enrollment in School System	1	3	10	16	70
Special Ed Classifications:					
Gifted & Talented	0	5	5	8	81
Educable Mentally Retarded	1	1	5	35	58
Trainable Mentally Retarded	1	2	10	27	60
Speech Impaired	1	2	8	16	73
Severely Emotionally Disturbed	1	0	7	27	65
Specific Learning Disability	1	1	10	17	71

SOURCE: B. Harry (1992). *Cultural diversity, families, and the special education system.* New York: Teachers College Press, p. 62. Reprinted by permission of the publisher, ©1992 by Teachers College, Columbia University. All rights reserved.

other teachers of adapting instruction to students' learning styles, skill levels, and interests and often act as advocates and helpers for their students, helping to get them through the school system to graduation (Grant & Sleeter, 1986).

A fifth aspect of grouping is vocational classes, which group students at the secondary level somewhat by interest. Even here, however, we find grouping roughly following social class, race, and gender lines. For example, Oakes (1985) found a distinct racial difference in vocational courses: Home economics and general industrial arts were by far the main vocational courses in White schools, whereas courses preparing students for specific blue-collar and clerical occupations were common in non-White and racially mixed schools. In spite of Title IX (an education amendment of 1972 that forbids schools from restricting access to courses and school activities based upon sex), one is also likely to find a gender difference, with home economics and clerical courses dominated by girls and industrial arts courses dominated by boys (DBS Corporation, 1982). Although enrollments in vocational courses depend largely on student choice, researchers find that other factors strongly affect what students choose. These factors include availability of courses at their school, how comfortable students feel with the gender composition that is usually in a given course, how useful students think the course will be in helping them attain what they consider is a realistic (although not necessarily desirable) future occupation, and the quality of guidance and encouragement they receive (Grant & Sleeter, 1986; Oakes, 1985; Valli, 1986).

A sixth aspect of grouping at the secondary level is bilingual education or English as a Second Language (ESL). Many bilingual programs at the secondary level are seen by local administrators as remedial in nature, designed primarily for the limited English proficiency student who needs to "catch up" or minimally develop "survival" English skills. In addition, many programs segregate language-minority students within the school, making it more diffi-cult for them to interact with Anglo students in English or to receive exposure to the curriculum that Anglo students are being taught. In some states where graduation requirements have recently been raised, bilingual and ESL classes are not counted for graduation. With the institution of minimum competency testing (in English), many language-minority students face the possibility of not receiving high school diplomas or of receiving "attendance diplomas" that will close opportunities for postsecondary education (Fernandez & Velez, 1985).

All of this suggests that when schools operate according to business as usual, students are grouped in ways that roughly parallel race, class, and gen-der lines and then are taught in ways that help channel them into roles cur-rently occupied by members of their race, class, and gender groups. Grouping is usually based on tests, teacher judgment, grades, and student choice, but as ethnographic studies of schools are revealing, all of these processes are often linked in subtle but strong ways to race, social class, and gender.

Other Patterns

Additional patterns in schools tend to mirror and help reproduce prevailing race, social class, and gender patterns. Viewing school systems from top to bottom, one finds the following staffing patterns: Superintendents are over-whelmingly White and male (95%). Twenty-seven percent (27%) of the princi-pals in the country are women, and although they make up 34% of the ele-mentary school principals, they only account for 12% of the secondary school principalships (American Association of School Administrators, 1989). Therefore, women and men of color in school administration tend to be ele-mentary school principals, central office staff, or administrators charged with duties related to Title IX, desegregation, and so forth. Over 90% of teachers are White, and this percentage is increasing. Over 80% of elementary school teachers are female; mathematics, science, and industrial arts teachers are predominantly male, whereas foreign language, English, and home econom-ics teachers tend to be female. People of color are often custodians and aides, and over 90% of secretaries are women. These patterns offer distinct role models and authority relationships for students.

In addition, the growing lack of people of color in teaching and adminis-tration means that fewer teachers are likely to identify with and advocate concerns particular to students of color. Furthermore, the preponderance of men in decision-making positions sometimes causes insufficient attention to be paid to the concerns of female students, whereas the preponderance of women at the elementary school level makes it difficult for many boys to identify with school and its requirements.

Extracurricular activities can also mirror existing societal patterns and reinforce segregation patterns, although situations vary from school to school. However, the following patterns are not uncommon. Middle- and upper-class students often dominate the activities, especially activities that are academically oriented. In racially mixed schools, especially if Whites are clearly in the majority, Whites tend to dominate. When White domination occurs, other students often feel unwelcome in activities. Students of color sometimes dominate some of the sports. At times, sports are race/class divided, with golf or swimming, for example, predominantly White and basketball predominantly Black. Boys' sports often receive a larger share of the budget than girls' sports and may receive better coaches, better playing schedules, and so forth. Probably the greatest change in extracurricular activities in the past several decades has been the development of girls' sports; the challenge now seems to be to make them qualitatively equal to boys' sports.

Student Culture

The preceding discussion centered on what schools do. But students do not respond to schools in a mechanical fashion. Researchers are increasingly aware that student cultures develop in ways that often help reproduce existing social patterns, make it difficult to change student behavior, and reaffirm to teachers that their own behavior toward students is correct. Often, great gaps exist between how teachers and students perceive each other and how they perceive themselves.

Everhart (1983), for example, studied boys in a White, working-class junior high school. The boys entered school uncertain about occupational goals, familiar mainly with working-class jobs and ways of life. The teachers perceived the students as academically average or below average, with most of them probably headed for working-class jobs. Classroom instruction was teacher dominated, rarely individualized, and routine, emphasizing the memorization of predigested material. To an observer, it was immediately apparent that students spent quite a bit of time goofing off, investing only as much effort in classwork as they needed to get by. On closer examination, however, Everhart found that the students actively engaged in creating a culture that would help make school livable. The students saw school as analogous to the work world, and the school offered much on which to base this analogy: It was clearly dominated by authority figures with whom the students could not identify; the work was routine and unrelated to the students' daily lives; most of the students' time was structured; and students were rewarded for accomplishing prescribed pieces of work. Without consciously connecting their interpretation of school to the labor market or their future life chances, the students attempted to control whatever fragments of time they could and to build relationships with each other. To the teachers, the students' behavior reaffirmed that they were not interested in academic work and were incapable of managing substantive decisions, so there was no point in challenging them. The teachers seemed unaware that the student culture was generated partly in response to what they offered the students; and the low level of academic work, accepted by both teachers and students, helped ensure the students a working-class future.

Gaskell (1985) offers a similar portrait of working-class girls in clerical courses. The girls chose the courses for several reasons: These courses offered more hands-on learning than did college-preparation courses and were therefore more fun; the students were treated more like adults than were academic students; and the courses would help the girls secure a secretarial job before settling down to raise a family. Many of the girls did not particularly like secretarial work, but given the world they grew up in, this option seemed like a more viable alternative than college preparation. In school, they developed a culture that rejected academics (academic kids being viewed as somewhat childish rather than mature). Their culture centered around building social relationships with each other and drew on traditional patterns of femininity for guidance in how to control bosses, handle male workers, make boring work fun, and so forth. To the outside observer, it seemed that these girls were predisposed to be traditional women, that they chose secretarial work because they liked it, and that the school had nothing to do with these things. From the inside, it was found that the girls developed their secretarial culture as a way of trying to make the best of what they saw as limited career options, to cope with male co-workers, and to attain some status for themselves in relationship to middle-class, college-bound students.

Student culture has relevance to "business as usual," because it helps shape many of the decisions students make about school and because it develops as much from within the school as from outside the school. Many teachers believe that all or most of their students' values and beliefs are generated only from outside; students who fail, turn off, drop out, or choose low-ability classes are doing so in spite of the school's attempt to give all an equal chance. These teachers often blame the students' home culture or society in general.

Although society and home certainly cannot be discounted, they do not determine student behavior. In a very real sense, students determine it as they make sense of the school experience they confront every day. All the patterns described here as business as usual present students with experiences that vary somewhat according to student race, social class, and gender, among other factors; the experiences that students have outside the school give them frameworks that also vary by race, social class, and gender, and students use these frameworks to interpret school life. There has always been a gap between teachers and students, resulting at least from age and role and often compounded by differences in cultural background. This gap has been recently expanded, as an increasing number of students come from homes that have alternative life styles and family arrangements. Some teachers bridge this gap and grasp the differences in student culture and life style fairly well; many do not, interpreting student behavior as part of the natural order of things that teachers need to control and to discourage from being reproduced. As the teaching staff in the United States becomes increasingly older and increasingly White, it is quite possible that the gap between teachers and students, and especially low socioeconomic-status students and students of color, will widen to become a chasm in many schools.

APPROACHES TO MULTICULTURAL EDUCATION

The problems we have just described have existed for a long time and have been recognized and contested by many educators. In fact, the progress that we have noted has come about largely through the efforts of educators, working in conjunction with community and social movements, to make schools, along with other social institutions, more fair and responsive to the needs of the students.

The reforms that educators have advocated bear different names but are directed toward common practices. Some of the more common names for these reforms are *multicultural education, nonsexist education, human relations, gender fair education, multiethnic education, ethnic studies, sex equity, bilingual/bicultural education, anti-racist teaching*, and *mainstreaming*. Multicultural education has emerged as an umbrella concept that deals with race, culture, language, social class, gender, and disability. Although many educators still apply it only to race, it is the term most frequently extended to include additional forms of diversity. For this reason, we will use the term *multicultural education* to refer to educational practices directed toward race, culture, language, social class, gender, and disability, although in selecting the term we do not imply that race is the primary form of social inequality that needs to be addressed. We see racism, classism, and sexism as equally important.

Educators have not advocated a single, unified plan for multicultural education. Responding to somewhat different issues in different schools, employing different conceptual views of school and society, and holding somewhat different visions of the good society, educators over the years have constructed different approaches to multicultural education.

Gibson in 1976 reviewed advocacy literature in multicultural education, identifying four approaches that led her to ultimately suggest a fifth. The four approaches she identified were education of the culturally different, or benevolent multiculturalism, which seeks to incorporate culturally different students more effectively into mainstream culture and society; education about cultural differences, which teaches all students about cultural differences in an effort to promote better cross-cultural understanding; education for cultural pluralism, which seeks to preserve ethnic cultures and increase the power of ethnic minority groups; and bicultural education, which seeks to prepare students to operate successfully in two different cultures. She proposed, as an alternative, "multicultural education as the normal human experience," which teaches students to function in multiple cultural contexts, ethnic or otherwise (such as regional).

Pratte's (1983) typology of approaches was similar. He identified the following four approaches: restricted multicultural education, which seeks to remediate deficiencies in culturally different students and teach majority students to tolerate minorities; modified restricted multicultural education, which seeks to promote full school services for all groups and promote equality among groups within the school; unrestricted multicultural education, which seeks to remediate ethnocentrism in all students by teaching them to identify with a plurality of cultural groups; and modified unrestricted multicultural education, which seeks to prepare all students for active citizenship in a racially diverse society.

Combined, these two typologies distinguish fairly well among the various approaches to multicultural education, but they have some limitations, the main one being that neither author fleshed out the theory undergirding each approach. (Each approach occupied a page or less in a journal.) A second limitation is that both typologies were applied only to race and missed or glossed over distinctions related to gender and social class. A third limitation is that the two typologies did not quite capture the range of practices we have observed in schools. Finally, a fourth limitation is that they tended to focus on issues related to cultural diversity more than social inequality.

Based on our own work as teachers, administrators, college professors, and ethnographic researchers, as well as on extensive reviews of the literature on multicultural education (Grant, 1992a, 1992b; Grant & Sleeter, 1985; Grant, Sleeter, & Anderson, 1986; Sleeter, 1991, 1992; Sleeter & Grant, 1987), we constructed our own typology of approaches to multicultural education. We will briefly introduce these approaches.

During the 1960s, in efforts to desegregate schools, many White educators "discovered" students of color and saw them as culturally deprived. This view was contested vigorously by those who argued that these students were different, not deficient, and that their cultural differences should be accepted by the school. This view has been paralleled by many special educators who argue that disabled students' differences should be accepted and built on. The approach that emerged—Teaching the Exceptional and the Culturally Different—focuses on adapting instruction to student differences for the purpose of helping these students more effectively succeed in the mainstream. This corresponds to Gibson's first approach and Pratte's first and second.

During about the same period, but building on the post–World War II Intercultural Education Movement, other educators argued that love, respect, and more effective communication should be developed in schools to bring people who differ closer together. This developed into the Human Relations approach, which corresponds to Gibson's second approach. It has often been applied to race, gender, and handicap.

The 1960s also saw the emergence of more assertive approaches to change the mainstream of America rather than trying to fit people into it. Ethnic studies, women's studies, and, to a lesser extent, labor studies were developed in an effort to focus attention on specific groups, raise consciousness regarding that group's oppression, and mobilize for social action. This was a portion of Pratte's second approach.

The Multicultural Education approach emerged during the early 1970s, continuing to develop as some educators have grown disenchanted with earlier approaches and as others have begun conceptualizing more complete and complex plans for reforming education. This approach links race, language, culture, gender, disability, and, to a lesser extent, social class, working toward making the entire school celebrate human diversity and equal opportunity. Both Gibson and Pratte described it as their third approach, and we have subsumed Gibson's fourth and fifth approaches under it.

Finally, the 1970s and 1980s saw the development of a fifth approach, which we are calling Education That Is Multicultural and Social Reconstructionist. In the 1990s this approach gained in recognition and credibility in part because it extends the Multicultural Education approach into the realm of social action and focuses at least as much on challenging social stratification as on celebrating human diversity and equal opportunity. Pratte's fourth approach leaned in this direction.

REFERENCES

Alsalam, N., & Rogers, G. T. (1991). *The condition of education 1991: Volume 2. Postsecondary education.* Washington, DC: U.S. Government Printing Office.

American Association of School Administrators. (1989). Personal communication.

The Americans with Disabilities Act: Where we are now. (1991, January/February). *The Disability Rag,* 11–19.

Anyon, J. (1981). Elementary schooling and distinctions of social class. *Interchange, 12,* 118–132.

Barlett, D. L., & Steele, J. B. (1992). *America: What went wrong?* Kansas City, MO: Andrews & McMeel.

Beulow, M. C. (1992, July 13). State doctors told to ask more about domestic abuse. *Kenosha News,* p. 1.

Bigler, P., & Lockard, K. (1992). *Failing grades.* Arlington, VA: Vandermere Press.

Bobo, L., Schuman, H., & Steeh, C. (1986). Changing racial attitudes toward residential integration. In J. Goering (Ed.), *Housing desegregation and federal policy* (pp. 153–169). Chapel Hill: University of North Carolina Press.

Campbell, P. (1984). The computer revolution: Guess who's left out? *Interracial Books for Children Bulletin, 15*, 3–6.

Congressional Quarterly Weekly Report. (1986, 8 November).

Cuban, L. (1984). *How teachers taught.* New York: Longman.

DBS Corporation. (1982). *Elementary and secondary schools survey.* Unpublished paper prepared for the U.S. Office of Civil Rights, U.S. Department of Education.

Dervarics, C. (1991). Landmark study confirms widespread job bias. *Black Issues in Higher Education, 8*(7), 1 & 4.

Deyhle, D. (1985). Testing among Navajo and Anglo students: Another consideration of cultural bias. *Journal of Educational Equity and Leadership, 5*, 119–131.

Everhart, R. (1983). *Reading, writing, and resistance.* Boston: Routledge & Kegan Paul.

Fennema, E. (1984). Girls, women, and mathematics. In E. Fennema & M. I. Ayer (Eds.), *Women and education* (pp. 137–164). Berkeley: McCutchan.

Fernandez, R. R., & Velez, W. (1985). Race, color, and language in the changing public schools. In L. Maldonado & J. Moore (Eds.), *Urban ethnicity in the United States: New immigrants and old minorities* (pp. 123–144). Beverly Hills, CA: Sage.

Gallup, G., Jr., & Hugick, L. (1990). *Racial tolerance grows, progress on racial equality less evident.* Los Angeles: Gallup Poll News Service.

Garcia, E. E. (1986). Bilingual development and the education of bilingual children during early childhood. *American Journal of Education, 95*, 96–121.

Gaskell, J. (1985). Course enrollment in the high school: The perspective of working-class females. *Sociology of Education, 58*, 48–59.

Gearheart, B. (1980). *Special education for the '80s.* New York: Merrill/Macmillan.

Gest, T. (1991, June 17). The new meaning of equality. *U.S. News & World Report*, p. 48.

Gibson, M. A. (1976). Approaches to multicultural education in the United States: Some concepts and assumptions. *Anthropology and Education Quarterly, 7*, 7–18.

Gliedman, J., & Roth, W. (1980). *The unexpected minority.* New York: Harcourt Brace Jovanovich.

Goodlad, J. I. (1984). *A place called school.* New York: McGraw-Hill.

Grant, C. A. (1992a). *Best practices in teacher preparation for urban schools.* Paper presented at the American Educational Research Association National Conference, San Francisco.

Grant, C. A. (Ed.). (1992b). *Research and multicultural education.* London: The Falmer Press.

Grant, C. A., & Sleeter, C. E. (1985). The literature on multicultural education: Review and analysis. *Educational Review, 37*, 97–118.

Grant, C. A., & Sleeter, C. E. (1986). *After the school bell rings.* Barcombe, England: Falmer Press.

Grant, C. A., Sleeter, C. E., & Anderson, J. E. (1986). The literature on multicultural education: Review and analysis, Part II. *Educational Studies, 12*, 47–71.

Guthrie, G. P. (1985). *A school divided.* Hillsdale, NJ: Lawrence Erlbaum.

Habeck, R. V., Galvid, D. E., Frey, W. D., Chadderden, L. M., & Tate, D. G. (1985). Economics and equity in employment of people with disabilities: International policies and practices. *Proceedings from the Symposium.* East Lansing, MI: University Center for International Rehabilitation.

Hacker, A. (1992). *Two nations: Black and white, separate, hostile, and unequal.* New York: Charles Scribner's Sons.

Harrington, M. (1984). *The new American poverty.* New York: Holt, Rinehart & Winston.

Harry, B. (1992). *Cultural diversity, families, and the special education system.* New York: Teachers College Press.

Hasazi, S., Gordon, L., & Roe, C. (1985). Factors associated with the employment status of handicapped youth exiting high school from 1979 to 1983. *Exceptional Children, 51,* 455–477.

Hate. (1992, May/June). *The Disability Rag,* 4–7.

Jackson, G., & Cosca, C. (1974). The inequality of educational opportunity in the Southwest: An observational study of ethnically mixed classrooms. *American Educational Research Journal, 11,* 219–229.

Jencks, C., Smith, M., Acland, H., Bane, M. J., Cohen, D., Gintis, H., Heyns, B., & Michelson, S. (1972). *Inequality: A reassessment of the effect of family and schooling in America.* New York: Harper & Row.

Johnson, M. (1991, March/April). What builders don't know. *The Disability Rag,* 12–17.

Kyle, C. L., Jr., Lane, J., Sween, A., & Triana, A. (1986). *We have a choice: Students at risk of leaving Chicago public schools.* Chicago: DePaul University Center for Research on Hispanics.

Lau v. Nichol, 414, U.S. 563 (1974).

Lucas, L. (1992). Does ability grouping do more harm than good? Don't ignore the potential of talented students. *On Campus, 11*(6), 6.

Mare, R. D., & Winship, C. (1984). The paradox of lessening racial inequality and joblessness among black youth: Enrollment, enlistment, and employment, 1964–1981. *American Sociological Review, 49,* 39–55.

McGowan, B. (1991). *Children welfare reform.* New York: National Center for Children in Poverty, Columbia University School of Public Health.

Mitchell, B. L. (1992). Does ability grouping do more harm than good? It creates labels that last a life time. *On Campus, 11*(6), 6–9.

Mithaug, D. E., Horiuchi, C. N., & Fanning, P. N. (1985). A report on the Colorado statewide follow-up survey of special education students. *Exceptional Children, 51,* 397–404.

National Center for Education Statistics, Office of Education Research and Improvement. (1991). Washington, DC: U.S. Government Printing Office.

National Commission on Children. (1991). *Beyond rhetoric.* Washington, DC: U.S. Government Printing Office.

No housing to refer people to. (1990, May/June). *The Disability Rag,* 7.

Oakes, J. (1985). *Keeping track: How schools structure inequality.* New Haven: Yale University Press.

Ogle, L. T., Alsalam, N., & Rogers, G. T. (1991). *The condition of education 1991: Volume 1. Elementary and secondary education.* Washington, DC: U.S. Government Printing Office.

Orfield, G. (1986). Hispanic education: Challenges, research, and policies. *American Journal of Education, 95,* 1–25.

Orum, L., & Vincent, A. (1984). *Selected statistics in the education of Hispanics.* Washington, DC: National Council of La Raza.

Page, R. N. (1991). *Lower-track classrooms.* New York: Teachers College Press.

Parenti, M. (1978). *Power and the powerless.* New York: St. Martin's Press.

Pratte, R. (1983). Multicultural education: Four normative arguments. *Educational Theory, 33,* 21–32.

Reeves, R. (1990, August 30). Who got what in the 1980's. *Kenosha News,* p. 10.

Riche, M. F. (1991). We're all minorities now. *American Demographics,* 26–34.

Rumberger, R. W. (1983). The influence of family background in education, earnings, and wealth. *Social Forces, 3,* 755–773.

Sadker, M., & Sadker, A. (1982). *Sex equity handbook for schools.* New York: Longman.

Shade, B. J. (1989). *Culture, style, and the educative process.* Springfield, IL: Charles C. Thomas.

Sidel, R. (1990). *On her own: Growing up in the shadow of the American dream.* New York: Penguin Books.

Siegel, S. (1986). *The right to work: Public policy and the employment of the handicapped.* Unpublished doctoral dissertation, San Francisco State University and University of California, Berkeley.

Sleeter, C. E. (1986). Learning disabilities: The social construction of a special education category. *Exceptional Children, 53,* 46–54.

Sleeter, C. E. (Ed.). (1991). *Empowerment through multicultural education.* Albany, NY: SUNY Press.

Sleeter, C. E. (1992). *Keepers of the American dream.* London: The Falmer Press.

Sleeter, C. E., & Grant, C. A. (1987). An analysis of multicultural education in the U.S.A. *Harvard Educational Review, 57,* 421–444.

Sleeter, C., & Grant, C. (1991). Race, class gender, and disability in current textbooks. In M. W. Apple & L. K. Christian-Smith (Eds.), *The politics of the textbook* (pp. 78–110). New York: Routledge.

Spring, J. (1976). *The sorting machine: National education policy since 1945.* New York: McKay.

Tippeconnic, J. W., III. (1991). The education of American Indians: Policy, practice, and future direction. In D. E. Green & T. V. Tonnesen (Eds.), *American Indians: Social justice and public policy* (pp. 180–207). Milwaukee, WI: University of Wisconsin System Institute for Race and Ethnicity.

Treiman, D. J., & Hartman, H. I. (1981). *Women, work, and wages: Equal pay for jobs of equal value.* Washington, DC: National Academy Press.

Trueba, H. T., Jacobs, L., & Kirton, E. (1990). *Cultural conflict and adaptation: The case of Hmong children in American society.* London: The Falmer Press.

U.S. Department of Commerce, Bureau of the Census. (1991a). *Current Population Reports*, Series P-70, No. 29. Washington, DC: U.S. Government Printing Office.

U.S. Department of Commerce, Bureau of the Census. (1991b). *Measuring the effect of benefits and taxes on income and poverty: 1990.* Washington, DC: U.S. Government Printing Office.

U.S. Department of Commerce, Bureau of the Census. (1991c). *Statistical Abstract of the United States 1991.* Washington, DC: U.S. Government Printing Office.

U.S. Department of Commerce, Bureau of the Census. (1991d). U.S. Department of Labor statistics. *Employment and Earnings.* Washington, DC: U.S. Government Printing Office.

U.S. Department of Commerce, Bureau of the Census. (1991e). *Workers with low earnings: 1964 to 1990.* Washington, DC: U.S. Government Printing Office.

U.S. Department of Health and Human Services. (1985). *Report to the secretary's task force on Black and minority health, Vol. 1, Executive summary.* Washington, DC: U.S. Department of Health and Human Services.

U.S. Department of Justice. (1990). *Correctional population in the U.S.* National Prison Statistics Series. Washington, DC: U.S. Government Printing Office.

Valli, L. (1986). *Becoming clerical workers.* Boston: Routledge & Kegan Paul.

Wolf, N. (1991). *The beauty myth: How images of beauty are used against women.* New York: William Morrow.

6

▼▼▼▼▼▼▼

Higher Education as a Public Good*

Stanley Aronowitz

1

Higher education has become a major public issue for the first time since the late 1960s, when student demonstrations and occupations forced open admissions in many public colleges and universities. There are three questions that define the debate: the commitment of legislative and executive authorities to maintaining public higher education at a level of funding adequate enough to enable institutions to offer a high-quality education to students; who should be admitted and who should be excluded from higher education (the so-called access debate); and finally, especially in recent years, the question of curriculum. These three questions are neither simple nor simplistic. Regarding the access debate, should higher education be a "right" like elementary and secondary schooling? Or should it be, like its European counterparts, a privilege reserved for those who have a requisite level of academic achievement? In this debate, one hears such comments as "After all, not everyone should be in college; what about the millions who work in factories or offices?" Curriculum has been thrust closer to center stage. The chief bone of contention is whether the once-presumed liberal arts should be available to every college student; indeed, should every student, regardless of the discipline, be required to imbibe at least a sampling of literature, philosophy, history, and the social sciences? Or as some have argued—and many institutions have agreed—should students in technical and professional areas like computer science, engineering, and even natural science largely be exempt from such encumbrances? This argument applies to both high-level technical universities, such as Carnegie Mellon, Rensselaer Polytechnic Institute, and Case, and to the large number of community colleges whose "mission" is now almost exclusively confined to preparing trained workers for the corporations with whom they have developed close relationships.

Higher education has become prominent on the political screen as the widespread perception that earning a bachelor's degree is the absolute precondition for obtaining a better niche in the occupational structure. But as postsecondary credentials have become a necessary qualification for nearly every technical (let alone professional) job, higher education costs—both tuition and living expenses—have skyrocketed. At the same time, more students and their families are seeking places in private colleges and universities and, with the exception of a handful of elite public research universities, interpret failure to secure admission to leading private schools as a major personal and economic defeat. The bare truth is that in the last decade of neoliberal economic and social ideologies, public postsecondary schools have taken a severe beating in the commonwealth. In the current environment, budget cuts and downsizing are prescribed by policymakers as the zeitgeist has shifted to the view that only the marketplace represents quality and anything connected to public goods that does not submit itself to the business environment is a secondhand article.

The effect of this persistent and merciless attack on public higher education has been to demoralize faculty, and prompt conservative-dominated legislatures to impose a regime of permanent austerity that, with the exception of a handful of public research universities (notably those of the University of California and of the Big Ten), has resulted in sharpening the distinction between the two research tiers of the academic system on the one hand and the "third tier" of public teaching institutions, both senior and community colleges, on the other. Former Berkeley Chancellor Clark Kerr's notorious proposal, first announced in 1958 and inscribed in the California state systems in the early 1960s, that the research tiers be fiercely defended from the horde by establishing a clear cleavage between those institutions that produce knowledge and those that transmit, has succeeded beyond his and his critics' wildest expectations. Today, this mantra has been advanced by the proposition that only certain teaching institutions and some private four-year colleges are "excellent" enough to qualify for the transmission task.

The Kerr plan was no mere speculation; it contained a detailed program to ensure the separation. Research university faculty members were to teach one or two courses a semester and even be able to purchase their teaching time with research grants. In contrast, the third-tier universities and colleges obliged faculty to teach three or four courses, and community colleges as much as five. The reward systems in the two tiers would be different insofar as publication would play a distinctly subordinate role in the third tier. At the same time, Kerr envisioned substantial salary differentials. The only means for moving upward in the new academic system would be through research, writing, and, of course, administration.

Yet creating tiers of higher education hit a snag in the 1960s. Two distinct movements for university reform gained momentum. The first was the insistent demands by black, Latino, and working-class students for access to the institutions as a sign of equality as well as equality of opportunity; the second was the profound dissatisfaction by mostly white, middle-class students in elite universities with the growing trend toward focusing on technical/scientific knowledge production in what Kerr called the "multiversity." At Berkeley and elsewhere, they came together in the early 1960s in a mass student movement in which these two quite different thrusts were merged in the struggle against the emergence of the corporate university. The success of the demand for extending higher education access to virtually any high school graduate depended, in part, on the authority of the civil rights movement that undergirded student protest and on the crisis of legitimacy of the national government in the wake of its unpopular Vietnam War policies. It was made feasible, as well, by the relative buoyancy of the war-suffused United States' economy, which enabled federal and state governments to supply the funds needed to expand the public university system.

Students made their protest on questions of curriculum and, for a time, forced faculty and university administrations to give some ground. Although the Berkeley Free Speech Movement was detonated by the policy of the technocratic Kerr administration barring "outside" political groups from the campus, its apogee was in the achievement of significant curricular reforms. In the UC system, Berkeley, San Diego, and Irvine students wanted the right to select their own courses and choose instructors to teach them. In some places, they demanded and won exemption from course requirements and from large introductory classes and protested the authoritarian pedagogical styles of some professors, which prompted the most obdurate among them to resign and go elsewhere. These struggles, which dominated many campuses until the emergence of the antiwar movement in the late 1960s, succeeded in changing higher education's culture for the next twenty years. Beginning with Harvard University's reimposition of the core curriculum in 1979 and the ebbing of the student movement, faculty and administration slowly regained the upper hand in the next two decades.

With the triumph of market principles in higher education, in which everything from student enrollments, curriculum, and tuition costs was determined by the sales effort, the job market, the ebbing of the black freedom movement, and the mass antiwar movement, the astounding expansion of public colleges and universities came to a screeching halt. Suddenly, in this most advanced of advanced industrial societies, corporate and government economists announced a "fiscal crisis" in public goods, including higher education. The "public" (read business, professional, and corporate farm interests) was simply unwilling to pay the bill for education, health, and other elements of the social wage. They suggested that the way out of the crisis was that user taxes be imposed on public goods; students and their families should be required to substantially pay for public higher education. If enrollees in the private schools were willing to pay large tuition fees, why not those in public universities?

Conservatives in and out of higher education had never accepted open admissions policies. By their lights, the democratization of access to public colleges—and to the elite and private schools as well—degraded the value of the degree. Changes in public higher education in the late 1960s were brought about by the entrance into colleges and universities of perhaps a million additional blacks, Latinos, and other racial minorities who, absent the civil rights movement, would never have reached their gates; there was considerable pressure on the Ivy League colleges and other private schools to undertake policies which, in effect, modified their traditions of cronyism, nepotism, and their meritocratic bias. Contrary to popular myth, neither the public nor the private sector was indiscriminate in its admissions policies; open admissions never meant that students with low grade-point averages and lower scores on the SAT and other standardized tests gained entrance to public senior colleges, let alone the private elite colleges and universities. Although these schools often provided remediation services to students, especially to those who failed the math sections of the SAT or did not take enough math to qualify, admission policies remained selective. In most states, open admissions had been confined to community colleges and some third-tier senior colleges.

Abetted by the media, which seem to swallow almost any attack on public higher education emanating from conservative education think tanks like the Hudson and Manhattan Institutes, the educational Right has mounted what may be the most concerted and coordinated attack against public goods in this century. With the possible exception of the widespread belief that charter schools and vouchers are needed to radically issue a wake-up call to public elementary and secondary education, in recent educational history, policy is more than ever driven by the conservative ideology of hierarchy and privatization.

2

The rise of mass public higher education in America was a result of several influences, chiefly those that resulted from the problems associated with the post-World War II era. Perhaps the most important piece of social engineering after the war was the Servicemen's Readjustment Act of 1944, popularly known as the GI Bill of Rights. At the urging of President Franklin D. Roosevelt, who feared mass unemployment in the postwar period, Congress passed a bill providing returning veterans with income support for a one-year period and funds to enter educational programs, including higher education. Between 1945 and 1952, a million veterans entered mostly private colleges and universities armed with the price of tuition and modest living expenses. All manner of institutions, including the Ivy Leagues and other elite schools, gladly accepted these veterans and the government money that accompanied them.

Public higher education has a long history. Founded in 1847 by Townsend Harris, the City College of New York was intended to provide an opportunity for "talented" young people of modest means to gain the benefits of a college education on a tuition-free basis. The municipal college movement spread slowly and was never really embraced by a large number of communities, but its example inspired parallel efforts at the state level. After the founding of City College, the most substantial event in the emergence of public higher education was the Morrell Act of 1862. Large tracts of federal land were supplied to states that were willing to found universities for the purpose of providing their people with general education in all areas of learning but chiefly scientific and technical research and assistance to agriculture and industry.

Within a half century, many Midwestern states and several in the Northeast and in the South established "land grant" colleges. Despite the intention of the Morrell Act, many of them remained glorified teachers colleges, but some, like the Universities of Michigan, Wisconsin, Illinois, and Indiana, took on characteristics identified with the modern research university. Together with the University of California at Berkeley and Cornell University, they—along with Harvard, MIT, and Princeton among the private schools—constituted the basis for the development of the modern research university, which came into its own with the government's rearmament program on the eve of World War II.

After World War II, the state universities and public municipal colleges also benefited from the largesse of the federal government. In fact, under the imperatives of the Korean War, which drafted more than a million men and women, the GI bill was extended. The Cold War provided a substantial boost to the research programs of public state universities. Having exploded a nuclear device by 1949, the Soviet Union accelerated its military nuclear and space programs which, among other windfalls, prompted the U.S. government to support higher education in a concerted attempt to stem the "Sputnik effect," the alleged Soviet superiority in space exploration and its perceived nuclear parity. By the late 1950s, the federal government had committed itself to long-term support for postsecondary schooling, especially to students seeking careers in natural science and technology, but also supported the humanities and social sciences. States were pouring substantial funds into higher education as well, and by 1960 the public sector was larger than the private sector; a decade later, it accounted for more than 70 percent of student enrollment.

After more than sixty years of public colleges and universities gradually supplanting private schools as the dominant sector of higher education, we are now witnessing the return of tradition. The private sector of post-secondary education is growing faster than the public and, perhaps more to the point, is widely perceived as superior. If the measure of quality is, for all practical purposes, equivalent to a school's ability to exclude students because of the institution's marketability, then the elite private schools have gained substantially on similarly placed public institutions. To be sure, some public systems such as the Big Ten and the University of California schools are still highly competitive, but private institutions such as Brown, Harvard, and Yale, for example, reject more than four of every five applicants; many others, such as the "little" Ivies, have similar records of exclusion.

The economic reasons for this state of affairs are not difficult to discern: faced with deregulation and the threat of globalization, Congress and state legislatures hurried to court the favor of business interests and deprogressivize taxes, made it difficult to raise public funds for public education by raising the standard by which such bills would be passed, and removed authority for new taxes to the voters. In California, Massachusetts, and many other states, the referenda (whose origin was in the Progressive Era's skeptical response to "bought" politicians of those years) were used to provoke what Richard Elman called "The Poorhouse State." In California, the Northeast, and the Southwest, for example, annual budget cuts, either in monetary or real terms, have been imposed by many state legislatures. The consequent systematic replacement of full-time professors with adjuncts, teaching assistants, and temporary professors in teaching the undergraduate curricula is rife. The slide in salaries for full-timers causes many of those with some lateral mobility to move on to private institutions. We witness the drying-up of funds for construction, and maintenance of aging physical plants.

But money tells only part of the story. Private colleges and universities mounted a huge public relations effort to persuade those parents and prospective students with resources to pay that the advantages they offer are worth the price of exorbitant tuition, especially in comparison with the costs of public education. They are brazenly attempting to capture disaffected students from public education and shed no tears when their appeal results in huge debt for families that can ill afford the price of private tuition. Needless to say, getting a good education is only part of the consideration. Above all, the private schools, especially the elite ones, offer prestige—which leads to effective job placement in the corporate world, valuable contacts among peers for future jobs, and a more comfortable student life exemplified in better facilities such as dorms, sports, and recreation centers.

Beyond these trumpeted advantages is the systematic attack against public higher education emanating from right-wing think tanks and conservatives whose views find a receptive ear in the media. For example, the New York media gave enormous and favorable publicity to a recent report on City University of New York (CUNY) by a mayoral commission headed by former Yale President Benno Schmidt, and among whose members were conservatives of all stripes as well as employees of the mayor's. The commission found the two hundred thousand students at CUNY "adrift" and in need of reform. It recommended major changes, among them further administrative centralization to ensure that the reform program would be effective. The report covered the erosion of faculty governance, since the faculty was judged a leading obstacle to changes anticipated by the report, and recommended provisions to undermine the faculty's professional autonomy; it also recommended "mission differentiation," a code term for creating several new tiers in the system to ensure that the top tier was protected against the community colleges, and took a hard look at tenure with a view to abolishing or severely restricting it. Currently the leader of the Edison Project, a for-profit corporation that organizes and consults with public schools around the country in search of privatization, Schmidt included Heather McDonald (a fellow of the Manhattan Institute, a conservative think tank) and an array of similarly oriented members on his commission. Shortly after issuing the CUNY report, which has become a blueprint for the new administration that took office at the end of 1999, Schmidt became vice-chair of CUNY's Board of Trustees.

The prospective transformation of CUNY from a beacon of open admissions for the city's minority and working-class population to a genuine competitor in the elite game that has swept through higher education would be a step into the pre-1960s when New York City's four colleges were held to a higher standard than nearly all of the area's higher education institutions. To gain entrance to tuition-free schools, students were required to earn grade-point averages (GPAs) of eighty-five or higher from a secondary school system that was second to none in the entire country. In fact, the four original city colleges and Baruch, the system's business college, still require high GPAs as well as passing grades on each of three "placement" (that is, admission) tests. The difference in the intervening forty years is that these grades are held in the majority by blacks, Latinos, and Asians and for this reason are considered by CUNY's detractors to be "inflated."

Curiously, the charge of grade inflation, which has been made and tacitly acknowledged by several Ivy League schools, has failed to diminish their prestige. What accounts for a school such as Princeton, which recently abolished the grade of A-plus, is that it rejects many more applicants than it accepts and has a sumptuous endowment; accordingly, Princeton retains its elite standing. Similarly, in an article on the alleged revival of Columbia University, *New York Times* reporter Karen Aronson pointed out that one of the major indicators that the school enjoys a revived reputation is that it admitted only 13.7 percent of applicants last year, a figure which placed it second only to Brown, whose rejection rate is 87 percent. In none of the recent reports of the booming private college industry has the question of educational quality figured in the evaluation of their successes. The measure of quality seems to rely heavily on whether school admission is considered a valuable commodity to prospective students; in other words, is it a product that can command high tuition and many applicants?

In fact, as a grim 1999 report from the University of Chicago attests, according to the university administration, this paragon of the vaunted Great Books curriculum was having trouble in its recruitment campaign precisely because, in the face of the zeitgeist pointing in the opposite direction, it retained too much academic rigor. Consequently, the board and the administration announced a new emphasis away from its classical educational focus and towards a more lenient academic program and added sports facilities and stronger placement services. Appalled members of the faculty and student body protested the shift, after which the university's president announced his resignation to take up teaching duties, but the board has neither retracted its program nor expressed any intention of modifying it. Despite its prestige, many on the faculty have discovered that even in matters of curriculum, the heart of faculty sovereignty, their powers are limited.

In the sciences, technologies, and graduate professional education, the two dozen or so leading public research universities are holding their own in this competition. Despite budget constraints imposed by state legislatures eager to reduce taxes for their business and upper-middle-class constituents, many have retained their ability to raise substantial research grants. For example, UC-Irvine and UC-San Diego are major recipients of grants for bioengineering from agencies such as the National Institutes of Health and the Centers for Disease Control; Cornell, Berkeley, and Illinois are leading research institutions in physics; and Penn State and Pittsburgh are among the most important of the technical science research institutions. Where the legislature has cut back on operating funds, the proceeds from research activity often manage to keep many programs in the humanities and arts alive.

The most severe problem institutions in public higher education are those in the tier below the two categories of research universities. Apart from the departments and schools of teacher education that, while not prospering in this age of academic austerity, have substantial social utility (even by conservative lights), many universities and community colleges are scrambling to find a "mission" sufficiently attractive to convince skeptical legislators that they have an economically viable role. The new mantra of higher education is that by training technically competent labor, but also by providing income to a large number of blue-collar, clerical, and professional workers, postsecondary schooling makes significant contributions to local and regional economies. Consequently, schools are making agreements with private corporations to provide curricula and teaching staff for dedicated skills training. Even when specific deals do not drive the curriculum, vocationalization does. As students get the message that a higher education credential is necessary for survival in this global economy, many feel they do not have the luxury to indulge their artistic, critical, or literary interests and must instead keep their collective noses to the technical grindstone. As a result, many social sciences departments are relegated to the status of providers of "breadth" requirements or are encouraged or forced to adopt vocational majors in order to prevent being closed down, and when majors have declined steeply, English departments are often little more than composition mills.

For the time being, there is no imminent threat of school closings in most state systems. However, university and college administrations in the third (nonresearch) tier are admonished by regents and state commissions of higher education to find ways to close budget shortfalls by raising tuition, making alliances with corporations or otherwise turning their predominantly liberal arts institutions into vocational schools, or adding more research capacity to their faculty and facilities. A history professor acquaintance tells me that once a broad general education school with a few scientific and technical programs, the third-tier Illinois public university in which he teaches now consists largely of business and technical majors. Similar trends are evident in New York, New Jersey, Colorado, and California. The separation of their "flagship" schools and their largely undergraduate and masters-level institutions is widening. For the latter, the message is clear: sink or swim. Needless to say, few administrators in public higher education are willing to risk the severe penalties of smaller enrollments and diminished income by retaining their liberal arts focus. The brute fact is that undergraduate humanities majors are few; only in fields like economics (because of its predominant business ties), political science (because it is understood as a good pre-law major), and sociology (because of the still lively interest in the social services as a profession) has there been some growth in student interest.

Even some private school students exhibit anxiety about the future and are demanding better placement services and sticking more closely to fields that have direct occupational outcomes rather than using their undergraduate schooling as a time of exploration and creative uncertainty. Some elite schools, public as well as private, remain beacons for English and other language majors; some, like Pittsburgh, have attractive undergraduate philosophy and history programs. But major state schools, such as the four SUNY research universities, Rutgers, and many in the UC system, report a decline in undergraduate majors in history, philosophy, and literatures. While most of these are in no imminent danger of becoming composition factories for technical majors even as they retain their highly rated Ph.D. programs, the so-called economic boom has failed to produce a new era of relaxation. Students remain enervated because, I suspect, they know what the media has ignored: there is a lot of work but few jobs—if by jobs we mean work that is accompanied by the amenities of security, benefits, and a career ladder that enables them to gain income and authority along with their experience. Moreover, they know from their own parents' experience that corporate downsizing has affected middle management and professionals as well as blue-collar workers.

The economic and social environment of the late 1990s is inimical to the development of a system of public higher education in which the goals are defined beyond the utilitarian uses of credentials and acquisition of job skills. Far from being citadels of education, many public colleges and universities are constituted as labor exchanges and not as public spaces where adults of all ages can take noncredit-bearing courses in world affairs, as well as craft and art forms such as pottery, or participate in forums and conferences of all sorts. As for one of the historic aims of public higher education, the development of citizens able to participate in key decisions affecting the polity, this role has been consigned to one of the "distribution" requirements of the first two years of a baccalaureate degree. The hard fact is that continuing and citizenship education are now conceived by administrators as a moneymaking activity and are most effective in private institutions. Threadbare, many public schools are bereft of these programs or offer only a limited range of skills-oriented courses.

3

With their victory in reimposing a core curriculum in most colleges and universities, education leaders in higher education are in the throes of a second stage of curriculum "reform" which has provoked considerable debate: is education for whom and for what? The dispute over the curriculum takes many forms. Feminist, black, Asian, and Latino educators responded to the imposition of core curricula that resuscitated the traditional literary canon as a site of privileged learning by insisting on the inclusion of global, postcolonial, and otherwise marginalized literatures and philosophy. But the so-called multicultural or diversity curriculum only peripherally addresses the central problem that afflicts public universities. The command from executive authorities in and out of the institution is that public schools justify their existence by proving value to the larger society, in most cases read "business interests." In turn, educational leaders such as presidents and provosts are inclined to seek a "mission" that simultaneously translates as vocationalization, which entails leasing or selling huge portions of its curriculum and its research products directly to companies.

As a result, the public research universities are dusting off one of Kerr's most important suggestions: undergraduates as well as graduate students should be recruited to participate in the research activities of the professoriat, especially in the sciences. Like sports, research now demands a considerable time commitment from the practitioner. In some places, notably UC universities such as San Diego and Irvine, schools are reducing the obligation of science and technology majors to the humanities and social sciences so they can more accurately mimic the practices of the great private technical universities. This, of course, raises the question of whether the public universities as public goods should maintain their obligation to educate students to citizenship as well as in job skills.

As a professor in UC-Irvine's school of social sciences, I can recall legislative hearings in the 1970s conducted by the chair of the higher education committee of the California State Assembly. The chair and other committee members were concerned that faculty members were avoiding undergraduate teaching in the service of their research and that the state universities were slighting programs aimed at educating for citizenship. The university administration appeared to bow to the legislators' stern warning that if they did not alter the situation, their budgets would feel heat. Unfortunately, as with all attempts by legislatures to micromanage education, it did not take long for the administration and the faculty to regain lost ground. Today, most UC campuses are monuments to technoscience, and with few exceptions at the undergraduate level, the humanities and social sciences are gradually being relegated to the status of ornaments and service departments.

In the third tier, the forms of privatization and vocationalization are far more explicit. For example, the New York telephone company Bell Atlantic developed relationships with public community and senior colleges throughout the state on condition that the schools agreed to enroll and train students for specific occupations needed by the company. While in most cases no money changes hands, the school benefits by additional enrollment and because it shows the legislature and other politicians that it is playing a role in increasing worker productivity and enhancing economic growth, and for these reasons should be rewarded with funds. In addition to a degree, the employees learn occupational skills that often lead to upgrading, and the company transfers the costs of training it would have to do anyway to the public. Ironically, the Communications Workers of America, the collective bargaining representative, takes credit for the program by including the right of certain high seniority members to an "education" in the contract—read here as upgrading opportunities without themselves assuming the cost of tuition.

The question at issue is whether schools should forge direct corporate partnerships and, in effect, sell their teaching staff—let alone hand over the curriculum to vocational ends. Needless to say, in the occupational programs I have examined, the liberal arts, especially English and history, play a service role; at Nassau Community College in Long Island, students are required to take a course in labor history, and their English requirement is confined to composition. Otherwise, the remainder of the two-year curriculum is devoted to technical subjects of direct applicability to the telephone industry. Third-tier public colleges and universities are under direct pressure to reduce their humanities and social sciences offerings to introductory and service courses in the technical and scientific curriculum. In effect, the prospective English or sociology majors face a huge obstacle to obtain a degree in their chosen discipline because there are often not enough electives to fulfill the major. As a result, we can observe the rush to mergers of social sciences departments in many third-tier public schools.

Sociology, anthropology, and political science departments are consolidating. At Cameron State University in Lawton, Oklahoma, the two philosophers on campus are now in the social sciences department, which includes the traditional disciplines, and teach courses such as business ethics. In order to maintain viability, the department has majors in occupational specializations such as the large major in social welfare, a vocational sequence designed to train counselors and low-level professionals in the criminal justice system—a thriving industry in the state. Absent a social and political theorist, these required courses are taught by a criminologist. With almost five hundred majors, the eleven full-time members of the department each teach more than 120 students in four course-loads a semester, in addition to academic and professional advisement of bachelor's and master's students. Many courses are taught by adjuncts. Since the university has many business majors, a favorite of dozens of third-tier schools, the humanities and social sciences departments are crucial for fulfilling the shriveling "breadth" requirements.

Economic pressures as much as the ideological assaults on the liberal arts account for the change in the curriculum that is in process in public higher education. Students and their families feel more acutely the urgency of getting a leg up in the race for survival. The relative luxury of the liberal arts might be reserved for the few who are liberated from paid work during their college years. The consequence is that the human sciences are squeezed from the bottom as well as the top as students demand "relevance" in the curriculum and lose their thirst for reflection.

It may safely be declared that only in the larger cities, and then not uniformly, have faculty and students successfully defended the liberal arts. At CUNY, a decade of determined faculty resistance has slowed, but not reversed, the trend. As the new century dawned, CUNY administration was preparing its version of distance learning, one of the more blatant efforts to end the traditional reliance on classroom learning in favor of a model that focuses on the use of technology to produce more standard packages of predigested knowledge. In addition, it is an answer to the fiscal crisis suffered by many public schools because the style of learning reduces the number and proportion of full-time faculty to adjuncts, transforms brick-and-mortar locations into cyberspace so that building and maintenance costs are reduced, and through standardization eliminates the mediation of a critical intellectual to interpret transmitted knowledge. The latter saving does not refer as much to cost as to the centralization of political and social control.

The bare fact is that neither the discourse nor the practices of critical learning are abroad in public higher education except as the rear-guard protests of a much-exhausted faculty and a fragment of the largely demobilized student body. Blindsided by the sixties, many educators went along with student demands for ending requirements and ended up with the marketplace in which demand-driven criteria determined curricular choices. In other words, neoliberalism entered the academy through the back door of student protest. For progressive educators, the task remains to demand a rigorous core of knowledge as a requisite of any postsecondary credential. Today, such a demand is a radical act. To capitulate to the "market" (which, arguably, wants something else because in a panic about an uncertain future, students and their parents really do not believe in the palaver of the "boom economy") is to surrender the idea of higher education as a public good. Educators would acknowledge that these institutions largely paid for by the working and middle classes should not promote critical thinking, should not explore the meaning of citizenship in the new neoliberal era, and should abhor the project of democratic appropriation of both Western and subaltern (marginal) traditions through attitudes of bold skepticism.

Perhaps it is too early to propose that public higher education be thoroughly decommodified and shorn of its corporate characteristics and that all tuition costs be paid by a tax system that must be reprogressivized. Perhaps the battle cry that at least in the first two years only science, philosophy, literature, and history (understood in the context of social theory) be taught and learned and that specializations be confined to the last two years, are so controversial, even among critics of current trends, that they remain too countercultural. Yet if higher education is to become a public good in the double meaning of the term—as a decommodified resource for the people and as an ethically legitimate institution that does not submit to the business imperative—then beyond access we would have to promote a national debate about what is to be taught—and what is to be learned—if citizenship and critical thought are to remain, even at the level of intention, at the heart of higher learning.

II

SCHOOLS FOR SALE: CONSUMERISM, CORPORATE CULTURE, AND PUBLIC EDUCATION

A major underlying theme of this book has to do with the interrelationships among educational institutions (the public schools in particular) and other significant sociocultural institutions. Public education is just that—a *public* institution—and as such is inevitably subject to all the various community influences, pressures, and concerns. By the same token, schools have their own agendas and inevitably interact with other institutions and in so doing have an impact on them. This is both a sociological reality and a historical fact. Although each institution and realm of our society and culture has its own unique character and dimensions, inevitably in our modern complex world they will, by necessity, interact with each other. School policies and practices, for example, are deeply affected by cultural values, religious beliefs, budget concerns, ideological debates, demographic considerations, and partisan politics, just to name some of the more general factors.

Historically, the establishment of public schools was, by no means, inevitable, but instead was the result of a long and controversial public and political battle concerning a number of ideological, economic, and cultural considerations. Indeed American public schools as presently defined (i.e., compulsory, universal, tax-supported, and supervised by a public agency) was not fully manifest until the early 20th century. The initial proposals for such a system in the early and mid-19th century were based on a number of what might be called *noneducational concerns*—the development of loyalty to and affirmation of the new and fragile democratic institutions, a newly unified American nation, and an equally new system of federalism. In addition, those proposing a public, tax-supported school system saw it as a way to deal with concerns for the moral and religious character of the people, the development of a uniquely American culture, and the preservation of the dominant culture. The public schools were, in effect, charged with the responsibility of being an important, if not paramount, agent for achieving a number of specific political, social, cultural, and economic goals.

Prominent among these other goals were, of course, issues related to the economy (e.g., the development of a reliable, compliant, and skilled workforce in an era of rapid industrialization and economic growth). It goes without saying that there has always been an intimate and powerful relationship between economic concerns and educational matters. (As exemplified in President Calvin Coolidge's famous adage from his Inaugural address: "The business of government is business").

Some of these economic concerns are rather obvious and, on the face of it, relatively if not deceptively benign. For example, communities must confront budgetary questions—how much money do the schools require and where do we get it—issues that are certain to generate controversy and conflict among competing interest groups. Some parents are likely to demand quality education (e.g., smaller classes and more curriculum choices) while many taxpayers are prone to demand lower costs (e.g., larger classrooms and fewer curriculum choices). In addition, other groups (e.g., politicians, real estate developers, and professional educators) have their own particular interests very much connected to the size and nature of the school budget.

Another example of the virtually inevitable strong ties between schools and the economy is the matter of job training. Obviously, businesses need trained workers, and parents want their children to be prepared to have a competitive edge when they enter the job market. There are any number of complex and controversial issues connected to this function—to what degree should the schools offer programs focused on specific vocational skills? How much influence should employers have on school policy? What is the relationship between general education and vocational education? For that matter, what is the difference, if any, between them?

These are difficult and controversial questions of educational policy that require the kind of specific research and analysis that can help in gathering accurate and relevant information. More important, they reflect a much broader and deeper struggle within our society. More specifically, they mirror our attitudes toward and beliefs about our various financial, industrial, and corporate structures and the values inherent in these structures. We as a people have had and continue to have mixed feelings about big business and its impact on us as a society and as a people. We often marvel at how the creative energy of the free market system and giant corporations has produced so much wealth and so many useful and playful products. At the same time, we often resent the power of these corporate giants to so arrogantly and completely dominate and control social and political institutions by dint of that very wealth.

By the same token, many of us admire and try to emulate the personal attributes and moral values associated with our economic system—hard work, perseverance, dedication, rugged individualism, personal freedom, self-confidence, soaring ambition, and material success. Yet we often register our fears about the personal and social costs of the relentless pursuit of personal freedom, ambition, and success. We have seen and continue to see, in the midst of unparalleled prosperity for many, continued poverty and misery for a great many more. Moreover, we are witness to a steady erosion of social responsibility, political involvement, and personal meaning as the obsession with self-advancement and materialism has intensified.

In the wake of the euphoria following the collapse of the regimes in Eastern Europe and the Soviet Union, there were assurances from many pundits that the world was on the threshold of a golden age of long-time, if not permanent, peace and prosperity. This would happen because all nations would now come to realize that the only roads to Utopia were the ones marked Global Economy, Free Market, and Liberal Democracy as designed by the wealthiest and most powerful superpower—the United States. What seemed to emerge from the cold war was less of a sense of victory of the forces of justice and liberty than the belief of the triumph of capitalism over socialism and that the ultimate criterion for a successful society was its material wealth rather than the ability to provide liberty and justice for all.

As we all know, however, things did not quite work out that way. In the years since the end of the cold war, the world continues to experience extraordinary poverty, hunger, and suffering. The gap between the haves and the have-nots continues to grow despite all the promises and in the face of an ever-expanding free market. Nor, of course, have we experienced the democratization and peaceful conditions that were to be the consequences of prosperity. Instead worldwide we have seen a dramatic increase in desperation and despair rooted in great numbers of people struggling with economic, cultural, and political oppression.

In our own country, we continue to experience significant unemployment and underemployment along with continued poverty and hardships for far too many of our people. Despite all the efforts of learned and earnest experts, economic fluctuations and uncertainties continue as exemplified in the incredible bull market in the 1990s and the equally dramatic collapse of the dot.com bubble. The reasons for all this are obviously multiple and complex, but it is clear that we must consider the possibility that a major contributing factor has been an even more intense and ruthless pursuit of ever more wealth and power by increasingly voracious global corporations.

As if this were not enough, our society is reeling under the shock of our latest round of business scandals, which go beyond even the most cynical notions of how far some people are willing to go to maximize profits. The degree of corruption and criminality recently revealed in such major corporations as Enron, Worldcom, and Arthur Anderson are stunning in their audacity and arrogance. They not only appear to violate the criminal code and accepted standards of business ethics, but to be serious breaches of some of our bedrock moral and community values such as good faith, trust, and honesty. These companies and others of their ilk have caused great pain and agony to their workers, stockholders, and pensioners. Perhaps even more serious damage has been done to the struggle to maintain our commitment to a moral framework based on compassion, social responsibility, and social justice.

An especially galling aspect of recent business excesses is the extraordinary way in which corporate executives are compensated by way of fantastically high salaries and lucrative severance packages. In the process, the ratio of the highest paid and lowest paid workers in American corporations has risen dramatically in the past decade. Ironically enough, at the very moment when the business community has been excoriating the schools for failing to tie educators' salaries to student outcomes we learn that many CEOs continue to receive substantial salary increases even when their companies experience financial downturns.

It goes without saying that what goes on in the business community profoundly affects us all in both the short and long terms. These effects certainly have an impact on our financial concerns, but also on our sense of purpose and meaning. Society's obsession with profits and possessions, our preoccupation with hard work and ambition, and the desperate ways we worry about our children's economic future have left many of us searching for other paths to a worthwhile and fulfilling life. The deep disillusionment with business as well as with all other cultural and social institutions has produced a great deal of cynicism, alienation, and self-centeredness—a development that may have especially serious consequences for the young and for our future.

This section of the book focuses on some of the direct consequences of the present state of the economy and corporate culture on the public schools. Clinton Boutwell (chap. 7, this volume) writes about how corporate America has dramatically changed its employment practices and how this threatens the long-standing social compact between schools and business. Two of the articles (those by Henry Giroux, chap. 8; and Alex Molnar, chap. 10) detail the ways in which many corporations have aggressively targeted schools as markets with the potential for becoming highly profitable. Both of these authors examine the ethical, cultural, social, and political dimensions of such business-sponsored policies and practices as the privatization of schools, exclusive contracts for vendors, direct marketing to students, and school vouchers.

Svi Shapiro's essay (chap. 9, this volume), writing within the context of the Littleton tragedy, takes this analysis further and discusses the moral and psychological effects on students of a culture dominated by competition and rigidly focused on achieving a greater level of personal success and social status. The section concludes with an article by David Purpel (chap. 11, this volume), who connects these matters to issues of educational policy and addresses the increasing sense of despair within the profession regarding the direction of these policies.

7
▼▼▼▼▼▼▼

Profits Without People*

Clinton E. Boutwell

Why—when corporations are shedding employees and reducing job opportunities as fast as they can—are business leaders demanding that educators produce a world-class work force? Could it be, Mr. Boutwell speculates, that one way to keep wages and incomes low is to have a huge supply of highly educated workers but a small demand for their services?

Louis V. Gerstner, Jr., had a busy year in 1993. He was recruited from RJR Nabisco to become the CEO of IBM. He was also the principal author of a book that berated American schools and teachers.[1] In that book, he held educators accountable for not increasing America's supply of world-class workers—those with high-tech skills and problem-solving abilities—that he claimed the corporations sorely needed.

Gerstner's recruitment to IBM turned out to be very propitious for him, though not for IBM's world-class employees. First, Gerstner was paid a bonus of $4,924,596 just to sign as CEO. Then he was given a stock package worth $10,820,880. That, plus some incidental incentives, brought Gerstner's total compensation package to more than $21 million.[2] For that kind of money, one would think that Gerstner would just take care of IBM's business and let educators take care of their own, especially when Gerstner's advice to educators was wrongheaded and disingenuously misleading.

Gerstner's own executive behavior gave the lie to the message of his book. IBM made its reputation and its huge profits by employing the high-tech researchers, engineers, and technical developers who represented the finest products of American schools—indeed, the very kind of graduates that Gerstner claimed the public schools were not supplying to business. Yet, in line with IBM's new "lean and mean" management strategy, Gerstner fired some 90,000 of those highly trained employees, about one-third of IBM's 270,000 workers. That was in addition to the other 183,000 high-quality employees that IBM fired before Gerstner arrived.[3]

Gerstner's actions were driven by the current conventional wisdom of business executives with regard to the new global economy, to wit: systemic restructuring of the world's industrial economies is proceeding rapidly, and corporations have to capitalize on the power of technology and use more sophisticated production processes to become more efficient. They need to build what the executives stylishly call a "new economy." Gerstner and his peers felt that American business had better get on the bandwagon or be left behind. These corporate executives believed that America's businesses had dilly-dallied and managed to lose America's competitive advantage through a series of ill-advised and inept decisions. The effects of those poor decisions were accelerated by a series of unwise government actions, especially certain tax policies and a military expansion.[4]

For at least two decades, the United States did little to protect its manufacturing base against intrusion from foreign competitors. But by 1980, America's core corporations had finally recognized the steady loss of competitive advantage to businesses in other countries, Japan and Germany in particular. In their panicky reaction to the new global economic challenge, these core corporations initiated a number of piecemeal actions.

America's business executives could have responded more effectively to changes occurring in the global economy. They could have cultivated new ideas and approaches to make the American economy competitive again. But they did not. Instead, they adopted simple-minded downsizing.

First, the core corporations and their subsidiaries began to shift factories and routine manufacturing work to low-wage areas within the U.S. When they ran out of places to move to in America, routine manufacturing companies began moving to Mexico, Malaysia, Ireland, and other low-wage foreign countries. Based on what one writer calls a "postindustrial fantasy," many thriving high-skill industries that manufactured such commodities as textiles, electronics, autos and auto parts, and hundreds of home consumer products were allowed either to move overseas or to come under the domain of other advanced industrial countries—Japan, Germany, the Netherlands, France, and others.[5]

Step by step, American executives began to dismantle the tacit compact they had with their workers and with the American public, thereby undermining much good will between themselves and their employees and customers. From 1947 through 1979 that compact had ensured better job security, wages, and fair prices for most American workers and consumers. To justify ending that compact, industry apologists and economic pundits argued that America was moving from an economy based on industry to an economy based on information. The policy elite argued that America's "Information Age" would generate high-wage, high-tech jobs to replace lost manufacturing jobs. The country witnessed a decline from 31 million manufacturing jobs in 1980 to 16.6 million manufacturing jobs in 1993, including the loss of tens of thousands of high-skill, high-quality jobs.[6]

When shipping the jobs to foreign countries did not solve the problem of foreign competition, the next set of executive decisions was to slash wages and lay off workers—a practice euphemistically referred to as "downsizing" and "right sizing." But foreign competitors met those actions with further price reductions. Thus in the 1980s America's core corporations began to merge, hoping to gain advantage from greater economies of scale. But computer-based manufacturing methods reduced the cost advantage of mass-produced goods, and foreign competitors continued to eat away at America's advantage. Corporate executives appeared to have run out of piecemeal solutions; all that was left was a complete abrogation of the social compact and the beginning of a serious restructuring of the American economy, a process that is still continuing.

AMERICA'S NEW ECONOMY

Restructuring America's economy to make it lean and competitive involves four basic elements. First, technological innovation is applied relentlessly in the workplace to replace or de-skill workers. Second, managerial processes are radically modified in order to organize the functions of employees and managers to maximize the efficiency of technological innovations. Third, economic interests, investments, and ownership are internationalized. Fourth, and most germane to our purposes, intellectual talent and ideas are internationalized.

Knowledge workers—including those from newly industrializing countries—and the intellectual products they create can be imported and exported by any country, including the U.S. Being a knowledge worker gives one the capability of moving anywhere in the world where one's intelligence, talent, and services are needed; it also means that one can command handsome salaries and perks. America's corporations are capitalizing on that worldwide intellectual potential to hire the best minds in the world or, at least, to snap up and control the intellectual products of those minds and so to reduce the work options for Americans.

Implementing the four elements of restructuring has made it possible for America's major corporations to regain much of the competitive advantage they had lost to businesses in other advanced industrial countries. However, in regaining that competitive advantage, American corporations have become not only lean but also mean.

America's corporate executives, such as IBM's Gerstner, discovered that they did not need a huge world-class work force. Therefore, the bottom line of corporate restructuring for Americans was the massive shedding of workers, a reduction in future job opportunities, and a concomitant plunge in income, benefits, and living standards for millions of households. For example, Xerox, AT&T, Bank of America, United Technologies, General Motors, and other Fortune 500 companies consigned more than 583,000 high-tech, highly skilled workers to the unemployment lines in 1993. By that same year the steel industry had shed 208,000 highly skilled employees since the late 1980s.[7]

In 1994 there was another round of cuts by powerful firms that typically employ highly skilled workers. For example, General Motors fired an additional 74,000 workers, AT&T fired 83,500, Sears fired 50,000, and GTE fired 32,150. AT&T cut another 77,800 employees in 1995, more than half of its 151,000 managers, and it eliminated another 40,000 high-tech and managerial jobs in 1996.[8] On top of that, the telecommunications industry as a whole plans to lop off another 100,000 highly skilled employees by the year 2000.[9]

Large numbers of highly skilled workers who received pink slips have been forced into low-wage, temporary, and contingent jobs. In 1994 two-thirds of all new jobs created in the U.S. were low-wage jobs that carried no benefits.[10] The Conference Board, the corporation's major research alliance, notes that the number of "contingent workers"—temporary hires, part-timers, independent contractors—was at an all-time high in 1995, constituting at least 10% of the work force. That is almost double the proportion of contingent workers in 1990.[11] Contingent workers receive pay that is comparable to that of full-time employees, but they do not receive the benefits that typically add about 40% to labor costs. A contingent work force is also more flexible: when business sags, the temps are the first to go.

Many of the new jobs being "created" are actually temporary jobs. In fact, at least a quarter of those employed today are temporary, part-time, or contract workers. The number of Americans working part time grew by 2.2 million between 1973 and 1996, reaching a total of 6.2 million. This growth was entirely a function of involuntary part-timers, those who would rather work full time. Moreover, hundreds of big companies have outsourced non-core functions—such as legal work, assembly, maintenance, repair, customer service, auditing, cafeteria services, and mailroom operations—to other companies.[12]

The total *number* of high-tech, highly skilled jobs is shrinking as America builds its "new economy." Projections from the Bureau of Labor Statistics through the year 2005, the most authoritative figures available, show clearly that highly skilled, high-tech jobs will be at a premium, while low-wage, low-tech jobs will become abundant.[13] One business magazine concluded:

> The country that invented mass production can no longer compete for routine manufacturing jobs. . . . [But] the hot industries of the 1980s—computers, finance, retailing, and defense—[also] are shedding workers at a furious pace.[14]

ALL DRESSED UP AND NOWHERE TO GO

Newspapers and the publications of professional organizations are filled with reports bemoaning the decline in good jobs. However, universities continue to produce large numbers of high-quality professional graduates. As Daniel Greenberg, publisher of the influential *Science and Government Newsletter*, reports, "The Ph.D. production system is obviously out of whack with the needs of the economy."[15] Both the National Science Foundation and the Bureau of Labor Statistics report that the number of scientists in the U.S. increased 12.6% between 1987 and 1992. Unfortunately, that growth produced such a glut that many science graduates end up with jobs for which their education overqualifies them. The lack of science and engineering jobs is forcing many Ph.D.s to become "migratory workers," moving from one low-paying technician's job to another.[16]

The pharmaceutical industry has cut more than 3,000 science jobs, and the chemical industry has cut 16,000.[17] Yet in 1993 American universities awarded a record 39,754 doctorates, up 2.3% from the previous high in 1992. This caused one critic to comment sarcastically, "The university system has never been particularly permeable to logic. . . . The university version [of featherbedding] will expire when the money runs out."[18]

A RAND Corporation report concluded that new doctoral degrees in science and engineering average 25% *above* appropriate employment opportunities. RAND charged that universities are oblivious to the job market, especially one that has no place for so many expensively trained graduates.[19] One investigator commented, "These bright, energetic scholars are all facing the same problem. Our universities are turning out more scientists with advanced degrees than our culture can absorb."[20] The problem is so severe that many experts recommend that requirements for doctoral degrees be broadened to provide graduates with training in business, education, and other fields that might enable them to switch careers.[21]

More people than scientists and engineers are caught in the supply/demand bind produced by corporate restructuring. Thousands from other professions face the same situation. Even graduates of America's most prestigious *business* schools, for example, are finding no guarantee of a job. MIT's

Sloan School of Management, one of the top two business schools in the U.S., had 4% of its graduates unable to find jobs after graduation; Northwestern University's Kellogg School had 4.5% unemployed; Dartmouth's Amos Tuck School had 11%; and an amazing 16% of the newly minted M.B.A. graduates of Stanford University were unable to find jobs. Less prestigious business schools fared even worse: 40% of the graduates of Ohio State's business school could not find jobs; the figure for the University of Georgia was 30%; for the University of Texas at Austin, 24%; and for Tulane University, 24%.[22]

As the American economy continues to restructure itself, all indicators show clearly that the demand for highly skilled, high-performance workers will never reach the levels needed by the old economy. In other words, millions of graduates will find *no* jobs awaiting them or will have to accept *substandard* jobs for which they will be overqualified. Educators working to help high school and college students "prepare for the world of highly skilled work" face a quandary: How can educators' efforts to prepare a world-class work force be reconciled with the increasingly obvious decline in world-class job opportunities?

Even with the glut of college graduates and highly skilled, high-tech workers, America's high schools continue to push students to take more academically challenging classes. They do so because they believe that such classes will prepare students for tomorrow's work force. Enrollment in these academically challenging subjects has increased dramatically. For example, by the middle of the 1980s, almost every state had increased the number of credits in math and science required for graduation. The Council of Chief State School Officers reported that the number of students taking math and science courses increased dramatically between 1982 and 1994. By the early 1990s, enrollment in upper-level math and science courses had risen in more than half of the states.[23] By 1994, 61% of all high school graduates had taken three years of challenging math, and 5% had taken three years of science.[24] At the same time, there was a commensurate enrollment decline in lower level math and science courses, as students became convinced that such classes were dead ends. In 1993 high school graduates earned an average of 2.6 more credits than students earned a decade earlier.

And the trend continued after 1993. In 1994, for example, 60% of high school graduates had completed three years of math, up from the 37% in 1982. Much of that increase involved academically challenging math courses. The percentage of students who had taken both algebra and geometry, for instance, went from 29% in 1982 to 50% in 1994. Participation in calculus classes more than doubled, from 4% in 1982 to 10% in 1994. Contrary to what some critics have averred, these courses were not watered down, a conclusion affirmed by an on-site study conducted by the Wisconsin Center for Education Research.[25]

Not only are high school students taking more challenging classes, but they are also entering college in record numbers—rising from 49.9% of males and 43.4% of females in 1970 to 58.7% of males and 64% of females in 1993. Moreover, 68% of seniors from the wealthiest families (the top economic quartile) were enrolled in college-prep courses. However, as more students became aware that a college education was required to earn decent wages, enrollment in college-prep courses increased dramatically, including a 21.8% increase in the number of high school seniors from the lowest economic quartile who were enrolled in college-prep programs.[26] All those young men and women who are entering and finishing college in record numbers are expecting to get high-paying jobs when they graduate, but some of them will be disappointed.

The soft demand for highly skilled workers has led to a continuing decline in wages since 1973. In the early 1970s, 25.9% of the work force between the ages of 25 and 64 had more than 12 years of schooling and earned an annual income of $38,117. By 1990, 52% of those in that age group had more than 12 years of schooling—25.7% had attended community college—and were earning only $32,892, a 17% drop from 1970 levels.[27] That trend continued through 1995, when annual wages declined another 2.5% for those with some college.[28]

Experts project that, of the millions of university graduates, only a mere 20% will be able to find the well-paying, challenging jobs for which they were trained. The evidence suggests that, for the few high-paying career opportunities that are available, only a small elite of university graduates will be needed.[29] Employers are hiring only those who offer something exceptional. A recent U.S. Census Bureau study concluded that "college graduates are having a hard time finding well-paid jobs." According to the study, the proportion of college graduates entering the better-paid occupations—executive, managerial, and professional specialties—*declined* from 53.6% in 1989 to 48.4% in 1991.[30] On the other hand, the proportion entering technical, sales, and administrative support and clerical jobs, which typically pay less, *increased* from 33.4% to 38.2%.[31] All other occupations stayed pretty much the same during that period.

SUPPLY AND DEMAND

Regardless of the turmoil and hardship they are producing in America, the captains of corporate power have a rationale for this frenzied drive to downsize. However, when stated baldly, it sounds strangely tautological. They argue that downsizing, cost-cutting, and consolidation are driven by the increasingly competitive global market and by dramatic technological changes. In turn, globalization and technology allow suppliers of goods and services to produce much more at lower cost. That situation, these executives argue, quickly creates excess production capacity throughout the world, which forces their companies to redouble their efforts to get costs even lower, which "logically" leads to even further downsizing.

More-independent analysts think there are other reasons for all the "cost-cutting" and employee shedding. They question why, when corporations are shedding employees and reducing job opportunities as fast as they can, business leaders are demanding that educators produce a world-class work force. Why would such business executives as IBM's Gerstner urge American educators to produce more and more students with high-tech skills, creative problem-solving abilities, and a spirit of teamwork—an education that would supposedly give America an even stronger world-class labor pool from which to *select* applicants—that is, a large *supply* of workers—is part of corporate America's plan? After all, by the rules of supply and demand, one way to keep wages and incomes low is to have a huge supply of highly educated workers but a small demand for their services. That way, businesses can get the pick of the litter pretty cheap and can scrap the rest.

Corporations have shed high-quality workers by the millions and have lowered wages for the rest. As a consequence, not only have America's corporations successfully regained a competitive advantage over their major foreign competitors, but they have seen profits increase to astronomical highs. However, the outcome of this corporate restructuring "success" for most Americans is fewer and fewer high-wage, highly skilled job opportunities.

There is additional evidence to suggest that increasing the labor pool and keeping wages low may be part of a corporate strategy. For example, job openings in 1996—including vacancies created by retirements, deaths, or resignations—were 20% fewer than a decade earlier, even with full economic recovery from our most recent recession.[32] However, more than 2.2 million new temporary jobs have been created, jobs paying an average wage of only $7.74 per hour, even though the overall average wage is almost $12 per hour. Eighty-six percent of all companies now farm out work they used to do. Those downsized workers who manage to find a new job also find themselves making at least 10% less than in their old job. With such a large pool of qualified workers, is it any wonder that fully 79% of currently employed workers say they are worried about their jobs?[33]

Indeed, in the inexorable process of building a "new economy," corporations in the U.S. have created a critical problem for the American people and for the education system. With encouragement from opportunistic business executives, anxious educators failed to heed the warnings implicit in that fundamental principle of economics: the law of supply and demand. Business leaders seem to have reasoned, "If educators provide a huge increase in the supply of qualified workers, even though we have a need for only a handful of them, then we will have a large field to choose from, and we will be able to control wages. Workers are more passive when they know they can be re-placed easily." Educators seem to have thought, "Here's our change to get business support."

Using an oversimplified, but not inaccurate, example, the problem can be illustrated as follows. If 100 workers are needed (*demand*) and if educators produce 100 qualified workers (*supply*), there is a balance between demand and supply. However, if business finds ways to eliminate the need for half of those 100 workers—for example, through technological innovation—and education continues to produce a supply of 100 qualified workers, an *imbalance* occurs. That is the situation developing nationwide in the U.S.

The American economy now has far fewer decent jobs than ever before, and the future holds even fewer challenging job opportunities for tomorrow's graduates.[34] As corporate America becomes lean, through corporate reengineering, downsizing, and the use of labor-saving technologies, it simultaneously reduces the overall *demand* for highly trained workers. At the same time that the number of jobs in high-quality occupations is declining severely, millions of new temporary, contingent, and contract jobs are being created with low wages and few benefits.[35] This is not a situation in which having an education is an advantage.

However, corporate America has been insistent in its demand that the education system produce a world-class work force. With help from business-oriented media, corporate executives have caused parents to become concerned about the schools and restive about their children's future. As a result, America's school and university educators have been scrambling to produce that world-class work force. Universities are redesigning their curricula to skew them toward technical training and professional applications. At the same time, high schools are trying to redefine how they prepare students for the future by setting new standards, reforming, restructuring, and reinventing.

Thus the education system is developing an ever-growing supply of workers with high-performance abilities. But that supply of well-qualified graduates (along with those employees displaced from their current jobs) will overwhelm the available demand for such workers. Millions of American college and high school students are being prepared for high-performance jobs that may never exist.[36] There is a glut of high-quality workers about to hit the U.S. economy.[37]

THE NEED FOR LESS-SKILLED WORKERS

The reduction of high-quality job opportunities is structural, not cyclical. Thus it is not just a question of waiting it out. Cyclical fluctuations are merely the typical ups and downs of a free-market economy, in which recession is

soon followed by a period of growth. Structural change results from a fundamental, long-term transformation of an economy. Structural changes are
more profound and permanent. America experienced such a transformation
when its basic economy shifted from agriculture to industry, a change that
began shortly after the Civil War.

The current dilemma arises because both the world in general and the
U.S. in particular are experiencing an even more profound transformation:
a shift from an economy based on mass production to a *techno-informational* economy. The techno-informational economy (often referred to as
the Information Age or the postindustrial economy) rests on the development of computer-based manufacturing and information systems technology. These developments allow businesses to reduce their dependence on
human resources.

At first, the profound structural changes occurring in the economy appeared to promise a great many interesting, high-wage, highly skilled jobs, as
well as an easier life for all. There were tangible signs all around of the benefits of the techno-informational revolution: computers, cellular telephones,
autos with computer chips, the Internet, faxes, high-definition television, organ transplants, rockets to the moon, and so on. Who could doubt that we
had truly entered a new age? For educators, this was pretty heady stuff. We
wanted and needed to get on the technology bandwagon, in terms of both au-
tomating schoolrooms and implementing 21st-century curricula. The promise was that, by getting more and better education, especially technologically
focused education, the lives of most American high school and university
graduates would be better. That promise may never be fulfilled.

As it turns out, the need for a greater supply of high-quality workers is a
myth perpetuated by the vested interests of businesses. Every caring educator
has believed the myth. But that myth will soon be exposed when 80% of
America's graduates, regardless of their high-tech training, will have to resign
themselves to menial, routine, dead-end jobs.[38] The fact is that there will be a
need for ever-greater numbers of less-skilled, low-wage workers.

Why is it that so many Americans continue to believe the myth and ignore
the growing jobs dilemma? One reason is that the jobs dilemma is *not* a matter of the total number of jobs or of employment rates. The U.S. economy is
known throughout the world as a "jobs machine," meaning that American
businesses hire lots of people and the country's unemployment rate is low in
comparison with the rates of most other advanced industrial nations.[39]

The *official* unemployment rate in the U.S. has averaged below 6% since
1994. Almost two million workers were hired in 1994, mostly in low-wage
jobs.[40] The only group that *increased* its unemployment rate was black teenagers, the last hired and first fired of all groups. However, these official figures convey an incomplete statistical view of employment in the U.S. One of
the reasons that the U.S. can claim that it has produced a lot of new jobs is

the way it determines who is and is not employed. In almost every other advanced industrialized country, anyone who wants a full-time job and is forced to work part time is counted as unemployed. In the U.S., a person working part time is counted as employed, a procedure that considerably reduces the overall unemployment numbers. If the U.S. counted its unemployed as the other industrial countries do, we would have 4.5 million more people unemployed, and our unemployment rate would be equal to or higher than the 11% rate in Europe.[41]

Be that as it may, the average monthly growth in new jobs was 247,000 in 1994, which totals almost three million jobs in one year. That number was up another million by 1995 and reached a total of 4.8 million by 1996. The Bureau of Labor Statistics projects that total employment will increase from 12.1 million in 1992 to 147.5 million by 2005.[42] That projected 22% rate of employment growth is slightly higher than the increase attained during the previous 13-year period, from 1979 to 1992.[43] So *absolute* job growth is not causing the jobs dilemma. Lack of growth in *high-quality* jobs is what's causing the problem.

WHAT LIES AHEAD

Unless there is a fundamental change in policy, millions of American high school and university graduates will be unable to find decent, challenging, well-paid work. This problem is due in large measure to the American education system's misguided commitment to producing world-class graduates without a reciprocal commitment from corporate America to make a sufficient number of high-quality jobs available. The vested interests of the business establishment and the historic mission of America's educational institutions seem to be working at cross purposes.

Some economists argue fatalistically that a high-quality labor supply will always exceed demand, especially given the current and projected technological capability of American businesses. Moreover, few scholars see any turning back from the economic restructuring taking place in America.

But what are the consequences of passive acquiescence to radical economic restructuring? To understand the implications of capitulation to "inexorable forces," instead of making political and economic decisions that might mitigate those "forces," the American public and America's educators need look no further than the dire predictions made about American society as it moves into the 21st century.

Ending the jobs dilemma will demand creative solutions and a push for *more* technologically driven economic growth. That growth will allow our economy to absorb a larger number of highly qualified graduates of universities and community colleges, as well as graduates of sophisticated school-to-work and apprenticeship programs. The challenge is to find *structural* ways to increase the number of employment opportunities for highly skilled, high-tech craft workers, as well as for other knowledge workers.

There is an advantage to education. It is reflected in the higher incomes and challenging occupations found among the elite American craft workers and other knowledge workers. The question we must answer as we prepare to enter a new century is how to expand such job opportunities.

NOTES

1. Louis V. Gerstner, Jr., et al., *Reinventing Education* (New York: Dutton, 1994).

2. "The Big Picture Out There: The Percent of U.S. Corporate R&D Spent Overseas," *Business Week*, 18 April 1994, p. 8.

3. "Big Blue's White Elephant Sale," *Business Week*, 20 February 1994, p. 36; and *Forbes*, 25 April 1994, p. 13.

4. For details, see Michael A. Bernstein and David E. Adler, eds., *Understanding American Economic Decline* (New York: Cambridge University Press, 1994).

5. David Friedman, "Why the Big Apple Is No Economic Model for L.A.," *Los Angeles Times*, 12 June 1994, p. M-1.

6. Robert E. Kutscher, "Historical Trends, 1950–92 and Current Uncertainties," *Monthly Labor Review*, November 1993, p. 7.

7. "Downsizing Continues," *Business Week*, 19 January 1993, p. 26.

8. "For a Pink Slip, Press 2," *Business Week*, 27 November 1995, p. 48; and "AT&T Offers Buyouts to More Than Half Its Managers," *Los Angeles Times*, 16 November 1995, p. D-1. Primarily managerial, professional, and white-collar positions were cut, positions that represent a savings of $50,000 each. Upon hearing the announcement of AT&T's cuts, Wall Street investors pushed up the price of the company's shares by $1.25—to $64.50.

9. Jube Shiver and Karen Kaplan, "AT&T Split into Three Firms to Cost 40,000 Jobs," *Los Angeles Times*, 3 January 1996, pp. A-1, A-9; and "The Bloodletting at AT&T Is Just Beginning," *Business Week*, 15 January 1996, p. 30.

10. "Strong Employment Gains Spur Inflation Worries," *Washington Post*, 17 May 1994, pp. A-1, A-9.

11. "Use of Contingent Workers Rising, Report Says," *Los Angeles Times*, 15 September 1995, p. D-4.

12. Sometimes outsourcing work can be deadly. Prior to the airline crash that killed more than a hundred people, ValuJet had its planes maintained by outside contractors, who apparently failed to do high-quality work. The airline temporarily shut down after the Federal Aviation Administration questioned its maintenance quality control. See "FAA Shake-Up Is Scheduled, Hinson Says," *Los Angeles Times*, 18 June 1996, p. A-15.

13. George T. Silvestri, "Occupational Employment: Wide Variations in Growth," *Monthly Labor Review*, April 1994, pp. 56–84. Entry-level jobs, the least skilled of all, may also be in short supply soon. The Bureau of Labor Statistics forecast suggests that, when the new welfare law forces recipients to get jobs after two years on welfare, there may not be any jobs for them to get, regardless of how hard they try. See "Welfare Bill May Deplete Job Supply," *USA Today*, 28 July 1996, p. 27.

14. "Downsizing Continues," *Business Week*, 19 January 1993, p. 26.

15. Daniel S. Greenberg, "So Many Ph.D.s," *Washington Post National Weekly Edition*, 5–12 June 1995, p. 24.

16. Ibid.

17. Boyce Rensberger, "No Help Wanted: Young Scientists Go Begging," *Washington Post National Weekly Edition*, 9–15 January 1995, pp. 5, 7.

18. Greenberg, op. cit.

19. Lee Dye, "Blame Federal Grant System for America's Ph.D. Glut," *Los Angeles Times*, 29 March 1995, p. D-4.

20. Ibid.

21. Jerry Glasser, "Nascent MBAs Take Their Show on the Road," *Business Week*, 5 September 1994, p. 37.

22. Ibid.

23. Meg Sommerfeld, "Upper-Level Math, Science Enrollment Is Up, Study Says," *Education Week*, 11 October 1995, p. 10.

24. Ibid.

25. Debra Viadero, "Studies Chart Big Boost in Course Taking," *Education Week*, 30 September 1995, pp. 1, 16.

26. "Moving Ahead," *Education Week*, 13 September 1994, p. 4.

27. *Commission on the Future of Worker-Management Relations: Fact Finding Report* (Washington, D.C.: U.S. Departments of Labor and Commerce, May 1994), pp. 12, 17. These figures are for male workers. The 17% drop in wages was partially offset by the entrance of women into the work force in great numbers. Women's wages rose from $21,530 in 1971 to $23,161 in 1990.

28. Dean Baker and Lawrence Mishel, "Profits Up, Wages Down," Economic Policy Institute, Washington, D.C., September 1995, p. 5.

29. Stanley Aronowitz and William DiFazio, *The Jobless Future* (Minneapolis: University of Minnesota Press, 1994), pp. 325–27.

30. "Job Market Jitters," *Education Week*, 10 November 1993, p. 3. A more recent study, which indicated a tiny 1.1% increase in hiring of new college graduates, states that the increase was the lowest in 14 months and came nowhere near to making up for the huge loss of job opportunities reported by the Census Bureau. See "Downsizing Slows but Sheepskin Set Is Still Scrambling," *Business Week*, 22 August 1994, p. 20.

31. Mary McClellan, "Why Blame the Schools?," *Research Bulletin No. 12*, Phi Delta Kappa Center for Evaluation, Development, and Research, Bloomington, Ind., March 1994, pp. 1–6.

32. Aaron Bernstein, "This Job Market Still Has Plenty of Slack," *Business Week*, 24 June 1996, p. 36.

33. Ibid.

34. Neal H. Rosenthal, "The Nature of Occupational Employment Growth, 1983–1993," *Monthly Labor Review*, June 1995, pp. 45–54.

35. Ibid.

36. Aronowitz and DiFazio, pp. 325–27.

37. Jeremy Rifkin, *The End of Work: The Decline of the Global Labor Force and the Dawn of the Post-Market Era* (New York: Tarcher/Putnam Books, 1995), pp. 3–15 and *passim*.

38. Ibid.

39. Herrhausen Society, *Work in the Future* (Stuttgart, Germany: Schaffer-Poeschel Verlag, 1994), p. 4; see also *Employment Outlook* (Paris: Organization for Economic Co-operation and Development, July 1994), chap. 2.

40. "Labor Markets Hit a Slow Boil but Inflation Keeps Its Cool," *Business Week*, 22 August 1994, p. 21. The high-growth jobs were in such service areas as personal supply, health care, and the retail trade, while hiring in the juicy jobs in finance and manufacturing was slight.

41. Lester C. Thurow, "America Reverts to the 19th Century," *Los Angeles Times*, 29 January 1996, p. B-9.

42. The year 1992 is used here because that is the base year the Bureau of Labor Statistics established for its very precise projection of employment opportunities through the year 2005.

43. Silvestri, pp. 52–53.

8
▼▼▼▼▼▼▼

Kids for Sale: Corporate Culture and the Challenge of Public Schooling*

Henry A. Giroux

School is . . . the ideal time to influence attitudes, build long-term loyalties, introduce new products, test markets, promote sampling and trial usage and—above all—to generate immediate sales.
> —Cited in Consumer Union Education Services,
> *Captive Kids: Commercial Pressures on Kids at Schools*

PREPARING CITIZENS OR CONSUMERS

One of the most important legacies of American public education has been providing students with the critical capacities, knowledge, and values that enable them to become active citizens striving to build a stronger democratic society. Within this tradition, Americans have defined schooling as a public good and a fundamental right.[1] Such a definition rightfully asserts the primacy of democratic values over corporate culture and commercial values. Schools are an important indicator of the well-being of a democratic society. They remind us of the civic values that must be passed on to young people in order for them to think critically, to participate in power relations and policy decisions that affect their lives, and to transform the racial, social, and economic inequities that limit democratic social relations. Yet as crucial as the role of public schooling has been in American history, it is facing an unprecedented attack from proponents of market ideology who strongly advocate the unparalleled expansion of corporate culture.[2]

Influential educational consultants such as Robert Zemsky of Stanford University and Chester Finn of the Hudson Institute now "advise their clients in the name of efficiency to act like corporations selling products and seek 'market niches' to save themselves." They are advised to adopt such strategies so as to meet the challenges of the new world economic order.[3] School leaders are now drawn from the ranks of corporate executives, employing a managerial style that describes school systems as "major companies," students as "customers," and learning as a measurable outcome. One example of the new corporate school leader was highlighted in a recent article in *The New York Times*. Under the byline, "Applying Corporate Touch to a Troubled School System," the article focuses on Andre J. Hornsby, the new superintendent of the Yonkers school district, the fourth largest in New York City. Touted as a model for the type of leadership now in vogue among urban school systems, the *Times* describes him as "arrogant, autocratic, an egomaniac . . . adamant that poor minority children can overcome their socioeconomic hurdles, driven to raise scores on standardized tests using cookie-cutter curriculums, and assuming an almost militaristic take-charge approach." Without skipping a beat the article then goes on to point out that one of Mr. Hornsby's first initiatives was to impose additional work loads on his teachers, which prompted a strike, and at his initiative prompted a successful court battle to prevent extra resources from being distributed to "eight school districts the courts identified as being in most need." It seems that in spite of Mr. Hornsby's concern for poor students, he preferred to distribute the extra money among all school districts, "a tactic favored by the predominantly white school board that hired him."[4] Hornsby appears typical of a corporate leadership model that has nothing to say about inequality, wields power autocratically, reduces curricula to the language of standards and testing, and makes sure that teachers have little control over the conditions of teaching and learning.

The advocates of corporate culture no longer view public education in terms of its civic function; rather it is primarily a commercial venture in which the only form of citizenship available for young people is consumerism. In what follows, I argue that reducing public education to the ideological imperatives of the corporate order works against the critical social demands of educating citizens to sustain and develop inclusive democratic identities, relations, and public spheres. Underlying this analysis is the assumption that the struggle to reclaim the public schools must be seen as part of a broader battle over the defense of children's culture and the public good. At the heart of such a struggle is the need to challenge the ever-growing influence of corporate power and politics.

The corporatizing of public education has taken a distinct turn as we approach the twenty-first century. No longer content merely to argue for the application of business principles to the organization of schooling, the forces of corporate culture have adopted a much more radical agenda. Central to this agenda is the attempt to transform public education from a public good, benefiting all students, to a private good designed to expand the profits of investors, educate students as consumers, and train young people for the low-paying jobs of the new global marketplace. And the stakes are high. According to the *Education Industry Directory*, the for-profit education market represents $600 billion in revenue for corporate interests.[5] And this is an expanding market, "larger than either the military budget or social security."[6] The lure of such big profits has attracted a range of investors including former junk bond wizard Michael Milken along with an increasing number of corporate players such as Apple, Sony, Microsoft, Oracle, and the *Washington Post*.[7]

But the corporate takeover of schools is not rationalized in the name of profits and market efficiency alone; it is also legitimated through the call for vouchers, privatized choice plans, and excellence. Although this discourse cloaks itself in the democratic principles of freedom, individualism, and consumer rights, it fails to provide the broader historical, social, and political contexts necessary to render such principles meaningful and applicable, particularly with respect to the problems facing public schools.

While a wide range of marketplace-based approaches to schooling exist, all share a faith in corporate culture that overrides defending public education as a noncommodified public sphere, a repository for nourishing the primacy of civic over corporate values, and as a public entitlement that is essential for the well-being of children and the future of democracy.

THE POLITICS OF PRIVATIZATION

Privatization is the most powerful educational reform movement to come since the *Sputnik* crisis caused a panic among educators in the 1950s when schools rushed to prepare a new generation of scientists to lead the American space race against the Russians. The movement is funded by an array of conservative institutions such as the Heritage Foundation, the Hudson Institute, and the Olin Foundation.[8] Capitalizing on their wealth and media influence, these foundations have enlisted an army of conservative pundits, many of whom served in the Department of Education under Presidents Reagan and Bush. Some of the better-known members of this reform movement include Chester Finn, Jr., Lamar Alexander, Diane Ravitch, David Kearns, and William Bennett. Providing policy papers and op-ed commentaries, appearing on television talk shows, and running a variety of educational clearinghouses and resource centers, these stalwart opponents of public education relentlessly blame the schools for the country's economic woes. Diane Ravitch and others cite low test scores, a decline in basic skills, and the watering down of the school curriculum in order to legitimate the ideology of privatization with its accompanying call for vouchers, privatized charter schools, and the placing of public schools entirely under the control of corporate contractors.[9] More specific reforms simply recycle right-wing ideology critiques calling for the replacement of teacher unions and "giving parents choice, back-to-basics and performance-driven curriculums, management 'design teams' and accountability."[10]

Underlying the call for privatization is a reform movement in which public education is seen as "a local industry that over time will become a global business."[11] As a for-profit venture, public education represents a rapidly growing market and a lucrative source of profits. The importance of such a market has not been lost on conservatives such as Chester Finn, Jr., and David Kearns, both of whom have connections with for-profit schooling groups such as the Edison Project and the North American Schools Development Corporation, respectfully. At the level of policy, by all reports the right-wing assault has been quite successful. More than twenty-eight states have drafted legislation supporting vouchers, choice programs, and contracting with for-profit management companies, such as the Edison Project and Sabis International Schools. But the public's perception of such ventures appears to be less enthusiastic, and rightly so. Many firms, such as Educational Alternatives Inc., which took over the Hartford and Baltimore public schools, have had their contracts canceled as a result of numerous public complaints. The complaints range from the way in which such firms deal with children with learning disabilities and engage in union busting to the charge that their cookie-cutter standardized curriculum and testing packages fail to provide the quality of educational results that such companies initially promised.[12]

But there is more at stake in the privatization of public schooling than issues of public versus private ownership or public good versus private gain. There is also the issue of how individual achievement is weighed against issues of equity and the social good, how teaching and learning are defined, and what sorts of identities are produced when the histories, experiences, values, and desires of students are delineated through corporate rather than democratic ideals.

Within the language of privatization and market reforms, there is a strong emphasis on standards, measurements of outcomes, and holding teachers and students more accountable. Privatization is an appealing prospect for legislators who do not want to spend money on schools and for those Americans who feel that they do not want to support public education through increased taxes. Such appeals are reductive in nature and hollow in substance.

Not only do they remove questions of equity and equality from the discussion of standards, they appropriate the democratic rhetoric of choice and freedom without addressing issues of power. In their refusal to address the financial inequities that burden the public schools, the ideas and images that permeate this corporate model of schooling reek with the rhetoric of insincerity and the politics of social indifference. Educational theorist Jonathan Kozol captures this sentiment well. He writes:

> To speak of national standards and, increasingly, of national exams but never to dare speak of national equality is a transparent venture into punitive hypocrisy. Thus, the children in poor rural schools in Mississippi and Ohio will continue to get education funded at less than $4,000 yearly and children in the South Bronx will get less than $7,000, while children in the richest suburbs will continue to receive up to $18,000 yearly. But they'll all be told they must be held to the same standards and they'll all be judged, of course, by their performance on the same exams.[13]

Because they have no language of social responsibility, the advocates of privatization reject the assumption that school failure might be better understood within the political, economic, and social dynamics of poverty, joblessness, sexism, race and class discrimination, unequal funding, or a diminished tax base. Rather, student failure, especially the failure of poor minority-group students, often is attributed to a genetically encoded lack of intelligence, a culture of deprivation, or simply to pathology. Books such as *The Bell Curve*[14] and films such as *Dangerous Minds* and *187* reinforce such representations of African American and Latino urban youth and in doing so reinforce and perpetuate a legacy of racist exclusions. Similarly, the informalities of privatization schemes in which schools simply mimic the free market, with the assumption that its regulatory and competitive spirit will allow the most motivated and gifted students to succeed, deepen such racist exclusions. A shameful element of racism and a retrograde social Darwinism permeates this attitude, one that relinquishes the responsibility of parents, teachers, administrators, social workers, businesspeople, and other members of the wider society to provide *all* young people with the cultural resources, economic opportunities, and social services necessary to learn without having to bear the crushing burdens of poverty, racism, and other forms of oppression.

The excessive celebration by privatization's advocates of an individual's sovereign interests does more than remove the dynamics of student performance from broader social and political considerations; it also feeds a value system in which compassion, solidarity, cooperation, social responsibility, and other attributes of education as a social good get displaced by defining education exclusively as a private good. If education is about, in part, creating particular identities, what dominates the corporate model is a notion of the student as an individual consumer and teachers as the ultimate salespeople.[15] Education scholar David Labaree is right in arguing that such an educational model undermines the traditional notion that education is a public good that should benefit all children and must be viewed as central to the democratic health of a society. But when viewed as a private good whose organizing principle is simply to mimic the market, education as the experience of democracy is transformed into a discourse and ideology of privilege driven by narrow individual interests. Labaree is quite clear on this issue:

> In an educational system where the consumer is king . . . education . . . is a private good that only benefits the owner, an investment in my future, not yours, in my children, not other people's children. For such an educational system to work effectively, it needs to focus a lot of attention on grading, sorting, and selecting students. It needs to provide a variety of ways for individuals to distinguish themselves from others—such as by placing themselves in a more prestigious college, a higher curriculum track, the top reading group, or the gifted program.[16]

In this framework education becomes less a social investment than an individual investment, a vehicle for social mobility for those privileged to have the resources and power to make their choices matter, and a form of social constraint for those who lack such resources and for whom choice and accountability betray a legacy of broken promises and an ideology of bad faith.

The privatization model of schooling also undermines the power of teachers to provide students with the vocabulary and skills of critical citizenship. Under the drive to impose national curricula uniformity and standardized testing, privatizing school advocates devalue teacher authority and subvert teacher skills by dictating not only what they teach but also how they should teach. California, for example, is drafting legislation that mandates both the content of school knowledge and "more specific guidelines for when and how to teach various principles in the core subjects."[17]

In this perspective teaching is completely removed from the cultural and social contexts that shape particular traditions, histories, and experiences in a community and school. Hence, this model of educational reform fails to recognize that students come from different backgrounds, bring diverse cultural experiences with them to the classroom, and relate to the world in different ways. Importance is no longer placed on having teachers begin with those places, histories, and experiences that actually constitute students' lives in order to connect whatever knowledge they learn to existing frameworks of reference. Rather, teaching in the corporate model translates educational exchange into financial exchange, critical learning into mastery, and leadership into management. This perspective lacks the ability to acknowledge students' histories, the stories that inform their lives, and the educational imperative of weaving such information into webs of meaning that link the everyday with the academic. Corporate education opposes such a critical approach because it cannot be standardized, routinized, and reduced to a prepackaged curriculum; on the contrary, a critical and transformative educational practice takes seriously the abilities of teachers to theorize, contextualize, and honor their students' diverse lives. It is far removed from a corporate educational system based on an industrial model of learning that represents a flagrant violation of the democratic educational mission.

A debilitating logic is at work in the corporate model of teaching with its mandated curriculum, top-down teaching practices, and national tests to measure educational standards. Infused with the drive toward standardized curricula and teaching, "teachers and communities shorn of the capacity to use their own ideas, judgments and initiative in matters of importance can't teach kids to do so."[18] Such approaches have little to do with teaching students to develop critical skills and an awareness of the operations of power that would enable them to both locate themselves in the world and to intervene in and shape it effectively.[19] On the contrary, corporate educational policies undermine such critical approaches by defining teaching less as an intellectual activity and more as a standardized, mechanical, and utterly passive mode of transmission. Sociologist Stanley Aronowitz argues that such a system largely functions to "measure" student progress while simultaneously reproducing a tracking system that parallels the deep racial and economic inequalities of the larger society. He writes:

> Where once liberal, let alone radical, educators insisted that education be at the core an activity of self-exploration in which, through intellectual and affective encounters, the student attempts to discover her own subjectivity, now nearly all learning space is occupied by an elaborate testing apparatus that measures the student's "progress" in ingesting externally imposed curricula and, more insidiously, provides a sorting device to reproduce the inequalities inherent in the capitalist market system.[20]

The main role of the teacher-turned-classroom manager is to legitimate through mandated subject matter and educational practices a market-based conception of the learner as simply a consumer of information. Yet such reforms have support, in spite of a long tradition of critique of the ways in which teachers are being shorn of their skills and increasingly treated "more and more as impersonal instruments in a bureaucratic process than as thoughtful and creative intellectuals whose personal vision of education really matters."[21] Moreover, within the standardized teaching models proffered by corporations, it is difficult to offer students the opportunity to think critically about the knowledge they gain, to appreciate the value of learning as more than the mastery of discrete bits of information, or how to use knowledge as a form of power to fight injustices in a market-based society founded on deep inequalities of power. Given the vested interests that conglomerates have in turning students "into consumers and avenues to a vast consumer base," it is highly improbable that schools will be allowed to foster resistance to corporate ideologies. And this fact becomes increasingly more likely as corporations control publishing companies, magazines, newspapers, and other knowledge-producing sources. For example, *New York Times* writer Russell Baker writing about Michael Milken's foray into for-profit education speculates about whether a Milken School would allow teachers and students to critically examine the financial corruption that marked a number of business scandals in the 1980s, including the way in which Milken used his power as a junk bond dealer and financial adviser to downsize companies and eventually throw thousands of people out of work. In response to such an inquiry, Baker writes that a former colleague says "Absolutely not." He concludes that "Such concerns seem borne out in a book produced by a Milken-backed publishing house, Knowledge Exchange. Its *Business Encyclopedia* approvingly cites Milken's role in the junk-bond market without mention of the economic and social devastation associated with it."[22]

One could raise the censorship issue about a number of corporations that have made heavy investments in gaining a share of the education market. For example, Disney has been criticized in a number of quarters for preventing critical news commentators and stories from being aired on its radio stations.[23] In light of such allegations, it is conceivable that Disney would exercise the same type of censorship on curricular materials used in the schools that were critical of, let us say, its outsourcing of the production of its clothing and toys to sweatshops in such countries as Haiti, Burma, Vietnam, and China.[24] In addition, if such conglomerates can slash "surplus teachers" in order to become more cost effective, they can easily legitimate and select teaching materials that contribute positively to their public relations campaigns.

Finally, it is no small matter that the project that fuels privatization not only celebrates competitive, self-interested individuals attempting to further their own needs and aspirations but also takes place within a dialogue of decline, a jeremiad against public life. In doing so it actually undermines the role that public schools might play in keeping the experiences, hopes, and dreams of a democracy alive for each successive generation of students.

The major objective of privatization is that public schools conform to the needs of the market and reflect more completely the interests of corporate culture—in essence, the private sector should control and own the public schools. While this represents the most direct assault on schooling as a public sphere, the program does not stop there. A different but no less important and dangerous strategy of the corporate dismantling and takeover of public schools is the promotion of educational choice, vouchers, and charters as a way of both opening public schools to private contractors and using public tax monies to finance private forms of education. Both approaches treat education as a private good, and both transform the student's role from citizen to educational consumer. But the real danger at work in privatization, as educational theorist Jeffrey Henig points out, is not simply that students who transfer into private schools will drain money from the public schools but that they will further a process already at work in the larger society aimed at eroding "the public forums in which decisions with social consequences can be democratically resolved."[25]

COMMERCIALIZATION IN SCHOOLS

Corporate culture can be seen not only in the placement of public schools in the control of corporate contractors. It is also visible in the growing commercialization of school space and curricula. Strapped for money, many public schools have had to lease out space in their hallways, buses, rest rooms, monthly lunch menus, and school cafeterias, transforming such spaces into glittering billboards for the highest corporate bidder.[26] School notices, classroom displays, and student artwork have been replaced by advertisements for Coca-Cola, Pepsi, Nike, Hollywood films, and a litany of other products. Invaded by candy manufacturers, breakfast cereal makers, sneaker companies, and fast food chains, schools increasingly offer the not-so-subtle message to students that everything is for sale including student identities, desires, and values. Seduced by the lure of free equipment and money, schools all too readily make the transition from advertising to offering commercial merchandise in the form of curricula materials designed to build brand loyalty and markets among a captive public school audience. Although schools may reap small financial benefit from such school-business transactions, the real profits go to the corporations that spend millions on advertising to reach a market of an estimated 43 million children in school "with spending power of over $108 billion per year and the power to influence parental spending."[27]

The commercial logic that fuels this market-based reform movement is also evident in the way in which corporate culture targets schools not simply as investments for substantial profits but also as training grounds for educating students to define themselves as consumers rather than as multifaceted social actors. As schools struggle to raise money for texts, curricula, and extracurricular activities, they engage in partnerships with businesses that are all too willing to provide free curriculum packages; as in the case of companies such as Channel One that provide each school with $50,000 in "free" electronic equipment, including VCRs, televisions, and satellite dishes, on the condition that the schools agree to broadcast a ten-minute program of current events and news material along with two minutes of commercials.[28] A number of companies want to capitalize on cash-poor schools in order to gain a foothold to promote learning as a way to create "consumers in training." For example ZapMe, a Silicon Valley company, "gives schools free personal computers and Internet access in exchange for the right to display a constant stream of on-screen advertisements. Participating schools must also promise that the system will be in use for at least four hours per school day."[29]

The marriage of commercialism and education often takes place in schools with too few resources to critically monitor how learning is structured or to recognize the sleight-of-hand that appears to be a generous offer on the part of corporations. A few examples will suffice. In a recent cover story, *Business Week* magazine reported on the adoption of a McDonald's-sponsored curriculum package by the Pembroke Lakes elementary school in Broward County, Florida. Commenting on what one ten-year-old learned from the curricula, *Business Week* claimed that "Travis Licate recently learned how to design a McDonald's restaurant, how a McDonald's works, and how to apply and interview for a job at McDonald's thanks to [the] seven-week company sponsored class intended to teach kids about the work world."[30] When Travis was asked if the curriculum was worthwhile, he responded: "If you want to work in a McDonald's when you grow up, you already know what to do. . . . Also, McDonald's is better than Burger King."[31] According to the Center for Commercial-Free Public Education, Exxon developed a curriculum that teaches young students that the Valdez oil spill was an example of environmental protection. The center also cites a Nike-sponsored curriculum that teaches students to learn how a Nike shoe is created but fails to address "the sweatshop portion of the manufacturing process."[32] McGraw-Hill recently published an elementary-school math textbook full of advertisements for products such as Nike, Gatorade, and Sony PlayStations. Another company offers a math exercise book that "purports to teach third-graders math by having them count Tootsie Rolls."[33] Such curricula have little to do with critical learning and a great deal with producing debased narratives of citizenship, suggesting to students that the only roles open to them are defined through the ethos of consumerism. The version of citizenship presented in this commercial educational system debases public life and privatizes learning by removing it from noncommercial values and considerations.[34]

Many school systems not only accept corporate-sponsored curricula, they also lease out space in their hallways, on their buses, and even on book covers. Cover Concepts Marketing Services, Inc., for example, provides schools with free book covers strategically designed to promote brand-name products that include Nike, Gitano, FootLocker, Starburst, Nestlé, and Pepsi. The covers are distributed to over 8,000 public schools and reach an audience of over 6 million high school, junior high, and elementary school students.[35] In Colorado Springs, Colorado, Palmer High School allows Burger King and Sprite to advertise on the sides of its school buses. In Salt Lake City, Youthtalk Advertising Agency places acrylic-faced advertising billboards in school rest rooms and cafeterias. It is estimated by the company that over "80,000 students are exposed to the ads while standing at urinals and sitting in toilet stalls."[36]

A number of public and private schools are also allowing corporations to harness students as captive audiences for market research during the school day. Trading student time for industry resources, many schools forge partnerships with corporations in which students become the objects of market-based group research. Corporations give the schools money, equipment, or curricula for the right to use students to take taste tests, experiment with different products, or answer opinion polls in which they are asked questions that range from "where they got their news [to] what television shows they like."[37] Some educators eager to justify such blatant acts of commercialism argue that these practices constitute a genuine learning experience for students; in doing so they often appear to be merely echoing the words of research consultants who claim that such market-based approaches are actually empowering for kids. For example, Martha Marie Pooler, the principal of Our Lady of Assumption elementary school in Lynnfield, Massachusetts, agreed to accept $600 for her school in exchange for a corporation using students in a cereal taste test. She justified this type of corporate intrusion by claiming that the test had educational benefits in that it was similar "to conducting a science-class experiment."[38] Pooler is part of a growing number of educators who refuse to face the serious ethical dilemmas involved in allowing companies to conduct market research on children who should be learning critical knowledge and skills that, at the very least, would enable them to refuse to participate in such exploitative behavior. Not only do the students have no say in participating in such market driven tests, they, along with the teachers, appear powerless as the school shifts its priorities from education to marketing products. Andrew Hagelshaw, a senior program director of the Center for Commercial-Free Public Education in Oakland, California rightfully argues that "companies are turning schools into sales agents for their products . . . [and are] going to change the priorities from education to . . . consumption."[39] The National Association of State Boards of Education recently argued that schools that offer captive audiences of children in classrooms as fodder for commercial profit are engaging in practices that constitute both an act of "exploitation and a violation of the public trust."[40] Such violations of the public trust present a major challenge to those educators, parents, and concerned citizens who want to protect children from corporate intrusion into their lives.

Schools are being transformed into commercial rather than public spheres as students become subject to the whims and practices of marketers whose agenda has nothing to do with critical learning and a great deal to do with restructuring civic life in the image of market culture.[41] Civic courage—upholding the most basic noncommercial principles of democracy—as a defining principle of society is devalued as corporate power transforms school knowledge so that students are taught to recognize brand names or learn the appropriate attitudes for future work in low-skilled, low-paying jobs. They are no longer taught how to connect the meaning of work to the imperatives of a strong democracy. What links Channel One, Nike, Pepsi, the Campbell Soup Company, the McDonald Corporation, and a host of others is that they substitute corporate propaganda for real learning, upset the requisite balance between the public and the private, and in doing so treat schools like any other business.

Underlying the attempt to redefine the meaning and purpose of schooling as part of a market economy rather than a fundamental feature of substantive democracy is a model of society in which "consumer accountability [is] mediated by a relationship with an educational market [rather than] a democratic accountability mediated by a relationship with the whole community of citizens."[42] Most disturbing about the market approach to schooling is that it contains no special consideration for the vocabulary of ethics and values. British educator Gerald Grace insightfully argues that when public education becomes a venue for making a profit, delivering a product, or constructing consuming subjects, education reneges on its responsibilities for creating a democracy of citizens by shifting its focus to producing a democracy of consumers.[43]

Growing up corporate has become a way of life for American youth. This is evident as corporate mergers consolidate control of assets and markets, particularly as they extend their influence over the media and its management of public opinion. But it is also apparent in the accelerated commercialism in all aspects of everyday life, including the "commercialization of public schools, the renaming of public streets for commercial sponsors, Janis Joplin's Mercedes pitch, restroom advertising, and [even the marketing] of an official commercial bottled water for a papal visit."[44] Although it is largely recognized that market culture exercises a powerful educational role in mobilizing desires and shaping identities, it still comes as a shock when an increasing number of pollsters report that young people, when asked to provide a definition for democracy, answered by referring to "the freedom to buy and consume whatever they wish, without government restriction."[45]

Couched in the language of business competition and individual success, the current educational reform movement must be recognized as a full-fledged attack on both public education and democracy itself. Social critic David Stratman's warning that the goal of such a movement "is not to raise the expectations of our young people but to narrow, stifle, and crush them"[46] needs to be taken seriously by anyone concerned about public education. This is particularly true if public education is to play a fundamental role in placing limits on market culture, affirming the language of moral compassion, and expanding the meaning of freedom and choice to broader considerations of equity, justice, and social responsibility.

As market culture permeates the social order, it threatens to diminish the tension between market values and democratic values, such as justice; freedom; equality; respect for children; and the rights of citizens as equal, free human beings. Without such values, children are relegated to the role of economic calculating machines, and the growing disregard for public life that appears to be gaining ground in the United States is left unchecked.

History has been clear about the dangers of unbridled corporate power. Four hundred years of slavery; ongoing although unofficial segregation; the exploitation of child labor; the sanctioning of cruel working conditions in coal mines and sweatshops; and the destruction of the environment have all been fueled by the law of maximizing profits and minimizing costs, especially when civil society offers no countervailing power to hold such forces in check. This is not to suggest that corporations are the enemy of democracy but to highlight the importance of a strong democratic civil society that limits the reach and effects of corporate culture.[47] John Dewey correctly argues that democracy requires work, but that work is not synonymous with democracy.[48]

Educational critic Alex Molnar rightfully cautions educators that the market does not provide "guidance on matters of justice and fairness that are at the heart of a democratic civil society."[49] The power of corporate culture, when left to its own devices, respects few boundaries and even fewer basic social needs, such as the need for uncontaminated food, decent health care, and safe forms of transportation. This was made clear, for example, in recent revelations about the failure of tobacco companies to reveal evidence about the addictive nature of nicotine. In direct violation of broader health considerations, these corporations effectively promoted the addiction of young smokers to increase sales and profits. Moreover, as multinational corporations increase their control over the circulation of information in the media, little is mentioned about how they undermine the principles of justice and freedom that should be at the center of our most vital civic institutions. Developing a vocabulary that affirms non-market values such as love, trust, and compassion is particularly important for the public schools, whose function, in part, is to teach students about the importance of critical dialogue, debate, and decision making in a participatory democracy.

One recent incident at a public school in Evans, Georgia, provides an example of how corporate culture actually can be used to punish students who challenge the corporate approach to learning. Greenbrier High School decided to participate in an Education Day as part of a larger district-wide contest sponsored by Coca-Cola executives. Each school that entered the contest sponsored rallies, heard speeches from Coke executives, analyzed the sugar content of Coke in chemistry classes, and gathered for "an aerial photograph of the students' bodies dressed in red and white and forming the word 'coke.' The reward for winning the district-wide contest—five hundred dollars."[50] Two students decided to disrupt the photo shoot by removing their shirts to reveal Pepsi logos. Both students were suspended on the grounds that they were rude. What students learned as a result is that the individual right to dissent, to freely express their opinions and ideas, and to challenge authority, when addressed within the context of commercial culture, is a punishable offense. Choice in this context is about choosing the right soft drink, not about the right to question whether schools should be turned into advertising billboards for corporate interests.

EDUCATION AND THE IMPERATIVES OF DEMOCRACY

Challenging the encroachment of corporate power is essential if democracy is to remain a defining principle of education and everyday life. In order to mobilize such a challenge educators need to create organizations capable of providing an alternative conception of the meaning and purpose of public education, one that links education to expanding and deepening democracy itself. Educators must also create political coalitions that have the power and resources to produce legislation that limits corporate power's ascendancy over the institutions and mechanisms of civil society. This project requires that educators and students provide the rationale and mobilize the possibility for the creation of enclaves of resistance, new public cultures, and institutional spaces that highlight, nourish, and evaluate the tension between civil society and corporate power while simultaneously emphasizing citizen rights rather than consumer rights.

Educators, families, and community members need to reinvigorate the language, social relations, and politics of schooling. We must analyze how power shapes knowledge, how teaching broader social values provides safeguards against turning citizenship skills into workplace-training skills, and how schooling can help students reconcile the seemingly opposing needs of freedom and solidarity. As educators, we need to examine alternative models of education that challenge the corporatization of public schools. For example, pioneering educators such as Deborah Meier, Ted Sizer, James Comer, and organizations like the Rethinking School Collective, among others, are working hard to link educational policies and classroom practices to expand the scope of freedom, justice, and democracy.

In strategic terms, in order to revitalize public dialogue, educators need to take seriously the importance of defending public education as an institution whose purpose is to educate students for active citizenship.[51] Schooling is a site that offers students the opportunity to be involved in the deepest problems of society and to acquire the knowledge, skills, and ethical vocabulary necessary to actively participate in democratic public life. Educators need to come together locally and nationally to defend public schools as indispensable to the life of the nation because they are one of the few remaining public spheres where students can gain the knowledge and skills they need for learning how to govern, take risks, and develop the knowledge necessary for deliberation, reasoned arguments, and social action. At issue is providing students with an education that allows them to recognize the dream and promise of a substantive democracy, particularly the idea that as citizens, as historian Robin Kelley points out, they are "entitled to public services, decent housing, safety, security, support during hard times, and most importantly, some power over decision making."[52] Social critics Carol Ascher, Norm Fruchter, and Robert Berne capture the gravity of such a project in their claim that

> the urgency to solve the inequities in schooling is perhaps the most important reason for continuing the struggle to reform public education. For we will not survive as a republic nor move toward a genuine democracy unless we can narrow the gap between the rich and the poor, reduce our racial and ethnic divides, and create a deeper sense of community.[53]

But more is needed than defending public education as central to developing and nourishing the proper balance between democratic public spheres and commercial power, between identities founded on democratic principles and identities steeped in forms of competitive, self-interested individualism that celebrate their own material and ideological advantages. Given the current attempts by state legislators to limit the power educators have over the curriculum and classroom teachers, it is politically crucial that such educators be defended as public intellectuals who provide an indispensable service to the nation. Such an appeal cannot be made merely in the name of disinterested scholarship and professionalism, but in terms of such educators' civic duty to provide students with the knowledge and skills they need to participate in and shape ongoing public conversations about crucial political, social, and cultural issues. Educators in our nation's schools represent the conscience of a society; they shape the conditions under which future generations learn about themselves and their relations to others and the world, and they also employ teaching practices that are by their very nature moral and political rather than simply technical. And at their best, such practices bear witness to the ethical and political dilemmas that animate the broader social landscape.

Organizing against the corporate takeover of schools also suggests fighting to protect collective bargaining and health benefits for teachers, developing legislation to prevent untrained teachers from assuming classroom responsibilities, and working to put more power into the hands of faculty, parents, and students. Educators at the public school level are under massive assault in this country. Not only are they increasingly losing their autonomy and capacity for imaginative teaching, they bear the burden, especially in the urban centers, of overcrowded classes, limited resources, and hostile legislators. Such educators need to form alliances with parents, social movements, and progressive legislators around a common platform that resists the corporatizing of schools, reducing teachers' skills, and limiting learning to the narrow dictates of efficiency and standardization. Local and national committees can be organized to protect public schools from becoming subject to the whims and interests of corporations. Such organizations can put pressure on legislators to pass laws to ban commercial logos and brand name advertisements on school property, including in books, on the walls of schools, and on the sides of buses. Steve Manning highlights the role that parents in Seattle played in organizing against the commercialization of the public schools. He writes:

> In Seattle, parents organized a series of "commercialism walk-throughs" of the city's schools, collecting as many examples of commercial material as they could. Their findings helped to stop a proposed district wide policy that would have allowed corporate advertising in schools, and led to the formation of a school/community task force to study the issue.[54]

Such actions need to be publicized and links need to be developed between parents and social movements around the country who can learn from each other how to stop such commercialization from shaping school policies.

The growing corporate influence on American education reflects a crisis of vision regarding the meaning and purpose of democracy at a time when "market cultures, market moralities, market mentalities [are] shattering community, eroding civic society, [and] undermining the nurturing system for children."[55] Yet such a crisis also represents a unique opportunity for progressive educators to reaffirm the meaning and importance of democracy—radically defined as a struggle to combine the distribution of wealth, income, and knowledge with a recognition and positive valuation of cultural diversity—by reasserting the primacy of politics, power, and struggle as an educational task. Educators need to confront the march of corporate power by resurrecting a noble tradition, extending from Horace Mann to Martin Luther King, Jr., in which education is affirmed as a political process that encourages people to identify themselves as more than consuming subjects and democracy as more than a spectacle of market culture. Evidence of such struggles can be seen in school districts across the country where students, parents, and community activists are fighting against the commercialization of schools. Steven Manning of the Open Society Institute in New York reports that student activist Sarah Church led a successful campaign to prevent Pepsi-Cola from contracting an exclusive vending deal with Berkeley High School in exchange for a $90,000 electronic scoreboard for the football stadium. He also highlights the passing of the Commercial Free Schools Act by the San Francisco School Board. As he points out, the "act bars the district from signing exclusive beverage contracts or adopting educational materials that contain brand names."[56]

Finally, it is worth remembering that the debate about public education is really about what form the relationship between corporations and public life is going to take in the next century. The meaning and purpose of such a debate has not been lost on students. During the first week of March 1998, students from over 100 colleges held a series of "teach-ins" protesting the intrusion and increasing involvement of corporations in public and higher education.[57] For those who work in such institutions as well as for those concerned about the plight of children in this country, it is time to provide an example through our own actions of the meaning and importance of civic courage.

NOTES

1. John Dewey, *Democracy and Education* (New York: Free Press, 1916); Henry Giroux, *Schooling and the Struggle for Public Life* (Minneapolis: University of Minnesota Press, 1988); David Sehr, *Education for Democracy* (Albany: State University of New York Press, 1996).

2. Michael Jacobson and Laurie Masur, *Laurie Marketing Madness* (Boulder, Colo.: Westview, 1995); Alex Molnar, *Giving Kids the Business* (Boulder, Colo.: Westview, 1996); Consumer Union Education Service, *Captive Kids: A Report on Commercial Pressures on Kids at School* (Yonkers, N.Y.: Consumer Union Education Services, 1998).

3. Cited in Stanley Aronowitz, "The New Corporate University," *Dollars and Sense* (March/April 1998), p. 3

4. All quotes cited in Randall C. Archibold, "Applying Corporate Touch to a Troubled School District," *The New York Times* (Tuesday, October 12, 1999), p. A28.

5. Cited in Peter Applebome, "Lure of the Education Market Remains Strong for Business," *New York Times*, January 31, 1996, p. A1.

6. Cited in Russell Baker, "The Education of Mike Milken: From Junk-Bond King to Master of the Knowledge Universe," *The Nation*, May 3, 1999, p. 12.

7. See Russell Baker's commentary on Milken's launching of Knowledge Universe, with revenues of $1.2 billion, and an insatiable reach for buying everything that appears to have any potential for making a profit in the educational marketplace. In ibid., pp. 11–18.

8. Phyllis Vine, "To Market, to Market," *The Nation*, September 8–15, 1997, pp. 11–17.

9. David W. Kirkpatrick, *Choice in Schooling: A Case for Tuition Vouchers* (Chicago: Loyola University Press, 1990); Diane Ravitch, *Debating the Future of American Education* (Washington, D.C.: Brookings Institute, 1995). Many of these reports are produced by right-wing think tanks with a vested interest in the privatization movement. For example, see Paul Pekin, "Schoolhouse Crock: Right-Wing Myths Behind the 'New Stupidity,'" *Extra!* (January/February 1998), pp. 9–10. For an excellent rebuttal of the charge that American public education is in a state of disastrous decline, see David Berliner and Bruce Biddle, *The Manufactured Crisis* (Reading, Mass.: Addison Wesley, 1995); Gerald Bracey, "What Happened

to America's Public Schools? Not What You Think?" *American Heritage* (November 1997), pp. 39–52.

10. Cited in Vine, "To Market, to Market," p. 12.

11. Cited in ibid., p. 11.

12. For a summary of the historical failures of privatization, see Carol Ascher, Norm Fruchter, and Robert Berne, *Hard Lessons: Public Schools and Privatization* (New York: The Twentieth Century Fund, 1996). For a specific analysis of the failure of Education Alternatives, Inc., in Baltimore and Hartford, see Molnar, *Giving Kids the Business,* esp. chap. 4, pp. 77–116. Also, see Vine, "To Market, to Market," pp. 11–17; Bruce Shapiro, "Privateers Flunk Schools," *The Nation*, February 19, 1998, p. 4.

13. Jonathan Kozol, "Saving Public Education," *The Nation,* February 17, 1997, p. 16.

14. Richard J. Herrnstein and Charles Murray, *The Bell Curve* (New York: The Free Press, 1994).

15. This is particularly true as schools engage in market-sponsored contests in which teachers spend valuable teaching time coaching kids how to collect cash receipts, sell goods to their friends and neighbors, or learn the rules for bringing in profits for companies who then offer prizes to schools. See Molnar, *Giving Kids the Business*, esp. chap. 3.

16. David Labaree, "Are Students 'Consumers'?", September 17, 1997, p. 48.

17. Kathleen Kennedy Manzo, "California School Board Infusing Pedagogy Into Frameworks," *Education Week,* March 11, 1998, p. 7.

18. Deborah W. Meier, "Saving Public Education," *The Nation*, February 17, 1997, p. 24.

19. Alan O'Shea, "A Special Relationship? Academia and Pedagogy," *Cultural Studies* 12:4 (1998), pp. 521–522.

20. Stanley Aronowitz, "Introduction," in Paulo Freire, *Pedagogy of Freedom: Ethics, Democracy, and Civic Courage* (Lanham, Md.: Rowman and Littlefield, 1998), pp. 4–5.

21. Svi Shapiro, "Public School Reform: The Mismeasure of Education," *Tikkun* 13:1 (Winter 1998), p. 54. See also Henry A. Giroux, *Teachers as Intellectuals* (Westport, Conn.: Bergin and Garvey Press, 1988); Stanley Aronowitz and Henry A. Giroux, *Education Still Under Siege* (Westport, Conn.: Bergin and Garvey Press, 1993).

22. Baker, "Education of Mike Milken," p. 17.

23. I take up this issue in Henry A. Giroux, *The Mouse That Roared: Disney and the End of Innocence* (Lanham, Md.: Rowman and Littlefield, 1999).

24. Russell Mokhiber and Robert Weissman, *Corporate Predators* (Monroe, Me.: Common Courage Press, 1999), p. 168.

25. Jeffrey Henig, "The Danger of Market Rhetoric," in Robert Lowe and Barbara Miner, eds., *Selling Out Our Schools* (Milwaukee: Rethinking Schools Institute, 1996), p. 11. See also Jeffrey Henig, *Rethinking School Choice* (Princeton, N.J.: Princeton University Press, 1994).

26. Consumer Union, *Captive.*

27. Phyllis Sides, "Captive Kids: Teaching Students to Be Consumers," in *Selling Out Our Schools: Vouchers, Markets, and the Future of Public Education* (Milwaukee: Rethinking Schools Publication, 1996), p. 36.

28. For an extensive analysis of Channel One, see Henry A. Giroux, *Disturbing Pleasures: Learning Popular Culture* (New York: Routledge, 1994), esp. chap. 3, pp. 47–67.

29. Steven Manning, "Classrooms for Sale," *New York Times*, March 4, 1999, p. A27; see also, Steven Manning "Zapped," *The Nation,* September 27, 1999, p. 9.

30. Cover story, "This Lesson Is Brought to You By," *Business Week,* June 30, 1997, p. 69.

31. Ibid.

32. Cited in Editors, "Reading, Writing . . . and Purchasing," *Educational Leadership* 56:2 (1998), p. 16.

33. Manning, "Classrooms for Sale," p. A27.

34. For a brilliant analysis of how citizenship is being privatized within an expanding corporate culture, see Lauren Berlant, *The Queen of America Goes to Washington* (Durham, N.C.: Duke University Press, 1997).

35. Consumer Union, *Captive Kids*, p. 9.

36. Ibid., p. 26.

37. Mary B. W. Tabor, "Schools Profit From Offering Pupils for Market Research," *New York Times,* April 5, 1999, pp. A1, A16.

38. Ibid., p. A16.

39. Cited in Steven Manning, "How Corporations Are Buying Their Way into America's Classroom," *The Nation* (September 27, 1999), p. 12.

40. Tabor, "Schools Profit From Offering Pupils for Market Research," p. A16.

41. This issue is taken up in great detail in Molnar, *Giving Kids the Business.* For a more general analysis of the relationship between corporate culture and schooling, see Joe Kincheloe and Shirley Steinberg, eds., *KinderCulture: The Corporate Construction of Childhood* (Boulder, Colo.: Westview, 1997).

42. Gerald Grace, "Politics, Markets, and Democratic Schools: On the Transformation of School Leadership," in A. H. Halsey, Hugh Lauder, Phillip Brown, and Amy Stuart Wells, eds., *Education: Culture, Economy, Society* (New York: Oxford, 1997), p. 314.

43. Ibid., p. 315.

44. R. George Wright, *Selling Words: Free Speech in a Commercial Culture* (New York: New York University Press, 1997), p. 181.

45. Ibid., p. 182.

46. David Stratman, "School Reform and the Attack on Public Education," *Dollars and Sense* (March/April 1988), p. 7.

47. Nor am I suggesting that corporations cannot play a fundamental role in expanding democratic values. See, for example, the role of groups such as Business Leaders for Sensible Priorities, that have lobbied to decrease military spending in favor of investing in public resources such as schools, health care, and the like. See the powerful ad placed by the group against increases in military spending in *New York Times,* March 24, 1999, p. A21.

48. Dewey, *Democracy and Education.*

49. Molnar, *Giving Kids the Business,* p. 17.

50. This issue is explored in Ken Saltman, "Collateral Damage: Public School Privatization and the Threat to Democracy," Ph.D. Diss., Pennsylvania State University, May 1999, p. 92.

51. A number of books take up the relationship between schooling and democracy; some of the more important recent critical contributions include: Elizabeth A. Kelly, *Education, Democracy, & Public Knowledge* (Boulder, Colo.: Westview, 1995); Wilfred Carr and Anthony Hartnett, *Education and the Struggle for Democracy* (Philadelphia: Open University Press, 1996); Sehr, *Education for Public Democracy*; James Fraser, *Reading, Writing and Justice: School Reform as If Democracy Matters* (Albany: State University of New York Press, 1997); see also Giroux, *Schooling and the Struggle for Public Life*; and Henry A. Giroux, *Pedagogy and the Politics of Hope* (Boulder, Colo.: Westview, 1997).

52. Robin D. G. Kelley, "Neo-Cons of the Black Nation," *Black Renaissance Noire* 1:2 (Summer/Fall 1997), p. 146.

53. Ascher, Fruchter, and Berne, *Hard Lessons*, p. 112.

54. Manning, "Classrooms for Sale," p. A27.

55. Cornel West, "America's Three-Fold Crisis," *Tikkun* 9:2 (1994), p. 42.

56. See Steven Manning, "How Corporations Are Buying Their Way Into Classrooms," op. cit., p. 15.

57. "Short Subjects," *Chronicle of Higher Education*, March 13, 1998, p. A11.

9

▼▼▼▼▼▼▼

The Littleton Tragedy*

Svi Shapiro

The tragic events at Columbine High School in Littleton, Colorado (sadly repeated at places as far apart as Santee, California and Pearl, Mississippi) broke through, if only for a few moments, the usual discourse of educational concerns in this country. Suddenly we found ourselves attending to issues that were not about academic skills and test scores, accountability of teachers, and the measurement of our state's or country's educational performance. We were looking at what was happening in schools from a perspective that had little to do with those things that typically filled the nation's discussion about education. What burst to the surface was an ugly and disturbing brew of issues and concerns that, most of the time, remained buried under the all-consuming focus on kids and schools' academic achievement scores. We were now compelled to confront issues of alienation, competition and social isolation, rage and hostility, and the search for meaning in a violent and cynical world. Here was a very different perspective on what was happening among at least some of our youth.

The question of school community looms large in the Littleton tragedy. Talk to any group of high school students and the issue of social groups and cliques in their school is a central concern for them. For those who study the culture and sociology of schools (or make movies about it), likewise, the issue of sub-cultures and social divisions is a preeminent dimension of the moral and relational character of educational institutions. Yet for most others who are concerned with what schools do—legislators, policy makers, media commentators—the social milieu within which our kids live out their school lives seems like trivial stuff having little real bearing on matters of serious educational importance. How surprising then it was to find that the social relationships in school are the locus of so much emotion—and, for some, so much anger, bitterness and pain. From Columbine High School we learn that school cliques are places of privilege and power, inclusion and isolation. We learn that behind the veneer of the well-organized, efficient suburban school is a social context in which young people routinely deal with each other in ways that demean the other, and where differences of appearance or orientation become the vehicle for insults, "put downs" and threats. For the undergraduate class I taught a few days after the shootings many of my students, themselves not long out of high school, easily recognized the environment of hostility and intolerance among social groups. It was not hard for them to identify with the anger over privileged athletes and cheerleading favorites. For many these invidious comparisons are the day to day stuff of social relations in high school. They readily recognized too the way such divisiveness can become degrading or dehumanizing when the student "other" comes from a racial minority, is gay, or appears or talks in ways that are outside of the cultural mainstream. While they certainly did not endorse the destructiveness and killing they could understand how the competitiveness and intolerance of the high school environment produced intense frustration and even rage.

These students also found it relatively simple to see how the ever-increasing focus on success and achievement in our schools left less and less room for a meaningful focus on community and respect for others. Our national preoccupation (obsession) with increased test scores, higher academic competencies and the like leaves little serious space for developing relationships of care and concern among young people. Getting ahead and doing well is the preeminent agenda of high schools, not learning how we might create loving communities in which differences are respected and cherished. Indeed, part of the poignancy of the moment is hearing political leaders suddenly forced to attend to issues of education that are not about the value of the internet, the information superhighway, or technology, or their concern for more competitive standards and selective procedures in our schools. Education, they discover, is ultimately about something much more precious and profound. It is about the making of a world; about kids learning what it means to be human and questioning the ways that individuals can live together. In short, and in its most profound sense, education is not a transmission belt for acquiring technical skills or a competitive edge over one's peers. It is about developing selves that have the moral, spiritual and cognitive capacities to live in just, compassionate and responsible communities. The

Littleton disaster revealed how far many of our schools are from taking seriously such concerns.

It has been said that schools are mirrors of our society. Certainly the salience of social divisions, invidious distinctions, and cruel and insensitive behavior are the inevitable price paid for a culture where so much attention is paid to hierarchy and comparing human worth. Indeed the moral economies of schools surely cannot be separated from the relentless emphasis, in the wider culture, on winning and losing, becoming "someone" by distinguishing oneself from those who are left behind as "nobodies." The typical insecurities of adolescent identity are now appropriated and exploited to an unprecedented degree by the market, which powerfully and continually sells not just products to young people, but the importance of fitting in and achieving acceptance. The booming adolescent market (now the largest segment of the consumer market) is nothing if not a series of markers for what it takes to be "in" and to be "cool." And by design it is a place where such status is always insecurely held; the market ensures that what it takes to be accepted is a moving target—today's fashion, style, etc. changes rapidly into what is, tomorrow, outmoded and embarrassing. The inevitable awkwardness and fears of youth become the fodder for a market which shamelessly and exploits these anxieties, turning huge profits by instilling an obsessive concern for how individuals measure up in comparison with their peers, reinforcing the importance of discrimination and ranking among young people.

Of course, critical social commentators have made clear that young people are not mere shills for the culture industry, passively and unquestioningly being manipulated by style elites. Indeed, as in Littleton, youngsters also rebel against the dictates of society and institutions. The so-called "trench coat mafia" is but one more in a long series of examples of kids contesting who gets to be honored, conferred privileges and a measure of power by the institution. Every high school has them—students who feel themselves alienated from the official norms of success and recognition; kids who reject and turn on its head the sanctioned and legitimized values of the school hierarchy. Such students resist the behaviors, attitudes, and appearance of the student mainstream. They create, through their own dress, language and rituals, a "subculture" of style that resists the institutional norms. They express, sometimes aggressively, their anger and frustrations at how power and privilege are distributed in the school. At Littleton we know this culture produced not just the more typical forms of non-conformity and deviance, but an explosion of rage and destruction. Yet this too could be predicted. What came together at Columbine High School was an outlook borne of intense hostility towards the pecking order of status and value at the school, the high emotionality surrounding issues of identity and recognition typical of the adolescent years, with the easy accessibility to violence that now characterizes American society. Of course the insanity of the ready availability of guns—handguns, semiautomatic weapons, assault weapons and so on—is apparent to more and more of us (in 1996, the last year that statistics are available, 4643 children and teenagers were killed with guns—13 every day, the same number killed at Littleton). Yet, political influence undercuts the possibility of the kind of draconian gun legislation passed in countries like Australia and the United Kingdom after their own killing outrages. Of course accessibility to weapons is only part of the story here—one that cannot be separated from the pervasive influence and glorification of violent images found throughout our culture. Those who argue that video games, movies, newsreel images, etc. do not in themselves cause more violent behavior are probably correct. But they are right only so long as we are looking for—as is so typically the case in our media—some straightforward cause and effect influence. Certainly human behavior is shaped in more complex and multidimensional ways. We have to see these electronic and media images as part of a cultural process that much more subtly and invisibly shapes how we think and feel (what the media scholar George Gerbner refers to as a "glacial like" process). The cultural commentator Zygmunt Bauman was probably right when he described our culture as one engaged in a process of "adiaphorization"—the steady erosion of moral sensitivity towards human suffering. It is impossible to think that kids (like those involved in the Littleton killing) who immersed themselves in hours of violent and destructive video game images were not themselves desensitized to the real consequences of violence. And this desensitization, we have learned, is more pronounced and effective the younger the age at which this exposure is begun.

Yet the dangerous brew we have described contained one other powerful element which impelled this destructive rampage. The extent and nature of today's youth alienation, it seems, is of a qualitatively different character than in past generations. Social scientists and therapists argue that the disaffection of teens now is deeper and is associated with more dysfunctional problems—depression, addictions, violence including suicide. They argue that many of the most sensitive kids, while deploring conditions in the world, have no belief that things could be made better. Jeffrey Arnett, author of the book "Metalheads: Heavy Metal Music and Adolescent Alienation," describes attitudes this way: "the only alternative was to live your own life the best you could. Institutions were corrupt, and the hell with it." Arnett adds that such kids had no sense of a purposeful future that contained the possibility of meaningful commitment and action. Wayne Wooden, whose book "Renegade Kids, Suburban Outlaws" explores the lives of suburban middle-class teens, says, "Today's group is full of gloom and doom, and nothing is worth saving. Some have so internalized their bleakness that they strike out and back, using the very instruments of rage and power that the broader culture is using." These views are supported by other surveys of teens which show an absence of hopeful vision or a sense that their lives can purposefully affect and improve the quality of our nation or world. It is in this context of disbelief and nihilism that one can understand the appeal of dark and fascistic imagery and ideology to at least some kids. In the absence of any inspiring vision of human possibility, such ideologies offer powerful and—through the internet—easily available images that speak to the isolation and rage of many young men like those at Columbine. These images connect both the sense of impotence and the desire for action through the promise of destruction and mayhem unleashed on a world that seems to offer nothing but hurt and pain. Its promise is not of social change or amelioration—seen as futile—but only the catharsis of hitting back. And, of course, while the world is seen as irredeemably corrupt, the ideology will always emphasize the loathsomeness of particular categories of people—gays, Blacks, Jews. Such groups carry a special onus for the world's oppressiveness. Much of this was, sadly, in evidence in this case. Finally, this hate-filled world offered its own twisted version of connection and solidarity. In the face of an institution in which there was no inclusive and loving community, ostracism, ridicule and marginalization produced their own tragic version of communal identification—one built around hate and the fantasies of revenge.

Of course the psychological pundits will point to the usual culprits in explaining this tragedy: the lack of time and involvement of adults, especially parents, with kids; the lack of open and honest dialogue between kids and adults; the easy availability of drugs and alcohol; the stress that teens feel because of overly scheduled or academically pressured lives, or their isolation from others; physical abuse and poor supervision by parents. Certainly all of these are important and worth worrying about. Yet we must be careful that we don't end up with what Russell Jacoby once called "social amnesia"—that peculiarly American tendency to avoid or deny the distinctly social lessons of what is happening. Littleton speaks to the kind of *cultural* world inhabited by our children—a "socially toxic" world which is thrilled by violence, where compassionate, caring relationships take a back seat to the quest for individual success and status, and where the values of materialism and consumerism far outweigh any commitment to lives of ethical purpose and spiritual meaning. To "remember" the social context of this tragedy means to confront what is really at stake in a politics that goes beyond the usual agendas—a politics that seeks to address the abyss of meaning that torments so many of us including, so tragically, our children.

10

▼▼▼▼▼▼▼

Commercial Culture and the Assault on Children's Character*

Alex Molnar

Americans live what author Leslie Savan has referred to as sponsored lives.[1] Virtually every facet of life in the United States now comes with sponsorship of some sort. From the radio programs we listen to and the television programs we watch to the clothes we wear and the leisure activities we pursue, we are surrounded by commercials. According to Savan, television-watching Americans see about one hundred commercials a day.[2] Add other commercial venues such as billboards, shopping carts, clothing labels, and city buses, and the number of ads that clamor for attention from each American reaches 16,000 a day.[3]

In American commercial culture anything can be turned into a product and put up for sale—and everything has a price, from dog food to automobiles, from hair spray to time-share condos, from companionship to political action. Increasingly, people are defined by what they purchase and valued for what they possess.

It would be impossible for a cultural impulse as strong as the commercialism that now lies at the heart of American life not to affect the character of children. Anyone who has seen the highly stylized ads for children's clothing in the relentlessly upscale *New York Times Magazine*, or watched a soft drink commercial on television, or listened to an athletic shoe ad on the radio knows that Madison Avenue has designs on America's children.[4] Indeed, Madison Avenue probably sends more messages to children about who they are and who they should strive to be than all of the character educators in all of America's schools combined. Yet, surprisingly, the literature on character education, despite its focus on morals, values, and social dissolution, is largely mute on the subject of commercialism, which is a corrosive phenomenon that comes between parents and children, threatens nonmaterial human relationships, and undermines democratic values.

Modern character education is driven by a broadly based consensus that the United States is in a period of moral decline. Unlike character education advocates in the 1960s and 1970s, who attempted to help students "clarify" their values[5] or to progress toward a higher level of moral reasoning,[6] contemporary character educators such as Thomas Lickona, Jacques Benninga, and Edward Wynne[7] advocate instruction in "core" ethical values. They also link the development of children's character to civic renewal.

The ascendant view links character education in its most fundamental aspects to a vision of society that assumes that the independent value-based behavior of individuals is the best explanation for social virtue or moral decay. This popular view helps explain the success of William Bennett's *Book of Virtues*.[8] Although character educators discuss the need to promote civic renewal and promote collaborative endeavor,[9] the implicit conception of character advanced by the modern character education movement assumes that each individual is able to choose to do good regardless of context or circumstance. This is a view that resonates with Americans' attachment to the ideal of the rugged individualist as master of her or his own destiny—a person willing and able to stand against the tide in defense of personal conviction and enduring values. In America's mercantile culture the ideal of the rugged individualist has been transformed into the ideal of the savvy consumer who controls the marketplace by making well-informed, independent decisions about what sort of mouth wash, candy bar, or stereo to buy.

Since context and circumstance are left unaccounted for in the epistemology of contemporary character education, it is hardly surprising that character education can offer only a rudimentary and simplistic understanding of how powerful cultural phenomena influence the social boundary markers that shape and define the moral understanding and ethical behavior of children. In practical terms, this deficiency no doubt often results in children regarding the well-intentioned exhortations built into character education programs as out of touch with the real world that they inhabit.

This probably explains, at least in part, why it is so difficult to document any lasting impact of character education on children's ethical behavior.[10] To be sure, children seem to have no trouble learning to *identify* what proper behavior (as defined by the character educator) is or in swearing allegiance to it.

However, identifying and giving verbal endorsement to behavior preferred by character education programs is not the same as actually behaving that way.

If children are able to tell character educators what they want to hear while they go on behaving in ways defined as sensible by their economic, social, and cultural milieu, they are also happy to tell anyone who asks that advertisements have no effect on their behavior at all.[11] They do this despite the fact that children as a group tend to demand the same products from jeans and sneakers to soft drinks and hair gel.

American children have learned the meta-message of commercial culture very well, i.e., that consuming is the best way to express one's individuality and celebrate one's uniqueness. As Savan has noted, advertisers ". . . have learned that to break through . . . they have to be as cool, hip, and ironic as the target audience likes to think of itself as being."[12] Small wonder that children (and adults) in America are often part of what David Riesman called a "lonely crowd"[13]—a crowd that represents the negation of both the individual and genuine community. Members of the Riesman's lonely crowd define themselves by their possessions and express their individuality by looking, smelling, and thinking like everyone else. In this world, people are asked to believe that fads, for example, emerge from a magical confluence of independent judgments rather than being the result of deliberate promotion by advertisers.[14]

If character educators were to take seriously their rhetoric about promoting enduring values and democratic civic engagement, they would devote a good deal of time to the analysis of commercial culture and to what Vance Packard labeled "the hidden persuaders."[15] The underlying emotional content of advertising deployed for the express purpose of manipulating behavior is inherently and profoundly antidemocratic. If the strength of a democracy rests on a foundation of reasoned judgments made by people capable of genuine human attachments, then anyone who has observed the extent to which commercialism has infiltrated and corrupted the American political process cannot help but be alarmed. Candidates are now "packaged" and marketed to the public like any other product, political programs are built on illusory rather than real differences, and political debate is a lexicon of corrupted meanings.

The father of modern mass advertising, Edward Bernays (Sigmund Freud's nephew), pointed the way. After he had been hired by the American Tobacco Company, Bernays drew on the psychological research of A. A. Brill that suggested that, for women, smoking represented emancipation. Using that knowledge, Bernays transformed cigarettes into "torches of liberty," and arranged for ten young women to march in the 1929 Easter parade on Fifth Avenue in New York smoking their "torches of liberty" to protest against women's inequality.[16] Orwell's vision of a world in which good is bad, love is hate, and peace is war arrived long before 1984 for America's marketers.

While character educators busy themselves decrying the "apathy, distrust, cynicism, and dishonesty"[17] of America's young people the commercial tide rising in American schools promotes precisely these qualities and debases the humanity of everyone it touches. Every school day children all over the United States are subjected to dishonest propaganda supplied by a variety of corporate interests. There is no altruistic impulse in commercialism—marketing to children is big business.

When Michael Milken, the junk bond king, was let out of prison, he said that he wanted to be involved in education because he considered it to be one of the biggest moneymakers for American business.[18] He is right. According to Consumers Union, elementary school children spend around $15 billion a year and also influence the spending of another $160 billion. Teenagers spend an estimated $57 billion of their own money and another $36 billion of their families' cash.[19]

The attempt to mine childhood for commercial advantage is nothing new. As early as 1929, concern about the influence of corporations on school curriculum was strong enough for the National Education Association to impanel a "Committee on Propaganda in the Schools."[20] However, the subsequent NEA report and other mild efforts by professional educators to set boundaries around commercial activities in the schools have been ineffectual in the face of the commercial onslaught.

In 1959, Saatchi & Saatchi, the New York advertising agency, created the first television ad aimed exclusively at children. The only problem was that there was nowhere on television to show it. Not willing to let the star of their commercial, the Trix rabbit, go homeless, Saatchi & Saatchi invented Saturday morning children's television so that their ad would have programming to interrupt.[21] Thirty years later, when Channel One was brought to life with millions of high-voltage advertising dollars, the "vast wasteland" of American commercial television spread to the classroom.

Sheila Harty's 1979 book, *Hucksters in the Classroom*,[22] documented the extent to which corporate propaganda was being used in the nation's schools in the areas of nutrition, nuclear power, the environment, and economics. Yet, as alarming as they were, the practices Harty detailed were only a prelude to the unparalleled commercial onslaught that was to come.

In the 1980s, a Rubicon of sorts was crossed. Not only did the volume of advertising reach new levels of intrusiveness—often under the guise of helping cash-strapped schools fill in the gap left by missing tax dollars—but marketing efforts were unashamedly characterized as legitimate contributions to curriculum content, as helpful teaching aids, and as a good way of promoting school-business cooperation.

It was not long before a commercial wave broke over the schools. In homes across America, parents may have discovered that their daughters and sons had been given a "Gushers" fruit snack, told to burst it between their teeth, and asked by their teacher to compare the sensation to a geothermic eruption (compliments of General Mills). Children were taught the history of the potato chip (compliments of The Potato Board and the Snack Food Association). Adolescent girls learned about self-esteem by discussing "good hair days" and "bad hair days" in class (compliments of Revlon). Tootsie Roll provided a lesson on "The Sweet Taste of Success." Exxon sent out a videotape, "Scientists and the Alaska Oil Spill," to help teachers reassure students that the Valdez disaster was not so bad after all. And Prego spaghetti sauce offered to help students learn science by comparing the thickness of Prego sauce to that of Ragu.

One or two examples of dishonest, self-serving, corporate material might be laughed off as aberrations. But it is hardly a laughing matter when, by their sheer volume, sponsored materials threaten to turn the school curriculum into a booming, buzzing confusion; when the energy and focus of a school are diverted from the education of children to the promotion of commercial interests; when the trust parents have that what their children are being taught is important information, honestly presented, is routinely violated; and when children are encouraged to associate a particular product with personal worth and success.

By 1990, the situation was bad enough for Consumers Union to call for schools to be made ad-free zones.[23] In 1995, a Consumers Union report, *Captive Kids*, documented a commercial assault that was continuing unabated.[24]

School-related debates over sex education, religious values, censorship, drug use, and, yes, *character* regularly find their way into the media. However, the ethical problems created by using corporate-sponsored materials in the schools rarely rise to the surface. In part, this is because of the extent to which commercial values have now assumed the status of common sense. And, in part, it is because, as right wing radio personality Rush Limbaugh discovered, it is about power.

The "BOOK IT!" program sponsored by Pizza Hut awards a free pizza to children who meet their reading goals. Limbaugh had criticized the offer (justifiably) as little more than "bribes for books." During his May 25, 1995 radio show, he learned that the "BOOK IT!" program was sponsored by Pizza Hut, a company for which he did commercials. In response he proclaimed: "I'm demonstrating my independence. Just because I do a Pizza Hut commercial does not mean that I have been purchased hook, line, and sinker."[25]

It took only one day for Limbaugh to adjust his attitude: "Since the program ended yesterday, I have been in, and my staff have been in, almost hourly contact with the officials at Pizza Hut. . . . Now, I've got my mind right, ladies and gentlemen. I've had it 'splained to me by a number of different people and I'm prepared here to do a mea culpa because I didn't understand what the whole thing was about yesterday."[26]

What it was about was power. And Limbaugh was taught that the people paying the piper call the tune. As comical or inconsequential as the programs they purchase may sometimes seem, sponsorship dollars come from powerful special interests that are very serious about pressing for advantage, whether on our airwaves or in our schools.

The pervasiveness of commercial activities now carried out in the school has helped to blur the distinction between promoting special privilege and advancing the general welfare in education and has transformed children into commodities along the way. There is now little talk of valuing children for their own right—just because we love them. Quite the contrary. At a time when poor children have killed each other for a pair of over-priced, over-hyped sports shoes, they are forced to watch advertising messages for high-priced sneakers in school. At a time when American children are increasingly overweight and at risk of coronary disease, they have been taught how the heart functions by a poster advertising junk food and they have been served high-fat meals by the fast-food concessionaires that run their school cafeterias. And at a time when many children are literally made sick by the air they breathe they are told that some of the country's biggest polluters are their friends. At a time when young people hunger for real connections and genuine relationships, they are fed illusions.

The promotional materials distributed by one company, Scholastic, illustrate the ethical bankruptcy of America's commercial culture. Scholastic promotes itself as "... the *only* publishing pipeline covering the entire pre-K to 12th grade marketplace."[27] For the right price, Scholastic will develop marketing vehicles such as single-sponsor magazines, inserts, and special sections, contests, posters, teaching guides, videos, software, research, and books. When it promotes itself to potential clients, Scholastic gives examples of past school-based ad campaigns such as: "*Discover Card* and Scholastic Give Teens Extra Credit," "*Minute Maid* Puts the Squeeze on the Competition with a Summer Reading Program," and "To Billy Joel, *CBS Records* and Scholastic History Is Hot."[28]

Mother Jones magazine contacted Modern Talking Pictures, another firm that specializes in helping corporations put messages into schools and classrooms, and pretended to be representing a potential client concerned about the bad publicity that nuclear power had been getting.

Mother Jones: This is the company's pet project. They're very concerned about putting out material that will help correct the antinuclear bias in most educational materials. So we don't want much tampering with the material. Is that a problem?

Modern Talking Pictures: I understand exactly what you're saying. We wouldn't want to write anything our client didn't want us to. It would have to be factual, of course.

MJ: Of course.

MTP: But we try to be sensitive to our client's aims. . . . We wouldn't want to write anything that makes the sponsor unhappy.

MJ: Now, we're talking national—we want to get this into every school in the country. Can you handle that?

MTP: We've done that for a lot of our corporate clients—Proctor & Gamble, IBM. . . . We know how to get materials into the hands of educators.

MJ: I understand there's quite a demand for these kinds of materials now.

MTP: Educators just eat them up.[29]

Even more insidious is the saga of Old Joe Camel, the corporate dromedary that pitches Camel cigarettes, and *Weekly Reader*, a venerable children's newspaper that has been a staple in American classrooms for decades. Since 1991, *Weekly Reader* has been owned by K-III Communications, a subsidiary of Kohlberg, Kravis, Roberts & Company, a major shareholder in RJR Nabisco whose R.J. Reynolds division is the corporate home of Old Joe.[30]

Old Joe is a bad actor, but children love him. Introduced in 1988, the Old Joe ad campaign puts the cartoon camel on billboards, phone booths, baseball caps, and T-shirts. Often he is pictured on a motorcycle or in a pool hall surrounded by girl camels. Like Ronald McDonald, he also hangs out at promotional events. It did not take long for observers to begin wondering who the intended target of the Old Joe cartoon campaign was. Research has suggested an answer. Between 1988 and 1991, Camel sales to children rose from $6 million to $476 million a year.[31]

Either Old Joe is an unguided marketing missile or he is doing exactly what he is supposed to do. Critics point out that people rarely start smoking after the age of eighteen and charge that with the shrinking of more health-conscious adult market for their product, R.J. Reynolds is trying to build an early customer base.

Research published in the *Journal of the American Medical Association* revealed, among other things, that 91 percent of six-year-olds could match Old Joe with a cigarette (about the same number that could pair Mickey Mouse with the Disney Channel); that teenagers were more likely to respond favorably to Old Joe than adults; and that, although only 9 percent of adult smokers identified Camel as their brand, 33 percent of school-age smokers did.[32]

When Old Joe was featured on the cover of an issue of *Weekly Reader* with the headline "Are Camel Ads Attracting Kids to Smoking?", some people saw a double message and wondered about *Weekly Reader's* motives. They had reason to be concerned. In 1995, *Education Week* reported that researchers evaluating tobacco-related articles in *Weekly Reader* and another weekly children's magazine between 1989 and 1994 found that 68 percent of the *Weekly Reader* stories included the tobacco industry's views as compared to 32 percent in the other magazine. More significantly, the researchers found that after *Weekly Reader* was purchased by K-III, the number of articles on tobacco-related topics that contained an anti-smoking message declined dramatically. Before K-III owned *Weekly Reader*, 65 percent of its tobacco-related stories contained an anti-smoking message; after K-III took over, only 24 percent of the stories did.[33]

While all of this is going on, character educators tut tut and cluck cluck about the moral crisis that has overtaken our *young*. As adults wring their hands and decry youthful cynicism, school children are routinely treated as resources to be exploited for adult advantage. Wendell Berry exposes the underlying moral rot:

> It seems that we have been reduced almost to a state of absolute economics, in which people and all other creatures and things may be considered purely as economic "units," or integers of production, and in which a human being may be dealt with, as John Ruskin put it, "merely as a covetous machine." And the voices bitterest to hear are those saying that all this destructive work of mindless genius, money, and power is regrettable but cannot be helped.[34]

Despite the obvious ethical problems with using schools to make sales pitches to children and their families, it is rare to hear education, business, or community leaders voice either ethical or educational objections to school-based commercialism. Instead, they are apt to support the idea that commercial activities in the school are legitimate "partnerships" between the public schools and the business community.

The danger to our democracy and our children posed by commercialism is great. As Ralph Nader argues,

> Any culture that surrenders its vision and its self-sustaining human values to the narrow judgment of commerce will be neither free nor just. . . . The commercialistic cocoon enveloping children with the "entertainment" of violence, addiction, and low-grade sensuality reflects the displacement of more nurturing values by a "marketing madness."[35]

A character education movement that genuinely valued children would, at the very least, demand an end to commercial activities in the schools and an end to the dubious co-marketing plans that educational organizations have entered into with any number of businesses. Even these basic steps are unlikely, however, so long as character education remains so philosophically muddled, so conceptually empty, so attached to lists of "good" behaviors, and so silent in the face of the corrupting influence of entrenched corporate power. How much easier it is to simply tell children to "do the right thing."

NOTES

1. Leslie Savan, *The Sponsored Life: Ads, TV, and American Culture* (Philadelphia: Temple University Press, 1994).

2. Ibid., p. 1.

3. Ibid.

4. See, for example, James U. McNeal, *Kids as Customers: A Handbook of Marketing to Children* (New York: Lexington Books, 1992).

5. See, for example, Louis E. Raths, Merrill Harmin, and Sidney B. Simon, *Values and Teaching* (Columbus, Ohio: Charles E. Merrill, 1966).

6. See, for example, F. Clark Power, Ann Higgins, and Lawrence Kohlberg, *Lawrence Kohlberg's Approach to Moral Education* (New York: Columbia University Press, 1989).

7. See Thomas Lickona, *Educating for Character: How Our Schools Can Teach Respect and Responsibility* (New York: Bantam Books, 1991); Jacques Benninga, "Schools, Character Development, and Citizenship," this volume; and Edward A. Wynne, "The Moral Character of Teaching," in Allan Ornstein, ed., *Teaching: Theory into Practice* (Boston: Allyn and Bacon, 1995), pp. 190–202.

8. William J. Bennett, ed., *The Book of Virtues: A Treasury of Great Moral Stories* (New York: Simon and Schuster, 1993).

9. A good window on the conventional wisdom of the modern character education movement is provided by materials made available by the Character Education Partnership, an organization based in Alexandria, Virginia, that describes itself in its brochure as "A nonpartisan coalition of organizations and individuals who are concerned about the moral crisis confronting America's youth and dedicated to developing moral character and civic virtue in our young people as one way of promoting a more compassionate and responsible society." The brochure goes on to assert, among other things, that "We are a compassionate society if we demonstrate in our life together an active concern for the welfare of others," and "We are a responsible society if we guard the fundamental rights of all citizens to carry out the obligations of citizenship by working toward a common vision of the common good." Character Education Partnership, *Character Education: Questions & Answers* (Alexandria, Va.: Character Education Partnership, n.d.).

10. James S. Leming, "In Search of Effective Character Education," *Educational Leadership* 51 (November 1993): 63–71.

11. Hugh Rank, *The Pitch* (Park Forest, Ill.: Counter Propaganda Press, 1991).

12. Savan, *The Sponsored Life*, p. 6.

13. David Riesman, Nathan Glazer, and Reuel Denney, *The Lonely Crowd: A Study of the Changing American Character* (Garden City, N.Y.: Doubleday, 1955).

14. See Vance Packard, "The Psycho-Seduction of Children," in Vance Packard, *The Hidden Persuaders* (New York: Pocket Books, 1963).

15. Packard, *The Hidden Persuaders*.

Age of Academe (New York:

17. Character Education Partnership, *Character Education: Questions & Answers*, p. 1.

18. Alex Molnar, *Giving Kids the Business: The Commercialization of America's Schools* (Boulder, Colo.: Westview Press, 1996).

19. Ibid., p. 21.

20. Edwin C. Broome, "Report of the Committee on Propaganda in the Schools," presented at the meeting of the National Education Association in Atlanta, Ga., July 1929.

21. WBZ-TV, Boston, Mass. A broadcast interview with a spokeswoman for Saatchi & Saatchi, November 13, 1995.

22. Sheila Harry, *Hucksters in the Classroom: A Review of Industry Propaganda in Schools* (Washington, D.C.: Center for the Study of Responsive Law, 1979).

23. Consumers Union, *Selling America's Kids: Commercial Pressures on Kids of the 90s* (Yonkers, N.Y.: Consumers Union, 1990).

24. Consumers Union, *Captive Kids* (Yonkers, N.Y.: Consumers Union, 1995).

25. Fairness and Accuracy in Reporting, "A Word from the Sponsor," *EXTRA! Update* (October 1995), p. 3.

26. Ibid.

27. Scholastic, Inc., *Experience the Power of Trust with Scholastic*, promotional brochure (New York: Scholastic, Inc., n.d.).

28. Ibid.

29. "Kiddie Corps," *Mother Jones* (July–August 1992): 14.

30. Jessica Porter, "Study Chides *Weekly Reader's* Tobacco Coverage," *Education Week*, 15 November 1995.

31. Geoffrey Cowley, "I'd Toddle a Mile for a Camel," *Newsweek*, 23 December 1991, p. 70.

32. Ibid.

33. Porter, "Study Chides *Weekly Reader's* Tobacco Coverage."

34. Wendell Berry, "Economy and Pleasure," in Charles I. Schuster and William V. Van Pelt, eds., *Speculations: Readings in Culture, Identity, and Values* (Englewood Cliffs, N.J.: Prentice-Hall, 1993).

35. Ralph Nader, "Foreword," in Michael F. Jacobson and Laurie Ann Mazur, *Marketing Madness: A Survival Guide for a Consumer Society* (Boulder, Colo.: Westview Press, 1995).

Goals 2000: The Triumph of Vulgarity and the Legitimation of Social Injustice*

David E. Purpel

I believe that the policies, procedures, and programs represented in the Goals 2000 legislation represent a significant crystallization of recent trends in educational thought so much so that they can be used as a telling if not chilling index of a quite clear social and cultural consensus on a number of critically important professional and public issues. This legislation, its support, and the nature of the critical response to it tell us a great deal about the present state of the continuous debate on the basic direction of American society and the role of public education in the determination and shaping of the direction. In this essay, I want to comment on those aspects of the legislation that seem to have provoked the least negative response, as it is my assumption that these are the aspects that represent the greatest amount of consensus by the public and the profession. Like the dog in the Sherlock Holmes story, what is significant here is the absence of barking and howling, or more precisely, the particular rhythms and qualities of the barking and the silences.

It is quite clear that the passage of the law was not a matter of great public interest. It received little attention in the media, and it certainly was not highlighted as one of the major political battles of the Clinton administration as were health care and welfare reform. It is premature to fully gauge mainstream professional reactions but my impression is that it has been relatively tepid and that the criticisms tend to focus on the meagerness of the funds involved and the high degree of federal involvement in curriculum decisions. Time will tell whether this relative indifference represents a shrewd insight into what might turn out to be toothless legislation with marginal consequences, or a gross miscalculation of the far-reaching consequences of landmark educational policy making. However, the debate and eventual passage of this program is a permanent record of what seems to constitute a clear current consensus (public and professional) on what ought to be both the purposes of education and the basic curriculum orientation.

What is particularly revealing about this legislation is that it represents an effort to integrate educational policy into a clear, unambiguous, and coherent social, economic, political, and cultural agenda. This is not a program directed at education "for its own sake" but is openly and proudly presented as an instrument of a particular set of government policies. Indeed, there is little indication that those who proposed the legislation make *any* distinction between education and socioeconomic policy, although there is no ample evidence of a close analysis of the relationship between proposed curriculum policies and economic goals.

CURRICULUM THEORY

Although the legislation does not obviously attempt to delve into serious curriculum theorizing, it does deal quite decisively, if rather heavy-handedly, with what we have come to believe is a complex and perplexing issue, namely the question about what should be taught. After all the debates and struggles and all the painstaking and heated debates on the nature of knowledge, on what knowledge is of most worth, on whether we should strive to be child-centered or subject-centered, on whether we can integrate critical pedagogy with eco-feminism, on the place of the arts, on the balance of the body, mind, and spirit, and all the other countless and important controversies, proposals, projects, and critiques, finally the President and the Congress have cut through all these knots and conundrums and have decided. One clear winner is the ever popular and remarkably resilient gaggle of conventional disciplines—"English, mathematics, science, foreign languages, civics and government, arts, history, and geography." Another winner is the much unloved and critically abused "mastery and competence" approach to learning which says something about the comparative influence of Madeline Hunter and Paulo Freire on American consciousness. The losers include many of the areas that progressive and humanistic educators have emphasized over the years: interdisciplinary studies, critical thinking, constructivism, service learning, education for democracy, education for personal expression, education for social responsibility, esthetics education, moral education, multicultural education, environmental education, physical education, health education, and sexuality education, to mention a few prominent ones. This is not to say that these areas are dead and buried but the legislation makes its priorities crystal clear and one doesn't have to be clairvoyant to figure out how the United States Government sees the difference between the truly important and the merely interesting components of the curriculum. The harsh reality is that there is now official sanction and anointment for a particular curriculum perspective, a reality made poignant if not tragic given that this perspective is culturally narrow and intellectually shallow.

This poignancy is magnified when we consider what seems to be the utter irrelevance and futility of the sum total of the profession's efforts to sophisticate the public dialogue on these issues. After decades of articles, books, experiments, debates, investigations, and critiques, and with a heritage of brilliant and imaginative pedagogical theories we are told that the best we can do is to turn to a dreary collection of depressing clichés and anachronisms. Apart from the ideological concerns, this legislation surely must be seen as totally devoid of any kind of semi-serious educational theorizing or reasoning or to put it another way, it is written as if there is *no* tradition of educational discourse. In this regard, we in the profession must confront what appears to be our humiliating and shameful failure to penetrate the consciousness of mainstream American intellectual and political thought. How do we as a profession account for the failure to at least ameliorate the effects of political cynicism and public naïveté? To what degree is the profession complicit by dint of those who pander to the powerful? To what degree is the profession incompetent by dint of its failure to establish a framework of a sophisticated public discourse of education? To what degree is the profession derelict in its responsibility to engage the public in genuine dialogue on the social, political, economic, cultural, and moral dimensions of educational policy and practice? Ultimately, as we have seen in the case of Goals 2000, educational policy is determined by those in power, but the ease by which vulgar and shallow educational thought has triumphed tells us that we must work a great deal harder and smarter to insist that such decisions be made with full knowledge of the complexities involved. In this way we can maintain hope in the educability of the public and reenergize our sense of the purpose and importance of our work.

SOCIOECONOMIC POLICY

Not much ambiguity here. The words "productive" and "competiti
pear with amazing regularity as if to reassure everyone that this pi
cational legislation is for real, that is, it is specifically designed
real and heavily competitive world of the global economy. The
economic contexts for the significance of the legislation had b
lished and astonishingly enough largely accepted. We are

America is in a desperate struggle for economic dominance, if not survival with other more disciplined and hard-working nations. We are in this predicament and in danger of losing even more ground in part because of slackness and mediocrity in our schools, as it is clear that our competitor nations are outdistancing us in intellectual achievements, particularly in the crucial areas of science, technology, and mathematics. What is urgently needed then is to stiffen our will, increase standards, demand more work from our students and teachers, and to carefully scrutinize and monitor educational achievement. The problem is a lack of sufficiently trained cadres of hardworking, productive, technologically savvy workers, and the solution is for the schools to cull out those with promise and motivate, train, test, and produce them. The cry became: "The nation is at risk—fix the schools."

This readily accepted myth represents policies that serve a number of purposes. First, it co-opts the public schools to accept their primary task to be that of feeding and sustaining the interests of international capitalists who require a lot of hardworking, productive, technologically savvy workers, and a great number of people who believe that this is the only right and proper purpose of education. Secondly, it distracts us into believing that our social and economic problems are rooted in our schools rather than in our social and economic policies and institutions, thereby avoiding rather messy and troubling questions on what constitutes a just and equitable system of distributing wealth and privilege. Thirdly, it provides a convenient justification to impose more control, uniformity, and orthodoxy in a culture very unsure and uneasy about dissent, difference, and pluralism. The "nation at risk" myth suggests that we simply can't afford 1960s style experimentation and counterculturalism in a period of economic crisis. In addition, the myth encourages the best friends of those who want to maintain their power, namely, fear and anxiety and their companions, suspicion and divisiveness. The message is clear—the future belongs to the willing and the talented and for them it holds fame and fortune. Such people need only follow directions. For those who insist on slovenliness, laziness, and surliness the future is bleak and threatening, and they are advised to get out of the way and be prepared to take their just desserts. For those who are willing but who have limited talents the future is extremely uncertain, and such people are well advised to be obedient, work harder, lay low, be alert, and stay on guard.

It is by now clear that we are immersed in a more virulent form of capitalism in which national boundaries, social contracts, and moral frameworks become increasingly irrelevant. It is a time of downsizing, bottom-line thinking, mergers, intense competition, and an era when greed is masked as freedom, and hustling becomes a creative activity. The effects on our community have been staggering—persistent unemployment and underemployment; an ever-widening gap between have and have-not nations; greater pollution and erosion of natural resources; increasing disparities in income; a shortage of meaningful jobs; intense pressures on families to earn a living wage; homelessness; poverty; welfare bashing; the rationing of medical care; and many other manifestations of a cruel and relentless economic order. This triumphant and unchallenged order must be seen as the driving force of not only Goals 2000 but of virtually all current official efforts at school reform, and indeed, we are well advised to examine the substance of this economic grounding rather than focusing only on the procedural and curricular dimensions of this legislation. This legislation is not primarily about advancing knowledge, or expanding intellectual and creative horizons, nor is it about the pursuit of meaning and the nurturing of the soul; it is, instead, concerned with the deployment of human resources into immense struggles for economic dominance, privilege, and hegemony. Goals 2000 is not directed at individual empowerment or social democracy but is instead designed to supply the arsenal of human resources needed for the bloody economic wars being fought by transnational corporations, national economies, and financial entrepreneurs.

President Clinton summed up this point rather well in his 1994 State of the Union speech in which he endorsed public school choice and chartering, "as long as we measure every school by one high standard: Are our children learning what they need to know to compete and win in the global economy?" What a commentary on our society when the President, in a major policy address to the nation, enunciates our basic educational policy as one that reduces the purposes of education to the promotion of material success and the intensification of international economic competition.

MORAL VISION

The kind of economic policy which drives the Goals 2000 program has had an enormous influence not only on material issues, as I have already indicated, but also on our relationships with each other and on our basic human values. It is a time when meritocracy has shifted from being a term of accusation and dread to one of approbation and celebration, a time of a reenergized and revalidated social Darwinism. Our new post-industrial society and post-modern culture require highly skilled, tough-minded, highly sophisticated people who can and do change intellectual, cultural, and moral loyalties easily and joyfully. All bets are off, traditional loyalties and allegiances are suspect, communities and credos are all problematic, it's all flow and go. Presumably, the good news is that what will or, at least should, count is not family or social connections or previous conditions of mastery but sheer talent, and for that reason we must not discriminate by the outmoded cultural categories of race, class, and gender but by the more democratic and hip ones of cybernetic literacy, language fluency, and entrepreneurial chutzpa. This consciousness is well expressed in the well-nigh universally accepted shibbo-leth of "leveling the playing field," that is, the importance of reducing socially artificial barriers to achievement. Indeed, this concept is reflected in the Goals 2000 legislation with its references to the development of "opportunity standards," defined in the act as "the criteria for, and the basis of, assessing the sufficiency or quality of the resources, practices, and conditions necessary at each level of the education system . . . to provide all students with an op-portunity to learn the material in voluntary national content standards or State content standards" (Goals 2000, 1994). Presumably, once we have es-tablished and controlled for the independent variables (e.g., quality and quantity of educational resources) we can get on with judging children on the critical dependent variable of achievement. The metaphor of a playing field is very likely used to evoke images of enjoyable contests among willing, fair-minded folks who relish the opportunity to display and hone their skills with other evenly matched and motivated folks. Everyone is expected to play by the rules, to try hard, to be fair, and to accept the outcome with grace. Level-ing the playing field is about removing irrelevant, unfair, and preventable barriers to fair competition. So, what is wrong with this picture?

Let's take a closer look at this metaphor and examine the consequences of games played on a level playing field under the assumption that miraculously there is a political will to do this leveling and that we are successful at achiev-ing the goal. Such games still involve competition, contestants of enormously varied interests, abilities, and competitiveness, winners and losers, ranking, and differential rewards which in this case have enormous consequences. The spoils go to the victor and this is to be celebrated because the victory is "fair," that is, based on the inherent and demonstrable superiority of the winner. The major moral tragedy here is that such a contest requires and structures losers, for indeed the game cannot be played without losers and its primary purpose is to identify them as part of the process of distributing the wealth. What we have here is a variation of the age-old process of powerful groups imposing a system of hierarchy and privilege and simultaneously providing a discourse of pragmatic justification and social inevitability for what is at base a cruel and callous policy of calculated legitimated inequality. Presumably the myth of equality of *opportunity* allows us to believe that both the victors and the losers deserve their fate and that the community has fulfilled its re-sponsibilities by removing "artificial" barriers to "genuine" competition. What, in fact, the community has done is to mask a system in which human beings are required to compete even if they are averse to competing and to compete in contests even if it requires them to display skills in which they are uninterested, lacking, or both. The penalty for not engaging in these compul-sory contests is the same, if not worse, as coming in dead last in the games themselves. The consequences are *intended* to be very serious, namely, one's socioeconomic standing in the community. Put another way, they involve the matter of whether you will be rich or poor, hungry or well fed, and whether you will have a home or not.

One of the major technological problems of our society, therefore, becomes how to develop a "fair" system of affording privilege, legitimating inequality, and evading the Golden Rule. As usual, the intellectual and professional classes have been eager to stoop to the task and have developed a stunning array of sophisticated modes of judging people's worth which goes under more euphemistic terms like measurement and assessment. Accountability and evaluation become indispensable dimensions of a cruel but fair meritocracy in which our compelling moral responsibility is shifted from creating a more just and loving community to the moral imperative of providing reliable and valid techniques to maintain an inherently unfair society. If nothing else, Goals 2000 is an epiphany to the evaluation and sorting process, an official enshrinement of valid and reliable rituals of ultimate judgment, and an iconization of testing. So much for the traditions of education for play, creativity, and growth; so much for nurturing respect and compassion for each other; so much for the notion of public education as an instrument for nourishing a democratic community with liberty and justice for all.

Goals 2000 is an apt metaphor for a cultural vision of personal achievement, materialism, individuality, survival of the fittest, ruthless competition, political realism, and detached technology. It is a vision that discourages solidarity among peoples, since people are not seen as family members but as competitors. It is a vision that is so powerful that educators find themselves having to work very hard to make convincing and persuasive arguments on the importance of caring and compassion. The fact that nourishing the impulse to care is seen as an intriguing and interesting educational innovation and that the presence of guns is now accepted as commonplace in the school is powerful testimony to the desperation and divisiveness in our culture. The response of Goals 2000 to our social and cultural crises is to define the major educational problem to be that of low productivity and to locate the solution in raising educational achievement and to formalize and institutionalize a national policy of even more testing, sorting, discriminating, classifying, allocating, and channeling of children in order that we might "compete and win in the global economy."

SO WHAT'S NEW?

As I've already mentioned, the public response to Goals 2000 has been something less than heated, and indeed, seems to have been one of the major nonevents of 1994. I believe that this in part represents a "so what?" reaction to what is by now the emergent and familiar public consensus on what constitutes the essential process and purpose of education. This consensus has now been formally ratified by the President and Congress. There has been some professional and public criticism, most of which has centered on the issues of federal control and the imposition of uniform educational standards. What is truly extraordinary in the reaction, however, is the explicit and implicit acclaim with which the public and profession have lavished on the broad goals themselves, even in criticizing them as unrealistic and romantic.

A typical form of criticism begins with a disclaimer on criticizing the goals themselves and then proceeds to take the legislation to task for not providing sufficient funds for these well-intentioned goals or for not recognizing the structural problems that are barriers to achieving these lofty aspirations. Writing as guest editor of a special issue of the *Phi Delta Kappan* mostly devoted to a critical symposium on Goals 2000, Evans Clinchy describes the contributors to the symposium as "transformationists" and clearly their articles are thoughtful and insightful critiques of major elements of the legislation. However, in the very beginning of his lead article, Clinchy has this to say: ". . . this new national mission may at first glance appear to be *no more than a list of obviously desirable goals and generally non-controversial aims. . . .* Indeed, the question here is not whether these . . . goals are worth pursuing but whether the Clinton Administration and the Congress understand what the goals imply and thus what it will take to actually achieve them" [emphasis added] (Clinchy, 1995).

What Clinchy characterizes as "transformationist" critique for the most part turns out to be essentially grounded in serious concerns about pedagogical, curricular, and organizational issues, with only occasional references to fundamental social and cultural concerns and none to economic ones. Therefore, what is not new here is the endorsement of an educational policy thoroughly folded into the interests of the dominant industrial, financial, and business interests and totally integrated into the ideology of the free market system (i.e., capitalism). Moreover, what is also constant in the reactions, both pro and con, is the implicit ratification of the existing social, political, and economic paradigm, at least by default, by the vast majority of the profession.

To the extent that there is strong criticism from the profession, my impression is that it tends to focus on the issues of an unimaginative curriculum, an overdetermined degree of testing, and on the matter of the federal imposition of educational uniformity. I have already made reference to the dreariness of the curricular orientation represented in Goals 2000, and, as depressing as it may be, there is the reality that it is an orientation that has persisted and prevailed both in the schools and in the public consciousness as virtually inevitable, if not incomparable. The status of the sacred five subjects (English, science, history, mathematics, and foreign languages) has reached a level of near permanence and has remained basically unchallenged as the starting point of curricular discussions for several decades. Again, Goals 2000 does not represent an abrupt change in what constitutes the prevailing views on curriculum but has simply affirmed a political reality: namely, that the struggles for serious and fundamental reexamination of the curriculum have had little or no impact on broad educational policy. And surely the emphasis on testing and accountability is hardly a surprise in an era when we are supposed to cheer "authentic assessment" and "portfolios" as progressive ways of rendering to Caesar his insistence on ranking and judging children.

What does appear to be new and ominous is the rather large foot of the federal government in the door of educational regulation, not withstanding the clearly disingenuous and promiscuous use of the term "voluntary" in the legislation. I agree with those who see this as a dangerous and potentially devastating blow to our vital principles and traditions of teacher autonomy, community involvement, and student participation, and as an important aspect of an irresistible tide of centralized rigidity, uniformity, and control. The dangers here are very real and involve the possibility of the total politicization of education by the federal government, the erosion of pluralism, diversity, and experimentation, and an escalation of bureaucratic interference, harassment, meddling, and Mickey Mousing. As dreadful as these policies may be, they basically represent a continuation, perhaps at a somewhat more intense level, of well-established, basically uncontested, and generally accepted educational policies and practices. Through a combination of various factors and forces—for example, the homogenization of American culture, the near uniformity in college admissions requirements, the enormous mobility of American workers and families, the existence of a de facto national curriculum (see above), accreditation and certification requirements, the textbook and testing industry, and so on, to all intents and purposes the public schools in the United States are virtually uniform in all the most important respects. One very important exception to this uniformity, however, is the area of allocated resources. Indeed, because we as a society have wanted to be able to move from school to school easily, we have arranged an organization, curriculum, and culture of public education of easily recognizable and assembled interchangeable parts. There surely are vigorous programs in many communities that allow for significant parental and/or teacher involvement, but they, for the most part, still work within the framework of these interchangeable parts. The enthusiasm for state mandated accountability as a mode of imposing uniform standards is as real as it is depressing, and the striking similarity of these standards across the states should not be in the least surprising.

WHAT'S GOING ON HERE?

For me, the main issue here is not so much about clarifying the new dangers to public education that Goals 2000 poses but rather to be alert to the old dangers of public education to our vision of a just and loving community.

What Goals 2000 represents, extends, magnifies, and cements is an essentially unchallenged educational paradigm that mirrors and seeks to extend a cruel and unjust cultural vision. I believe that critics are right to point out that the legislation seriously erodes the vitality of grass roots, local involvement in the public schools, surely an extremely important dimension of a democratic society. I also agree with the critics who lament the rather crude emphasis on test results that seriously undermines efforts at stimulating critical thinking, individual expression, and human creativity. And, as I've indicated, Goals 2000 accentuates an extremely unwise and self-defeating growth in uniformity, rigidity, and overregulation. However, as important and vital as these criticisms are, they do not go nearly far enough in interpreting the social, political, and cultural significance of the meaning of this latest round of educational reform. We get more insight into the bedrock issues from the critics who correctly point out that our political leaders are very reluctant to confront the real financial and political cost of actually trying seriously to meet the goals, for example, by failing to discuss the impact that programs directed at the virtual elimination of drugs and violence would have on federal and state budgets or by avoiding discussion of what it really takes to reduce poverty, so necessary even for the relatively modest goal of equal opportunity.

Disingenuousness, however, is not the exclusive prerogative of politicians. It is also very much in evidence among educators who seek to distance schooling from the social, cultural, economic, and political divisions in which they are embedded. The operative present visions (educational and otherwise) actually require, structure, and ensure inequality and poverty in their insistence on hierarchy, competition, and meritocracy. Key to the understanding of why education is such a hotly debated issue is the well-understood tenet that it is a critically important mode of attaining an edge in achieving privilege in a society that embraces and legitimates an unequal distribution of wealth. It seems to me that this is *the* critical axis that our educational institutions turn on, and astonishingly enough, the least questioned and resisted. I certainly prefer that teachers and parents work at the local and school levels to improve educational programs but not if the programs maintain and accentuate the present system of structured inequality and poverty. I also love to support imaginative, child-centered, developmentally appropriate, and thought provoking curricula but my concern for an education that fosters a just and loving community is far greater. Perhaps we do not have to choose between local control and justice or between a humane curriculum and equality, but we must make the connection very, very clear because the reality is that our dominant public and professional discourse is very muddy on these relationships. Actually, the politicians (as in Goals 2000) tend to be much more up front in their insistence on connecting education to the needs of business, government, and the military. It seems that many professionals are invested in reifying education such that it can be separated from ideologi-

cal concerns, operating from the myth that good education is good education, good teaching is good teaching, and good schools are good schools regardless of the political and economic contexts.

WHAT SHOULD WE DO?

There are, as I see it, three major problems here: (1) the triumph of the reac-
tionary educational reform movement as reflected in the ho-hum reaction to
the passage of the Goals 2000 project; (2) the timidity and modesty of
oppositional forces as reflected in the mildness of the criticisms of Goals
2000; and (3) the sense of futility and despair as reflected in the near absence
of alternative social, economic, and cultural visions to the one represented in
Goals 2000. The energy that is created from the interaction of triumph, timidity, and despair is surely entropic and hence can only magnify our crises of
poverty, inequity, and polarization. What needs to be done is, therefore,
quite clear and very difficult: to reinstill our visions, dreams, and hopes for
creating a loving and just world and to recover our confidence in the human
capacity to overcome the obstacles to them. This is not the time to be timid
precisely because there is so much timidity. This is not the time to be despair-
ing especially because there is so little hope out there. This is not the time to
preserve the status-quo particularly because there is so little effort to work for
social and cultural transformation.

   Let's put it another way—we don't need professional and intellectual
classes to ratify and legitimate policies that engender and sustain social injustice, poverty, and privilege or to add to the sense of their inevitability and im-
mutability. If there ever was a time for those who aspire to leadership and responsibility to speak out with passion and conviction on our shared vision of
an end to poverty, unnecessary human suffering, to homelessness, to humiliation, to authoritarianism, and to anything else standing in the way of a life of
meaning and dignity for all people, this is surely it. There is an extraordinary
vacuum in the public sphere needing to be filled with a greater understanding
of the moral, social, and cultural consequences of our educational policies
and with an educational vision that is grounded in a commitment to a world
of peace, love, and community. As educators our responsibility is surely not
to carry out current educational policies and practices, however oppressive
they may be, but to uphold and nourish the cherished principles that inform
our deepest dreams and highest aspirations. As responsible professionals, we
are uniquely positioned to affirm the capacity of education to contribute to a
consciousness of compassion and justice. However, this is a time when we
need to talk less about our educational goals and more about our moral aspirations, less about our professional role as educators and more about ethical
responsibilities as citizens. We need to stop accommodating to the forces of

institutional control and instead renew our commitment to the spirit of joyous community. To paraphrase Rabbi Hillel, if we as a profession do not support education, who will? If we are only for our profession, what are we? If not now, when?

REFERENCES

Goals 2000: Educate America Act. Public Law 103-227—March 31, 1994.

Clinchy, Evans. "Sustaining and Expanding the Educational Conversation" in *Phi Delta Kappan*, March 20, 1995.

III
▼▼▼▼▼▼▼

MARGINALITY AND DIFFERENCE:
THE FRACTURED COMMUNITY

> *Every migrant knows in his heart of hearts, that it is impossi-*
> *ble to return. Even if he is physically able to return, he does*
> *not truly return, because he himself has been so deeply*
> *changed by this emigration. . . . Today, as soon as very early*
> *childhood is over, the home can never again be home, as it*
> *was in other epochs. This century, for all its wealth and with*
> *all its communication systems, is the century of banishment.*
> *(Berger, 1984, pp. 65–67)*

Berger's powerful words take us into the unifying theme of
Part II of this book—a theme now of immense significance in
the United States as well as elsewhere in the world. For Berger
and others, homelessness is the defining condition of humankind in the contemporary era. Many adults as well as young
people feel estranged from the context in which they make their
lives. Their sense of connection to where they live, work, and
go to school is at best ambivalent and at worst filled with hostility. This sense of alienation marks their children's experience of
education. Schools for many, as we know from so much research, do not reflect who one is, the community that shapes
one's identity, or the knowledge and experience that constitutes
one's culture. From this perspective, we see a world deeply
scarred by what has been called *the poison of separation*. Our
lives and our cultures are pervaded by fragmentation. Too little

do we connect the life world that provides us with a sense of meaning and place to the public world of which schools are a great mediator. The educational process neither reflects nor seems to value the social world within which the identity of so many young people is formed and nurtured. Schooling ignores or even opposes those things that provide the substance of young people's life world. For many young people, school provides little that connects to those things that constitute their dreams, concerns, hopes, and fears and the emotional and spiritual resources that feed these. Globalization with its increasing migration of workers and their families has exacerbated the extent to which so many feel themselves to be strangers and outsiders barely tolerated and often resented by long-time residents. We find ourselves in a world that excludes, sometimes brutally, whole categories of people from any real participation in the collective making of the material or cultural conditions of their lives. Many of us live in a society of which we do not feel a part in any meaningful way. Groups of people cast into the role of *surplus populations* find their lives, experiences, values, and ways of life demeaned and invalidated by those who hold superior political, economic, and cultural power. This world of separation and invalidation places human beings on a path of fatal dissonance with the institutions that provide a context for their lives. Such institutions seem to express neither civic legitimacy nor democratic purpose. Instead they are seen and experienced as repositories of arbitrary and unjust political and cultural power. Cynicism, hostility, and even violence become inevitable expressions of discontent by those whose lives and experiences seem neither reflected nor valued in the practices of formal education.

Those like philosopher Maxine Greene have made eloquently clear that in the United States alienation and freedom have too often represented opposite sides of the same coin. *Freedom* in this country has always meant a freedom *from*. It has meant bourgeois or *laissez-faire* freedom in which obligation, duty, and responsibility to the state or community are minimal. Individuals are expected to become self-sufficient beings, unconstrained in their geographical and social mobility, and by the moral ties that bind them to others. *Individuality, autonomy*, and *independence* are the watchwords of the American ideology—the heart of the promise of American life. This promise has been enormously appealing to generations of immigrants from lands in which lives were stunted or thwarted by repressive traditions, state coercion, or economic scarcity. Yet we have paid a heavy price for this type of freedom, founded as it is on separation and a weak sense of human interdependence or social solidarity. Cultural critics have pointed to the sport utility vehicle (SUV) as an apt metaphor for this attitude, with its promise of powerful and rugged independence and its contempt for the safety of others on the road or the social and economic consequences of its excessive fuel demands. To an extraordinary extent, American society offers individual freedom but denigrates common bonds and collective ties and responsibilities. However much we might wax nostalgic or sentimental about such social connections (or laud them when they are demonstrated by our soldiers, police, or emergency workers), the price for entry into the relative security of middle-class life is often the dissolution of social ties. Success or achievement is attained primarily through the often ruthless, competitive, and egoistic drives demanded by the economic marketplace. As one of our essays in this section demonstrates, it is precisely here that a revalidation of those reproductive concerns with relationship, care of others, and social responsibility looms especially important in an educational vision that might prepare people for the ethical transformation of our culture, away from its overwhelming emphasis on individual success and achievement.

Success in America means abandonment of those communal ties that might limit the headlong rush for personal achievement. It means shredding the traditions of language, beliefs, and values that stand in the way of conforming to the White, male, Christian, heterosexual, middle-class standards that constitute American normalcy. For many, winning one's place in the American mainstream means submission to a brutal process of alienation. One must, in the first place, forfeit those ethnically, linguistically, and racially mediated cultures that are eschewed by the dominant culture. In other words, one must dissolve those historically constituted ties through which whole groups of human beings learned to locate themselves in the world. Doing so, one must not simply abandon social ties, but also eliminate important aspects of one's subjectivity. One must give up parts of oneself whether this be the sense of ethnic pride or kinship, assimilate to prevailing forms of religious belief, or embrace acceptable political, cultural, or sexual identities. The price of some minimal degree of economic well-being or security is frequently denial, shame, and a distancing from one's existential roots.

This insistence on cultural homogenization has often been accompanied by a process in which dominant groups rationalize their positions of privilege through myths about their intellectual or cultural superiority and the purported inferiority of those that have been marginalized. The recent revival of talk about the unequal distribution of intelligence among different racial groups is witness to this. Yet as our readings also make clear, the process of exclusion or marginalization is neither smooth nor conflict-free. Indeed both individually and collectively, human beings have resisted the Faustian bargain in which the price of economic survival is a denial of one's cultural community and one's identity. This has never been more evident in the recent upsurge of political movements organized around issues of identity. The demands of such movements for cultural recognition and inclusion have meant powerful new forms of democratic struggle. It has given deeper meaning to the idea of social justice in a pluralistic society. Identity struggles in the United States mirror similar struggles in many other parts of the world as globalization has meant the creation of new linguistic, religious, and cultural communities in existing societies. Such movements have forced us to think anew about the acceptance and valuing of strangers in our midst. In education, for example, students and their parents continue to struggle to preserve and validate ethnic, cultural, religious, and sexual identities over which schools frequently ride roughshod. Such struggles have not been without success as educational policies have been promulgated that recognize and support racial, linguistic, ethnic, or other minorities in the preservation of their communal forms and cultures. Still the success of such policies is often exaggerated in the discourse of a right-wing backlash. More often we continue to witness a system that falls far short of adequately respecting human and cultural differences. Indeed as these readings show, we have only begun to see how the prevailing logic of educational practice—even where it is internal to be ameliorative—confirms and reproduces the traditional structures of hierarchy, exclusion, and prejudice. More generally, we refuse to confront the way in which educational policies reflect questions of power—cultural, economic, and political. Exploring the enduring and pervasive forms of personal and collective alienation inside as well as outside the school means persisting in identifying how educational institutions discount the voices of, and exclude from meaningful participation, too many of their students.

The readings in this section explore and illustrate these themes. For example, they look at the dilemma of a parent anxious to both affirm and develop the particularistic traditions of a minority religious community while not shredding the ties of a democratic community through pursuing only the socially fragmenting concerns of separate cultural identities. In a similar vein, another writer examines the way that the strong assimilationist tendency of American society, together with the militant advocacy of nativist organizations, has made the preservation of foreign languages a near impossibility. The threat, this writer contends, is less a Babel-like society than a society without cultural memory. A third writer considers the major reasons given for the superior educational attainments of White students. In particular he looks at the way standardized tests are an insidious form of institutionalized racism that obscures the crucial distinction between academic performance and academic achievement as measured by these tests. Such tests, with their claim to objectivity, obfuscate the way school continues to stigmatize particular racial identities.

In a seminal piece, the educational philosopher Jane Roland Martin (chap. 12, this volume) considers the way that schooling forces on many students the loss of linguistic and cultural identity. Alienation from home—a narrative of existential loss—is frequently the sad concomitant to success in school, she argues. Martin's piece is also a commentary on the exclusion from educational legitimacy of forms of knowledge that articulate the socially relational dimensions of human existence. This piece receives amplifi-

cation in the following examination of the process of socialization connected to masculinity. The author argues that the so-called *war against boys*
in America has misconstrued the real problem. Masculinity continues to
construct males in such a way that only a limited definition of allowable humanity is possible. The author argues that we need to speak not of masculinity in the singular, but of a pluralized notion of *masculinities*. In the final
piece in this section, the author reflects on pedagogy that concerns itself
with gay and lesbian issues. Drawing on the antigay prejudice and heterosexist bias that was the context for the murder of Matthew Shepard, the
piece considers the process of engaging the assumptions of students' own
sexuality. The author offers a path to consider *the nexus among gender,
power, and authority* that shapes the inequities manifested in sexism, racism,
and heterosexism. In the teaching experience he draws from, the writer
urges students to take seriously their actions in the world and the contributions they might make to a more just and free world.

All the writings in this section reflect an important shift in our view of cultures and human behaviors that do not conform to what has been considered
normal. In place of the widely held assumption that other kinds of people are
deficient or abnormal, we begin to use a language of *difference* that seeks to
treat all human beings with dignity and equal value. No human practices, values, or beliefs can easily set themselves up as the standard by which everyone
should be judged or measured. Through the work of postmodern critics, such
as Michel Foucault, we see how claims about what is normal usually cloak
the power of one group or another to impose its views about the supposedly
proper way to live, speak, think, feel, or value. It becomes increasingly apparent how the discourse of normality masks the power to control others who
are different because of race, nationality, religion, gender, sexual preference,
language, class, physical appearance, and mental or physical ability. From
the perspective of difference, a socially just world is impossible without a significantly deepened appreciation of the worth and dignity of all people, and a
radically expanded affirmation of the meaning and value of human diversity.

REFERENCE

Berger, J. (1984). *And our faces, my heart, brief as photos*. New York: Pantheon.

Becoming Educated: A Journey of Alienation or Integration?*

Jane Roland Martin

In his educational autobiography *Hunger of Memory*, Richard Rodriguez (1982) tells of growing up in Sacramento, California, the third of four children in a Spanish-speaking family. Upon entering first grade he could understand perhaps 50 English words. Within the year his teachers convinced his parents to speak only English at home and Rodriguez soon became fluent in the language. By the time he graduated from elementary school with citations galore and entered high school, he had read hundreds of books. He went on to attend Stanford University and, 20 years after his parents' decision to abandon their native tongue, he sat in the British Museum writing a PhD dissertation in English literature.

Rodriguez learned to speak English and went on to acquire a liberal education. History, literature, science, mathematics, philosophy: these he studied and made his own. Rodriguez's story is of the cultural assimilation of a Mexican-American, but it is more than this, for by no means do all assimilated Americans conform to our image of a well-educated person. Rodriguez does because, to use the terms the philosopher R. S. Peters (1966, 1972) employs in his analysis of the concept of the educated man, he did not simply acquire knowledge and skill. He acquired conceptual schemes to raise his knowledge beyond the level of a collection of disjointed facts and to enable him to under-

---

stand the "reason why" of things. Moreover, the knowledge he acquired is not "inert": It characterizes the way he looks at the world and it involves the kind of commitment to the standards of evidence and canons of proof of the various disciplines that comes from "getting on the inside of a form of thought and awareness" (Peters, 1961, p. 9).

Quite a success story, yet *Hunger of Memory* is notable primarily as a narrative of loss. In becoming an educated person Rodriguez loses his fluency in Spanish, but that is the least of it. As soon as English becomes the language of the Rodriguez family, the special feeling of closeness at home is diminished. Furthermore, as his days are increasingly devoted to understanding the meaning of words, it becomes difficult for Rodriguez to hear intimate family voices. When it is Spanish-speaking, his home is a noisy, playful, warm, emotionally charged environment; with the advent of English the atmosphere becomes quiet and restrained. There is no acrimony. The family remains loving. But the experience of "feeling individualized" by family members is now rare, and occasions for intimacy are infrequent.

Rodriguez tells a story of alienation: from his parents, for whom he soon has no names; from the Spanish language, in which he loses his childhood fluency; from his Mexican roots, in which he shows no interest; from his own feelings and emotions, which all but disappear as he learns to control them; from his body itself, as he discovers when he takes a construction job after his senior year in college.

John Dewey spent his life trying to combat the tendency of educators to divorce mind from body and reason from emotion. Rodriguez's educational autobiography documents these divorces, and another one Dewey deplored, that of self from other. Above all *Hunger of Memory* depicts a journey from intimacy to isolation. Close ties with family members are dissolved as public anonymity replaces private attention. Rodriguez becomes a spectator in his own home as noise gives way to silence and connection to distance. School, says Rodriguez, bade him trust "lonely" reason primarily. And there is enough time and "silence," he adds, "to think about ideas (big ideas)" (p. 47).

What is the significance of this narrative of loss? Not every American has Rodriguez's good fortune of being born into a loving home filled with the warm sounds of intimacy, yet the separation and distance he ultimately experienced are not unique to him. On the contrary, they represent the natural end point of the educational journey Rodriguez took.

Dewey repeatedly pointed out that the distinction educators draw between liberal and vocational education represents a separation of mind from body, head from hand, thought from action. Since we define an educated person as one who has had and has profited from a liberal education, these splits are built into our ideal of the educated person. Since most definitions of excellence in education derive from that ideal, these splits are built into them as well. A split between reason and emotion is built into our definitions of excellence too, for we take the aim of a liberal education to be the development not of mind as a whole, but of rational mind. We define this in terms of the acquisition of knowledge and understanding, construed narrowly (Martin, 1981b). It is not surprising that Rodriguez acquires habits of quiet reflection rather than noisy activity, reasoned deliberation rather than spontaneous reaction, dispassionate inquiry rather than emotional response, abstract analytic theorizing rather than concrete storytelling. These are integral to the ideal of the educated person that has come down to us from Plato.

Upon completion of his educational journey Rodriguez bears a remarkable resemblance to the guardians of the Just State that Plato constructs in the *Republic*. Those worthies are to acquire through their education a wide range of theoretical knowledge, highly developed powers of reasoning, and the qualities of objectivity and emotional distance. To be sure, not one of Plato's guardians will be the "disembodied mind" Rodriguez becomes, for Plato believed that a strong mind requires a strong body. But Plato designed for his guardians an education of heads, not hands. (Presumably the artisans of the Just State would serve as their hands.) Moreover, considering the passions to be unruly and untrustworthy, Plato held up for the guardians an ideal of self-discipline and self-government in which reason keeps feelings and emotion under tight control. As a consequence, although he wanted the guardians of the Just State to be so connected to one another that they would feel each other's pains and pleasures, the educational ideal he developed emphasizes "inner" harmony at the expense of "outward" connection. If his guardians do not begin their lives in intimacy, as Rodriguez did, their education, like his, is intended to confirm in them a sense of self in isolation from others.

Do the separations bequeathed to us by Plato matter? The great irony of the liberal education that comes down to us from Plato and still today as the mark of an educated person is that it is neither tolerant nor generous (Martin, 1981b). As Richard Rodriguez discovered, there is no place in it for education of the body, and since most action involves bodily movement, this means that there is little in it for education of action. Nor is there room for education of other-regarding feelings and emotions. The liberally educated person will be provided with knowledge about others, but will not be taught to care about their welfare or act kindly toward them. That person will be given some understanding of society, but will not be taught to feel its injustices or even to be concerned over its fate. The liberally educated person will be an ivory tower person—one who can reason but has no desire to solve real problems in the real world—or else a technical person who likes to solve real problems but does not care about the solutions' consequences for real people and for the earth itself.

The case of Rodriguez illuminates several unhappy aspects of our Platonic heritage, while concealing another. No one who has seen Frederick Wiseman's film *High School* can forget the woman who reads to the assembled students a letter she has received from a pupil in Vietnam. But for a few teachers who cared, she tells her audience, Bob Walters, a sub-average student academically, "might have been a nobody." Instead, while awaiting a plane that is to drop him behind the DMZ, he has written her to say that he has made the school the beneficiary of his life insurance policy. "I am a little jittery right now," she reads. She is not to worry about him, however, because "I am only a body doing a job." Measuring his worth as a human being by his provision for the school, she overlooks the fact that Bob Walters was not merely participating in a war of dubious morality but was taking pride in being an automaton.

High School was made in 1968, but Bob Walter's words were echoed many times over by 18- and 19-year-old Marine recruits in the days immediately following the Grenada invasion. Readers of *Hunger of Memory* will not be surprised. The underside of a liberal education devoted to the development of "disembodied minds" is a vocational education whose business is the production of "mindless bodies." In Plato's Just State, where, because of their rational powers, the specially educated few will rule the many, a young man's image of himself as "only a body doing a job" is the desired one. That the educational theory and practice of a democracy derives from Plato's explicitly undemocratic philosophical vision is disturbing. We are not supposed to have two classes of people, those who think and those who do not. We are not supposed to have two kinds of people, those who rule and those who obey.

The Council for Basic Education has long recommended, and some people concerned with excellence in education now suggest, that a liberal education at least through high school be extended to all. For the sake of argument let us suppose that this program can be carried out without making more acute the inequities it is meant to erase. We would then presumably have a world in which no one thinks of him- or herself as simply a body doing a job. We would, however, have a world filled with unconnected, uncaring, emotionally impoverished people. Even if it were egalitarian, it would be a sorry place in which to live. Nor would the world be better if somehow we combined Rodriguez's liberal education with a vocational one. For assuming it to be peopled by individuals who joined head and hand, reason would still be divorced from feeling and emotion, and each individual cut off from others.

The world we live in is just such a place. It is a world of child abuse and family violence (Breines & Gordon, 1983), a world in which one out of every four women will be raped at some time in her life (Johnson, 1980; Lott, Reilly, & Howard, 1982). Our world is on the brink of nuclear and/or ecological disaster. Efforts to overcome these problems, as well as the related ones of poverty and economic scarcity, flounder today under the direction of people who try hard to be rational, objective, autonomous agents but, like Plato's guardians, do not know how to sustain human relationships or respond directly to human needs. Indeed, they do not even see the value of trying to do so. Of course, it is a mistake to suppose that education alone can solve this world's problems. Yet if there is to be hope of the continuation of life on earth, let alone of a good life for all, as educators we must strive to do more than join mind and body, head and hand, thought and action.

REDEFINING EDUCATION

For Rodriguez, the English language is a metaphor. In the literal sense of the term he had to learn English to become an educated *American*, yet in his narrative the learning of English represents the acquisition not so much of a new natural language as of new ways of thinking, acting, and being that he associates with the public world. Rodriguez makes it clear that the transition from Spanish to English represented for him the transition almost every child in our society makes from the "private world" of home to the "public world" of business, politics, and culture. He realizes that Spanish is not intrinsically a private language and English a public one, although his own experiences made it seem this way. He knows that the larger significance of his story lies in the fact that education inducts one into new activities and processes.

In my research on the place of women in educational thought (1982, 1985), I have invoked a distinction between the productive and the reproductive processes of society and have argued that both historians of educational thought and contemporary philosophers of education define the educational realm in relation to society's productive processes only. Briefly, the reproductive processes include not simply the biological reproduction of the species, but the rearing of children to maturity and the related activities of keeping house, managing a household, and serving the needs and purposes of family members. In turn, the productive processes include political, social, and cultural activities as well as economic ones. This distinction is related to the one Rodriguez repeatedly draws between public and private worlds, for in our society reproductive processes are for the most part carried on in the private world of the home and domesticity, and productive processes in the public world of politics and work. Rodriguez's autobiography reveals that the definition of education as preparation solely for carrying on the productive processes of society is not a figment of the academic imagination.

Needless to say, the liberal education Rodriguez received did not fit him to carry on all productive processes of society. Aiming at the development of rational mind, his liberal education prepared him to be a consumer and creator of ideas, not an auto mechanic or factory worker. A vocational education, had he received one, would have prepared him to work with his hands and use procedures designed by others. They are very different kinds of education, yet both are designed to fit students to carry on productive, not reproductive, societal processes.

Why do I stress the connection between the definition of education and the productive processes of society? *Hunger of Memory* contains a wonderful account of Rodriguez's grandmother telling him stories of her life. He is moved by the sounds she makes and by the message of intimacy her person transmits. The words themselves are not important to him, for he perceives the private world in which she moves—the world of childrearing and homemaking—to be one of feeling and emotion, intimacy and connection, and hence a realm of the nonrational. In contrast, he sees the public world—the world of productive process for which his education fit him—as the realm of the rational. Feeling and emotion have no place in it, and neither do intimacy and connection. Instead, analysis, critical thinking, and self-sufficiency are the dominant values.

Rodriguez's assumption that feeling and emotion, intimacy and concession are naturally related to the home and society's reproductive processes and that these qualities are irrelevant to carrying on the productive processes is commonly accepted. But then, it is to be expected that their development is ignored by education in general and by liberal education in particular. Since education is supposed to equip people for carrying on productive societal processes, from a practical standpoint would it not be foolhardy for liberal or vocational studies to foster these traits?

Only in light of the fact that education turns its back on the reproductive processes of society and the private world of the home can Rodriguez's story of alienation be understood. His alienation from his body will reoccur so long as we equate being an educated person with having a liberal education. His journey of isolation and divorce from his emotions will be repeated so long as we define education exclusively in relation to the productive processes of society. But the assumption of inevitability underlying *Hunger of Memory* is mistaken. Education need not separate mind from body and thought from action, for it need not draw a sharp line between liberal and vocational education. More to the point, it need not separate reason from emotion and self from other. The reproductive processes *can* be brought into the educational realm thereby overriding the theoretical and practical grounds for ignoring feeling and emotion, intimacy and connection.

If we define education in relation to *both* kinds of societal processes and act upon our redefinition, future generations will not have to experience Rodriguez's pain. He never questions the fundamental dichotomies upon which his education rests. We must question them so that we can effect the reconciliation of reason and emotion, self and other, that Dewey sought. There are, moreover, two overwhelming reasons for favoring such a redefinition, both of which take us beyond Dewey.

All of us—male and female—participate in the reproductive processes of society. In the past, many have thought that education for carrying them on was not necessary: These processes were assumed to be the responsibility of women, and it was supposed that by instinct a woman would automatically acquire the traits or qualities associated with them. The contemporary statistics on child abuse are enough by themselves to put to rest the doctrine of maternal instinct. Furthermore, both sexes have responsibility for making the reproductive processes of society work well. Family living and childrearing are not today, if they ever were, solely in the hands of women. Nor should they be. Thus, both sexes need to learn to carry on the reproductive processes of society just as in the 1980s both sexes needed to learn to carry on the productive ones.

The reproductive processes are of central importance to society, yet it would be a terrible mistake to suppose that the traits and qualities traditionally associated with these processes have no relevance beyond them. Jonathan Schell (1982, p. 175) has said "The nuclear peril makes all of us, whether we happen to have children of our own or not, the parents of all future generations" and that the will we must have to save the human species is a form of love resembling "the generative love of parents." He is speaking of what Nancy Chodorow (1978) calls nurturing capacities and Carol Gilligan (1982) calls an "ethics of care." Schell is right. The fate of the earth depends on all of us possessing these qualities. Thus, although these qualities are associated in our minds with the reproductive processes of society, they have the broadest moral, social, and political significance. Care, concern, connectedness, and nurturance are as important for carrying on society's economic, political, and social processes as its reproductive ones. If education is to help us acquire them, it must be redefined.

THE WORKS OF GENDER

It is no accident that in *Hunger of Memory* the person who embodies nurturing capacities and an ethics of care is a woman—Rodriguez's grandmother. The two kinds of societal processes are gender-related and so are the traits our culture associates with them. According to our cultural stereotypes, males are objective, analytical, rational, interested in ideas and things. They have no interpersonal orientation: they are not nurturant or supportive, empathetic or sensitive. Women, on the other hand, possess the traits men lack (Kaplan & Bean, 1976; Kaplan & Sedney, 1980).

Education is also gender-related. Our definition of its function makes it so. For if education is viewed as preparation for carrying on processes historically associated with males, it will inculcate traits the culture considers masculine. If the concept of education is tied by definition to the productive processes of society, our ideal of the educated person will coincide with the cultural stereotype of a male human being, and our definitions of excellence in education will embody "masculine" traits.

Of course, it is possible for members of one sex to acquire personal traits or qualities our cultural stereotypes attribute to the other. Thus females can and do acquire traits incorporated in our educational ideal. However, it must be understood that these traits are *genderized*: that is, they are appraised differently when they are possessed by males and females (Beardsley, 1977; Martin, 1981a, 1985). For example, whereas a male will be admired for his rational powers, a woman who is analytical and critical will be derided or shunned or will be told that she thinks like a man. Even if this latter is intended as a compliment, since we take masculinity and femininity to lie at opposite ends of a single continuum, she will thereby be judged as lacking in femininity and, as a consequence, judged abnormal or unnatural. Elizabeth Janeway (1971, p. 96) has said, and I am afraid she is right, that "unnatural" and "abnormal" are the equivalent for our age of what "damned" meant to our ancestors.

Because his hands were soft Rodriguez worried that his education was making him effeminate.[1] Imagine his anxieties on that score if he had been educated in those supposedly feminine virtues of caring and concern and had been taught to sustain these intimate relationships and value connection. To be sure, had his education fostered these qualities, Rodriguez would not have had to travel a road from intimacy to isolation. I do not mean to suggest that there would have been no alienation at all; his is a complex case involving class, ethnicity, and color. But an education in which reason was joined to feeling and emotion and self to other would have yielded a very different life story. Had his education fostered these qualities, however, Rodriguez would have experienced another kind of hardship.

The pain Rodriguez suffers is a consequence of the loss of intimacy and the stunting of emotional growth that are themselves consequences of education. Now it is possible that Rodriguez's experience is more representative of males than females. But if it be the case that females tend to maintain emotional growth and intimate connections better than males do, one thing is certain: educated girls are penalized for what Rodriguez considers his *gains*. If they become analytic, objective thinkers and autonomous agents, they are judged less feminine than they should be. Thus, for them the essential myth of childhood is every bit as painful as it was for Rodriguez, for they are alienated from their own identity as females.

When education is defined so as to give the reproductive processes of society their due, and the virtues of nurturance and care associated with those processes are fostered in both males and females, educated men can expect to suffer for possessing traits genderized in favor of females as educated women now do for possessing traits genderized in favor of males. This is not to say that males will be placed in the double bind educated females find themselves in now, for males will acquire traits genderized in their own favor as well as ones genderized in favor of females. Whereas the traits educated females must acquire today are *all* genderized in favor of males. On the other hand, since traits genderized in favor of females are considered lesser virtues, if virtues at all (Blum, 1980), and the societal processes with which they are associated are thought to be relatively unimportant, males will be placed in the position of having to acquire traits both they and their society consider inferior.

One of the most important findings of contemporary scholarship is that our culture embraces a hierarchy of values that places the productive processes of society and their associated traits above society's reproductive processes and the associated traits of care and nurturance. There is nothing new about this. We are the inheritors of a tradition of Western thought according to which the functions, tasks, and traits associated with females are deemed less valuable than those associated with males. In view of these findings, the difficulties facing those of us who would transform Rodriguez's educational journey from one of alienation to one of the integration of reason and emotion, of self and other, become apparent.

It is important to understand the magnitude of the changes to be wrought by an education that takes the integration of reason and emotion, self and other, seriously. Granted, when girls today embark on Rodriguez's journey they acquire traits genderized in favor of the "opposite" sex; but if on account of trait genderization they experience hardships Rodriguez did not, they can at least console themselves that their newly acquired traits, along with the societal processes to which the traits are attached, are considered valuable. Were we to attempt to change the nature of our educational ideal without also changing our value hierarchy, boys and men would have no such consolation. Without this consolation, however, we can be quite sure that the change we desire would not come to pass.

TOWARD AN INTEGRATED CURRICULUM

Just as the value structure I have been describing is reflected in our ideal of the educated person, so too it is reflected in the curriculum such a person is supposed to study. A large body of scholarship documents the extent to which the academic fields constituting the subjects of the liberal curriculum exclude women's lives, works, and experiences from their subject matter or else distort them by projecting the cultural stereotype of a female onto the evidence.[2] History, philosophy, politics; art and music; the social and behavioral sciences; even the biological and physical sciences give pride of place to male experience and achievements and to the societal processes thought to belong to men.

The research to which I refer reveals the place of women—or rather the absence thereof—in the theories, interpretations, and narratives constituting the disciplines of knowledge. Since the subject matter of the liberal curriculum is drawn from these disciplines, that curriculum gives pride of place to male experience and achievements and to the societal processes associated with men. In so doing, it is the bearer of bad news about women and the reproductive processes of society. Can it be doubted that when the works of women are excluded from the subject matter of the fields into which they are being initiated, students of both sexes will come to believe, or else will have their existing belief reinforced, that males are superior and females are inferior human beings? Can it be doubted that when in the course of this initiation the lives and experiences of women are scarcely mentioned, males and females will come to believe, or else believe more strongly than ever, that the ways in which women have lived and the things women have done through history have no value?

At campuses across the country projects are underway to incorporate the growing body of new scholarship on women into the liberal curriculum. Such efforts must be undertaken at all levels of schooling, not simply because women comprise one half of the world's population, but because the exclusion of women from the subject matter of the "curriculum proper" constitutes a hidden curriculum in the validation of one gender, its associated tasks, traits, and functions, and the denigration of the other. Supporting our culture's genderized hierarchy of value even as it reflects it, this hidden curriculum must be raised to consciousness and counteracted (Martin, 1976). Introduction of the new scholarship on women into the liberal curriculum proper—and for that matter into the vocational curriculum too—makes this possible, on the one hand because it allows students to understand the workings of gender and, on the other, because it provides them with the opportunity to appreciate women's traditional tasks, traits, and functions.

In a curriculum encompassing the experience of one sex, not two, questions of gender are automatically eliminated. For the value hierarchy under discussion to be understood, as it must be if it is to be abolished, its genderized roots must be exposed. Furthermore, if intimacy and connection are to be valued as highly as independence and distance, and if emotion and feeling are to be viewed as positive rather than untrustworthy elements of personality, women must no longer be viewed as different and alien—as the Other, to use Simone de Beauvoir's expression (1961).

Thus, we need to incorporate the study of women into curricula so that females—their lives, experiences, works, and attributes—are devalued by neither sex. But simply incorporating the new scholarship on women in the curriculum does not address the alienation and loss Rodriguez describes so well. To overcome these we must seek not only a transformation of the content of curriculum proper, but an expansion of the educational realm to include the reproductive processes of society and a corresponding redefinition of what it means to become educated.

The expansion of the educational realm I propose does not entail an extension of a skill-oriented home economics education to males. Although it is important for both sexes to learn to cook and sew, I have in mind something different when I say that education must give the reproductive processes of society their due. The traits associated with women as wives and mothers—nurturance, care, compassion, connection, sensitivity to others, a willingness to put aside one's own projects, a desire to build and maintain relationships—need to be incorporated into our ideal. This does not mean that we should fill up the curriculum with courses in the three C's of caring, concern, and connection. Given a redefinition of education, Compassion 101a need no more be listed in a school's course offerings than Objectivity 101a is now. Just as the productive processes of society have given us the general curricular goals of rationality and individual autonomy, so too the reproductive processes yield general goals. And just as rationality and autonomy are posited as goals of particular subjects, e.g., science, as well as of the curriculum as a whole, so nurturance and connection can be understood as overarching educational goals and also as the goals of particular subjects.

But now a puzzling question arises. Given that the standard subjects of the curriculum derive from the productive processes of society, must we not insert cooking and sewing and perhaps childrearing into the curriculum if we want caring, concern, and connection to be educational objectives? Science, math, history, literature, auto mechanics, refrigeration, typing: these are the subjects of the curriculum now and these derive from productive processes. If for subjects deriving from productive processes we set educational goals whose source is the reproductive processes of society, do we not distort these subjects beyond recognition? But then ought we not to opt instead for a divided curriculum with two sets of subjects? One set might be derived from the productive processes of society and foster traits associated with those, with the other set derived from the reproductive processes of society and fostering their associated traits. Is this the only way to do justice to both sets of traits?

If possible, a replication within the curriculum of the split between the productive and reproductive processes of society is to be avoided. So long as education insists on linking nurturing capacities and the three C's to subjects arising out of the reproductive processes, we will lose sight of their *general* moral, society, and political significance. Moreover, so long as rationality and autonomous judgment are considered to belong exclusively to the productive processes of society, the reproductive ones will continue to be devalued. Thus, unless it is essential to divide up curricular goals according to the classification of a subject as productive or reproductive, we ought not to do so. That it is not essential becomes clear once we give up our stereotypical pictures of the two kinds of societal processes.

Readers of June Goodfield's *An Imagined World* (1981) will know that feeling an emotion, intimacy, and connection can be an integral part of the processes of scientific discovery.[3] Goodfield recorded the day-to-day activities of Anna, a Portuguese scientist studying lymphocytes in a cancer laboratory in

New York. Anna's relationship to her colleagues *and* to the cells she studied provides quite a contrast to the rationalistic, atomistic vision of scientists and scientific discovery most of us have. To be sure, some years ago James Watson (1969) made it clear that scientists are human. But Watson portrayed scientific discovery as a race between ambitious, aggressive, highly competitive contestants while Goodfield's Anna calls it "a kind of birth." Fear, urgency, intense joy: loneliness, intimacy, and a desire to share: these are some of the emotions that motivate and shape Anna's thoughts even as her reasoned analysis and her objective scrutiny of evidence engender passion. Moreover, she is bound closely to her colleagues in the lab by feeling, as well as by scientific need, and she empathizes with the lymphocytes she studies as well as with the sick people she hopes will one day benefit from her work.

If scientific activity can flourish in an atmosphere of cooperation and connection, and important scientific discoveries can take place when passionate feeling motivates and shapes thought, then surely it is not necessary for science education to be directed solely toward rationalistic, atomistic goals. And if nurturant capacities and the three C's of caring, concern, and connection can become goals of science teaching without that subject being betrayed or abandoned, surely they can become the goals of *any* subject.

By the same token, if rational thought and independent judgment are components of successful childrearing and family living, it is not necessary to design education in subjects deriving from the reproductive processes of society solely around "affective" goals. That they can and should be part and parcel of these activities was argued long ago, and very convincingly, by both Mary Wollstonecraft and Catharine Beecher (Martin, 1985) and is a basic tenet of the home economics profession today.

Thus, just as nurturance and concern can be goals of any subject, rationality and independent judgment can also be. The temptation to institute a sharp separation of goals within an expanded educational realm corresponding to a sharp separation of subjects must, then, be resisted so that the general significance of the very real virtues we associate with women and the reproductive processes of society is understood and these virtues themselves are fostered in everyone.

CONCLUSION

In becoming educated one does not have to travel Rodriguez's road from intimacy to isolation. His journey of alienation is a function of a definition of education, a particular ideal of the educated person, and a particular definition of excellence—all of which can be rejected. Becoming educated can be a journey of integration, not alienation. The detailed task of restructuring an ideal of the educated person to guide this new journey I leave for another occasion. The general problem to be solved is that of uniting thought and action, reason and emotion, self and other. This was the problem Dewey addressed, but his failure to understand the workings of gender made it impossible for him to solve it.

I leave the task of mapping the precise contours of a transformed curriculum for another occasion too. The general problem to be solved here is that of giving the reproductive processes of society—and the females who have traditionally been assigned responsibility for carrying them on—their due. Only then will feeling and emotion, intimacy and connection be perceived as valuable qualities so that a journey of integration is possible.

Loss, pain, isolation: It is a tragedy that these should be the results of becoming educated, the consequences of excellence. An alternative journey to Rodriguez's requires fundamental changes in both educational theory and practice. Since these changes will make it possible to diffuse throughout the population the nurturant capacities and the ethics of care that are absolutely essential to the survival of society itself, indeed, to the survival of life on earth, they should ultimately be welcomed even by those who would claim that the loss, pain, and isolation Rodriguez experienced in becoming educated did him no harm.

NOTES

1. Quite clearly, Rodriguez's class background is a factor in this judgment. Notice, however, that the form his fear takes relates to gender.
2. This scholarship cannot possibly be cited here. For reviews of the literature in the various academic disciplines see past issues of *Signs: Journal of Women in Culture and Society*.
3. See also Keller (1983).

REFERENCES

Beardsley, E. (1977). Traits and genderization. In M. Vetterling-Braggin, F. A. Elliston, & L. English (Eds.), *Feminism and philosophy* (pp. 117–123). Totowa, NJ: Littlefield.

Blum, L. (1980). *Friendship, altruism, and morality*. London: Routledge & Kegan Paul.

Breines, W., & Gordon, L. (1983). The new scholarship on family violence. *Signs*, 8(3), 493–507.

Chodorow, N. (1978). *The reproduction of mothering*. Berkeley: University of California Press.

de Beauvoir, S. (1961). *The second sex*. New York: Bantam.

Gilligan, C. (1982). *In a different voice*. Cambridge: Harvard University Press.

Goodfield, J. (1981). *An imagined world*. New York: Harper & Row.

Janeway, E. (1971). *Man's world, woman's place*. New York: Morrow.

Johnson, A. G. (1980). On the prevalence of rape in the United States. *Signs*, 6(1), 136–146.

Kaplan, A. G., & Bean, J. P. (Eds.). (1976). *Beyond sex-role stereotypes*. Boston: Little, Brown.

Kaplan, A. G., & Sedney, M. A. (1980). *Psychology and sex roles*. Boston: Little, Brown.

Keller, E. F. (1983). *A feeling for the organism*. San Francisco: W. H. Freeman.

Lott, B., Reilly, M. E., & Howard, D. R. (1982). Sexual assault and harassment: A campus community case study. *Sign*, 8(2), 296–319.

Martin, J. R. (1976). What should we do with a hidden curriculum when we find one? *Curriculum Inquiry*, 6(2), 135–151.

Martin, J. R. (1981a). The ideal of the educated person. *Educational Theory*, 31(2), 97–109.

Martin, J. R. (1981b). Needed: A new paradigm for liberal education. In J. F. Soltis (Ed.), *Philosophy and education* (pp. 37–59). Chicago: University of Chicago Press.

Martin, J. R. (1982). Excluding women from the educational realm. *Harvard Educational Review*, 52(2), 133–148.

Martin, J. R. (1985). *Reclaiming a conversation: The ideal of the educated woman*. New Haven: Yale University Press.

Peters, R. S. (1966). *Ethics and education*. London: Allen & Unwin.

Peters, R. S. (1972). Education and the educated man. In R. F. Dearden, P. H. Hirst, & R. S. Peters (Eds.), *A critique of current educational aims*. London: Routledge & Kegan Paul.

Rodriguez, R. (1982). *Hunger of memory*. Boston: David R. Godine.

Schell, J. (1982). *The fate of the earth*. New York: Avon.

Watson, J. D. (1969). *The double helix*. New York: New American Library.

English-Only Triumphs,
but the Costs Are High*

Alejandro Portes

The surge of immigration into the United States during the past 30 years has brought a proliferation of foreign languages, and with it fears that the English language may lose its predominance and cultural unity may be undermined. Several conservative national organizations, including the powerful U.S. English, have been established to combat this trend. U.S. English describes the cultural threat in somber tones:

"Where linguistic unity has broken down, our energies and resources flow into tensions, hostilities, prejudices and resentments. These develop and persist. Within a few years, if the breakdown persists, there will be no retreat. It becomes irrevocable, irreversible. Society as we know it can fade into noisy Babel and then chaos."

What is the likelihood of such a catastrophe? Every period of high immigration has given rise to nativist movements warning of cultural disintegration, and thus calling for the immediate linguistic assimilation of foreigners. Almost a century before the emergence of the U.S. English organization, President Theodore Roosevelt wrote: "We have room for one language here and that is the English language; for we intend to see that the crucible turns our people out as Americans, and not as dwellers in a polyglot boarding house."

These fears are proving unfounded.

NEW "THREATS" TO ENGLISH

German, Polish, and Italian immigrants were targeted as threats to cultural unity in the past, as migrants from Mexico, Russia and China are today. The agents vary, but the perceived threat is the same. In the past, these fears have proven unfounded. In no other country, among 35 nations compared in a detailed study by sociologist Stanley Lieberson and his colleagues, did foreign languages fade as swiftly as in the United States. Linguists such as Joshua Fishman and Calvin Veltman have documented how this process takes place. First-generation immigrants learn as much English as they can, but continue to speak their mother tongue at home. The second generation grows up speaking the mother tongue at home, but English in school and at work. By the third generation, English becomes the home language and the transition to monolingualism is completed.

Illustrative of this trend, the 1990 census found that 92 percent of the U.S. population spoke only English. The remaining 8 percent were almost exclusively first-generation immigrants undergoing the initial stages of linguistic assimilation. Immigration accelerated during the 1990s, raising the question of whether language assimilation continues to be as swift today as it was in the past. In part to address this question, Rubén G. Rumbaut and I surveyed a large sample of children of immigrants—the new second generation—attending public and private schools in Miami/Fort Lauderdale and San Diego, two of the metropolitan areas most affected by contemporary immigration. The resulting Children of Immigrants Longitudinal Study (CILS) collected data on over 5,200 students from 77 different nationalities attending eighth and ninth grades in 1992–93. We followed the sample and reinterviewed 82 percent of them three years later, when most were about to graduate from high school.

Miami is the main entry and settlement area for immigrants from Cuba, Nicaragua, Haiti, and other Caribbean and South American countries. San Diego is a primary destination for migrants from Mexico, El Salvador, the Philippines and Southeast Asia. Despite this diversity, the patterns of language assimilation were uniform. At the time of the first survey, 94 percent of respondents spoke English fluently by the age of 14, and the figure rose to 98 percent three years later. The overwhelming majority not only knew but preferred English, with 72 percent preferring English over their native tongue in middle school and 88 percent preferring it by senior high school. Remarkably, more than 95 percent of Cuban-American children attending private bilingual schools in the heart of the Cuban enclave in Miami preferred English.

LOSING MOTHER TONGUES

Relatively few retained their parental tongues. If one defines fluency as the ability to speak, understand, read, and write well, no second-generation group was fluent in its mother tongue by age 17. Less than one-third of the sample (29 percent) were able to communicate easily in both English and a foreign tongue. English-Spanish bilingualism was the most common, but most Latin-American children (65 percent) had lost fluency in their parental language. Among other nationalities, more than 90 percent of the children lacked native language fluency. Languages that literally disappeared in this second-generation sample included Chinese, French, Haitian Creole, Korean, Portuguese, Philippine Tagalog and Vietnamese. By age 17 on the average, the majority of these youths had become exclusively English-speaking.

IS COMPLETE LANGUAGE ASSIMILATION DESIRABLE?

These trends raise the question of whether complete language assimilation—acquisition of fluent English and abandonment of native languages—is desirable. There are good reasons for this concern.

Seventy years ago, the case for exclusive English speaking was buttressed by the scholarship of the time that considered migrant children's retention of their native language as a sign of intellectual inferiority. Madorah Smith, a prominent psychologist in the 1930s, declared bilingualism to be a hardship devoid of any advantage. In her view, echoed by most of her colleagues, "An important factor in the retardation of speech is the attempt to make use of two languages." The studies that supported this conclusion commonly paired poor immigrant children with middle-class native-born Americans. The studies also did not distinguish between fluent bilinguals and limited bilinguals whose command of one language or the other was poor.

BILINGUAL STUDENTS BETTER?

This perception started to change in the 1960s, with a study of French-Canadian children conducted by psychologists Elizabeth Peal and Wallace E. Lambert. They compared a sample of monolingual 10-year-old children with a group of fluent bilinguals matched by sex, age and family status. Contrary to the common wisdom of the time, this study found that bilinguals outperformed their monolingual counterparts in almost all cognitive tests. Similar results were subsequently obtained by other psychologists with any number of language combinations including English-French, English-Chinese, German-French and English-Spanish. The association of bilingualism with better cognitive development raised the question of cause and effect. Did brighter children perform better in school and retain their parental languages better, or did bilingualism itself produce enhanced cognitive performance?

In an attempt to shed light on this relationship, psychologists Kenji Hakuta and Rafael Diaz examined Puerto Rican students in New Haven, Connecticut. They discovered that bilingualism at an early age influenced subsequent cognitive development. Linguists contributed a series of studies that sought to clarify the nature of this relationship. According to Werner Leopold, bilinguals' enhanced cognitive performance is explained by their having more than one conception for a concrete thing, thus liberating them from the "tyranny of words." For another linguist, Jim Cummins, bilinguals are able "to look at language, rather than through it, to the intended meaning."

Although all of these studies were based on small samples, sociologists working with larger samples have reinforced these findings. For example, Rumbaut and Cornelius compared fluent bilingual students with limited bilinguals of the same national origin and with English monolinguals in the entire San Diego school system in the late 1980s. Without exception, fluent bilinguals outperformed limited bilinguals and English-only students in standardized tests and grade point averages, even after statistically controlling for parental status and other variables.

GREATER SELF-ESTEEM

More recently, our CILS study in south Florida and southern California confirmed the positive association between bilingualism and better academic performance. We also found that children who were fluent bilinguals in the early high school years had significantly higher educational aspirations and self-esteem three years later.

There are positive social aspects of bilingualism as well. Retaining the parental tongue allows children to better understand their cultural origins. This, in turn, reinforces their sense of self-worth. Bilingualism also increases communication between immigrant youths and their parents, reducing the generational conflicts commonly found in families in which parents remain foreign monolinguals and the children have shifted entirely to English. Family cohesion and open communication enable parents to better guide their children.

Family cohesion is also important for immigrant communities. Immigrant children—now numbering 13.8 million—already make up one-fifth of the American population under age 18. Their presence is even greater in those metropolitan areas where immigrants concentrate. Due to low average incomes, immigrants cluster in central city areas and their children attend neglected public schools. There they are exposed to behavior and role models that are not conducive to school achievement. Parental guidance and control are often the only counterweights to the lure of youth gangs and drugs. How many in this growing population will assimilate "downward" into the urban underclass or move upward into the middle-class mainstream largely depends on how much solidarity, guidance, and support their families can provide.

The importance of bilingualism is underlined by statistical analyses Lingxin Hao and I conducted on the CILS survey. Fluent bilinguals are more likely than English-only speakers who are similar to them in age, sex, national origin, time in the United States, and other factors to have greater solidarity and less conflict with their parents, as well as higher levels of self-esteem and ambition.

ENGLISH-PLUS

There is a final argument for an "English-plus" approach. Economic globalization and the expansion of the immigrant population in the United States have resulted in a growing labor market for skilled bilingual workers. This demand ranges from multinational corporations to government agencies to retail outlets. As Saskia Sassen has noted, New York and, to a lesser extent, other American metropolitan areas have become "global cities" with a primary economic function of coordinating and managing financial and information flows worldwide. The pressure of linguistic assimilation results in a growing shortage of bilingual and multilingual personnel, often in the very cities experiencing accelerated immigration. As a Miami business leader recently tellingly observed, "There are 600,000 Hispanics in this area and my firm has difficulty finding a bilingual person capable of writing a proper business letter in Spanish."

The individual and family advantages of fluent bilingualism combine with the growing requirements of the American labor market to make it preferable to either form of monolingualism. The question is whether school programs can be put in place to bring about this outcome or whether forces of assimilation will continue to prevail.

THE BILINGUAL EDUCATION DEBATE

In 1998, California voters approved by an overwhelming margin Proposition 227, the so-called English for the Children initiative. Its primary proponent, millionaire Ronald Unz, made this argument: "Inspired in part by the example of my own mother, who was born in Los Angeles into a Yiddish-speaking immigrant home but had quickly and easily learned English as a young child, I never understood why children were being kept for years in native-language classes, or why such programs continued to exist."

Unz was motivated to action by the spectacle of immigrant children confined, year after year, to inferior foreign language classes and unable to learn

English. He proposed instead to shift them to English-immersion classes following the model of his erstwhile Yiddish-speaking mother. In public school bureaucracies, bilingual education had come to mean remedial education in foreign languages that led to both inferior schooling and delayed learning of English. Not surprisingly, many immigrant parents lobbied in favor of Proposition 227 as a means to obtain proper education for their children.

The system against which Unz and his supporters rallied is not bilingual education at all, but a well-intentioned albeit misguided security blanket thrown at immigrant children. The terminological confusion of calling this "bilingual education" has clouded the issue in the public mind. True bilingual education for immigrant students involves vigorous instruction in English, along with deliberate efforts to preserve the parental tongue through teaching of selected topics in that language. For native English speakers, true bilingual instruction starts early, in grammar school if possible, and is followed by regular teaching of certain subjects in the chosen foreign language.

True bilingual education is currently practiced in only a handful of "dual language" schools, either private or public "magnet" units. These schools obtain remarkable results, both sustaining fluency in two languages among foreign students and creating it among native English speakers. Moreover, maintaining bilingual fluency in high school requires only one or two hours per day rather than half the total class time. In the CILS sample, the only group in which fluent bilinguals predominated were Cuban-American students attending private bilingual schools in Miami. These schools combine regular teaching of most subjects in English with one or two hours of daily instruction in Spanish.

In part as a result of the success of these schools, the U.S. Department of Education has called for a significant expansion of magnet language programs in public school systems across the country. In defense of this position, former secretary of education Richard W. Riley noted the sharp difference between American students, most of whom end up as English monolinguals, and European students, who commonly speak two or more languages fluently. Riley saw no reason why American children could not equal the linguistic accomplishments of their European peers. There is indeed no psychological reason why Riley's vision cannot be realized. The obstacles are rather social and political.

The strong assimilationist bent of American society, supported by the militant advocacy of nativist organizations, has rendered the preservation of foreign languages a near impossibility. Only in large ethnic enclaves, such as that of Cubans in Miami or in a few elite schools, have such efforts proven successful. Linguist Joshua Fishman has noted that Americans generally approve of foreign languages learned in Paris or in elite universities, but disapprove of immigrants' efforts to pass their languages on to their offspring. The implementation of this ideology by school systems across America has led to the present situation in which activists treat acquisition of English and preservation of foreign languages as a zero-sum game. Fluent bilingualism is a casualty. The result is a massive loss of a cultural resource that should be the birthright of immigrant children. Additional costs are added burdens in the upbringing of these children and unnecessary shortages of fluent multilingual workers. English-only is winning, but its costs are high for immigrant families, the communities where they settle, and society as a whole.

RECOMMENDED RESOURCES

Fishman, Joshua A. *Language Loyalty in the United States.* The Hague: Mouton, 1966.

Hakuta, Kenji. *Mirror of Language: The Debate on Bilingualism.* New York: Basic Books, 1986.

Leopold, Werner F. *Speech Development of a Bilingual Child: A Linguist's Record.* New York: AMS Press, 1970.

Lieberson, Stanley, Guy Dalto, and Mary Ellen Johnston. "The Course of Mother Tongue Diversity in Nations." *American Journal of Sociology* 81 (July 1975): 34–61.

Mouw, Ted, and Yu Xie. "Bilingualism and the Academic Achievement of First- and Second-Generation Asian-Americans." *American Sociological Review* 64 (April 1999): 232–52.

Peal, Elizabeth, and Wallace E. Lambert. *The Relation of Bilingualism to Intelligence.* Washington, D.C.: American Psychological Association, 1962.

Portes, Alejandro, and Lingxin Hao. "E Pluribus Unum: Bilingualism and Loss of Language in the Second Generation." *Sociology of Education* 71 (October 1998): 269–94.

Rumbaut, Rubén G., and Wayne A. Cornelius. *California's Immigrant Children: Theory, Research, and Implications for Educational Policy.* La Jolla, Calif.: Center for U.S.-Mexican Studies, University of California, San Diego, 1995.

14

▼▼▼▼▼▼▼

What About the Boys?*

Michael Kimmel

You've probably heard there's a "war against boys" in America. The latest book of that title by Christina Hoff Sommers claims that men are now the second sex and that boys—not girls—are the ones who are in serious trouble, the "victims" of "misguided" feminist efforts to protect and promote girls' development. At the same time, best-selling books like William Pollack's *Real Boys* and Dan Kindlon and Michael Thompson's *Raising Cain* sound the same tocsin. Writing from the therapists' point of view, they warn of alarming levels of depression and suicide, and describe boys' interior lives as an emotionally barren landscape, with all affect suppressed beneath postures of false bravado. They counsel anguished parents to "rescue" or "protect" boys—not from feminists, but from a definition of masculinity that is harmful not just to boys, but to girls and other living things.

In part, both sides are right. There *is* a crisis among boys. But the discussion in the popular media misdiagnoses the cause of the crisis. Consequently their proposed reforms would make it even harder for young boys to negotiate the difficult path to a manhood of integrity, ethical commitment, and compassion. At least the therapists get that part right. But in part, both sides are also wrong, because on most measures boys—at least the middle class white boys everyone seems concerned about—are doing just fine, taking their places in an unequal society to which they have always felt entitled. However, the unchecked crisis among boys has real consequences for all of us.

The current empirical discussion about where the boys are and what they are doing encompasses three phenomena—numbers, achievement, and behavior. These three themes frame the political debate about boys as well. The prevalent data on boys seem to suggest that there are fewer and fewer boys in school compared to girls, that they are getting poorer grades, and that they are having increasing numbers of behavioral problems. We hear about boys failing at school, where their behavior is increasingly seen as a problem. We read that boys are depressed, suicidal, emotionally shut down. Therapists caution parents about boys' fragility, warn of their hidden despondency and depression, and issue stern advice about the dire consequences if we don't watch our collective cultural step. According to these critics, the salutary effects of paying attention to girls have been offset by increasing problems related to boys. It was feminists, we are told, who pitted girls against boys. Though we hear an awful lot about *males*, we hear very little about *masculinity*, about what that biological condition actually means. Addressing the issue of masculinity will, I believe, enable us to resolve many of these debates, and move forward in a constructive way to create equity in our schools for boys as well as girls.

WHAT DO BOYS NEED?

Introducing the concept of masculinity into the discussion addresses several of the problems associated with the "what about the boys?" debate. For one thing it enables us to explore the ways in which class and race complicate the picture of boys' achievement and behaviors. For another, it reveals that boys and girls are on the same side in this struggle, not pitted against each other. Further, challenging those stereotypes, decreasing tolerance for school violence and bullying, and increasing attention to violence at home actually enables both girls and boys to feel safer at school.[1]

For example, when Thompson and Kindlon describe the treatment that *boys* need, they are really describing what *children* need. Adolescent boys, they inform us, want to be loved, have sex, and not be hurt.[2] Thompson and Kindlon counsel parents to use the following guidelines for their sons: allow them to indulge their emotions; accept a high level of physical activity; speak their language and treat them with respect; teach that empathy is courage; use discipline to guide and build; model manhood as emotionally attached; and teach the many ways in which a boy can be a man.[3] It becomes clear that what they advocate is exactly what feminist women have been advocating for girls for some time.

Focusing on masculinity allows us to understand what is happening to boys in school. Consider again the parallel for girls. Carol Gilligan's astonishing and often moving work on adolescent girls describes the extent to which assertive, confident, and proud young girls "lose their voices" when they hit adolescence. At the same moment, William Pollack notes, boys become *more* confident, even beyond their abilities. One might even say that boys *find* their voices during adolescence, but they are the inauthentic voices of bravado, constant posturing, foolish risk-taking, and gratuitous violence. The "boy code" teaches them that they are supposed to be in power, and thus they begin to act as if they are. They "ruffle in a manly pose," as William Butler Yeats once put it, "for all their timid heart."

What's the cause of all this posturing and posing? It's not testosterone, but privilege. In adolescence both boys and girls get their first real dose of gender inequality: girls suppress ambition, boys inflate it. Recent research on the gender gap in school achievement bears this out. Girls are more likely to undervalue their abilities, especially in the more traditionally "masculine" subjects of math and science. Only the ablest and most secure girls take such courses. Thus, their numbers tend to be few, and their grades high. Boys, however, possessed of this false voice of bravado and often facing strong family pressure are correspondingly likely to *overvalue* their abilities and, unlike girls, to remain in programs in which they are less qualified and less able to succeed. Consequently, their grades and other assessment scores may be negatively affected.

This difference, not some putative discrimination against boys, accounts for the fact that girls' mean test scores in math and science are now approaching those of boys. Too many boys who overvalue their abilities remain in difficult math and science courses longer than they should, thus pulling the boys' mean scores down. By contrast, the few girls whose abilities and self-esteem are sufficient to enable them to "trespass" into a male domain skew female data upwards.

A parallel process is at work in the humanities and social sciences. Girls' mean test scores in English and foreign languages, for example, also outpace those of boys. Again, this disparity emerges not as the result of "reverse discrimination" but because the boys bump up against the norms of masculinity. Boys regard English as a "feminine" subject. Pioneering research in Australia by Wayne Martino found that boys are uninterested in English because such an interest might call into question their (inauthentic) masculine pose. "Reading is lame, sitting down and looking at words is pathetic," commented one boy. "Most guys who like English are faggots." The traditional liberal arts curriculum is seen as feminizing; as Catherine Stimpson recently put it sarcastically, "real men don't speak French."

Boys tend to hate English and foreign languages for the same reasons that girls love them. In English, they observe, there are no hard and fast rules; rather, students express their opinion about the topic, and everyone's opinion is equally valued. "The answer can be a variety of things, you're never really wrong," observed one boy. "It's not like math and science where there is one set answer to everything." Another boy noted:

> I find English hard. It's because there are no set rules for reading texts. . . . English isn't like math where you have rules on how to do things and where there are right and wrong answers. In English you have to write down how you feel and that's what I don't like.[4]

Compare this with the comments of a girl in the same study:

> I feel motivated to study English because . . . you have freedom in English—unlike subjects such as math and science—and your view isn't necessarily wrong. There is no definite right or wrong answer and you have the freedom to say what you feel is right without it being rejected as a wrong answer.[5]

It is not the school experience that "feminizes" boys, but rather the ideology of traditional masculinity that keeps boys from wanting to succeed. "The work you do here is girls' work," one boy commented to a researcher.[6] "It's not real work."

CULTURAL EXPECTATIONS FOR BOYS

Some of the recent books for boys do accept the notion that masculinity—not feminism, not testosterone, not fatherlessness, and not the teaching of evolution—is the key to understanding boyhood and its current crisis. Thompson and Kindlon, for example, write that male peers present a young boy with a "culture of cruelty"[7] in which they force him to deny emotional neediness, "routinely disguise his feelings," and thus end up feeling emotionally isolated. Therapist William Pollack calls it the "boy code" and the "mask of masculinity"—a kind of swaggering posture that boys embrace to hide their fears, suppress dependency and vulnerability, and present a stoic, impervious front.

What is that "boy code"? Twenty-five years ago, psychologist Robert Brannon described the four basic rules of manhood.[8]

1. **No sissy stuff.** Masculinity is the repudiation of the feminine.
2. **Be a big wheel.** Masculinity is measured by wealth, power, and status.
3. **Be a sturdy oak.** Masculinity requires emotional imperviousness.
4. **Give 'em hell.** Masculinity requires daring, aggression, and risk-taking in our society.

Different groups of men—based on class, race, ethnicity, sexuality—express these four rules in different ways. There are as sizable, in fact greater, distinctions among different groups of men as there are differences between women and men. What it means to be 71-year-old black, gay man in Cleveland is probably radically different from what it means to be a 17-year-old white, heterosexual boy in Iowa.

Despite biology and the traditional cliché "boys will be boys," there's plenty of evidence that boys will not necessarily be boys everywhere in the same way. Few other Western nations would boast of violent, homophobic, and misogynist adolescent males and excuse them by virtue of this expression. If it's all so biological, why are European boys so different? Are they not boys?

We therefore should not speak of masculinity in the singular, but of *masculinities*, in recognition of the different definitions of manhood that we construct. By pluralizing the term, we acknowledge that masculinity means different things to different groups of men at different times.

But at the same time, we can't forget that all masculinities are not created equal. All American men must also contend with a singular vision of masculinity, a particular definition that is held up as the model against which we all measure ourselves. What it means to be a man in our culture is defined in opposition to a set of "others"—racial minorities, sexual minorities, and above all women. The sociologist Erving Goffman once wrote:

> In an important sense there is only one complete unblushing male in America: a young, married, white, urban, northern, heterosexual, Protestant, father, of college education, fully employed, of good complexion, weight, and height, and a recent record in sports. . . . Any male who fails to qualify in any one of these ways is likely to view himself—during moments at least—as unworthy, incomplete, and inferior.

I think it's crucial to listen to those last few words. When we don't feel we measure up or, more accurately, when we feel that we do not measure up—we are likely to feel unworthy, incomplete, and inferior. It is, I believe, from this place of unworthiness, incompleteness, and inferiority that boys begin their efforts to prove themselves as men. And the ways in which they do it—based on misinformation and disinformation—cause problems for both girls and boys in school.

Underlying many of these anti-feminist complaints may be the most depressing and widespread assumption that "boys will be boys." This accompanies a defeatist posture, a hopeless resignation: boys are this way and will not change. And the way these boys "are" is violent, predatory beasts; uncaged, uncivilized animals.

Personally I find such images insulting; yes, I'd even use the term "male bashing." And when we assume that the propensity for violence is innate, the inevitable fruit of that testosterone cocktail determined in utero, that only begs the question. We must still decide whether to organize society so as to maximize boys' "natural" predisposition toward violence or to minimize it. Biology alone cannot support the claim that boys will be boys, and by helplessly shrugging our collective shoulders, we abrogate our social responsibility.

Besides, one wants to ask, which biology are we talking about? Therapist Michael Gurian demands that we accept boys' "hard wiring," which, he informs us, is competitive and aggressive: "Aggression and physical risk taking are hard wired into a boy."[9] Gurian claims to like a kind of feminism that "is not anti-male, accepts that boys are who they are, and chooses to love them rather than change their hard wiring."[10]

That's too impoverished a view of feminism—and of boys—for my taste. Simply accepting boys and this highly selective definition of their hard-wiring demands far too little of us. Feminism specifically asks us *not* to accept those behaviors that are hurtful to boys, girls, and their environment—because we can do better than this part of our hard-wiring might dictate. We are also, after all, hard-wired toward compassion, nurturing, and love, aren't we?

I'm reminded of a line from Kate Millett's pathbreaking book, *Sexual Politics*, published 30 years ago:

> Perhaps nothing is so depressing an index of the inhumanity of the male supremacist mentality as the fact that the more genial human traits are assigned to the underclass: affection, response to sympathy, kindness, cheerfulness.

The question, to my mind, is not whether or not males are hard-wired, but rather which hard-wiring elements we choose to honor as a society, and which we choose to challenge. In this way we can further expand the opportunities for boys by removing the limitations imposed by traditional masculinity standards. We can also make school a safer place for all students to learn to the best of their abilities.

NOTES

1. S. McGee Bailey and P. B. Campbell, "The Gender Wars in Education" in WCW *Research Report*, 1999/2(X)O.
2. D. Thompson and M. Kindlon, *Raising Cain: Protecting the Emotional Life of Boys* (New York: Ballantine Books: 1999) pp. 195–6.
3. Thompson and Kindlon, pp. 241–256.
4. W. Martino, "Gendered Learning Practices: Exploring the Costs of Hegemonic Masculinity for Girls and Boys in Schools" in *Gender Equity: A Framework for Australian Schools* (Canberra: Ministerial Council on Education, Employment, Training, and Youth Affairs, 1997) p. 133.
5. Martino, 1997, p. 134.

6. M. Mac an Ghaill, *The Making of Men: Masculinities, Sexualities, and Schooling* (London: Open University Press, 1994) p. 59.

7. M. Thompson and D. Kindlon, p. 89.

8. R. Brannon and D. David, eds., *The Forty-Nine Percent Majority* (Reading: Addison Wesley, 1976).

9. M. Gurian, *The Wonder of Boys* (New York: Tarcher/Putnam, 1996) p. 53.

10. M. Gurian, p. 53–4.

15

▼▼▼▼▼▼▼

Race and the Achievement Gap*

Harold Berlak

That there is a race gap in educational achievement is not news. Large numbers of the nation's children leave school, with and without high school diplomas, barely able to read, write, and do simple math. But the failures of the schools are not evenly distributed. They fall disproportionately on students of color.[1]

Even when parents' income and wealth is comparable, African-Americans, Native Americans, Latinos, and immigrants for whom English is not a first language lag behind English-speaking, native born, white students. The evidence for the gap has been documented repeatedly by the usual measures. These include drop-out rates, relative numbers of students who take the advanced placement examination, who are enrolled in the top academic and "gifted" classes and/or admitted to higher-status secondary schools, colleges, graduate and professional programs. And last but certainly not least are the discrepancies in scores on standardized tests of academic achievement, on which teachers' and students' fate so heavily depend.

How is this achievement gap to be explained? This essay focuses first on the general question and then separately on the statistical gap in standardized test scores. It then discusses the crucial distinction between academic performance and academic achievement as measured by standardized tests. Though often spoken of as though they are one, they are clearly different.

The failure to separate out the difference clouds and confounds educational and policy issues and misleads us in efforts to explain and eradicate the race gap in academic performance.

EXPLANATIONS OVER THE YEARS

Over the years, the major reasons given for the claimed superior attainments of whites in cultural, artistic, and academic endeavors were overtly racist. It was said that the explanation lay in the superior genes of white northern European, Anglo-Americans. As the social sciences developed in the latter years of the 19th and the 20th centuries, "scientific" tracts defending white supremacy appeared with regularity. By the 1930s, the eugenics movement (which posited a biological basis for the superiority of whites) managed to gain a foothold in North American universities. And, it is relevant to add, all the leaders of this overtly racist movement were the leaders of the newly emerging field of scientific mental measurement. Many were the same men who testified before Congress in the early 1920s and lent scientific credence to the racist immigration exclusion acts which barred or greatly restricted immigration from Asia, Latin America, and southern and eastern Europe. The eugenics movement was considered a respectable academic discipline until it was discredited following the defeat of the Third Reich and the immensity of the crimes committed in the name of Nordic racial purity.[2]

In 1969, the scientific case for racism was revived by an article published in the *Harvard Educational Review* by University of California-Berkeley education professor Arthur Jensen. Based on his statistical analysis of I.Q. test scores, he concluded that African Americans were genetically inferior to whites in general intelligence. His racist thesis was widely disseminated and discussed in the popular press and in respectable academic and policy circles. In time, Jensen's conclusions were thoroughly discredited by a spate of books and articles.[3] In 1994, once again using standardized test data, Charles Murray and Richard Hernstein in *The Bell Curve* claimed to have proven that the inferior place of black and brown people in the social, political, and economic order was rooted in biology. The arguments for the genetic superiority of the white race were again dismembered and discredited by many geneticists and biologists.[4]

Recently a more subtle form of "scientific" racism has gained some respectability. The inferiority of the Black and brown races is now said to lie not necessarily in genetics but in culture and history. This more quietly spoken academic version of the master-race ideology has also been thoroughly dismantled, yet racist explanations for the race gap persist.[5]

Once all "scientific" arguments supporting racism are dismissed how is the ever-present gap in academic school performance to be explained? Numerous social and behavioral scientists have addressed this question.

A statistical study by Professor Samuel Meyers Jr. at the Roy Wilkins Center for Human Relations and Social Justice at the University of Minnesota sought to determine whether poverty was a primary cause of the poor performance of Black students on the Minnesota Basic Standards Test.[6] Passing this test was scheduled to become a prerequisite for a high school diploma in 2000. In a 1996 trial run in Minneapolis, 75 percent of African-American students failed the math test, and 79 percent failed in reading, compared to 26 percent and 42 percent, respectively, for whites.

The researchers found that, contrary to expectations, test scores were *not* statistically related to school poverty, neighborhood poverty, racial concentration, or even ranking of schools (except in the case of whites). They did find that African Americans, American Indians, and Hispanics were underrepresented in the top ranked schools.[7] African-Americans were 4.5 times as likely to be found in schools ranked low in math and twice as likely to be found in schools ranked lowest in reading.

For both white and students of color, success on the tests was positively correlated to how an individual had been tracked. Only 6.9 percent of students of color compared to 23 percent of white students had access to "gifted and talented" programs. This study suggests that tracking and the quality of the academic opportunities available in the school affects both the test score gap and the gap in academic performance generally. While these correlational studies are suggestive, they do not examine basic causes nor explain the pervasiveness and stability of the gap over prolonged periods of time.

A set of experimental studies conducted by Stanford University professor Claude Steele, an African-American psychologist, sought to explain the circumstances and situations that give rise to the race gap in test scores.[8] He and colleagues gave equal numbers of African-American and white Stanford sophomores a 30-minute standardized test composed of some of the more challenging items from the advanced Graduate Record Examination in literature. Steele notes all the students were highly successful students and test-takers since all Stanford students must earn SAT scores well above the national average in order to be admitted to the university.

The researchers told half the students that the test did not assess ability, but that the research was aimed at "understanding the psychological factors involved in solving verbal problems." The others were told that the test was a valid measure of academic ability and capacity. African-American students who were told that the test was a true measure of ability scored significantly lower than the white students. The other African-American students' scores were equal to white students'. Whites performed the same in both situations.

The explanation Steele offers is that Black students know they are especially likely to be seen as having limited ability. Groups not stereotyped in this way do not experience this extra intimidation. He suggests that "it is serious intimidation, implying as it does that if they should perform badly, they

may not belong in walks of life where their tested abilities are important—
walks of life in which they are heavily invested." He labels this phenomenon
"stereotype vulnerability."

In another study, Steele and colleagues found, to their surprise, that students most likely to do poorest on the tests were not the least able and prepared academically. To the contrary, they tended to be among the more
highly motivated and academically focused.

While Steele's research provides a plausible psychological explanation for
the gap, it does not probe the historical, social, and cultural factors that have
created and continue to sustain these stereotypes. We are left with no explanation of how "stereotype vulnerability" is created by and also shapes everyday life in society and at school.

The previously cited studies focus on the gap in standardized test scores.
The next study cited is one of a large number of recent "qualitative" studies—
observational, historical, and ethnographic studies—that illuminate relationships of culture, gender, and race to the social relations within the classroom
and school.[9]

Signithia Fordham, an African-American anthropologist, studied a
Washington, D.C., public high school and focused on how the "hidden" and
explicit curriculum shapes student aspirations and achievements, and how
students of differing cultural, racial, and social backgrounds respond to the
schooling experience.[10] Hers is a multifaceted, complex study, including inter-
views, participant observation, questionnaires, and field notes gathered over
a 4-year period. She concludes that for African-American students, patterns
of academic success and underachievement are a reflection of processes of resistance that enable them to maintain their humanness in the face of a stigma-
tized racial identity. She shows that African-American adolescents' profound
ambivalence about the value and possibility of school success is manifest as
both conformity and avoidance. Ambivalence is manifest in students' motivation and interest in schoolwork, which of course includes mastery of standardized test-taking skills. The following two quotes are taken from inter-
views with two African-American men. The first is from a young lawyer
employed in a Washington D.C. firm who had been a National Merit finalist
and whose test scores were among the top 2% in his state.

Commenting on why he was disappointed with his career, he observed: "I
realized that no matter how smart I was [in school] or how hard I was willing
to work [in the law firm] that it wasn't going to happen for me. . . . Don't get
me wrong, integration has been great for my life. Without it, I would be playing on a much more restrictive field, [but] there's no doubt in my mind that I
would be much more successful today if I were white."

A high-performing, African-American high school student offers the following view of why African Americans often underperform in school, and
also expresses his doubts that his own school success will be rewarded.

"Well, we supposed to be stupid . . . we perform poorly in school 'cause we all have it thought it up in our heads we're supposed to be dumb so we might as well go ahead and *be* dumb," he said. "And we think that most of the things we learn [at school] won't help us in life anyway. . . . What good is a quadratic equation gonna do me if I'm picking up garbage cans?"

Fordham found that even the most academically talented African-American high school students expressed profound ambivalence toward schooling and uncertainty that they will reap the rewards of school success. Virtually all African Americans she interviewed indicated that a central problem facing them at school and in larger white society is the widely held perception by whites that African-Americans are less able and intelligent and their continuing need to confront and deal with this reality in everyday experience.

These three studies taken together suggest three related explanations for the race gap in academic achievement and in test scores. First, is students' perceptions of the opportunities in the wider society and the realities of "making it." Second, are the educational opportunities available in the educational system itself—within school districts, schools, and within each classroom. Third, are the cumulative psychic and emotional effects of living in a social world saturated with racist ideology, and where racist practices and structures are pervasive and often go unnamed.

GAP IN TEST SCORES

There has been long-standing concern over the race gap in test scores. What is almost always overlooked is the size and educational significance of the test score gap. Most people assume that the statistical gap in scores between persons of color and whites is enormous. It is not. Depending on the test the difference varies but hovers in the range of 10%.[11] This difference in average scores has persisted over time, regardless of the type of test, whether it is an "IQ" test norm-referenced or proficiency test, regardless of a test's publisher, or educational level of the test-taker, be it kindergarten or graduate school.[12]

Figure 15.1 illustrates graphically an 8% difference in California's CBEST, a standardized test of basic literacy required of principals, teachers, and virtually any adult who works professionally with children in school. It is first important to note that the distributions of scores are highly overlapping. In practical terms, the difference gap amounts to a mere handful of test items. In Fig. 15.1, the gap is an average of 3.2 multiple-choice test item on a fifty-item multiple-choice test.[13] (The number will vary according to the number of items on the test.) From an educational point of view, such differences have little if any significance. Because of the way the tests are normed and cut scores set, however, minor differences in the number of correct answers on a multiple-choice test create grossly inflated failure rates for persons of color. On CBEST (see Fig. 15.2), for example, African-American test-takers are 3.5

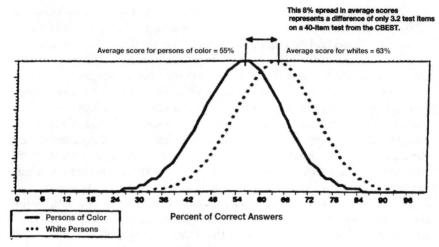

FIG. 15.1.   Difference of scores on CBEST.

times more likely to fail the test than whites, Latino/Hispanics more than twice as likely, and Asian Americans more than 1.5 times as likely to fail than whites (see Fig. 15.2).[14]

Numerous researchers have carefully documented the highly disproportionate adverse impact on students of color of standardized achievement testing.[15] An argument might be made that these differences in test scores, while small, nevertheless represent real differences in performance, and that tests, though imperfect, eliminate those most likely to perform poorly at school or on the job. Steele's study suggests the opposite—that the more talented students are at greater risk of failure. There is no evidence to support the claim that standardized tests are valid and credible measures of academic achievement or intellectual capacity. Further, there is no demonstrable connection between observed academic performance and standardized test scores. Test scores do not predict future success in school, the university, or in the workplace. Some standardized tests, the SAT for example, do correlate statistically to future grades. But this correlation is short lived.[16] What standardized achievement tests appear to predict best are parents' wealth and scores on other similarly constructed tests. As reported by Peter Sacks, socio-economic class accounts for approximately 50% of the variance in SAT test scores. He

	Number eliminated	percent failing
African Americans	11,200	63.0
Latinos	15,600	50.6
Asians	23,800	47.0
Whites	125,900	19.7

FIG. 15.2.   Number and percentages of first-time failures on CBEST 1985–95.

estimates that for every additional $10,000 in family income, a person on average gains 30 points on the SAT.[17]

Among the more commonly heard explanations for the gap in standardized test scores is that the tests themselves are culturally and racially biased. What this has usually been taken to mean is that the bias is lodged in the content or language of individual test items. In the early years of mental measurement, the racism of the test items was often blatant. In more recent years, major test publishers have made efforts to review and eliminate items with overt cultural and racial bias. Though item bias remains, it is implausible to conclude that all the publishers in all their tests knowingly or unknowingly managed to create tests with an almost identical ratio of biased to unbiased items. The fact that scores on all commercially produced tests show the same eight to ten percent gap suggests that the gap cannot be fully explained by racial or cultural bias lodged in individual test items. Rather, the bias is *systemic* and *structural*—that is, built into the basic assumptions and technology of standardized testing in the way the tests are constructed and administered, the way results are reported, and in the organizational structure and administrative rules of the accountability system itself.

There is perhaps no clearer illustration of how the differences among the races are greatly exaggerated and distorted than the numerical scales used to report results. There is, as I have noted, about a 10 percent difference in scores between white and nonwhite students. On a 100 point scale, this 10 percent difference constitutes a gap of ten points. However, California's Academic Performance Index or API (which is based entirely on students' scores on the Stanford 9 Achievement Test) creates a 200 to 1000 point scale, and a 10 percent difference in scores morphs into a formidable 100 points. The SAT, the most commonly used test for college admissions, and also frequently used (inappropriately) to rank states' academic performance, creates a 400 to 1600 point scale. On this scale, a ten percent difference is transformed to a 120 point chasm.

A major goal of social reformers of the 20th century was the elimination of legalized segregation. We still live in a society that is separate and unequal. To achieve social and economic justice, the goal for the 21st century must become the elimination of institutionalized racism in all sectors of social, economic, cultural, and political life—in business, housing, employment, law enforcement, the courts, health-care institutions, and, of course, schools. What makes institutionalized racism so pernicious and difficult to eradicate is that racist practices are often invisible because they are accepted as standard operating procedures within our institutions.

Standardized tests are a particularly invidious form of institutionalized racism because they lend the cloak of science to policies that have denied, and are continuing to deny, persons of color equal access to educational and job opportunities. An educational accountability system based on standardized testing though predicated on "standardized" measurements which are purportedly neutral, objective, and color-blind, perpetuates and strengthens institutionalized racism.

NOTES

1. *Still Separate, Still Unequal, A Research Brief*. Oakland, CA: Applied Research Center, May, 2000. www.arc.org.

2. See Stephen Selden *Inheriting Shame: The Story of Eugenics in America*. New York: Teachers College Press, 1999.

3. Steven J. Gould, "Jensen's Last Stand," *New York Review of Books*, 1980; Leon J. Kamin, *The Science and Politics of IQ*. New York 1974; Daniel M. Kohl, "The IQ Game: Bait and Switch," *School Review* 84:44 1976, John Wiley.

4. Russell Jacoby and Naomi Glauberman (eds.) *The Bell Curve Debate*. New York: NY Times Books/Random House, 1995.

5. Cultural supremacy arguments are dismantled in Jared Diamond, *Guns, Germs and Steel*. New York: Norton, 1997.

6. Samuel L. Myers Jr. and Cheryl Mandala *Is Poverty the Cause of Poor Performance of Black Students on Basic Standards Examination?* Roy Wilkins Center for Human Relations and Social Justice, Univ. of Minnesota. Paper presented at the 1998 American Educ. Research Assoc. Annual Meeting, June, 1997.

7. Schools were ranked in terms of resources, education and experience of staff, number, depth and range of academic course offerings.

8. Claude M. Steele, "A threat in the air: How stereotypes shape the intellectual identities," *American Psychologist*, 52, 1997. Also see "Stereotyping and its threat are real," *American Psychologist*, 53, 1998.

9. These include Lisa Delpit (1995) *Other People's Children*. New York: The New Press; Joyce E. King (1996), "The Purpose of Schooling for African American Students," In J. King, E. Hollins and W. C. Hayman eds. *Preparing Teachers for Cultural Diversity*. New York: Teachers College Press; Gloria Ladson Billings (1999) *The Dream Keepers Successful Teachers of African-American Children*. San Francisco: Jossey-Bass; Ann Berlak and Sekani Moyenda (2001) *Taking it Personally: Racism in Schools*. Philadelphia: Temple Univ. Press.

10. Fordham, Signithia (1996) *Blacked Out, Dilemmas of Race, Identity, and Success at Capital High*. Chicago: University of Chicago Press.

11. Most of the data are from court records in Civil Rights challenges to standardized tests. See Walter Haney, George Madaus, and Amelia Keritzer *Charms Talismanic: Testing Teachers for the Improvement of American Education*, Review of Educational Research 14, 1987.

12. See Robert Linn "Assessments and Accountability," *Educational Researcher* 29:2 2000. He cites data from the Florida high school competency test, given annually since 1977 to illustrate a common pattern. When first a test is introduced, scores rise markedly for several years for whites and persons of color, level off, and over time decline slightly. However, the gap in test performance between the races remains virtually constant over time.

13. In CBEST, 10 of the 50 items on the math and language section are not scored. They are used in creating items for a future version of CBEST. Eight percent of 40 items equals 3.2 items.

14. On some tests, particularly in mathematics and engineering, some Asian populations outperform whites.

15. These include: Linda McNeil *Contradictions of School Reform; The Educational Costs of Standardized Testing*. New York: Routledge, 2000; George F. Madaus, "A Technological

and Historical Consideration of Equity Issues Associated with Proposals to Change the Nation's Testing Policy," *Harvard Educational Review*, 64:1, 1994; Diana C. Pullin, "Learning to Work: The Impact of Curriculum and Assessment Standards on Educational Opportunity," *Harvard Educational Review*, 64:1, 1994.

16. Some achievement tests, the college entrance SAT for example, predict academic grades at the next level, but only in the very short run.

17. See Peter Sacks, *Standardized Minds*. Cambridge, MA: Perseus Books 2000. The concluding paragraph, slightly revised, is taken from Deborah Meier, "Educating a Democracy: Standards and the future of public education," *Boston Review*, Dec 1999/Jan 2000.

16

▼▼▼▼▼▼▼

What Matthew Shepard Would Tell Us: Gay and Lesbian Issues in Education*

Doug Risner

"We just don't have any gay kids in my school."
—High School Principal

Of the many provocative topics in my undergraduate social foundations of education course, no discussion brings more anger, tears, confusion, and hostility than our readings and discussion about gay and lesbian issues. Within a spiraling curriculum that interrogates race, social class, gender and their myriad intersections, gay and lesbian issues in educational policy and practice remain the most volatile in this class. Knowing such, I continue to experiment with different pedagogical approaches that focus not only on the roots of sexism, discrimination, bigotry, and hate, but also on the ways in which these students as future educators are ethically obligated to confront their own attitudes and beliefs about gays and lesbians in schools—their students, their students' parents or family members, their fellow teachers and administrators.

Current teacher training programs in higher education in the US focus upon discipline-specific competency classes and methods coursework, usually supplemented with one course in educational psychology and one in social/philosophical foundations of education. The vast majority of teacher preparation emphasizes *what* is to be taught and *how* (most efficiently) to teach it. Conversely, foundations courses emphasize for future teachers the *why* of democratic public education, for what purposes, in whose benefit, to what ends. And therefore, the course centralizes the aims of freedom, equality, human dignity, diversity, and social justice. Because students receive only one semester of such coursework, much needs to happen in a very short period of time.

For this reason, I use a multi-dimensional spiral progression, rather than a linear approach to social issues and their intersections with educational theory and practice. The helical structure of the spiral allows critical social problems of race, class, and gender to stand as a central pole, a cylinder around which the students' reflections and questions wind gradually, simultaneously receding from and drawing near, each time (hopefully) more informed. Advancing and retreating in a methodological coil enables students to see not only the interrelatedness and complexity of social constructions of privilege and marginality, but also to reflect upon their own place within these hierarchical structures that inevitably dominate and oppress.

CONFRONTING DIFFERENCE AND HATE

Having spent a good deal of class time on issues of sexism and gender inequity in education, we extrapolate more fully the prejudice and bias women experience in US culture and the ways in which dominant patriarchal structures and sexism often lead to homophobia. In order to begin discussion about bigotry and hate directed toward gay, lesbian, and bisexual people, as well as their contemporary manifestations in schools, I turn to the senseless and brutal death of college student, Matthew Shepard. I do so not so much for its horrific detail or its public notoriety, but because the tragedy moves us as educators to reconsider what our past educative efforts have accomplished and, more importantly, where we might necessarily position our labors in the present.

In 1998, Shepard, who was gay, died after being tied to a fence outside Laramie, Wyoming, where he was pistol-whipped, beaten, and then left for dead in the freezing night by his killers. What we can learn from Shepard's highly publicized death, we could most likely learn from any number of others who suffered viciously horrific murders because they were gay: Brandon Teena, raped and shot to death in 1993; Billy Jack Gaither, beaten and set on fire in 1999; Danny Overstreet, gunned down in 2000; JR Warren, gang-beaten and run over with a car in 2000; or Army Pfc. Barry Winchell, bludgeoned to death with a baseball bat while sleeping in 1999. I chose the Shepard case not because it was the most brutal or the most senseless, but rather because of its intense national reaction and what can be learned from such a response.

I do not focus on the evil consciousness responsible for Shepard's murder because frankly that kind of wickedness is beyond my comprehension, and also because attending to such trivializes the significance and power of education. While I in no way wish to diminish the inhumanity of these violent acts of cruelty, I do not dwell on such evil that I simply cannot understand or explain. However, if we look at Shepard's death and all that surrounds it, as a symptom of our larger cultural and educative failures and accomplishments, we are moved to respond, rather than to fall into despair. The national response to this hate-motivated murder teaches us many things about understanding difference. At the same time, the tragedy encapsulates for students the confusion and frustration that accompanies issues of sexual orientation in our culture and the divide this social dissonance deeply cuts in our society and schools.

Following Shepard's death, outrage was voiced throughout the US. Proclamations were made, petitions signed, vigils organized, memorials given, and hate crimes legislation demanded by those who found Shepard's death a needless and senseless atrocity. And at the same time, those in opposition to homosexuality responded with anti-gay protests—picketing rallies and memorial services across the country, posting Internet messages on websites such as godhatesfags.com. Anti-gay protesters at Shepard's funeral shouted epithets at mourners and carried signs reading "Fags Deserve Death" and "Matthew Shepard Burns in Hell." Some conservative religious leaders offered sympathy, but also used Shepard's death to warn their congregations of the "dangers" of homosexuality.

The cultural divide widened as attorneys for the two defendants in the case sought to argue what has become known as the "gay panic" defense, in which straights fearing unsolicited homosexual advances act out of self-defense. This strategy, one not dissimilar from "she asked for it" type defense tactics employed for alleged rapists, portrays the victim as provoking and inciting, as in the Shepard case, his own violently fatal attack.

Public debate often revolved around notions that Shepard brought the attack on himself or at best "should have known better." Conservative talk radio positioned Shepard's death to reaffirm gay rights as "special rights"—unnecessary and without merit. Although state lawmakers in Wyoming had rejected hate crimes measures four previous times since 1995, four months after Shepard was beaten to death, an emotionally charged move to pass a hate crimes bill was thought to surely be ratified; however, the Wyoming State Legislature defeated the measure in early 1999.

The social dissonance in the national response to Matthew Shepard's murder resolves some of our questions, but also gives rise to new ones. As a culture we have an intense sense of justice and solidarity, one that shows both collective support and respect for human life, and the impulse for "the good." While at the same time, the impulse for hate, opportunism, division, self-preservation, and blame (not to mention evil) flourishes in reciprocal fashion. It is within this profound confusion that we must begin to imagine things otherwise, radically different. Because it should be abundantly clear that as a society we are highly adept at simultaneously holding two highly contradictory narratives in our collective heads and hearts.

In tandem, the Shepard tragedy allows students to see the unrelenting power of a society that focuses heavily on difference and the pejorative categorization of such. Discrimination, in a consumer capitalist culture, directed toward those who are different or perceived to be different, develops because the ethical vision of the culture socializes citizens to view difference as a fearful threat, a menace people are obliged to compete with, to commodify, to divide and conquer. Understanding homophobia in this context reveals that these fears may on one level be more about difference and competition in a generic sense, rather than specifically about sexuality, or challenges to heterosexuality. This view of difference, its discrimination and homophobic attitude, is the product of a "where's Waldo?" enculturation process rooted in rigid categorization, emphasizing dissimilarity and hierarchy. Although seemingly benign, this discriminatory vision of the world is pervasively potent from a very young age. Elmo and his Sesame Street cohorts have taught us well to discern "which of these things is not like the other?" Given that the voice of Elmo is in reality that of a gay black male, this kind of socialization is especially incriminating.

DOMINANT CULTURE: HETEROSEXISM AND HOMOPHOBIA

Though undergraduate students sometimes comprehend the racist and sexist systems operating in US culture, they rarely and, I might add, then only reluctantly comprehend the heterosexist underpinnings and assumptions characteristic of the world in which they live. Although the murderers' motivation for Shepard's death facilitates deeper understanding of the ways in which anti-gay prejudice and heterosexist bias develop socially in the US, I still find it necessary to engage the students on an even more profound level, their own sexuality. To achieve this kind of engagement, I ask students to complete the following survey that I adapted from Martin Rochlin (1985).

Heterosexual Questionnaire

1. When and how did you first decide you were heterosexual?
2. What do you think caused your heterosexuality?

3. Is it possible that your heterosexuality is just a phase you may grow out of?

4. Is it possible that your heterosexuality stems from a neurotic fear of members of the same sex?

5. To whom have you disclosed your heterosexuality? How did they react?

6. The great majority of child molesters are heterosexuals (95%). Do you really consider it safe to expose your children to heterosexual teachers?

7. Why do heterosexuals place so much emphasis on sex?

8. If you've never slept with a person of the same sex, how do you know you wouldn't prefer that?

9. Does your employer know you are heterosexual? Are you openly heterosexual when with your family members? roommates? co-workers? church members?

10. With 50% of first-time heterosexual marriages ending in divorce, and over 60% of second heterosexual marriages also ending in divorce, there seem to be very few happy heterosexuals. Techniques have been developed to change your sexual orientation; have you considered aversion therapy to treat your heterosexuality?

Although students have a fair amount of difficulty answering many of the survey questions, their understanding of heterosexual bias and heterocentric assumptions that characterize the culture in which they live greatly expands in attempting the exercise. In order for future educators to understand the nature of this kind of marginalization, and gay issues more specifically, I find it helpful to outline the manner in which the dominant culture not only organizes political, social, and economic privilege for some, but also separates, discredits, and discriminates against others.

Simply put, when we refer to the dominant culture and its ideology we are referencing the assumptions, ideas, concepts, and values that prevail in the central ways in which we organize our lives. Although usually associated with the "taken-for-granted" socio-political realm, or more plainly, people and their relationship to power, dominant ideology powerfully colors societal opinion, behavior, and worldview. At the same time, the unquestioned nature of dominant culture allows a commanding control that unfortunately benefits some people at the expense of others, in this case at the cost of gays and lesbians.

Friend (1986) defines the systemic practice of valuing and privileging heterosexuality as superior over homosexuality as heterosexism. Heterosexist prejudice holds a bias in favor of heterosexual people and discrimination against bisexual and homosexual persons. Gay men and lesbians encounter discrimination, stigmatization, prejudice, and violence based upon their sexual orientation or perceived sexual orientation. Oppressed segments of the population often serve as falsely depicted stereotypes, unjustly ridiculed scapegoats, and blameworthy villains solely by virtue of their perceived cultural and social differences. As a system of domination and discrimination, pervasive heterosexism shapes the political, economic, social, religious, familial, and educational spheres in American culture. Jung and Smith (1993) contend that at the center of heterosexist prejudice is the organizing belief that heterosexuality is the normative form of human sexual relations. As such, the standard measurement used to evaluate and judge all other sexual orientations is defined as heterocentrism.

Homophobia, as first defined by sociologist Weinberg (1972), is the irrational fear and hatred of homosexuality, either in oneself or in others. A more expansive understanding of homophobia advances the definition to include disgust, anxiety, and anger directed toward homosexuality (MacDonald, 1976). Herek (1984) asserts that homophobia is frequently considered appropriate and utilitarian by individuals who possess it, inasmuch as homophobia is frequently a primary defining characteristic of contemporary masculinity in our culture. Boys learn from a very young age that there is no worse slur or taunt than being called a sissy, fag, or queer. What's more, young children who use these epithets rarely know what the words actually mean, other than their expressly pejorative connotations.

Though often precipitated by heterosexism, homophobia does not fundamentally or logically indicate a relationship between the two. Whereas heterosexism is similar to racism and sexism, homophobia is analogous to racial bigotry and misogyny. Without critical examination, fear and hatred of homosexuality often reproduces exponentially. In addition, pervasive homophobic prejudice, customarily associated with heterosexuals, negatively affects all persons, institutions, and cultures.

More specifically, homophobia and homophobic discrimination often emerge from the dominant cultural construction of heterocentrism, and therefore all persons, heterosexuals, gay men, lesbians, bisexuals, and transgendered persons to some degree and in various contexts, experience the hegemony (or unquestioned ruling power) of the heterocentrist center. Because heterocentrism 1) defines the ways in which people regard homosexuality, 2) frames routinely performed heterosexist biases, and 3) maintains a myriad of disparaging moral judgments about gay men and lesbians, the underpinnings of heterocentrism and heterosexual hegemony situate gays in the marginalized fringe.

While forms of resistance have and continue to challenge preponderant controlling ideas, such as the civil and human rights movements, feminism, environmental groups, and the gay and lesbian movement, the prevailing influence in American culture remains largely based on "white" masculine, heterosexual values and practices. Furthermore, the nexus among gender, power, and authority gives rise to subsequent inequities manifested in sexism, racism, and heterosexism. As such, dominant culture normalizes this narrow perspective as a widely held worldview and thereby carves its socially accepted center, subsequently situating or marginalizing "others" (women, racial minorities, gays) on the cultural fringe. Like sexism and racism, systems of heterosexism reinforce dominant ideological assumptions and messages that constitute the characterization of sexual minority groups.

A recent survey finds that nearly 70 percent of lesbian, gay, and bisexual students face verbal, sexual, or physical harassment or physical assault while at school (*Gay, Lesbian, Straight Education Network*, 2001), and nearly half of all gay and lesbian youth suffer violence from their families, peers, and strangers (Edwards, 1997). Unfortunately, many gay and lesbian students, unable to escape the pervasive nature of heterocentrism and homophobic prejudice in American culture and schools, internalize negative feelings about themselves (Gonsiorek, 1987). In its most recent study, the *American Journal of Public Health* finds that teenagers with same-sex attractions are twice as likely as their heterosexual counterparts to attempt suicide. Massachusetts Safe Schools Program for Gay & Lesbian Students has shown important statistical links between levels of student harassment experienced and attempted student suicide. According to the Human Rights Watch, a non-profit advocacy and research organization, millions of gay teenagers may be subjected to such widespread harassment and teacher indifference in US schools that they do not receive an adequate education.

Plotting the margin (gays, women, minorities) and center (straights, men, whites) in this manner allows students to address more thoroughly 1) the important links between sociocultural attitudes about homosexuality/homophobia and recurrent manifestations in educational practice and policy, and 2) each student's own relationship to and role in the dominant ideology of margin and center. Given the sobering assessment of current school climate, teacher indifference, and the tragic consequences that ensue for gay and lesbian youth, a fundamental shift in the way we view ourselves and our students, as difficult, controversial, and painful as it may be, is not only necessary, but obligatory given the highly problematic world in which we live and teach.

GAY AND LESBIAN YOUTH

Whether educators' work is rooted in K–12 instruction, school administration, higher education, research, counseling, or policy, it is absolutely crucial to realize that gay teens and young adults are in our schools and programs. As educators, our opportunities for making a better, more just world and eradicating hateful prejudice remains before us. To be sure, speaking openly with children about sexual orientation is perceived as problematic in the homophobic culture in which we find ourselves, although research shows that children and adolescents have far less difficulty accepting alternative family structures and sexual difference than might be supposed (Chasnoff and Cohen, 1996). A recent study of US high school seniors finds that 85 percent of seniors believe that gay men and lesbians should be accepted by society (Gilbert, 2001). Despite the apparent support for gay students, however, the survey found that US high schools remain a largely hostile environment for gay and lesbian youth. What is more, many parents, teachers, and administrators are frequently uncomfortable even in the limited discussions our culture currently presents. These obstacles, though certainly tangible and substantial, should not diminish or trivialize our deepest commitments and sincerest concerns for developing humanizing pedagogies that prioritize the safety and well-being of all students.

Regrettably, even when we are made aware of profound injustices and abuses, we frequently distance ourselves from the real dilemmas at hand—explaining away the necessary and ethically responsive action as someone else's problem—in someone else's classroom or school. For example, a high school principal, aware of my research interests, recently said to me, "we just don't have any gay kids in my school." Research, of course, strongly suggests that the principal's assessment of his student body is statistically impossible (Besner and Spungin, 1995). Common sense would indicate that although no students have publicly identified themselves as gay or lesbian, in all likelihood a school of 1000 pupils would have, by conservative estimates, a minimum of thirty non-heterosexual students. Other estimates might put the number of gay, lesbian, and bisexual teens in his school as high as 100. Unfortunately, this kind of dominant attitude assumes that discussion of sexual orientation has as its sole aim the support of gay and lesbian people only, without any benefit or interest to heterosexual persons. This perspective, which universalizes heterosexuality or, more simply, assumes that everyone is heterosexual, eliminates the need for discussion of gay issues, and in doing so also eliminates vast possibilities for greater understanding of sexuality and sexual difference, the reduction of prejudice, and the confrontation of bigotry and hate.

For those in K–12 environments, as well as those teaching and researching within academia, it is of utmost importance that we realize the significant impact that addressing sexual orientation issues in our own locales—our own classrooms, our faculty meetings, our communities, and through our authority positions as teachers and role models, can have. By not only acknowledging, but also acting upon the educative potential schools hold for reducing homophobia and anti-gay stigmatization, the profession has the ability to

play a profoundly important leadership role in re-shaping our culture's negative messages about difference and prejudice.

In particular, young boys' avoidance and denial of their homosexual orientation is facilitated by countless diversions perpetrated by a pervasively
heterocentric culture, especially when considering the overwhelmingly ridiculed status of sissy boys in American society. While there is vast individual
variation, young gay males tend to begin homosexual activity during early or
mid-adolescence; similar feelings and activity for lesbian females does not begin until around age twenty (Lipkin, 1994). For male K–12 educators—
straight, gay, or bisexual—this profound opportunity for confronting homophobia in middle and high schools seems particularly cogent, especially when
we take seriously the vulnerability of gay and bisexual male teens.

Because adolescents are only beginning to possess the capacity for abstract
thought and formal reasoning skills to cognitively integrate their sexual experiences, educators must realize that gay male adolescents are extremely vulnerable to gendered criticism, homophobic attitudes, anti-gay slurs, and the
absence of positive gay male role models. Young gay males may also suffer
from internalized homophobia learned throughout childhood in which self-
hate, low self-esteem, destructive behavior, and further confusion characterize their underlying attitudes and conduct. Moreover, gay adolescents and
teens often have far fewer resources available to them for understanding homosexuality and same-sex attraction in a balanced and unbiased manner. Social support networks for the young gay male are rare. What is more, the embarrassment, humiliation, and contempt of being labeled the pansy, the fag,
or the queer demand that he actively "prove" his heterosexuality over and
over again. This kind of environment is stressful and often threatening, particularly since these are young people struggling to claim and affirm their sexual orientation in a frequently hostile social atmosphere. Teachers, aware of
it or not, have a profound impact on this environment.

Certainly these issues are in no way limited to the education profession.
However, these concerns should compel each of us as teachers to ask ourselves about the choices we make consciously or unconsciously, the behaviors we tolerate or ignore, the [in]actions we take or avoid, and the world we
create by doing so—for what purposes, for what ends? Not talking honestly
and genuinely about sexual orientation, prejudice, and anti-gay violence
not only nurtures a suspicious cultural perspective of sexual difference, but
also makes matters worse by unnecessarily magnifying issues of sexual orientation more than is worthwhile or appropriate. Minimizing such in se-
crecy and denial energizes a deleterious and discriminatory homosexual mythology, one that is harmful to all in education. In order to make our
schools and our teaching more humane, let us instead confront sexual orientation pedagogically, mine the larger social ramifications more candidly,

and learn from our lessons more sincerely, as taught to us by Matthew Shepard's senseless death.

WHAT CAN EDUCATORS DO?

The approach I urge students to contemplate asks them not only to consider seriously their actions in the world, but also that they believe their actions do actually matter and, therefore, have the potential for making a more just and liberating world in the here and now. Although I in no way forecast a quick and painless end to our deeply rooted social problems, I attempt to communicate this approach with a fervent sense of support on one hand, but also with a profound sense of urgency on the other. From this renewed questioning and our response to such, we are compelled to commit ourselves to take action against these and other oppressive practices. There is much to be learned by questioning our own complicity with the domination and privilege of the white, middle class inner circle. The internal contradictions and dissonances we harbor, when attended to and pestered further, may be in actuality our utmost source of energy and hope.

Unfortunately, the enormity of our social ills all too often paralyzes our daily capability for considering and creating a better world. In undergraduate teacher training programs, courses in social foundations are particularly at risk for producing socially conscious yet deeply discouraged pre-service teachers—more fully aware, but equally as numb. It is essential that cultural workers in educational foundations not only help their students "describe the world, but to take a stand in shaping its construction" (Hytten 1998, 253). Given the extent of continued discrimination, bigotry, hate, and its violence, as well as the difficult nature of contemplating the need for such vast cultural change, I offer students some insights on how this kind of approach might sensibly unfold for themselves and their schools.

Invariably, the frustration that many of these future teachers experience by the middle of the semester is accompanied by a desperate need to know what specifically can be done to help gay, lesbian, and bisexual students/colleagues as the course draws to a close. Before offering the students some particular suggestions for confronting anti-gay prejudice and harassment in schools, I attempt to make clear that this overarching framework emerges from identifying one's intimate connection to the whole of these critical issues in education. Exhuming one's "taken for granted" assumptions about the world is often characterized by intense struggle, sometimes disheartening limitation, but always one of ethical obligation. Praxis—critical reflection and responsive action—requires that educators consider seriously their actions in the world and that they believe their actions in schools actually have the potential for making a more just and loving world in the here and now. Having said that, I recommend some concrete suggestions in this arduous, yet compelling task. I briefly present them here for further contemplation and informed action (Griffin 1995, 61–63).

Teachers can:

- Evaluate and monitor their own attitudes and actions about homo/heterosexuality. Stop behaviors that either encourage a prejudiced or hostile environment for gay and lesbian students, or condone any antigay actions by any student.
- Inventory their own heterosexist beliefs, assumptions, and actions that unnecessarily and unintentionally create an environment of shame, humiliation, or embarrassment for gay and lesbian students and teachers.
- Refrain from assuming that all students are heterosexual. Some probably are lesbian, gay, or bisexual. Others may be questioning their sexual identity.
- Realize the fact that learning about gays and lesbians does not cause young people to become gay, though it might encourage those who are struggling with their sexual identity to feel better about themselves. Present positive gay and lesbian role models.
- Use homophobic remarks in class and in after-school practices as "teachable moments."
- Understand the necessity of *age appropriate approaches* to sexual orientation and alternative lifestyles. View the award-winning documentary film, *It's Elementary*, for guidance.
- Be available and prepared to talk with students or other teachers who are (1) questioning their sexual orientation, or (2) expressing homophobic beliefs. Many closeted gays use homophobic slurs and antigay epithets to buttress an outwardly heterosexual persona.
- Identify and readily make available pertinent resources for students and parents who need them, such as Parents and Friends of Lesbians & Gays (PFLAG, www.pflag.org) and the Gay Straight Alliances (GSA), an extension of the Gay, Lesbian, Straight Education Network (GLSEN, www. glsen.org).
- Develop support networks with other teachers, parents, and administrators concerned about the well-being and safety of gay, lesbian, and bisexual students.
- Request that teachers' associations provide programs about homophobia and how to meet the needs of lesbian, gay, and bisexual students.
- Invite a guest, former student, counseling professional, or current faculty member who is gay or lesbian to speak about gay and lesbian issues for their students.
- Post informational items that address gay and lesbian issues in your classrooms. Display, in a place of visual prominence, the Pink Trian-

gle—universally associated with safe zones for gay, lesbian, and bisexual people.

- Understand more fully your authority and power as a positive role model for students and the respect you inherently garner from your students. Contemplate the fact that what you don't say is just as important as what you do.
- Challenge *Zero Tolerance* policies that do not address sexual orientation, anti-gay harassment, and hate-based violence in schools.
- (For gay, lesbian, and bisexual educators.) Try to be as open and candid as you safely can about who you are. All youth need to know gay adults who are leading satisfying, productive, and meaningful lives.
- (For heterosexual educators.) Give unwavering support for your gay and lesbian colleagues by speaking out against antigay attitudes, actions, and policies.

Encourage administrators to:

- Establish non-discrimination and anti-harassment policies that include sexual orientation. Ensure that all teachers, parents, and students understand what actions are unacceptable, and what procedures are to be followed when the policies are violated.
- Establish non-discrimination and anti-harassment policies in the local, regional, state, and national education organizations that govern educational programs.
- Provide teachers with anti-homophobia education and gay and lesbian issues programming focused on the needs of gay, lesbian, and bisexual students.
- Initiate and develop strategies for addressing homophobia among parents.
- Be open and forthright in their attitudes, behavior, and conduct that openly address the physical, mental, and spiritual safety and well-being of gay/lesbian, and bisexual teachers, staff, and students.

Encourage parents to:

- Know their child's school or university program—its teachers, administrators, department head, and faculty. Inquire about its policies on discrimination, harassment, and sexual orientation. Talk to other parents.
- Challenge their own prejudices and biases about gay, lesbian, and bisexual people, and evaluate how they condone or reaffirm antigay prejudice in their children.

- Understand that for adolescent boys and male teens, there is an especially great deal of social stigmatization and harassment for those who do not conform to cultural norms of masculinity. Explore the ways in which they support or discourage their son's interests and aptitudes, regardless of gender norms.
- Understand that a teacher's sexual orientation does not determine his or her ability to be an effective and respected professional.
- Contact a local chapter of Parents and Friends of Gays and Lesbians (PFLAG) if necessary for information and support.
- Contemplate the difficult and arduous struggle their child suffers and endures as a gay, lesbian, or bisexual person.
- Show sensitivity, caring, and support, regardless of their personal belief system, if their son or daughter comes out to them as a gay, lesbian, or bisexual. Remember that sexual orientation is a leading and contributing factor to teen depression, drop out rate, and suicide.

REFERENCES

Besner, F., & Spungin, C. (1995) *Gay & Lesbian Students: Understanding Their Needs.* Philadelphia: Taylor & Francis.

Chasnoff, D., & Cohen, H. (1996) *It's Elementary: Talking About Gay Issues in Schools.* Ho-ho-kus, NJ: New Day Films, 1996.

Edwards, A. (1997) Let's stop ignoring our gay and lesbian youth. *Educational Leadership,* April.

Friend, R. (1986) The individual and social psychology of aging: clinical implications for lesbians and gay men. *Journal of Homosexuality,* 14, 307–331.

Gay, Lesbian, Straight Education Network (GLSEN) (2001) Report of School Climate for Gays & Lesbians. www.glsen.org

Gilbert, D. (2001) *High school climate for gay youth survey.* Clinton, NY: Zogby International/ Hamilton College.

Gonsiorek, J. (1987) *Homosexuality and Psychotherapy: A Practitioner's Handbook of Affirmative Models.* New York: Haworth Press, Inc.

Griffin, P. (1995) Homophobia in sport: Addressing the needs of lesbian and gay high school athletes. In G. Unks (Ed.), *The Gay Teen: Educational Practice and Theory for Lesbian, Gay, and Bisexual Adolescents.* New York: Routledge. 53–66.

Herek, G. (1984) Beyond "homophobia": a social psychological perspective on attitudes towards lesbians and gay men. *Journal of Homosexuality,* 10, 1–21.

Hytten, K. (1998) The ethics of cultural studies. *Educational Studies,* 29(3), 247–265.

Jung, P., & Smith, R. (1993) *Heterosexism: An Ethical Challenge.* Albany, NY: State University of New York Press.

Lehne, G. (1976) Homophobia among men. In D. David & R. Brannon (Eds.), *The forty-nine percent majority: The male sex role,* pp. 66–88. Reading, MA: Addison-Wesley.

Lipkin, A. (1994) The case for a gay and lesbian curriculum. *The High School Journal,* 77, 1.

MacDonald, A. (1976) Homophobia: Its roots and meanings. *Homosexual Counseling Journal,* 3(1), 23–33.

Rochlin, M. (1985) The heterosexual questionnaire. In G. Back (Ed.), *Are You Still My Mother.* West Hollywood, CA: Warner Books.

17
▼▼▼▼▼▼▼

A Parent's Dilemma:
Public vs. Jewish Education*

Svi Shapiro

The time for decision always seemed to be far off. It would be six years from the beginning of kindergarten before my daughter would complete her elementary schooling—a seemingly endless period of time during which I would surely find the clarity of thinking to decide on the future course of her education. Yet fifth grade at B'nai Shalom Day School had arrived far more rapidly than I wanted. I would now have to seriously confront my own commitments to public education, and to Jewish education—to say nothing of my ambivalence about private schooling and the privileges of class, the rootlessness of a postmodern America, and the comforts of parochial communities.

For leftist academics, there is always the danger of allowing the particularities of one person's life to become lost in the much grander narratives of moral, ideological, and political considerations. This is, after all, a decision about where my eleven-year-old daughter Sarah is to spend her sixth grade. Nor, as I have reminded myself many times, can I hold her needs hostage to my own heavily worked concerns about the course of social justice and identity in this country.

We live in Greensboro, North Carolina. This is not New York or Philadelphia. The Jewish community (well established and comfortable as it is) exists as a very small island in an overwhelmingly dominant Christian milieu. This is what is sometimes referred to as the New South—middle class, moderately conservative. Greensboro is a city of several colleges and universities; we recycle garbage; our mayor is a woman and an environmentalist. Despite a notorious 1979 shoot-out involving the Ku Klux Klan, this is not Klan country.

To grow up Jewish here is certainly a minority experience. But it is far from the culturally marginalizing and politely silent experience I had growing up Jewish in England in the 1950s. Here, Jewish holidays are visibly and positively commented on in the local media, the television stations wish their viewers a happy Chanukah, and the downtown Christmas decorations are referred to as the "Festival of Lights." Even our supermarkets consult with our Conservative rabbi on Jewish dietary laws and culinary tastes.

The Jewish day school my daughter attends is a quite beautiful institution. Its enrollment is about 190 students—fairly remarkable in a city of about 1,200 Jewish families. Recently celebrating its twenty-fifth anniversary, the school provides a warm, very *haimish* Jewish environment, where holidays and Shabbat are richly celebrated, and the Hebrew language ubiquitous. Its religiosity is traditional though non-dogmatic, and it affirms the notions of *tikkun olam*. While I find the pedagogy too conventional, my daughter has found the place to be nurturant and loving. She has, for the most part, found delight in being there—a place where schooling has sustained her, not opposed her life.

What was at stake in my choice of Sarah's schooling was no abstract pedagogic exercise. I want my daughter's heart and soul to be shaped and nurtured by a *Yiddishkeyt* that would ensure her allegiance to a Jewish identity. As spiritually or historically compelling as this might be, I make no claim that this is not, at root, a selfish act. Such an education would ensure my continuing ability to recognize my own self in my daughter's being—the natural, if not entirely laudable, desire of most parents. Until now, my decision has been richly repaid; she has indeed absorbed not only some of the knowledge and culture of Jewish life, but more significantly its texture and feel. She senses its importance and its uniqueness. The joys and significance of this belong not only to the private sphere of family life, but also for her to the sphere of communal participation. Jewish life exists not merely in home or synagogue, but richly and vibrantly in the everyday, Monday-through-Friday world from which, for most of us, it is abstracted.

The mobilization of support for a politics that eviscerates public institutions is bound up with the widely felt hostility in modern societies toward the state, with all of its impersonality, inefficiency, and waste. It is precisely this perception that has fueled the relentless drive of the Right to gut almost everything that has the word "public" in it.

At the heart of this assault is an ideology that lionizes the marketplace and scorns society's attempts to ameliorate social injustice. In this view, the marketplace and market forces are regarded as the only legitimate means to allocate resources and to assign economic or cultural values. The resultant push for smaller government and a balanced budget has the effect of drastically reducing the scope and scale of the social safety net. It means ever more drastic cutbacks in society's supports to the elderly, children, the unemployed, the poor, and the sick.

So, our culture continues to foster self-interest and a lack of concern for the common good. Where the marketplace alone is to be arbiter of economic investment and social values, attempts are made to eliminate or reduce publicly financed education and culture. Prisons become one of the few areas of public investment. And where public policy collides with the imperatives of the market, as in environmental and consumer regulation, then the latter need be scaled back if not eradicated.

The political discourse that has sought to achieve these ends is not without its own conflicts and contradictions. It is clear, for example, that many people subscribe to the notion of smaller, less wasteful government, but also support a state that lessens the hazards and dangers of the free market. In this sense the state is, paradoxically, both the focus of much popular anger and repository of much of our needs and aspirations as a community. It irks us with its demands and intrusiveness, but it also instantiates our collective responsibilities and obligations. For all of its flaws, the state embodies some notion of a shared purpose; its ultimate client purports to be the public good, not simply the desirous ego.

The irony is that those conservatives who have often been the loudest in their condemnation of the decline of community and an ethic of responsibility have pursued a politics that has sought to allow the standards and ethics of the market to exert ever more freedom and dominance in our social, economic, and cultural lives. In working to ensure a world in which private interests and profits are less and less hindered by broad public responsibilities, and where the public arena is endlessly demeaned and savagely attacked, these free-marketeers have helped create a society that more and more resembles a predatory jungle. The violence of the Oklahoma bombing and the shut-down of the federal government, with its callous layoffs of workers and undelivered unemployment checks, are the most recent visible evidence of a discourse which has effectively trashed the public domain.

Sadly, it is often only when cuts in services and benefits are directly felt that individuals become more critical of what is happening on a broader level. Until then, the politics of racism and division succeed in legitimating the Right's social policies. A bunker mentality spreads, which calls for a social ethic of each for him or herself; individualism, separateness, and isolation frame our disposition toward the rest of the world. All of this has been given added impetus by corporate behavior in the 1980s and 1990s, replete with lay-offs, downsizing, closings, and relocations. It is a world that mocks any notions of obligation or commitment to workers, consumers, or community. Nothing really counts except the hunt for immediate profitability. Public accountability is a barrier to be subverted by whatever means necessary.

Yet in spite of all of this, there is still a deep hunger for communal life and the public good in America. Despite the shift to the Right, large majorities continue to affirm the importance of protecting our environment, maintaining investments in public libraries and cultural resources, and ensuring the availability of health care. Sometimes it becomes crystallized in ways that seem narrow or even repressive (protecting "our" flag). Yet behind these can be heard a cry for a society in which our collective concerns, not just our private interests, are honored, and where there is a strong sense of the public good instantiated in our civic world and in our social institutions.

Perhaps nowhere has this struggle been more focused than around the institutions of public education. Indeed, all of our societal schizophrenia around questions of public and private, marketplace and equity, democracy and capitalism, are in evidence there. In its most ideal rendering, public schooling represents a space where all of our children may be educated; a place where the rights of citizenship take precedence over the privileges or disadvantages of social and economic life. Understood in this way, public education becomes a crucial element in the making of a democratic civil society. It is an indispensable site for the nurturing of a new generation in those attitudes and values that ensure the possibility of meaningful democratic life.

Public school brings together in one setting children who, regardless of their class, race, gender, or ethnicity, may acquire the capacity for critical intelligence, the sense of community, and the cultural literacy that are requisites for democracy. As many political commentators have pointed out, the current crisis of democracy in the United States is closely related to the decline of meaningful public spaces where citizens can engage in a thoughtful and critical consideration of our society's pressing issues and concerns. In a world where commercial malls and presidential debates simulate real public interaction and involvement, there is a growing urgency to preserve those places where notions of equity, community, citizenship, and the public good still have validity.

Sadly, the reality of public schools has always been a long way from its democratic promise. The fundamental ideal of a place where the offspring of all citizens might meet and come together as a community has always been upset by the harsh realities of privilege, inequity, and racism. The historic struggles to eradicate the effects of a racially segregated system of public education are well known. Less obvious have been the continuing pernicious effects of class and race in maintaining schools vastly different in their resources, funding, expectations of students, and educational climate. Jonathan Kozol, among others, vividly documented the horrendous conditions that beset schools in poor and underfunded districts, producing debilitating and demoralizing third-world environments for kids in many of this nation's cities.

This public sphere mirrors the increasing polarization of wealth and opportunity found in the wider society. Urban schools with their violence, high drop-out rates, low achievement, and poor morale exist as altogether different institutions from those in suburban areas that function as conduits to good colleges and economic well-being.

Far from equalizing opportunities for diverse groups of students, education typically reinforces the already existing advantages and disadvantages found in the larger culture. The bitter irony of the process is that it occurs under the apparently well-meaning rhetoric of educational theories that promise to teach to the intellectual and emotional differences among students. Yet, in practice, the effect is usually to rationalize racism and classism. The ubiquitous grouping and tracking of students becomes little more than a way of affirming the "cultural capital" of some individuals and invalidating that of others. It takes only a cursory look at many schools to see how education dignifies the knowledge and experiences of some young people and silences and marginalizes that of others.

Typically, schooling represents a process of mindless absorption of knowledge separated from any notion of existential or social meaning. Successful learning comes to be seen as a regurgitation of bits and pieces of knowledge abstracted from a context that might provide them with relevance to the lives, hopes, interests, and dreams of kids' lives. And the "hidden curriculum" of schooling is such that the emphasis on achievement, individual success, and competition undermines efforts to build communities of respect and care. Indeed, where the latter are taken seriously, they must confront the contradictions not only of school culture but that of the larger social milieu. The daily grind of public school life with its boredom, alienation, and bureaucratic regimentation are the resonant features of contemporary, adolescent popular culture.

In my struggle to decide the fate of my fifth-grade daughter, I am mindful of the desperate need to sustain the promise of public life in this country. The withdrawal of the middle class from public institutions is the certain vehicle for their demoralization and decline. Not only in this country but in other places such as the United Kingdom, the turn toward more individualistic lifestyles and privatized institutions, promoted by conservative governments, has turned the public space into one of neglect and decay. Whether in health care, housing, or in education, the story is one of double standards—where publicly provided institutions or systems are synonymous with the poor, and where standards are increasingly inferior as compared to those found in the private domain.

In wrestling with whether to send my daughter to a public school, I feel compelled to weigh my own moral responsibility as to whether I am to be part of the flight from our public world into the safety and privileges of a private institution. A commitment to progressive politics would seem to demand commitment to those public institutions where we may share, to some degree, our lives with those who inhabit economic, cultural, or racial worlds quite different from our own.

Among all these concerns, one is of particular significance to me. How do we reconcile a commitment to public education with the need to recognize and affirm cultural, religious, or other differences? For many on the Left, this validation of difference has been central to the contemporary struggle to deepen the meaning of democratic life. It has been seen as a critical feature of democracy in a "postmodern" world. The struggle to recognize the multiplicity of voices and the diversity of histories and experiences of those who inhabit our nation and world has been a key focus of progressive educators.

And there has been increasing recognition of the ways that education has for so long denied the contributions and presence of many kinds of people. Whether because of class or race or ethnicity or gender or religion or nationality, it has become clear just how much we have ignored or invalidated the knowledge and traditions of others—those who fall outside the constructed norms of the culture. As educators, we have come to see how this process demeans and silences our students as the classroom becomes a place that is quite foreign to their homes, neighborhood, or communities.

In this regard, the emergence of a "multicultural" awareness in our schools is an important and liberating phenomenon. It is certainly a mark of progress that children are being taught to question the notion that "Columbus discovered America" with all its ethnocentric and racist assumptions about civilization; or that history, social studies, and English are beginning to be taught in more expansive and inclusive ways. Even where there are good-faith efforts, multiculturalism too often becomes trivialized—a matter of food, fiestas, and dressing up. It offers a very superficial appreciation indeed of what difference has meant to communities often denigrated or despised by those in the mainstream of society. Whatever its limitations, these efforts represent real cracks in the wall of cultural assumptions that have confronted generations of young people, shutting out or silencing those whose language, history, beliefs, and culture have been made to seem peripheral to the society.

Yet even where difference is valued and the plural nature of cultures in America is celebrated, the texture of the particular cultures recognized by our public schools is likely to be "thin." For my daughter, no multicultural environment can offer the judaically rich, evocative, and full experience that would be available to her in a Jewish day school. Only in that environment does Jewishness become a form of life that colors moral expression, joyful celebration, the moments of soulful reflection and sadness, and the days and seasons of the calendar. Jewishness becomes more than an abstract focus of intellectual discussion: the living vehicle through which my daughter can construct her identity and articulate her ethical and spiritual commitments.

Such a voice is a matter of both the heart and the mind, and only a pedagogic environment that is flooded with the resonance of Jewish memory and experience can nurture it. Nor is a deep sense of value about Jewish life easily available outside of a context which integrates it into a community's daily practice—one that draws in some way from the moral and spiritual meanings of our people's historical wisdom. The "thick" texture of Jewish life—the pervasive sounds of Hebrew, the smell of challah, the *niggunim* and Israeli songs, the benching after meals—are the resources upon which are built an identity that contains an enduring commitment to Jewish life and continuity.

The intensity of this experience, however, holds the potential danger of nurturing parochial or arrogant attitudes. Such schooling may produce a *shtetl* consciousness that shuns or disparages anything foreign—one that later fuels the intolerance of "*goyim*-bashing," or the self-righteousness that underlays so much of the American-Jewish support for chauvinistic, right-wing Israeli politics.

While at B'nai Shalom, much hard work goes toward developing a sense of social responsibility and celebrating the values of human community and global connectedness, the school my daughter attends is nevertheless a sheltered, limited community that is separated from much that other children must confront and deal with in their lives. Certainly its ambiance is too competitive, oriented to the goals of individual success and achievements. Its selectivity as a Jewish and predominantly middle- and upper-middle-class institution ensures that it is the kind of secure and cohesive community so appealing to parents. Yet in this sense it also provides a powerful, if disturbing, answer to some of the dilemmas of a postmodern world.

In their observations of postmodern society, there is a surprising convergence among both left- and right-wing critics. At the center is the belief that the world we have entered is one in which barriers—spatial, moral, political, intellectual, and aesthetic—have collapsed. Even the boundaries of gender appear permeable in an age in which sexual borders are easily crossed and labile. Our age is one of unfixity, uncertainty, and flux.

There is much to celebrate in all of this. The unfixing of boundaries, verities, and distinctions has given us the promise of a world that is more fluid, open, and free. Yet there is a price to pay—one, I believe, that has traumatic consequences for the young. And in this the conservative critique finds a powerful resonance in the anguish of many parents, by no means all of whom can be dismissed as simply and predictably right wing.

It is quite clear that the desire for discipline and structure in the raising of the young now hits a powerful chord across a wide range of parents. This desire emanates from the increasing recognition of a world in which a moral and spiritual homelessness is the prevailing sensibility. More and more there is the sense of being uprooted from the stabilities of place, family, and normative communities. The postmodern world is one in which individuals increasingly feel as if they are in exile—existentially and morally adrift in a world that constantly disrupts and dissolves any sense of situatedness in an enduring web of meaning and community. Indeed, far from acknowledging the pain of so much alienation, we are urged by Madison Avenue as well as the hipper cultural critics to enjoy the tumultuous ride.

In ways that distort the broad concern for the disintegration of ethical life and the erosion of the sense of social responsibility, talk of tradition, values, and discipline is mistakenly understood as only a discourse of the Right. Yet a world in which all that is solid melts—moral commitment, identity, community, social connection—is a matter that confronts all of us. And nowhere is this more painfully so than in regard to the upbringing of our own children. Daily, all of us, especially parents, are forced to confront the fall-out from the postmodern condition—the self-destructiveness of adolescent suicide, drugs, alcoholism and compulsive dieting, widespread depression and generalized rage, and a cynical detachment from social institutions. However manipulative or distorting, conservative discourse succeeds because it speaks to the widespread anguish of an older generation.

In this context of disintegration, rootlessness, and the culture of images, Jewish schooling offers a sense of possibility not easily found elsewhere. Here there is the hope of nurturing an identity grounded in the Jewish people's long history—a history rich with the struggles for a world of justice and freedom. Here, too, is the real possibility of transmitting what it means to be a "stranger in the land"—developing personalities empathic to the pain of exclusion and human indignity.

Jewish "memory" roots us in a temporal community of unbelievable human tragedies, celebrations, suffering, courage, and the will for physical and spiritual survival. And such history makes powerful claims on the living—an insistence on the vision of *tikkun olam*; to act as if we ourselves had experienced the bondage of Egypt. Far from the Disney World theme park of historical images, Jewish pedagogy can offer a deep sense of historic and communal identification. Such identification is one of connectedness to an enduring moral and spiritual vision.

The religious sensibility forged in this history is one that continually demands that we create and recognize boundaries—distinctions within our world between ways of living that express the sacred and those that are profane. Judaism is a religion of everyday life that constantly seeks to make sacred the so-called ordinary, taken-for-granted acts of daily existence. Those of us who grew up in Orthodox homes know the rigidity and frequently stultifying nature of halakhic Judaism. Yet, at the same time, one can find here a powerful rejoinder to the dehumanization and degradation of our common world—one that insists that we seek to make holy human life and behavior, as well as the whole environment that makes life possible.

Certainly Judaism, like all religions, can become dogmatic and reified; a series of mindless rituals and practices. Yet I have reason to believe that B'nai Shalom offers my daughter the beginning of a deeper set of meanings that points to the limits and boundaries that structure our relationship to the world as one of respect, consciousness of the needs of others, and responsibility toward them. In this school's Judaism there is, too, a sense of celebration and festivity—one that seeks to teach the young something about experiencing lives of joy, wonder, and appreciation. It is, I believe, in this synthesis of social responsibility and joyful mindfulness that we can find the beginnings of a meaningful response to the rampant cynicism and nihilism of our culture.

It is true that the school offers an environment that is only very cautiously questioning or critical of the injustices of our world. And I am concerned lest it limit the importance of developing the critical mind and spirit—the lifeblood of a democratic culture. But beyond the need for our young to be educated to enable them to challenge their world, there is a need for the sense of hope and possibility that the world can be changed and transformed. And this, I believe, happens best in an environment where we feel a deeply shared, and inspiring, sense of connected fate. For Jews, there is our long history of struggle in a harsh world of brutality and oppression, and the will to maintain our hope for a better world.

Without this communal rootedness and affirmation of a way of life there is, I think, little emotional capacity to act in the world—at least not where acting means trying to transform the moral character of our lives and the political shape of our society. There is only disconnected apathy and cynicism— the world of the young so well reflected in the recent popular movies, *Slacker* and *Clueless*.

The Right is correct to argue that without an internalized discipline the self becomes passive, unable to act in the world. Yet the discipline that empowers is not that of the obedient drone but the structure that comes from participation and responsibility in the life of a meaningful and enduring community.

These are not easy times. Such communities are not easy to find. All of us must somehow find the capacity for commitment in a world where all beliefs seem uncertain, visions uncertain, and social relations fragile or broken. Yet the need to find a place in which our commitments are shared and our identities confirmed is the necessary ground of our being as moral agents in the world.

Let me be clear that my real interest is not in what is referred to today as "Jewish continuity." The continuation of a set of practices and rituals is of no particular significance to me. The ultimate value of Jewish education is not found in my daughter's capacity to read or speak Hebrew, or her knowledge of Judaica, but in whether she will become a human being deeply concerned for the worth and dignity of all the lives that share our world. My hope is that her Jewish education will be a powerful vehicle for developing such a way of being. The particular here, I hope, will provide a gateway to the universal.

Yet I worry that my desire for this education will also boost the arguments of those who favor "school choice." These are often no more than thinly veiled attempts to promote educational policies that are elitist, racially separatist, or religiously fundamentalist, and have little to do with creating a more compassionate or respectful civic culture. As I wrestle with my daughter's future, I feel the strong and inescapable claims of the particular in a world that more and more demands a recognition of our universal connectedness and responsibilities.

GLOSSARY

Yiddishkeyt	Jewishness
Goyim	Non-Jews
Challah	Sweet-tasting bread eaten on the Jewish Sabbath
Niggunim	Traditional melodies
Tikkun Olam	To heal and repair the world
Heimish	Familiar and inviting environment
Benching	Grace said after meals
Shtetl	Small town in Eastern Europe with vibrant Jewish community
Halakhic Judaism	Religious practice followed by orthodox Jews

CRITIQUE AND HOPE:
MORAL AND SPIRITUAL
PERSPECTIVES ON EDUCATION

The basic purpose of this book is to present a critical analysis of some of the most pressing and significant issues of educational policy and practice in their relationship to broader social, cultural, economic, and political phenomena. By *critical* we mean a searching and thorough examination of the wider and deeper ramifications and implications of particular ideas and policies. This examination, sadly enough, has revealed a number of serious and troubling problems in education as well as in the larger social and cultural realms. Many of these problems are so deeply rooted and entrenched that they seem intractable, if not inevitable. Ironically enough, this pessimism has generated another severe problem—that of an increasing sense of cynicism, futility, and despair, which, of course, only makes matters worse.

A powerful example of this can be seen in the current dearth of innovation from the field of curriculum, normally a fertile source of creative and imaginative ideas on the substance and nature of the instructional program. There is not only a reduction of such ideas, but even more telling is the growing lack of professional and public interest in developing new curricula. It is as if all the perplexing questions about what we should teach have been resolved and all the intense controversies surrounding that issue settled so that there is no compelling need to inquire into other possibilities. Clearly these matters have not been resolved and probably never will be. Yet at the same time they cannot simply be ignored, and we can only bemoan the reality of the relatively inert state of serious dialogue about them.

There are a number of explanations for this state of affairs. First of all, there has been a deepening understanding of the power of the so-called *hidden curriculum*, sometimes called the *tacit* or *implicit curriculum*. These terms refer to the total impact of the whole range of the school experience, including but not at all limited to formal course offerings. These include such things as rules and regulations (e.g., rules of discipline, dress codes, and attendance policies); theoretical assumptions on such matters as the nature of knowledge and on how students learn; and moral values as reflected in such matters as competition, deference to authority, and social responsibility. These attitudes and values get expressed in the whole range of school life; in textbooks curriculum materials and classroom discussion; at lunchtime, recess, as well as before, during, and after school; and in human relationships—student–student, teacher–student, administrator–teacher, parent–teacher, and so on. Clearly the dimensions of the hidden curriculum are derived from and mirror the values, beliefs, and attitudes of the larger society and culture and hence are much more difficult to change than say the contents of the ninth-grade algebra course.

A related reason for the apparent decline in the vitality of curriculum is the virtual standardization of the formal curriculum (conventionally defined as the study of English, Mathematics, Science, History/Geography, and Foreign Languages). This is largely a function of the proliferation of high-stakes testing, which is almost always done through standardized tests. The power of these tests has been greatly intensified by recent federal legislation that has dramatically changed the politics of public education. The movement from a situation in which school policies and programs were largely determined at a local level and with considerable teacher discretion to one in which the federal government has become the dominant player represents a radical shift in the center of gravity of the politics of American education. Basically, the conventional curriculum has been promulgated as official and made permanent by dint of public acquiescence, professional impotence, and federal mandate.

Part of the tragedy of this lies in the irony that many, if not most, educators and much of the public do not consider critical curriculum questions to be resolved and likely would welcome fresh thinking on them. The utter failure of the educational profession to provide authoritative expertise (e.g., in the manner of science and medicine) has created a vacuum in leadership that partisan politicians, ideologues, and interest groups have been only too willing to fill. In part this represents a trend toward disenchantment with some of our most cherished traditional assumptions of how to effect social and educational change. These traditions include major reliance on the efficacy of empirical inquiry (which has become increasingly suspect), the rightness of democratic processes (which continues to be eroded by the power of centralized business and government), and the imperative of social responsibility (which has been undermined by the obsession with personal success).

The continuing disillusionment with the ability of these processes to effect social, cultural, and educational transformation has contributed to a growing sense of cynicism and powerlessness, if not paralysis and despair, among those working for such change. Once again we see a phenomenon in the world of education that mirrors events and attitudes in the broader context of American life where we also find disillusionment and a sense of powerlessness. It seems that every major sociocultural institution has had its reputation tarnished and its moral authority weakened by significant illegal and/or unethical behavior. Certainly the integrity of our democratic institutions (up to and including the criminal justice system and the electoral process) has been compromised as have entire industries (tobacco and asbestos come to mind). We have experienced a seeming increase in serious ethical infractions not only in business, but also in such highly respected professions as law, medicine, science, and even among the clergy. All these outrages have occurred despite existing laws, safeguards, regulation, and the clarity and veneration of traditional ethical and moral standards. These moral and legal violations are not only sickening and depressing in a society grounded in the rule of law and deeply felt moral traditions, but they also strike even deeper into our souls. In an era of rampant consumerism and materialism, along with the maniacal (often fruitless) pursuit of personal success, many people have found themselves questioning the effects of what appears more and more to be a life full of the possibility of emptiness and meaninglessness.

Over the past two decades, doubts of the viability of a life based on consumerism and material possessions have produced an extraordinary explosion of public interest in religious, spiritual, and moral ideas and formulations. At the very least, this would seem to represent an effort to seriously reflect on the likelihood of finding meaning and fulfillment by traveling on the paths of consumerism or by climbing the ladder of socioeconomic advancement. Beyond that, it also seems part of a movement directed at finding a spiritual and moral grounding that can inform and direct the quest for personal meaning and a just and loving community. Moreover, this moral and spiritual quest seems directed at seeking energizing forces that can overcome the understandable pessimism and sense of powerlessness that is so destructive to our deeply felt need for hope and possibility.

This movement has certainly influenced the educational profession and that part of the public interested in educational programs focused on creating a more just and humane world. Again there is nothing particularly new about the moral and spiritual life of schools. However, what is new is the way in which there is less and less reliance on approaching this concern through the formal curriculum. It seems clearer and clearer that the power of the hidden curriculum is far greater and far more enduring than the formal list of courses and syllabi and sooner or later overrides any and all school- or system-wide changes. Instead of going the route of trying to make changes in a system already locked into a set of fundamental and controlling assumptions, many educators have taken the view that it would be more appropriate and efficacious to reexamine the traditional discourse (language) that permeates the field of education. The current educational language is full of references to competition, achievement, grades, standardization, rules, discipline, motivational techniques, order, sorting, and accountability. It is a language of stability and stasis largely directed at helping students to be conventionally successful and responding to the needs of the state and of commerce. It is not a language of moral and spiritual quest nor is it one that is particularly concerned with the concerns of those engaged in the struggle for a just and loving community. The conventional language accepts and validates the myth of the *American Dream* and with it the concept of meritocracy, which justifies a society composed of winners and losers all the while insisting on its claims of objectivity and neutrality. It is a language of functionality and instrumentalism, not a language of the kind of hopes and dreams that emerge from the spirit.

The operational language of the profession is typically one of caution, accommodation, and practicality. If we are to succeed in dismantling the current educational regime of testing, standardization, sorting, and creating more caring, thoughtful, and humane schools, it is unlikely to come about by invoking a discourse that stresses caution, meritocracy, and neutrality. Nor is it likely to come about by simply invoking a language heavily flavored with moral and spiritual images for major social and educational transformation. In addition to moral direction and spiritual energy, it will inevitably require significant participation in the political process at all levels—community, local, state, regional, and national.

It is important to point out that we are currently undergoing a significant, if not radical, transformation in our educational system as well as in other institutions. Indeed much of these changes have been embedded in rhetoric strongly laced with moral and religious language. If nothing else, this demonstrates that major changes in social and cultural institutions can take place when there is strong ideological and political leadership. It is also a powerful example of the danger of promoting change for its own sake for the authors in this book have made it abundantly clear that the recent changes in education are, at best, highly problematic. Moreover, it reminds us that there are many moral and spiritual frameworks, and we need to be thoughtful about choosing those that resonate with the goals of achieving a more just and loving world. The articles in the following section offer a number of intriguing perspectives on developing a different discourse of education—one that is informed by our highest aspirations and deepest hopes.

The essay by Harold Berlak (chap. 18, this volume) chronicles and analyzes the process by which the federal government is using standardized testing in its zeal to become the controlling force in American public education. Svi Shapiro (chap. 19, this volume) also examines the widespread impact of the testing movement with particular emphasis on its moral significance. Nel Noddings' essay (chap. 20, this volume) explores the possibilities of developing a school program in a moral framework grounded in a profound concern for caring. Dwayne Huebner (chap. 21, this volume) wrestles with the challenge of creating a spiritual discourse for schools—one that would totally change our perspective on what schools are and could be. Michael Lerner (chap. 22, this volume), writing from a different religious context, describes ways in which spiritual language can co-exist and contribute to school and classroom practice. The section concludes with an essay by David Purpel (chap. 23), who discusses the relationship between spirituality and the need to promote and sustain hope for genuine educational transformation.

18
▼▼▼▼▼▼▼

From Local Control to Government and Corporate Takeover of School Curriculum: The *No Child Left Behind Act* and the *Reading First* Program*

Harold Berlak

INTRODUCTION

The *No Child Left Behind Act* signed into law in January 2002 by George W. Bush is the latest chapter in a historical conflict between business efforts to shape public education so that it serves their best interests, and the struggles by democratic movements to resist corporate control and create and sustain public schools that serve children's best interests and strengthen democracy.

This essay is in two parts. Part one is a history and analysis of the radical shift in federal educational policy over the last 40 years, a shift that fundamentally altered the balance of power—from a time when local educational authorities, principals, teachers, and teacher educators exerted considerable influence over the curriculum and learning process, to today when federal and state governments together with mainline corporations and numerous corporate funded think tanks, foundations, and NGOs such as the Business Roundtable, the Broad Foundation, and the Education Trust are the dominant force.

The second part focuses on a new federal program included in Title I of the *No Child Left Behind Act* called *Reading First*. It exemplifies how federal and state government together with major business interests exercise cultural control over schooling by controlling how basic reading is taught to the nation's

children. The essay concludes with a set of questions that ought to be asked
by the public, parents, teachers, principals, and community leaders about the
teaching of reading in their own communities.

I. THE ROUTE TO FEDERAL AND CORPORATE DOMINANCE

On October 4, 1957, the belief in U.S. invincibility was shattered when Soviet
scientists put Sputnik, the first man-made satellite, into orbit. Not much larger
than a basketball, it was visible to the naked eye as it circled the earth, and
quickly became a living symbol of the former Soviet Union's scientific and
technological prowess and of the failures of America's own unfortunately
named space program, "Vanguard." The launch of Sputnik inflicted more
than a psychic wound; it was taken as a threat to the survival of the US. *Time
Magazine* reflecting the temper of the times noted the following week that if the
Soviets had rockets powerful enough to launch a 184.3 pound satellite into orbit, they were capable of delivering nuclear warheads to the US heartland. The
New York Times response was a series of articles suggesting that among the
primary reasons for the US losing the "race to space" was the failure of the federal government to invest in technical and scientific education.

Over the next thirty or so years of the Cold War, real and imagined threats
from the Soviet Union profoundly changed the political, social, and economic life and the cultural landscape of the American nation, including its
educational policies and practices. Less than a year after the Sputnik launch,
Congress passed NDEA, the National Defense Education Act. This legislation was the first in a series of legislative moves that turned on its head a
foundational assumption of US democracy since Colonial times—that
schooling of the young was to be a strictly local affair, and pedagogical and
curricular decisions were to be left to teachers, principals, districts, and locally elected governing boards. There was no cabinet level federal office of
education nor was there much federal support for pre-collegiate education.
State governments rarely intruded on what were then presumed to be local
district and school-level prerogatives.

There were exceptions, notably the textbook adoption states, including
California, Texas, and the former Confederate states, where local school and
district curriculum and pedagogical choices were constrained by a list of state
approved texts districts and schools were permitted to purchase with state
funds. Many states also published so-called curriculum "frameworks" or
"guidelines." However, books and other materials that departed from the
mandated state texts and curriculum frameworks could be purchased using
local and in many cases state funds. Teachers, committees of teachers, and local officials made these curriculum choices. The states' curriculum prescrip-

tions were frequently ignored. State education departments often lacked the legal mandates or the bureaucratic apparatus required for enforcing the curriculum mandates.

NDEA aimed to shape local educational priorities in science education, technology mathematics, and modern foreign language, areas considered critical for defeating the communist menace and defending democracy. NDEA also channeled funds into schools, and colleges for interdisciplinary area studies, language development, teacher education, school counseling, libraries, educational media, and for guaranteed low-interest student loans. In spite of President Eisenhower's lukewarm support, the bill breezed through Congress with bipartisan support including from the junior senator from Massachusetts, John F. Kennedy, who two years later became president, and from Senator Barry Goldwater, the conservative Republican icon from Arizona who was defeated by Lyndon Johnson in the 1964 presidential election. Among the few in opposition was Senator Strom Thurmond, the hardcore states' rights segregationist from South Carolina who opined (correctly as it turned out) that NDEA marked the beginning of the end of the sacred principles of states' rights and local control of schools.

To address these concerns about local control, the following restriction was incorporated into NDEA. "Nothing in this act shall be construed to authorize any agency or employee of the United States to exercise any direction, supervision, or control over the curriculum, program of instruction, administration, or personnel of any educational institution or school system." There was also built into the act another protection against greater centralization of state authority. Federal funds flowed directly from the federal government to the local institution and/or local jurisdiction, bypassing the states' educational bureaucracies.

Lyndon Johnson succeeded to the presidency upon Kennedy's assassination and was elected to a full term as president in 1964. Though Kennedy is often remembered as the consummate politician, at the time of his assassination little of his highly acclaimed "New Frontier" program had made it through Congress. Johnson, a former senator from Texas and Democratic majority leader, was able to navigate an extraordinary number of highly controversial bills through a Congress stalemated by an alliance between Southern Democrats, who bitterly opposed voting rights and school desegregation, and Senate Republicans. Major pieces of legislation were passed creating educational and job opportunities, protecting voting, civil, and workers' rights, the environment, occupational and public health. Under Johnson the historic 1964 Civil Rights Act became law, a federal agency, the Commission on Civil Rights, was granted the power to enforce its provisions, and "affirmative action" was first advanced as a legitimate remedy for past and current injustices. This collection of programs and initiatives promoting civil rights and social justice Johnson called "The Great Society."

In 1965 Johnson signed the *Elementary and Secondary Act*, or ESEA, that replaced NDEA as the most important federal legislation authorizing expenditures for elementary and secondary schools and teacher education. It was the centerpiece of the Great Society plan to increase educational opportunities for children of the poor who were designated by the legislation as "disadvantaged." As with NDEA, prohibitions designed to preserve local control were written into ESEA. The federal government was forbidden to intervene in local school policies, in local pedagogical and curriculum decisions, and ESEA funds flowed directly from the federal government to the local institutions or jurisdictions in effect diluting the authority of state officials and state departments of education.

ESEA was passed at about the same time that Lyndon Johnson was escalating the Vietnam War and when public resistance to the war was widespread and growing. The anti-war, civil rights, and Black power movements were giving birth to the Cultural Revolution of the sixties and early seventies. A youthful, countercultural movement then called the "New Left" openly questioned the power structure, basic cultural values, and attitudes, and challenged sexual orthodoxies. The feminist movement was reborn with calls for abortion rights, political and economic equality for women. Other identity movements—La Raza, Native and Asian American, Latino, gay rights movements—emerged challenging corporate and white male dominance of the political process, the culture, and the economy.

Demands for political and economic democracy extended to public schools. There were calls for forms of teaching and learning that stimulate student creativity, develop imagination and critical thinking, teach democratic values, and encourage active participation in the political process. These were coupled with calls for more direct community, parent, and student participation in decision making, for Black and women's studies, and for an inclusive multicultural curriculum that acknowledges the role of non-European cultures and women in the formation of American society and culture.

As the decade of the sixties came to a close, the costs of the war in terms of dollars and American lives overshadowed all other public issues. Vietnam turned into a quagmire that in time destroyed the Johnson presidency, and talk of the War on Poverty and equality of opportunity largely disappeared from the American political scene. Guns once again triumphed over butter. While a number of Great Society programs including ESEA were enacted and survived, they were rarely funded at levels that had any hope of achieving the Great Society promises.

ESEA has been reauthorized every five to seven years since 1965. Over time it has been amended and its scope broadened. In 2001 it was rewritten by the Bush Administration to advance a right wing education agenda, and renamed the *No Child Left Behind Act* (NCLB). The act authorizes the vast majority of federal K–12 education programs including Indian education, teacher training, Head Start, early literacy, school libraries, bilingual education, technology, and school safety. Title I remains the flagship of the act. In 2003 Title I granted $11.7 billion in federal funds to schools that serve low income children, 64 percent of whom are students of color, in approximately 47,000, nearly half of the nation's public schools.

Though federal dollars account for about 7% of the nation's expenditures for elementary and secondary education, the lowest percentage among the developed democratic nations, these dollars have an enormous clout, particularly in times when states are in budget crisis—as most are. The federal hand rests especially heavy on schools and districts that depend most heavily on ESEA funds, those that serve communities with high proportions of poor children, African-American, Latino, and/or immigrants for whom English is a second language.

NDEA and ESEA brought federal dollars and federal oversight to the schools. While federal funds clearly skewed local priorities, there was not until the late eighties an effort to impose federal control over the content of the curriculum and approaches to teaching and learning. A large measure of control of curriculum content and teaching methods remained with schools and teachers.

By 2003 only vestiges of local control remain. Virtually all federal education grants now arrive with many strings. Once a school, district, or state accepts federal dollars, the Bush Administration claims the right to override state and local school curriculum decisions. The tentacles of federal authorities extend far beyond the curriculum. A provision of the act requires, for example, that schools receiving any Title I funds must provide assurances that they employ only "highly qualified" teachers, and teacher education programs conducted by colleges and universities and other institutions must also conform to what a federal panel considers "highly qualified." The federal government in effect has assumed the power to standardize the teacher education curriculum, fundamentally change existing teacher education programs, and override state teacher credentialing laws.

The second section of this paper focuses on the new Title I program, *Reading First*, as a case in point of how federal and corporate power in 2003 is exercised over the teaching of early reading in the nation's classrooms.

How did the U.S., where local control and democracy are celebrated, come to a place where federal government can exert so much control over the nation's schools? The explanation for this historic turnaround is found in the cultural changes and the political developments that accompanied and followed in the wake of the Vietnam War, and the response to these changes by those who hold political and economic power.

The social justice, liberation, and identity movements of the sixties provoked a cultural and political backlash. Corporate America feared the growing influence of the peace, countercultural, liberation, environmental, and consumer protection movements on American politics. It is uncontestable that large corporations have the most to lose by democratization of American politics and a government that actively protects the public interest. Many if not most liberals put off by "identity politics," feminism, and affirmative action abandoned social democracy along with the Great Society and shifted to the right. Christian fundamentalists considered the sixties a moral assault by the godless left on their most cherished values and beliefs about family, sexuality, and country. By the late seventies the far right had gained full control of the Republican Party and in 1980 chose former California Governor Ronald Reagan as its candidate for President.

Reagan was elected espousing the virtues of individualism, small government, low taxes, restoration of family values, and national pride. He vowed to dismantle the Department of Education as a cabinet level agency and return control of education to the states and the American people. As president he showed almost no interest in public education and during his eight-year tenure introduced no significant federal legislation.

During Reagan's presidency, however, the movement that led to centralized government, curriculum control, and national testing was launched by his first Secretary of Education Terrel Bell. With nominal support by Reagan, Bell commissioned what he called the "National Commission on Excellence in Education." Bell, a former Utah chief state education officer and a one-time superintendent of public schools, though thoroughly conservative on social and educational issues, was not an extreme right winger, nor a strong partisan for corporate interests. The eighteen-member Commission he appointed included several public school educators, superintendents of schools, principals, three college presidents, two distinguished academics, several state and local education officials, one former governor, and a single teacher. A retired Chairman of the Board of Bell Laboratories was the sole member with corporate credentials.

In 1982 the Commission produced a twenty-nine page report called *A Nation at Risk*. In words intended to shock it declared:

> Our Nation is at risk. Our once unchallenged preeminence in commerce, industry, science, and technological innovation is being overtaken by competitors throughout the world. This report is concerned with only one of the many causes and dimensions of the problem, but it is the one that undergirds American prosperity, security, and civility. . . .
>
> [T]he foundations of our society are presently being eroded by a rising tide of mediocrity. What was unimaginable a generation ago has begun to occur—others are matching and surpassing our educational attainments. . . . If an unfriendly foreign power had attempted to impose on America the mediocre educational performance that exists today, we might well have viewed it as an act of war. We have, in effect, been committing an act of unthinking, unilateral educational disarmament.

This overwrought rhetoric with its military metaphors preceded a set of rather unremarkable recommendations that were rarely cited and soon forgotten. The report would likely have been ignored had it not been for its overheated rhetoric and the fact that the nation was in the depths of its severest economic crisis since the 1930s. The report named the schools as the chief culprit for the failures of economy, affirmed conservative educational values, and called for a new commitment to excellence and the "basics." There was, however, no mention of vouchers, privatization of schools, public funds for religious schools, national standards, or national testing. The report in fact affirmed that education was primarily local concern, and the federal government had a supportive role to play in providing for the needs of "socioeconomically disadvantaged, students of color, language minority, and the handicapped" and for "protecting constitutional and civil rights of students and school personnel."[1]

A Nation at Risk offered no general prescriptions for national policy and made no grand recommendations for federal legislative action. It also had almost no effect on school governance or curriculum. The report however accomplished two things. First it made education a national issue by linking school reform to the health of the national economy. Second, it introduced the language of excellence and high standards into the language of school reform.

A Nation at Risk unleashed a torrent of other reports by all the major think tanks and foundations, national professional educational associations, advocacy groups, the national associations of governors, and chief state educational officers. Virtually all invoked the language of excellence and accepted without question the view that the first and central purpose of schooling is to serve the economy, which was usually taken as synonymous with serving US corporate needs and interests. At the time the media compared the US's economic stagnation with Japan's miracle of double-digit growth. The implication was that Japan's success was explained by its educational system with its no nonsense emphasis on discipline and mastery of the basics, as compared to US schools which had lost their way during the sixties in the pursuit of unattainable and unwise progressive social goals.

Reagan's vice president and successor, George H. Bush, attempted to capitalize on *A Nation at Risk*'s link between school reform and the economy. He proposed the first radical shift in the relationship of the federal government to states and local schools in the nation's history. During his campaign, Bush had been portrayed by the press as experienced in foreign policy, but lacking background and interest in domestic policy. His campaign manager, the former Republican governor of Tennessee, Lamar Alexander, urged Bush to make education his issue. Bush pledged to become the "Education President." After his election Lamar Alexander, who had a reputation as an educational reformer, was named Secretary of Education. Alexander had worked closely with fellow Southern governor Bill Clinton on a committee of the National Governors Association that was convened to respond to *A Nation at Risk*'s call for educational reform. The two were among the chief authors of a report, *Time for Results*, which urged national goals and standards.

In September 1989 Secretary Alexander, together with Governor Bill Clinton, assembled the first national "Education Summit" in Charlottesville, Virginia. It was cosponsored by the National Governors Association and cochaired by Clinton. In attendance were governors, state and federal legislators, chief state education officers, and several CEOs of major corporations who were also among the leaders of the *Business Roundtable* (BRT). BRT is a national organization with branches in every state. On its governing board sit the CEOs of the nation's 219 largest corporations. The avowed purpose of the BRT is to speak with one voice on a wide variety of public issues including public education. It is important to note whose voices were missing— scholars, researchers, parents, local educational officials, local labor and community leaders, practicing local school administrators, and teachers.[2]

The Summit took a position on reforming public schools that is indistinguishable from the positions adopted that same year by the BRT and National Governors Association: that standardized curriculum content standards tied to centralized testing and sanctions is the key to school reform. The Summit formed a "National Goals Panel" and adopted six National Education Goals designed "to guide reform of the nation's schools" by setting "high standards" and recommended that Congress authorize a panel to advise on "the desirability and feasibility of national standards and tests." Alexander subsequently assembled a thirty-member "National Council on Education Standards and Testing" co-chaired by a Republican and a Democratic governor.

At a Washington press conference in January 1992, the Council announced publication of *Raising Standards for American Education: A Report to the Congress and the American People*. Its chief recommendation was preordained: install national testing tied to standards. The word "standards" took on a particular meaning in the report. These are not broadly stated principles or guidelines but detailed prescriptions of curriculum content that all students are expected to master K–12. These "content standards" were in fact the same as what had previously been called curriculum "frameworks" or "guidelines." The important difference is that federal and state government was now prepared to use its bureaucratic power to force compliance to its mandates.

The report anticipated and made an effort to deflect the argument that national testing is an assault on state and local control by asserting that its plan for testing was "national" but not "federal" and was voluntary because the report claims states are under no obligation to join the program. The claim that national testing is not compulsory is disingenuous. Most states are in no position to forgo 7% of their annual public school budgets. Once states sign on to the program they are required to adopt content standards linked to tests and districts, schools, teachers, and students have no choice but to comply belying the claim that national testing does not infringe on local prerogatives.

G. H. Bush incorporated the key testing recommendations of the *Raising Standards For American Education* report into a legislative proposal he named *America 2000*. His reign as education president came to an abrupt end when the key national testing proposals of the bill were blocked in the education committee of the House by the Black Caucus and a coalition of civil rights, children's, and fair testing advocates.

As president, Clinton resurrected the Bush/Alexander plan repackaged and renamed it *Goals 2000: The Educate America Act*. It included a revised version of the six National Educational Goals adopted at the 1989 Summit. Several parts of Clinton's proposal were signed into law in the spring of 1995. Federal funds were allocated to develop "content standards" and states and schools were eligible for Goals 2000 grants on the condition that they develop content standards linked to testing. But Clinton's key proposal for national testing in math and reading for the 4th and 8th grades was eliminated from the bill by an odd alliance of progressive Democrats and far right wing Republicans led by the then senator John Ashcroft.

It was George W. Bush who finally managed to get through Congress a much revised version of national testing first proposed by his father. Along with other changes, national testing was incorporated into the *No Child Left Behind Act*, the 2002 reauthorization of ESEA.

II.   TEACHING READING AND *READING FIRST*

Controversies Over Reading Curriculum

When the words "literacy" or "fundamentals" are introduced into conversation, what come immediately to mind are not math, geography, history, or the arts, but reading. It is difficult to exaggerate the cultural and political significance of how reading is taught in the early grades. Reading is important not only for the obvious reasons that it is crucial for survival in daily life and for success at school, but also for the less obvious reasons that how basic reading is taught sets the tone of a school and shapes the entire primary school curriculum, as well as students' cultural beliefs and basic attitudes toward learning and knowledge—including how they perceive their own intellectual capacities and potential.

Controversies over approaches to teaching reading are not new. They persist over time because they are deeply rooted in profound differences in basic cultural and political beliefs and values about what children can and should read; about the importance of race, gender, culture, and language differences in the selection of content and teaching methods; and about the role schools should play fostering cultural diversity and democracy.

There are three identifiable approaches to teaching reading in U.S. schools:

Direct phonics instruction. According to the National Reading Panel (*which is described below*) there are two aspects to direct phonics instruction: (1) systematic acquisition of a sequence of discrete phonic skills, and (2) their application to reading.[3] The assumption of a systematic phonics-based approach is that all students need direct instruction in a *predetermined* sequence of letter/sound relationships. Racial, cultural differences and differences in home language are seen as relatively unimportant.

Whole language (also referred to as a *literature-based* or *constructivist*) approach emphasizes the importance of learning from context and drawing upon learners' previous experience and their capacity to use visual and textual clues. The assumption is that most children brought up in print rich communities grasp the elements of phonics—the association of spoken language with alphabetic symbols—from their daily life, their active experience with books, and conversations about books with peers and adults. This approach usually employs systematic phonics instruction, but rejects the idea that all children must master a fixed sequence of discrete phonetic skills *before* they are capable of reading "real" books.

A critical literacy emphasis requires children to go beyond taking meaning from print, to develop the capacity to become critical of experience and the texts they read, and to learn to observe and make critical judgments on both the texts they read and the world around them. There is no fine line between critical literacy and whole language perspectives; both stress the need for children to compose their own texts, to raise questions, to attend to differences in situation and context, and to connect texts with lived experience. Both assume that race, culture, language, and prior experience matter in the choice of curriculum materials and classroom activities. What distinguishes whole language from critical literacy is the latter's emphasis on democratic education—preparing students to become actively engaged in the social and political life in their communities advancing democracy and social justice.

Many variations of these three emphases coexist today, sometimes within a single school. Some version of direct phonics instruction is the most commonly used approach in U.S. classrooms and becoming more common as *Reading First* programs are adopted. Though fully developed "whole language" reading and writing programs are few, curriculum and methods associated with this approach are nevertheless widely used and accepted. Aspects of a critical literacy approach exist in schools, but living examples of such practices in the US are confined to a relatively small number of independent progressive schools, and within some alternative public schools, special programs, and charter schools.

For many years liberals and conservatives alike assumed that despite these deep divisions, the choice of teaching methods and materials was a local matter, left to teachers and educators at the school and district levels. Today, if schools and districts are to receive Title I funds, they must be prepared to accept federal controls over reading curriculum and methods. *Reading First* in effect federalizes curriculum decisions transferring control from local boards, communities, and teachers, to a state and/or federal government authority. The act's testing provisions and its *Reading First* program have a major impact on how schools teach reading.

Reading First

Reading First was modeled on a program that was introduced in Texas by G. W. Bush when he was governor. It was incorporated into NCLB based on a presumption that a highly structured phonics approach would ensure that every child will read by the third grade. It provides substantial federal grants to improve reading instruction[4] with the condition that the teaching materials, books, assessments, and professional development must be grounded in "scientifically-based" research, a term that appears at least 111 times in the text of the NCLB Act. What this means in practice is that a federal panel and the Department and the Secretary of Education must certify that the approach to teaching reading and the professional training offered to teachers are all "scientifically-based," that is to say consistent with what the Bush administration claims are the findings of the 2000 National Reading Panel report.

What are the grounds for the Bush Administration's claim that systematic direct phonics instruction is the only "scientifically based" approach to teaching reading?

In 1997, Congress authorized the creation of a National Reading Panel (NRP) whose charge was to identify best practices in reading instruction. The panel was appointed by the director of the National Institute for Child Health and Human Development (a part of NIH, the National Institute of Health) in consultation with the Secretary of Education. The chief of the branch that commissioned the NRP report was G. Reid Lyon, Ph.D. Lyon, a specialist in learning disabilities and self-proclaimed reading expert, is a long time advocate for direct, sequential, phonics instruction, and he has served as Bush's educational advisor on reading instruction since his days as governor. He had testified to a congressional committee in 1997, *prior* to the appointment of the Reading Panel, that science has definitively proven the superiority of direct phonics instruction in early reading.

Congress mandated that the National Reading Panel be composed of "leading scientists in reading research, representatives of colleges of education, reading teachers, education administrators, and parents." In fact, there were 12 university professors, eight of them academics in several areas, but none who questioned G. Reid Lyon's narrow perspective on educational and social scientific research. One person represented parents, and there were no teachers of early reading. There was a middle school teacher and one principal, Joanne Yatvin,[5] a former teacher and the only panel member who openly held a different perspective on early reading instruction. When the report of the National Reading Panel was released in April 2000, Ms. Yatvin refused to sign, charging that the Panel had deliberately misrepresented the evidence they did examine, and contrary perspectives on reading and reading research and literacy were systematically excluded.[6]

The NRP report was released in April 2000, together with a 32-page summary booklet and according to the news release, a video "ideal for parents, teachers, and anyone concerned about reading instruction and how to better teach children to read." Secretary Paige cited the findings of the National Reading Panel as the "scientific foundation" of the *Reading First* program.[7]

What Did the National Reading Panel Report Conclude?

Grand claims about what science says should be greeted with skepticism, particularly in an area as complex and contentious as reading, where there are vested interests within and outside of government, billions of dollars in products and services at stake, and deeply held ideological and cultural differences with respect to child development, learning, teaching, and the purposes of public education.

Although government sources and the Secretary of Education repeatedly claim the NRP report proved that structured phonics instruction is scientific and beyond question, a reading of the full NRP report reveals that this claim is false. Though the Panel was heavily weighted to favor direct phonics instruction, an unequivocal endorsement of heavy phonics is nowhere to be found in the report. The 32-page government summary of the NRP report in one place reads, "Teachers must understand that systematic phonics instruction is only one component—albeit a necessary component—of a total reading program. . . ."[8] The full report which runs over 500 pages includes numerous caveats against heavy-handed emphasis on phonics drills. In several places the report urges "balance" and increased opportunities for early readers to be "immersed in print" and to have ready access to real books and quality literature. The official summary booklet reads "systematic phonics produces significant benefits for students kindergarten through sixth grade," blatantly contradicting the full report which states "there were insufficient data to draw any conclusions about the effects of phonics with normally developing readers above first grade."[9]

Among the more alarming limitations of using the NRP report and the official summary as a guide to policy is that the panel chose to ignore a large body of research on reading and language that did not fit their criteria for what constitutes scientific research. The panel restricted its analyses and conclusions to what is known as "experimental research," that is research that assigns "subjects" randomly to an "experimental" or to a "control" group, and where all variables and outcomes are expressed and measured in quantitative terms. The NRP's definition of scientific research eliminated most of the research on reading—studies of teaching of reading as it occurs in natural settings, virtually all the established forms of systematic observational and interview research, and most, if not all, quantitative and qualitative studies conducted by linguists, cultural anthropologists, sociologists, reading researchers, and cognitive, developmental, and clinical psychologists.

Among the studies never considered were those that focused on the connections between writing and learning to read, student attitudes and motivation, and the impact of "print-rich" and "print-poor" social environments on learning to read. Ignored also were close-in interview and case studies of students with special developmental needs, qualitative longitudinal studies, research on the impact of race, racism, culture, and language on early language acquisition and reading. Finally, the panel failed to consider the gross inequities between rich and poor schools, the effects of the continuing failure to provide all children with the tools, human and material resources, necessary for learning. These include availability and quality of physical facilities, books, teaching materials, trained teachers, places to read, access to tutoring, and well-provisioned school and public libraries.[10]

Reading First and NCLB Testing Provisions

To continue to receive *Reading First* funding, schools are required to show "Annual Yearly Progress" (AYP)—the minimum gains in test scores as specified by government regulation—in reading and math for grades three through eight and, beginning in 2005, tests for grades 10 to 12. Each state has some latitude in choosing its plan and procedures for setting content standards and statewide testing, but the state plan must be deemed acceptable to federal authorities.

Beginning in 2002–03 states must also participate in biennial National Assessments of Educational Progress (NAEP) in reading for fourth- and eighth-graders, and use the data to ". . . examine the relative rigor of state standards and assessments against a common metric."[11] According to the plan NAEP test scores will ultimately serve as the national standard for measuring teaching quality, students' academic achievement, and for distributing rewards and applying sanctions.

NAEP are non-commercial standardized tests that the federal government administers to a national sample of students. NAEP currently do not provide scores for individual students or schools. NAEP results are released by the federal government to the public as a "report card" on the nation's public schools. Data are disaggregated by poverty, race or ethnicity, disability, and English proficiency.

The use of NAEP as the standard is problematic. The tests were never designed to be used for the purpose NCLB Act requires,[12] and the proficiency levels set by NAEP are arbitrary and set excessively high. On the 2000 NAEP reading assessment, for example, only 32% of U.S. fourth graders reached the "proficient" level or above, but U.S. nine year olds in a 27-nation comparison ranked second.[13] In addition, NAEP are afflicted with the same validity and reliability problems that plague the standardized tests now mandated by most states. Neither is correlated to actual academic performance nor has significant predictive value.

What is the effect of the act's testing provisions that rely on standardized tests to measure reading proficiency? There is a large body of independent research that suggests that the negative consequences of NCLB testing policies far outweigh the presumed benefits, and that should these policies continue the effects will be devastating in terms of the quality of teaching and learning, increasing dropouts and the "achievement gap." The best proponents can do is point to some very modest five- to ten-point gains in test scores, but the gains are predictably erratic and flatten over time. Nor is there any evidence that suggests that a few points gain in test scores translate to observable improvements in reading or school quality.

The educational significance of shifts up and down of a few points on standardized tests will likely continue to be debated by policy makers, the public, and the press. However there is little dispute over the effects of government mandated testing on the quality and breadth of the school curriculum. The pressures to raise standardized test scores translate to increased time and resources devoted to test preparation. Whatever does not contribute directly to short-term gains in test scores—writing, literature, critical thinking, civic education, interdisciplinary studies, the arts, physical education, and multicultural curriculum and bilingual education that are not add-ons, but integral to the entire curriculum—is marginalized. Standardized curriculum and testing extinguishes unpopular and dissenting perspectives and discourages curriculum innovation and community initiatives to develop educational programs that serve students, community, and local needs.

Whole language and critical literacy approaches to reading and language instruction and professional development are under attack and being supplanted with programs federal officials view as "scientifically based." Schools under great pressure to raise test scores increasingly adopt commercially available packaged programs such as *Open Court* and *Reading Mastery* (formerly called DISTAR) and similar highly scripted programs that focus almost entirely on teaching children to read through an intense focus on phonics. Such programs are heavily promoted as meeting the "scientifically based" requirement of the NCLB Act and therefore, it is assumed, consistent with the recommendations of the National Reading Panel report. The term "scientifically based" serves as a code word that indicates to state officials and local districts that the program is likely acceptable to federal officials and therefore fundable under the NCLB Act.

U.S. Department of Education Secretary Paige and Bush's educational advisor G. Reid Lyon readily endorse the use of such highly structured programs even though the NRP report explicitly cautions against "phonics programs [that] present a fixed set of lessons scheduled from the beginning to end of the school year," and "the lack of flexibility and developmental and cultural appropriateness offered by *commercial* programs."[14] (Italics added) The educational interests of all children—particularly those who are poor and of color—are compromised as decisions about testing and reading programs are made based on the political influence of major corporations including the highly concentrated textbook and test publishing industry. Among Bush's confidants and generous campaign contributors is Harold McGraw III, CEO of McGraw-Hill, which is the nation's largest producer of standardized tests, school textbooks, and instructional materials, including two of the best known highly scripted phonics programs, *Open Court* and *Reading Mastery*.

Reading First, Testing, and the Achievement Gap

There is nothing in the NRP report to support the claim that a direct instruction phonics approach is effective with poor children or children of color, or that such programs will close the achievement gap. The reason, noted earlier, is that studies that focused on race, culture, differences in learning styles, and family income were eliminated on the grounds they did not meet the panel's criteria for science.[15] It is also indisputable that poor children and children of color are the first in line for a truncated, narrow curriculum because they are disproportionately in the lowest scoring schools. The highly prescriptive commercial packages greatly restrict the ability of schools and classroom teachers to use their own observations and judgment in selecting teaching materials and teaching methods that are responsive to individual, cultural, and language differences.

Standardized tests used by NCLB to assess reading progress serve as gatekeepers determining, for example, eligibility for promotion, access to advanced classes, and special programs. The limitations of this form of assessment are especially troubling because standardized tests disproportionately exclude students of color, the poor, and those not raised in standard English-speaking households. Because the technology of standardized tests inflates differences that often have little or no educational significance, and because there are no demonstrable connections between performance on a standardized reading test and real academic performance, the use of standardized testing to measure reading proficiency and assess school and teacher competence serves as a form of institutional racism.

CONCLUSION

The *No Child Left Behind Act* and its *Reading First* program are defining examples of the social policies of the Bush presidency that serve corporate interests first, without a pretense that government is to serve as an arbiter or moderator between the corporate interest and the public interest. The federal government under Bush, father and son, and Clinton has become an unabashed advocate for the corporate educational agenda, and the use of governmental bureaucratic authority to impose its will.

Horace Mann, the 19th century educator considered the founding father of US public education, sought to convince business leaders of his day that a system of free public schools open to all was in their self-interest. He also spoke of his vision of public education as "the great equalizer" and "the great balance wheel of the social machinery" that would lead to the disappearance of poverty and with it the "rancorous discord between the haves and have-nots."[16] The *No Child Left Behind Act* as currently written and enforced cannot and will not advance this vision of the common school. Rather the effect of the corporate and government alliance that produced the act is to impose a regressive and standardized view of culture, curriculum, learning, and knowledge that is inimical to a free society.

Democratic reforms of schooling cannot occur without adequate funding and restoring power to local communities, parents, teachers, and students. This requires legislative action to reverse the damage visited upon public education by the *No Child Left Behind Act* as well as other laws that regulate public education nationally and within each state. New legislation, state and federal, is essential to put an end to the use by government of standardized tests as the definitive measure of school quality, teacher effectiveness, and student achievement.

These changes cannot occur on their own. They will come about only in response to persistent pressure by national and local coalitions and tactical alliances that cut across political party, social class, racial, and even ideological lines. Many coalitions of citizens, students, teachers, parents, child advocates, civil liberties and civil rights leaders, and fair test advocates now exist. The resistance to current policies is growing and will continue to grow and become more militant and well organized as the pernicious effects of mandated testing and other *No Child Left Behind* provisions become evident.

As a nation we will continue to differ profoundly on how schools ought to educate, what an educated person ought to know, and how best to teach the young to read. In a democracy we cannot allow federal and state officials, government appointed boards, and panels of experts remote from communities, classrooms, and students to make these choices and thereby control our and our children's futures.

QUESTIONS

Citizens, parents, and public officials must continue to raise questions about how testing is being used and how reading is being taught in their local schools. These include:

1. Does the reading program adequately address students' developmental, learning, and cultural differences? What is the mix of approach(es) to beginning reading in the school? Are there exceptions? To what extent are teachers being required to follow a fixed sequence of instruction? Is test preparation displacing writing, oral language, drama, and other aspects of a balanced reading and language program?

2. Section 1905 of NCLB states the following. "Federal officials may not mandate, direct, or control a state, local educational agency, or school's specific instructional content, academic achievement standards and assessments, curriculum or program of instruction."[17] Is this provision to preserve local community control being violated in your local school or district? Are parents and students told of their rights to waivers, exemptions, or modifications and accommodations in assessment practices? Are teachers and counselors allowed to explore the options with parents?

3. What are the claims being made about whether material and programs used are "scientifically based"? Are these claims critically examined? Are there independent reviews of such claims?

4. Are there adequate numbers of up-to-date texts, teaching materials, and school and public library collections? Are libraries accessible? Are the required texts and book collections reflective of the backgrounds and cultures of the students?

5. Are standardized tests being used as the only or primary measures of reading proficiency? Are the assessments used helpful to teachers and students?

6. Is there an independent assessment of the effects of standardized testing programs and curriculum on school climate, student engagement in learning, dropout rates, teacher morale, and turnover?[18]

NOTES

1. A Nation At Risk. (1983). http://www.ed.gov/pubs/NatAtRisk/risk.html
2. For an account of the role of the BRT in shaping federal state policy see unpublished dissertation Emery, K. (2002). The Business Roundtable and Systemic Reform, University of California Davis.
3. *Report of the National Reading Panel: Teaching Children to Read: Summary Booklet.* (1999). Washington, DC: National Institute of Child Health and Human Development. p. 8.
4. This figure was $900 million for 2002, see the No Child Left Behind web site: http://nclb.gov/start/facts/readingfirst.html. Critics note that this amount does not represent additional funds, rather funds are taken from existing federal programs. Support for purchase of library books is one example.
5. Yatvin, J. (2002). "Babes in the Woods: The Wanderings of the National Reading Panel." *Phi Delta Kappan*, January. pp. 364–369.
6. Coles, G. (2003). *Reading the naked truth: Literacy, legislation, and lies.* Portsmouth, NH: Heinemann; Garan, E. M. (2002). Resisting reading mandates: How to triumph with the truth. Portsmouth, NH: Heinemann; Metcalf, S. (2002). Reading between the lines. *The Nation* January, 28.
7. See http://www.ed.gov/PressReleases/04-2002/04022002.html
8. *Report of the National Reading Panel: Teaching Children to Read: Summary Booklet.* (1999). Washington, DC: National Institute of Child Health and Human Development. p. 11.
9. *Report of the National Reading Panel: Teaching Children to Read: Summary Booklet.* p. 9. *Report of the National Reading Panel: Teaching Children to Read: Report of the Subgroups* (1999). Washington, DC: National Institute of Child Health and Human Development. p. 2–116.
10. For more detailed critique and analysis see Coles, *op cit*. Garan, op cit., Krashen, S. (2000). "More Smoke and Mirrors: A Critique of NRP Report." *Phi Delta Kappan* 83 (2).
11. *No Child Left Behind: A Desktop Reference.* (2002). Washington, DC: Office of the Undersecretary. Available at http://www.ed.gov/offices/OESE/reference.html.
12. Linn, R. L. (1998). *Standards-Based Accountability: Ten Suggestions. Policy Paper.* Center for Research in Evaluation, Standards and Student Testing, General Accounting Office, *Educational Achievement Standards: NAGB's Approach Yields Misleading Interpretations.* (1993). Washington, DC: Author, June, Report GAO/PEMD-93-12; National Academy of Sciences, *Grading the Nation's Report Card: Evaluating NAEP and Transforming the Assessment of Educational Progress.* (1999). Washington, DC: National Academy Press. Jones, L. V. (1997). *National Tests of Educational Reform: Are They Compatible?* Princeton, NJ: Policy Information Center, Educational Testing Service. Available at www.ets.org/search97cgi/s97_cgi.
13. Bracey, G. (2003). *NCLB—A Plan for the Destruction of Public Education: Just Say 'No'* February Available online at http://nochildleft.com/2003/feb03no.html
14. *Report of the National Reading Panel: Teaching Children to Read: Report of the Subgroups.* (1999). Washington, DC: National Institute of Child Health and Human Development. p. 2–97.

15. Coles, G. *op cit*. Chapter 6. pp. 86–114.

16. Cremin, L. A. (1962). *The transformation of the school: Progressivism in American education, 1876–1957*. New York: Alfred A. Knopf. p. 9.

17. Manzo, K. K., & Hoff, D. J. (2003). Federal influence over curriculum exhibits growth. *Education Week*, February 5. p. 1.

18. I thank Ann Berlak for her careful critical reading and invaluable suggestions.

19
▼▼▼▼▼▼▼

Public School Reform:
The Mismeasure of Education*

Svi Shapiro

This past summer the legislature in my home state of North Carolina passed into law the so-called "Excellent Schools Act." While this legislation will certainly affect the lives of students and teachers here, the significance of what has been enacted goes well beyond the borders of North Carolina. In many ways the legislation reflects and crystallizes much of the thinking as well as the public discourse on education in this country at this time. Certainly the act is of a piece with the White House's current push to mandate national tests to measure educational standards in our public schools. The North Carolina legislation included the following items:

- Increased attention to state-mandated performance standards throughout K–12 schooling.
- Incentives for teachers and schools to achieve these standards; for teachers who exceed them in the classroom by 10 percent or more there are bonuses of $1500: for schools that meet their goals teachers would receive $750.
- Teachers in schools where students are doing poorly in the classroom will have to take a general knowledge test (if they do not pass it they get two more chances before losing their jobs).

- Local boards of education are able to decide whether a teacher should get tenure after four years in the classroom. In addition there is a "streamlining" of the appeals process for removing teachers, primarily through limiting the appeals process.
- Related legislation has also placed a Damocles sword over the heads of school principals who fail to ensure high or rising scores on achievement tests; failure to do so leads to the possibility of suspension or removal from their position.

The bill was originally proposed by Democratic governor Jim Hunt, considered one of the national leaders in public school reform. It was supported by both Democrats and Republicans in the state. Harold Brubaker, Republican Speaker of the House, summed up support in these words: "for the first time ever we are holding educators to the kind of accountability and performance measures people in the private sector are faced with on a daily basis."

In return for these changes teachers were promised a 6.5 percent increase in salaries and a long-term commitment by the governor to raise the pay of North Carolina teachers at least up to the national average (the state like most in the South has languished in standards of pay). The key concern at the center of the proposed changes, however, is the effort to ensure that public schools more fully reflect and conform to the needs of business, and that the criteria used to judge business success or effectiveness are more completely and consistently employed in public education. No one has expressed this more often and more persuasively than President Clinton, who has argued that the most important reason for school reform is the "need to be competitive in the 21st century." As the language of "performance goals" more and more dominates the public debate on schooling so the business concern with output and productivity comes to define our vision for school success. At school, as in the workplace, success is understood only in the most immediate and crude terms of empirically verifiable and quantifiable data, especially as schools become focused on tests that measure student performance in ways that are standardized and intellectually reductionist. As Alfie Kohn has noted, "The emphasis [at school and work] is on results, on turning out a product, on quantifying improvements on a fixed series of measures such as sales volume or return on investment." We have entered an era where, to an unparalleled degree, the language and thinking of business shape the thinking and vision of education.

Of course one does not need to be a genius to grasp the detrimental effect of all this on the lives of teachers and students. Under the regime of increasing standardization, schooling becomes simply the search for prefigured "right" answers, and the capacity to regurgitate bits of information that are on somebody else's list of what is intellectually correct or appropriate. Worst of all is the notion that only those things that can be measured in some kind of precise and quantifiable way have educational value. The arts or other creative areas of the curriculum which do not easily lend themselves to this "regime of measurement" are bound to lose out and be marginalized (or try to transform themselves into some grotesque form of measurable competencies which is now commonly the case).

Where teachers' livelihoods are made dependent on improvements in test scores, it will be only the most exceptional among them that will seek to make their classrooms places that are creative and expansive in their practices. Focusing on what is most shallow and homogenized in teaching negates those learning possibilities that emphasize the development of a critical intelligence, the stimulation of our imagination, or the quest to make meaning out of our own experience. All of these depend on cultivating attitudes that question so-called correct answers or knowledge and to seek, instead, what is unfamiliar, even irreverent or subversive. Real education encourages students in the search for the unpredictable or the unexpected. It helps us transcend the "givenness" or the taken-for-granted in our intellectual or cultural world.

Critical observers of schooling in this country have long noted how public schools have been shaped by industrial images—classrooms as factories, students as raw materials, teachers as workers, the pedagogic process as one of inputs and outputs subject to behavioral and technical manipulation. Today, under the pressures of both the White House and the state house, the concern to fit schools to such a vision has rarely seemed so apparent. And rarely have more "progressive" visions of education seemed so marginalized. This pressure has been fomented by the sense of panic about falling school standards that has suffused the public discourse on education since the publication of the 1983 "Nation at Risk" report. Hardly a day seems to go by without the publication of yet another report claiming that test scores in math, science, or reading have dropped, or that other countries continue to outscore the U.S. in measures of school achievement. It seems not to matter that careful scholars like Gerald Bracey or David Berliner have refuted the veracity of many of these claims. They have shown, for example, that invidious comparisons with SAT scores makes no sense when it is recognized how much more socially diverse is the present population of SAT test takers compared to the limited and disproportionately privileged groups taking it in earlier times. Nor does this country do especially badly in comparison to most other nations. Perhaps most significant is how little correlation there is between these measures and levels of economic growth or productivity. It is paradoxical indeed that while schools were blamed for the economic plight of the 1970s, the present economic boom is little credited to education.

Part of what is so debilitating about the North Carolina reforms and their counterparts elsewhere is the reduction of teachers' work to the crudest kinds of monetary incentives. Of course this is not about the reasonableness and justice of teachers being paid a little better. There has always been a great hypocrisy in the language we use to describe the value of those who help raise our children and how much society is prepared to pay those who do such work. No, the problem is the notion that better teaching can be paid off like piecework; count up the test results and give bonuses to the most effective workers. This vulgar notion that good teaching is reducible to higher scores on the test is surely the most limited of ways to think about the nature and purpose of teaching. The pressure to convert the breadth and complexity of children's development to the crude simplicity of a numerical score is a trivializing and insensitive travesty apparent to most teachers who understand just how little is captured by this about human intelligence, creativity, or sociability.

Finally, we are talking about a process that further accentuates the competitive culture of schools. In this regard critics of schooling have long rejected the claim that schools are ideologically or morally neutral institutions. They have, especially, noted the centrality of individualist and competitive values in what is sometimes referred to as the "hidden curriculum" of education. Schools in this view are a primary mechanism for inculcating the necessity and inevitability of a success-oriented, achievement-centered, hierarchical and egoistic culture. Schools provide the vehicle for sorting and legitimating what will ultimately become the class and other social divisions of American society—giving an intellectual rationale for how we allocate and distribute material and symbolic rewards. Within this context standardized tests are of enormous consequence. They provide a common-sense legitimacy to notions about the unequal distribution of intellectual capabilities. They offer a "scientific" justification for the hierarchical and unequal relationships between human beings. The ubiquitous "bell-curve" upon which an individual's success and failure is plotted gives an apparent naturalness and inevitability to the social and cultural divisions of our world. And certainly to the extent that they are attended to with increased concern, even alarm, they reinforce the culture's obsession with winning, "getting ahead," and the pursuit of individual success.

Whether they like it or not, in the present climate teachers and school administrators are forced to give inordinate attention to those things that differentiate and rank students, rather than concern themselves with developing an ethic of care and mutuality. From my own experience in working with teachers, this emphasis is at least an uncomfortable one. Many teachers are animated by a moral impulse to bring young people to a greater appreciation of the social relations of care, compassion, and mutual concern. The intense emphasis on standardized testing which now permeates our schools, however, promotes the opposite feelings; the culture of individual success always implies doing better than one's neighbor—sometimes at any cost. Whether or not we wish to acknowledge it, this is a process that encourages students to lie, cheat, or do "whatever is necessary" in order to do well. The self-interested ethic of the marketplace becomes the ethic of the classroom. It is a short distance from this to what Charles Derber has called the culture of "wilding"—a culture whose driving force is an unbridled concern with increasing one's own share of the pie.

Especially damaging in all of this is the pernicious myth of meritocracy. How we perform on these standardized tests is, we are to believe, a matter of individual ability and intelligence and the level of effort particular students can bring to bear on the task. Absent or silent in this view are the effects of the social context on how students relate to, or achieve, in school. Yet there is absolutely no doubt that school success is, in reality, overwhelmingly influenced by this context. We have known for many years that the single most important predictor of school achievement is one's social class. One only has to look at the numbers put out by the Educational Testing Service related to SAT performance:

Annual Family Income	SAT scores
Under $10,000	873
10,000–20,000	948
20,000–30,000	962
30,000–40,000	993
40,000–50,000	1015
50,000–60,000	1033
60,000–70,000	1048
70,000–80,000	1062
80,000–100,000	1090
over 100,000	1130

Sociologists, socio-linguists, and others have given us a significant understanding of why this is so. Though complex, it is a process that brings together the differential expectations of teachers, the attitudes of students towards the institution of school, the cultural and linguistic knowledge that students bring with them from home and the streets, as well as the educational and economic resources available in the community. Far from an innocent vehicle for impartially discerning merit among students, it turns out that schools are deeply implicated in the cultural and material inequities of class, race, gender, and region; who does well in school and who does badly is much better explained by the social circumstances within which our kids grow up than by whether their teachers are especially talented or even hard-working. In this sense North Carolina's intention to punish teachers where students do poorly, or to make them take a general knowledge test, is laughable were it not so insulting and threatening to teachers. The most realistic way to avoid such consequences is for teachers to find jobs in the upscale suburbs or neighborhoods of our cities.

Of course one may well ask why it is that such knowledge is excluded from the framing of the public debate—and legislation—on education. There is no easy response to this question. Certainly, however, part of the answer lies in our culture's deeply-rooted attempt to deny the existence or salience of social class in the shaping of our lives and experience. Instead we have a latter-day myth of "rugged individualism"—the notion that each person's success or failure is entirely explained by their own talents and efforts. In the face of the overwhelming reality that school success is more dependent on a child's social class than on any other single factor, placing the onus on the efforts of the individual teacher or student is a massive exercise in cultural denial and ideological confusion.

Particularly sad in the distortion of educational values and goals implicit in recent reforms is their effect on teachers' motivations and aspirations. The idealistic intentions that usually bring people into education—a desire to make some contribution to a better world, to improve the lives of kids, to offer a caring environment for children, and so on—become perverted by the limited pursuit of higher test scores and the crass exploitation of a few extra dollars for achieving "better" results. What sense of vocation can teachers be expected to bring to their work in a climate that stresses such crude, reductionist, and narrowly-defined educational goals? Like so many other areas, teaching has become not only a de-skilled craft but also a degraded one.

It is certainly paradoxical that at a time when there is so much talk about improving the professional quality of public school teaching, reforms increasingly limit and circumscribe the work of teachers. While on the one hand there seems to be an effort to decentralize power in school systems—so that greater decision-making possibilities exist at the local school level and among teachers themselves, the increasing centrality of standardized tests in guiding the curriculum means that the real power over pedagogy remains far removed from the actual work of teachers. Teachers, in effect, can have more say over less and less things that really matter in the educational process. Some of the most acute observers of the public school scene have noted for several years now that teachers are treated more and more as impersonal instruments in a bureaucratic process than as thoughtful and creative intellectuals whose personal vision of education really matters. Their concern with meaning and imagination becomes irrelevant as teaching is controlled by external test results and text-books, instructional materials, or software which manage the teaching process and curriculum content—all of which attempt to produce, in the words of Michael Apple, "teacher-proof" classrooms!

More insidious than these, however, are attempts, such as those in the North Carolina law, to weaken the tenure, job security, and appeal rights of teachers. While ostensibly making it easier to "weed-out" poor teachers, such changes in the professional security of teachers will undermine the confidence of those who might wish to break from the "daily grind" of test-driven classrooms to create more daring and challenging environments for their students. This country has a long history (some of which is vividly reconstructed in recent Hollywood movies) of the authoritarian exclusion of such teachers. As local school boards increasingly have the power to terminate teachers' contracts, right-wing activists will have greater opportunities to eradicate from the schools teachers who provide any kind of a liberal or dissenting view of culture or history in America. It would be politically naive in this context to expect anything less. One only has to look at the continuing battles around matters of curriculum, textbooks, literature, issues of sexuality, and so on to understand how attempts to weaken tenure laws can only increase the threat to teachers who are committed to classrooms where students might encounter ideas and beliefs that contradict traditional or more conventional worldviews. More conformity in classroom instruction rather than more compelling, interesting, or provocative teaching is the certain consequence of such changes.

We have come to understand from our recent studies of culture and literature that it is often the silences in our discourse—what is not said—that tell us what we truly value. While a steady public drumbeat calls us to connect education with competition and individual success, schooling seems ever more remote from what John Dewey called "the making of a world" that is democratic. One looks in vain in the discourse of teaching "excellence" for a concern with education as a potentially powerful vehicle for the renewal of a culture of active and meaningful citizenship: one in which education has a principal role in nurturing the skills, values, and commitments necessary to a culture in which individuals care about, and participate in, the making of a society that is just, compassionate, and free. For our schools to serve such democratic ends, rather than act as the training sites for the techno-corporate world, would mean a transformation in both our vision of educational purpose and in the practices of the classroom. When schools become places concerned with the meaning of citizenship and democracy rather than test scores and success, the educational agenda comes to be about matters of self and social awareness and the care for life. Schools are understood, preeminently, as places where students learn to critically examine the institutions, beliefs, values, and behaviors that constitute our world so that they understand the ways we promote or impede a world that treats human beings with dignity and respect. Students are encouraged to become critically conscious individuals able, as the great Brazilian educator Paolo Freire described it, to "problematize" our world—to question what is familiar or taken-for-granted in how we as human beings, both individually and collectively, understand and act toward others.

The impulse for such a concern is an ethical one. It is the quest for a world that is more just, more compassionate, more loving, more democratic, more free. It is the struggle for a world in which unnecessary suffering is reduced and joyful existence expanded. In this sense the critical citizenship we seek in our schools relies on the nurturing of an ethical sensibility that reveres life, seeks a world of dignity and caring, and sanctifies creation. While often marginalized, a powerful and rich educational tradition speaks, both philosophically as well as practically, to this notion of education for critical citizenship. It articulates a view of education that is inseparable from the quest for a renewal of the American values of democracy and community. It insists that literacy today must be a critical literacy that teaches students to understand the underlying moral and ideological meanings that permeate our cultural "texts," from books to movies, from fashions to popular music. It is an education that is about nurturing the sense of social responsibility, developing an awareness and respect for our differences as human beings, and the capacity to engage in the determination of our shared future. It means an education that teaches us, above all else, to care about the fate of human beings and of the earth itself—a concern for unnecessary poverty and violence, for racism and prejudice, for the destructive and wasteful uses of our material resources, and for the inviolable sanctity of life. Such a language and vision offers a significantly different agenda for educational reform than the present, corporate-driven approach to our schools. More than anything it reminds us of the significance of the public nature of these institutions as sites for the potential renewal of that sense of mutuality, community, and human agency in the seeking of a more just and compassionate commonwealth.

While the juggernaut of testing and competition continues its relentless shaping of our schools we can hear the rumblings of alternative educational discourses and agendas. Parents continue to tell pollsters the importance they attach to their children's schools being caring environments. The "Character Education" initiative promoted by the Clinton administration and various professional groups has promoted the importance of civic values in kids' education—though in ways that seem to emphasize moral conformity and the acceptance of authority rather than the feisty anti-authoritarianism required of a democratic culture. Religious and communal groups struggle with how to address issues of sexuality in schools, though typically here in ways that emphasize its dangers and evils rather than its pleasures. And in pedagogy itself educators try to promote some degree of creativity and meaningfulness in student learning by promoting a more integrated approach to the curriculum, or by emphasizing a "constructivist" approach to knowledge where the process of understanding rather than simply getting the answer right is paramount.

Yet all of this offers little to an educational vision which truly foregrounds the struggle for an education that prepares human beings to grapple with the transformation and repair of our world. There is little here that helps us break out of the deadly language of "excellence," "basic skills," "competencies," and "standards" that has dominated the goals of education in the last two decades. Such a change will mean that we see education as, in the first place, inextricably connected to the social, moral, and spiritual vision of our nation and our world. In this sense education is never morally or ideologically neutral. It can only be about maintaining and reproducing the world as it is, or about challenging and changing it. Notwithstanding the present hype about peace and prosperity, our world continues to be a place filled with the unnecessary suffering of violence and wars, poverty, meaningless work or unemployment, intolerance and racism, dangerous concentrations of political and economic power, the despoliation of the planet, civic withdrawal and isolation, and the dehumanizing commodification of everyday life. In such a context any education that does not define its purpose, preeminently, as the quest for lives of greater moral and spiritual meaning, and communities more caring, just, and democratic, is, surely, irresponsibly misdirected or dangerously distracted.

Care and Moral Education*

Nel Noddings

Increased interest in moral education in the past few years has led to vigorous debate among moral educators. In addition to the ongoing dialogue between cognitive-developmentalism and character education,[1] the ethic of care has been introduced as a perspective on moral education.[2] Because the ethic of care has roots in both feminism and pragmatic naturalism, and because moral education is at its very heart, it holds interest for educators as well as philosophers.

AN ETHIC OF CARE AND ITS SOURCE

Like deontological ethics—ethics of duty and right—the ethic of care speaks of obligation. A sense that *I must* do something arises when others address us. This "I must" is induced in direct encounter, in preparation for response. Sometimes we, as carers, attend and respond because we want to; we love the ones who address us, or we have sufficient positive regard for them, or the re-quest is so consonant with ordinary life that no inner conflict occurs. In a similar fashion, the recipients of such care may respond in a way that shows us that our caring has been received. When this happens, we say that the rela-

---

tion, episode, or encounter is one of natural caring. The "I must" expresses a desire or inclination—not a recognition of duty.

At other times, the initial "I must" is met by internal resistance. Simultaneously, we recognize the other's need and we resist; for some reason—the other's unpleasantness, our own fatigue, the magnitude of the need—we do not want to respond as carers. In such instances, we have to draw on ethical caring; we have to ask ourselves how we would behave if this other were pleasant or were a loved one, if we were not tired, if the need were not so great. In doing this, we draw upon an ethical ideal—a set of memories of caring and being cared for that we regard as manifestations of our best selves and relations. We summon what we need to maintain the original "I must."

Now why should we do this? Why, that is, do we recognize an obligation to care? If we were Kantians, we would trace our obligation to reason, to a commitment that logic will not allow us to escape. But in the ethic of care we accept our obligation because we value the relatedness of natural caring. Ethical caring is always aimed at establishing, restoring, or enhancing the kind of relation in which we respond freely because we want to do so.

An ethic of care does not eschew logic and reasoning. When we care, we must employ reasoning to decide what to do and how best to do it. We strive for competence because we want to do our best for those we care for. But reason is not what motivates us. It is feeling with and for the other that motivates us in natural caring. In ethical caring, this feeling is subdued, and so it must be augmented by a feeling for our own ethical selves.

Kant subordinated feeling to reason. He insisted that only acts done out of duty to carefully reasoned principle are morally worthy. Love, feeling, and inclination are all supposed by Kant to be untrustworthy. An ethic of care inverts these priorities. The preferred state is natural caring; ethical caring is invoked to restore it. This inversion of priority is one great difference between Kantian ethics and the ethic of care.

Another difference is anchored in feminist perspectives. An ethic of care is thoroughly relational. It is the *relation* to which we point when we use the adjective "caring." A relation may fail to be one of caring because the carer fails to be attentive or, having attended, rejects the "I must" and refuses to respond. Or, it may fail because the cared-for is unable or unwilling to respond; he or she does not receive the efforts of the carer, and therefore caring is not completed. Or, finally, both carer and cared-for may try to respond appropriately but some condition prevents completion; perhaps there has been too little time for an adequate relation to develop and the carer aims rather wildly at what he or she thinks the cared-for needs. A relational interpretation of caring pushes us to look not only at moral agents but at both the recipients of their acts and the conditions under which the parties interact.

Of course, the adjective "caring" is often used to refer to people who habitually care. There are people who attend and respond to others regularly and who have such a well-developed capacity to care that they can establish caring relations in even the most difficult situations. But, at bottom, the ethic of care should not be thought of as an ethic of virtue. Certainly, people who care in given situations exercise virtues, but if they begin to concentrate on their own character or virtue, the cared-for may feel put off. The cared-for is no longer the focus of attention. Rather, a virtue—being patient, or generous, or cheerful—becomes the focus, and the relation of caring itself becomes at risk.

From this very brief exposition of an ethic of care, we can see that moral education is at its very heart. We learn first how to be cared for, how to respond to loving efforts at care in a way that supports those efforts. An infant learns to smile at its caregiver, and this response so delights the caregiver that he or she seeks greater competence in producing smiles. Caregiver and cared-for enter a mutually satisfying relation. Later, the child learns to care for others—to comfort a crying baby, pet a kitten, pat a sad or tired mother with a murmured, "Poor mommy!"

The source of adult caring is thus two-fold. Because we (lucky ones) have been immersed in relations of care since birth, we often naturally respond as carers to others. When we need to draw on ethical caring, we turn to an ethical ideal constituted from memories of caring and being cared for. Thus the ethic of care may be regarded as a form of pragmatic naturalism. It does not posit a source of moral life beyond actual human interaction. It does not depend on gods, nor eternal verities, nor an essential human nature, nor postulated underlying structures of human consciousness. Even its relational ontology points to something observable in this world—the fact that I am defined in relation, that none of us could be an *individual*, or a *person*, or an entity recognizably human if we were not in relation.

It is obvious, then, that if we value relations of care, we must care for our children and teach them how to receive care and to give care. Further, our obligation does not end with the moral education of children. Contrary to Kant, who insisted that each person's moral perfection is his or her own project, we remain at least partly responsible for the moral development of each person we encounter. How I treat you may bring out the best or worst in you. How you behave may provide a model for me to grow and become better than I am. Whether I can become and remain a caring person—one who enters regularly into caring relations—depends in large part on how you respond to me. Further, ethical caring requires reflection and self-understanding. We need to understand our own capacities and how we are likely to react in various situations. We need to understand our own evil and selfish tendencies as well as our good and generous ones. Hence moral education is an essential part of an ethic of care, and much of moral education is devoted to the understanding of self and others.

THE COMPONENTS OF MORAL EDUCATION

Modeling, the first component of moral education in the care perspective, is important in almost every form of moral education. In the character education tradition, for example, it is central because exemplars constitute the very foundation of moral philosophy.[3] In the care perspective, we have to show in our modeling what it means to care.

There is a danger in putting too much emphasis on the modeling component of caring. When we focus on ourselves as models, we are distracted from the cared-for; the same peculiar distraction occurs, as we have seen, when we concentrate on our own exercise of virtue. Usually, we present the best possible model when we care unself-consciously, as a way of being in the world. When we do reflect, our attention should be on the relation between us and the cared-for: Is our response adequate? Could we put what we have said better? Has our act helped or hindered? We do not often reflect on our observers and what our behavior conveys to them. And this is as it should be.

But sometimes we must focus on ourselves as models of caring. When we show a small girl how to handle a pet, for example, our attention may be only peripherally on the pet. Our focal attention is on the little girl and whether she is learning from our demonstration. Similarly, as teachers, we often properly divert our attention from a particular student to the whole class of watchers. What does our behavior with this particular student convey to the class about what it means to care? As I said earlier, the shift of focus has its dangers and carried too far, it actually moves us away from caring.

In quiet moments, in the absence of those we must care for, reflection is essential. Not only should we reflect on our competence as carers, but we can now also consider our role as models. If I am, as a teacher, consistently very strict with my students "for their own good," what am I conveying? One teacher may emerge from such reflection satisfied that caring rightly forces cared-fors to do what is best for them. Another may emerge appalled that her efforts at care may suggest to students that caring is properly manifested in coercion. If the two get together to talk, both may be persuaded to modify their behavior, and this observation leads logically to the second component of moral education in this model.

Dialogue is the most fundamental component of the care model. True dialogue is open-ended, as Paulo Freire wrote.[4] The participants do not know at the outset what the conclusions will be. Both speak; both listen. Dialogue is not just conversation. There must be a topic, but the topic may shift, and either party in a dialogue may divert attention from the original topic to one more crucial, or less sensitive, or more fundamental.

The emphasis on dialogue points up the basic phenomenology of caring. A carer must attend to or be engrossed in the cared-for, and the cared-for must receive the carer's efforts at caring. This reception, too, is a form of attention. People in true dialogue within a caring relation do not turn their attention wholly to intellectual objects, although, of course, they may do this for brief intervals. Rather, they attend non-selectively to one another. Simone Weil described the connection this way:

> The love of our neighbor in all its fullness simply means being able to say to him: "What are you going through?" It is a recognition that the sufferer exists, not only as a unit in a collection, or a specimen from the social category labeled "unfortunate," but as a man, exactly like us. . . . This way of looking is first of all attentive. The soul empties itself of all its own contents in order to receive into itself the being it is looking at, just as he is, in all his truth.
>
> Only he who is capable of attention can do this.[5]

The other in a dialogue need not be suffering, but carers are always aware of the possibility of suffering. If the topic-at-hand causes pain, a caring participant may change the subject. Dialogue is sprinkled with episodes of interpersonal reasoning as well as the logical reasoning characteristic of intellectual debate.[6] A participant may pause to remind the other of her strengths, to reminisce, to explore, to express concern, to have a good laugh, or otherwise to connect with the other as cared-for. Dialogue, thus, always involves attention to the other participant, not just to the topic under discussion.

Dialogue is central to moral education because it always implies the question: What are you going through? It permits disclosure in a safe setting, and thus makes it possible for a carer to respond appropriately. Dialogue provides information about the participants, supports the relationship, induces further thought and reflection, and contributes to the communicative competence of its participants. As modes of dialogue are internalized, moral agents learn to talk to themselves as they talk to others. Such dialogue is an invitation to ever-deepening self-understanding. What do I really want? What was I trying to do when I acted as I did? What (good or evil) am I capable of? Am I too hard on myself? Am I honest with myself? One important aim of dialogue with others or with self is understanding the "other" with whom one is in dialogue.

Dialogue as described here rejects the "war model" of dialogue. It is not debate, and its purpose is not to win an argument. It may, of course, include intervals of debate, and both participants may enjoy such intervals. But throughout a dialogue, participants are aware of each other; they take turns as carer and cared-for, and no matter how great their ideological differences may be, they reach across the ideological gap to connect with each other.

One organization that has put aside the "war model" of dialogue is a group of women on opposite sides of the abortion issue; they call themselves

Common Ground. (Actually, several organizations using this name have sprung up around the country, but the one to which I refer here is in the San Francisco Bay Area.) The purpose of Common Ground is not for each side to argue its own convictions and effect a glorious victory over ignorant or evil opponents. Rather, the explicit primary goal is to "reject the war model of the abortion argument and fully recognize that human beings, not cardboard cut-outs, make up the 'other side'."[7] The women of Common Ground describe themselves as "frustrated and heartsick at what the abortion controversy has done to traditionally female values such as communication, compassion, and empathy." But can an issue like abortion be resolved through communication, compassion, and empathy? That question misses the whole point of the approach being discussed here. The point of coming together in true dialogue is *not* to persuade opponents that our own position is better justified logically and ethically than theirs. The issue may never be resolved. The point is to create or restore relations in which natural caring will guide future discussion and protect participants from inflicting and suffering pain. Many of the women of Common Ground continue their advocacy roles in pro-life or pro-choice organizations because advocacy/adversary roles are the only ones widely accepted in American politics. But their advocacy functions are deepened and softened by the goal of Common Ground—to maintain caring relations across differences. Strategies that participants might once have considered against faceless adversaries are now firmly rejected.

Common Ground may well achieve desirable practical outcomes beyond a cessation of violence and name-calling. Already, women of opposing views on abortion have agreed on other goals: providing aid to existing children who are needy, helping poor mothers, defending women who are deserted or abused. Energies have been diverted from condemning and fighting to accomplishing positive, cooperative goals and, more important, to the establishment of relations that will allow ideological opponents to live constructively with their differences.

Talk, conversation, and debate are used in every form of moral education, but often the focus is on justifying moral decisions. Cognitive programs of moral education concentrate on helping students to develop moral reasoning. In sorting through dilemmas, students learn to justify the positions they take and to judge the strength of other people's arguments. It is certainly worthwhile to exercise and strengthen students' powers of reason, but advocates of the care perspective worry that students may forget the purpose of moral reasoning—to establish and maintain caring relations at both individual and societal levels. Of course, advocates of a cognitive approach to moral education may deny that caring relations are central to moral reasoning. They may argue, instead, that the purpose of moral reasoning is to figure out what is right. This involves an evaluation of principles and selection of the one that should guide moral action. If this were done regularly by everyone, they might argue, we would achieve a just society and reduce individual suffering considerably. But care advocates worry about principles chosen and decisions made in abstract isolation, and we worry, too, about the assumption that what is right can be determined logically, without hearing what others are actually going through.

The theoretical differences between care and justice perspectives are too many and too deep to explore here. However, one point is especially relevant to the present discussion. There is some evidence that students exposed to cognitive approaches often come to believe that almost any decision can be justified, that the strength of their arguments is what really counts.[8] Cognitivist educators are not happy with this result, but to change it, they have to lead students toward concepts that help to anchor their thinking. They usually depend on a procedural mechanism to determine right or wrong. Care theorists more often line up with consequentialists here. In trying to figure out what is right, we have to find out what is good for the people involved. But this does not make us utilitarians, either. We do not posit one stable, abstract, universal good and try to produce that for the greatest number. Rather, we must work to determine what is good for this person or these people and how our proposed action will affect all of those in the network of care. Dialogue is the means through which we learn what the other wants and needs, and it is also the means by which we monitor the effects of our acts. We ask, "What are you going through?" before we act, as we act, and after we act. It is our way of being in relation.

A third component of moral education in the care perspective is practice. One must work at developing the capacity for interpersonal attention. Simone Weil thought that this capacity could be developed through the "right use of school studies"—especially subjects like geometry.[9] But all of us know people who are wonderfully attentive in an intellectual field and almost totally insensitive to people and their needs. To develop the capacity to care, one must engage in caregiving activities.

In almost all cultures, women seem to develop the capacity to care more often and more deeply than men. Most care theorists do not believe that this happens because of something innate or essential in women. Care theorists believe that it happens because girls are expected to care for people, and boys are too often relieved of this expectation. This is an open question, of course, but the hope of moral educators is that both sexes can learn to care. Indeed, most care theorists oppose any position that confines caring to women because it would tend to encourage the exploitation of women and undermine our efforts at moral education. Caring is not just for women, nor is it a way of being reserved only for private life.

What sort of practice should children have? It seems reasonable to suggest that, just as girls should have mathematical and scientific experience, boys should have caregiving experience. Boys, like girls, should attend to the needs of guests, care for smaller children, perform housekeeping chores, and the like. The supposition, from a care perspective, is that the closer we are to the intimate physical needs of life, the more likely we are to understand its fragility and to feel the pangs of the inner "I must"—that stirring of the heart that moves us to respond to one another.

Similarly, in schools, students should be encouraged to work together, to help one another—not just to improve academic performance. Teachers have a special responsibility to convey the moral importance of cooperation to their students. Small-group methods that involve inter-group competition should be monitored closely. Competition can be fun, and insisting that it has no place whatever in cooperative arrangements leads us into unnecessary confrontation. But, if competition induces insensitive interactions, teachers should draw this to the attention of their students and suggest alternative strategies. Such discussions can lead to interesting and fruitful analyses of competition at other levels of society.

Many high schools—more independent than public—have begun to require community service as a means of giving their students practice in caring. But a community service requirement cannot guarantee that students will care, any more than the requirement to "take algebra" can ensure that students will learn algebra in any meaningful way. Community service must be taken seriously as an opportunity to practice caring. Students must be placed in sites congenial to their interests and capacities. The people from whom they are to learn must model caring effectively, and this means that they must be capable of shifting their attention gently and sensitively from those they are caretaking, to those they are teaching. Students should also participate in a regular seminar at which they can engage in dialogue about their practice.

The last component of moral education from the care perspective is confirmation.[10] To confirm others is to bring out the best in them. When someone commits an uncaring act (judged, of course, from our own perspective), we respond—if we are engaging in confirmation—by attributing the best possible motive consonant with reality. By starting this way, we draw the cared-for's attention to his or her better self. We confirm the other by showing that we believe the act in question is not a full reflection of the one who committed it.

Confirmation is very different from the pattern found in many forms of religious education: accusation, confession, forgiveness, and penance. Accusation tends to drive carer and cared-for apart; it may thereby weaken the relation. Confession and forgiveness suggest a relation of authority and subordinate and may prevent transgressors from taking full responsibility for their acts. Further, confession and forgiveness can be ritualized. When this happens, there is no genuine dialogue. What happens does not depend on the relation between carer and cared-for, and the interaction is not aimed at strengthening the relation. Hence it has little effect on the construction of an ethical ideal in either carer or cared-for, since this ideal is composed reflectively from memories of caring and being cared for.

Confirmation is not a ritual act that can be performed for any person by any other person. It requires a relation. Carers have to understand their cared-fors well enough to know what it is they are trying to accomplish. Attributing the best possible motive consonant with reality requires a knowledge of that reality and cannot be pulled out of thin air. When carers identify a motive and use it in confirmation, the cared-for should recognize it as his or her own. "That is what I was trying to do!" It is wonderfully reassuring to realize that another sees the better self that often struggles for recognition beneath our lesser acts and poorer selves.

PHILOSOPHICAL ISSUES

The model of moral education discussed here is based on an ethic of care. That ethic has an element of universality. It begins with the recognition that all people everywhere want to be cared for. Universality evaporates when we try to describe exactly what it means to care, for manifestations of caring relations differ across times, cultures, and even individuals. In roughly similar settings and situations, one person may recognize a cool form of respect as caring, whereas another may feel uncared for without a warm hug.

Because of its beginning in natural attributes and events, caring may properly be identified with pragmatic naturalism. John Dewey started his ethical thought with the observation that human beings are social animals and desire to communicate. The ethic of care begins with the universal desire to be cared for—to be in positive relation with at least some other beings. We note that human beings do in fact place a high value on such relations, and so our most fundamental "ought" arises as instrumental: If we value such relations, then we ought to act so as to create, maintain, and enhance them.

As Dewey filled out his moral theory, he moved rapidly to problem solving—surely one aim of communication. As we fill out an ethic of care, we concentrate on the needs and responses required to maintain caring relations. The difference need not be construed as a gender difference, but it may indeed be the case that the care orientation arises more naturally and fully from the kind of experience traditionally associated with women. Dewey himself once remarked that when women started to do philosophy, they would almost surely "do it differently." This observation in no way implies that a gender difference must forever divide philosophical thinking. Mutual influence, critical reciprocity, may produce models that incorporate elements of both perspectives. However, it may be years before female philosophies are themselves fully developed. Will we finish up at the same place by a different route? Or will even the endpoint be different? These are intriguing questions for contemporary moral philosophy.

Whereas there is an element of universality in the ethic of care, we cannot claim universality for the model of moral education. Probably all moral educators incorporate modeling and practice in their educational programs, but many would reject confirmation, and some would reject the focus on dialogue, emphasizing instead commandment and obedience. Proponents of caring do not regard the lack of universality as a weakness. On the contrary, many of us feel that insistence on universal models is a form of cultural arrogance. Here we differ strongly with Kohlbergians on at least two matters: First, we see no reason to believe that people everywhere must reason or manifest their caring in identical ways; second, although we put great emphasis on intelligent action, we reject a narrow focus on reason itself. It is not just the level and power of reasoning that mark moral agents as well developed but the actual effects of their behavior on the relations of which they are part. Moreover, it is not so much the development of individual moral agents that interests us but the maintenance and growth of moral relations, and this is a very different focus.[11]

Care advocates differ also with certain aspects of character education. Although we share with Aristotelians and others who call themselves "communitarians" the conviction that modern moral philosophy has put far too much emphasis on individual moral agents wrestling in lonely isolation with logically decidable moral problems, we also fear the Aristotelian emphasis on social role or function. This emphasis can lead to hierarchies of virtue and demands for unwavering loyalty to church or state. Different virtues are expected of leaders and followers, men and women, bosses and workers. Further, educational models tend to suppose that communities can arrive at consensus on certain values and/or virtues.

Early in this century, the Character Development League sought to inculcate in all students a long list of virtues including obedience, industry, purity, self-reliance, courage, justice, and patriotism.[12] Probably both Kohlbergians and care advocates would agree that school children should have many opportunities to discuss such virtues and that they should read and hear inspiring stories illustrating the exercise of virtue. But to rely on community consensus is to lean on a wall made of flimsy material and colorful paint. If we all agree that honesty is somehow important, we probably disagree on exactly how it is manifested and how far it should be carried. Whereas Kant would have us never tell a lie and Charles Wesley spoke approvingly of the ancient father's statement "I would not tell a wilful lie to save the souls of the whole world,"[13] most of us would lie readily to save a life, a soul, or even the feelings of someone, if doing so would cause no further harm. Indeed, we might feel morally obligated to do so.

From a care perspective, we might begin with *apparent* consensus but with the frankly acknowledged purpose of uncovering and developing an appreciation for our legitimate differences. The need to do this—to respond to the universal desire for care (for respect, or love, or help, or understanding) underscores the centrality of dialogue. We must talk to one another. Sometimes we are successful at persuading them, sometimes they persuade us, and sometimes we must simply agree to go on caring across great ideological differences. Unless we probe beneath the surface of apparent consensus, we risk silencing divergent and creative voices. We risk also allowing a core of powerful authorities to establish a fixed set of approved virtues and values.

A central question today in debate over the introduction of values education is exactly the one alluded to above: Whose values? One group would press for its own; another would press for consensus. Care theorists would answer, "Everyone's!" But, with cognitivists, care theorists would subject all values to careful, critical scrutiny and, with character educators, we would insist that the effects of our choices on our communities and the effects of our communities on our choices be treated with appreciation. We would insist that our community—nation, town, classroom, family—stands for something, and we would attempt to socialize our children to the stated standards.[14] But we would do this with a respectful uncertainty, encouraging the question *why*, and recognizing our responsibility to present opposing alternatives as honestly as we can. Despite sometimes irresolvable differences, students should not forget the central aim of moral life—to encounter, attend, and respond to the need for care.

This reminder is well directed at moral educators as well. Although we differ on a host of issues in moral philosophy and psychology, as educators, we have a common aim—to contribute to the continuing moral education of both students and teachers. With that as our aim, we, too, should reject the war model and adopt a mode of constructive and genuine dialogue.

NOTES

1. See Larry P. Nucci, ed., *Moral Development and Character Education* (Berkeley: McCutchan, 1989).

2. See Nel Noddings, *Caring: A Feminine Perspective on Ethics and Moral Education* (Berkeley and Los Angeles: University of California Press, 1984); also *Women and Evil* (Berkeley and Los Angeles: University of California Press, 1989); and *The Challenge to Care in Schools* (New York: Teachers College Press, 1992).

3. For the foundation of this approach, see Aristotle, *Nicomachean Ethics*, trans. Terence Irwin (Indianapolis: Hackett, 1985).

4. Paulo Freire, *Pedagogy of the Oppressed*, trans. Myra Bergman Ramos (New York: Herder and Herder, 1970).

5. Simone Weil, "Reflections on the Right Use of School Studies with a View to the Love of God," in *Simone Weil Reader*, ed. George A. Panichas (Mt. Kisco, N.Y.: Moyer Bell Limited, 1977), p. 51.

6. See Nel Noddings, "Stories in Dialogue: Caring and Interpersonal Reasoning," in *Stories Lives Tell: Narrative and Dialogue in Education*, ed. Carol Witherell and Nel Noddings (New York: Teachers College Press, 1991), pp. 157–70.

7. Stephanie Salton, "Pro-life + pro-choice = Common Ground," *San Francisco Chronicle*, August 30, 1992, A15.

8. Instructors at the University of Montana, which now requires all undergraduates to take two courses in ethics, have noted this unfortunate result of the dilemma approach.

9. Weil, "Right Use of School Studies."

10. Confirmation is described in Martin Buber, *I and Thou*, trans. Walter Kaufmann (New York: Charles Scribner's Sons, 1970).

11. The relational perspective is described in psychological terms in Carol Gilligan, *In a Different Voice* (Cambridge: Harvard University Press, 1982); see also Mary F. Belenky, Blythe M. Clinchy, Nancy R. Goldberger, and Jill M. Tarule, *Women's Ways of Knowing* (New York: Basic Books, 1986).

12. See James Terry White, *Character Lessons in American Biography for Public Schools and Home Instruction* (New York: The Character Development League, 1909).

13. Quoted in Sissela Bok, *Lying: Moral Choice in Public and Private Life* (New York: Vintage Books, 1979), p. 34.

14. Even Lawrence Kohlberg acknowledged the need to socialize children. See Kohlberg, "Moral Education Reappraised," *The Humanist* 38 (Nov.–Dec., 1978): 13–15. In this article Kohlberg accepts the need to "indoctrinate." I do not think we need to indoctrinate. We socialize but always encourage students to ask *why*.

21

▼▼▼▼▼▼▼

Education and Spirituality*

Dwayne Huebner

How can one talk about the education, specifically, curriculum, and also talk about the spiritual? The problem is one of language and of the images that are both a source and consequence of that language. With what language tools and images (metaphors, ideas) do we describe, envision, and think critically about education? Thanks to Macdonald, Pinar, Apple, and a variety of other curriculum writers who stand on their shoulders, we no longer have the horrendous hegemony of technical language (drawing primarily on learning theory and ends/means structures) usurping discussion of education. Nevertheless, that language orientation is strongly established, embodied in educational architecture, materials, methods, organizations, and teacher education. Breaking out of that language is difficult, however, for the structures and processes which shape education—themselves derivatives of that language—force conversation into that technical mode. Our very locations and practices are framed by the language tools and images we would like to overcome.

We depend upon the language, practices, and materials as if they were the givens with which we have to work. We have forgotten or suppressed that imagination is a foundation of our so-called "givens." Our languages, practices, and resources are merely the embodied or materialized images in which

*Copyright © 1991 by Corporation for Curriculum Research Publishers. From "Education and Spirituality" in *Journal of Curriculum Theorizing*, Vol. 11, No. 2, pp. 13–34. By Dwayne Huebner. Reprinted by permission.

we chose to dwell. Other images, in which we could dwell, are currently un-embodied in worldly structures and abandoned. But embodied images are no more a reality than are unembodied images a mere figment of an "unreality." Embodied, or materialized images, and the language patterns associated with them, are more directly related to our sensory systems and our relations with powerful people. However, our sensory systems, and our social/political systems, are in touch with but a small part of the reality of the universe. The complicated and expensive technologies of modern physics take us into the strange world of electromagnetic frequencies, matter and anti-matter, particles and waves that several years ago were far beyond our wildest dreams, rooted only in the imaginations of science fiction writers. The mysterious crop circles throughout the globe also indicate the limited contact of our sensory systems, and their congruent language resources, with a larger, more encompassing reality. Religious and meditative communities point to other limitations of our sensory systems, and to alternative social/political structures.[1]

Can education be re-imagined? This does not mean inventing new language, new practice, new resources, new buildings. It means having a different view of people, of our educational spaces and resources, of what we do and what we say—a view that will enable us to critique the embodied images, see obstacles, and recognize alternatives.

My vocational history indicates how one person became aware of the problem and tried to solve it—a move from secular to religious education. I recall my first year or two of teaching in elementary schools. Piaget had not yet influenced educational language—although the research on concept development was underway. Aware of that beginning research, I wishfully thought that I could do a better job of planning and teaching if I knew what was going on in the heads of my students. I wanted to discover what was going on inside heads, through my own research or that of others. Several years later I began to question the educator's dependency on the research enterprise and realized the absurdity of my wishful thinking. It had the same quality as the question, "What do you do until a cure is found for the disease that we have?" Do you stop living and working and wait until there is more knowledge? Can action be postponed until more is known? If so, we have an infinite regress of waiting as new problems emerge. Is empirically based knowledge necessary before one can teach? Is there wisdom independent of research, yet open to that research? People have been teaching for centuries without research based knowledge. Obviously, they have not been without wisdom.

What do we do until a cure is discovered? We live and work, talk and play, laugh and cry, love and hate with our friends and neighbors. Our students share with us the human condition. They are our neighbors, if not our friends. The language of teacher/student—specifically the language of teacher/learner—hides that neighborliness and the student's strangeness. We and our students are part and parcel of the same mysterious universe.

It is a universe in which we know more than we can say, and often say more than we know, to quote Polanyi. It is much fuller, deeper, stranger, more complex, mysterious than I and, I am bold to say, we can ever hope to know. I know that

> The world is charged with the grandeur of God.
> It will flame out, like shining from shook foil,
> It gathers to a greatness like the ooze of oil
> Crushed. Why do men then now not reck His rod?
> Generations have trod, have trod, have trod;
> And all is seared with trade; bleared smeared with toil;
> And bears man's smudge, and shares man's smell; the soil
> Is bare now, nor can foot feel being shod.
> And for all this, nature is never spent;
> There lives the dearest freshness deep down things;
> And though the last lights from the black west went,
> Oh, morning at the brown bring eastward springs -
> Because the Holy Ghost over the bent
> World broods with warm breast, and wish, ah, bright wings.[2]

We may differ in our choice of words. Hopkins writes from within the Christian tradition, and feels comfortable with the word "God" and the words "Holy Ghost." Others may not or do not, and for me, in this paper, it matters not.

There is more than we know, can know, will ever know. It is a "moreness" that takes us by surprise when we are at the edge and end of our knowing. There is a comfort in that "moreness" that takes over in our weakness, our ignorance, at our limits or end. It is a comfort that cannot be anticipated, a "peace that passeth all understanding." Call it what you will. Hopkins calls it the Holy Ghost. One knows of that presence, that "moreness," when known resources fail and somehow we go beyond what we were and are and become something different, somehow new. There is also judgment in that "moreness," particularly when we smugly assume that we know what "it" is all about and end up in the dark or on our behinds. It is this very "moreness" that can be identified with the "spirit" and the "spiritual." In fact Kovel defines "spirit" as what "happens to us as the boundaries of the self give way."[3] Spirit is that which transcends the known, the expected, even the ego and the self. It is the source of hope. It is manifested through love and the waiting expectation that accompanies love. It overcomes us, as judgment, in our doubts, and in the uncomfortable looks of those with whom we disagree, particularly those with whom we disagree religiously. One whose imagination acknowledges that "moreness" can be said to dwell faithfully in the world.

If one dwells "faithfully" in the world, what images of education, specifically curriculum, are possible? I speak as one who tries to dwell as a Christian, because that is my religious tradition, and because I am more familiar with its many qualities, quirks, and its language than I am that of other traditions. Those in other traditions are invited to attempt the same, thereby enriching the ensuing conversation.

I use the word image in the sense of a view of a landscape. I assume that there is an educational landscape that may be envisioned (or imaged) in many ways. Different images of the same landscape enable us to see different possibilities, different relationships, and perhaps enable us to imagine new phenomena in that educational landscape.

A new image must be articulated or described so others can move within the landscape as they did in the past, but with greater freedom and new awareness of their choices and limitations. The current images of the educational landscape provide the comfort of the already known, even old familiar problems. A different image must not disorient those who feel that comfort. An image of the educational landscape that makes room for or includes the spiritual cannot be too alienating. It must welcome the experienced educator and the stranger. An image that lets the spiritual show needs to use most of the current categories of education. However, once inside that image, the educational landscape should appear differently, showing limitations in current educational practices and perhaps opening up new options for action. Traditional curriculum concerns need to be addressed—namely the goal or meaning of education, the social and political structures of education, content, teaching, and evaluation. However, an image of education that permits the spiritual to show will depict these dimensions differently. An image that acknowledges the spiritual shows other problems and tasks more clearly, such as moral and spiritual values, and the need for spiritual or religious disciplines for the teacher.

THE GOAL OF EDUCATION

The bewitching language of psychology and the behavioral sciences has skewed our view of education. The language of ends and objectives, which guides educational practice and decision making, is used to depict a future state of affairs. The process whereby an individual moves from one state of being to another and develops new capacities or competencies is identified as "learning"—a term so much a part of the coin of the realm that it blocks the imagination. We ask how "learning occurs," thus hiding the fact that we dwell in a near infinite world, that our possibilities are always more than we realize, and that life is movement, change, or journey. "Learning" too quickly explains and simplifies that movement or journey.

The "moreness" in the world, spirit, is a moreness that infuses each human being. Not only do we know more than we say, we "are" more than we "currently are." That is, the human being dwells in the transcendent, or more appropriately, the transcendent dwells in the human being. To use more direct religious imagery, the spirit dwells in us. Our possibilities are always before us. Our life is never a closed book, until death. In the Judeo-Christian tradition, there is no better image than Augustine's "our hearts are restless until they repose in Thee."[4] Kovel defines spirit as "connoting a relation between the person and the universe; while soul is the more self-referential term, connoting the kind of person who undergoes that relation. In a sense, soul cuts even closer home than spirit, because while spirits can be—and are—seen everywhere, soul refers to who we are and, necessarily, to what we make of ourselves. We may define soul, therefore, as the spiritual form taken by the self."[5]

What has this to do with education? The fact that we partake of the transcendent means that we are never complete, until death. We can always be more than we are. Within the Christian tradition, we are always open to a "turning"; to forgiveness, redemption, and the new being which results. The future is before us as open and new if we are willing to turn away from what we are and have, if we are willing to let the past in us (the self) die. Life is a journey of constantly encountering the moreness and constantly letting aspects of us die that the new may be born within us. It is not necessarily a comfortable journey, and moments of rest and peace are often more infrequent than we might want.

"Learning" is a trivial way of speaking of the journey of the self. The language of growth and development is a rather mundane way of talking about the mystery of participating in the transcendent, or in uniquely Christian language, the mystery of incarnation, death, and resurrection.[6] We do not need "learning theory" or "developmental theory" to explain human change. We need them to explain our fixations and neuroses, our limits, whether imposed by self or others. The question that educators need to ask is not how people learn and develop, but what gets in the way of the great journey—the journey of the self or soul. Education is a way of attending to and caring for that journey.

Educators and students are blinded by social and cultural systems and do not recognize their participation in the transcendent, in their ever open future. The journey of the self is short circuited or derailed by those who define the ends of life and education in less than ultimate terms. We are always caught in our proximate goals (our idols) or in the limitations imposed by others (our enslavements). Infrequently do we look beyond these limits or notice how life has been restricted by the social/cultural context. We are reminded of unrealized possibilities through social criticism, through art that points to other ways of seeing and being, through the stranger in our midst who illustrates that we too could be different, through worship and confession, and perhaps by divine discontent.

Our caughtness in systems that restrict our ultimate journey points to the fact that the journey is never a solitary one. In spite of this culture's bias toward privacy and individualism, we cannot be human beings without others.[7] We journey with others. Some precede us, some accompany us, some follow us. Consequently, we have paths, maps, models, scouts, and co-journeyers. We must be thankful for and wary of these co-journeyers. They show us the way and lead us astray. Life with others is never a substitute for the individuation required of us. Others cannot take our journey. Yet being with others on the journey is a source of hope, comfort, and love—all manifestations of the transcendent. It is also the source of the ever present possibility of domination. Given this existential fact, it is essential that our image of the educational landscape show the social/political structures of education.

The image of journey also shows the possibility of falling off the trail, deviating from the journey, being caught in byways and dead ends. In the Biblical tradition this is known as sin, a word much distorted in some circles, but which means falling away from God or off the path toward God. This risk in the educational landscape is best noticed when the problems of content come into view.

THE SOCIAL/POLITICAL STRUCTURE OF EDUCATION

An image of the educational landscape that allows the spiritual to be noticed points to the ultimate goal of education—the journey of the soul. The question that needs answering is why human beings try to derail that journey for their own purposes? Why do we try to shape the journey of others to fit cultural molds—whether of class, race, economic setting? Why do we try to shape the journey of others to maintain the present distribution of power, subjugating some people to the whims and fancies of others? Once we have in view the ultimate aim of education, then the misuses of power in the human world, and in education, are clearly seen. In the social/political context—e.g., the ordinary context of life—the journey of life is predefined for many, severely restricted for others, and the ultimate journey to God encouraged for only a few.

What must the image of the educational landscape contain to enable us to think about the constraints within which we work as teachers and educators? Joel Kovel's *History and Spirit* helps explore this as he renews the language of spirit in this culture, removing it from the restrictions of any one religious tradition.[8] Walter Wink's *Engaging the Powers*[9] is most helpful in thinking about this problem from within a Christian perspective. In Biblical language, the journey and the corresponding commitment to God, is restrained, redirected, and derailed by the principalities and powers—the forces that no longer serve God, but serve false gods and human beings. The principalities and powers bring us into their spheres of interest, where we serve their ends, rather than the ultimate end. Bob Dylan's "You Gotta Serve Someone" depicts the problem. The pursuit of our journey to God is short-circuited by the pursuit of lesser ends or outcomes, which are manifestations of the principalities and powers. They restrict and impede the religious journey, condition human life to the mundane world, or fixate human life before the journey is completed. Fortunately, educators now have ample depictions of the restrictive forces operating in education[10] and ideas to think about those restrictions. References to "education as liberation" or "education as self realization" acknowledge and seek to overcome these principalities and powers in the ordinary structures of education. The idea of liberal education, which frees one from the limits of a particular culture and society in order to take on the awesome responsibility of freedom, also acknowledges and seeks to overcome the restrictions of the principalities and powers. However, the articulation of these ideas is often merely another political claim, albeit liberal or progressive, rather than a religious claim, and hence often another effort to restrict the journey.

Wink calls attention to the domination systems of this world, and speaks of a world free from domination, obviously a utopian ideal, but also a central religious image in Christianity and other religious traditions. In the world controlled by domination systems redemption is through violence. Wink calls this the "myth of redemptive violence," which is implicit in almost all of the images of mass media and popular culture (Popeye, Superman, Robocop, etc.), as well as in the military systems that, by the threat of violence, keep peace in the world (and sell their excess arms to nations of the third world). In a domination-free world the redemptive myth is that of redemptive love. According to Wink the myth of redemptive violence is deeply ingrained in each of us—we have internalized the principalities and powers, or as Pogo said many years ago, "We have met the enemy, and they are us." Because the myth of redemptive love (in the Christian tradition, the "story" of redemptive love) is not deeply ingrained in our characters (a major failure of religious traditions), our educational system short circuits the journey of the self or leads it to dead ends.

The organization of the school, the selection of content, and teaching itself clearly illustrate this. The school is the one social institution constructed with children and youth in mind, yet they are often alienated in and from that institution. Others dwell in it and make it their own. Schools are a major institution of the principalities and powers, and a major source for teaching the myth of redemptive violence—that the world can be corrected and redeemed through power (including the power of knowledge) and might, but not through love. This criticism has been common enough in educational crises since the sixties, and I need not dwell on it. The influence of the principalities and powers in education is seen more clearly, as problems of curricular content are brought into focus.

THE CONTENT OF EDUCATION

In current images of the educational landscape teachers and curriculum people ask what is to be taught. The question is asked prematurely, for there is a prior realm of thinking and imagining, which if by-passed, ignores a crucial starting point. Even the prior thinking of epistemology brackets questions of spirituality.[11]

Where do we start to think about the content of education? The religious journey, the process of being educated, is always a consequence of encountering something that is strange and different,[12] something that is not me. That which is "other" and strange can be part of the I. In the infant the "other" is the hands, the sounds made, the feet that move; in childhood it might be feelings; in adolescence sexuality. The internal "otherness" continues throughout life as shadow, as thoughts, dreams, yearnings, and desires that frighten, shock, or stir us. Usually we think of the "other" as something in the external environment that is unknown, strange, new. Hovering always is the absolute "other," Spirit, that overwhelms us in moments of awe, terror, tragedy, beauty, and peace. Content is the "other." Knowing is the process of being in relationship with that "other." Knowledge is an abstraction from that process.

When the world no longer appears as "other," no longer seems strange, or has no strangeness, education appears to come to an end. Woe is that day, of course, for the power of knowledge has become prejudice, and the power of influence has become ownership, bringing all "otherness" into a relationship of domination. The whole world still seems new and strange to the young child, and education happens easily and naturally. This is curiosity. With age, less and less seems new or strange, and education appears less natural and frequent. Curiosity seems to end. The problem is not that education is just for the young, or that curiosity is a phenomenon of children and youth. The problem is that our controlling tendencies result in the hermetic environment, self or socially constructed, and we fail to recognize, or we forget, our relationship with and indebtedness to the absolute "Other" often manifested through the neighbor and the strange. The cause is not the decay of curiosity. It is idolatry and slavery. Educators, and people still being educated by the otherness of the world, easily slip into conditions of idolatry and slavery. The protection against this, of course, is criticism—calling attention to how our attention and our journey have become fixated or overpowered, a theme addressed later.

This image of the educational landscape helps us notice our traps, our limits, our idols, our slaveries. How does it help us plan? How can we use the image of the "other," the stranger, to design environments that educate? The topic is too vast for this paper, and I can only call attention to a few characteristics. First of all, it is crucial not to reify educational content, the otherness of the world, as if it were merely stuff made by human beings. To forget that knowledge and objects of culture are manifestations of and outcroppings from the creativity of the human species is a disastrous mistake. Priority must be given to human beings and the natural order. Then we can see more clearly how human kind participates in the continual creation of the world. We can also see how the "creations" of human kind sometimes bring us closer to extinction. Hopefully, then, our students can see, more easily, their own journey as a participation in the continual creation (or destruction) of the world.

Content is, first of all, "other" human beings. Others see the world differently, talk differently, act differently. Therefore they are possibilities for me. They point to a different future for me, another state on my journey. I could be like them. By being different they bring my particular self under criticism. What I am, I do not have to be. What they are, I could be. Other people call attention to a future that is not just a continuation of me, but a possible transformation of me. Through the presence of the "other" my participation in the transcendent becomes visible—the future is open if I will give up the self that is the current me and become other than I am. As content, other people are sources of criticism and new possibility.

Beside criticism and possibility, the "other" as content provides an opportunity to listen and speak with a stranger. Not only are the visions of my own journey shifted, perhaps reformed or transformed, but my party of co-journeyers is also enlarged. Strangers become neighbors. I have others to listen me into consciousness of self and the world. I have the gift of other stories of the great journey. Through conversation, I have a chance to refine my way of talking about the world, and to participate in the refinement of theirs. Through the caring act of listening and speaking, I have a chance to participate in the mystery of language. In listening and speaking, the transcendent is present as newness comes forth, as forgiveness is given and received, and as the poetic shaping of the world happens.

Whereas I have referred to the "otherness" primarily in terms of human beings, it is crucial to give the same credibility and respect to nature. Our habits do not include thinking about how the possibilities of the natural world intertwine with ours, or how we might carry on "conversations" with non-human "others." Hence the increased destruction of the natural world. The religious response to the ecological crisis, the interest in how other cultures (Native Americans for instance) respect the land and its occupants, and the emerging paradigms of the new physics and other sciences indicate how the world view is gradually shifting to see nature and human beings as part of the same creation. The thinking of educators has not kept pace with these changes, in part, because of dominant economic interests that view nature as resource and commodity.

When we shift our focus from the content which is "other" people, to the content which is the outcropping of their creativity and actions—symbols, bodies of knowledge, works of art, institutions, technologies, products, and practices—we face problems too numerous for an essay. The strangeness persists, the "otherness" is still there. These are parts of the world still "other" to the student. How does the presence of this cultural object bring me under criticism? What new possibilities does it offer me? How can my life be different because of it? What new paths, maps, scouts, and co-journeyers are before me? What new conversations can I enter? What new stories of the great journey are available? But ownership also exists, in that these outcroppings of human creativity are usually in the possession of other people or other communities. These outcroppings are available as gifts, or they may be stolen or purchased. The teacher should be a gift giver. However, there are segments of the educational community, particularly at the graduate level, where one has to purchase the symbolic "other," perhaps by paying dues for belonging to that community of cultural ownership.

Wink suggests that all human constructions (institutions, structures of knowledge, etc.) have vocations and spiritual dimensions. They serve God. They can also serve Caesar or mammon. They have the possibility to free people for their journey, or to tie them into structures of idolatry or slavery. All content areas of the curriculum need to be looked at with this in view, a task much too complicated for this essay. Phenix does this in some ways in *Realms of Meanings*.[13] Foshay looked at the spiritual in mathematics.[14] Noddings and Shore explore aspects of this in their work on intuition.[15]

From within this image, planning appears different. The question is not what does this "other" mean to the student, for meaning is an operation from within the current self. Rather, the question is how will the student be different because of this "other." For people already captivated by idols, or fixated to other aspects of self and world, the question is, what must be given up, or in Christian language, what part of oneself must die so new life becomes possible? Those familiar with the Christian Gospels may recall that in Mark the followers of Jesus exclaimed, after an exorcism, "What is this? A new teaching—with authority! He commands even the unclean spirits, and they obey him."[16] Teaching is, in part, a form of exorcism, the casting out of the "unclean spirit" so new vitality and life is possible. But we must be exceedingly careful, for the power to destroy seems easier than the power to give. Too frequently teachers ask "How do we motivate?" or "What threats (such as grades and testing) can we use?" More appropriate questions are—"How can this student see himself or herself anew in this content?" and "How can one be supported while one gives up one's old self to become a new self?" The first question must be answered esthetically, for it requires attention to the presentation of the "other" in a way that "grips" the student. The answer to the second question is of a "pastoral" nature because dying to one's self, giving up a part of one's self or past, entails grief work, and requires a community of life wherein one can die and know that life will not be lost, but found.

The second step in the planning process is that of displaying the fascination and structure of the "other." The student is invited in and begins to recognize new power and pleasure of self. "Playing with" is the image because play is nonthreatening and gradually introduces one into the rules, habits, and forms of the content. This should be a "playing with" that gradually introduces the student to more complexity, and to the feeling of more power or more pleasure. Many of the achievements of the post Sputnik period with respect to math and science were of this kind—displaying structure as an invitation to "come and play" so the student could feel enhanced. This is not to imply that education is never work. However, the word "work," in school and in society, has come to mean a form of losing self for others, of alienation, not of finding myself, my power, my future, and my journey. Similarly, the significance of the word "study" has been destroyed. Students study to do what someone else requires, not for their own transformation, a way of "working" on their own journey, or their struggle with spirit, the otherness beyond them. Just as therapy is work, hard work, but important for the loosening of old bonds and discovering the new self, so too should education as study be seen as a form of that kind of work.

TEACHING

Teaching has been seen as a set of skills, as particular kinds of action. Teachers are not replaceable cogs in an educational machine, nor is teaching carrying out a set of tactics and strategies owned by others. Teaching does require skills, and hence depends, at times, on reproducible knowledge. However, if teaching is restricted to that image, there are few ways of thinking about the spiritual aspects of teaching and the teacher. Teaching needs to be grounded in a life. It is not a way of making a living, but a way of making a life. The spiritual dimensions of teaching are recognized by acknowledging that teaching is a vocation.[17] When that is acknowledged other dimensions of teaching will also be seen more clearly.

A vocation is a call. In the religious traditions it is a call from God, or a call to serve God. But the religious meaning need not be invoked here. A teacher is called to a particular way of living. Three voices call, or three demands are made on the teacher. Hence the life that is teaching is inherently a conflicted way of living. The teacher is called by the students, by the content and its communities, and by the institution within which the teacher lives. Depending upon the institution, teachers feel this conflict differently. For elementary school teachers the call of the students is probably more dominant. College and university teachers hear the call of content and its communities as primary. Of course, given the institutional binds that teachers feel, few ever feel called by the institution. But it is there, if only fully responded to by those aspiring to administrative posts. Each of these calls places demands or obligations on the one who would live the life of a teacher.

That part of the teaching life that is a response to the call of the student results in the work of love; to the call of content, the work of truth; to the call of the institution, the work of justice. As in all vocations, these works are easily distorted by the principalities and powers. Spiritual warfare is inherent in all vocations.

The work of love is obvious. The teacher listens to the student and speaks with great care, that the gift of language, jointly shared, may reassure and disclose a world filled with truth and beauty, joy and suffering, mystery and grace. The teacher makes promises to the student. The journey of the student is filled with hope, rather than despair; more life, rather than less. The teacher introduces the student to the "otherness" of the world, to that which is strange, and assures the student that the strangeness will not overpower but empower. If the encounter with the "other" requires that old ways of knowing, relating, and feeling be given up, the teacher assures the student that during the resulting vulnerability no harm will come and that the grief will be shared. If the student is temporally disabled by the loss, the teacher may step in to fill the void. If some dying of the self happens, the past will not be forgotten, but celebrated and integrated as useful memory. If idols are given up, the teacher promises the security of the spirit that is the source of all transcendence. If the security of slavery is thrown overboard, the teacher will help the student find new communities in which power is shared. These positive images, derived in part from the redemptive myth of love, disclose the negative power of the social/political context wherein the life that is teaching is lived.

The work of truth is a work of stewardship. Responding to a particular discipline or content area the teacher is called to keep it truthful and useful. The language and other symbols of the content are easily distorted, tarnished and stained by the principalities and powers. They lose their luminosity—their power to disclose. They hide more than they reveal. They become idolatrous, ends in themselves, and no longer point to the spirit that enlivens human beings. The teacher's work of truth is to keep vitality and signs of transcendence in the language and symbols. The content that makes up the curriculum is part of creation and a source for its continuance. Thus the deadness must be rooted out, and those parts that have become idols, criticized and renewed or placed in the museum of the past—to be beheld as that which once gave and celebrated life. To be called to the work of truth is to recognize that the "other" also has a vocation of honoring spirit and participates in the transcendent. Thus that part of the "other" by which it is criticized, transformed, improved, and made more serviceable must also be available for the student. In science, this is done by making accessible not only the outcroppings of the scientists, the theories and technologies, but also the methods, procedures, and communities through which a science renews itself.

The work of justice is the third call, the call of the institution within which the teaching life is lived. The institution of the schools is the meeting ground of conflicting interests. It is not and cannot be a neutral place. The teacher lives and works in an almost unbearable conflict zone among those competing interests. The present form of the institution is shaped by the balance of interests. To assume that the present order and structure are givens is to yield unthinkingly to the principalities and powers of the past.

The school as an institution also has a vocation. It serves students, the communities with interest in the curriculum content, the teachers, and those who support it economically. Its vocations become tainted when justice does not prevail among these competing interests, and one or more of the interests, or some other power, gets control. Justice, which is never an absolute value, always requires the adjudication of competing claims.

Teaching is a vulnerable form of life, for the teacher works among these competing interests. Teachers often fall away from the vocation of teaching and become mere functionaries as they do the work demanded by others in workbooks, schedules, exams, grading, and what have you. It is often easier to deny the vulnerability, the competing interests, and to fall into the form demanded by the principalities and powers, those in control. Teachers lose hope, accept idols and enslavement, and burn out. Teachers give up teaching as part of their own spiritual journey, to pick up the journey at the end of the school day, the beginning of summer, or the end of their career.

The work of justice requires acknowledging the impotency of the isolated individual and the danger of the closed classroom door. Teachers called to the work of justice need alliances and coalitions of those called to the same vocation. The struggle for justice in schools requires sensitivity to pain and unfairness. Such sensitivity brings under question curriculum materials, teachers' skills, and institutional practices like grading, grouping. The pain of teachers, unable to respond to the call of some students, is often too much, and they seek relief by hardening their hearts.

CRITICISM

The fourth rubric in traditional curriculum planning, after goals, content, and teaching, is evaluation. The process involves stepping back and asking how we are all doing in this educational enterprise. Students and teacher are evaluated because they are the weakest politically and most at the mercy of the principalities and powers. Students move on. Teachers can be replaced.

Thus they are the scapegoats in the domination system. The school's procedure, materials, and basic organization have longer lives.

An image of the educational landscape that makes room for the spiritual suggests other ways of thinking about evaluation. In *The Protestant Era,*[18] Tillich calls attention to the necessity for continuous protest against form. Form gradually loses its vocation, becomes idolatrous, and no longer points to the transcendent. Continual protest against form is necessary for reformation and renewal of vocation. Others speak of the necessary dialectic of creation and criticism. Forms created by human beings soon become idols or enslave others. Criticism calls attention to what is still beautiful, truthful, transparent for God, filled with the possibilities of transcendence and the promise of life. It also calls attention to the breakdown of vocation and the fading of luminosity.

The dialectic of criticism and creation is hidden by the idea of evaluation. Evaluation is the act of those already in power to determine the effectiveness of their power. Some forms of evaluation are used appropriately in the instructional process for diagnostic purposes. This is criticism of instructional materials and techniques based upon teacher and student sensitivity to their failure to serve students. Such evaluation should result in different materials or procedures, a reforming of method to fit the student.

However, the power of existing evaluation instruments points to the impotency of other participants in the schooling process to criticize and reform education. In some ways, the discipline problems of students are forms of criticism; the lunch room, coffee break, and after school conversations among teachers are forms of criticism; parent complaints can be forms of criticism. However, the possibilities to reform schools and classrooms are not in the hands of those who live there for a variety of reasons. Hence criticism is removed as part of the creative process and becomes merely carping and blowing off steam. This is a denial of the spirit in those who work in the educational landscape, for criticism is also part of the creative power of the spirit.

CONCLUSION

I have briefly sketched an alternative image of some of the basic principles of curriculum and instruction, drawing upon sources and images that make room for the spiritual aspects of human life. Much more needs to be done. Two problem areas can be seen more clearly through this image.

First, recent discourse about moral and spiritual values in the classroom is incorrectly focused. That discourse assumes that there is something special that can be identified as moral or spiritual. This assumption is false. Everything that is done in schools, and in preparation for school activity, is already infused with the spiritual. All activity in school has moral consequences. The very highlighting of the need to teach moral and spiritual values in schools implies a breakdown not in the spirituality and morality of the student, but a breakdown in the moral activity and spirituality of the school itself, and of the people in control of the school. Those in control of the schools cover over their own complicity in the domination system by urging the teaching of moral and spiritual values. They do not urge that the moral and spiritual climate of the schools, which they control, be changed. That teachers do not feel the freedom to be critical and creative is a sign of their enslavement to other principalities and powers. The need is not to see moral and spiritual values as something outside the normal curriculum and school activity, but to probe deeper into the educational landscape to reveal how the spiritual and moral is being denied in everything. The problem of the schools is not that kids are not being taught moral and spiritual values, the problem is the schools are not places where the moral and spiritual life is lived with any kind of intentionality.

It is also quite clear to me that it is futile to hope that teachers can be aware of the spiritual in education unless they maintain some form of spiritual discipline. This needs to be of two kinds. Given the inherent conflicts involved in teaching and the inherent vulnerability of their vocation, teachers need to seek out communities of faith, love, and hope. Teachers can deal with conflict and vulnerability if they are in the presence of others who radiate faith and hope and power. To be in the company of co-journeyers is to be enabled to identify personal and collective idols, to name oppression, and to undergo the continuing transformation necessary in the vocation of teaching. The second discipline is a disciplining of the mind, not in the sense of staying on top of all the educational research and literature, but in the sense of developing an imagination that has room for the spiritual. When teachers examine the educational landscape we should see what is there and hear the call to respond with love, truth, and justice. We should also see the principalities and powers, the idols and the spiritual possibilities hidden behind all of the forms and events that are taken for granted. Teachers should be able to see that

> nature is never spent;
> There lives the dearest freshness deep down things;
> And though the last lights from the black west went,
> Oh, morning at the brown brink eastward springs—
> Because the Holy Ghost over the bent
> World broods with warm breast, and with, ah, bright wings.

NOTES

1. For example in the Christian traditions see Stanley Hauerwas and William H. Willimon, *Resident Aliens* (Nashville: Abingdon Press, 1989) and Dietrich Bonhoeffer, *Life Together*, trans. John W. Doberstein (New York: Harper and Row, 1954).

2. Gerald Manley Hopkins, "The Grandeur of God," in *The Oxford Book of English Mystical Verse* (Oxford: Clarendon Press, 1953).

3. Joel Kovel, *History and Spirit: An Inquiry into the Philosophy of Liberation* (Boston: Beacon Press, 1991).

4. *The Confessions of St. Augustine, Book One*, trans. J. Sheed (New York: Sheed and Ward, 1943).

5. Kovel, *History and Spirit*, p. 33.

6. Other religions have other ways of talking about this mystery. The work of Ken Wilber has been the most helpful in bringing together the multitude of religious and psychological perspectives. See "The Spectrum of Development" in *Transformations of Consciousness*, eds. Ken Wilber, Jack Engler & Daniel Brown (Boston: New Science Library, 1986), pp. 65–106.

7. See John MacMurray, *Persons in Relation* (New York: Harper, 1961).

8. Kovel, *History and Spirit*.

9. Walter Wink, *Engaging the Powers* (Philadelphia: Fortress Press, 1992).

10. See, among others, the works of Michael Apple.

11. I explored this in two previous essays. See Dwayne Huebner, "Spirituality and Knowing," in *Learning and Teaching The Ways of Knowing* (Chicago: National Society for the Study of Education, 1985), pp. 159–173, and "Religious Metaphors in the Language of Education," *Phenomenology & Pedagogy: A Human Science Journal*, Vol. 2, No. 2 (1984); also in *Religious Education*, Vol. 80, No. 3 (Summer, 1985), pp. 460–472.

12. The best psychological analysis of this process is Robert Kegan, *The Evolving Self* (Cambridge: Harvard University Press, 1982).

13. Phillip Phenix, *Realms of Meaning* (New York: McGraw-Hill Book Co., 1964).

14. Arthur W. Foshay, "The Curriculum Matrix: Transcendence and Mathematics," *Journal of Curriculum and Supervision*, Vol. 6, No. 4 (Summer, 1991), pp. 277–293.

15. Nel Noddings and Paul J. Shore, *Awakening the Inner Eye: Intuition in Education* (New York: Teachers College Press, 1984).

16. Mark 1:27

17. See Dwayne Huebner, "Teaching as a Vocation" in *Teacher Renewal: Professional Studies, Personal Choices* (New York: Teachers College Press, 1987). A revised form is available in *The Auburn News*, Fall 1987 (New York: Auburn Theological Seminary).

18. Paul Tillich, *The Protestant Era* (Chicago: University of Chicago Press, 1948).

22

▼▼▼▼▼▼▼

The Spiritual Transformation
of Education*

Michael Lerner

Nowhere have liberals more consistently missed the mark than in the way they approach education. Over and over again, their focus is narrowly extrinsic and superficial.

Liberals correctly point out that teachers need better pay, that the teacher student ratio needs to decrease so that one teacher has enough time to work with individual students, and that school buildings themselves need to be upgraded.

All this is true, and the liberals' program should be quickly adopted.

But then, in order to show that they are "tough-minded," liberals have joined with conservatives to demand "performance" skills as demonstrated by early and frequent tests to ensure that students acquire the necessary skills to succeed in the economic marketplace. "We are showing that we really care for students and really care about the possibility of equal opportunity," they argue, "when we insist on quality schools teaching the skills that will be needed for economic success." They often strike a chord with parents who have been convinced that the system is unchangeable, and that the smart thing to do is to position your own child in such a way that she will be most successful in the competitive marketplace. If the market demands skill X, and the parents believe that the market will always remain the arbiter of their children's success, they will demand that schools teach X.

If the goal of education is to ensure your competitive advantage in the marketplace, you will educate in the way that we currently educate. The consequences: huge amounts of unhappiness, a population that has few of the skills that would make it possible for them to access the richness of a spiritual life, and a society that thinks being rational means being selfish, materialistic, and cynical.

As Emancipatory Spirituality becomes more prevalent, more and more people will begin to demand a fundamentally different kind of educational system.

If your goal is to create a human being who is loving, capable of showing deep caring for others, alive to the spiritual and ethical dimensions of being, ecologically sensitive, intellectually alive, self-determining, and creative, there are ways of restructuring education to foster this kind of person.

In describing an educational system with a true "new bottom line," I am seeking to provide a vision of what the goal of educational reform could be if it were inspired by Emancipatory Spirituality. None of this will seem particularly plausible given the current bottom line of "making it" and using education for that purpose. So the picture being presented here may seem disconnected from the immediate struggles likely to be waged in the coming years. Yet from my standpoint, it is the absence of a compelling vision that inexorably leads so much "educational reform" into narrowly technocratic tinkerings with a fundamentally misguided system.

The task of Emancipatory Spirituality is not to present minor educational reforms within the context of contemporary "realistic politics." So I present a more sweeping alternative, as I have in the case of medicine and law, in the hopes that a vision of what the world could be might help generate a new commitment to transformation. I realize that what I'm presenting here is no more likely to become reality in the next thirty years than is a legal system that eliminates the adversarial pose or a medical system that gives prominence to the spiritual dimension of healing. So if the picture I draw seems utopian, it is meant to be utopian in exactly the sense that it seems utopian today to envision a society with a new bottom line of love or caring. Yet before you dismiss the picture I'm painting, remember how utopian it seemed a mere fifty years ago to talk about full equality for women, African Americans, or other minority groups. Yesterday's utopian visions can become the realities of today or tomorrow.

Of course, there may be other objections to building an educational system that seeks to foster loving human beings. Consider, for example, this objection: "You are talking about indoctrination of your values, and thereby undermining the two-hundred-year struggle of liberals and progressives to get religious indoctrination out of schools. What you are advocating is dangerous."

This line of argument seems persuasive only to the extent that we are unwilling to acknowledge to ourselves and understand our own experience of schooling. One reason the whole enterprise of this book may feel counter-intuitive to many people is that we have been so deeply educated into a set of values that tells us that the social system we have is the inevitable outgrowth of human nature and that its values are really not values at all but the manifestations of the further development of rationality. What I've shown in this book is that the alleged ideological neutrality of contemporary social and economic institutions is actually a thin veneer covering a powerful commitment to competitive individualism, scientism, materialism, and selfishness—and that a spiritual world would seek to replace the dominant values with other values (described in chapter five).

The alleged neutrality of contemporary education is a sham that covers up the systematic indoctrination of students into the dominant religion of the contemporary world: the slavish subordination of everyone to the idols of the marketplace and its "common sense" that all people should seek to maximize their own advantage without regard to the consequences for others, that all that is real is what can be validated through sense observation, that it's only human nature for people to compete with each other and seek "individual excellence," and that schooling should aim to promote economic success, which is available to anyone who has accumulated the requisite skills and who has the requisite intelligence.

Once one recognizes that public schools today are set up to teach the dominant values in this society, it seems a bit less outrageous to suggest that there are other values around which schooling should be structured. And that is precisely what I'm about to do.

ELIMINATE THE SAT AND OTHER ODIOUS FORMS OF TESTING

Nothing eliminates a sense of connection to others more effectively than the way contemporary schooling teaches students that their own success depends on their ability to do better than others. And nothing reinforces this more than the current approach to testing. Limited testing for diagnostic purposes may be of some use in some subject matters, but objective testing in schools has become something very different—a method to provide a supposedly objective warrant for re-creating a hierarchical system of rewards.

Perhaps the most destructive of all the tests is the IQ test, with its claim to measure a socially constructed but supposedly inherent quality called intelligence. The assumption that intelligence can be measured is the result of massive societal indoctrination: people did not think of themselves or each other as differentially intelligent in societies without tests. Many people believe the validity of IQ tests is a reflection of the degree to which they have internalized the dominant message that testing is meant to reinforce: you deserve to be where you are. As Peter Gabel wrote in an editorial in TIKKUN (October/November 1995), "We have created a society where we are addicted to feeling dumb, inadequate, and like failures, no matter how inaccurate and even childish the 'measures' which create and reinforce this impression."

The whole warrant for testing lies on the empirical foundation that all forms of emerging spirituality seek to challenge: that what is real is what is publicly observable and repeatable under controlled conditions. From this limited perspective, that which cannot be tested is not real, and hence is not worthy of our attention. Over and over again, the use of testing has had a mind-corroding effect, because as a social practice, it begins to legitimate this pernicious doctrine about reality in mass consciousness. Anything that cannot be "measured" in these kinds of ways is dismissed as purely subjective and as not worthy of our attention or respect.

This same kind of fallacious reasoning leads people to say that love and caring should not be at the core of our educational system, or that awe and wonder cannot really be taught, because there is no objective way to measure them. That this is seen as obvious is a testimony to how destructive the pervasiveness of testing has become in our society.

Consider the SATs, the primary test determining entrance to colleges. They do not measure your capacity to be creative or caring or to connect to the deepest truths in literature, philosophy, or art. What they do measure, Peter Gabel points out, is "your capacity to think like a machine—by which I mean to think without employing the faculty of human understanding (or more accurately, while suppressing the faculty of human understanding)—under highly abusive competitive and authoritarian social conditions."

Gabel goes on to capture this brilliantly:

"The abusive conditions consist of herding together in one room young people who since early childhood have been conditioned like rats to believe that love and approval depend on the quick and correct public answering of magical questions, and then subjecting them under extreme time pressure to what they are told is the one Big Test that will determine the degree of cultural validation they will get for the rest of their lives."

What Gabel means by "thinking like a machine" is this: the SAT measures meaningless thought, thought that has been purposely separated from the actual emotional situations and ethical and spiritual concerns that fill our real lives. The multiple-choice format is meant to test the ability of the student to "disconnect him or herself from any such understanding and adopt a hypothetical rather than an engaged relationship to reality."

Of course, those who do best on these kinds of tests are those who are best able to make this kind of disconnection. The tests will accurately predict who will succeed in the universities and the alienated institutions of a society that separates skills from moral or emotional wisdom.

The kinds of people who are selected to be trained to be our scientists and engineers, our doctors and our university professors, are people who have learned how to close their eyes to the ethical, spiritual, and emotional damage they are doing to the planet, to each other, and to themselves as they work within the framework of the society as currently constituted. If, by chance, some of them manage to maintain an ounce of ethical and spiritual sense, it is only by accident or by their consciously working to resist some of the most degrading aspects of the education they receive. But the empathic understanding of human longings; the connection with a sense of stewardship or responsibility for the planet, the ability to experience empathy, caring, or love for others—these are precisely what gets stamped out as attention is focused more and more on objective testing. Though this kind of detachment is an ingredient in every aspect of the educational system and the institutions into which we graduate, "the trial by fire that we all must go through in late adolescence," says Gabel, cements this pervasive cultural distortion into consciousness. It is, concludes Gabel, "brutalizing to the soul of everyone who is subjected to it because it requires that we alienate ourselves from everything that matters to us in order to be recognized by the prevailing criteria of merit as deserving, worthy, intelligent members of our community."

It becomes clear how people who have been selected by such criteria of merit could be able to both "know" that the current arrangements of the world are leading to ecological destruction and nevertheless explain to themselves that they have to be realistic and focus on the requirements of their job and self-advancement.

Challenging the world seems as pointless as challenging the SATs—"it's just how it is, so we might as well do well at it." In other circumstances people join fascist parties; in the current world they do nothing more than attend to their business and ignore the larger social context and the larger spiritual, ethical, and ecological crises facing our world.

Moreover, those who have succeeded by the criteria of the SAT and other objective tests feel that they have an "objective validation" that may offset the other messages they've internalized that tell them they do not deserve love and caring. So they frantically cling to the validity of the tests and are furious at anyone who dares challenge them. With fervor equal to that of any religious fundamentalist, many of these people dismiss those who would dare question the validity of this system as not only irrational, but evil. I remember having that feeling myself when my own high 700s came back in both math and English. So now I could show everyone that I was in the top 1 percent of students nationwide! Within months, I was attending an Ivy League school filled with others who had similarly proven their capacities, and we all thought we were so very special. Many of us went on to take positions of power in the society, feeling perfectly justified in having much more money and power than others—after all, our scores had proven our worthiness. It was only years later that I thought more clearly about the tremendous cost to me and to others of competing so desperately for this kind of validation and of the ways it had guaranteed mutual estrangement and loneliness for us all.

I don't mean to suggest that testing can never be useful. I'd like the people who perform surgery to be tested on their capacities to do that, though I don't care much about whether they get tested on their math skills in high school or their ability to memorize formulas for bio-chem prerequisites. I'd like the person who flies my airplane to be tested on his or her capacity to do that, and that will probably involve some skills in reading and deciphering complicated computer information. I'm happy if the very few professions where measurable skills are required teach those measurable skills and test on them, but I don't want to see five year olds or twenty year olds who have no interest or intention of ever using those skills to find that their chances of getting into college or grad school are decreased because they show no interest in or capacity to perform well on "objective" standardized tests.

In a spiritually balanced society, measurable skills will play the same role that, say, the tests measuring a carpenter or an architect might play today. We certainly need good carpenters and good architects, and part of what that means involves the ability to demonstrate intersubjectively verifiable skills. I don't want everyone to have to learn how to be a good carpenter or architect, I don't want the skills that are common to the architect and the airplane pilot and the machinist to be imposed on the rest of us, who probably would get through life very well with not much more than the capacity to do algebra plus instruct a computer to consult its memory bank to answer most (not all) of the other questions that are intersubjectively verifiable.

For a further discussion of the distortions brought to us by objective testing, please consult *The Big Test*, by Nicholas Lemann and *Standardized Minds*, by Peter Sacks.

MULTIPLE FORMS OF INTELLIGENCE

Another way to understand what's so wrong with the SATs, the IQ tests, and many other objective tests is to recognize that there is no one right way to understand the world. There are multiple forms of intelligence, and that insight underlies the work of people like Daniel Goleman (in his book, *Emotional Intelligence*), Michael Murphy (in his emphasis on cultivating somatic understanding), Jurgen Habermas, and many who have talked about left and right brain functions. The same insight is captured by those who talk about the aesthetic imagination and how different it is from linear forms of knowledge.

Important work by Carol Gilligan has helped us understand that gender differences may foster different visions of knowledge and intelligence. Masculine approaches emphasize "objective," distanced, and abstract ways of knowing, whereas feminine approaches may be more "subjective," relational, concrete, and focused on specific contexts. I tend to doubt whether these differences are ultimately rooted in sex differences, because much of the spiritual wisdom I've been seeking to reclaim in this book fits the feminine side of this dichotomy. But it has been developed by both men and women throughout spiritual history.

Part of our Western conception of knowledge was shaped by a Hellenistic culture that saw perfection in the form of a God who was the unmoved mover, totally self-contained, needing nothing else in the world. Knowledge was a way to see the world the way God saw the world—a way that involved universal, abstract, and disconnected knowledge.

Judaism was in open conflict with that Hellenistic worldview. Jewish theology (now articulated in strains of Christianity and Islam as well) saw God as a Being who had a fundamental need for relationship with human beings, who cared about our lives, who had emotions and did not feel totally complete as long as the world was filled with cruelty and injustice. From that very different and non-Western approach, relationship to others is central, and knowledge is shaped by how it affects our human relationships. Non-Western forms of knowledge also put a greater emphasis on the link between study and action in the world. Again, the Biblical view of knowing is directly linked to intimacy and action.

In part, what is at stake here is an expanded sense of the goals of knowledge. If real knowledge involves cultivating the ability to love and receive the love of the universe, to be attuned to the spiritual and ethical realities of life, to be deeply connected to the presence of Spirit, and to understand how the world needs to be healed and how best to do so, then this will require a greatly expanded notion of intelligence.

I don't intend to try to develop a spiritual theory of knowledge here, but only to remind you that the attack on SATs and IQ tests is the tip of a deeper iceberg that questions the significance of the kinds of knowledge that could possibly be measured in a nonrelational context. As with all things spiritual, the point is not to delegitimize the type of knowledge that could conceivably be tested (mathematical skills or the ability to remember the definitions of words), but to insist that our education system needs a profound transformation so it can ultimately reflect a better balance among the different forms of knowledge. Western rational models of knowledge can take their place alongside somatic, emotional, aesthetic, and spiritual ways of knowing (compare with Don Rothenberg's instructive essay, "Transpersonal Studies at the Millennium").

BUT DON'T YOU NEED OBJECTIVE CRITERIA
FOR EXCELLENCE?

Sometimes yes, sometimes no.

Excellence must be related to what our human goals are. If our goal is to find the person best able to construct a nuclear weapon, yes we might be able to do that without trying to ascertain his or her moral or loving capacities. But that produces a certain kind of expert: the kind that has never been asked to develop his or her moral and loving capacities. Such people are all too good at "just following orders," while the science and technology they produce is used to undermine our chance of survival on this planet. It is a human disaster to separate the moral and spiritual from the technical when we assess excellence.

When it comes to moral and spiritual excellence, there is no "objective test." We have no choice but to use our own spiritual and moral intuitions when assessing how well others are doing.

Of course, this has the potential to be abused. Who does the choosing when it comes to moral or spiritual excellence—and how can we trust that the choosers will not be bribed or corrupted or become enamored of their own power, no matter how high the moral and spiritual principles they articulate? This was precisely the kind of thing that happened in the former Soviet Union when people who articulated wonderful principles actually used those principles as fig leaves to cover their own elitism, hunger for power, and inevitable human fallibility. Won't the same thing happen if people are empowered to make subjective judgments of others?

This is an important objection, though not decisive because "objective" criteria themselves are biased toward those who are best at being out of touch with their feelings, least connected to the spiritual dimension of reality, and most agile at separating their "personal" moral judgments from their sense of what they should be doing in the public arena to achieve success and recognition. It's not that "objective" criteria are morally neutral—they just reflect a different set of moral priorities. And the people they select for positions of power can be every bit as morally obtuse as any other system of selection.

Still, it behooves us to take important steps to block against the possibilities of corruption, favoritism, and abuse. There are two ways this can be built into the system of rewards and advancement. First, if decisions are going to be made evaluating people's spiritual and ethical capacities, these judgments should be made not by a long-standing committee of professional evaluators, but rather by the relevant communities out of which people emerge. So, for example, a neighborhood high school might seek to create its own criteria for moral and spiritual excellence and then provide some rankings based on its assessments of how well different students are doing.

This, too, may have its problems—the imposition of local prejudices under the guise of moral or spiritual evaluation. To protect people against that, there need to be alternative tracks in which people could seek to have their ethical and spiritual talents evaluated. For example, students should turn to their religious, ethnic, social action, or other voluntary communities and ask that they make such evaluations. The idea here is to create a series of options so that no one community would get too much power and begin to operate with its own form of "political correctness" that can stifle rather than enhance individual creativity and eccentricity.

The principle is clear: We want to preserve the subjectivity of evaluation that comes from our teachers and peers. We want to value the kinds of moral, spiritual, and loving capacities that will never be measurable but that are just as real and sometimes even more relevant to our central goal: to create loving, caring, spiritually alive, and morally and ecologically attuned human beings. And we want to achieve this in ways that do not allow political correctness or community totalitarianism to undermine the process or make it feel as unsafe as the current "objective tests" do to most who confront them.

EDUCATION FOR AWE AND WONDER
AT THE SACRED

Let awe and wonder be the first goals of education. Let our teachers be judged on how successful they are at generating students who can respond to the universe, each other, and their own bodies with awe, wonder, and radical amazement at the miracles that are daily with us. I don't mean teaching students *about* awe and wonder—as a new subject matter, memorizing facts and passing objective tests. (Ludicrous as it sounds, I once had a course on Eastern religions in my undergraduate days at Columbia University in which the entire focus was precisely this kind of ridiculous memorizing of facts, none of which I could remember the week after the course concluded.) Rather, I mean we should teach students to actually embody awe and wonder in the ways that approach their own experience of the universe.

Educating for awe and wonder would require a whole new pedagogy.

It would begin with a focus on integrating "knowledge about" (in the external left-brain sense) with a deeper right-brain emotional and experiential focus.

Students in kindergarten through sixth grade should spend a significant part of their school time in natural settings. (Urban students could be bussed from their metropolitan centers to parks or country settings.) In those settings, teachers should combine free play with instruction aimed at eliciting a way to see the grandeur of the universe. Yes, that way of seeing can be taught, and if you start young enough, you can succeed. It's difficult in this society, where media cynicism conveyed to children in the cartoons they see at ages three to five may already preclude it—but remember, I'm trying to describe what could happen in a society where a powerful pro-spirituality movement supports rather than undermines our spiritual consciousness.

On the days students spent inside classroom buildings, the focus would be on art, music, storytelling, history, science, and theater. Science would be taught through experimentation with nature, and reading would be taught in noncoercive ways, free from the anxiety that so many parents and teachers transmit as they approach this arena today.

The more education is seen as "useless" (that is, not aimed at achieving some future economic success), the more successful it would actually be, because students would be able to learn for the joy of learning, not to fulfill internalized parental expectations or to ensure future marketability. But when I say it would be successful, I mean successful in creating human beings capable of participating in a society based on love, caring, solidarity, and awe.

Grade schools should be places where students can experiment with a wide variety of different activities to see what grabs them and speaks to their souls. So, we'd have lots and lots of free time in which students might wander in and out of rooms dedicated to providing opportunities for them to delve into a wide variety of activities: art, drama, music, archaeology, history, literature, poetry, biology, chemistry, physics, astronomy, ecology, cooking, computers, mathematics, dance, movie-making, mechanical and woodworking shop, health, and much more. Let students explore without feeling that they need to master some specific skill or talent by the time they are eleven!

In the upper grades, students would be rewarded for the extent to which they could pioneer new avenues for manifesting and deepening awe and wonder. Their goal would be to learn to see the sacred in the ordinary.

The person who was most grateful and most awe-filled would be the person most likely to succeed in building a fulfilling life and most likely to have the qualities of soul desired by the institutions that eventually do the hiring and promotion at every level of the society.

I do *not* favor teaching a specific religion or a specific concept of God in our public schools—nor is that implied in teaching awe, wonder, or awareness of the sacred. There are good reasons to prevent schools from being committed to any particular religious tradition, and they do not have to do so in order to teach awe and wonder.

But it does make good sense to teach students about all the different religious and spiritual traditions—all the manifold ways people have responded to awe and wonder and the sacred throughout human history.

There is much to gain from having students who have been exposed to the wide variety of religious and spiritual traditions, both those rooted in native peoples and those that developed in class societies. First Amendment purists rightly worry about the slippery slope to indoctrination, but today we've seen the opposite extreme and the destructive consequences of students graduating from high school without ever having been exposed to the rich spiritual heritage of the human race. But teaching about religion without religious indoctrination can be tricky; it requires the kind of sensitivity and respect for spiritual differences that would be a central value of societies seeking to embody Emancipatory Spirituality.

Well, you might think, then let's teach spirituality in a kind of anthropological mode: "strange lands and peoples." But this distancing actually teaches nothing more than the capacity to distance. If you want to expose children to the range of spiritual wisdom of the human race, you have to allow for some level of experience and advocacy of different traditions. And the legitimate fear, of course, is that students will be co-opted into some spiritual trip other than the ones being introduced by parents at a stage in their lives when they are ill prepared for it.

However, nothing is as destructive to spiritual wisdom as the attempt to present spirituality in "neutral" or "objective" and distanced ways. It's like teaching music by teaching music theory to students who are never given a chance to listen to actual music. Whatever they are learning, it's not music. Similarly, you can't teach about spiritual or religious traditions without any experiential exposure.

To ensure that religious traditions are presented in the fullness of their spiritual richness, they need to be presented by people who are excited about their perspective and are good at communicating what it is that excites people who are part of that tradition. I don't expect that classroom teachers in any given school could do that with equal commitment and without communicating their own biases. So, one way the "exposure to world religions and spiritual traditions" course might work is this: students would view a set of video tapes prepared by different religious and spiritual communities on a set of specific questions, adjusted for grade level and growing sophistication, beginning in eighth grade and continuing through high school.

These tapes would present advocates of different religious and spiritual traditions and would show forms of worship, the history of the traditions, their philosophical underpinnings, and their music, dance, and silence. Starting in eleventh grade, students would be given Internet capacities (and whatever else technological breakthroughs make possible) to connect to practitioners of different traditions so they could pose their various questions, explore their own thinking, and, if they so chose, find out how they could pursue a particular spiritual practice outside of school. One option presented in this panoply of possibilities would be the voice of those who argue for a nontheistic approach to awe and wonder.

Using videotapes and the Web are very imperfect ways of introducing spiritual and religious voices, but they may be temporarily necessary as a transition to a more trusting and loving society. In the meantime, as a Jew, I don't wish to have Jewish children taught these subjects by a classroom teacher who may give a covert messages that "the real" approach to Spirit is only through Jesus, Mohammed, or Buddha. The technology approach can be monitored for fairness and balance (though it should not be neutered or made "safe" in the sense of eliminating the potential for students to find themselves attracted to other spiritual traditions than the ones in which they have been raised).

The main focus of spiritual education in schools will not be this introduction to other spiritual traditions, but the focus on generating an aliveness to the sacred in students themselves. And the key to that is to have teachers who are alive to the sacred themselves and who are allowed to use their own creativity and spontaneity to open this awareness to their students.

One element of this training is: teach students how to be alone with their own thoughts and feelings. In part, this can be learned through instruction in meditation and other techniques of inner awareness. The goal is to learn how to be fully aware of one's own experience in a gentle and nonjudgmental way, and to lovingly and nonjudgmentally observe all that is happening both outside and particularly inside oneself.

Schools can begin to teach this consciousness from the earliest grades, and by the time students are in high school, they can learn fairly sophisticated techniques of meditation, compassionate awareness, and spiritual aliveness. This capacity for mindfulness is a fundamental prerequisite for increasing one's capacity to notice the wonder of the universe that appropriately elicits radical amazement and joy.

There's an important societal benefit to teaching mindfulness and the development of an inner life: the development of inner resources to resist totalitarianism in all its overt and subtle forms.

We used to be afraid of external power-driven maniacal dictators, but today we are growing equally fearful of a gentle totalitarianism that gets indoctrinated through the media, the World Wide Web, and the globalized marketplace. For this reason, it is a high priority for people to develop the capacity to maintain their own perspectives and not allow the community to undermine their own views. Helping your children develop the capacity for meditation and for attention to their own inner lives will allow them to resist the various forms of totalitarian mind control that can sometimes present themselves as democratic or even spiritual. Here we encourage a regulative principle that should follow every lesson: to thine own self be true!

Thus educated, students will have the ability to develop their own private space, fully resistant to the demands of public space. This capacity will also provide a foundation for resisting the potential abuses in implementing Emancipatory Spirituality. The spiritual approach must always insist on the limits of our own knowledge, a deep humility about the appropriateness of the means to our ends, and a willingness to recognize that even the highest spiritual goals can and often have been misused for destructive purposes. For these reasons, we must resist every attempt to allow any spiritual system to colonize every aspect of personal life and to insist that the personal and political should never be fully coextensive.

EDUCATION FOR LOVE, CARING, AND COOPERATION

One of the tired old saws of the educational reductionists is that schools can't substitute for a good and loving home environment. The underlying assumption is an old version of the public-private split: school is the public realm where spirit, emotion, and ethics have no place; whereas home is the private arena where all this "nonobjective, nonverifiable" material can be addressed. To protect the sanctity of the home, schools should stay away from "private matters."

I respect the importance of a realm separate from the public sphere. As I've argued in the previous section, the cultivation of an inner life is meant to foster our capacity to have that separate realm, not to undermine it. But love, caring, and cooperation are not only matters for inner life, but also for our lives together in society, so we all have a stake in ensuring that each person in this society is encouraged to develop loving capacities. In chapters two and three, I showed how much contemporary family life, schooling, and the world of work are structured to undermine or limit our loving.

There is no reason to believe that schools that support love, caring, and cooperation will undermine the love and caring available in families and communities. On the contrary, as I've shown here and in *The Politics of Meaning*, a society that puts selfishness and materialism at the center of its values and at the center of its schooling constantly undermines the capacity of families and communities to teach love; and a society that values and teaches the importance of love will serve as an important accessory to parental attempts to foster loving children.

In a loving society, schools themselves will be embodiments of loving energy, just as in the medical and legal arenas. There is no reason to want schools to be impersonal and bureaucratic factories pouring out little beings with narrowly defined and testable skills. Far better that they should turn out beings who are bursting with love and caring for others.

A loving education requires teachers who are capable of demonstrating love and caring in their own being and in the way they interact with each other and with students.

Moreover, teachers will have transcended the mistaken notion that love is a zero sum game and that the more you give the less you have. Teachers will know and embody the opposite truth—that love is a capacity that develops and deepens the more it is used and manifested.

I've already seen a few experiments with fostering a more caring environment in some schools, and they have been powerful. At one school, students were rewarded for the degree to which they showed cooperation and caring for each other. Each day began with students being asked to give examples of behavior they had seen the previous day in which some fellow student had been generous or caring toward someone else. Each week the school had a schoolwide assembly (approximately eight hundred students), and the actions of generosity or caring of at least five students were publicly described in a sensitive (not overly bombastic) and supportive way, and those students were rewarded with a book or video. At the end of each semester, two students at each grade level were selected for their acts of kindness and generosity, and their families were given a free weekend vacation at a vacation resort.

Though the model of rewards and material incentives may ultimately be transcended as Emancipatory Spirituality becomes more widespread throughout the society, rewarding cooperation and caring behavior in the classroom had a remarkable impact. I spoke to students aged twelve to sixteen who were deeply motivated in their school work, successful at their studies, and highly motivated to care for other students. They saw their success in "we" terms: "we are learning" and "we can figure out how to make sense of our world together."

One of the features of this kind of learning is that students are encouraged to work in small groups at every level, including working together on papers, tests, and end-of-term projects. I witnessed this at some schools in Israel and saw how well it fostered a sense of community. I had originally worried that this kind of community learning might eliminate students' ability to think as individuals, but, to the contrary, I found that it made it easier for them to express their individuality because they felt more supported and less scared of embarrassment at revealing themselves to be inadequate. These students went on to become capable scientists, electronic specialists, doctors, college professors, teachers, social workers, etc. The group experience they had in school did not make them incapable of functioning on their own. It did not reduce their individual creativity but actually fostered creativity, and it did not produce a passivity that is often feared if people are not taught to compete.

One feature of a cooperative learning environment is that students are encouraged to be mentors to younger students. At the beginning of the school year, students aged twelve to fifteen are paired with students aged eight to eleven and assigned to work with them and assist them in learning. The mentors feel enormous pride in helping the younger students succeed in "getting" the skills they are taught. One of their central tasks is to help those students feel good about themselves and their capacities. To do that, the older students have a supervision seminar with a teacher who helps them think about what younger students need to feel good about themselves and how to foster that.

Growing up in this system, students end up feeling enormous excitement about the possibility of becoming a mentor and deep gratitude at the opportunity to help someone else.

The joy of giving to others can become a central aspect of the experience of school, something quite absent from schools that focus on developing lone individuals who see everyone else as potential competitors for scarce rewards.

Schools that educate for caring and cooperation will teach a very different perspective on what it is to be a human being.

In many schools today the history of the human race is framed as a struggle for survival, and the main events taught are wars and the successions to power of kings, queens, presidents, and political parties. History and literature classes focus too often on self-aggrandizing individuals, ruling elites, and the cultures they have formed. But what distinguishes human beings from other animals is not our cruelty but our capacity to be creative, caring, innovative, and conscious of our ability to heal and transform.

In a world increasingly alive to Spirit, students will learn about the great movements of cooperation throughout our evolution as humans. The powerful accomplishment of developing language, the incredible achievement of mastering fire, the wonder of developing agriculture and cooking, and the emergence of science and technology—all of these will be taught with a sense of wonder at the amazing things people can do when they cooperate and when they share information, learning, and experimentation. The levels of cooperation necessary to protect human infants, and the wide variety of ways people have found to raise children, will be part of the exciting story of the history of cooperation that has been central to the survival of our species.

Of course, history cannot be told in a Pollyannaish way—it must also describe the distortions, the cruelty, and the ways that humanity has sometimes gone astray. Truth is, the course of human history has been rocky and filled with unnecessary pain and cruelty. Suffering is real and should not be hidden. The shadow side of human history must be fully acknowledged. In a society that tilts toward spirituality, it's very important to teach the history of the ways that religious and spiritual traditions have functioned as bulwarks of oppression and cruelty.

It is one thing to acknowledge the shadow; quite another thing to be taught that the shadow is ontological, built into the structure of necessity, an unchanging and necessary feature of what it is to be human, and hence a good reason to develop personalities and styles of behavior aimed at protecting oneself from everyone around. That kind of negative expectation is usually self-fulfilling and should not be part of the educational systems of the future.

It will take several generations to get to the place where schools are fully successful at educating for caring, cooperation, and love. One major obstacle is that many students come from homes in which they are not given enough love and recognition. Students who have been deprived of adequate recognition and support come to school in various stages of woundedness, and in the contemporary world teachers are given neither the tools nor the time to address the wounds.

As Emancipatory Spirituality becomes an increasingly powerful force in our society, more and more schools will begin to take a central transitional task seriously: helping to heal the psychic wounds of children and teens. Until these wounds are healed, educators face an almost impossible burden.

Yet today we are far from even acknowledging that this healing is a societal necessity. So, the first thing that needs to happen is the acknowledgment that differences in capacities to learn are usually differences in levels of fear and emotional pain. This kind of pain creates huge "attention deficits" whose cure is less likely to be found in drugs than in changes in the way we parent and the way we educate. Today students are burdened by fears of physical deprivation (not enough food, clothing, and shelter), fears of emotional deprivation (not enough recognition for being someone who deserves love and attention), and fears of spiritual repression (not enough support to see the world as magical and alive, filled with miraculous beauty). However, if educational systems can work in tandem with parents to overcome these fears and create space for students to pursue their interests in wonder and joy, those students are likely to be far more successful at learning.

Differences in innate capacities may exist. I'd be willing to accept that hypothesis if, after a thousand years of living in a loving, caring, and spiritually alive society, there continued to be marked differences in people's capacity to learn subjects they really wished to learn. But in our own society, there's ample evidence that much of what we see as an innate range of intelligences and capacities may actually reflect a range of levels of pain and coping strategies for that pain. Many students who have trouble learning are not "less intelligent" but are less capable of handling the pain they've experienced as a result of the twin traumas of having their spiritual awareness denied or debunked and having their need for recognition systematically thwarted. On the other hand, while some students who do well in school today are healthier psychologically, most are not, but only are better at coping and denying or repressing their most fundamental needs—a capacity for which we are well rewarded in schools and professional training but which will eventually explode in the form of spiritual pain, social alienation, or psychological depression.

So, in the transition to a society congruent with Emancipatory Spirituality, we must seek to create caring schools that see their first priority as developing an environment in which students are supported to recover from psychic and spiritual wounds. This can be done in a vulgar way (some of the educational reform attempts of the 1960s and 1970s had a kind of "laissez faire," or "students always know what's in their best interest," ideology that undermined their otherwise strong commitment to creating social healing, and schools have consistently responded to struggling students by "dumbing down" material, making it even less interesting, never questioning the way the material is taught) or in a sophisticated way (for example, rewarding a commitment to learning, because in a society that values caring and coopera-tion, one person's knowledge benefits everybody). That's why, even though I favor students having a wide variety of options to experiment with all kinds of interests, I also favor providing them with competent teachers who can, in fact, show them the difference between a well-made poem and a sloppy one, or between historical or literary thinking that is rigorous and thinking that is shallow. To be loving is not to be sloppy, and avoiding objective tests doesn't mean that there are no standards.

In the transition period to a more spiritually oriented world, schools will provide a variety of ways for students to learn about how they may have been taught misinformation (for example, that they are not smart, that they do not deserve to be loved, that if they see things in different ways than others do they are not being mature, and that if they don't like the way things are in the adult world they are not being adult).

At every grade level there will be time, energy, and classes devoted to teaching students how to understand the tensions their own parents may be facing in the larger world, the stresses that sometimes evince irrational or even hurtful behavior, the ways students learn to internalize negative feelings and act them out on each other, and the ways they can recognize when they feel bad about themselves and about others and how to overcome some of the hurt involved.

As a peripheral addition to a curriculum, this kind of focus would almost certainly have little impact. That's why it must be introduced in contexts where school systems recognize it as an urgent need and as a basic prerequi-site for making schools successful. In the current world, where people have good reason to be suspicious of schools and schooling, they would likely re-sist such efforts and feel that the school was meddling in their private lives. But as a movement for social healing begins to win more public support, more and more parents will be open to the idea that a public school system could be their ally, not a hurdle on the path to getting their children a good start in the competitive market.

In the current climate in which the materialism and selfishness of the mar-ketplace has infiltrated and shaped the agenda of schools, attempts to intro-duce this focus will face ridicule and derision at first. But as the struggle for an Emancipatory Spirituality heats up, more and more parents will feel em-powered to demand changes in the way we educate our children. More and more parents will begin to feel critical of the school system not because of its failure to help their children get high scores on objective tests, but rather be-cause the schools have failed to support their own efforts to raise children who are loving, caring, and morally, spiritually, and ecologically sensitive and alive. As parents begin to demand a new bottom line from their local school systems, the impact of these struggles will strengthen the resolve of people in law, medicine, and other spheres to struggle for a new bottom line.

Won't parents object to a decrease in their authority if schools start to break down the barrier between public and private in this way?

Some will.

Some will feel immensely threatened and fearful that their personal distortions might be revealed by their children, and they will fight tooth and nail to keep these kinds of discussions from taking place in schools. They will be panicked at the thought that their own failures will be exposed and that they will be publicly shamed. In response, they will scream about the dangers of schools becoming instruments of totalitarian control, they will imagine that the last vestiges of freedom are about to be eliminated, and they will argue that teachers should stay out of anything connected to love, caring, and cooperation and should focus exclusively on "the basics" of reading, writing, and computer skills.

Incidentally, the same kinds of arguments were used just a few decades ago to argue that teachers should not bring feminist consciousness into public schools. The notion that the teaching of history or literature should be changed to include the experience of women was seen as subversive and revolutionary, and it was argued that those who sought to "impose" their feminist agenda on schools would actually subvert the entire educational system. These changes certainly were a bit of a shock to many teachers, and many schools have not yet integrated this new understanding into their curricula or the way subject matter is taught. But today thousands of schools have succeeded in reshaping the way people teach so as to include more understanding of the experience of women and more validation of the potential for equality in social and economic institutions. The same kind of change will take place as spiritual values enter the public arena—and there will be similar struggles, similar fears, and eventually a similar triumph of the spiritual orientation.

One reason the spiritual orientation will eventually triumph is that parents will eventually feel grateful that their children feel better about themselves as they learn categories to explain their world, categories that empower them to succeed as learners. In the transition period, where parents are still tied to oppressive forms of work, the potential support they can get from schools, particularly in fostering the psychic health of children, will ultimately be acknowledged and welcomed (after a few decades in which it is likely to be resisted and denounced).

As the movement for Emancipatory Spirituality becomes more present in public discourse, more and more parents will realize that their children need the kind of caring that can only be gotten in an atmosphere in which competition and the values of the cut-throat marketplace are not at the center of the educational venture. Witnessing the societal dysfunction and the tremendous unhappiness that pervades our schools today, more and more parents will begin to opt for a spiritually oriented school system.

I imagine that this will be hotly contested for the next fifty years at least, but as Spirit becomes a more central force in other arenas, parents who support spiritually oriented education will become more and more successful.

As Emancipatory Spirituality becomes a shared goal of tens of millions of people, the separation between teachers and parents will decrease, and they can build real alliance based on shared values and can work together in the best interest of the children. Instead of fearing that teachers will steal parental prerogatives, parents and teachers will share information, strategize together, and do their best to show children that they are cared for, respected, recognized, and valued as embodiments of Spirit.

EDUCATION FOR TOLERANCE AND DIVERSITY

There is no one right way.

No one has the only way to God, to love, or to spiritual truth.

But one thing is certainly wrong: to demean others and to not recognize them as intrinsically valuable and worthy of respect and caring. It is wrong to prevent others from realizing their fullest potential, as long as they realize that potential in ways that are not hurtful to others.

This is the opposite of moral relativism. Moral relativism teaches that every path is equally good. We need to teach that the path of demeaning others, not recognizing their value, not treating them with respect and caring—all of these are wrong. We have a positive moral obligation to help others.

But there is no necessary right way to implement this objective value. There are many ways, many paths.

Riane Eisler talks about one path—what she calls Partnership Education to distinguish it from the "dominator model," which has been so deeply embedded in previous forms of education. Boys and girls will be taught to see each other as equally valuable and to overcome the long history of education that devalued the contributions and wisdom of women and that dismissed caring and caretaking work as "merely women's work." Students will learn that caretaking work "is the highest calling for both women and men, that nonviolence and caretaking do not make boys 'sissies,' and that when girls are assertive leaders, they are not being 'unfeminine' but are expressing part of their human potential."

One element in partnership education is respect for difference, starting with respect for the differences between the female and male halves of humanity. "They will have mental maps that do not lead to the scapegoating and persecution of those who are not quite like them. They will learn to regu-

late their own impulses, not out of fear of punishment and pain, but in anticipation of the pleasure of responsible and truly satisfying lives and relationships" (Eisler, TIKKUN, January/February 2000).

That's why it's important to teach the experimental method in school—the
possibility of trying different approaches, learning how to assess outcomes,
and then deciding, based on the evidence, how to proceed. At each stage in
this process, one's own intuitive capacities are brought to bear, not only in
framing the experiment but also in assessing the outcomes.

To figure out what kind of supports you need to build a bridge, you look
for one kind of evidence. To figure out how to be most caring toward people
who have suffered childhood emotional wounds, you look for a very different
kind of evidence. Assessing evidence in the second case may often depend on
empathic intuition. The Greek philosopher Aristotle pointed out that the
kind of evidence you seek is always shaped by the kind of issues you confront.

The importance of an experimental method is that it suggests that our conclusions about the best way to maximize love, caring, and ethical, spiritual,
and ecological sensitivities are almost always tentative, subject to refinement
and reformulation.

In such a world, there will be a wide variety of options for how to live and
how to teach. We will recognize alternative ethical and spiritual traditions
and alternative visions of how best to achieve shared goals, and we will make
space for diversity of goals as well.

Not everyone sees the good life in the same way, nor should they. So, we
want to build an ethos of mutual respect and tolerance.

Sharon Welch teaches about this two-sided spiritual approach: an absolute commitment to our highest ideals and infinite suspicion of our own motives—because we don't have all the answers, and we need to be circumspect.
Henry Giroux calls this task developing a provisional ethic. In the language
of the spiritual tradition, we must have a deep sense of humility rather than
the kind of self-righteousness that has all too frequently dominated the practice of religious and political movements.

In this context, we seek not a single path but a multicultural plurality of
paths and a societal respect for difference. As I argue for my particular perspective, I'm committed to building a society and a school system in which a
wide diversity of traditions are taught. But diversity doesn't mean tolerance
for everything, and so I'll side with an active intolerance for intolerance.

It is central to my spiritual vision that every human being is a reflection of
the God energy of the universe (in Biblical terms: created in the image of
God). If so, then every person's story is worth hearing. So history, literature,
and many other fields of intellectual inquiry must be reshaped to reinclude
the experience of those who have been previously marginalized or ignored:
women, ethnic and religious minorities, gays and lesbians, and others whose
perspective has not been fully heard in public discourse.

Ecologists are teaching us to expand that consciousness to include the story and needs of other species and of the entire planet. Our schools must become places in which the voices of all are heard and treated with respect. But to treat with respect does not mean to listen uncritically or without one's own perspective. Genuine respect involves an encounter between an I and a Thou. To have such an encounter, one's own "I" must be developed and fostered. Turning ourselves into mush out of fear that we might be imposing our own views should we hold them too strongly actually undermines the possibility of genuine dialogue and real respect.

If we take this qualification into account, classrooms can become meeting points, bringing people with different histories and cultural backgrounds together. In fact, we should seek to use new technologies to allow people from all different cultures to interact. Imagine, for example, if for a few hours each week students participated in a global classroom in which they met twenty students from every part of the world, and through simultaneous translations, were able to learn from each other.

The key, of course, is that the communication be real—not passive acceptance of some "lesson" to be taught by a teacher, but rather active engagement in which the goal was to allow people to speak and tell their real stories to each other. Accompanying this kind of direct encounter could be a more structured lesson in which students learned about others' culture, history, and literature.

Multiculturalism must not be taught as a branch of postmodernist relativism. Emancipatory Spirituality insists on multicultural education precisely because we hold the objective, universally applicable "master narrative" that all human beings are precious and sacred, deserving of respect and love, entitled to the fullest opportunities to develop their intellectual and creative capacities, and entitled to be supported in freely choosing and shaping their own life paths.

There's nothing relative, however, about our underlying ethical stance—that every human being deserves love and compassion, and that a good society is one that promotes not just the "opportunity" for people to be loving, joyous, intellectually alive, and creative beings, but also the actuality of that (in short, we are not talking about the opportunity to compete for self-actualization, but rather about creating a world in which everyone does, in fact, get to self-actualize—provided that this self-actualization does not come at the expense of others).

Learning about the diversity of experience and insight from all the world's peoples may provide a foundation for another central value of Emancipatory Spirituality: a humility about the limits of our knowledge and understanding, and an openness to learn from others. The more we learn from others, the greater chance we have of strengthening our sense of mutual connection and interdependency, shared interests, and shared moral vision.

One danger is that the forces behind the globalization of capital will advocate for a form of multicultural education whose hidden goal is to subvert differences and to convince people across cultural boundaries that they can overcome the negativity, rivalries, and hatreds of the past through the universal religion of consumption, materialism, and cynicism. Emancipatory Spirituality, on the other hand, will oppose the homogenizing aspects of the new global melting pot and will instead champion the importance of preserving difference and multiplicity of cultural heritages—within the context of a shared respect for every person on the planet and a commitment to the notion that everyone has a part of the truth and is partly a manifestation of God's presence.

EDUCATION FOR CITIZENSHIP

Building a democratic society is one of the elements in the central spiritual belief that every human being is a partial embodiment of Spirit. One of the keys to building democratic participation is to learn to see other human beings as fundamentally deserving of love, caring, and respect.

An equally important tool is to provide students with the capacity to think for themselves, to evaluate the ideas of others, and to view the world with a critical perspective that enables them to recognize that the world can be transformed and that they can be agents of that transformation.

Through the works of Paulo Freire, Maxine Green, Herb Kohl, Ira Shor, Henry Giroux, and Svi Shapiro, a powerful movement for critical pedagogy has taught us that students today are trained to learn specific ideas, but they are not taught how to participate in a democratic society. A democratic society requires the ability to look at any given reality critically and to imagine alternatives to that reality.

Developing this kind of critical consciousness becomes increasingly difficult as young minds are shaped by television and the Internet, where the dominant message is: you can make changes in your life, but beyond that, "reality" must stay the same; don't expect to change it.

Contemporary education all too often puts the mind to sleep. Spiritual education wakes it up and teaches us to recognize that every aspect of reality can be fundamentally healed and transformed, and that each of us is the agent of that transformation. Spiritual education is about learning how to look at all that exists, including all that we are being taught, with a lovingly critical attitude. Or, to put it in the words of Maxine Green, it is about making the familiar strange and the strange familiar—a kind of shaking up of our ordinary attitudes and assumptions so the things we take most for granted can be questioned.

The danger in the rest of my prescriptions for education is that they may be taken as a new "content" that can be used to deaden the mind just as well as the old content—because every content and every set of values can be transformed from something spiritually alive into a new ideology, a new dogma, a new religion.

So much of contemporary education is based on a kind of banking method: you get a certain course material and you put it in the mind bank; when you have enough of these courses in the bank, you are supposedly educated and ready to graduate and teach others. This produces people who know a lot but who can't think critically. They can operate complex technology, do careful scientific research, or analyze a novel, a poem, or a painting. They can teach someone how to read; they can even be psychotherapists, lawyers, or doctors, but they are unable to ask themselves what kind of a world they want to live in or how their activity contributes to building that kind of world. They are unable to understand how their own activity contributes to the creation of the status quo, much less how that status quo might be shifted.

So pedagogy itself must change. It must be directed at engaging the student in asking critical questions and learning to see the possibilities in every given actuality. Even the deepest spiritual truths are of little value if taught as a new catechism. Unless students are awakened to do their own thinking and exploring, much of the rest of what we teach is going to be useless, no matter how wonderful its content.

It's not enough to see through the phoniness or moral vacuity of what is—we must also learn how to act in the world to change it. For that reason, students must be given opportunities to become involved in social change activities as part of their education. Reflecting on that activity, learning to think about the strengths and weaknesses of their own actions, can be an important element in preparing students for participation in democratic transformation.

Emancipatory Spirituality adds another element into the mix: we want students to be lovingly critical—to bring a spirit of compassion and love to the act of criticism and the practice of social transformation. We need not approach contemporary reality drenched in anger and upset, but rather with a deep knowledge that what has happened so far in history and in the organization of our society can provide us with a springboard for a deep healing and transformation of all that is.

When students learn to look at reality as filled with opportunities for change, they avoid the frustration that often accompanies pedagogy that is laden with critique and not balanced with celebration. Sure, there is much to generate anger—the injustice and suffering of millions, the irresponsible destruction of the life support system of the planet, the willful obliviousness of advanced industrial societies about the hurtful consequences of our narcissism and self-indulgence. But we also have much to celebrate in being alive, being conscious, and watching the world develop the tools that will make a much higher level of spiritual evolution and social solidarity possible. Teaching students to see both the importance and necessity of social transformation, giving them the tools to think critically and act powerfully, while nurturing their ability to celebrate the universe and acknowledge all that is good in what we have already accomplished as a human race provide the kind of balancing a spiritually sensitive education must achieve.

23
▼▼▼▼▼▼▼

Social Justice, Curriculum, and Spirituality*

David E. Purpel

There are moments when I find the culture's extraordinary reluctance to respond honestly to the realities of social injustice to be ironic and troubling, but most of the time I am horrified and outraged. As I write, we have just finished a Presidential campaign that the press criticized as dull; in which the incumbent glowed about his tough stand on crime and his pride in "ending welfare as we know it"; while one of his opponents delighted in attacking affirmative action and immigration and the other candidate seemed to be overcome with anguish over the public deficit. There was virtually no mention of poverty or racism; no reference to hunger and homelessness; no sense of outrage at unnecessary human suffering. Instead of debate on the plight of the homeless there were ploys to attract soccer moms; the war on poverty had been replaced by a crusade for middle-class tax relief.

Meanwhile, mainstream educators seem to be focused on devising more sophisticated testing and tighter control mechanisms, and many educational critics are engaged in fierce battles over the fate of the universe and the nature of deconstructionism. Some educational visionaries would have us believe that what we really need in education is an end to dualistic thinking and a consciousness of spiritual oneness with nature and the universe. While politicians spin, educators test, critics reflect, and theorists parse, there are people eating dog food, teenagers turning tricks, children dealing in drugs, and families living in boxes. I say all this because I believe that it is intolerable that there be any educational discourse without continuous reference to the presence of the pain and suffering that is rooted in human greed, irresponsibility, and callousness.

THE RISE AND FALL OF CURRICULUM

Although the field of curriculum theory has been declared moribund, it is perhaps fairer to say that it appears that many theorists have given up on the notion that reforming the formal school curriculum is the key to social, if not educational reform. In response to this disenchantment with curriculum development, much of what goes on in the name of curriculum discourse today tends to be mostly highly theoretical and ideological in nature. The vacuum of dialogue on what should we teach has been largely filled with discussion of instructional and assessment issues. Indeed, it would appear that even the politicians have discovered the language of the hidden curriculum as they call for an education that responds to the concerns of competing in the global economy and for "a return to values." The once powerful demands for more demanding science, history, and math courses as well as for a more academic curriculum now seem like part of ancient history.

Herbert Kliebard has helped to clarify how the various curriculum controversies have been played out in the schools historically. It is his position that the story of twentieth century American school curriculum can be seen as the struggle among four broad competing educational groups:

"First there were the humanists, the guardians of an ancient tradition tied to the powers of reason and the finest elements of Western cultural heritage. . . ." [The second group] "led the drive for a curriculum reformed along the lines of a natural order of development of the child" . . . based on scientific data. [Third, there are] "the social efficiency educators . . . also imbued with the power of science but, their priorities lay with creating a coolly efficient, smoothly running society. . . ."

Finally, there were the social meliorists who felt that "new social conditions did not demand an obsessional fixation on the child and on child psychology; nor did the solution lie in simply ironing out the inefficiencies in the existing social order. The answer lay in the power of the schools to create a new social order" (Kliebard 1986, 23–25).

Kliebard's conclusion is that none of these orientations ever became dominant as the schools tried to accommodate to pressures from each of these groups: "In the end, what became the American curriculum was not the result of any decisive victory by any of the contending parties, but a loose, largely unarticulated, and not very tidy compromise" (Kliebard, 25).

This typology helps us to see that the continuity of our educational concerns as important aspects of these orientations can be easily detected in contemporary dialogue on educational policy. Surely, for example, the debate on multicultural education reflects the agenda of what Kliebard calls "the humanists," and certainly critical pedagogy is very much in the tradition of the "social meliorists." However, there are other forces in American culture that influence the curriculum which are not as apparent in this formulation. For example, the persistence of the arts and athletics in the standard curriculum over time cannot be explained entirely or even largely by these four orientations. There is also the recurring phenomenon of using the curriculum as a vehicle for promoting nationalism (patriotism) and/or ideology (democracy), and the term "social efficiency" only begins to suggest the current obsession with competing in the global economy.

Underneath and cutting across these four approaches and their variations are what I would term fundamental educational imperatives in which we are called upon, nay commanded, to earnestly and conscientiously pursue certain ideals. The most familiar and enduring cultural formulation of such imperatives urges us to seek "the Truth, the Good, and the Beautiful." Others would want to add to these commandments the injunction to pursue Meaning. These commandments are so profoundly revered and have become so powerfully internalized that they have come to constitute the spiritual foundation of education. Put another way, no matter what the specific educational goals may be, there is the underlying demand that we reach these goals without violating the canons of these fundamental imperatives.

Today, perhaps the single most powerful and pervasive of these educational commandments is "Thou Shalt Seek the Truth." In modern times, truth has come to be typically defined as accurate and precise knowledge; information that can be verified through empirical and/or logical processes. The triumph of Enlightenment thought is testimony to the primacy of this imperative, with its basically unchallenged demands for precision, proof, reason, analysis, detachment, and skepticism. We are enjoined to seek this kind of Truth, however difficult and unsettling it may be and regardless of the consequences presumably in the faith that the Truth will make us free. Not only is this pursuit presented as a moral and aesthetic imperative, but a pragmatically essential dimension of creating a progressive civilization. If nothing else, American education is about preserving and enhancing the intellectual and aesthetic processes of pursuing this kind of Truth. Critics and defenders of the educational status quo unite in their dedication to the values of critical rationality insofar as they give us valid information and knowledge that at least approaches the Truth. Our schools and universities constantly test for accuracy and precision, for right answers, and for the presence of compelling evidence. Indeed, the mottoes of two of our oldest and most prestigious universities—Harvard and Yale—are simply and boldly translated as *"Truth."*

This is surely not to say that the school curriculum centers on the acquisition of knowledge for its own sake, or that universities are singularly committed to the search for Truth. What I am saying is that whatever the social and cultural goals may be (job training, national solidarity, human development, social change, personal fulfillment, etc.), we are deeply committed to pursuing them within a context of intellectual integrity, i.e., we all want to be sure to be accurate, precise, rational, and knowledgeable. Indeed, at the cost of appearing to be gratuitous, I want to reaffirm my own strong commitment to an education strongly rooted in reason and rationality.

Having said all that, it is also clear that such an education is not without criticism. There are those who insist on the validity and significance of other ultimate goals such as wisdom or goodness. It is also clear that although knowledge and intellectual acuity may be necessary, they are surely not sufficient conditions for wisdom and goodness. Our history has made it painfully clear that smart people can do hateful things and that the impulse to be cruel and callous is not significantly mitigated by acquiring knowledge or analytic skills. Even more troubling is the phenomenon of people deliberately utilizing knowledge (truth) for destructive purposes. The design and production of Zyklon B, napalm, and land mines require the same degree of intellectual mastery as the design and production of antibiotics and computers. Manipulation requires as much insight as does enlightenment; knowledge of how people learn is as useful to the wizards of Madison Avenue as it is to the gurus of Sesame Street.

There is, of course, another strong educational tradition that seeks to go beyond the pursuit of information and knowledge, namely that of the pursuit of Meaning. In this tradition, knowledge is an important dimension of this pursuit, and Truth is thought to be metaphysical in nature. Abraham Joshua Heschel expresses this orientation eloquently:

> Socrates taught us that a life without thinking is not worth living. . . . Thinking is a noble effort, but the finest thinking may end in futility. . . . The Bible taught us that life without commitment is not worth living; that thinking without roots will bear flowers but no fruit. . . . Our systems of education stress the importance of enabling the student to exploit the power aspect of reality. . . . We teach the children how to measure, how to weigh! We fail to teach to revere, how to sense wonder and awe . . . , the sense of the sublime, [and] the sign of the inward greatness of the human soul. (Heschel 1955, 36, 216)

POSTMODERNISM: THE WORM IN THE APPLE

It is surely not for me to enter into the seemingly interminable and torturous scholarly debate about the meaning and significance of this concept except to be clear on what I make of all this hullabaloo. Beyond all the smoke of battle and prolixity is the harsh reality of a very serious crisis of authority. We have come to see more and more clearly how much of our understanding of the world is contingent on such matters as history, culture, gender, class, and, above all, language, and how much we have been confusing universal truth with particularist interpretation. The very tools of Enlightenment thinking itself have, ironically enough, undermined its most basic and profound project—that of affording human liberation through reason, objectivity, science, technology, and detachment, a project now described by many postmodernists as delusional.

This critique goes beyond eroding our epistemological grounding (as fundamental as that is) and extends to questioning the nature of and commitment to our core moral aspirations. It would appear that not only have we committed the sin of being wrong about the nature of Truth, but we have compounded that sin by utilizing these errors in such a way as to provide privilege and advantage to some. What is involved is not only the sin of intellectual arrogance but the evil of political oppression. Walter Brueggemann (1994) puts it this way:

> The practice of modernity . . . has given us a world imagined through the privilege of white, male, Western, colonial hegemony with all its pluses and minuses. It is a world that we have come to trust and take for granted. It is a world that has wrought great good, but also has accomplished enormous mischief against some for the sake of others. The simple truth is that this constructed world can no longer be sustained, is no longer persuasive or viable, and we are able to discern no larger image to put in its place. . . . The imagined world of privilege and disparity is treasured by all who live in the advantaged West. It is treasured more by men than women, more by whites than blacks, but all of us in the West have enormous advantage. (18–20)

The notions of the social construction of knowledge, the close relationships between power arrangements and constructions of reality, and the problematics of essentialist formulations, although surely not new, have had a profound effect on all cultural institutions, including education. What we face amounts to an intellectual and moral crisis that comes in a most importune time of enormous peril from the forces of greed, divisiveness, and hatred. What we urgently need is a common understanding of our plight and a common vision that can save us from ourselves. In a time when we seek community, we are confronted with the realities of its ambiguities and problematics; at a time when we long for authentic identity, we are required to face the indictment of essentialism; in a time when we feel impelled to speak out at the injustices inflicted on marginal groups, we must deal with the ways in which the definition of these groups has been deconstructed; and in a time when we search for the moral vision to sustain us through despair and cynicism, we must confront new insights on how ideology impinges on our moral quests.

The implications for education are deeply troubling, for as we have indicated, underlying the various curricular approaches has been the profound
commitment to the pursuit of Truth in the more restricted sense of critical rationality and/or the metaphysical sense of ultimate meaning. Much of postmodern thought would seem to undermine both of these quests. If truth is an
illusion and meaning a delusion, then what are we to teach other than basic
literacy, numeracy, and the conversation-ending assertions of postmodernism? How do we make a rational and coherent plan for education when many
brilliant theorists make a compelling case that rationality and moral coherence are no more than charming fictions?

ENTER SPIRITUALITY

It is hardly surprising that in an atmosphere of political, moral, and intellectual crisis we as a culture would look to the spiritual as a path toward sanity
and hope. The extraordinary surge of interest in matters religious and spiritual is as deep as it is broad, expressing itself not only in religious fundamentalism and New Age spiritualism, but in such movements as liberation theology, feminist theology, and Jewish renewal as well as in such phenomena as
alternative approaches to healing and to organizational management.

This interest has also manifested itself in education, as reflected in the recent publication and popularity of a growing number of articles and books
on spirituality and education. There are a growing number of authors like
Dwayne Huebner, Jeffrey Kane, Kathleen Kesson, James Moffett, Ron
Miller, Parker Palmer, and Douglas Sloan who are writing directly on issues
at the intersection of education and spirituality. There are also other major
curriculum theorists whose works surely are spiritual in nature even though
they do not necessarily use religious or spiritual language as their primary
form of discourse. For example, Nel Noddings' daring and challenging work
on caring and compassion speaks to matters of the spirit and to the centrality
of human connectiveness, while Jane Roland Martin's focus on nurturance,
relationship, and responsibility is a powerful affirmation of the deep inner
impulses for love and intimacy.

However, proclaiming the bond between education and spirituality does
not begin to resolve our problems, since that only begs further questions.
Whose spirituality? Which spirituality? How are we to accept the authority of
particular spiritual orientations? In other words, the same critiques that have
rendered other educational formulations problematic require us to examine
critically the claims for a spiritually grounded education. Indeed, the history
of religious and spiritual expression requires us to be specially alert to its particular problematics, e.g., the possibilities of dogmatism, zealotry, authoritarianism, and irrelevance. The whole notion of an education based on spiri-

tual beliefs goes totally counter to what we have learned about the danger and implausibility of visions that emerge from "grand narratives."

And yet the power of the spirit is the very energy we need lest we fall into the paralysis and cynicism that are the consequences of moral despair and intellectual confusion. Even as intellectuals scoff at facts as fictions, reform efforts as self-serving, and moral visions as pretentious, there is vast and needless human suffering in our midst. Millions of human beings are malnourished and maltreated; millions of people do not have adequate housing, medical care, and education; and the gap between rich and poor has grown to obscene proportions. Even more disheartening is the way that we as a people, nation, and profession have failed to begin to fully accept the depth and gravity of this human suffering, never mind taking responsibility for it. The problem is surely not rooted in a lack of understanding, knowledge, and information. There can be no doubt whatsoever that we know about the suffering and that we have the material and intellectual resources to significantly relieve if not eliminate it. However, the great irony and shame is that we cannot utilize the extraordinary knowledge and expertise that we have accumulated to meet our most profound moral commitments. This is largely but not entirely because the spirits of greed, suspicion, hate, and division are so pervasive and dominant in our culture.

The reality of immense human suffering is made even more unspeakable by its origins in human stupidity and cupidity, as our failure to redress these sins provides proof enough of our capacity to do evil. Surely, we have enough understanding of the intellectual underpinnings of our efforts at creating a just and loving society to make some judgments about them. As far as modernism is concerned, my view is that now is the time to proclaim that the long run has finally arrived and that it is terrible. And as far as postmodernism is concerned, all I have to say is that the misery and suffering of millions of people is not a socially constructed metaphor but is as real and certain as misery and suffering.

How then do we go on with our commitments in a time when we have clear responsibilities and fuzzy authority, and how do we generate hope and vision in an era of uncertainty, despair, and disenchantment? This is not merely a challenge that educators must address but one that requires creative and thoughtful responses from all aspects of our society and culture. One very helpful response has been presented by Walter Brueggemann in his book *Texts Under Negotiation*, in which he struggles with the implications of postmodernism for another influential cultural institution, the Christian church. After acknowledging the power and influence of postmodern thinking, he goes on to offer some suggestions on how the Church can sustain its efforts in the light of this disquieting critique without in any way loosening its commitment to its worldview based on divine creation and ultimate redemption:

... It is not, in my judgement, the work of the church ... to construct a full alternative world, for that would be to act as preemptively and imperialistically as all those old construals and impositions. Rather, the task is a more modest one, [namely] ... to *fund*—to provide the pieces, materials, and resources, out of which a new world can be imagined. Our responsibility, then, is not a grand scheme or a coherent system, but the voicing of a lot of little pieces out of which people can put life together in fresh configurations. (Brueggemann 1994, 22)

He goes on to urge his colleagues to create places of meeting where people can come together to share their "funds" but not to make

claims that are so large and comprehensive that they ring hollow in a context of our general failure, demise, and disease. It is rather a place where people come to receive new materials, or old materials freshly voiced, that will fund, feed, nurture, legitimate, and authorize a *counterimagination of the world* ... an imagination that is not at all congenial to dominant intellectual or political modes. [emphasis in original] (Brueggemann, 23)

A MODEST FUNDING PROPOSAL

I want to move past all the postmodern handwringing about the nature of reality and truth as a troubling, interesting, and useful critique but one that is marginally relevant and fundamentally distracting to our moral responsibilities. Surely, the suffering and the pain are real enough, and there is no great mystery about what is required to ease that suffering. In spite of this, one of the horrible ironies of the past few decades is a serious erosion in concern for social justice, e.g., concern for the poor and the homeless. Much of the responsibility for this lies with those who have chosen to see the poor as irresponsible, unskilled, and/or an impediment to the demands of a highly competitive global economy. However, the erosion has been heightened by the neglect of many of those who have traditionally been active in drawing attention to the plight of the poor, a neglect that is not so much the result of a change in moral conviction as it is a consequence of being distracted by other important concerns. Among such concerns are postmodern thought, cybernetics, and the ecological crisis, all matters of enormous import and significance. There are undoubtedly important connections among issues of social justice, computers, ecology, and postmodernism, but my view is that priority for social justice has been significantly eroded, if not superseded. I reject the notion that we cannot pursue social justice till we get our epistemology right as well as the notion that issues of social justice must be seen only in the perspective of the fate of the universe. My point is not to discount the importance of such powerfully significant issues as the nature of truth, the impact of technology, or the preservation of the planet, but only to argue that we not be held hostage to them or not allow ourselves to be distracted from our non-negotiable, permanent, and solemn responsibility to work for the elimination of unnecessary human suffering.

At the same time, and in spite of the devastating postmodern critique, the commitment in the academy and among educators (conservatives as well as radicals) to the pursuit of knowledge and critical rationality seems as passionate and relentless as ever. The dedication to being rational, precise, accurate, perceptive; the solemn vows to conduct careful research and thoughtful inquiry; and the devotion to creating new knowledge and discovering the laws of nature constitute the ultimate raison d'être of contemporary formal education. One way or another, educators pay homage to this Holiest of Grails, for whether it's vocational education or critical pedagogy, whether it's a book report or a dissertation, a manifesto or a monograph, we want it to be grounded in the name of the Spirits of rationality, knowledge, and inquiry and meet their demands for accuracy, precision, and reliability.

My intention is by no means to reject these Spirits as false gods, only to put them in perspective and in their proper place. Let us begin with an examination of the aesthetic values of pursuing knowledge and understanding for their own sake. My sense is that even as educators and scholars embrace pragmatism and functionalism and as they make eloquent and poetic claims for the benefits of increased knowledge and understanding (e.g., as necessary for citizenship or for personal meaning) there remains an abiding love and passion for the search and accumulation of knowledge and understanding per se. This seems reasonable enough as an educational goal for the relatively limited number of people with that highly specialized sensibility, but hardly plausible as the Ground Zero of all curriculum being.

There is also the problematic nature of the pragmatic claims for knowledge since it has become eminently clear that even though highly knowledgeable and understanding people tend to be richer, more powerful, and more famous, they are also among the most dangerous and evil. This is certainly and emphatically not to say that smart equals bad, but only to say that it is often the case that people use their smarts to do bad things. Power in the United States is not in the hands of the illiterate and intellectually dense; I dare say that we would find a disproportionate number of highly educated (or, at minimum, highly schooled) among the movers and shakers of Wall Street, Madison Avenue, Capitol Hill, Hollywood, and all the other power centers of our society and culture. It must also be said that many of the people who genuinely do serious good are also very knowledgeable and understanding. And that, my friends, is the whole point.

At the very least, the persistence of such claims suggests that increasing knowledge and understanding is supposed to have some consequence over and above the fun and profit of simply finding and having it. The very simple and obvious "truth of the matter" is that education for increased knowledge and understanding should be grounded in a deeper commitment to pursue a larger good than studying for its own sake. My own explanation as to why heightened understanding and knowledge continues to be used for bad things is that we have not demanded that, if and when it is to be used, it be used *only* for good things. I believe that there are three basic reasons why we haven't made such demands:

1. Some of us genuinely like finding truth for its own sake.
2. Some of us really want to do bad things.
3. Some of us don't know the difference between good and bad.

To those in Group One, I offer respectful tolerance; to those in Group Two, I have only contempt; but to those in Group Three, I offer some suggestions.

My most basic recommendation is that we ground our education *not* in the pursuit and adoration of truth, knowledge, understanding, insight, critical rationality, interpretive schema, or analytic tools, but rather in a relentless and whole-hearted quest for the attitude formerly known as *agape*. I say this because I have come to see the wisdom in that all-time, oldest, and corniest of all clichés that it is only unconditional and dispassionate love that can truly overcome unnecessary human suffering. It is a wisdom that persists across time and space in spite of vulgarization and oversimplification and in the face of scorn, ridicule, and cynicism, including more than my fair share. I am convinced that a people grounded in a consciousness of *agape* would end most human misery even as I realize that such a statement is somewhat tautological as it can also be said that human misery is rooted in lack of human caring and compassion. I am also very much aware that a project for an education based on nourishing a human consciousness of agape is incredibly ambitious if not outrageously pretentious or just plain impossible. However, I do not see such a project as any less ambitious, impractical, pretentious, or possible than the Enlightenment project of human freedom through increased knowledge, understanding, and insight. Indeed, I believe that developing the capacity for understanding and insight alongside a commitment to nourishing the capacity for love is a whole lot more practical than teaching people only to be critical and thoughtful.

Mary Daly's definition is helpful:

> In the fullest sense, *agape* is God's love. It is generous love, not appetitive in the sense that there is need to satisfy that in oneself which is incomplete, not stimulated by or dependent upon that which is loved. It is indifferent to value, seeking to confer good, rather than to obtain it. It is therefore, spontaneous and creative, and it is rooted in abundance rather than in poverty. (Daly 1973, 210)

The idea that we as a people could attain such a consciousness seems remote, if not the stuff of delusion and fantasy. However, the idea that all people have the capacity for the development of an equally intense critical consciousness seems no less daunting and improbable. A major difference is that most educators as a matter of faith readily accept the call to work as if people have both the need and the potential to develop a critical consciousness, continually pressing students to stretch and expand their critical skills. Indeed, the educational project for the development of a critical consciousness is deeply embedded in the whole array of our curricular and instructional repertoire. It has been well organized and its elements subdivided into any number of categories, e.g., literacy and numeracy; the sciences and the humanities; writing skills, analytic and interpretive skills; research skills; reliance on theories of cognitive development; and the use of laboratories for experiments. The point here is that schools and universities approach the task of developing intellectual acumen not as a special program but as a Spirit that is to energize and permeate all aspects of its academic program with at least the implicit understanding that the effect of all the particular intellectual skills adds up to something more than the sum of its parts, i.e., a critical consciousness.

What I am suggesting here is parallel to that approach, i.e., not a special program or course in moral education or caring (although these are not unreasonable possibilities) but a larger, deeper, and more endemic commitment to the project of nourishing and demanding the enhancement of the human capacity to love. In doing so we also encounter problematics parallel to that of the commitment to develop critical consciousness, e.g., issues of definition, resistance, and complexity. As educators and citizens, we have the responsibility to continue to engage these issues and problems as difficult and perplexing as they are. It surely is not that we are without resources in such an endeavor for one of the marvels of human life is that people over time and across space have seriously and profoundly involved themselves with the question of how we are to live with each other with justice and love. As a result we have an extraordinary heritage of powerfully enduring ideas, images, and visions of love and social justice as well as the legacy of remarkable children, men, women, and groups who have endeavored to embody them.

It is easy enough to realize that many of these visions have been betrayed, that many of these formulations conflict with each other, and that much misery has been inflicted in their names. This is a reality that we must not ever deny or rationalize and one that represents a human potential for stupidity and cruelty that we dare not discount nor minimize. At the same time, and without blinking from the horrors of some of our best intentions, it must also be acknowledged that in spite of all the turmoil and divisiveness, there really does exist an important space of common moral affirmation in which there is a very large degree of consensus, even if some of this is limited to rhetoric. It is a space worthy of passionate embrace and zealous protection that is no less real but perhaps more vulnerable than the privilege, domination, and greed occupied by the space of human conflict. These items of consensus are admittedly general, perhaps ambiguous and even vague; yet their very persistence in spite of the intellectual and empirical battering they have taken is nothing short of miraculous.

Perhaps the most basic and most profound is our belief in the preciousness of life itself and, in that context, our affirmation of the right of every person to a life of dignity and respect. I really do believe that we believe this even though there are reservations to this commitment. For example, there are those who say that certain people, like serial killers, child molesters, and rapists, should be excluded from this affirmation by virtue of the unforgivable nature of their crimes. I admit to my own deep ambivalence about forgiving and affirming such people, but I am clear that we should not let the worst of the world shape our moral visions and am equally clear that the vast majority of us are not vicious and hateful criminals. As educators, we can surely affirm the dignity of children, even if we are perplexed and grieved when some of them act out in anger and violence. At the very least, we can reaffirm our commitment to enhancing the dignity of those students who are not hateful and continue to struggle with how to respond to those who are.

These reservations notwithstanding, the roots for the affirmation of life with dignity run very deep and wide in our history and in our religious, spiritual, and moral traditions. They are embraced, surely in a variety of discourses, by people of all faiths, colors, denominations, classes, genders, ethnicities, creeds, and epistemological preferences. Such affirmation is reflected in the Bible, the Koran, the Declaration of Independence, the U.S. Constitution, the Gettysburg Address, and the Pledge of Allegiance, although regretfully, they are not exactly prominent in Goals 2000. Indeed, the United Nations Universal Declaration of Human Rights (which all member nations are required to uphold) begins with this assertion:

"*Whereas* recognition of the inherent dignity and of the equal and inalienable rights of all members of the human family is the foundation of freedom, justice, and peace in the world, . . ." Later on in the preamble, the statement goes on to require that "every individual and every organ of society, keeping this declaration constantly in mind, shall strive by teaching and education to promote respect for these rights and freedoms and by progressive measures, national and international, to secure their universal and effective recognition and observance."

However, educators bent on connecting curriculum-making with such stirring discourse need to be reminded of the dangers of grand narratives and magisterial programs. As Walter Brueggemann points out in support of his notion of

> funding the pieces, materials, and resources out of which a new world can be imagined. . . . What is yearned for among us is not new doctrine or new morality, but new world, new self, new future. The new world is not given whole, any more than the new self is given abruptly in psychotherapy. It is given only a little at a

time, one miracle at a time, one poem at a time, one healing, one promise, one commandment. Over time these pieces are stitched together into a sensible collage, stitched together, all of us in concert, but each of us idiosyncratically, stitched together in a new whole—all things new. (Brueggemann 1994, 24–25)

I would like to suggest a few such pieces of the collage that certainly can give us direction and an agenda. Firstly, the concepts of agape or unconditional love are at once daunting and controversial, laden with so much baggage that it can be a non-starter. We might begin more modestly and perhaps more realistically by taking Charity James' suggestion of substituting the concept of "respect" for the notion of agape as a goal of education. She has this to say:

Swami Muktananda teaches that the true *dharma* (way, path, religion in the non-dogmatic sense) is to "welcome one another with great respect and love." I find this helpful because respect is more difficult for the ego to fool around with than is love or compassion. It seems to be a truly manageable proposition to build an institution and a process on an ethic of uncompromised mutual respect. And of course if we make (and encourage) the steady practice of respecting others, the privilege, the great attainment, of loving will increasingly flow toward us. (James 1980, 8)

This adds up to respect for life itself and for the affirmation of human dignity for all. In order to move such an affirmation beyond mere rhetoric, I suggest that we can agree on some minimum standards of what it means concretely to affirm human dignity. These standards not only help to define basic human dignity, but they also serve as part of the conditions under which individuals can find meaning and fulfillment. I want to suggest standards that are not only consistent and resonant with our consensual moral commitments, but are also eminently and immediately technologically, logistically, and materially doable. They are simultaneously simple and profound, traditional and radical, spiritual, and material:

Every person should have enough to eat. Every person should have adequate shelter. Every person should have proper health care. Every person should be afforded dignity and respect. Every person has the responsibility to participate in efforts to ensure that these requirements are met.

Notice that I have *not* said every person should have the opportunity to *pursue* adequate diet, shelter, and health—these are not areas that are to be left to chance or the market, nor are they to be rationed as scarce commodities or awarded as prizes, but instead are the inherent and inviolable rights afforded by membership in our community. There are important questions, of course, as to what constitutes adequate diet, shelter, and medical care, and there are legitimate questions concerning the conditions under which individuals can be said to forfeit these rights. Important as these questions are, they are still marginal ones and are no excuse to put everything else on hold. The uncontested dignity of the vast majority of human beings should not be held hostage to the very few who try our patience. In summary then, we can, at least partially, fund what Brueggemann calls "that which can help us to imagine a new world" by grounding our educational program in the commitment to respect human life by ensuring adequate food, shelter, and health care for all, with the understanding that there are unsettled questions, problems, and policies that need to be debated within that commitment.

For educators, generally speaking, this would mean that the Spirit of this commitment would pervade the rhetoric, consciousness, and energy of the schools to the point that it would be taken for granted and assimilated as much as the Spirits of critical rationality and the accumulation of knowledge are. Indeed, the decisions on content selection and instructional emphases would be largely driven by the concern for which bodies of knowledge, which research skills, which resources, and which attitudes are most likely to further the commitment to human dignity.

More particularly, schools would be required to examine their policies, rules, and regulations on the basis of their consonance with this commitment. To make them consonant would surely mean drastic changes in these policies and rules, which by itself tells us a great deal. For example, what does it mean to have a grading system at all in a situation where we are endeavoring to promote deep and profound respect and dignity for all? Imagine the impact on the schools if all students, faculty, and staff were required to treat each other with utmost respect. Imagine what the effect would be if that policy was considered as vital and enforced as firmly as the policies forbidding violence and drugs in the school. How affirming this would be for those educators who have devoted their lives to honoring their students as precious and unique beings.

This is surely not to say that such a process is without controversy and difficulty since it would certainly and very quickly generate any number of torturous and anguishing dilemmas since we would have to constantly consider what most deeply and truly constitutes and enhances human dignity. However, this is not essentially different from the complex and contradictory problems that educators face currently, the difference being one of focus and priority. Moreover, it cannot be but enormously beneficial that educational discourse be driven by the heuristic of vigorous dispute and argument over which educational policies are most likely to enhance human dignity!

Further, we would need an educational psychology less concerned with instruction, measurement, and evaluation and more with the conditions under which people can learn to love and respect themselves and each other. We would need to have more research that delves into the human impulses for community, compassion, and social justice, and there would need to be more analysis and understanding of the forces that disrupt those impulses. Our history needs to be enriched with more of the language, stories, and images of the costly and courageous struggles for social justice that sanctifies our past, gives energy to the present, and provides hope for the future. Our art can be the vehicle not only for self-expression and the evocation of form, but also as the creative and imaginative processes that can give voice, shape, and image to the community of justice, love, and joy for which we so ache. Indeed, our failure to create communities of justice and love is not so much a reflection of the failure of the intellect, but of the failure of the imagination to envision a life where both freedom and equality can flourish.

The commandments to seek Truth and the processes that facilitate it would be replaced by the commandments to seek Justice and the arts and sciences that yield it. To pursue the pleasures of the mind while there are bodies in pain is to be seen as aberrational rather than quaint, more as an indication of self-indulgence than as a sign of grace. We must be mindful, however, that both minds and bodies are terrible things to waste. The capacity for love can only mature when it is nurtured and enhanced by the enormous powers of human rationality, imagination, and creativity. In this way, education becomes the integration of body, mind, and spirit.

A LAST WORD

I accept as a matter of course that life is extremely complicated, contradictory, and messy, and I have spent a great deal of my career learning, teaching, and writing about the incredible tangle of ambivalence, uncertainty, and perplexity that is involved in dealing with educational issues. I have, inevitably, also come to learn about the problematics of problematics, particularly in their capacity to obscure and paralyze and so I come not to praise complexity but to give it a rest. Some very important issues are quite clear and eminently simple:

No person should have to go hungry, homeless, or without health care. We have the material and logistical capacity to make this possible. In spite of this, millions endure the pain and humiliation of hunger, homelessness, and poor health.

I would submit that these facts be the dominant and underlying elements of *all* discussions and debates on educational policies and practices. The realities of widespread unnecessary human suffering should replace issues of competing in the global economy, of accountability, of computer instruction, of school-based management, of multicultural education, even of critical pedagogy, eco-feminism, and spirituality as the starting and ending points of any and all educational dialogue. It is inconceivable to me that we could do otherwise than be constantly aware of and attentive to the shameful way we have reneged on our most profound commitments and responsibilities to our brothers and sisters.

Let us not ask how the problems of human misery illumine and demonstrate the importance of our favorite specialized projects like success in the global economy, accountability, computer instruction, school-based management, multi-cultural education, critical pedagogy, eco-feminism, or spirituality. Let us, instead, reaffirm our commitment to human dignity for all and insist that before anything else, all people should have enough to eat, adequate shelter, and proper health care. I believe very strongly that there are educational processes that can significantly contribute to these goals and that we should concentrate our energies on them as our number one priority. There is no number two.

It may be useful to see this task and responsibility as "spiritual" rather than "educational" since it does raise and reflect the most profound questions of existence. What is the origin of this intense impulse for social justice that is so pervasive across time and space? Why do we have this urge to seek meaning and to link the details of our everyday world with visions of the sacred? Asking and responding to such questions are spiritual acts in themselves. When we sense the pain of suffering, the ache of responsibility, and the joy of justice, we are surely in the presence of Mystery.

Heschel (1955) helps us to clarify this phenomenon:

> To the speculative mind, the world is an enigma; to the religious mind, the world is a challenge. The speculative problem is impersonal; the religious problem is a problem addressed to the person. The first is concerned with finding an answer to the question: what is the cause of being? The second, with giving an answer to the question: What is asked of us? . . . In spite of our pride, in spite of our acquisitiveness, we are driven by an awareness that something is asked of us; that we are asked to wonder, to revere, think, and to live in a way that is compatible with the grandeur and mystery of living. What gives birth to religion is not intellectual curiosity but the fact and experience of our being asked. (Heschel, 111–112)

Within this Mystery is an astonishing Truth: We are asked to regard each other as sisters and brothers, to be their keepers, to strive to respect, if not love them, at minimum not to hurt them, and surely to provide for them. An education grounded in that Mystery and Truth is light years away from the mean-spirited and vulgar spirit of our operating educational model. Nor, it must be said, does this educational vision guarantee a cosmic consciousness. Yet it provides a perspective that is both practical in its application and idealistic in its hopes; doable in its possibilities and daring in its aspirations; traditional in its roots and radical in its critique.

The opportunity to develop a pedagogy of human dignity is an awesome one for it goes beyond our *professional* obligations to our *human* responsibilities as co-creators of our world. What makes it so exhilarating is its very awesomeness, i.e., the opportunity to match human capacities with a sacred vision, to engage in a task that is grand *and* realizable, and to make the educational process truly redemptive, not merely profitable.

REFERENCES

Brueggemann, Walter. 1994. *Texts under negotiation: the Bible and postmodern imagination.* Minneapolis: Fortress Press.

Daly, Mary. "*Love*" in *Dictionary of history of ideas.* vol. 2, 1973. New York: Charles Scribner.

Heschel, Abraham Joshua. 1955. *God in search of man.* New York: Farrar, Straus, and Giroux.

James, Charity. *Spirituality and education.* Unpublished manuscript, 1980.

Kliebard, Herbert. 1986. *The struggle for the American curriculum.* Boston: Routledge and Kegan Paul.

GLOBALIZATION AND EDUCATION:
THE 21st-CENTURY CHALLENGE

In the final section of this book, we look at the issue of global-ization—arguably the most significant concern facing human-kind in the new century. Some would note, however, that glob-alization is not really that new—that the process by which human beings and societies become ever more interconnected with one another has been developing for hundreds of years. Although this is clearly accurate, nothing really resembles the extraordinary explosion of links and connections that now binds societies and nations together and that has occurred in the last decades of the 20th century. Certainly there is nothing comparable to the compression of time and space that new technologies have made possible in the last few years. Such technologies have begun to radically undermine the existing borders, boundaries, and identities that marked our world, as well our definitions of who we are. To a degree previously un-imaginable, a world system has emerged that has begun to eclipse the old system of autarchic nation states. Of course this process has occurred in ways that are asymmetrical in terms of power and cultural influence. As a result, globalization con-fronts the world with unprecedented stresses and tensions that, at least in the United States, made the events of September 11, 2001, a moment in which the new global condition burst upon a largely unaware population.

Of course this is not to say that American workers were unaware of the way that, throughout the 1980s and 1990s, a new economic order was emerging that gave unprecedented power to transnational economic interests to reshape work and employment. Workers in manufacturing especially suffered a devastating loss of jobs as the new regime of unrestricted free trade made it possible for companies to move their businesses to wherever labor was cheapest, and legislation affecting things like work conditions and the environment was the least onerous to companies. In some respects, there was a *race to the bottom* as big business could pursue the biggest profits through setting up shop in places where workers could be paid the least. The new regime of global flexibility was also manifest in finance, where banking and other interests could speculate in international currencies through almost instantaneous movements of vast, often unimaginable, sums of money made possible through recently developed information technologies. All of this meant a world in which there was, simultaneously, unprecedented opportunities to amass huge sums of wealth while, for many working- and middle-class people, extraordinary economic uncertainty. Massive layoffs, financial bubbles, industrial sweat shops, communal and environmental deterioration, and company mergers and buyouts are the fallout of the brave new world of the global economic system. Although there was certainly convincing evidence in some areas that globalization had provided new jobs and opportunities, it was also undeniably certain that the world witnessed horrifying levels of human exploitation and social inequality. U.N. surveys in the 1990s indicated that one half of the world's population lived on less than $2 a day, and that one third of the world's population had a life expectancy of under 40 years.

Alongside the problems of economic insecurity and the terrible levels of poverty in many parts of the world (women, it should be noted, bore the brunt of the latter, representing fully 70% of the world's 1 billion poor), critics of globalization argued that the new global order represented a major threat to democracy. With corporations becoming transnational—neither restricted by nor beholden to the polity of a particular country, major economic decisions being made by international bodies like the WTO or the IMF usually behind closed doors with representatives of labor or environmental organizations largely excluded—the policies and agenda that shaped the everyday lives of citizens were now formulated outside of their influence and scrutiny. In other words, the core features of a democracy in which citizens could participate and shape the conditions that affected their lives were being seriously undermined. Indeed more than this, the very locus of civic activity—the nation state—was being sidelined as the major economic players on the international scene saw the entire planet as the potential stage for their activities. Of course it is this fact that has been central to much of the international protests against globalization. Such protests have brought together, in an unprecedented way, labor unions, environmental groups, and fair trade activists across the world who have protested the lack of democracy in the emerging global order as well as the growing inequities between the haves and have-nots resulting from neoliberal economic policies. As educators, globalization requires now that we think again about education's responsibilities in the making of a democratic culture. We must now consider what it means to educate for a global citizenship in which questions of the rights of consumers and workers, as well environmental responsibilities, must be looked at on a planetary scale. Of course such a vision of citizenship places a new emphasis on universal human rights that cannot be separated from questions of economic and social justice. Among the latter, special attention is required concerning the misery of so many children and young people disfigured by poverty, child labor, military conscription, and sexual exploitation.

The occasional disruptions of such protests pale, of course, when compared to the horrific violence of international terrorism in this era of globalization. Yet again it is important to locate this violence in the context of the economic and cultural changes such globalization is producing. We have already alluded to the terrible levels of material deprivation and economic hopelessness that grip so many people in the world—especially among the young. Poverty in the world is, of course, not new in human history. What is new, however, is the pervasive exposure of people all over the world to the bombardment of tantalizing and seductive images that offer a view of how others live, especially in the affluent West. The relentless emphasis on buying, wealth, sex, and violence simultaneously feeds the desires, fantasies, frustrations, and resentments of many around the world. This insidious spectacle of the West, and America in particular, becomes the focal point for the pent-up fury of those who are outraged by its cultural, economic, and political influence. Of course we are not suggesting here that forms of religious fanaticism really offer a viable or humane, let alone democratic, response to the crisis of our increasingly global culture. The very opposite certainly seems to be the case, compounding the problems that beset so many people and unleashing new forms of violence, hatred, and authoritarianism.

In the affluent world, the infusion of unfamiliar cultures has also brought a new intolerance. Borders have become more permeable not just to goods and money, but also to people. Globalization has brought with it huge influxes of migrant workers looking for jobs and economic possibility. Such movements of people into hitherto settled communities have stimulated new fears and hostilities—anxieties about the presence of strange cultures and religious practices, unfamiliar faces and languages, and competition for jobs. Throughout Europe and North America, such developments have been the catalyst for extreme right-wing parties that express the angst of the local populations. The spread of fear, intolerance, bigotry, and absolutist approaches to religious belief makes new demands on the work of educators. The latter are challenged to respond to the rising culture of fear and apprehension with renewed emphasis on the value of diversity, pluralism, tolerance, and compassion toward others in our midst. Beyond this is the importance of developing a more complex understanding of the interconnected and relational nature of all culture and human identity as we seek to combat all forms of absolutism and essentialism.

Our readings focus on a number of these themes. Naomi Klein's piece (chap. 24, this volume) from her influential book on globalization looks at the process of enforced casualization—the way that jobs are being reshaped away from full-time, secure employment into part-time, temporary, and freelance labor, which allows corporations to keep overheads down and have minimal responsibilities to their employees. David Held (chap. 27, this volume) examines a central element of the current ideology—the belief that economic growth is the key to meeting human needs and alleviating poverty. His article provides a contrary picture of the devastating effects of unrestricted growth on human communities and well-being as well as on the environment. In his chapter, Held argues that the contemporary forms of globalization necessitate new forms of democratic polity—"a community of democratic communities" that reflects the need for transnational, cross-border structures of political action. These new political communities would recognize that we now live in a complex, interconnected world that requires radically different forms of citizenship and civic cultures. Edmund O'Sullivan (chap. 25, this volume) argues that the fundamental educational task of our time is to make "the choice for a sustainable global planetary habitat of interdependent life forms over and against the global competitive market-place." O'Sullivan asserts that educational institutions have been major *apologists* for industrial society and part of the hegemonic process that mediates the fantasies of consumer culture. Zygmunt Bauman (chap. 26, this volume) reflects on the explosion of politics and thought around issues of identity in recent times. There is, he argues, a paradoxical relationship between such concerns and the process of globalization; as established political institutions are sapped of their capacity to have much effect on things, so alternative modes of collective action emerge. These communities of identity offer a sense of security, confidence, and meaning in a world that seems to escape effective control and encourages privatization and individualization. Identity builders, says Bauman, seek pegs on which they can hang together their individually experienced fears and anxieties. Finally, Svi Shapiro (chap. 28, this volume) considers the lessons of September 11. Condemning the lack of serious engagement in schools with the events of this day, Shapiro suggests a number of important moral and political implications that include looking at the meaning of modernity on traditional cultures, the connection between rage and social injustice, the dangers of demonizing the other, and the need to regain our sense of value for public service. Of course only some of these articles directly relate to education. Yet it is our belief that all of them raise issues that are of immense significance in the world that will confront our children. It is surely our task as educators to find ways to address these concerns in preparing young lives for this new world. We can do no less.

24

▼▼▼▼▼▼▼

Threats and Temps*

Naomi Klein

A sense of impermanence is blowing through the labor force, destabilizing everyone from office temps to high-tech independent contractors to restaurant and retail clerks. Factory jobs are being outsourced, garment jobs are morphing into homework, and in every industry, temporary contracts are replacing full, secure employment. In a growing number of instances, even CEOs are opting for shorter stints at one corporation after another, breezing in and out of different corner offices and purging half the employees as they come and go.

Almost every major labor battle of the decade has focused not on wage issues but on enforced casualization, from the United Parcel Service workers' stand against "part-time America" to the unionized Australian dockworkers fighting their replacement by contract workers, to the Canadian autoworkers at Ford and Chrysler striking against the outsourcing of their jobs to non-union factories. All these stories are about different industries doing variations on the same thing: finding ways to cut ties to their workforce and travel light. The underbelly of the shiny "brands, not products" revelation can be seen increasingly in every workplace around the globe. Every corporation wants a fluid reserve of part-timers, temps, and freelancers to help it keep overheads down and ride the twists and turns in the market. As British management consultant Charles Handy says, savvy companies prefer to see them-

---

selves as "organizers" of collections of contractors, as opposed to "employment organizations."[1] One thing is certain: offering employment—the steady kind, with benefits, holiday pay, a measure of security, and maybe even union representation—has fallen out of economic fashion.

BRANDED WORK: HOBBIES, NOT JOBS

Though an entire class of consumer-goods companies has transcended the need to produce what it sells, so far not even the most weightless multinational has been able to free itself entirely from the burden of employees. Production may be relegated to contractors, but clerks are still needed to sell the brand-name goods at the point of purchase, especially given the growth of branded retail. In the service industry, however, big-brand employers have become artful at dodging most commitments to their employees, expertly fostering the notion that their clerks are somehow not quite legitimate workers, and thus do not really need or deserve job security, livable wages, and benefits.

Most of the large employers in the service sector manage their workforce as if their clerks didn't depend on their paychecks for anything essential, such as rent or child support. Instead, retail and service employers tend to view their employees as children: students looking for summer jobs, spending money or a quick stopover on the road to a more fulfilling and better-paying career. These are great jobs, in other words, for people who don't really need them. And so the mall and the superstore have given birth to a ballooning subcategory of joke jobs—the frozen-yogurt jerk, the Orange Julius juicer, the Gap greeter, the Prozac-happy Wal-Mart "sales associate"—that are notoriously unstable, low-paying, and overwhelmingly part-time.

What is distressing about this trend, is that over the past two decades, the relative importance of the service sector as a source of jobs has soared. The decline in manufacturing, as well as the waves of downsizing and cutbacks in the public sector, have been met by dramatic growth in the numbers of service-sector jobs to the extent that services and retail now account for 75 percent of total U.S. employment.[2] (See Table 10.2.) Today, there are four and a half times as many Americans selling clothes in specialty and department stores as there are workers stitching and weaving them, and Wal-Mart isn't just the biggest retailer in the world, it is also the largest private employer in the United States.

And yet despite these shifts in employment patterns, most brand-name retail, service, and restaurant chains have opted to put on economic blinders, insisting that they are still offering hobby jobs for kids. Never mind that the service sector is now filled with workers who have multiple university degrees, immigrants unable to find manufacturing jobs, laid-off nurses and teachers, and downsized middle managers. Never mind, too, that the students who do work in retail and fast food—as many of them do—are facing higher tuition costs, less financial assistance from parents and government, and more years in school. Never mind that the food service workforce has been steadily aging over the last decade so that more than half are now over twenty-five years old. Or that a 1997 study found that 25 percent of non-management Canadian retail workers had been with the same company for eleven years or more and that 39 percent had been there for between four and ten years.[3] That's a lot longer than "Chainsaw" Al Dunlap lasted as CEO of Sunbeam Corp. But never mind all that. Everyone knows that a job in the service sector is a hobby, and retail is a place where people go for "experience," not a livelihood.

Nowhere has this message been more successfully absorbed than at the cash register and the takeout counter, where many workers say they feel as if they are just passing through even after logging a decade in the McWork sector. Brenda Hilbrich, who works at Borders Books and Music in Manhattan, explains how difficult it is to reconcile the quality of her employment with a sense of personal success: "You're stuck with this dichotomy of 'I'm supposed to do better but yet I can't because I can't find another job.' So you tell yourself, 'I'm only here temporarily because I'm going to find something better.' "[4] This internalized state of perpetual transience has been convenient for service-sector employers who have been free to let wages stagnate and to provide little room for upward mobility, since there is no urgent need to improve the conditions of jobs that everyone agrees are only temporary. Borders clerk Jason Chappell says that the retail chains work hard to reinforce feelings of transience in their workers in order to protect this highly profitable formula. "So much of the company propaganda is convincing you that you're not workers, that it's something else, that you're not working class. . . . Everyone thinks they are middle class even when they're making $13,000 a year."[5]

I met with Chappell and Hilbrich late one night in October 1997, at a deli in Manhattan's financial district. We chose this place because it was close to the Borders outlet at the base of the World Trade Center where they both work. I had heard about the pair because of their successful efforts to bring a union to Borders, part of a flurry of labor organizing inside the large chains since the mid-nineties: at Starbucks, Barnes & Noble, Wal-Mart, Kentucky Fried Chicken, McDonald's. It seems as if more and more of the twenty-something-going-on-thirty-something clerks working for the superbrands are looking around—at the counters in front of them where they serve Sumatran coffee, and at the best-selling books, and made-in-China sweaters—and are acknowledging that, for better or worse, some of them aren't going anywhere fast. Laurie Bonang, who works at Starbucks in Vancouver, British Columbia, told me that "people our age are finally realizing that we get out of university, we're a zillion dollars in debt, and we're working in Starbucks. This

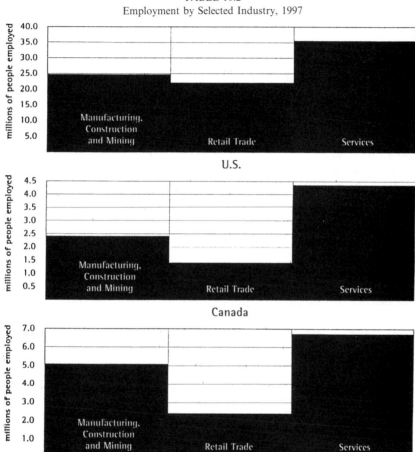

TABLE 10.2
Employment by Selected Industry, 1997

Source for U.S. figures: "Employment and Earnings," Bureau of Labor Statistics. Source for Canadian figures: "Annual Estimates of Employment, Earnings and Hours 1985–1997," Statistics Canada. Source for U.K. figures: Office for National Statistics.

isn't how we want to spend the rest of our lives, but for right now the dream job isn't waiting for us anymore. . . . I was hoping that Starbucks would be a stepping stone to bigger and better things, but unfortunately it's a stepping stone to a big sinkhole."[6]

As Bonang told her story, she was painfully aware that she is living out one of the most hackneyed pop-culture clichés of our branded age: this is the stuff of *Saturday Night Live*'s "Gap Girls" skit, circa 1993, in which bored, underemployed mall chicks ask each other: "Didja cinch it?" Or of the Starbucks "baristas" who rattle off long trains of coffee adjectives—grande-decaf-low-fat-moccacino—in movies like *You've Got Mail*. But there is a reason why the most vocally unhappy service-sector workers are the ones working for the highest-profile global retailers and restaurants. Large chains such as Wal-Mart, Starbucks, and the Gap, as they have proliferated since the mid-eighties, have been lowering workplace standards in the service sector, fueling their marketing budgets, imperialistic expansion, and high-concept "retail experiences" by lowballing their clerks on wages and hours. Most of the big-name brands in the service sector pay the legal minimum wage or slightly more, even though the average wage for retail workers is several dollars higher.[7] Wal-Mart clerks in the U.S., for instance, earn an average of $7.50 an hour, and since Wal-Mart classifies "full time" as twenty-eight hours a week, the average annual income is $10,920—significantly less than the industry average.[8] Kmart wages are also low and the benefits are considered so substandard that when a 172,000-square-foot Super Kmart opened in San Jose, California, in October 1997, the local city council voted to endorse a boycott of the retailer. Council member Margie Fernandes said that the low wages, minimal health benefits, and part-time hours are far below those provided by other area retailers, and that these are not the kind of jobs the community needs. "San Jose is a very, very expensive place to live and we need to make sure the people who work here can afford to live here," Fernandes explained.[9]

McDonald's and Starbucks staff, meanwhile, frequently earn less than the employees of single-outlet restaurants and cafés, which explains why McDonald's is widely credited for pioneering the throwaway "McJob" that the entire fast-food industry has since moved to emulate. At Britain's McLibel Trial, in which the company contested claims made by two Greenpeace activists about its employment practices, international trade unionist Dan Gallin defined a McJob as "a low skill, low pay, high stress, exhausting and unstable job."[10] Though the activists on trial for libel were found guilty on several counts, in his verdict Chief Justice Rodger Bell ruled that in the matter of McJobs the defendants had a point. The chain has had a negative impact on food-service wages as a whole, he wrote, and the allegation that McDonald's "pays its workers low wages, helping to depress wages for workers in the catering trade in Britain has been proved to be true. It is justified."[11]

As we have seen in Cavite, the brand-name multinationals have freed themselves of the burden of providing employees with a living wage. In the malls of North America and England, on the high street, in the food court, and at the superstore, they have managed a similar trick. In some cases, particularly in the garment sector, these retailers are the very same companies that are doing business in the export processing zones, meaning that their responsibilities as employers have been sharply reduced at both the production and service ends of the economic cycle. Wal-Mart and the Gap, for instance, contract out their production to EPZs dotting the Southern Hemisphere, where goods are produced mostly by women in their teens and twenties who earn minimum wage or less and live in cramped dorm rooms. Those goods—sweatshirts, baby clothes, toys, and Walkmans—are then sold by another workforce, concentrated in the North, which is also largely filled with young people earning approximately minimum wage, most in their teens and early twenties.

Though in many ways it is indecent to compare the relative privilege of retail workers at the mall with the abuse and exploitation suffered by zone workers, there is an undeniable pattern at work. In general, the corporations in question have ensured that they do not have to confront the possibility that adults with families are depending on the wages that they pay, whether at the mall or in the zone. Just as factory jobs that once supported families have been reconfigured in the Third World as jobs for teenagers, so have the brand-name clothing companies and restaurant chains given legitimacy to the idea that fast-food and retail-sector jobs are disposable and unfit for adults.

As in the zones, the youthfulness of the sector is far from accidental. It reflects a distinct preference on the part of service-sector employers, achieved through a series of overt and covert management actions. Young workers are consistently hired over older ones, and workers who have been on staff for a few years—building up higher wages and seniority—often report losing precious shifts to new batches of younger and cheaper clerks. Other anti-adult tactics have included the targeting of older workers for harassment—the issue that served as the catalyst for the first strike at a McDonald's outlet. In April 1998, after witnessing a verbally abusive supervisor reduce an elderly co-worker to tears, the teenage workers at the Golden Arches in Macedonia, Ohio, walked off the job in protest. They didn't return until management agreed to undergo "people skills" training. "We get verbally harassed, and physically too. Not me, but basically just the elderly woman," teen striker Bryan Drapp said on *Good Morning America*. Drapp was fired two months later.[12]

Brenda Hilbrich of Borders contends that justifying low wages on the grounds that young workers are just passing through is a handy self-fulfilling prophecy—particularly in her field, bookselling. "It doesn't have to have a high turnover," she says. "If the conditions are good and you're making a nice salary, people actually like working in the service industry. They like working with books. A lot of people who have left have said, 'This was my favorite job, but I had to go because I can't make enough money to live.' "[13]

The fact is that the economy needs steady jobs that adults can live on. And it's clear that many people would stay in retail if it paid adult rates, the proof being that when the sector does pay decently, it attracts older workers, and the rate of staff turnover falls in line with the rest of the economy. But at the large chains, which seem at least for now to have bottomless resources to build superstores and to sink millions into expanding and synergizing their brands, the idea of paying a living wage is rarely considered. At Borders, where most clerks earn wages in line with other bookstore chains but below the retail average, company president Richard L. Flanagan wrote a letter to all his clerks, addressing the question of whether Borders could pay a "living wage" as opposed to what it reportedly pays now—between US$6.63 and $9.27 an hour. "While the concept is romantically appealing," he wrote, "it ignores the practicalities and realities of our business environment."[14]

Much of what makes paying a living wage seem so "romantic" has to do with the rapid expansion described in Part II, "No Choice." For companies whose business plans depend upon becoming dominant in their market before their nearest competitor beats them to it, new outlets come before workers— even when those workers are a key part of the chain's image. "They expect us to look like a Gap ad, professional, clean and neat all the time, and I can't even pay to do laundry," says Laurie Bonang of Starbucks. "You can buy two grande mocha cappuccinos with my hourly salary." Like millions of her demographic coevals on the payrolls of all-star brands like the Gap, Nike, and Barnes & Noble, Bonang is living inside a stunning corporate success story— though you'd never know it from the resignation and anger in her voice. All the brand-name retail workers I spoke with expressed their frustration at helping their stores rake in, to them, unimaginable profits, and then having to watch that profit get funneled into compulsive expansion. Employee wages, meanwhile, stagnate or even decline. At Starbucks in British Columbia, new workers faced an actual wage decrease—from Can$7.50 to $7 an hour—during a period when the chain was doubling its profits and opening 350 new stores a year. "I do the banking. I know how much the store pulls in a week," Laurie Bonang says. "They just take all that revenue and open up new stores."[15]

Borders clerks also maintain that wages have suffered as a result of rapid growth. They say that their chain used to be a more equitable place to work before the neck-and-neck race with Barnes & Noble took over corporate priorities; there was a profit-sharing program and a biannual 5 percent raise for all workers. "Then came expansion and corresponding cuts," reads a statement from disgruntled employees at a downtown Philadelphia outlet of Borders. "Profit sharing was dropped, raises were cut. . . ."[16]

In sharp contrast to the days when corporate employees took pride in their company's growth, seeing it as the result of a successful group effort, many clerks have come to see themselves as being in direct competition with their employers' expansion dreams. "If Borders opened thirty-eight new stores a year instead of forty," reasoned Jason Chappell, sitting next to Brenda Hilbrich on the vinyl seats of our deli booth, "they could afford to give us a nice wage increase. On average it costs $7 million to open a superstore. That's Borders' own figures. . . ."

"But," Brenda interrupted, "if you say that directly to them, they say, 'Well, that's two markets we don't get into.' "

"We have to saturate markets," Chappell said, nodding.

"Yeah," Brenda added. "We have to compete with Barnes & Noble."

The retail clerks employed by the superchains are only too familiar with the manic logic of expansion.

BUSTING THE McUNION

The need to prevent workers from weighing too heavily on the bottom line is the main reason that the branded chains have fought off the recent wave of unionization with such ferocity. McDonald's, for instance, has been embroiled in bribery scandals during German union drives, and over the course of a 1994 union drive in France, ten McDonald's managers were arrested for violating labor laws and trade-union rights.[17] In June 1998, the company fired the two young workers who organized the strike in Macedonia, Ohio.[18] In 1997, when the employees at a Windsor, Ontario, Wal-Mart were about to hold an election on joining a union, a series of not-so-subtle management hints led many workers to believe that if they voted yes their store would be shut down. The Ontario Labour Relations Board reviewed the process and found that the behavior of Wal-Mart managers and supervisors before the vote amounted to "a subtle but extremely effective threat," which caused "the average reasonable employee to conclude that the store would close if the union got in."[19]

Other chains have not hesitated to make good on the threat to close. In 1997, Starbucks decided to shut down its Vancouver distribution plant after workers unionized. In February 1998, just as a union certification for a Montreal-area outlet of McDonald's was being reviewed by the Quebec Labour Commission, the franchise owner closed down the outlet. Shortly after the closure, the labor commission accredited the union—cold comfort, since no one works there anymore. Six months later, another McDonald's restaurant was successfully unionized, this one a busy outlet in Squamish, British Columbia, near the Whistler ski resort. The organizers were two teenage girls, one sixteen, the other seventeen. It wasn't about wages, they said—they were just tired of being scolded like children in front of the customers. The outlet remains open, making it the only unionized McDonald's in North America, but at the time of writing, the company was on the verge of having the union decertified. Fighting the battle on the public-relations front, in mid-1999 the fast-food chain launched an international television campaign featuring McDonald's workers serving up shakes and fries under the captions "future lawyer," "future engineer," and so on. Here was the true McDonald's workforce, the company seemed to be saying: happy, contented, and just passing through.

During the late 1990s, the process of turning the service sector into a low-wage ghetto advanced rapidly in Germany. The German unemployment rate reached 12.6 percent in 1998, primarily because the economy could not absorb the massive layoffs in the manufacturing sector that occurred after reunification—four out of five East German factory jobs were lost. To make up for the shortfall, the service sector was touted by the business press and the political right wing as the economic panacea. There was just one catch: before the mall could step in to save the German economy, the minimum wage would have to be substantially lowered and benefits such as long holidays for all workers would have to be dismantled. In other words, good jobs with security and a living wage would have to be turned into bad jobs. Then Germany too would enjoy the benefits of a service-based economic recovery.

It is one of the paradoxes of service-sector employment that the more prominent a role it plays in the labor landscape, the more casual service-sector companies became in their attitude toward providing job security. Nowhere is this more in evidence than in the industry's increasing reliance on part-timers. (See Table 10.2.) Starbucks, for instance, staffs its outlets almost exclusively with part-timers while only one-third of Kmart's workforce is full-time. Workers at the ill-fated Montreal-area McDonald's cited as their principal reason for unionization the fact that they often couldn't get shifts longer than three hours.

In the U.S. the number of part-timers has tripled since 1968, while in Canada, between 1975 and 1997, the growth rate of part-time jobs was nearly three times the rate of full-time jobs.[20] But the problem is not the part-time nature of work per se. In Canada, only one-third of part-timers want but cannot find full-time jobs (which is an increase from one-fifth in the late eighties). In the U.S., only one-quarter want full-time jobs but can't find them. The vast majority of part-timers are students and women, many of whom are juggling childcare and paid work. (See Table 10.2.)

But while many workers are indeed drawn to flexible work arrangements, their definition of what constitutes "flexibility" is dramatically different from the one favored by service-sector bosses. For instance, while studies have shown that working mothers define flexibility as "having the ability to work less than full-time hours at decent wages and benefits, while still working a regular schedule,"[21] the service sector has a different view of part-time work, and a different agenda. A handful of brand-name chains, including Starbucks and Borders, bolster low wages by offering health and dental benefits to their part-timers. For other employers, however, part-time positions are used as a loophole to keep wages down and to avoid benefits and overtime; "flexibility" becomes a code for "no promises," making the juggling of other commitments—both financial and parental—more challenging, not less. At some retail outlets I've researched, the allotment of hours is so random that the ritual of posting next week's schedule prompts the staff to gather around anxiously, craning their necks and hopping up and down as if they are checking to see who got the lead in the high-school musical.

Furthermore, the "part-time" classification is often more a technicality than a reality, with retail employers keeping their part-timers just below the forty-hour legal cutoff for full-time—Laurie Bonang, for instance, clocks between thirty-five and thirty-nine hours a week at Starbucks. For all intents and purposes, she has the duties of a full-time employee, but under forty hours the company does not have to pay overtime or guarantee full-time hours. Other chains are equally creative. Borders instituted a company-wide thirty-seven-and-a-half-hour work week for all employees, and Wal-Mart caps its work week at thirty-three hours, defining base "full time" as twenty-eight hours. What all of this means in the lives of workers is a scheduling roller coaster that in many ways is more demanding than the traditional forty-hour week. For instance, the Gap—which defines full-time as thirty hours a week—has a system of keeping clerks "on call" for certain shifts during which time they aren't scheduled or paid to work but must be available to come in if the manager calls. (One worker joked to me that she had to buy a beeper in case a folding crisis flared up in Gap Kids.)

Starbucks has been the most innovative in the modern art of supple scheduling. The company has created a software program called Star Labor that allows head office maximum control over the schedules of its clerks down to the minute. With Star Labor, gone is anything as blunt and imprecise as a day or evening shift. The software measures exactly when each latte is sold and by whom, then tailor-makes shifts—often only a few hours long—to maximize coffee-selling efficiency. As Laurie Bonang explains, "They give you an arbitrary skill number from one to nine and they plug in when you're available, how long you've been there, when customers come in and when we need more staff, and the computer spits out your schedule based on that."[22] While Starbucks' breakthrough in "just-in-time" frothing looks great on a spreadsheet, for Steve Emery it meant hauling himself out of bed to start work at 5 a.m., only to leave at 9:30 a.m. after the morning rush had peaked and, according to Star Labor, he was no longer working at maximum efficiency. Wal-Mart has introduced a similar centralized scheduling system, effectively reducing employee hours by pinning them precisely to in-store traffic. "It's done just like we order merchandise," says Wal-Mart CEO David Glass.[23]

The vast gulf between employee and employer definitions of "flexibility" was the central issue of the United Parcel Service strike in the summer of 1997, the largest U.S. job action in fourteen years. Despite profits of $1 billion in 1996, UPS had kept 58 percent of its workers classified as part-time and was rapidly moving toward an even more "flexible" workforce. Of the 43,000 jobs UPS had created since 1992, only 8,000 were full time. The system worked well for the courier company, since it was able to ride the peaks and valleys of the delivery cycle that sees heavy pickups and deliveries in the morning and evening but lulls during the day. "There's too much downtime in between to hire full-time workers," explained UPS spokesperson Susan Rosenberg.[24]

Building up a part-time workforce had other cost-saving benefits. Before the strike, the company paid its part-timers roughly half the hourly wage of its full-timers for performing the same tasks.[25] Furthermore, the union claimed that 10,000 of the company's so-called part-timers were, like Laurie Bonang at Starbucks, actually working between thirty-five and thirty-nine hours a week—just under the cutoff that would require overtime pay, full benefits, and the higher wage scale.

Some service-sector companies have made much of the fact that they offer stock options or "profit-sharing" to low-level employees, among them Wal-Mart, which calls its clerks "sales associates"; Borders, which refers to them as "co-owners"; and Starbucks, which prefers the term "partners." Many employees do appreciate these gestures, but others claim that while the workplace democracy schemes sparkle on a corporate Web site, they rarely translate into much of substance. Most part-time workers at Starbucks, for instance, can't afford to buy into the employee stock-option program since their salaries barely cover their expenses. And where profit-sharing schemes are automatic, as at Wal-Mart, workers say their "share" of the $118 billion of annual sales their company hauls in is laughable. Clerks in the Windsor, Ontario, outlet of Wal-Mart, for example, say they only saw an extra $70 during the first three years that their store was open. "Never mind that from the viewpoint of the boardroom, the pension plan's best feature was that it kept 28 million more shares in firm control of company executives," writes *The Wall Street Journal*'s Bob Ortega of the Wal-Mart plan. "Most workers *perceived* that they could cash in, so the cost of the plan paid off in spades by helping keep the unions out and the wages low" (italics his).[26]

FREE WORK: MORE FAKE JOBS, COURTESY OF THE SUPERBRANDS

One thing you can say about the retail and service industries: at least they pay their workers a little something for their trouble. Not so for some other industries that have liberated themselves from the chains of social-security forms with such free-market gusto that many young workers receive no pay from them at all. Perhaps predictably, the culture industry has led the way in the blossoming of unpaid work, blithely turning a blind eye to the unglamorous fact that many people under thirty are saddled with the mundane responsibility of actually having to support themselves.

Writing about his former job, which involved hiring unpaid interns to send faxes and run errands for *Men's Journal* magazine, Jim Frederick notes that many of his applicants had already worked for nothing at *Interview*, CBS News, MTV, *The Village Voice*, and so on. " 'Very impressive,' I would say. By my quick calculations they had contributed, conservatively, five or six thousand dollars' worth of uncompensated work to various media conglomerates."[27] Of course, the media conglomerates—the broadcasters, magazines, and book publishers—insist that they are generously offering young people precious experience in a hard employment market—a foot in the door on the old-fashioned "apprenticeship" model. Besides, they say, sounding suspiciously like McDonald's managers the world over, the interns are just kids—they don't really *need* the money.

And getting two "unreal" jobs for the price of one, most interns subsidize their unpaid day job by working in the service industry at night and on weekends, as well as by living at home to a later age. But in the U.S.—where it has become commonplace to hop from one unpaid culture job to the next for a year or two—a disproportionate number of interns, as Frederick observes, appear to be living off trust funds, seemingly without any immediate concerns about earning a living. But just as the service-sector employers will not admit that the youthfulness of their workforce might have something to do with the wages they pay and the security they fail to offer, you will never catch a television network or a publisher confessing that the absence of remuneration for internships might also have something to do with the relative privilege of those applying for these positions at their companies. This racket is not only exploitative in the classic sense, it also has some very real implications for the future of cultural production: today's interns are tomorrow's managers, producers, and editors and, as Frederick writes, "If you can't get a job unless you've had an internship, and you can't take an internship unless you can get supported by daddy for a couple of months, then the system guarantees an applicant pool that is decidedly privileged."[28]

Music video stations such as MTV have been among the more liberal users of the unpaid internship system. When it was first introduced, the music video channel represented a managerial coup in low-cost, high-profit broadcasting since the stations primarily play videos that are produced out of house and supplied by record labels. While some stations, including Canada's MuchMusic, now pay licensing and royalty fees to broadcast videos, these pale in comparison to the production costs of the videos in a single top 30 countdown. Inside the stations, on air-hosts, producers, and technicians work alongside unpaid, mostly student, interns who sometimes are rewarded with jobs and sometimes stay at the station for many months, hoping for their big break. Which is where the legendary success stories come in—the famous V.J. who started off answering phones, or the greatest success story of them all: the tale of Rick the Temp. In 1996, Rick won the annual "Be a Temp at MuchMusic Contest" and was welcomed to the station with cross promotional fanfare and branded giveaways. One year later, Rick was on the air in his new job as V.J., but the kicker was that even after he became a big star, he kept the moniker Rick the Temp. There was Rick on TV, interviewing the Backstreet Boys, and although he was always paid for his work, for would-be interns, his success served a daily advertisement for the glory and glamour that awaits if you donate your labor as a gift to a major media company.

TEMPS: THE RENTED WORKER

Rick the Temp isn't just the Great White Hope for unpaid interns. He also represents the pinnacle of another subcategory of New Age workers: the temps. And temps, it must be said, need all the hope they can get. The use of temp labor in the U.S. has increased by 400 percent since 1982 and that growth has been steady.[29] Annual industry revenue among American temp firms has increased by about 20 percent every year since 1992, with the firms pulling in revenues of $58.7 billion in 1998.[30] The mammoth international temp agency Manpower Temporary Services rivals Wal-Mart as the largest private employer in the U.S.[31] According to a 1997 study, 83 percent of the fastest-growing American companies are now outsourcing jobs they once hired people to perform—compared with 64 percent just three years before.[32] In Canada, the Association of Canadian Search, Employment & Staffing Services estimates that more than 75 percent of businesses use the services of the $2 billion Canadian temp industry.

The most dramatic growth, however, is taking place not in North America but in Western Europe, where temp agencies are among Europe's fastest-growing companies.[33] In France, Spain, the Netherlands, and Germany, hiring workers on long-term temporary contracts has become a well-trampled back entranceway to the labor market, allowing employers to sidestep tough laws that provide generous employee benefits and make firing without just cause far more difficult than in the United States. France, for instance, has become the second-largest temp-services market after the U.S., making up 30 percent of worldwide temp revenue. And though temping accounts for only 2 percent of all the country's jobs, according to France's labor minister, Martine Aubry, "86 per cent of new hires are on short-term contracts."[34] Manpower Europe, an outpost of the U.S.-based temp firm, saw its revenue in Spain jump a staggering 719 percent in just one year, from $6.1 million in

1996 to $50 million in 1997. Italy didn't legalize temp agencies until 1997, but when it did, Manpower Europe rushed in to open thirty-five offices in 1998.[35]

Every day, 4.5 million workers are assigned to jobs through temp agencies in Europe and the U.S., but since only 12.5 percent of temps are placed on any given day, the real number of total temporary employees in Europe and the U.S. is closer to 36 million people.[36] More significant than soaring numbers, however, is a major shift under way in the nature of the temporary work industry. Temp agencies are no longer strictly in the business of farming out rent-a-receptionists when the secretary calls in sick. For starters, temps are no longer all that temporary: in the U.S., 29 percent stay at the same posting for a year or more.[37] Their agencies, meanwhile, have become full-service human resource departments for all your no-commitment staffing needs, including accounting, filing, manufacturing, and computer services. And according to Bruce Steinberg, director of research at the U.S.-based National Association of Temporary and Staffing Services, "a quiet evolution is taking place throughout the staffing services industry"—rather than renting out workers, the agencies are "providing a complete service solution."[38] What that means is that more companies are contracting out entire functions and divisions— work previously performed in-house—to outside agencies charged not only with staffing but, like the contract factories in the export processing zones, administration and maintenance of the task as well. For instance, in 1993 American Airlines outsourced the ticket counters at twenty-eight U.S. airports to outside agencies. Around 550 ticketing-agent jobs went temp and, in some cases, workers who had earned $40,000 were offered their same jobs back for $16,000.[39] A similar reshuffling took place when UPS decided to turn over its customer-service centers to outside contractors—5,000 employees earning $10 to $12 an hour were replaced with temps earning between $6.50 and $8.[40]

As Tom Peters says, "You're a damn fool if you own it!"[41] Bruce Steinberg concurs: by amputating whole divisions and sloughing them off on "managed services arrangements, the business can concentrate its time, energy and resources on core business while staffing service practices its core competency of managing workers."[42] Hiring and managing workers, in other words, is not the base of a healthy company but a specialized task—somebody else's "core competency" that is better left to the experts, while the real business is tended to by an ever-shrinking number of workers, as the next chapter will show.

YES, BUT . . . WON'T BILL GATES SAVE US?

Any discussion of the plight of corporate temps, UPS couriers, outsourced GM workers, Gap greeters, MTV interns, and Starbucks "baristas" leads inevitably to the same place: Yes, but . . . what about all the great new jobs in the growing high-tech world? For my generation of workers, the legendary riches awaiting technology workers in Seattle and Silicon Valley are the "yes, but" answer to any and all grievances about employment exclusions. Standing in contrast to all the downer stories about layoffs and McJobs is this shimmering digital mecca where fifteen-year-olds design video games for Sega, where AT&T hires hackers just to keep an eye on them, and where scores of young workers become millionaires from their lavish stock options. Yes, but . . . Bill Gates will make it all okay, won't he?

It was Microsoft, with its famous employee stock-option plan, that developed and fostered the mythology of Silicon Gold, but it is also Microsoft that has done the most to dismantle it. The golden era of the geeks has come and gone, and today's high-tech jobs are as unstable as any other. Part-timers, temps, and contractors are rampant in Silicon Valley—a recent labor study of the region estimates that between 27 and 40 percent of the Valley's employees are "contingency workers," and the use of temps there is increasing at twice the rate of the rest of the country. The percentage of Silicon Valley workers employed by temp agencies is nearly three times the national average.[43]

And Microsoft, the largest of the software firms, didn't just lead the way to this part-time promised land, it wrote the operating manual. For more than a decade, the company has been busily closing ranks around the programmers who got there first, and banishing as many other employees as it can from that sacred inner circle. Through extensive use of independent contractors, temps, and "full-service employment solutions," Microsoft is well on its way to engineering the perfect employee-less corporation, a jigsaw puzzle of outsourced divisions, contract factories, and freelance employees. Gates has already converted one-third of his general workforce into temps, and in the Interactive Media Division, where CD-ROMs and Internet products are developed, about half the workers are officially employed by outside "payroll agencies," who deliver tax-free workers like printer cartridges.[44]

Microsoft's two-tier workforce is a microcosm of the job market's New Age new deal. At the center is the high-tech dream: permanent, full-time employees, with benefits and generous stock options, working and playing on the youthful corporate "campus." These Microserfs are cultishly loyal to their corporation, its soaring stock price, and its staggering 51 percent operating profit margin ("Show me the money!" they roared at the annual staff meeting in Seattle's Kingdome Stadium in fall 1997).[45] And why shouldn't they be loyal? They earn an average of $220,000 a year, and that's not even factoring in the top five superrich executives.

Orbiting around this starry-eyed core are between 4,000 and 5,750 temporary workers.[46] The temps work side by side with members of the core group—as technicians, designers, and programmers—and perform many of the same jobs. About 1,500 have been with the company for so long they have taken to calling themselves "permatemps." The only way to tell the temps from the "real" Microserfs is by the color of their badges: blue for perms, orange for permatemps.

Like the fleet of part-timers who give UPS the "flexibility" to employ workers only during peak hours, and the contract workers in Cavite who provide their factory owners with the "flexibility" to send them home during dry spells, what thousands of temps means for Microsoft is the freedom to expand and contract its workforce at will. "We use them," says Microsoft personnel officer Doug McKenna, "to provide us with flexibility and to deal with uncertainty."[47]

Trouble began in 1990 when the Internal Revenue Service challenged Microsoft's classification of orange badges as independent contractors, ruling that these people were actually employees of Microsoft and the company should be paying their payroll tax. Based in part on this finding, in 1993 a group of employees classified by Microsoft as contractors launched a lawsuit against the company, claiming they were regular workers and deserved the same benefits and stock options as their permanent colleagues. In July 1997, Microsoft lost the landmark case when an eleven-judge Court of Appeals panel ruled that the freelancers were "common law" employees and had the right to the company's benefits program, to its pension, and to its stock-purchasing plan.[48]

Microsoft's response to this setback, however, has not been to add freelancers to its payroll but simply to work more assiduously to marginalize the temps. To this end, the company has moved away from hiring "independent contractors" directly. Instead, after employees have been scouted, interviewed, and selected by Microsoft, they are instructed to register with one of five payroll agencies that have special arrangements with the company. MicroTemps are then hired through an agency that acts as the official employer: cutting paychecks, withholding income taxes, and sometimes providing bare-bones benefits. Laird Post, a principal with management consultant Towers Perrin in Seattle, Washington, explains the legalities of this new arrangement. "It's hard to rationalize legally that the person is not an employee unless they are an employee of someone else"—in Microsoft's case, that someone else is the payroll agency.[49] To make sure that the temps will never again be confused with actual Microsoft workers, they are barred from all extracurricular company functions, including taking part in late-night pizza meals and after-hours parties. And in June 1998 the company introduced a new policy requiring temps who have been on an assignment with the company for a year or more to take a thirty-one-day break before they can take another "temporary" post.[50] As Sharon Decker, Microsoft's director of contingency staffing, explains, "We are refocusing a lot of policies we had in place so everyone understands how a temp should be treated and what is appropriate."[51]

In addition to staffing its campus with permatemps, in 1997 Microsoft initiated a series of moves to disentangle itself from other earthly and cumbersome aspects of running a multibillion-dollar company. "Don't get caught with useless fixed assets," Bob Herbold, Microsoft's chief operating officer, says, explaining his staffing philosophy to a group of shareholders.[52] According to Herbold, pretty much everything but the core functions of programming and product development fall into the "useless fixed assets" category—including the company's sixty-three receptionists, who were laid off, losing benefits and stock options, and told to reapply through the Tascor temp agency. "We were overpaying them," Herbold said.[53]

In the same stroke, Microsoft sliced and diced its Redmond campus and parceled out the pieces (along with employees who wanted to hold on to their jobs) to outside "vendors": Pitney Bowes took over the mail room; the print and copy center is now operated by Xerox personnel; the CD-ROM factory was sold to KAO Information Systems; even the company store was outsourced to Benussen Deutsch & Associates. In this latest round of restructuring, 680 jobs were cut from the payroll and $500 million slashed from the operating budget.[54] With all these contractors on the campus, Herbold noted, "just managing the outsourcers is quite a task"—and there was no reason for Microsoft to get saddled with that useless fixed asset. In a stroke of divestment genius, Microsoft contracted out the task of managing the contractors to Johnson Controls, which also takes care of the campus facilities. "Our revenue has gone up 91 percent and our head count has actually decreased 19 percent," Bob Herbold says proudly. And what did Microsoft do with the savings? "We're plowing them into R&D and we're plowing them into profit, obviously."[55]

"FREE AGENT NATION"

It must be said that many of Microsoft's high-tech freelancers are hardly defenseless victims of Bill Gates's payroll concoctions, but are freelancers by choice. Like many contractors, the "software gypsies," as high-tech freelancers are sometimes called, have made a conscious decision to put independence and mobility before institutional loyalty and security. Some of them are even what Tom Peters likes to call a "Brand Called You."

Tom Peters' latest management-guru idea is that just as companies must reach branding nirvana by learning to let go of manufacturing and employment, so must individual workers empower themselves by abandoning the idea of being employees. According to this logic, if we are to be successful in the new economy, all of us must self-incorporate into our very own brand—a Brand Called You. Success in the job market will only come when we retrofit ourselves as consultants and service providers, identify our own Brand You equities and lease ourselves out to targeted projects that will in turn increase our individual portfolio of "braggables." "I call the approach Me Inc.," Peters writes. "You're Chairperson/CEO/Entrepreneur-in-Chief of your own professional service firm."[56] Faith Popcorn, the management guru who came to prominence with her 1991 best-seller, *The Popcorn Report*, goes so far as to recommend that we change our names to better "click" with our carefully designed and marketed brand image. *She* did—her name used to be Faith Plotkin.

Even more than Popcorn or Peters, however, it is a man named Daniel H. Pink who is the dean at Brand You U. Pink has seen the growth in temporary and contract work, as well as the rise in self-employment, and has declared the arrival of "Free Agent Nation." Not only is he writing a book by that title, but Pink himself is a proud patriot of the nation. After quitting a prestigious White House job as Al Gore's chief speechwriter, Pink went on a journey in search of fellow "free agents": people who had chosen a life of contracts and freelance gigs over bosses and benefits. What he found, as he relayed in a cover article in *Fast Company*, was the sixties. The citizens of Pink's nation are marketing consultants, headhunters, copywriters, and software designers who are all striving to achieve a Zen-like balance of work and personal life. They practice their yoga positions and play with their dogs in their wired home offices, while earning more money—by jumping from one contract to the next—than they did when they were tied to one company and paid a fixed salary. "This is the summer of love revisited, man!" we hear from Bo Rinald, an agent representing a thousand freelance software developers in Silicon Valley.[57] For Pink's free agents, the end of jobs is the baby-boomer dream come true: free-market capitalism without neckties; dropped out of the corporate world in body but plugged-in in spirit. Everyone knows that you can't be a cog in the machine if you work from your living room. . . .

A younger—and, of course, hipper—version of Free Agent Nation was articulated in a special work issue of *Details* magazine. For Gen-Xers with MBAs, the future of work is apparently filled with stunningly profitable snowboarding businesses, video-game companies, and cool-hunting firms. "Opportunity Rocks!" crowed the headline of an article that laid out the future of work as a nonstop party of extreme self-employment: "Life without jobs, work without bosses, money without salaries, lives without limits."[58] According to the writer, Rob Lieber, "The time of considering yourself an 'employee' has passed. Now it's time to start thinking of yourself as a service provider, hiring out your skills and services to the highest, or most interesting, bidder."[59]

I admit to being lured by the sirens of free agency myself. About four years ago, I quit my job as a magazine editor to go freelance, and like Pink I've never looked back. Of course I love the fact that no one boss controls my every working hour (that privilege is now spread around to dozens of people), that I'm not subject to the arbitrary edicts of petty managers, and, most important, that I can work in my pajamas if I feel like it. I know from firsthand experience that freelance life can indeed mean freedom, just as part time, for others, can live up to its promise of genuine flexibility. Pink has a point when he says of free agency, "This is a legitimate way to work—it isn't some poor laid-off slob struggling to find his way back to the corporate bosom."[60] However, there's a problem when it's people like Pink—or other freelance writers overly euphoric about working in their pajamas—who hold themselves up as living proof that divestment from corporate employment is a win-win formula. And it does seem as if most of the major articles about the joys of freelancing have been written by successful freelance writers under the impression that they themselves represent the millions of contractors, temps, freelancers, part-timers, and the self-employed. But writing, because of its solitary nature and low overhead, is one of the very few professions that are genuinely compatible with homework, and study after study shows that it is absurd to equate the experience of being a freelance journalist, or having your own advertising company, with that of being a temp secretary at Microsoft or a contract factory worker in Cavite. On the whole, casualization pans out as the worst of both worlds: monotonous work at lower wages, with no benefits or security, and even less control over scheduling.

The bottom line is that the advantages and drawbacks of contract and contingency work have a simple correlation to the class of the individuals doing the work: the higher up they are on the income scale, the more chance they have to leverage their comings and goings. The further down they are, the more vulnerable they are to being yanked around and bargained even lower. The top 20 percent of wage earners tend to more or less maintain their high wages whether they are in full-time jobs or on freelance contracts. But according to a 1997 U.S. study, 52 percent of women in nonstandard work arrangements are being paid "poverty-level wages"—compared with only 27.6 percent in the full-time female worker population being paid those low wages. In other words, most nonstandard workers aren't members of Free Agent Nation. According to the study, "58.2 per cent are in the lowest quality work arrangements—jobs with substantial pay penalties and few benefits relative to full-time standard workers."[61] Furthermore, the real wages of temp workers in the U.S. actually went down, on average, by 14.7 percent between 1989 and 1994.[62] In Canada, nonpermanent jobs pay one-third less than permanent jobs, and 30 percent of nonpermanent employees work irregular hours.[63] Clearly, temping puts the most vulnerable workforce further at risk, and no matter what *Details* says, it doesn't rock.

Moreover, there is a direct cause-and-effect relationship between the free agents skipping and hopping on the top rungs of the corporate ladder, and the agents hanging off the bottom who have been "freed" of such pesky burdens as security and benefits. Nobody is more liberated, after all, than the CEOs themselves, who, like Nike's cabal of Über-athletes, have formed their own Dream Team to be traded back and forth between companies whenever some star power is needed to boost Wall Street morale. Temp CEOs, as writer Clive Thompson calls them, now shuttle from multinational to multinational, staying for an average term of only five years, collecting multimillion-dollar incentive packages on the way in, and multimillion-dollar golden handshakes on the way out.[64] "Companies are changing executives like baseball managers," says John Challenger, executive vice president of the outplacement firm Challenger, Gray & Christmas. "The replacement will typically arrive like a SWAT team and sweep out the old and restaff with his or her own people."[65] When "Chainsaw" Al Dunlap was appointed CEO of Sunbeam in July 1996, Scott Graham, an analyst at Oppenheimer & Co., commented, "This is like the Lakers signing Shaquille O'Neal."[66]

The two extreme poles of workplace transience—represented by the contractor in Cavite afraid of flying factories, and the temp CEO unveiling restructuring plans in New York—work together like a global seesaw. Since the CEO superstars earn their reputation on Wall Street through such kamikaze missions as auctioning off their company's entire manufacturing base or initiating a grandiose merger that will save millions of dollars in job duplication, the more mobile the CEOs become, the more unstable the position of the broader workforce will be. As Daniel Pink points out, the word "freelance" is derived from the age when mercenary soldiers rented themselves—and their lances—out for battle. "The free lancers roamed from assignment to assignment—killing people for money."[67] Granted it's a little dramatic, but it's not a half-bad job description for today's free-agent executives. In fact, it is the precise reason CEO salaries skyrocketed during the years that layoffs were at their most ruthless. Ira T. Kay, author of *CEO Pay and Shareholder Value*, knows why. Writing in *The Wall Street Journal*, Kay points out that the exorbitant salaries American companies have taken to paying their CEOs is a "crucial factor making the U.S. economy the most competitive in the world" because without juicy bonuses company heads would have "no economic incentive to face up to difficult management decisions, such as layoffs." In other words, as satirist Wayne Grytting retorted, we are "supporting those executive bonuses so we can get . . . fired."[68]

It's a fair enough equation, particularly in the U.S. According to the AFL-CIO, "the CEOs of the 30 companies with the largest announced layoffs saw their salaries, bonuses, and long-term compensation increase by 67.3 per cent."[69] The man responsible for the most layoffs in 1997—Eastman Kodak CEO George Fisher, who cut 20,100 jobs—received an options grant that same year estimated to be worth $60 million.[70] And the highest-paid man in the world in 1997 was Sanford Wiell, who earned $230 million as head of the

Travelers Group. The first thing Wiell did in 1998 was announce that Travelers would merge with Citicorp, a move that, while sending stock prices soaring, is expected to throw thousands out of work. In the same spirit, John Smith, the General Motors chairman implementing those 82,000 job cuts discussed in the last chapter, received a $2.54 million bonus in 1997 that was tied to the company's record earnings.[71]

There are many others in the business community who, unlike Ira T. Kay, are appalled by the amounts executives have been paying themselves in recent years. In *Business Week*, Jennifer Reingold writes with some disgust, "Good, bad, or indifferent, virtually anyone who spent time in the corner office of a large public company in 1997 saw his or her net worth rise by at least several million."[72] For Reingold, the injustice lies in the fact that CEOs are able to collect raises and bonuses even when their company's stock price drops and shareholders take a hit. For instance, Ray Irani, CEO of Occidental Petroleum, collected $101 million in compensation in 1997, the same year that the company lost $390 million.

This camp of market watchers has been pushing for CEO remuneration to be directly linked to stock performance; in other words, "You make us rich, you get a healthy cut. But if we take a hit, then you take one too." Though this system protects stockholders from the greed of ineffective executives, it actually puts ordinary workers at even greater risk, by creating direct incentives for the quick and dirty layoffs that are always sure to rally stock prices and bring on the bonuses. For instance, at Caterpillar—the model of the incentive-driven corporation—executives get paid in stocks that have consistently been inflated by massive plant closures and worker wage rollbacks. What is emerging out of this growing trend of tying executive pay to stock performance is a corporate culture so damaged that workers must often be fired or shortchanged for the boss to get paid.

This last point raises the most interesting question of all, I think, about the long-term effect of the brand-name multinationals' divestment of the jobs business. From Starbucks to Microsoft, from Caterpillar to Citibank, the correlation between profit and job growth is in the process of being severed. As Buzz Hargrove, president of the Canadian Auto Workers, says, "Workers can work harder, their employers can be more successful, but—and downsizing and outsourcing are only one example—the link between overall economic success and the guaranteed sharing in that success is weaker than ever before."[73] We know what this means in the short term: record profits, giddy shareholders, and no seats left in business class. But what does it mean in the slightly longer term? What of the workers who fell off the payroll, whose bosses are voices on the phone at employment agencies, who lost their reason to take pride in their company's good fortune? Is it possible that the corporate sector, by fleeing from jobs, is unwittingly pouring fuel on the fire of its own opposition movement?

NOTES

1. "A Conversation with Charles Handy," *Organizational Dynamics*, Summer 1996, 15–26.

2. For instance, in Canada, "between 1976 and 1997, the proportion of Canadians working in goods-producing industries shrank to 27 percent from 36 percent, according to Statistics Canada. Meanwhile, the proportion of the population working in the service industries rose to 73 per cent from 65 per cent." *Report on Business Magazine*, April 1998, 74.

3. Donna Smith and Carole Lusby, "Analysis of Educational Needs Assessment of Retail Employees," Ryerson Polytechnic University, 14 February 1997.

4. Personal interview, 7 October 1997.

5. Personal interview, 7 October 1997.

6. Personal interview, 24 November 1997.

7. In the U.S., the average hourly wage for a retail worker was $8.26.

8. Ortega, *In Sam We Trust,* 361. In Canada, Wal-Mart employees earn Can$8 an hour and have an average annual income of around $12,000.

9. *San Francisco Chronicle*, 3 October 1997, A19.

10. Dan Gallin is general secretary of the International Union of Food, Agricultural, Hotel, Restaurant, Catering, Tobacco and Allied Workers Association (IUF) based in Geneva. He offered the definition in an interview on the McSpotlight Web site. A good illustration of the place where trademark law interferes with public discourse about the reality of the corporate political landscape is in the McDonald Corporation's threat to sue the Oxford Dictionary (among several other parties) over the word "McJobs." Not only has McDonald's, which employs over 1 million people worldwide, played a huge role in pioneering the low standards now equated with the word "McJobs," but it has also decided to restrict our ability to have a public discussion about the impact of the McJobs phenomenon.

11. Verdict delivered 19 June 1997.

12. *Good Morning America*, 16 April 1998, interviewer Kevin Newman with guests Bryan Drapp and Dominic Tocco.

13. Personal interview, 7 October 1997.

14. Letter addressed to "Borders Booksellers, Musicsellers, and Cafe Staff," from Richard L. Flanagan, President, Borders Stores, 30 May 1997.

15. Personal interview, 24 November 1997.

16. "Why Store 21 Tried to Unionize," Borders Books & Union Stuff Web site.

17. Source: Dan Gallin, general secretary of the International Union of Food, Agricultural, Hotel, Restaurant, Catering, Tobacco and Allied Workers Association (IUF), McSpotlight Web site.

18. *Globe and Mail*, 13 June 1998.

19. Ontario Labour Relations Board, File No. 0387-96-R. Decision of Janice Johnston, vice chair, and board member H. Peacock, 10 February 1997.

20. The number of part-time workers in the U.S. in 1997 was 23.2 million. *Handbook of U.S. Labor Statistics*, Bureau of Labor Statistics, 1998. According to Harry Pold, labor force researcher at Statistics Canada, between 1975 and 1997, part-time employment in Canada increased by 4.2 percent and full-time employment increased by a rate of only 1.5 percent ("Employment & Job Growth," Labour & Household Surveys Analysis Division, 1998).

21. Andrew Jackson, "Creating More and Better Jobs Through Reduction of Working Time," policy paper for Canadian Labour Conference, February 1998.

22. Personal interview, 24 November 1997.

23. Ortega, *In Sam We Trust,* 351.

24. *USA Today*, 5 August 1997, B1.

25. Ibid.

26. Ortega, *In Sam We Trust*, xiii.

27. Jim Frederick, "Internment Camp: The Intern Economy and the Culture Trust," *Baffler*, no. 9, 51–58.

28. Ibid.

29. U.S. Department of Labor.

30. "Staffing Services Annual Update," National Association of Temporary and Staffing Services, 1999.

31. In fact, Manpower, which employs over 800,000 workers, is a larger employer than Wal-Mart, which employs 720,000, but since Manpower's workers aren't out working every day, on any given day Wal-Mart has more workers on the payroll than Manpower.

32. *USA Today,* 5 August 1997, B1.

33. Helen Cooper and Thomas Kamm, "Europe Firms Lift Unemployment by Laying Off Unneeded Workers," *Wall Street Journal,* 3 June 1998.

34. Ibid.

35. Ibid.

36. Cooper and Kamm, "Europe Firms Lift Unemployment."

37. United States Bureau of Labor Statistics.

38. Bruce Steinberg, "Temporary Help Annual Update for 1997," *Contemporary Times*, Spring 1998.

39. Bernstein, "Outsourced—And Out of Luck."

40. Ibid.

41. Peters, *The Circle of Innovation*, 240.

42. Steinberg, "Temporary Help Annual Update for 1997."

43. Chris Benner, "Shock Absorbers in the Flexible Economy: The Rise of Contingent Employment in Silicon Valley," May 1996. Published by Working Partnerships USA.

44. Leslie Helm, "Microsoft Testing Limits on Temp Worker Use," *Los Angeles Times*, 7 December 1997, D1.

45. Ibid.

46. Microsoft won't divulge how many temps it uses but the 5,750 figure comes from the National Writers Union, which came to it by counting the number of E-mail addresses at Microsoft that begin with the "a-" prefix. The "a" stands for "agency" and is on all the temps' accounts.

47. Helm, "Microsoft Testing Limits."

48. TechWire, 26 July 1997.

49. *Business Insurance*, 9 December 1996, 3.

50. Kevin Ervin, "Microsoft Clarifies Relationship with Temporary Workers," Knight Ridder Tribune Business News, 24 June 1998.

51. Alex Fryer, "Temporary Fix at Microsoft?" *Seattle Times*, 16 December 1997, A1.

52. Remarks by Bob Herbold, Seattle, Washington, 24 July 1997. From transcript.

53. Helm, "Microsoft Testing Limits."

54. Jonathan D. Miller, "Microsoft cutting back? In one sense it has, official says," *Eastside Journal* (Bellevue WA), 17 July 1997.

55. Remarks by Bob Herbold, Executive Vice President and Chief Operating Officer, Microsoft Corporation Annual Shareholders' Meeting, 14 November 1997, Seattle, Washington.

56. Peters, *The Circle of Innovation*, 184–85.

57. Daniel H. Pink, "Free Agent Nation," *Fast Company*, December 1997/January 1998.

58. "Opportunity Rocks!" *Details*, June 1997, 103.

59. Ron Lieber, "Don't Believe the Hype," *Details*, June 1997, 113.

60. "How We Work Now," *Newsweek*, 1 February 1999.

61. "Nonstandard Work, Substandard Jobs: Flexible Work Arrangements in the U.S.," Economic Policy Institute, Washington, DC.

62. Benner, "Shock Absorbers in the Flexible Economy."

63. *Employment and Unemployment in 1997: The Continuing Jobs Crisis*, Canadian Labour Congress.

64. Clive Thompson, "The Temp," *This Magazine*, February 1998, 32.

65. *San Francisco Examiner*, 27 April 1998, D27.

66. *Wall Street Journal*, 22 May 1998 (on-line).

67. Pink, "Free Agent Nation."

68. *Wall Street Journal*, 23 February 1998, A22.

69. "Runaway CEO Pay," on AFL-CIO's Executive PayWatch Web site.

70. "Executive Excess '98: Fifth Annual Executive Compensation Survey" (Boston: United for a Fair Economy), 23 April 1998.

71. *Globe and Mail*, "Report On Business," 21 April 1998.

72. Jennifer Reingold, "Executive Pay," *Business Week*, 20 April 1998, 64–70.

73. From "Corporate Success, Social Failure, Corporate Credibility," a speech given to the Canadian Club of Toronto, 23 February 1998.

25

▼▼▼▼▼▼▼

Education and the Dilemmas
of Modernism: Towards an
Ecozoic Vision*

Edmund O'Sullivan

In my introductory Prologue, I have made a preliminary assessment of the role of educational institutions in our current crisis. Let me draw the reader's attention to Thomas Berry's criteria for assessing educational institutions: "All human institutions, programs, and activities must now be judged primarily by the extent to which they inhibit, ignore or foster a mutually enhancing human–earth relationship" (personal communication, 23 February 1990).

With these criteria in mind, we can say that the modernist educational venture in all its forms is incredibly deficient in the understanding of human–earth relationships. Since formal conventional educational institutions are tailored to the needs of the consumer industrial society, it should not be surprising that our society's present direction aligns itself with programs and procedures that ignore and inhibit human–earth relationships. This is indeed the case, and it is important that we consider the role of educational institutions in our present crisis. We must do this, for, if we neglect the historical role of educational institutions, we will be rendered blind to its impact.

Our educational institutions have been apologists for the industrial society and they are part of a broad hegemonic process for consumer dream structures. Optimism and belief in the consumer industrial society are still a part of everyday education. Here is an instance of that optimism from a 1957 Canadian textbook on the topic of the development of Canadian education: "Disregarding world factors beyond our immediate frame of reference and control, we may look to a bright future for Canadian education. Achievements during the short period of our history have been encouraging to say the least. They should be even more impressive during the next stage of Canadian development" (Phillips 1957: 66).

Although the optimism of the late 1950s and 1960s reversed itself in the 1970s and 1980s, this turnaround had virtually nothing to do with questioning the economic industrial order and its attendant morbidity. Educational institutions were chided for their permissiveness and laxity in failing to teach the basics for a fluidly functioning industrial order. As frequently as in the past, education became the whipping boy for the changing business cycle (O'Sullivan 1980; Quarter and Matthews 1987); the scapegoat for letting down the exigencies of the plundering industrial economy. This is the gist of the recent "back to the basics" movement (O'Sullivan 1980). The basics are the core literacy subjects of reading, writing and mathematics that are seen as prerequisites for the functioning of the industrial order.

Coming into the twenty-first century, we can see how progress through science, technology and the industrial order geared to the exploitation and consumption of the earth's resources became the major motif for the economic order of the twentieth century. Carnegie and Rockefeller had the evolutionary philosopher William Spencer lecture across the United States, making the connection between Darwin's ideas on the "survival of the fittest" and the world of industry and business. Social Darwinism became part of the apologetic ideology for the industrial order that has led us to our present state of environmental morbidity (Hofstadter 1955). The industrialists, aided by the "captains of consciousness" (modern advertisers), introduced this century to the marvels of endless industrial product consumption (Ewen 1976). Educational institutions have immersed themselves in the fulfillment of the needs of the industrial order. The history of American education will follow the ethos of science, technology and corporate capitalism up to the highest levels of education (Noble 1977).

One of the major apologists and proponents of this educational format was the educational historian Lawrence Cremin (1964; 1976). He observed that although there is tremendous diversity in American education, its fundamental goals are in the interest of creating equal opportunity. Equal opportunity education was defined as a fair chance for all to participate in the industrial order of democratic capitalism. Nowhere in this historical educational perspective is there a questioning of the potential down-side of the industrial order or its underlying assumptions. Even when criticism was made of the modern educational system by Marxist-oriented scholars and historians (be they from America, France, Great Britain or Australia), it was a criticism that says our present industrial order reproduces unequal opportunity and unequal access to industrial goods and services (Apple 1979; Bourdieu and

Passeron 1977; Bowles and Gintis 1976; Connell et al. 1983; de Lone 1979; Katz 1968). The focus of their criticism in no way comes to terms with issues of what the industrial order is doing to the natural world on its own terms. Thus, we can readily see that all received western educational traditions, even when they differ from one another in specifics, share some common assumptions about the appropriateness of the industrial order's exploitation of the natural world for human consumption.

In the 1980s, the response to our current educational crisis was to accelerate the scenario of the new world order of globalization. In general, the answer to the problems produced by the technological industrialism of the terminal cenozoic is more industrial technique (Ellul 1964). The supposedly new panaceas are the computer and genetic engineering (Rifkin and Perlas 1983; O'Sullivan 1983; 1985). Added to the advance of computerization and genetic engineering is the larger arc of the "global competitive marketplace." The global marketplace is now the centerpiece of our current educational ventures, and we are being asked to restructure our schools to help students to become competitive in that emergent global sphere. This is our newest version of educational reform. It has an old ring to it; the linking of schools directly to the needs of industry and business. The only difference is that, today, the yardstick is now stretched to global proportions. We have seen this business–education marriage. It has been a marriage that has contributed to the detriment of our natural world and habitat. Part of our task and challenge will be to extricate ourselves from the industrial trance state that we have been in since the beginning of the twentieth century.

THE NEED TO CHOOSE BETWEEN VISIONS

I would like to venture the thesis that the fundamental educational task of our times is to make the choice for a sustainable global planetary habitat of interdependent life forms over and against the global competitive marketplace. We are now living in a watershed period comparable to the major shift that took place from the medieval into the modern world. We are at another vast turning point, and we are in need of a cosmological story that can carry the weight of planetary consciousness into where we are now moving. To move towards a global planetary education, it will be necessary to have a functional cosmology that is in line with the vision of where this education will be leading us. Drawing from the work of Thomas Berry (1988), I refer to this postmodern period as the "ecozoic" period. This choice for an "ecozoic vision" can also be called a "transformative" perspective because it posits a radical restructuring of all current educational directions. The educational framework appropriate for this movement must then not only be visionary and transformative, but clearly must go beyond the conventional educational outlooks that we have cultivated for the last several centuries.

THE COSMOLOGICAL CONTEXT

Contemporary education lacks a comprehensive cosmology. This is one of the central ideas that I will be developing in this book. When education has been drawn from the sciences, its attention has been directed to the social sciences as distinguished from the natural sciences. In most cases, educational theory and practice have borrowed from the sciences of psychology, sociology and, to a lesser extent, anthropology. Modern educational theory lacks a comprehensive and integrated perspective that has in the past been identified as a cosmology. Thus, contemporary educational theory and practice carry with them the same blinders that have plagued modern scientific specialization coming out of the post-Newtonian period. To be sure, modern western educational thought has attempted to identify itself with humanism, but it has done so without providing a renewal of an acceptable cosmology. What I am working towards in this book is an articulation and presentation of a cosmology that can be functionally effective in providing a basis for an educational program that would engender an ecologically sustainable vision of society in the broadest terms; what can be called a planetary vision. This new cosmology, at its mythic and visionary level, could initiate and guide the new order of earth's existence into an emerging ecozoic era. As I have already indicated, we are now at the end of the cenozoic era of the planet earth's 4.5 billion-year history. This era is rapidly ending. Not only the human aspect but, even more so, the functioning of the entire planet is being altered. All living beings are being altered in the most extensive transformation that has taken place on the planet earth in the last 65 million years. So extensive is the dissolution of the life systems of the earth during the past century that the viability of the human being can no longer be taken for granted.

The long-term survival of our species, and of other species that share our living planet, depends on understanding the depth of what is happening to the planet at present. It is essential to admit that what is occurring is nothing less than biocide. It also depends on rekindling a relationship between the human and the natural world that is far beyond the exploitative relationships of our current industrial mode. A different kind of prosperity and progress needs to be envisioned which embraces the whole life community. All our human institutions, professions, all our programs and activities, need to function now in this wider life community context.

It is time to evoke the emergence of a new earth period that can be identified as the ecozoic era. Even now the shift is beginning to take place in which a relationship of mutual enhancement between humans and the natural world is regarded not only as possible but essential to planetary survival. We have seen this in the various manifestations of the ecology movement and also in coexisting social justice and human rights movements. How do educators fit in with this momentous change?

Now the whole question of the educator's role in dealing with planetary crisis becomes prominent. Educators, for the most part, see themselves as practitioners who are teaching their students to function within the social order. At this historical moment, almost all educational institutions are geared towards teaching the skills necessary for dealing with the needs of the consumer–industrial phase of this terminal cenozoic period. Within this context, we can clearly say that education is part of the problem rather than part of the solution. What is needed is a radical change in perspective within educational institutions to deal with the magnitude of the problems that we are currently facing at a planetary level.

Educators have not been prepared for this momentous undertaking. They have carried out their educational tasks in the technological and industrial world that is presently our dying heritage. To cope with the magnitude of our present problems, educators must see their work within a wider historical perspective. Because educators are strongly encouraged to deal with immediate practical problems, the historical perspective that is being suggested may, at first, appear beyond their competencies. In spite of this reservation, I feel it is absolutely necessary that they ponder the broad sweep of evolutionary history that I present in my introduction. History helps us to develop perspective and, what is more, it may be an aid in changing our perspective. I have already suggested that, in biological terms, the planet earth is at the end of the cenozoic period. This period is fast coming to a close by the plundering industrial economy that humans have imposed on the planet during these past two centuries. Truly, we now have a choice either to listen to the voices of the terminal cenozoic or to follow other emergent voices that take us in the direction of transformative education.

ASSESSING THE FORCES:
THE CENOZOIC–ECOZOIC TENSION

If the terminal decade of the twentieth century is a transitional moment, as I have indicated in Chapter 1, then it is very important to examine the fluctuating and conflicting forces that we are privy to in our educational venture. We know that transitional moments are fraught with ambiguities and contradictions. This is to be expected. A more pressing need is that we make a clear assessment of these forces so that we do not become simply prey to their twists and turns and that we exercise the power of choice while venturing into new and emergent directions. One of the preparations for the future is a sober assessment of the past, to see how the forces of the past are operating in the present moment. We have done some of this work in Chapter 1, but a more extended treatment is now warranted. This brings us to the present trends that have historical roots in North American education.

TABLE 25.1
Educational Visions

Features	Progressive Technozoic	Conservative	Ecozoic Transformational
Educational world view/ history	Modern	Anti-modern	Postmodern
Orientation to community and natural world	Exploitive	Traditional	Reflexive/interactive
View of time	Evolutionary	Cyclical/static	Time developmental
View of space	Pluralistic	Organic essentialist	Organic/interactive
Pre-eminent metaphor	Mechanistic	Anthropological organic (human body)	Biocentric (i.e. organic web of life) "circle of life"
View of conflict	Superficial/ ameliorative	Deviant/anarchic	Creative
Contemporary educational features	Progressive	Traditional	Emergent

My concentration on the North American educational context is consistent with my framing of this work in what I have labeled "northern privilege." I shall examine three main currents that are operating in this cenozoic–ecozoic tension: the progressive technozoic, the conservative organic and the transformative ecozoic. It is my assessment that both the conservative organic and the progressive technozoic, for all their differences, rest solidly within the "terminal cenozoic vision." With that *caveat*, I hope that the reader will come away with the conclusion that my categories reveal more than they conceal; enlighten rather than obfuscate. Table 25.1 is a summary of the work of the rest of this chapter.

THE PROGRESSIVE TECHNOZOIC VISION

Educational World View/History.   Education history in North America is strongly influenced by the political economy of the United States of America. Even when this educational thrust is in Canada, it still bears the features of American educational hegemony. There is a public commitment to the development of "democratic citizenry." There is also an abiding commitment to the idea of progress and its integral linkage to the technological–industrial society. This, in a nutshell, is the core of the progressive technozoic vision. It is the thesis of this book that this educational vision is now in a terminal phase and it is, thus, being called the terminal cenozoic. The vision is, therefore, a vision in decline. The major problem with this dream structure is that its contemporary proponents do not see its terminal qualities. For purposes of clarity and comparison, I shall discuss each of the prototype visions and what I judge to be some of their distinguishing features. It is important for the reader to understand that my treatment here on educational currents is schematic rather than historically accurate and exhaustive. It is my view that the educational vision of "progressive technozoic" education is deeply embedded in the modernist dream of the "terminal cenozoic" and must now be subject to a thorough critical re-evaluation. To do this, it is appropriate to begin with a sense of its educational history in North America.

First, the sense of the tension in the progressive technozoic stream is exemplified in the educational thinking of John Dewey and Edward Thorndike. In reading Lawrence Cremin's historical work, *The Transformation of the School* (1964), one is impressed that, at the turn of this century, the educational philosopher Dewey and the educational psychologist Thorndike were two of the more salient figures in the burgeoning educational reform that was to inaugurate twentieth-century education. Both Dewey and Thorndike responded to the needs of a newly industrialized and increasingly urbanized society. Dewey's reform commentaries were ordinarily addressed to those involved in elementary education, whereas Thorndike's suggestions were geared to those in the secondary level (Cremin 1964).

Dewey and Thorndike complemented one another and, combined, they provided the matrix of an educational vision that allied itself, at a fundamental level, with the march of progress that was catapulting the educational world view into the educational venture of twentieth-century capitalism. For Dewey (1963: 216), the idea of progress was to be coupled with its twin sister "development": "The aim of education is growth or development, both intellectual and moral. Ethical and psychological principles can aid the school in the greatest of all constructions—the building of free and powerful character. Education is the work of supplying the conditions that will enable the psychological functions to mature in the freest and fullest manner."

Dewey's progressive developmentalism has a contemporary ring, relating to cognitive developmental psychology as seen in the work of such theorists as Bruner, Piaget and Kohlberg (see O'Sullivan 1990). For example, Kohlberg has a deep allegiance to Dewey's ideas when applying cognitive developmental stage theory to education.

Dewey and contemporary proponents can be understood as the liberal wing of progressivism. The interest in Thorndike's (Cremin 1964) ideas take us further into a feature of education called the basics or "back to the basics." Unlike Dewey, Thorndike was not a philosopher, and he allied all his ideas to empirical studies. He would be labeled in contemporary terms as an "educational psychologist." His ultimate impact on educational practice and theory was as profound and far-reaching as that of his contemporary, Dewey. Thorndike's vigorous empiricism also sparked his interest in the educational testing movement that was booming in the 1920s. Like many other psychometricians, he embarked on an elaborate program of testing and classification of learners. It appeared that the psychological approach generated by Thorndike lent its support to many school practices in North America throughout the twentieth century. In line with "basic education" fare, Thorndike's position was most consistent with curriculum methods that emphasized drill and repetition.

Moving from settings of learning that are based within school systems, there is also the field of adult education. Although there have been pioneers in the area of adult education who have linked their work to working-class and what is today called popular education, it must be conceded that the formal field of adult education has developed in a manner that has excluded popular movements, citizen groups, farmers and the education of labor within the terms of those movements. Some of those popular movements included the pioneer work of Moses Cody in Canada, Raymond Williams in Britain and Myles Horton at the Highlander School in the United States (Welton 1995). At the end of the war, movements such as these would not have been counted as adult education. In the post-war era, professional middle-class educators emerged who took as their task the management of the learning process in formal and professional settings. The professionalization of adult education in the post-war era until the 1980s proceeded almost entirely without a critical social perspective. Michael Collins, in commenting on conventional adult education as a field, sees it aligned with the "cult of efficiency" (Collins 1991; 1995). In this light, the vocation of the field seemed to be preoccupied with personal and career development techniques. Much of the field falls into the category of a corporate pedagogy exemplified in such things as competency-based education and human resource development. There is an emphasis in this field on "instrumental reason" as the prime mode of rationality.

The post-war direction of adult education relied heavily on the discipline of psychology. Following from this is its emphasis on the individual learner. Two of the major architects of this emphasis are Alan Tough and Malcolm Knowles. They developed the notion of the "self-directed learner" with the emphasis on the individual as the unit of analysis (Knowles 1986; Tough 1981). Their work proceeded on the assumption that the individual is the primary source of his or her own learning experiences. Within this learning paradigm of the individual, they further developed the idea of "learning contracts." This formulation for adult learning has been immensely popular and well received within professional adult education circles. It has been implemented in many institutional settings, including hospitals, business firms, colleges, public schools and prisons. The model is, in the final analysis, trapped in its individualistic framework and thus is blind to the power dynamics of institutions. Thus this model works knowingly or unknowingly on behalf of the power of institutions.

From this capsule summary, we can draw the conclusion that throughout the history of North American education there has been an interweaving of the forces of progressivism and technology. This has been the yin and yang for "liberal progressive reform" and "back to the basics" reform; the upswing of the business cycle allied to the former, the downswing of the business cycle to the latter (Quarter and Matthews 1987).

The 1960s were probably the most economically expansive decade of the twentieth century. This period witnessed a renaissance in liberal-progressive thinking, while the 1990s showed a failing economy allied to "quality education" and "back to the basics" rhetoric. Educational criticism heard nowadays contains no fundamental questioning of the contemporary consumer–industrial order. The "back to the basics" movement is designed to prepare students for the exigencies of the new global economic order as played out in the arena of the "global competitive marketplace." The bottom line is to turn out learners who can compete in this dream of the global technosphere.

Orientation to Community and Natural World. Throughout the twentieth century, one can conclude that the progressive technozoic vision has aligned itself to the technological order of the contemporary nation-state. In its most contemporary form, we see the new global competitive marketplace of the multinational corporations. Within this venue, we see schools as the preparation ground for this new industrial economic order. Here the jargon goes something like "the schools must prepare new learners to be competitive in the new global economic community." There are no questions asked on the planetary sustainability of this direction. This position accepts uncritically the demands of the global market on competition and consumption. The attitude towards the natural world is fundamentally *exploitative*. It appears that our local and national community life must be geared to this global marketplace. There is no depth of reflection on how pursuit of this dream of the global marketplace may have dramatic and negative impacts on our natural habitat and biosphere. There is very little emphasis on the development of local community life and the sense that these communities also have a profound impact on the quality of our lives. Historically, this progressive technozoic model of change has been in place since the breakdown of "traditional" societies. The idea of the market community has its origins in nineteenth-century thought. The parallels are made in the following observation of Holland and Henriot (1984: 24): "The ideal of a well-balanced society in nineteenth and twentieth-century Europe and North America was a 'market' environment in which unrelated parts interacted competitively through 'free enterprise' (economics), liberal democracy (politics), and 'free thought' (culture)."

Because of its enmeshment within the "terminal cenozoic dream," the trajectory of the progressive technozoic vision, when moving towards this world marketplace, ignores the impact that this pursuit has on the environment and the exigencies of our natural habitat. In short, pursuit of the competitive marketplace must now be seen as antithetical to a viable habitat; an insult to the natural world. Local community life within this world economic community is not an end in itself but only a means to an end. That is why along with the growth of this global economic marketplace there has been corresponding destruction to community life lived at local levels (Daly and Cobb 1989). The "wonderworld" of this competitive global community is becoming the "wasteworld" of the local community.

View of Time. There is a type of "manifest destiny" mentality in the progressive technozoic vision. The concepts of growth, development and competition are placed in an evolutionary framework. The time-line of this vision is linear and evolutionary. There is a kind of unfolding of destiny, and the best approach is to embrace the changes that destiny dictates. Change is viewed as "progress" and proceeds along a continuum in which societies and communities are gradually moving onwards and upwards. As Ronald Reagan said long ago in his General Electric advertisements: "progress is our most important product." This forwards, onwards and upwards movement of history frequently makes light of the past. The past is the enemy of the future. This is the notion of progress in the idea of the "progressive form." Progress, in its contemporary form, is the movement into the global competitive marketplace.

View of Space. The dominant idea of space within this vision can be labeled "pluralistic." Pluralism here means that there is no idea of a collective relational whole that is seen governing each part. Thus, we see a cluster of freely operating or isolated parts. We are talking here of a "pluriverse" rather than a universe; a "pluriverse" whose foundation engenders the fundamental motif of "competition":

> Functional regions are distinct and unrelated (e.g.; economics, politics, and culture). It is assumed in this model that the "common good" is not the direct object of social concern, but results indirectly from the self-actualization of all of the parts. In economic terms, an "invisible hand" guides competition in the "free market" system for the benefit of all. In political terms, the parts are actuated as interest groups; in cultural terms they express themselves through "free thought." In this view, a healthy society is marked by individualism and innovation; it thrives in an expanding, competitive market. (Holland and Henriot 1984: 29)

In this atmosphere of pluralistic atomism, it is the role of the educational system to prepare the learner for the newly emergent market that is expanding beyond the nation-state into the sphere of the transnational corporations.

Pre-eminent Metaphor. Machines as an analogue for the understanding of human behavior and institutions have been part of the fabric of scientific and social explanation in the modern world. Mechanistic explanation is based on the principles of analysis and atomism. The whole can be understood as the sum of its individual parts. You can understand the clock by taking it apart and rebuilding it from its constituent components. It is felt by some of the ecological critics that the view of the world in mechanistic terms has been one of the major factors in the deterioration of our relationship to the natural world (Berman 1981; Merchant 1980). We can also see how the metaphor of mechanism operates at the level of the organization of the schools. Much of the development of modern bureaucratic organizations has as its foundation a nonorganic perspective of how parts of an organization relate to one another. There is no intrinsic relationship of parts; parts are held together by an authoritarian hierarchy and discrete horizontal status divisions.

View of Conflict. Although the rhetoric of competition and combat is given center stage, we nevertheless see that when it comes to questioning the fundamental tenets of this vision there is an ameliorating emphasis on gradualism and incremental change. Therefore, any conflictual challenges to the hegemony of this system of thinking are considered to be unnecessary and therefore superficial. When ecologists make fundamental critiques of the governing global market economy as antithetical to the functioning of the biosphere, these criticisms are labeled as precipitous and an overreaction. There is a cure within this system for everything. Anything that has been done can be undone. Technology can solve the problems created by technological innovation. Within the broad spectrum of this line of thinking, there is zero tolerance for conflict and critique that challenges this system's integrity. Therefore, in societies like our own, the whole area of social conflict is closely managed by politicians, business persons and, ultimately, the educator who acts as the apologist of this system. Managing the challenge of social conflict and keeping it at the level of superficial change is the *sine qua non* of liberal progressive thought. Within this system, the most powerful social force is inertia. Technology and science can solve our so-called "exaggerated environmental crisis." As it is frequently put in ironic terms within this vision, "What's the problem?"

Contemporary Educational Features. Because of the pluralism of this educational space, educational trends are as varied as they are unrelated to one another. Their one common feature is that they all appear to accept uncritically the direction of educational change that leads us into the global competitive marketplace. The techniques are as variable as they are fragmented. For the global competitive educator, we have the global cafeteria of techniques and approaches. On the theoretical side we have the emergent area of educational theory called by its followers "cognitive science." Cognitive science is an amalgam of research and theory and partly an offshoot of post-Piagetian research. It is also combined with recent developments in computer simulation. In relation to education, it may be said that there is an assumption that the improvement of education is related to an improved and adequate science of the mind. A specific development of this type of science is the attempt to make links between the area of cognitive developmental psychology and computer systems simulation. Ulric Neisser (1967) gives an indication of the machine-metaphorical use of the computer as a guide to human understanding: he perceives that the task of the psychologist trying to understand human cognition is analogous to that of a person trying to discover how a computer is programmed. Particularly, if the program seems to store and reuse information, the researcher would like to know by what "routines" or "procedures" that it is done. There have been many developments in the area of cognitive science that could be assessed over the past twenty-five years. There is also a growing skepticism about many of the attempts at simulation of the mind through machine analogues (O'Sullivan 1983). For our purposes, it is sufficient to say that this total approach proceeds with all of its variations on the assumption that the mind is independent from the natural world. It remains, therefore, locked in the Cartesian split that puts the mind over nature rather than in the natural world. There is also a penchant within this direction somehow to exceed the ordinary feats of the mind by creating organisms or machines such as robots. Here again we see a certain hubris that "nature didn't do it right the first time." However, some positive features are indicated in some of the directions of "cognitive science." For example, the cultural historian William Irwin Thompson ventures a more biocentric direction for cognitive science. In a series of edited essays entitled *Gaia: A Way of Knowing* (1987), Thompson attempts to connect the earlier work of Gregory Bateson in *Steps in an Ecology of Mind* (1972) and *Mind in Nature* (1980) to the recent work on the mind as a self-regulating autopoetic structure embedded in the natural world. This is an attempt to locate the direction of cognitive science in a "biocentric" as opposed to a "technocentric" path. This emergent direction is not center stage as of yet, and conventional cognitive science still reigns.

My overall assessment of cognitive science is that it continues to see the mind outside nature and possesses the hubris that it is for the "human mind" to correct nature through the development of the technologies of the human mind. Where one of those technologies is the wedding of the mind to robotics, a note of caution is certainly warranted (Mander 1991).

Having discussed cognitive science, it is important to note that one of the more prominent directions of educational psychological theory and research extols the virtue of a view of the learner as independent of the natural world. Cognitive science is just one of the many innovations in educational research that competes for the attention of educators who desperately try to find one technical solution after another to deal with the declining effectiveness of schools in the lives of students at all levels of education. In this light, teachers are constantly hoping the next panacea will be the real thing. So we have the seeming endless parade of new techniques and workshops that extol the latest idea that promises a way out of the dilemmas of survival in the terminal cenozoic. All do their thing in the guise that whatever technique is being touted, it is scientifically based and will contribute to our uncritical forward advance through technology. This is progress and it is a progress that is extolled by the conventional advance of science and technological breakthrough. The question that I pose to you here is, "What if the breakthrough is contributing to the breakdown rather than alleviating it?" C. A. Bowers makes an important critical observation about our unreflective use of science and technique in education:

> The vast number of techniques being promoted as essential to professional growth also has another effect, namely the fostering of a nihilistic attitude where everything begins to be seen as of equal value. Without a deeper knowledge that allows issues, trends, and techniques to be put into a more reflective perspective, each technique loses its distinctness and special merit, particularly when teachers begin to realize that each year brings new disseminators with even more "advanced" techniques and learning skills. What may have been found to be useful from a previous workshop, like individualized instruction or performance objectives, disappears from the list of workshop topics as new topics are added. (Bowers 1993b: 86–7)

Bowers then goes further and criticizes the progressive technocratic tradition in education for its total lack of understanding of the ecological crisis. Speaking again about the proliferation of techniques he stresses their tendency to foster an ecological myopia:

> It also becomes part of a professional hypnosis where the events in the larger world beyond the classroom are not and cannot be fully grasped as related to what goes on in the classroom. This is particularly the case when social and environmental events cannot be related to the technique. How does the teacher connect the loss of forest cover with the classroom techniques derived from brain research, or the warming of the earth's atmosphere with "Proactive Classroom Management?" (Bowers 1993b: 87)

As educators, we can no longer move along this path uncritically, and criticism is forthcoming from many circles. One area of criticism comes from the conservative critique of modern education. It is to this tradition or vision that we now turn.

THE CONSERVATIVE VISION

There have always been reactions to the modernist vision of evolutionary progress. Even at the onset of industrialism, with all its entrancement, there were very vocal critics of the project of modernism embedded in the techno-logical industrialism of the late cenozoic. The visionary poetry of William Blake is replete with criticism of both the Enlightenment and the fundamen-tal tenets of the industrial revolution. There has also been a long history of "anti-modern" reaction to the historical directions of modernism. This type of reaction has many turns and nuances, sometimes bringing together pecu-liar bedfellows. What is common to all the reactions, to the ideal of industrial progress, is an abhorrence of some of the negative features of the modern world as well as, frequently, nostalgia. Two of those anti-modern features co-alesce in the vision of conservatism and romanticism. We will focus on the conservative dimension since it has been the most dominant form of anti-modernism in contemporary educational contexts.

From the "conservative" side, there is an attempt to conserve the forces and institutions that were bypassed by the developments of modernism. Fre-quently, the conservative reaction is embedded in a position of elitism and hi-erarchy where there are attempts to defy some of the democratic directions of the modern world. For example, the institution of the Catholic Church was one of the main counter-positions to modernism in both the late nineteenth century and the first half of the twentieth century. There is an anti-modernist critique which labels modernism as the destroyer of traditional community values such as authority and obedience to traditional rules and customs. Thus, one aspect of the conservative critique of modernism is the perception that there is the erosion of a "sense of community." The other side of the re-action to modernism can be labeled the romantic revolt. The romantic revolt is highly critical of the modern dimensions of science and technology that have led to a disembodied thinking. This critique of rationalism is centered on modern thought, indicating that there is an inability to include the emotions in the development of the intellect. A further criticism is located in a sense of the loss of a body awareness and in the reification of the mind as distinct from the natural world. This results in the exclusion of vital organic processes in highly mechanistic views of the world. Thus, in both its conservative and romantic guises, a critique of modernism has always been forthcoming. Especially in its conservative aspects, the conservative–romantic vision commends the virtues of the institutions of the past. Nothing succeeds like the past.

Educational World View/History.   Nothing illustrates the amalgam of conservative and romantic writing on education better than the work of Henry Adams, a cultural historian, writing and reflecting on our arrival into the twentieth century. In a series of essays under the title *The Education of*

Henry Adams (1931 [1918]), he reflects on the possible negative features of the dynamic industrial–technical inventiveness that he witnessed in the development of the machine technologies that were being extolled at the World's Fair of 1896. He was a historian of medieval western culture, and we can see in his writing a kind of nostalgia for what was being lost in the exodus from the medieval world synthesis. We see in the core of his writings—as in those of many of the other critics of modernism—a deep suspicion towards the many directions of the modernist spirit. In our century newer forms have appeared. There has been a deep suspicion about the developments of modern technology in the work of such writers as Jaques Ellul (1964) and George Grant (1983); a wariness towards the democratization of the masses as seen in the writing of Ortega y Gasset (1957); and a protest against the general direction of education towards vocational technological ends. In the latter context, we see education critiqued because it allies itself to the forces of the modern world of industry and technology and conforms its mandate to their needs. Robert Maynard Hutchins, in defining a "liberal education," gives us a sense of why contemporary education has become problematic.

> What is Liberal education? It is easy to say what it is not. It is not specialized education, not vocational, professional or preprofessional. It's not an education that teaches a man to do any specific thing. . . . I am tempted to say that it is education that no American can get in an educational institution nowadays. We are all specialists now. Even early in High School we are told that we must begin to think that we are going to earn a living, and the prerequisites that are supposed to prepare us for that activity become more and more the ingredients for our educational diet. I am afraid that we shall have to admit that the educational process in America is either a rather pleasant way of passing the time until we are ready to go to work, or a way of getting ready for some occupation, or a combination of the two. What is missing is education to be human beings, education to make the most of our human powers, education for our responsibilities as members of a democratic society, education for freedom. (Hutchins 1959: v)

And where does this conservative tradition suggest that we go to find this type of liberal education? Hutchins suggests that we find it in "the great books of the western world." When you look carefully at the suggested "great" books, you realize that they are male-authored. We see here that the journey into our past is limited only to our western cultural past, a past devoid of women. That this particular approach continues to have a contemporary attraction and ring was seen in the recent interest in Alan Bloom's *The Closing of the American Mind* (1987). His book is the most recent embodiment of the "great books tradition" of the western world. As one critic of his work puts it, "he believes that questions about the content of education (i.e., curriculum) were settled some time ago; perhaps once and for all with Plato, but certainly not later than Nietzsche" (Orr 1992: 97). Along with his cultivation of the life of the mind through the classics of western literature, there is a scurrilous attack on American youth culture. It is, in Bloom's opinion, morally deficient and intellectually slack. These are just two negative characteristics among the numerous qualities of youth culture that he finds repugnant. In this most contemporary version of the conservation of our best male western authors, we become aware that there is nowhere in this critique of modern educational institutions a mention of issues of social justice, poverty and ecological degradation that plague the modern mind as well as the modern landscape. What is present, as with his predecessors in this tradition, is an unreflective ethnocentric eurocentrism coupled with blind gender bias. As the same critic put it:

> It is widely acknowledged that the classics of the Western tradition are deficient in certain respects. First, having been composed by white males, they exclude the vast majority of human experience. Moreover, there are problems that this tradition has not successfully resolved, either because they are of recent origin, or because they are regarded as unimportant. In the latter category is the issue of the human role in the natural world. . . . Whatever timeless qualities human nature may or may not have, Western culture has not offered much enlightenment on the appropriate relationship between humanity and its habitat. (Orr 1992: 98)

This is not to say that certain aspects of a conservative perspective have no merit in addressing our present ecological crisis. For example, C. A. Bowers (1993b) identifies two lines of conservatism, an anthropocentric and an ecological strain. The tradition of Adler, Bloom and others is categorized in Bower's work as anthropocentric, and he makes the same criticism of this direction that I am making here. He further identifies a tradition of conservatism that he calls "ecological conservatism." This is a tradition that has a deep cultural critique of our modern technological culture regarding its effects on the natural habitat. Bowers (1993b) names Edward Schumacher, Wendell Berry and Gary Snyder as exemplars of this tradition. I do not discuss this direction here, which Bowers correctly identifies as an ecologically oriented perspective, because the writers in this line of thinking have not addressed themselves to the issues of education in the formal sense. For myself, this tradition is more in line with what I will later be calling the "ecozoic transformational"; a direction that certainly has elements of ecological conservatism within it.

Orientation to Community and Natural World.   The conservative position has an orientation towards the natural world that is simultaneously anthropocentric and traditional. It is anthropocentric in that it locates all educational objectives within the human mind. Thus, the location of educational enrichment is housed within the cultivating powers of human thought. It is the task of education to provide educational stimulus for enriching that mind. At the level of school organization (as well as the community of the school) there is the fostering of community structures that are based on tradition and hierarchy. Edward Wynne, who locates himself within the conservative tradition, suggests a list of "traditional values" that should be incorporated into modern schooling. They are as follows:

1) The acceptance of traditional hierarchy
2) The exercise of strong adult control over children and adolescents
3) The priority given to immediate good conduct over more elaborate ratiocination
4) Great emphasis on the life of collective entities
5) Reverence for the knowledge of the past
6) The reservation of a sphere of life for sacred activities, beyond the day to day business of buying, selling, and producing
7) The equality of all community members as children of God, despite their temporal, material, and intellectual differences. (Wynne 1987: 130–2)

Although this particular catalogue of traditional conservative values might not receive universal acclaim, there are some elements of Wynne's traditionalism that apply to all. First, there is a nostalgia for a past that maintains order through hierarchy. Second, the sacred is located solely within the "human community." Third, there is no attention at all given to the effects that the human community is having on our natural habitat. Fourth, the human community is bound by and best regulated by traditions of the past. The way out of our present malaise is a return to the traditions of the past which, incidentally, go as far back only as the Judaeo-Christian past and the advent of western culture.

View of Time. Time in the conservative world view is cyclical and static. There is within this perspective of time an organic biological basis for temporality that is static because of the underlying belief that nothing changes in society in any fundamental or transformative manner. The expression *"plus ça change, plus c'est la meme-chose"* is apt. Change is a cycle that repeats itself in patterns of growth–decline, birth–maturity–death, and so on. We see these change patterns in nature's rhythms, for example in the cycles of the seasons of the year. Since there is no compelling forward direction of history, as in the progressive perspective, there is no desire to bring on some glorious future. What is present is a painstaking observation of the best of antiquity. Thus, the traditional preoccupation with the past is everywhere evident.

View of Space.   If the progressive view of space was atomistic and particularistic, the conservative position espouses a form of "organic essentialism." By organic, I mean here a view that society is some kind of organic unity where the whole of society is greater than the sum of its parts. By essentialist, I mean that there are some deep structural essences that are seen to be underlying all social processes. A great deal of natural law theory exemplifies the idea that there are deep structural essences that can be seen to integrate the complexities of human societies.

Pre-eminent Metaphor.   The pre-eminent conservative metaphor is the human body as an organic totality. Using the human body as a metaphor of understanding, there is a hierarchy that is established among the parts of the body with priority given to the head. The metaphor being organic in principle, there is an understanding that the human body grows, decays and regenerates and the various parts are organically related to one another with the internal functions and external operations controlled by the head. This type of organic understanding places a strong emphasis on the hierarchical arrangements of parts and the ordering of parts based on established authoritarian structures. Hierarchy is seen as a natural underlying structure of all institutional life. Thus Edward Wynne (1987), in outlining his conservative educational viewpoint, maintains that hierarchy is a fact in all continuing organizations in our era, including schools: "Today, there is much discussion to the effect that teachers should not properly be 'authority' figures. However, parents and children alike recognize the necessary truth that teachers must play an authority role, and they are puzzled by the confusion resulting from attempts to conceal the reality of hierarchy" (Wynne 1987: 130).

What is emphasized within this view is that the ordering of the parts is based on laws activated at the top of the structure. Thus, any type of change activated from a position other than from the top of the hierarchy is seen as deviant. This is how conflict is viewed in hierarchical systems.

View of Conflict.   In traditional systems of hierarchy, conflict is viewed within these structures as deviant and anarchic in the pejorative sense. Within hierarchical systems, there is a very marked emphasis on "law and order." The most appropriate response to the disorder of things is either to cushion its effects and absorb it into the present system or to reject the conflictual elements outright as in excommunication. Using the human body as metaphor, one can utilize the example of the transplant. When an organ is transplanted into the human body it is either accepted or rejected and expelled. A challenge to the body is either absorbed into the system or rejected. Thus we see, within the workings of traditional hierarchical organization, a very powerful emphasis on "law and order," with order and harmony as the basic social virtues. Holland and Henriot give us a very clear example of the working structure using the traditional western Catholic Church:

A landed aristocracy, hierarchically structured through nobility, high clergy, constituting a ruling elite. At best, this form of leadership served as a paternalistic guardian of the "common good" exercising a *noblesse oblige* toward lower classes. At worst, it collapsed into despotic absolutism. In either case, its reaction to a challenge to the status quo was the same—absorption or suppression. Such rule was justified on ideological grounds by appeals to the "divine right of kings," demands of "social order," the preservation of "tradition" and "sound doctrine," and the assertion that "this is the way things have always been done." (Holland and Henriot 1984: 34)

Contemporary Educational Features. In the past, the preservation of the conservative traditional ethos in education was seen in the development of private elite schools. These schools housed the children of the power elite. In the traditional systems of "elite education" there was a very strong emphasis on the value of hierarchy because it was considered the foundation for a just and ordered society. Children were inculcated into a hierarchical structure of order that they were to submit to with obedience. Furthermore, they were learning to understand that they were to be inheritors of a system where they would be the ones to give orders to others who would be their subjects. Thus, the children of the privileged acquired a sense of entitlement that they were to be the inheritors of a system of order that placed them at the top of the hierarchy. Pupils would learn the powers of governance that they would eventually apply to those who, by the very natural order of things, were below them. In contemporary education, the elite school system is only one embodiment of the traditional conservative vision. In the last ten years, there has also been a popular movement within the discourse of public education that propounds the virtues of traditionalism, conservatism and hierarchy. Edward Wynne is a vocal proponent of traditional hierarchical education within this public sphere. His description of effective schools serves as a clear example:

Effective schools are led, we are told, by vigorous principals who clearly make known their values and policies. When necessary, these principals display determination and courage and press toward their goals in the face of resistance. Furthermore, teachers in such schools respect their principals, follow directions, and expect similar obedience from students. Such leadership does not imply poor communication or disengagement between followers and leaders. In effective schools, adults are unquestionably in control. Fair, firm, and appropriate discipline is applied. Such insistence has nothing to do with oppression. It is simply regarded as an acceptance of traditional, transitional adult responsibility and as a means of transmitting wholesome values to young persons. (Wynne 1987: 132)

Wynne's articulation of a traditional conservative vision for schooling is a contemporary reaction to the breakdown of traditional authority in the development of modernist progressive education. There is absolutely no sense that there are problems that we are facing today that are truly unique to our historical period; namely the scope and magnitude of our ecological crisis. There is no mention, whatsoever, of this incredible degradation of the natural world as a problem to be dealt with as an educational challenge. One of the more prominent problems with the conservative vision is an extreme anthropocentrism. There is a total lack of response to the natural habitat in the discourse of modern conservative thinkers. Conservation is not the conservation of the natural habitat. Conservation within the contemporary discourse of educational theory is the maintenance of the authority structures of western male white culture.

THE TRANSFORMATIVE ECOZOIC VISION

In this book, I am attempting to develop what I consider as an emergent form, a "transformative vision." This transformative vision contests and repudiates the viability of the global marketplace as it is currently being formulated within the transnational economic order. It is my view that this global marketplace vision cannot be a viable cultural planetary vision for the future. In essence, we are attempting to pursue a transformative ecozoic vision as an alternative to the global market vision. Here the current resurgence of the "terminal cenozoic" is seen in the educational reform criticism of the global competitive marketeers.

The educational field of "critical pedagogy" is one emergent educational forum that attempts to deal with the broad area of social justice issues that are embedded in inequities of power and resources along the lines of class, race and gender. In my own work, *Critical Psychology and Critical Pedagogy* (1990) and *Critical Psychology: An Interpretation of the Personal World* (1984), I attempt to show how these structures operate in educational contexts in areas such as school learning and popular movement education. The work in this area covers vital social justice concerns dealing with postcolonial and antiracist education (Dei 1995b), class analysis and gender inequity (O'Sullivan 1990; 1984; hooks 1994; Hart 1995). There is a development of resistance education (also called counter-hegemonic education) based on the work of Antonio Gramsci (1971), Paulo Freire (1970), bell hooks (1994) and others (Aronowitz and Giroux, 1993).

There are also some similar trends in a critical standpoint that is presently being formulated in the area of adult education. A compilation of these trends in adult education can be found in Michael Welton's edited *In Defense of the Life World: Critical Perspectives on Adult Learning* (1995) and Paul Wangoola and Frank Youngman's edited *Towards a Transformative Political Economy of Adult Education* (1996). Critical adult education is a counter-movement in adult education that is presently questioning the hegemony of conventional adult education that I have discussed under progressive techno-cratic education. What we see in these newer critical currents is a questioning of the vision of the global marketplace, gender and class inequity, and post-colonial perspectives that question the dominance of western cultural hegem-ony. There is a criticism of mainstream adult education, at the level of para-digm, from the point of view of critical social theory that can be found in the works of Jack Meizerow (1995), Michael Welton (1995), Mechhthild Hart (1995) and Michael Collins (1991; 1995).

Probably one of the most prominent omissions in the critical pedagogical approach to education at this juncture of its formulations is its lack of atten-tion to ecological issues. My major criticism is the pre-eminent emphasis on inter-human problems frequently to the detriment of the relations of humans to the wider biotic community and the natural world. The general direction of critical perspectives is towards anthropocentrism. The criticism of anthro-pocentrism is by no means a reason for dismissal of the vital concerns that critical perspectives pose for contemporary education. These issues must be taken forwards and fused into wider biocentric concerns. This will be a major challenge of this book in its final chapters.

Holistic education is another emergent trend in education which chal-lenges the fragmentation of modernism that comes to us under a scientific an-alytical and instrumentally rational world view (J. Miller 1996). John Miller, one of the major architects of holistic education in North America, signals some of the features of holism in his introductory comments to the topic in *The Holistic Curriculum*:

> Holistic education attempts to bring education into alignment with the funda-mental realities of nature. Nature at its core is interrelated and dynamic. We can see this dynamism and connectedness in the atom, organic systems, the bio-sphere, and the universe itself. Unfortunately, the human world since the Indus-trial Revolution has stressed compartmentalization and standardization. The result has been the fragmentation of life. (J. Miller 1996: 1)

Holistic educators are also very critical of the instrumental technocratic emphasis of contemporary education to the exclusion of very core aspects of life such as creativity and spirituality. Declining to identify themselves within a religious framework, there are several current treatments of education which identify spirituality as a core feature for all educational endeavors (Palmer 1993; Purpel 1989; Moffett 1994). In criticizing the shallow rational-ism and value-neutral nature of modernist education, holistic educators at-tempt to root education in an ethical framework that goes beyond the broken surface of our lives today to a hidden wholeness. In this type of education, the intellect and spirit are integral parts of one another.

As with critical pedagogy, holistic educators are sharply critical of modernist education but for very different reasons. My conclusion is that they complement one another and should be allied. Attempting to make this alignment will be another goal of an expanded and integral "transformative ecozoic education."

Finally, an emergent area labeled "global education" deserves mention. Here I am not speaking of global perspectives that prepare us for the global marketplace, but of global education perspectives that carry a planetary consciousness. The approaches to global education that I am speaking of here bear the closest resemblance to what I am calling transformative ecozoic education, in that they wed a holistic education to a planetary consciousness while maintaining a critical perspective. There are numerous instances. Budd Hall and I have done some preliminary work in the area of adult education, attempting to articulate a transformative vision in this field of adult education (Hall and O'Sullivan 1995). There is also the groundbreaking work in global education of David Selby (1995) and Graham Pike (Pike and Selby 1988) from England. The pioneering of Thomas Lyons (Lyons and O'Sullivan 1992) at the Ontario Teachers' Federation is another example. Working with teachers in the Province of Ontario, Lyons has articulated an educational vision that takes into consideration a broad cosmological perspective and combines it with an integral vision of education that includes global planetary concepts, social justice and human rights sensitivities, peace perspectives and environmental concerns.

Educational World View.   At this point I would like to outline the broad features of a transformative vision that will be articulated in greater depth in the last section of this work. I have already suggested, through historical scholarship, that the loss of a cosmological sense has had profound consequences for the modern world. There is also an indication that the absence of a functional cosmology has profoundly affected the western mind-set in its treatment of the natural world. We have now reached the point where it is possible to open up a discussion on the redevelopment of enchantment or re-enchantment. There have been counter-movements to the disenchantment of the world going all the way back to Newton. Prophetic voices, from the very outset, could see the far-reaching implications of the potential down-side of the scientific world. William Blake, the mystical poet, was one of the first voices to see the underside of the Industrial Revolution. Blake was very perceptive in his poetic criticism and directed his critical gaze at Newton:

Now I a fourfold vision see
And a fourfold vision is given to me
Tis fourfold in my supreme delight
And threefold in soft Beaulah's night

And twofold Always May God us keep
From Single Vision & Newton's sleep!
(William Blake in Schorer 1946: 5)

In the Blakean world, Newton's single vision is the principle of analysis that partitioned the natural world and left it in fragments. Sleep connoted the hypnotic character that this fragmentation would have on the perception of his contemporaries as well as on posterity. The power of this type of criticism was no contest for the powerful world view that Newton and Descartes spawned. Even into the nineteenth century, the Romantic movement would attempt to launch devastating critiques in literary circles. This in no way undercut the magnetic power of the industrial–scientific world synthesis. It is the devastating ecological crisis that has brought into question the integrity and desirability of our industrial–scientific world order. When we speak of a re-enchantment of the natural world, we are stretching ourselves to a new cosmological vision of our world. This is a world in which we can feel at home in the universe. David Griffin (1988a) gives several conditions for this cosmological reorientation: "The formal conditions for such a postmodern cosmology, in which our understanding of humanity and nature are integrated with practice in view, include reinserting humanity and life as a whole back into nature, and regarding our fellow creatures not merely as a means but as ends in themselves" (38).

The theoretical physicist David Bohm deepens our understanding of the meaning of re-enchantment. Reflecting on the cosmological implications of the theory of relativity he conjectures:

We speak of a whirlpool but one does not exist. In the same way we can speak of a particle, but one does not exist: particle is the name for a certain form in the field of movement. If you bring two particles together, they will gradually modify each other and eventually become one. Consequently, the approach contradicted the assumptions of separate, elementary, mechanical constituents of the universe. In doing so, it brought in a view that I call unbroken wholeness or flowing wholeness. It has always been called seamless wholeness. The universe is one seamless, unbroken whole. (Bohm 1988: 23–4)

Our modern dilemma is that we cannot re-enchant the world with a pre-modern cosmos. A pre-modern cosmology would fly in the face of the amazing advances that we have made in modern science. Morris Berman is clear that nostalgia for the past is not the solution that we should be pursuing:

We cannot go back to alchemy or animism—at least that does not seem likely; but the alternative is the grim, scientific, totally controlled world of nuclear reactors, microprocessors, and genetic engineering—a world virtually upon us al-

ready. Some type of holistic, or participating, consciousness and a corresponding sociopolitical formation have to emerge if we are to survive as a species.
(Berman 1981: 23)

This desire for a creative hiatus is seen in all areas of the physical and social
sciences. David Bohm sounds a familiar call for change, remarking that our
entire world order has been dissolving away for over a century. His suggestion is to forge pathways beyond the modern temper:

> I suggest that if we are to survive in a meaningful way in the face of this disinte-
> gration of the present world order, a truly creative movement to a new kind of
> wholeness is needed, a movement that must ultimately give credence to a new
> order as was the modern to the medieval order. We cannot go back to the
> premodern order. A postmodern world must come into being before the mod-
> ern world destroys itself so thoroughly that little can be done for a long time to
> come. (Bohm 1988: 23–4)

I have been emphasizing that we are, at the present, in a transitional period
in need of a functional cosmology. The difficulty is that the term "cosmology" is so exclusively physical in its accepted meaning that it does not trans-
parently suggest the integral reality of the universe. For the same reason, the
term "geology" does not show the integral reality of the earth but only its
physical aspects. Now we do not have a terminology suited to a serious consideration of the earth. It is our task now to offer the reader a blueprint for a
new cosmological sense. In suggesting an alternative, the question must be
asked, "What will be the educational features of the transformative ecozoic
vision?" Here again, I will follow the conventions that I have adopted in the
previous sections.

Orientation to Community and Natural World.   There is both traditional wisdom and an emergent form of knowledge that comes from the ecological sciences that suggest a radically different view of the earth community. In the past decade, there has been a resurgence of interest in the world
views of Native American peoples that suggest a cosmology very different
from our traditional western scientific perspective. If we take away the ro-
manticization of native cultures (which seems also part of the current interest
in indigenous ways), there is much to be learned about a proper orientation
to the earth community from the traditional wisdoms of the native peoples of
the Americas (Sioui 1992). I say "wisdoms" because there is a tendency to
lump native cultures into a common soup while ignoring the incredible variety and splendor of differences that we see in the multiform presence of native
peoples on this continent (Burger 1990). One feature of sameness that seems
to cut across these differences is that of a common understanding that the
earth is not a dead resource for human consumption but a sacred community

and web of life of profound intricacy. Another feature that seems to be present is a profound intimacy with the natural processes of the earth. A third feature, although not universal, is an orientation to the earth in a nurturing form where the earth is seen as Mother. Finally, there is a mystical sense of the place of the human and other living beings.

Turning from indigenous world views of traditional peoples, we can also see a broadening of our sense of community as a result of the recent advances of space travel. In the Preface to the beautifully illustrated book, *The Home Planet*, the astronaut Russell Schweickart makes the following observation about the profound effect that his spaceflight had on his awareness of the planet earth:

> For me, having spent ten days in weightlessness, orbiting our beautiful home planet, fascinated by the 17,000 miles of spectacle passing below each hour, the overwhelming experience was that of a new relationship. The experience was not intellectual. The knowledge I had when I returned to Earth's surface was virtually the same knowledge that I had taken with me when I went into space. Yes I conducted scientific experiments that added new knowledge to our understanding of the Earth and the near-space in which it spins. But those specific extensions of technical details I did not come to know about until the data I helped to collect was analysed and reported. What took no analysis, however, no microscopic examination, no laborious processing, was the overwhelming beauty . . . the stark contrast between bright colourful home and stark black infinity . . . the unavoidable and awesome personal relationship, suddenly realized, with all life on this planet . . . Earth, our home. (Kelley 1988: Preface)

I beg the reader, at this point, to bear with me for a personal digression that has, I hope, didactic import. When I was a child, I had the incredible privilege of accompanying my father to Ireland, to his birthplace in County Cork, to spend three months in a farmhouse with no electricity and no plumbing. It was his house of birth and looked down on a salt-water lake with an abandoned castle on an island in the middle. The lake opened into a rapids that emptied into the Atlantic Ocean. The experience was of such significance for me that when I returned there with my wife some eighteen years later I had total recall of all the surroundings. The experience, for me, was rooted in the raw beauty of the natural world and its numinous presence. All my senses, at that time, seemed heightened. I returned many times to the memories of this period of my life as I was growing up. It was a very special place. It was, for me, an enchanted place. It was a sacred place. In mid-life I am now beginning to discover that this very earth which I call my home is a sacred place.

Indeed, the earth symbol is becoming a sacred symbol for me as for many others. Nevertheless, it is ironic that the perspective of the planet earth as our "home planet" comes out of the military–industrial complexes of the USA and the former USSR. The perspective of the earth from outer space moved the astronauts well beyond the parochialism of their nation-state consciousness:

> There is a clarity, a brilliance to space that simply doesn't exist on Earth, even on a cloudless summer's day in the Rockies, and nowhere else can you realize so fully the majesty of our Earth and be so awed at the thought that it's the only one of untold thousands of planets. (Gus Grissom, USA; cited in Kelley 1988: 18)

> What struck me most was the silence. It was a great silence, unlike any I have encountered on Earth, so vast and deep that I began to hear my own body; my heart beating, my blood vessels pulsating, even the rustle of my muscles moving over each other seemed audible. There were more stars in the sky than I had expected. The sky was deep black yet at the same time bright with sunlight. The Earth was small, light blue, and so touchingly alone, our home that must be defended as a holy relic. (Aleksei Leonov, USSR; cited in Kelley 1988: 24–5)

Reflecting on the astronauts' journey into outer space, James Lovelock (1988) brought to the scientific community a new understanding of the earth with his formulation of the "Gaia Hypothesis." I will not go into the technical details here, but the hypothesis ventures that in its totality the earth itself is a living entity. As Lovelock points out in this hypothesis, we can now see that the air, the ocean and the soil are much more than a mere environment for life; they are a part of life itself. He believes that the air is to life as the fur is to the cat or the nest for the bird. Lovelock contends that there is nothing unusual in the idea of life on earth interacting with the air, sea and rocks. He came to his initial idea for the "Gaia Hypothesis" when he observed an outside glimpse of the earth from outer space. Lovelock felt that this earth, in all its interactions and transformations, added up to a single giant living system with the capacity to keep itself in a state most favorable for the life upon it. It is within this wider context that we are beginning to appreciate the earth as a very special place. It is, in some very special ways, unique to our universe. The more that we explore the expanses of space, the more we are coming to recognize the incredible and exceptional beauty of our planet. There may be no other planet that has monarch butterflies, symphonic music, flowers. Our planet is inviting us to a new understanding of ourselves and our place within the earth and the larger cosmos. Louise Young, in her beautifully crafted essays on *The Blue Planet*, makes the point that we are still far from knowing the truth about our home in space but we are slowly moving towards deeper realizations:

> Less than a century ago the earth was believed to be the very embodiment of stability, the unchanging background against which the drama of movement and growth and life was enacted. Men spoke confidently of the "solid earth"

and the "everlasting hills." Now we know that nothing is static—not the earth itself or any part of it. If we could watch a time-lapse movie of the planet's history, we would see an amazing drama of change and development: mountains being created and destroyed, sea floor ejected along the ocean ridges and consumed again at the trenches, canyons being carved by turbulent rivers, new continents split from old ones and set adrift to wander around the planet. This information has caused a revolution in our understanding of the earth and the revolution is still in progress. Those of us who know the planet that we live on must look at it anew with unjaded eyes like those of a child. (Young 1983: 5)

We are coming to understand that we are living in a period of the earth's history that is incredibly turbulent and in an epoch in which there are violent processes of change that challenge us at every level imaginable. The pathos of human life today is that humans are totally caught up in this incredible transformation and have a most significant responsibility for the direction it will take. The terror here is that we have it within our power to make life extinct on this planet. Because of the magnitude of this responsibility for the planet, all our educational ventures must finally be judged within this order of magnitude. This is the challenge for all areas of education. For education, this realization is the bottom line. What do I mean here by bottom line? For me, the bottom line is that every educational endeavor must keep in mind the magnitude of our present moment when setting educational priorities. This demands a kind of attentiveness to our present planetary situation that does not go into slumber or denial. It poses momentous challenges to educators in areas heretofore unimagined. Education within the context of "global transformation" keeps concerns for the planet always at the forefront.

This broadening of perspective has given us a new sense of this planet in which we inhabit, and one of the most profound symbols of our time is the symbol of the planet earth seen from space. Joseph Campbell suggests that this earth symbol broadens our sense of community: "When you see the earth from the moon, you don't see any divisions there of nations or states. This might be the symbol for the new mythology to come. That is the country that we are going to be celebrating. And those of the people that we are one with" (Campbell 1988: 32).

Finally, recent developments in the ecological sciences have also given us a broadened sense of the living earth community. Instead of thinking of the world as a set of constituent parts as in a clock, we now have an emergent sense that humans are not separated constituent parts of a dead earth. We are creatures who are embedded in the "web of life." This growing awareness helps us to see the human species and the human community in a larger biotic context. We are a species among other species, not a species above other species. Our western hierarchical view of the human above other species and above the natural world itself is being fundamentally challenged. Bill Devall and George Sessions (1985) see the emergence of a deep ecological perspective as a way of developing a new balance and harmony between individuals, communities and all of nature. I would say that an ecozoic vision must have as its fundamental premise this broadened sense of community and the integral relationship that the humans have to have with it. The development of this consciousness must be one of the profound educational directions for the closing decade of the twentieth century.

View of Time. In my discussions of the conservative and technozoic progressive visions, I have treated time and space under separate headings. For the sake of symmetry, I will continue this distinction. Nevertheless, it must be said that with some of the current revelations of science it is more appropriate to speak in a dimension labeled space-time. Swimme and Berry clarify the idea of a "time-developmental" context as follows:

> We have, over these past few centuries, become aware that the universe has emerged into being through an irreversible sequence of transformations that have, in the larger arc of their movement, enabled the universe to pass from a lesser to a greater complexity in its structure and functioning as well as to a greater variety and intensity in its modes of conscious expression as this can be observed on the planet Earth. This sequence of transformations we might refer to as a time-developmental process. (Swimme and Berry 1992: 223)

View of Space as Space-Time Emergence. The universe is a unity that is a dynamic totality that cannot be explained by constituent parts. When I speak of unity, I mean that the way that one can understand the universe is that in all of its actions it operates as a seamless whole with a coherence that holds all things as an integral whole. This means that the various activities of the universe are interdependent and thus cannot be considered apart from one another. The universe acts in an integral manner. The systematic study of the universe as a whole demands a cosmological perspective that is interdisciplinary in nature. Our earlier treatment of modernism concluded that there is a veritable eclipse of cosmological thinking within this world view. Stephen Toulmin (1985), in his treatment of the cosmological sense, contends that the natural sciences have developed a systematic fragmentation and as a result it is no longer the professional business of any one discipline to think about "the Whole." It follows when discussing the universe as a totality or *whole* we are moving towards a more integral cosmological sense.

I submit to the reader that at all levels of analysis or integration of the universe, we are looking at an *interacting* and *genetically* related community of beings bonded together in an inseparable relationship in *space and time*. We are therefore talking about a universe that evolves in both space and time simultaneously. The universe, in the words of the physicist David Bohm, acts as a seamless whole. When we speak of a time-developmental universe we are attesting to the idea that the universe is an interacting and genetically related community bound together in an inseparable relationship (Bohm and Peat 1987). The universe acts in intelligible ways at all levels of interaction. When we speak of the emergence of the universe out of the primeval fireball, we are not talking about some random emergence. At all levels of interactivity there seems to be a creative ordering. The universe itself is the name of that creative ordering. We can then say that the sun and the earth and the planets are bonded relationships because the universe holds them together. The same may be said of our Milky Way galaxy in relation to all of the other known galaxies. Here again we say that the universe is doing this as a fact of its primordial irreducible activity. The universe attests to the idea that everything exists and can be understood only in the context of relationships. Nothing exists in isolation (Swimme and Berry 1992).

When I say that the universe acts as a unity in space and time, I am talking about a universe that is not only present to itself simultaneously but it is also present to itself over time. We are talking about a time-developmental universe. With a time-developmental perspective we have the notion of an evolutionary emergence. Carl Sagan, in his book *Cosmos* (1980), says that humans are the product of burnt-out stars. We are one of the many results of the evolution of the universe. Thus, the primordial energy of the fireball is the energy of all life. That same energy of the fireball is acting in the present evolution of the universe. Our universe as well as ourselves are time-developmental beings. Our present planet is the result of the evolution of the stars. We know that this process has occurred but we do not know exactly how this has come about. We can also say that the same energy that evolved in the stars has through time come to wear a human face (Swimme and Berry 1992).

What then do we mean when we say that the universe is an *interacting* and *genetically* related community of beings? When we say that the universe is an *interacting community*, we are attesting to the reality that the universe is an integral reality, all the elements of which are mutually present to one another through space and time. When we say that there is a mutual presence with every other part, we are talking about a mutuality of action (interaction). This mutual presence of each element to every other element can be in the present (i.e. simultaneously or spatially) or be a mutual presence that reveals itself over time. The idea of a temporal unfolding brings into the picture a mutual presence that has an evolutionary dimension that reveals a time-irreversible genetic sequence. This genetic process is also a testimony to the integral relatedness of the universe. Swimme and Berry (1992) see the story of the universe as an integral story, not just a string of occurrences through time. They note that in the human eye we have present the elementary particles that stabilized in the fireball; we have the elemental creations of the supernova; we have the molecular architecture of the early organisms. Thus, when we open our eyes and capture light, we are employing a procedure nearly identical to that invented by the plants to capture sunlight. The molecules of our eyes act simi-

larly to the molecules of the plant leaf because our molecular structures derived from theirs. Their contention is that all past acts of intelligence are
layered into present reality. In a similar vein, we may also say that the planet
earth is an integral unity where each being of the planet is implicated in the
existence and functioning of every other being of the planet. We now understand the planet as a self-regulating unity in which there is a "web of life" that
can only be understood as a totality. There is an incredibly intricate mystery
that links everything to everything else on the planet. As humans, we are influenced by the tiniest organisms that are present on the earth from the beginnings of the planet. Simultaneously we are having a profound effect on the
presence of all other beings on the earth. The intricate unity of all life processes on earth is characterized by Elisabet Sahtouris as a dance:

> The word "evolution" when used in talking about human dancing means the
> changing pattern of steps in any particular dance. A dance thus evolves when its
> step patterns change into new ones as the dance goes on. In exactly this sense,
> the evolution of Gaia's dance—Earth life—is changing patterns of steps in the
> interwoven self-organization of creatures and their habitats over time. . . . This,
> then is Gaia's dance—the endless improvisation and elaboration of elegantly
> simple steps into the awesomely beautiful and complex being of which we are
> the newest feature. (Sahtouris 1989: 74)

Thus, the unity of all beings on the planet exists not only in the present but
also in evolutionary time. As a species on this earth we are not the dance,
rather we are a part of the mysterious dance of all life.

Pre-eminent Metaphor.   This dance brings us to a consideration of the
pre-eminent metaphor for the ecozoic vision that I am about to develop. The
metaphor is what is frequently referred to in ecological circles as the "web of
life" or in the native traditions as the "circle of life." Here, we humans are not
seen as apart from the natural world as in the "mechanistic viewpoint" (the
progressive technozoic vision) or at the top of an evolutionary hierarchy as
when the human body is used to signal human pre-eminence by putting the
human as the head and brains of the evolutionary hierarchy (the conservative
vision). The "web of life" is an integral metaphor where life processes are seen
as a seamless whole. In the web we have a deep-rooted sense of the symbiotic
relationship of all living things with the human playing an integral but not
pre-emptive role in evolutionary significance. Native cultures have used a
term similar to the "web": the "circle of life." The significance of the circle is
that all beings exist within it and no one particular being has pre-eminence.
Within the "circle of life" there is a view that life must be understood in cycles. The cycles exist in sacred rather than secular time that melds the present
with the past and future. For example, vision quests and dreams for native
peoples reflect journeys back and forth between past and future.

View of Conflict. It is hard to ignore aspects of violence at all levels of the universe as we know it. The basic terms in cosmology, geology, biology, anthropology, sociology and psychology carry a heavy charge of tension and violence. Neither the universe as a whole nor any part of the universe is especially peaceful (T. Berry 1988).

Life emerges and advances by the struggle of the species for complete life expression. Humans have made their way amid the harshness of the natural world and have imposed their violence on the natural world. Among themselves, humans have experienced unending conflict. An enormous psychic effort has been required to articulate the human mode of being in its full imaginative, emotional and intellectual qualities, a psychic effort that emerges from and gives expression to that dramatic confrontation of forces that shape the universe. Thomas Berry (1988) notes that confrontation may give rise to the "tears of things" as described by Virgil, but the creative function would be difficult to ignore.

With the advent of the human, a new violence was released on the planet (T. Berry 1988). But if in prior ages the violence of the natural world in the larger arc of its unfolding could be considered benign, the violence associated with human presence on the planet remains ambivalent in its ultimate consequences. Creativity is associated with a disequilibrium, a tension of forces whether this be in the physical, biological or consciousness context. If these tensions often result in destructive moments in the planetary process, these moments have ultimately been transformed in some creative context. As human power over the total process has increased, however, and the spontaneities of nature have been suppressed or extinguished, the proper functioning of the planet has become increasingly dependent on human wisdom and human decision. The dependence began with human intrusion into the natural functioning of the land, that is, with agriculture and the control of water through irrigation. Since then a conquest mentality has been generated coextensive with the civilizational process. The conquest of the earth and its functioning was extended to the conquest of people and their lands. The sectioning of the earth and its human inhabitants is the dominant theme in the story of the planet over these many years, until now more than 160 nation-states have established their identity.

The military–industrial ventures of modern nation-states now wield a destructive power that has changed every phase of earthly existence. We have to understand that we are now facing for the first time the fact that the planet has become capable of self-destruction in many of its major life systems through human agency, or that at least it has become capable of causing a violent and irreversible alteration of its chemical and biological constitution such as has not taken place since the original shaping of the earth occurred. Thus, while we reflect on the turmoil of the universe in its emergent process, we must also understand the splendor that finds expression amid this sequence of catastrophic events, splendor that set the context for the emergent human age. This period of the human in its modern form that began perhaps 60,000 years ago, after some 2 million years of transitional human types, roughly coincides with the last glacial advance and recession. With the advent of the human, a new violence was released on the planet. Within human consciousness, terror becomes aware of itself. Born of a conviction that the world can be shaped in such a way that oneself or one's group can be finally protected from violence (T. Berry 1988), humans create enormous and monstrous violence without redeeming value—violence without creativity, destruction without integration. We are now amply aware that "whenever creativity is impeded, the ultimate result is not simply the absence of creativity, but an actual positive presence of destructiveness" (T. Berry 1988: 218). We are contending with these forces at the present moment, and we see in this creative hiatus the ancient tension between chaos and order (Briggs and Peat 1989). Our response must be both creative and definitive. We have not been this way before, and we will not be here at this creative moment again. This is the time-developmental context of conflict and creativity.

Contemporary Educational Trends.   We have not been this way before and thus it will be the objective of the rest of this book to present a positive blueprint for an "ecozoic education." An ecozoic vision can nevertheless suggest some trends in recent educational practice that will give a sense of emerging directions. My colleagues at the Transformative Learning Centre at OISE/UT are doing groundbreaking work to forge this vision in the area of adult education (Clover, Follen and Hall 1998). The educational vision that is suggested points to a profoundly holistic and integral education that moves beyond mechanistic atomism. A mechanistic map of the universe is no longer helpful to our understanding of how the world works. However much we compartmentalize for practical purposes, everything, in the final analysis, is woven into a multi-layered, multi-dimensional web of interaction and significance (Pike and Selby 1988). At its foundation, we may speak of universe education; an education that identifies with the emergent universe in its variety of manifestations from the beginning until now. In this broad context our conception of knowledge is synthetic and holistic. In contrast to the mechanistic principle of analysis that postulates the whole as the sum of its parts, a synthetic holism suggests that the whole is a holistic educational paradigm and holds that all things are part of an indivisible unity or whole (Miller 1996). In addition, this holistic perspective is time-developmental in nature. We see in holism that events are viewed dynamically and are systematically connected in time and space. Thus a holistic paradigm is an outlook that considers that all events can be seen from an evolutionary viewpoint. This is what we mean when we say that we act in a time-developmental universe. It is also a perspective that does not consider that knowledge can exist apart from the

431

physical world. Thought is part and parcel of the natural world since human life is embedded in nature. We would say that human thought is nature's way of reflecting on itself. Thus holistic education within our perspective includes within it *earth education*. By *earth education* we do not mean education about the earth, but the earth as the immediate self-educating community of those living and non-living beings that constitute the earth. With some of the above distinctions in mind we now go on to consider the sensitivities that must be developed within an integral and holistic frame of reference.

BIBLIOGRAPHY

Abbey, Edward. 1982. *Down the River*. New York: Dutton.

Abram, David. 1996. *The Spell of the Sensuous*. New York: Vintage Books.

Adams, Henry. 1931 (1918). *The Education of Henry Adams*. New York: Random House-Modern Library.

Adelson, Ann. 1995. *Now What? Developing Our Future*. Ph D Dissertation. University of Toronto.

Apple, Michael. 1979. *Ideology and the Curriculum*. London: Routledge and Kegan Paul.

Aronowitz, Stanley and Henry Giroux. 1991. *Postmodern Education*. Minneapolis: University of Minnesota Press.

— 1993. *Education Still Under Siege*. Toronto: OISE Press.

Barnet, Richard. 1993. 'The End of Jobs.' *Harper's Magazine* (September): 18–24.

Barnet, R. and John Cavanagh. 1994. *Global Dreams: Imperial Corporations and the New World Order*. Toronto: Simon and Schuster.

Basic Call to Consciousness: Akwesasne Notes. 1978. Rooseveltown, NY: Mohawk Nation.

Bateson, Gregory. 1972. *Steps in an Ecology of Mind*. New York: Ballantine.

— 1980. *Mind in Nature: A Necessary Unity*. New York: Bantam.

Bellah, R. 1985. *Habits of the Heart*. New York: Harper and Row/Perennial Library.

Berman, Morris. 1981. *The Reenchantment of the World*. Ithaca, NY: Cornell University Press.

— 1989. *Coming to Our Senses: Body and Spirit in the Hidden History of the West*. New York: Bantam.

Bernanos, Georges. 1937. *Diary of a Country Priest*. New York: Macmillan.

Berry, Thomas. 1988. *The Dream of the Earth*. San Francisco: Sierra Club Books.

— 1989. 'Twelve Principles for Understanding the Universe and the Role of the Human in the Universe.' *Teilhard Perspective* 22. 1 (July): 1–3.

— 1991. *Befriending the Earth: A Theology of Reconciliation Between Humans and the Earth*. Mystic, CT: Twenty-Third Publications.

— 1993. 'A Moment of Grace: The Terminal Decade of the Twentieth Century.' Madan Handa Memorial Lecture, Toronto.

Berry Wendell. 1978. *Home Economics*. San Francisco: North Point Press.

Bertell, Rosalie. 1985. *No Immediate Danger. Prognosis for a Radioactive Earth*. Toronto: Women's Educational Press.

Bhabha, Homi. 1990. 'The Other Question: Difference, Discrimination and the Discourse of Colonialism.' In *Out There: Marginalization and Contemporary Culture*, ed. Russell Ferguson, Martha Gever, Trinh Minh-Ha and Cornell West. Cambridge, MA: MIT Press.

Bickmore, Kathy. 1997. 'Teaching Conflict Resolution.' *Theory Into Practice* 36. 1 (Winter): 3–10.

Bloom, Alan. 1987. *The Closing of the American Mind*. New York: Simon and Schuster.

Bohm, David. 1988. 'Postmodern Science in a Postmodern World.' In *The Reenchantment of Science: Postmodern Proposals,* ed. David Griffin. New York: State University of New York Press.

Bohm, David and David Peat. 1987. *Science, Order and Creativity.* Toronto: Bantam.

Bottomore, T. (ed.) 1983. *A Dictionary of Marxist Thought.* Cambridge, MA: Harvard University Press.

Bourdieu, T. and J. C. Passeron. 1977. *Reproduction in Education, Society and Culture.* Beverly Hills, CA: Sage Publications.

Bowers, C. A. 1993a. *Critical Essays on Education, Modernity, and the Recovery of the Ecological Imperative.* New York: Teachers' College/Colombia Press.

— 1993b. *Education, Cultural Myths, and the Ecological Crisis.* Albany, NY: State University of New York Press.

Bowles, Samuel and Herbert Gintis. 1976. *Schooling in Capitalist America.* New York: Basic Books.

Brenes-Castro, Abelardo. 1988. *Declaration of Human Responsibilities for Peace and Sustainable Development.* Costa Rica: University of Peace.

— (ed.). 1996. *Una Experiencia Pionera: Programa Cultura de Paz y Demoicracia en America Central.* Costa Rica: University of Peace.

Briggs, John and David Peat. 1989. *Turbulent Mirror: An Illustrated Guide to Chaos Theory and the Science of Wholeness.* New York: Harper and Row.

Brown, Lester R. et. al. (eds). 1988. *State of the World, 1988: A Worldwatch Institute Report on Progress Toward a Sustainable Society.* New York: W. W. Norton.

— 1990. *State of the World, 1990: A Worldwatch Institute Report on Progress Toward a Sustainable Society.* New York: W. W. Norton.

— 1991. *State of the World, 1991: A Worldwatch Institute Report on Progress Toward a Sustainable Society.* New York: W. W. Norton.

— 1996. *State of the World, 1996: A Worldwatch Institute Report on Progress Toward a Sustainable Society.* New York: W. W. Norton.

Brown Jr, Tom. 1988. *The Vision.* New York: Berkeley Books.

Brundtland, H. 1987. *Our Common Future: The World Commission on Environment and Development.* Oxford: Oxford University Press.

Burger, Julian (ed.). 1990. *The Gaia Atlas of First Peoples.* New York: Anchor.

— 1993. 'An International Agenda.' In *State of the Peoples: A Global Human Rights Report on Societies in Danger,* ed. Marc Miller et al. Boston: Beacon Press.

Campbell, Joseph. 1988. *The Power of Myth.* New York: Doubleday.

Capra, Fritjof. 1983. *The Turning Point.* New York: Simon and Schuster.

Carson, Rachel. 1962. *Silent Spring.* Cambridge, MA: Riverside Press.

Chomsky Noam. 1989a. *Necessary Illusions.* Montreal: CBC Publications.

— 1989b. *The Washington Connection and Third World Fascism.* Montreal: Black Rose Press.

— 1997. *Media Control: The Spiritual Achievement of Propaganda.* New York: Several Stories Press.

Clarke, Tony. 1997. *Silent Coup: Confronting the Big Business Takeover of Canada.* Toronto: James Lorimer and Co.

Clarke, Tony and Maude Barlow. 1997. *MAI: The Multilateral Agreement on Investment and the Threat to Canadian Sovereignty.* Toronto: Stoddart.

Clay, Jason. 1993. 'Looking Back to Go Forward: Predicting and Preventing Human Rights Violations.' In *State of the Peoples: A Global Human Rights Report on Societies in Danger,* ed. Marc Miller et al. Boston: Beacon Press.

Clover, Darlene, Shirley Follen and Budd Hall. 1998. *The Nature of Transformation: Environmental Adult and Popular Education.* Toronto: University of Toronto Press.

Cobb, Edith. 1977. *The Ecology of Imagination in Childhood.* New York: Colombia University Press.

Cockburn, Alexander. 1994. 'Beat The Devil.' *The Nation* 1, 3: 405.

Cohn, Carol. 1987. 'In the Rational World of Defense Intellectuals.' *Signs* 12, 4.

Collins, Michael. 1991. *Adult Education as Vocation: A Critical Role for the Adult Educator.* New York: Routledge.

—— 1995. 'Critical Commentaries on the Role of Adult Educators.' In *In Defense of the Life World: Critical Perspectives on Adult Learning*, ed. Michael Welton. Albany, NY: SUNY Press.

Connell, Robert, D. Kessler, G. W. Dowsett and G. W. Ashenden. 1983. *Making the Difference: Schools, Families and Social Division.* Boston: George Allen and Unwin.

Cox, R. W. 1991. 'The Global Political Economy and Social Choice.' In *The New Era of Social Competition: State Policy and Market Power*, ed. D. Drache and M. Gertler. Montreal: McGill-Queens University Press.

Cremin, Lawrence. 1964. *The Transformation of The School.* New York: Vintage.

—— 1976. *Traditions of American Education.* New York: Basic Books.

Csikszentmihali, Mihaly. 1990. *Flow: The Psychology of Optimal Experience.* New York: Harper Perennial.

—— 1993. *The Evolving Self: A Psychology For The Third Millennium.* New York: Harper Perennial.

—— 1997. *Finding Flow: The Psychology of Engagement with Everyday Life.* New York: Basic Books.

Cushman, Phillip. 1990. 'Why is the Self Empty: Toward a Historically Situated Psychology.' *American Psychologist* 45, 5: 599–610.

Dalai Lama. 1982. *Essence of Refined Gold.* Ithaca, NY: Snow Lion Publications.

—— 1996. *The Good Heart: A Buddhist Perspective on the Teachings of Jesus.* Boston: Wisdom Publications.

Dale, Roger and Geoff Esland (eds.). 1976. *Schooling and Capitalism: A Sociological Reader.* London: Routledge and Kegan Paul.

Daly, Herman E. 1973. *Toward a Steady-State Economy.* San Francisco: Freeman.

Daly, Herman E. and John Cobb. 1989. *For the Common Good: Redirecting the Economy Toward Community, the Environment, and a Sustainable Development.* Boston: Beacon Press.

Davies, Paul. 1984. *God and the New Physics.* London: Penguin Books.

Dawson, Christopher. 1956. *The Dynamics of World History.* New York: Sheed and Ward.

de Chardin, Teilhard. 1959. *The Phenomenon of Man.* New York: Harper Torchbacks.

Dei, George. 1994. 'Anti-Racist Education: Working Across Differences.' *Orbit* 25, 2.

—— 1995a. *Drop Out or Push Out? The Dynamics of Black Students' Disengagement from School: A Report.* Toronto: Ontario Institute for Studies in Education.

—— 1995b. 'Indigenous Knowledge as an Empowerment Tool.' In *Empowerment: Towards Sustainable Development*, ed. N. Singh and V. Titi. Toronto: Fernwood.

—— 1996. *Anti-Racism Education: Theory and Practice.* Halifax, Nova Scotia: Fernwood.

de Lone, Richard. 1979. *Small Futures: Children, Inequality, and the Limits of Liberal Reform.* New York: Harcourt Brace Jovanovich.

Devall, Bill. 1988. *Simple in Means, Rich in Ends.* Salt Lake City: Peregrine Smith.

Devall, Bill and George Sessions. 1985. *Deep Ecology: Living as if Nature Mattered.* Salt Lake City: Peregrine Smith.

Devereux, Paul. 1996. *Re-Visioning the Earth: A Guide to Opening the Healing Channels Between Mind and Nature.* New York: Simon and Schuster.

Dewey, John. 1963. 'What Psychology Can Do For the Teacher.' In *John Dewey on Education: Selected Writings*, ed. R. Archambault. New York: Random House.

—— 1966. *Democracy and Education.* New York: Free Press.

Dialogue: Newsletter of the University of Peace. 1996. San Jose, Costa Rica: Peace University.

Diamond, Irene and A. Ornstein. 1990. *Reweaving the World: The Emergence of Ecofeminism.* San Francisco: Sierra Club Books.

Dillard, Annie. 1974. *Pilgrim at Tinker Creek.* New York: Harper and Row.

— 1983. *Teaching a Stone to Talk: Expeditions and Encounters.* New York: Harper and Row.

Distress Signals. 1986. Video. Director, John Waler. National Film Board of Canada (17 December).

Durning, Alan. 1991. 'Asking How Much is Enough?' In S*tate of the World, 1991: A Worldwatch Institute Report on Progress Toward a Sustainable Society,* ed. Lester R. Brown et al. New York: W. W. Norton.

— 1992. *How Much is Enough: The Consumer Society and the Future of the Earth.* New York: W. W. Norton.

Dyson, Freeman. 1985. *Weapons and Hope.* New York: Harper Colophon.

Ehrlich, Paul R. and Anne H. Ehrlich. 1981. *Extinction: The Causes and Consequences of the Disappearance of Species.* New York: Random House.

Eiseley, Loren. 1960. *The Immense Journey.* New York: Random House.

— 1972. *The Unexpected Universe.* New York: Harcourt Brace Jovanovich.

— 1978. *The Star Thrower.* New York: Times Books.

Eisler, Riane. 1988. *The Chalice and the Blade: Our History, Our Future.* San Francisco: Harper and Row.

— 1995. *Sacred Pleasure: Sex, Myth, and the Politics of the Body.* San Francisco: Harper San Francisco.

Eisler, Riane and David Loye. 1990. *The Partnership Way.* San Francisco: Harper and Row.

Ekins, Paul Hillman. 1992. *The Gaia Atlas of Green Economics.* Toronto: Anchor Books.

Eliade, Mircea. 1959. *Cosmos and History: The Myth of the Eternal Return.* New York: Harper Torchbooks.

Eliot, T. S. 1969. *The Complete Poems and Plays of T. S. Eliot.* London: Faber and Faber.

Ellul, Jaques. 1964. *The Technological Society.* New York: Vintage/Random House.

Environmental Education for Sustainable Societies and Global Responsibility. 1993. Environmental Education Treaty. Brazil.

Epp-Tiessen, Ester. 1990. 'Project Ploughshares.' Working Paper. Waterloo, Ontario.

Evereet-Green, Robert. 1997. 'Arts, Not IBM, Makes Kids Smarter.' *Toronto Star* (17 November).

Evernden, Neil. 1985. *The Natural Alien.* Toronto: University of Toronto Press.

Ewen, Stuart. 1976. *Captains of Consciousness: Advertising and the Social Roots of the Consumer Culture.* New York: McGraw Hill.

Fiske, John. 1978. *Reading Television.* London: Methuen.

Foley, Gruff. 1993. *Adult Education and Capitalist Reorganization.* Sydney, Australia: University of Technology

Fox, Matthew. 1983. *Original Blessing: A Primer in Creation Spirituality.* Santa Fe: Bear and Co.

— 1988. *The Coming of the Cosmic Christ.* San Francisco: Harper and Row.

— 1991. *Creation Spirituality.* San Francisco: Harper San Francisco.

Fox, Stephen. 1981. *John Muir and His Legacy: The American Conservation Movement.* Boston: Little, Brown.

Fox, Warwick. 1990. *Toward Transpersonal Ecology.* Boston: Shambhala.

Freire, Paulo. 1970. *The Pedagogy of the Oppressed.* New York: Seabury Press.

French, Marilyn. 1992. *The War Against Women.* Toronto: Summit.

Frye, Marilyn. 1983. *The Politics of Reality.* Freedom, CA: Crossing Press.

Galtung, Johann. 1982. *Environment, Development, and Military Activity.* Oslo: Universitetsforlaget.

Gare, Arran. 1995. *Postmodernism and the Environmental Crisis.* New York: Routledge.

Gayton, Don (ed.). 1996. *Landscapes of the Interior: Re-Explorations of Nature and the Human Spirit.* Gabriola Island, BC: New Society Publishers.

Georgescu-Roegen, Nicholas. 1971. *The Entrophy Law and the Economic Process.* Cambridge, MA: Harvard University Press.

Gerbner, George. 1970. 'Cultural Indicators: The Case of Violence in Television Drama.' *Annals of the American Association of Political and Social Science,* 338, 23.

Giddens, Anthony. 1990. *The Consequences of Modernity.* Stanford, CA: Stanford University Press.

— 1991. *Modernity and Self Identity: Self and Society in the Late Modern Age.* Stanford, CA: Stanford University Press.

— 1994. *Beyond Left and Right: The Future of Radical Politics.* Stanford, CA: Stanford University Press.

Gimbutas, Marija. 1974. *The Gods and Goddesses of Old Europe, 7000 to 3500 B.C.: Myths, Legends, and Cult Images.* London and Berkeley, CA: Thames and Hudson and University of California Press.

Ginsberg, Morris. 1973. 'Progress in the Modern Era.' In *Dictionary of the History of Ideas,* ed. Philip Wiener. New York: Charles Scribner and Sons: 633–50.

Gioseffi, Daniela (ed.). 1993. *On Prejudice: A Global Perspective.* New York: Anchor Books.

Glendinning, Chellis. 1995. *My Name is Chellis and I'm Recovering from Western Civilization.* Boston: Shambhala.

Goldson, Rose. 1977. *The Show and Tell Machine.* New York: Delta.

Gourevitch, Philip. 1995. 'Rwanda: A Case of Genocide.' *New Yorker* (March): 41–84.

Gramsci, Antonio. 1971. *Selections from Prison Notebooks.* New York: International Publishers.

Grant, George. 1983. *Modernity and Responsibility.* Toronto: University of Toronto Press.

Graveline, Fyre Jean. 1998. *Circle Works: Transforming Eurocentric Consciousness.* Halifax, Nova Scotia: Fernwood.

Griffin, David (ed.). 1988a. *The Reenchantment of Science: Postmodern Proposals.* New York: SUNY Press.

— (ed.). 1988b. *Spirituality and Society: Postmodern Visions.* New York: SUNY Press.

— (ed.). 1990. *Sacred Interconnections.* Albany, NY: State University of New York Press.

Griffin, Susan. 1978. *Woman and Nature: The Roaring Inside Her.* New York: Harper and Row.

— 1995. *The Eros of Everyday Life.* New York: Doubleday.

Grof, Stanislav. 1985. *Beyond the Brain.* Albany, NY: State University of New York Press.

Gutierrez, G. 1973. *A Theology of Liberation.* Marynoll, NY: Orbis Books.

Hall, Budd. 1996. 'Adult Education, Globalization and the Development of Global Civil Society.' World Congress of Comparative Education.

Hall, Budd and Edmund V. O'Sullivan. 1995. 'Transformative Learning: Contexts and Practices.' In *Empowerment: Toward Sustainable Development,* ed. N. Singh and V. Titi. Toronto: Fernwood.

Handa, Madan. 1982. *Manifesto for a Peaceful World Order: A Gandhian Perspective.* Toronto: Cosmic Way Publications.

Haraway, Donna. 1991. *Simians, Cyborgs and Women: The Reinvention of Nature.* New York: Routledge.

Harman, Willis. 1988. *Global Mind Change: The Promise of the Last Years of the Twentieth Century.* Indianapolis: Knowledge Systems Inc.

Hart, Mechhthild. 1995. 'Working and Education for Life.' In *Defense of the Life World: Critical Perspectives on Adult Learning,* ed. Michael Welton. Albany, NY: SUNY Press.

Henderson, Hazel. 1992. *Creating Alternative Futures.* Boston: Perigrine Books.

Herman, Edward and Noam Chomsky. 1988. *Manufacturing of Consent.* New York: Pantheon Books.

Herman, Judith. 1992. *Trauma and Recovery: The Aftermath of Violence from Domestic Abuse and Political Terror.* New York: Basic Books.

Heyward, Carter. 1989. *Touching Our Strength.* San Francisco: Harper.

Hillman, James. 1996. *The Soul's Code: In Search of Character and Calling.* New York: Random House.

Hofstadter, Richard. 1955. *Social Darwinism in American Thought.* New York: George Braziller.

Holland, Joe and Peter Henriot. 1984. *Social Analysis: Linking Faith and Social Justice.* Washington, DC: Orbis.

hooks, bell. 1994. *Teaching to Transgress.* New York: Routledge.

Hopkins, Gerard Manley. 1959. *The Journals and Papers of Gerard Manley Hopkins.* Toronto: Oxford University Press.

Hurtig, M. 1991. *The Betrayal of Canada.* Toronto: Stoddart.

Hutchins, Robert Maynard. 1959. *A General Introduction to the Great Books and to a Liberal Education.* Toronto: Encyclopaedia Britannica.

Hutchinson, David. 1998. *Growing Up Greedy.* New York: Teachers College Press.

Isla, Ana. 1996. 'Downplaying Ecological Stress: Debt-for-Nature Swaps.' Unpublished MS. Toronto.

Jantsch, Erich. 1984. *The Self-Organizing Universe: Scientific and Human Implications of the Emerging Paradigm of Evolution.* New York: Pergamon Press.

Jensen, Derrick. 1996. 'Listening to the Land.' In *Landscapes of the Interior: Re-Explorations of Nature and the Human Spirit,* ed. Don Gayton. Gabriola Island, British Colombia: New Society Publishers.

Kaplan, Robert D. 1994. 'The Coming of Anarchy.' *Atlantic Monthly* (February): 44–76.

Katz, Michael. 1968. *The Irony of Early School Reform.* Cambridge, MA: Harvard University Press.

Kaufman, Michael. 1997. 'Working with Young Men to End Sexism.' *Orbit* 28, 1: 14–17.

Keen, Sam. 1994. *Hymns to an Unknown God.* New York: Bantam.

Kelley, Kevin (ed.). 1988. *The Home Planet.* Don Mills, Ontario: Addison-Wesley.

Kennedy, Paul. 1993. *Preparing for the Twenty-First Century.* New York: Harper.

Knowles, Malcolm. 1986. *Using Learning Contracts: Practical Approaches to Individualizing and Structuring Learning.* San Francisco: Jossey-Bass.

Knudston, Peter and David Suzuki. 1992. *The Wisdom of Elders.* Toronto: Stoddart.

Korten, D. 1991. 'People Centered Development: An Alternative for a World in Crisis.' People Centered Development Forum, Manila, Philippines.

— 1995. *When Corporations Rule the World.* West Hartford, CT: Kumarian Press.

Kothari, Rajni. 1988. *Transformation and Survival: In Search of Humane World Order.* Delhi: Ajanta Publications.

Kropotkin, P. 1895. *Mutual Aid.* Brighton: Horizon Press.

La Chapelle, Dolores. 1988. *Sacred Land, Sacred Sex, Rapture of the Deep: Concerning Deep Ecology and Celebrating Life.* Silverton, CO: Fine Hill Arts.

Larkin, June. 1997. 'Confronting Sexual Harassment in Schools.' *Orbit* 28, 1.

Lasch, Christopher. 1978. *The Culture of Narcissism.* New York: W. W. Norton.

— 1989. 'Progress: The Last Superstition.' *Tikkun* 4, 3 (May/June): 27–30.

Latouche, Serge. 1993. *In the Wake of the Affluent Society: An Exploration of Post Development.* London: Zed Books.

Leopold, Aldo. 1949. *A Sand County Almanac.* New York: Oxford University Press.

Lerner, Michael. 1994. *Jewish Renewals: A Path to Healing and Transformation.* New York: Grosset/Putnam.

— 1996. *The Politics of Meaning.* Reading, MA: Addison-Wesley.

Lewy, Guenter. 1974. *Religion and Revolution.* New York: Oxford University Press.

Lifton, Robert Jay. 1993. *The Protean Self.* New York: Basic Books.

Livingstone, David (ed.). 1987. *Critical Pedagogy and Cultural Power.* South Hadley, MA: Bergin and Garvey.

Lopez, Barry Holstun. 1986. *Arctic Dreams.* New York: Charles Scribner and Sons.

Lorde, Audre. 1978. *The Uses of the Erotic: The Erotic as Power.* New York: Out and Out Books.

— 1990. 'Age, Race, Class, and Sex: Women Redefining Difference.' In *Out There: Marginalization and Contemporary Culture,* ed. Russell Ferguson, Martha Gever, Trinh Minh-Ha and Cornell West. Cambridge, MA: MIT Press.

Lovelock, James E. 1979. *Gaia: A New Look at Life on Earth.* New York: Oxford University Press.

— 1987. *Gaia: A Model for Planetary and Cellular Survival.* Boston, MA: Lindisfarne Press.

— 1988. *The Ages of Gaia: A Biography of Our Living Earth.* Boston, MA: Lindisfarne Press.

Lynn, Marion and Eimear O'Neill. 1995. 'Families, Power, and Violence.' In *Canadian Families: Diversity, Conflict, and Change,* ed. Ann Duffy and Mancy Mandell. Toronto: Harcourt Brace: 271–305.

Lyons, Thomas and Edmund V. O'Sullivan. (1992). 'Educating for a Global Perspective.' *Orbit* 1.

McDermott, R. (ed.). 1987. *The Essential Aurobindo.* Rochester, VT: Inner Tradition/Lindisfarne Press.

McGaa, Ed Eagle Man. 1990. *Mother Earth Spirituality: Native American Paths to Healing Ourselves and Our World.* San Francisco: Harper San Francisco.

McKibben, Bill. 1989. *The End of Nature.* New York: Random House.

MacMurray, John. 1957. *The Self as Agent.* London: Faber and Faber.

— *Persons in Relation.* 1961. London: Faber and Faber.

McPhail, Thomas. 1981. *Electronic Colonialism.* Beverly Hills, CA: Sage Publications.

Macy, Joanna. 1983. *Despair and Power in the Nuclear Age.* Philadelphia: New Society Publishers.

— 1989. 'Awakening to the Ecological Self.' In *Healing the Wounds,* ed. Judith Plant. Toronto: Between the Lines.

— 1991. *World as Lover, World as Self.* Berkeley, CA: Parallax Press.

Maitreya. 1988. *The Gospel of Peace.* Toronto: Universal Way Publications.

Mander, Jerry. 1991. *In the Absence of the Sacred: The Failure of Technology and the Survival of Indian Nations.* San Francisco: Sierra Club Books.

Mander, Jerry and Edward Goldsmith. 1996. *The Case Against the Global Economy.* San Francisco: Sierra Club Books.

Margulis, Lynn. 1987. *Microcosmos: Four Billion Years of Evolution from Our Microbial Ancestors.* London: George Allen and Unwin.

Margulis, Lynn and Karlene Schwartz. 1982. *Five Kingdoms: An Illustrated Guide to the Phyla of Life on Earth.* San Francisco: Freeman.

Mason, Mike. 1997. *Development and Disorder: A History of the Third World Since 1945.* Toronto: Between the Lines.

Max-Neef, Manfred E. A. and Martin Hopenhayen. 1989. 'Another Development: Human Scale Development.' *Development Dialogue* 1: 17–61.

Meizerow, Jack. 1995. 'Transformation Theory of Adult Learning.' In *Defense of the Life World: Critical Perspectives on Adult Learning,* ed. Michael Welton. Albany, NY: SUNY Press.

Menzies, Heather. 1989. *Fast Forward: How Technology is Changing Your Life.* Toronto: Macmillan of Canada.

Merchant, Carolyn. 1980. *The Death of Nature: Women, Ecology, and the Scientific Revolution.* New York: Harper and Row.

— 1995. *Earthcare.* New York: Routledge.

Merton, Thomas. 1967. *Mystics and Zen Masters.* New York: Delta Books.

— 1973. *The Asian Journals of Thomas Merton.* New York: New Directions Publication.

Metzner, Ralph. 1993. 'The Split Between Spirit and Nature in European Consciousness.' *Trumpeter* 10, 1.

Mies, Maria. 1986. *Patriarchy and Accumulation on a World Scale: Women in the International Division of Labor.* London: Zed Books.

Mies, Maria and Vandana Shiva. 1993. *Ecofeminism.* Halifax, Nova Scotia: Fernwood.

Milbrath, Lester W. 1989. *Envisioning a Sustainable Society: Learning Our Way Out.* Albany, NY: State University of New York Press.

Miles, Angela. 1996. *Integrative Feminisms: Building Global Visions.* New York: Routledge.

Miller, John. 1994. *The Contemplative Practitioner.* Toronto: OISE Press.

— 1996. *The Holistic Curriculum: Revised and Expanded Edition.* Toronto: OISE Press.

Miller, R. (ed.). 1993. *The Renewal of Meaning in Education.* Brandon, VT: Holistic Education Press.

Mitter, Swasti. 1986. *Common Fate Common Bond: Women in the Global Economy.* London: Pluto Press.

Mische, Patricia. 1989. 'Ecological Security in an Interdependent World.' *Breakthrough: A Publication of Global Education Associates* 1 (4) Summer–Fall.

Moffett, J. 1994. *The Universal Schoolhouse.* San Francisco: Jossey-Bass.

Montessori, Maria. 1973. *The Education of the Human Potential.* Madras, India: Kalakshetra Publications.

Moore, Thomas. 1992. *Care of the Soul.* New York: HarperCollins.

— 1994. *Soul Mates: Honoring the Mysteries of Love and Relationship.* New York: HarperCollins.

Mumford, Lewis. 1961. *The City in History: Its Origins, Its Transformations, and Its Prospects.* New York: Harcourt, Brace, and World.

Myers, Norman (ed.). 1984. *Gaia: An Atlas of Planet Management.* Garden City, NY: Anchor/ Doubleday.

Neisser, Ulric. 1967. *Cognitive Psychology.* New York: Appleton Century Crofts.

Nelson, Joyce. 1989. *Sultans of Sleaze.* Toronto: Between the Lines.

Nethardt, John G. 1972. *Black Elk Speaks: Being the Life Story of a Holy Man of the Oglala Sioux.* New York: Washington Square Press.

New Internationalist. 1990. 'The Poor Step Up Trade Wars.' 294 (February).

— 1991. 'Test Tube Coup: Biotechs Global Takeover.' 217 (March).

— 1992. 230 (April).

— 1997. 'Gene dream.' 293 (August).

Noble, David. 1977. *America by Design: Science, Technology, and the Rise of Corporate Capitalism.* New York: Oxford University Press.

— 1992. *A World Without Women: The Christian Clerical Culture of Western Science.* New York: Oxford University Press.

Nozick, Marcia. 1992. *No Place Like Home.* Ottawa: Canadian Council of Social Development.

Oliver, Donald W. and Kathleen Waldron Gershman. 1989. *Education, Modernity and Fractured Meaning: Toward a Process Theory of Teaching and Learning.* Albany, NY: State University of New York Press.

Oliver, Mary. 1992. *New and Selected Poems.* Boston: Beacon Press.

O'Neill, Eimear. 1998. 'From Global Economies to Local Cuts: Globalization and Structural Change in Our Own Backyard.' In *Confronting the Cuts: A Sourcebook for Women in Ontario,* ed. L. Ricciutelli, J. Larkin and E. O'Neill. Toronto: Inanna Publications and Education Inc.: 3–11.

Ornstein, Robert and Paul Ehrlich. 1989. *New World New Mind.* New York: Simon and Schuster.

Orr, David W. 1992. *Ecological Literacy: Education and the Transition to a Postmodern World.* Albany, NY: State University of New York Press.

Ortega y Gasset, José. 1957. *The Revolt of the Masses.* New York: W. W. Norton.

O'Sullivan, Edmund. 1980. 'Can Values Be Taught?' In *Moral Development and Socialization,* ed. E. Turiel. Boston: Allyn and Bacon.

— 1983. 'Computers, Culture and Educational Futures: A Critical Appraisal.' *Interchange* 4, 3 (Winter): 17–26.

— 1984. *Critical Psychology: An Interpretation of the Personal World.* New York: Plenum Press.

— 1985. 'Computers, Culture and Educational Futures: A Meditation on Mindstorms.' *Interchange* 16, 3 (Fall): 1–18.

— 1990. *Critical Psychology and Critical Pedagogy.* New York: Bergin and Garvey.

Otto, Rudolph. 1969. *The Idea of the Holy.* New York: Oxford University Press.

Palmer, Parker. 1993. *To Know as We are Known.* San Francisco: Harper and Row.

Paz, Octavio. 1995. *The Double Flame: Love and Eroticism.* New York: Harcourt Brace and Co.

Peterson, Scott. 1990. *Native American Prophesies: Examining the History, Wisdom and Startling Predictions of Visionary Native Americans.* New York: Paragon House.

Phillips, Charles. 1957. *The Development of Education in Canada.* Toronto: W. J. Gage and Co.

Pierce, Carol Wagner. 1994. *A Male/Female Continuum: Paths to Colleagueship.* Lacona, NH: New Dynamics Publications.

Pike, Graham and David Selby. 1988. *Global Teacher, Global Learner.* Toronto: Hodder and Stoughton.

Plant, Judith (ed.). 1989. *Healing the Wounds.* Toronto: Between the Lines.

Postel, Sandra. 1992. 'Denial in a Decisive Decade.' In *State of the World, 1992: A Worldwatch Institute Report on Progress Toward a Sustainable Society,* ed. Lester R. Brown et al. New York: W. W. Norton.

Prigogine, Ilya and Isabelle Stengers. 1984. *Order Out of Chaos: Man's New Dialogue with Nature.* New York: Bantam.

The Progress of Nations. 1997. New York: UNICEF.

Purpel, David. 1989. *The Moral and Spiritual Crisis in Education: A Curriculum for Justice and Compassion in Education.* Grangy, MA: Bergin and Garvey.

Quarter, Jack. 1992. *Canada's Social Economy.* Toronto: James Lorimer and Co.

Quarter, Jack and Fred Matthews. 1987. 'Back to the Basics.' In *Critical Pedagogy and Cultural Power,* ed. David Livingstone. Massachusetts: Bergin and Garvey: 99–119.

Ransom, David. 1992. 'Green Justice.' *New Internationalist* 30 (April).

Reed, Carole Ann. 1994. 'The Omission of Anti-Semitism in Anti-Racism.' *Canadian Woman Studies/les cahiers de la femme* 14, 2 (Spring): 68–71.

Regehr, E. 1996. 'Weapons and War: Arms Trade Control as Conflict Resolution.' *Project Ploughshares Monitor* (September).

Renner, Michael. 1991. 'Assessing the Military's War on the Environment.' In *State of the World, 1991: A Worldwatch Institute Report on Progress Toward a Sustainable Society,* ed. Lester R. Brown. New York: W. W. Norton.

Rifkin, Jeremy. 1981. *Entropy.* New York: Viking.

— 1991. *Biosphere Politics: A New Consciousness for a New Century.* New York: Crown.

— 1995. *The End of Work.* New York: Jeremy Tarcher/Putnam Books.

Rifkin, Jeremy and Nicanor Perlas. 1983. *Algeny.* New York: Viking.

Roberts, W. Bacher. 1993. *Get a Life: A Green Cure For Canada's Economic Blues.* Toronto: Get A Life Publishing House.

Roman, Leslie and Linda Eyre (eds.). 1997. *Dangerous Territories: Struggles for Difference and Equality.* London: Routledge.

Rosen, Edward. 1973. 'Cosmology from Antiquity to 1850.' In *Dictionary of the History of Ideas,* ed. Philip Wiener. New York: Charles Scribner and Sons.

Ross, Rupert. 1996. *Returning to the Teachings.* Toronto: Penguin Books.

Roszak, T. 1978. *Person/Plant: The Creative Disintegration of Industrial Society.* Garden City, NY: Doubleday.

Rowledge, D. and L. Keeth. 1991. 'We've Gotta Have It: Economic Growth as an Addiction.' *Environment Network News:* 3–5.

Runes, D. 1955. *The Dictionary of Philosophy.* New Jersey: Littlefield Adams.

Russell, Peter. 1983. *The Global Brain.* Los Angeles: J. P. Tarcher.

Ryan, J. C. 1992. 'Conserving Biological Diversity.' In *State of the World, 1992: A Worldwatch Institute Report on Progress Toward a Sustainable Society,* ed. Lester R. Brown. New York: W. W. Norton.

Sachs, Wolfgang. 1992. 'Development.' *New Internationalist* 202.

Sagan, Carl. 1980. *Cosmos.* New York: Random House.

Sahtouris, Elisabet. 1989. *Gaia: The Human Journey from Chaos to Cosmos.* New York: Pocket Books Collophon.

Said, Edward. 1979. *Orientalism.* New York: Vintage Books.

— 1993. *Culture and Imperialism.* New York: Alfred A. Knopf.

Sale, Kirkpatrick. 1980. *Human Scale.* New York: Coward McCann and Geohegan.

— 1985. *Dwellers in the Land: The Bioregional Vision.* San Francisco: Sierra Club Books.

Sardello, Robert. 1994. *Facing the World with Soul: The Reimagination of Modern Life.* New York: HarperCollins.

— 1995. *Love and the Soul: Creating a Future for Earth.* New York: HarperCollins.

Schaef, A. 1987. *When Society Becomes Addict.* San Francisco: Harper and Row.

Schiller, Herbert. 1983. *The World Crisis and the New Information Technologies.* San Diego: Paper.

Schorer, Mark. 1946. *William Blake: The Politics of Vision.* New York: Vintage Books.

Schweickart, Russell. 1988. Preface. In *The Home Planet,* ed. Kevin Kelley. Don Mills, Ontario: Addison-Wesley.

Seager, Joni. 1993. *Earth Follies: Coming to Feminist Terms with the Global Environmental Crisis.* New York: Routledge.

— 1995. *The New State of the Earth Atlas,* 2nd ed. New York: Touchstone.

Seed, John and Joanna Macy. 1988. *Thinking Like a Mountain: Towards a Council of All Beings.* Philadelphia: New Society Publishers.

Selby, D. 1995. *Earthkind: A Teachers' Handbook on Humane Education.* Stoke-on Trent: Trentum.

Sheldrake, Rupert. 1988. *The Presence of the Past: Morphic Resonance and the Habits of Nature.* New York: Times Books.

— 1994. *The Rebirth of Nature and God.* Rochester, VT: Park Street Press.

Shiva, Vandana. 1989. *Staying Alive: Women, Ecology and Development.* London: Zed Books.

— 1992. 'Global Bullies: Tread Gently on the Earth.' *New Internationalist* (April).

— 1995. *Monocultures of the Mind: Perspectives on Biodiversity and Biotechnology.* London: Zed Books.

Sioui, George. 1992. *Amerindian Autohistory: An Essay on the Foundation of a Social Ethic.* Montreal: McGill University Press.

Smart, N. 1997. *Dimensions of the Sacred.* London: Fontana.

Smith, Huston. 1992. *Forgotten Truth: The Common Vision of the World's Religions.* New York: Harper.

Smith, James. 1993. 'Foreword.' *New Internationalist* 308.

Spretnak, Charlene. 1978. *The Spiritual Dimension of Green Politics.* Santa Fe: Bear and Co.

— 1991. *States of Grace: The Recovery of Meaning in the Postmodern Age.* San Francisco: Harper and Row.

Starhawk. 1979. *The Spiral Dance: A Rebirth of the Ancient Religion of the Great Goddess.* San Francisco: Harper and Row.

— 1997. *The Pagan Book of Living and Dying.* San Francisco: Harper San Francisco.

Stone, Merlin. 1976. *When God Was a Woman.* New York: Harvest.

Storm, Hyemeyohsts. 1972. *Seven Arrows.* New York: Ballantine.

Storr, Anthony. 1988. *Solitude.* London: Fontana.

Suzuki, David and Peter Knudston. 1988. *Genethics: The Ethics of Engineering Life.* Toronto: Stoddart.

Swimme, Brian. 1984. *The Universe is a Green Dragon: A Cosmic Creation Story.* Santa Fe, NM: Bear and Co.

— 1996. *The Hidden Heart of the Cosmos.* Marynoll, New York: Orbis Books.

Swimme, Brian and Thomas Berry. 1992. *The Universe Story: An Autobiography from Planet Earth.* San Francisco: Harper and Row.

Taylor, Charles. 1991. *The Malaise of Modernity.* Toronto: Anansi.

'Test Tube Coup: Biotech's Global Takeover.' 1991. *New Internationalist* 217 (March).

Thich Nhat Hanh. 1992. *Touching Peace: Practicing the Art of Mindful Living.* Berkeley, CA: Parallax Press.

— 1994. *A Joyful Path: Community Transformation and Peace.* Berkeley, CA: Parallax Press.

— 1996. *Breathe! You Are Alive.* Berkeley, CA: Parallax Press.

Thomas, Lewis. 1975. *The Lives of a Cell: Notes of a Biology Watcher.* New York: Bantam.

— 1980. *The Medusa and the Snail: More Notes of a Biology Watcher.* New York: Bantam.

— 1984. *Late Night Thoughts on Listening to Mahler's Ninth Symphony.* New York: Bantam.

Thompson, William Irvin. 1987. *Gaia: A Way of Knowing.* Barrington, MA: Lindisfarne Press.

Tough, Alan. 1981. *Learning Without a Teacher.* Toronto: OISE Press.

Toulmin, Stephen. 1985. *The Return to Cosmology.* Berkeley, CA: University of California Press.

Turk, Jim. 1992. 'Training is the Answer.' In *Training for What? Labour Perspectives on Job Training,* ed. Nancy Jackson. Toronto: Our Schools/Ourselves Foundation.

Turner, Frederick. 1980. *Beyond Geography: The Western Spirit Against the Wilderness.* New York: Viking Press.

Unger, Roberto Mangabeira. 1975. *Knowledge and Politics.* New York: Free Press.

Wackernagel, M. and W. Rees. 1996. *Our Ecological Footprint: Reducing Human Impact on the Earth.* Gabriola Island, BC: New Society Publishers.

Walker, Alice. 1997. *Anything We Love Can be Saved: A Writer's Activism.* New York: Random House.

Wangoola, Paul and Frank Youngman. 1996. *Towards A Transformative Political Economy of Adult Education.* De Kalb, IL: Northern Illinois Press.

Waring, Marilyn. 1988. *If Women Counted: A New Feminist Economics.* San Francisco: Harper and Row.

Weber, Max, 1958. *The Spirit of Capitalism and the Protestant Ethic.* New York: Charles Scribner and Sons.

Weil, Andrew. 1997. *8 Weeks to Optimum Health.* New York: Alfred A. Knopf.

Welton, M. 1995. 'In Defense of the Lifeworld.' In *Defense of the Life World: Critical Perspectives on Adult Learning,* ed. Michael Welton. Albany, NY: SUNY Press.

Wexler, Philip. 1996. *Holy Sparks: Social Theory, Education and Religion.* Toronto: Canadian Scholar Press.

Wiener, Philip (ed.). 1973. *Dictionary of the History of Ideas.* New York: Charles Scribner and Sons.

Wilber, Ken. 1995. *Sex, Ecology, Spirituality: The Spirit of Evolution.* Boston: Shambhala.

— 1996. *A Brief History of Everything.* Boston: Shambhala.

— 1997. *The Eye of the Spirit: An Integral Vision for a World Gone Slightly Mad.* Boston: Shambhala.

Williams, Raymond. 1976. *Key Words: A Vocabulary of Culture and Society.* London: Fontana.

Willoya, William. 1962. *Warriors of the Rainbow: Strange and Prophetic Dreams of the Indian Peoples.* Happy Camp, CA: Naturegraph Publishers.

Wishik, Heather and Carol Pierce. 1995. *Sexual Orientation and Identity.* Lacona, NH: New Dynamics.

Wolf, E. C. 1988. 'Avoiding a Mass Extinction of Species.' In *State of the World, 1988: A Worldwatch Institute Report on Progress Toward a Sustainable Society,* eds. Lester R. Brown et al. New York: W. W. Norton.

Wolf, Sandra. 1994. *Engendering Equity: Transforming Curriculum.* Toronto: Ministry of Education of Ontario.

World Guide 1997/1998: Alternative Reference to Countries of the Planet. 1997. World of Women, Instituto Del Tercer Mundo.

Worster, Donald. 1977. *Nature's Economy: A History of Ecological Ideas.* Cambridge: Cambridge University Press.

Wynne, Edward. 1987. 'Managing Effective Schools: The Moral Element.' In *Educational Policy for Effective Schools,* ed. Mark Holmes. Toronto: OISE Press.

Yeats, William Butler. 1983. 'The Second Coming.' In *Modern Poetry,* ed. Maynard Mack. New York: New American Library.

Young, Louise. 1983. *The Blue Planet: A Celebration of the Earth.* New York: New American Library.

Zarate, Jose. 1994 'Racism and Indigeneous Education.' *Orbit* 25, 2.

26

▼▼▼▼▼▼▼

Identity in the Globalizing World*

Zygmunt Bauman

"There has been a veritable discursive explosion in recent years around the concept of 'identity,' " observed Stuart Hall in the introduction to a volume of studies published in 1996.[1] A few years have passed since that observation was made, during which the explosion has triggered an avalanche. No other aspect of contemporary life, it seems, attracts the same amount of attention these days from philosophers, social scientists and psychologists. It is not just that "identity studies" are fast becoming a thriving industry in their own right; more than that is happening—one may say that "identity" has now become a prism through which other topical aspects of contemporary life are spotted, grasped and examined. Established issues of social analysis are being rehashed and refurbished to fit the discourse now rotating around the "identity" axis. For instance, the discussion of justice and equality tends to be conducted in terms of "recognition," culture is debated in terms of individual, group or categorial difference, creolization and hybridity, while the political process is ever more often theorized around the issues of human rights (that is, the right to a separate identity) and of "life politics" (that is, identity construction, negotiation and assertion).

I suggest that the spectacular rise of the "identity discourse" can tell us more about the present-day state of human society than its conceptual and analytical results have told us thus far. And so, rather than composing an-

other "career report" of contentions and controversies which combine into
that discourse, I intend to focus on the tracing of the experiential grounds,
and through them the structural roots, of that remarkable shift in intellectual
concerns of which the new centrality of the "identity discourse" is a most salient symptom.

We know from Hegel that the owl of Minerva, the goddess of wisdom,
spreads its wings, prudently, at dusk; knowledge, or whatever passes under
that name, arrives by the end of the day when the sun has set and things are
no longer brightly lit and easily found and handled (long before Hegel coined
the tarrying-owl metaphor, Sophocles made clarity of sight into the monop-
oly of blind Teiresias). Martin Heidegger gave a new twist to Hegel's apho-
rism in his discussion of the priority of *Zuhandenheit* over *Vorhandenheit* and
of the "catastrophic" origin of the second: good lighting is the true blind-
ness—one does not see what is all-too-visible, one does not note what is "always there," things are noticed when they disappear or go bust, they must
first fall out from the routinely "given" for the search after their essences to
start and the questions about their origin, whereabouts, use or value to be
asked. In Arland Ussher's succinct summary, "The world as world is only revealed to me when things go wrong."[2] Or, in Vincent Vycinas's rendition,[3]
whatever my world consists of is brought to my attention only when it goes
missing, or when it suddenly stops behaving as, monotonously, it did before,
loses its usefulness or shows itself to be "unready" for my attempts to use it. It
is the awkward and unwieldy, unreliable, resistant and otherwise *frustrating*
things that force themselves into our vision, attention and thought.

Let us note that the discovery that things do not keep their shape once and
for all and may be different from what they are is an ambiguous experience.
Unpredictability breeds anxiety and fear: the world is full of accidents and
surprises, one must never let vigilance lapse and should never lay down arms.
But the unsteadiness, softness and pliability of things may also trigger ambition and resolve: one can make things better than they are, and need not settle
for what there is since no verdict of nature is final, no resistance of reality is
unbreakable. One can now dream of a different life—more decent, bearable
or enjoyable. And if in addition one has confidence in one's power of thought
and in the strength of one's muscles, one can also act on those dreams and
perhaps even force them to come true . . . Alain Peyrefitte has suggested that
the remarkable, unprecedented and unique dynamism of our modern capitalist society, all the spectacular advances made by "Western civilization" over
the last two or three centuries, would be unthinkable without such confidence: the triple trust—in oneself,[4] in others, and in the jointly built, durable
institutions in which one can confidently inscribe one's long-term plans and
actions.

Anxiety and audacity, fear and courage, despair and hope are born together. But the proportion in which they are mixed depends on the resources

in one's possession. Owners of foolproof vessels and skilled navigators view the sea as the site of exciting adventure; those condemned to unsound and hazardous dinghies would rather hide behind breakwaters and think of sailing with trepidation. Fears and joys emanating from the instability of things are distributed highly unequally.

Modernity, we may say, specialized in making *zuhanden* things into *vorhanden*. By "setting the world in motion," it exposed the fragility and unsteadiness of things and threw open the possibility (and the need) of reshaping them. Marx and Engels praised the capitalists, the bourgeois revolutionaries, for "melting the solids and profaning the sacreds" which had for long centuries cramped human creative powers. Alexis de Tocqueville thought rather that the solids picked for melting in the heat of modernization were already in a state of advanced decomposition and so beyond salvation well before the modern overhaul of nature and society started. Whichever was the case, human nature, once seen as a lasting and not to be revoked legacy of one-off Divine creation, was thrown, together with the rest of Divine creation, into a melting pot. No more was it seen, no more could it be seen, as "given." Instead, it turned into a *task*, and a task which every man and woman had no choice but to face up to and perform to the best of their ability. "Predestination" was replaced with "life project," fate with vocation—and a "human nature" into which one was born was replaced with "identity" which one needs to saw up and make fit.

Philosophers of the Renaissance celebrated the new breathtaking vistas that the "unfinishedness" of human nature opened up before the resourceful and the bold. "Men can do all things if they will," declared Leon Battista Alberti with pride. "We can become what we will," announced Pico della Mirandola with joy and relish. Ovid's Proteus—who could turn at will from a young man into a lion, a wild boar or a snake, a stone or a tree—and the chameleon, that grandmaster of instant reincarnation, became the paragons of the newly discovered human virtue of self-constitution and self-assertion.[5] A few decades later Jean-Jacques Rousseau would name *perfectibility* as the sole no-choice attribute with which nature had endowed the human race; he would insist that the capacity of self-transformation is the only "human essence" and the only trait common to us all.[6] Humans are free to self-create. What they are does not depend on a no-appeal-allowed verdict of Providence, is not a matter of predestination.

Which did not mean necessarily that humans are doomed to float and drift: Proteus may be a symbol of the potency of self-creation, but protean existence is not necessarily the first choice of free human beings. Solids may be melted, but they are melted in order to mold new solids better shaped and better fitted for human happiness than the old ones—but also more solid and so more "certain" than the old solids managed to be. Melting the solids was to be but the preliminary, site-clearing stage of the modern undertaking to make the world more suitable for human habitation. Designing a new—tough, durable, reliable and trustworthy—setting for human life was to be the second stage, a stage that truly counted since it was to give meaning to the whole enterprise. One order needed to be dismantled so that it could be replaced with another, purpose-built and up to the standards of reason and logic.

As Immanuel Kant insisted, we all—each one of us—are endowed with the faculty of reason, that powerful tool which allows us to compare the options on offer and make our individual choices; but if we use that tool properly, we will all arrive at similar conclusions and will all accept one code of cohabitation which reason tells us is the best. Not all thinkers would be as sanguine as Kant was: not all were sure that each one of us would follow the guidance of reason of their own accord. Perhaps people need to be forced to be free, as Rousseau suspected? Perhaps the newly acquired freedom needs to be used *for* the people rather than *by* people? Perhaps we still need the despots, though ones who are "enlightened" and so less erratic, more resolute and effective than the despots of yore, to design and fix reason-dictated patterns which would guarantee that people make right and proper uses of their freedom? Both suppositions sounded plausible and both had their enthusiasts, prophets and preachers. The idea of human self-construction and self-assertion carried, as it were, the seeds of democracy mixed with the spores of totalitarianism. The new era of flexible realities and freedom of choice was to be pregnant with unlikely twins: with human rights—but also with what Hannah Arendt called "totalitarian temptation."

These comments are on the face of it unrelated to our theme; if I made them here, I did it with the intention of showing that the ostensible unrelatedness is but an illusion, if not a grave mistake. Incompleteness of identity, and particularly the individual responsibility for its completion, are in fact intimately related to all other aspects of the modern condition. However it has been posited in our times and however it presents itself in our reflections, "identity" is not a "private matter" and a "private worry." That our individuality is socially produced is by now a trivial truth; but the obverse of that truth still needs to be repeated more often: the shape of our sociality, and so of the society we share, depends in its turn on the way in which the task of "individualization" is framed and responded to.

What the idea of "individualization" carries is the emancipation of the individual from the ascribed, inherited and inborn determination of his or her social character: a departure rightly seen as a most conspicuous and seminal feature of the modern condition. To put it in a nutshell, "individualization" consists in transforming human "identity" from a "given" into a "task"—and charging the actors with the responsibility for performing that task and for the consequences (also the side-effects) of their performance; in other words, it consists in establishing a "de jure" autonomy (though not necessarily a *de facto* one). One's place in society, one's "social definition," has ceased to be *zuhanden* and become *vorhanden* instead. One's place in society no longer comes as a (wanted or unwanted) gift. (As Jean-Paul Sartre famously put it: it is not enough to be born a bourgeois—one must live one's life as a bourgeois. The same did not need to be said, and could not be said, about princes, knights, serfs or townsmen of the premodern era.) Needing to *become* what one *is* is the feature of modern living (not of "modern individualization"— that expression being evidently pleonastic; to speak of individualization and of modernity is to speak of the same social condition). Modernity replaces the *determination* of social standing with a compulsive and obligatory *self*-determination.

This, let me repeat, holds for the whole of the modern era: for all periods and for all sectors of society. If so—then why has "the veritable explosion" of concerns with identity occurred in recent years only? What, if anything, happened that was new to affect a problem as old as modernity itself?

Yes, there is something new in the old problem—and this explains the current alarm about the tasks which past generations seemed to handle routinely in a "matter-of-fact" way. Within the shared predicament of identity-builders there are significant variations setting successive periods of modern history apart from each other. The "self-identification" task put before men and women once the stiff frames of estates had been broken in the early modern era boiled down to the challenge of living "true to kind" ("keeping up with the Joneses"): of actively conforming to the established social types and models of conduct, of imitating, following the pattern, "acculturating," not falling out of step, not deviating from the norm. The falling apart of "estates" did not set individuals drifting. "Estates" came to be replaced by "classes."

While the estates were a matter of ascription, class membership entailed a large measure of achievement; classes, unlike the estates, had to be "joined," and the membership had to be continuously renewed, reconfirmed and documented in day-by-day conduct. In other words, the "disembedded" individuals were prompted and prodded to deploy their new powers and new right to self-determination in the frantic search for "re-embeddedness." And there was no shortage of "beds" waiting and ready to accommodate them. Class allocation, though formed and negotiable rather than inherited or simply "born into" in the way the *estates*, *Stände* or *états* used to be, tended to become as solid, unalterable and resistant to individual manipulation as the premodern assignment to the estate. Class and gender hung heavily over the individual range of choices; to escape their constraint was not much easier than challenging one's place in the "divine chain of beings." If not in theory, then at least for *practical* intents and purposes, class and gender looked uncannily like "facts of nature" and the task left to most self-assertive individuals was to "fit in" into the allocated niche through behaving as its established residents did.

This is, precisely, what distinguished the "individualization" of yore from the form it has taken now, in our own times of "liquid" modernity, when not just the individual *placements* in society, but the *places* to which the individuals may gain access and in which they may wish to settle are melting fast and can hardly serve as targets for "life projects." This new restlessness and fragility of goals affects us all, unskilled and skilled, uneducated and educated, work-shy and hard-working alike. There is little or nothing we can do to "bind the future" through following diligently the current standards.

As Daniel Cohen has pointed out, "Qui débute sa carrière chez Microsoft n'a aucune idée de là où il la terminera. La commencer chez Ford ou Renault s'était au contraire la quasi-certitude de la finir au même endroit."[7] It is not just the individuals who are on the move but also the finishing lines of the tracks they run and the running tracks themselves. "Disembeddedness" is now an experience which is likely to be repeated an unknown number of times in the course of an individual life since few if any "beds" for "re-embedding" look solid enough to augur the stability of long occupation. The "beds" in view look rather like "musical chairs" of various sizes and styles as well as of changing numbers and mobile positions, forcing men and women to be constantly on the run, promising no rest and none of the satisfaction of "arriving," none of the comfort of reaching the destination where one can lay down one's arms, relax and stop worrying. There is no prospect of a "final re-embeddedness" at the end of the road; being on the road has become the permanent way of life of the (now chronically) disembedded individuals.

Writing at the beginning of the twentieth century, Max Weber suggested that "instrumental rationality" is the main factor regulating human behavior in the era of modernity—perhaps the only one likely to emerge unscathed from the battle of motivational forces. The matter of ends seemed then to have been settled, and the remaining task of modern men and women was to select the best means to the ends. One could say that uncertainty as to the relative efficiency of means and their availability would be, as long as Weber's proposition held true, the main source of insecurity and anxiety characteristic of modern life. I suggest, though, that whether or not Weber's view was correct at the start of the twentieth century, its truth gradually yet relentlessly evaporated as the century drew to its close. Nowadays, it is not the *means* that are the prime source of insecurity and anxiety.

The twentieth century excelled in the overproduction of means; means have been produced at a constantly accelerating speed, overtaking the known, let alone acutely felt, needs. Abundant means came to seek the ends which they could serve; it was the turn of the solutions to search desperately for not-yet-articulated problems which they could resolve. On the other hand, though, the ends have become ever more diffuse, scattered and uncertain: the most profuse source of anxiety, the great unknown of men's and women's lives. If you look for a short, sharp yet apt and poignant expression of that new predicament in which people tend to find themselves these days, you could do worse than remember a small ad published recently in the "jobs sought" column of an English daily: "Have car, can travel; awaiting proposi-tions."

And so the "problem of identity," haunting men and women since the ad-vent of modern times, has changed its shape and content. It used to be the kind of problem which pilgrims confront and struggle to resolve: a problem of "how to get there?" It is now more like a problem with which the vaga-bonds, people without fixed addresses and *sans papiers*, struggle daily: "Where could I, or should I, go? And where will this road I've taken bring me?" The task is no longer to muster enough strength and determination to proceed, through trials and errors, triumphs and defeats, along the beaten track stretching ahead. The task is to pick the least risky turn at the nearest crossroads, to change direction before the road ahead gets impassable or be-fore the road scheme has been redesigned, or before the coveted destination is moved elsewhere or has lost its past glitter. In other words, the quandary tor-menting men and women at the turn of the century is not so much how to ob-tain the identities of their choice and how to have them recognized by people around—but *which* identity to choose and how to keep alert and vigilant so that *another* choice can be made in case the previously chosen identity is with-drawn from the market or stripped of its seductive powers. The main, the most nerve-wracking worry is not how to find a place inside a solid frame of social class or category, and—having found it—how to guard it and avoid eviction; what makes one worry is the suspicion that the hard-won frame will soon be torn apart or melted.

In his by now classic statement of about forty years ago, Erik H. Erikson di-agnosed the confusion suffered by the adolescents of that time as "identity cri-sis" (a term first coined during the war to describe the condition of some men-tal patients who "lost a sense of personal sameness and historical continuity"). "Identity crisis" in adults, as Erikson put it, is a pathological condition which requires medical intervention; it is also a common yet passing stage in "nor-mal" personal development, which in all probability will come to its natural end as an adolescent matures. To the question of what the healthy state of a person should be, "what identity feels like when you become aware of the fact that you do undoubtedly *have* one," Erikson answered: it makes itself felt "as a *subjective sense* of an *invigorating sameness* and *continuity*."[8]

Either Erikson's opinion has aged, as opinions usually do, or the "identity crisis" has become today more than a rare condition of mental patients or a passing condition of adolescence: that "sameness" and "continuity" are feel-ings seldom experienced nowadays either by the young or by adults. Further-more, they are no longer coveted—and if desired, the dream is as a rule con-taminated with sinister premonitions and fears. As the two prominent cultural analysts Zbyszko Melosik and Tomasz Szkudlarek have pointed out,[9] it is a curse of all identity construction that "I lose my freedom, when I reach the goal; I am not myself, when I become somebody." And in a kaleido-

scopic world of reshuffled values, of moving tracks and melting frames, freedom of maneuver rises to the rank of the topmost value—indeed, the *meta*
value, condition of access to all other values: past, present and above all those
yet to come. Rational conduct in such a world demands that the options, as
many as possible, are kept open, and gaining an identity which fits too
tightly, an identity that once and for all offers "sameness" and "continuity,"
results in the closing of options or forfeiting them in advance. As Christopher
Lasch famously observed, the "identities" sought these days are such as "can
be adopted and discarded like a change of costume"; if they are "freely chosen," the choice "no longer implies commitments and consequences"—and
so "the freedom to choose amounts in practice to an abstention from
choice,"[10] at least, let me add, from a *binding* choice.

In Grenoble in December 1997, Pierre Bourdieu spoke of "précarité," which
"est aujourd'hui partout" and "hante les consciences et les inconscients." The
fragility of all conceivable points of reference and endemic uncertainty about
the future profoundly affect those who have already been hit and all the rest of
us who cannot be certain that future blows will pass us by. "En rendant tout
l'avenir incertain," says Bourdieu, "la précarité interdit toute anticipation
rationnelle et, en particulier, ce minimum de croyance et d'espérance en
l'avenir qu'il faut avoir pour se révolter, surtout collectivement, contre le
présent, même le plus intolérable." "Pour concevoir un projet révolutionnaire,
c'est-à-dire une ambition raisonnée de transformer le présent par référence à un
avenir projeté, il faut avoir un minimum de prise sur le présent"[11]—and the grip
on the present, the confidence of being in control of one's destiny, is what men
and women in our type of society most conspicuously lack. Less and less we
hope that by joining forces and standing arm in arm we may force a change in
the rules of the game; perhaps the risks which make us afraid and the catas-
trophes which make us suffer have collective, social origins—but they seem to
fall upon each one of us at random, as individual problems, of the kind that
could be confronted only individually, and repaired, if at all, only by individual efforts.

There seems to be little point in designing alternative modes of togetherness,
in stretching the imagination to visualize a society better serving the cause of
freedom and security, in drawing blueprints of socially administered justice, if
a collective agency capable of making the words flesh is nowhere in sight. Our
dependencies are now truly global, our actions however are, as before, local.
The powers which shape the conditions under which we confront our problems
are beyond the reach of all the agencies invented by modern democracy in the
two centuries of its history; as Manuel Castells put it—real power, the exterri-
torial global power, flows, but politics, confined now as in the past to the
framework of nation-states, stays as before attached to the ground.

A vicious circle, indeed. The fast globalization of the power network seems
to conspire and collaborate with a privatized life politics; they stimulate, sus-

tain and reinforce each other. If globalization saps the capacity of established political institutions to act effectively, the massive retreat from the "body politic" to the narrow concerns of life politics prevents the crystallization of alternative modes of collective action on a par with the globality of the network of dependencies. Everything seems to be in place to make *both* the globalization of life conditions *and* the "morcellement," the atomization and privatization of life struggles, self-propelling and self-perpetuating. It is against this background that the logic and the endemic illogicality of contemporary "identity concerns" and the actions they trigger needs to be scrutinized and understood.

As Ulrich Beck has pointed out, there are no biographical solutions to systemic contradiction—though it is such solutions that we are pressed or cajoled to discover or invent. There can be no rational response to the rising *précarité* of human conditions so long as such a response is to be confined to the individual's action; the irrationality of possible responses is inescapable, given that the scope of life politics and of the network of forces which determine its conditions are, purely and simply, incomparable and widely disproportionate.

If you cannot, or don't believe you can, do what truly matters, you turn to things which matter less or perhaps not at all, but which you can do or believe you can; and by turning your attention and energy to such things, you may even make them matter—for a time at least ... "Having no hope," says Christopher Lasch,

> of improving their lives in any of the ways that matter, people have convinced themselves that what matters is psychic self-improvement; getting in touch with their feelings, eating health food, taking lessons in ballet or belly-dancing, immersing themselves in the wisdom of the East, jogging, learning how to "relate," overcoming the "fear of pleasure." Harmless in themselves, these pursuits, elevated to a programme and wrapped in the rhetoric of authenticity and awareness, signify a retreat from politics. ...[12]

There is a wide and widening spectrum of "substitute pastimes," symptomatic of the shift from things that matter but about which nothing can be done to things that matter less or do not matter, but which can be dealt with and handled. Compulsive shopping figures prominently among them. Mikhail Bakhtin's "carnivals" used to be celebrated inside the home territory where "routine life" was at other times conducted, and so allowed to lay bare the normally hidden alternatives which daily life contained. Unlike them, the trips to the shopping malls are expeditions to *another world* starkly different from the rest of daily life, to that "elsewhere" where one can experience briefly that self-confidence and "authenticity" which one is seeking in vain in routine daily pursuits. Shopping expeditions fill the void left by the travels no longer undertaken by the imagination to an alternative, more secure, humane and just society.

The time-and-effort-consuming activity of putting together, dismantling and rearranging self-identity is another of the "substitute pastimes." That activity is, as we have already seen, conducted under conditions of acute insecurity: the targets of action are as precarious as its effects are uncertain. Efforts lead to frustration often enough for the fear of ultimate failure to poison the joy of temporary triumphs. No wonder that to dissolve personal fears in the "might of numbers," to try to make them inaudible in the hubbub of a boisterous crowd, is a constant temptation which many a lonely "identity-builder" finds it difficult to resist. Even stronger is the temptation to pretend that it is the similarity of individual fears that "makes a community" and so one can make company out of solitude.

As Eric Hobsbawm recently observed, "never was the word 'community' used more indiscriminately and emptily than in the decades when communities in the sociological sense became hard to find in real life";[13] "Men and women look for groups to which they can belong, certainly and forever, in a world in which all else is moving and shifting, in which nothing else is certain."[14] Jock Young supplies a succinct and poignant gloss: "Just as community collapses, identity is invented."[15] "Identity" owes the attention it attracts and the passions it begets to being a *surrogate of community*: of that allegedly "natural home" which is no longer available in the rapidly privatized and individualized, fast globalizing world, and which for that reason can be safely imagined as a cozy shelter of security and confidence, and as such hotly desired. The paradox, though, is that in order to offer even a modicum of security and so to perform its healing role, identity must belie its origin, must deny being just a surrogate, and best of all needs to conjure up a phantom of the self-same community which it has come to replace. Identity sprouts on the graveyard of communities, but flourishes thanks to its promise to resurrect the dead.

The "era of identity" is full of sound and fury. The search for identity divides and separates; yet the precariousness of the solitary identity-building prompts the identity-builders to seek pegs on which they can hang together their individually experienced fears and anxieties and perform the exorcism rites in the company of others, similarly afraid and anxious individuals. Whether such "peg communities" provide what they are hoped to offer—a collective insurance against individually confronted risks—is a moot question; but mounting a barricade in the company of others does supply a momentary respite from loneliness. Effective or not, something has been done, and one can at least console oneself that the blows are not being taken with hands down. As Jonathan Friedman put it, in our globalizing world "one thing that is not happening is that boundaries are disappearing. Rather, they seem to be erected on every new street corner of every declining neighbourhood of our world."[16]

Boundaries are not drawn to fence off and protect already existing identities. As the great Norwegian anthropologist Frederick Barth explained—it is exactly the other way round: the ostensibly shared, "communal" identities are by-products of feverish boundary-drawing. It is only after the border-posts have been dug in that the myths of their antiquity are spun and the fresh cultural/political origins of identity are carefully covered up by the genesis stories. This stratagem attempts to belie the fact that (to quote Stuart Hall again) what the idea of identity does *not* signal is a "stable core of the self, unfolding from the beginning to end through all the vicissitudes of history without change."[17]

Perhaps instead of talking about identities, inherited or acquired, it would be more in keeping with the realities of the globalizing world to speak of *identification*, a never-ending, always incomplete, unfinished and open-ended activity in which we all, by necessity or by choice, are engaged. There is little chance that the tensions, confrontations and conflicts which that activity generates will subside. The frantic search for identity is not a residue of preglobalization times which are not yet fully extirpated but bound to become extinct as the globalization progresses; it is, on the contrary, the side-effect and by-product of the combination of globalizing and individualizing pressures and the tensions they spawn. The identification wars are neither contrary to nor stand in the way of the globalizing tendency: they are a legitimate offspring and natural companion of globalization and, far from arresting it, lubricate its wheels.

NOTES

1. Stuart Hall, "Who needs 'identity'?", in Stuart Hall and Paul du Gay (eds.), *Questions of Cultural Identity* (London: Sage, 1996), p. 1.

2. Arland Ussher, *Journey through Dread* (New York: Devin-Adair, 1955), p. 80.

3. See Vincent Vycinas, *Earth and Gods* (The Hague: Martinus Nijhoff, 1969), pp. 36–7.

4. See Alain Peyrefitte, *La société de confiance. Essai sur les origines du développement* (Paris: Odile Jacob, 1998), pp. 514–16.

5. See Stevie Davies, *Renaissance View of Man* (Manchester: Manchester University Press, 1978), pp. 62ff.

6. See Jean-Jacques Rousseau, *The First and Second Discourses*, first published in 1749 and 1754, trans. Victor Gourevitch (New York: Harper and Row, 1986), pp. 148ff.

7. Daniel Cohen, *Richesse du monde, pauvretés des nations* (Paris: Flammarion, 1997), p. 84.

8. Erik H. Erikson, *Identity: Youth and Crisis* (London: Faber and Faber, 1974), pp. 17–19.

9. Zbyszko Melosik and Tomasz Szkudlarek, *Kultura, Tozsamosc I Edukacja* (Kraków: Impuls, 1998), p. 89.

10. Christopher Lasch, *The Minimal Self: Psychic Survival in Troubled Times* (London: Pan Books, 1984), p. 38.

11. Pierre Bourdieu, "La précarité est aujourd'hui partout," in *Contrefeux* (Paris: Liber-Raisons d'Agir, 1998), pp. 96–7. Translated as *Acts of Resistance* (Cambridge: Polity Press, 1998).

12. Christopher Lasch, *Culture of Narcissism* (New York: Warner Books, 1979), pp. 29–30.

13. Eric Hobsbawm, *The Age of Extremes* (London: Michael Joseph, 1994), p. 428.

14. Eric Hobsbawm, "The cult of identity politics," *New Left Review* 217 (1996), p. 40.

15. Jock Young, *The Exclusive Society* (London: Sage, 1999), p. 164.

16. Jonathan Friedman, "The hybridization of roots and the abhorrence of the bush," in Mike Featherstone and Scott Lash (eds.), *Spaces of Culture* (London: Sage, 1999), p. 241.

17. "Who needs "identity"?", p. 3.

27

▼▼▼▼▼▼▼

The Transformation of Political Community: Rethinking Democracy in the Context of Globalization*

David Held

In the first section of this chapter—a much shortened version of a chapter published in 1999—Held summarizes the development of modern ideas of the nation-state, the nation-state system and liberal democracy. He contrasts this with previously existing political arrangements in Europe and elsewhere. These possessed greater diversity within political communities, but greater homogeneity across them, although he recognizes this was partly due to the limited geographical extent of politics prior to the expansion of the European empires between the sixteenth and nineteenth centuries.

In Europe from the sixteenth century onward political power became increasingly concentrated within more strictly defined territorial borders. This reduced social, economic and cultural variation within these emerging states but increased diversity among them. By the eighteenth century this had become formalized in notions of territorially-defined sovereignty, initially embodied in the monarch, and emerging "national" identities highlighting shared features such as history, culture and language that united the people of one state and distinguished them from the people of other states. Alongside state-formation, the states system developed in a symbiotic relationship. Often seen as being enshrined in the Peace of Westphalia (1648), the "Westphalian system" culminated in ideas of sovereignty, sovereign equality among states, non-intervention in domestic affairs and states' consent as the basis of legal obligation becoming widely accepted principles. Within these confines, competing national interests, often resolved via war, rendered cooperation difficult and dangerous. Power and security were essential goals of foreign policy but ones that could only be acquired at the expense of others, ensuring confrontation and competition.

This framework of domestically centralized and homogeneous states coexisting in an international environment without central authority and where war is common and legitimate had a major effect on the development of democracy. The eighteenth-century advent of representative democracy—whereby people exercise democratic authority and accountability through elected representatives rather than direct participation—made democracy practical in these new, large states. Questions about who could participate in elections and other democratic practices were answered by reference to the state: those within its borders and sharing in a common identity were the democratic constituency. As importantly, politics in the states system identified members of other states as potential enemies and threats to security, thus justifying their exclusion from democratic processes. The hardening lines on the map that defined the limits of sovereignty neatly defined the state, the nation and the demos—those entitled to democratic representation and those to whom politicians are accountable. Those living in other states were different—"foreign"—and justifiably excluded.

Held concludes thus . . .

Accordingly, the heart or "deep structure" of the system of democratic nation states can be characterized by a number of striking features, which are, broadly: democracy in nation-states and non-democratic relations among states; the entrenchment of accountability and democratic legitimacy inside state boundaries and pursuit of reasons of state (and maximum political advantage) outside such boundaries; democracy and citizenship rights for those regarded as "insiders," and the frequent negation of these rights for those beyond their borders.

CHANGING FORMS OF REGIONAL AND GLOBAL ENMESHMENT

At the center of the dominant theoretical approaches to democratic politics is an uncritically appropriated concept of the territorial political community. The difficulty with this is that political communities have rarely—if ever—existed in isolation as bounded geographical totalities; they are better thought of as multiple overlapping networks of interaction. These networks crystallize around different sites and forms of power—economic, political, military, cultural, among others—producing diverse patterns of activity which do not correspond in any simple and straightforward way to territorial boundaries (Mann 1986: ch. 1).

The term "globalization" captures some of the changes which shape the nature of the political and the prospect of political community; unpacking the term helps create a framework for addressing some of the issues raised above. Globalization can be understood, I believe, in relation to a set of processes which shift the spatial form of human organization and activity to transcontinental or interregional patterns of activity, interaction and the exercise of power (see Held et al. 1999). It involves a stretching and deepening of social relations and institutions across space and time such that, on the one hand, day-to-day activities are increasingly influenced by events happening on the other side of the globe and, on the other, the practices and decisions of local groups or communities can have significant global reverberations (Giddens 1990). It is possible to distinguish different historical forms of globalization in terms of: (1) the extensiveness of networks of relations and connections; (2) the intensity of flows and levels of activity within these networks; and (3) the impact of these phenomena on particular bounded communities. It is not a case of saying, as many do, that there was once no globalization, but there is now; rather, it is a case of recognizing that forms of globalization have changed over time and that these can be systematically understood by reference to points 1–3 above. Such an historical approach to globalization contrasts with the current fashion to suggest either that globalization is fundamentally new—the "hyper-globalization school," with its insistence that global markets are now fully established (Ohmae 1990); or that there is nothing unprecedented about contemporary levels of international economic and social interaction since they resemble those of the gold standard era—the "skeptical school" (Hirst and Thompson 1996).

From the foundation of the International Telegraph Union in 1865, a plethora of international organizations developed with responsibility for regulating and ordering diverse domains of activity including trade, industrial infrastructure, agriculture, labor, public order and administration, elements of individual rights, health and research. At issue was not the creation of a single institution or authority to manage world affairs but rather the establishment of regulatory regimes for, in principle, the predictable and orderly conduct of pressing transnational processes. By 1914 many aspects of global affairs had been brought within the terms of these offices and rule systems. Accordingly, a new infrastructure for the regulations and control of economic, social and cultural affairs was slowly founded, stimulating telegrams, letters and packages to flood the international networks by the beginning of the twentieth century (Murphy 1994: ch. 2–3).

Virtually all countries in the world became enmeshed in and functionally part of a larger pattern of global flows and global transformations (Nierop 1994: 171). Goods, capital, people, knowledge, communications and weapons, as well as crime, culture, pollutants, fashions and beliefs, readily moved across territorial boundaries (McGrew 1992). Transnational networks, social movements and relationships extended through virtually all areas of human activity. The existence of interregional systems of trade, finance and production bound together the prosperity and fate of households, communities and nations across the world. Far from this being a world of "discrete civilizations," it became a fundamentally interconnected global order, marked by dense patterns of exchange as well as by power, hierarchy and unevenness.

Against this background, the meaning and place of political community, and particularly of the democratic political community, needs to be reexamined. At least two tasks are necessary in order to pursue this objective. First, it is important to illustrate some of the fundamental alterations in the patterns of interconnectedness among political communities and the subsequent shifts in the structure and form of political community itself. Second, it is important to set out some of the political implications of these changes.

1. Among the significant developments which are changing the nature of political community are global economic processes, especially growth in trade, production, and financial transactions, organized in part by rapidly expanding multinational companies. Trade has grown substantially, reaching unprecedented levels, particularly in the post-Second World War period.

Underpinning this economic shift has been the growth of multinational corporations, both productive and financial. Approximately 20,000 multinational corporations now account for a quarter to a third of world output, 70 per cent of world trade and 80 per cent of foreign direct investment. They are essential to the diffusion of skills and technology, and they are key players in the international money markets. In addition, multinational corporations can have profound effects on macroeconomic policy. They can respond to variations in interest rates by raising finance in whichever capital market is most favorable. They can shift their demand for employment to countries with much lower employment costs. And in the area of industrial policy, especially technology policy, they can move activities to where the maximum benefits accrue.

Although the rhetoric of hyper-globalization has provided many an elected politician with a conceptual resource for refusing political responsibility, globalization has significant and discernible characteristics which alter the balance of resources—economic and political—within and across borders. Among the most important of these is the tangible growth in the enmeshment of national economies in global economic transactions (that is, a growing proportion of nearly all national economies is involved in international economic exchanges with an increasing number of countries). As a result, the autonomy of democratically elected governments has been, and is increasingly, constrained by sources of unelected and unrepresentative economic power.

2. Within the realms of the media and culture there are also grounds for thinking that there is a growing disjuncture between the idea of the demo-

cratic state as an independent, accountable center of power bounded by fixed borders—in this case, a center of national culture, able to foster and sustain a national identity—and interlinked changes in the spheres of media and cultural exchange. A number of developments in recent times can be highlighted. English has spread as the dominant language of elite cultures throughout the world: it is now the dominant language in business, computing, law, science and politics. The internationalization and globalization of telecommunications had been extraordinarily rapid: international telephone traffic has increased more than fourfold between 1983 and 1995; there has been a massive increase in transnational cable links; there has been an explosion in satellite links; and the Internet has provided a remarkable increase in the infrastructure of horizontal and lateral communication capacity within and across borders. Moreover, substantial multimedia conglomerates have developed, such as the Murdoch empire and Time Warner. In addition, there has been a huge increase in tourism—for example, in 1960 there were 70 million international tourists, while in 1994 there were nearly 500 million. And in television and in film there are similar trends.

3. Environmental problems and challenges are perhaps the clearest and starkest examples of the global shift in human organization and activity, creating some of the most fundamental pressures on the efficacy of the nation-state and state-centric democratic politics. There are three types of problems at issue:

(i) The first is shared problems involving the global commons, that is, fundamental elements of the ecosystem—among the most significant challenges are global warming and ozone depletion;

(ii) A second category of global environmental problems involves the interlinked challenges of demographic expansion and resource consumption—pressing examples under this heading include desertification, questions of biodiversity, and threats to the existence of certain species;

(iii) A third category of problems is transboundary pollution such as acid rain, or river pollutants, or the contaminated rain which fell in connection with Chernobyl.

In response to the progressive development of, and publicity surrounding, environmental problems in the last three decades, there has been an interlinked process of cultural and political globalization as illustrated by the emergence of new cultural, scientific and intellectual networks; new environmental movements with transnational organizations and transnational concerns; and new institutions and conventions such as those agreed on in 1992 at the Earth Summit in Brazil. Not all environmental problems are, of course, global; such an implication would be entirely false. But there has been a striking shift in the physical and environmental conditions—that is, in the extent and intensity of environmental problems—affecting human affairs in general. These processes have moved politics dramatically away from an activity which crystallizes first and foremost around state and interstate concerns. It is clearer than ever that the fortunes of political communities and peoples can no longer be simply understood in exclusively national or territorial terms.

4. Changes in the development of international law have placed individuals, governments and non-governmental organizations under new systems of legal regulation. International law recognizes powers and constraints, and rights and duties, which have qualified the principle of state sovereignty in a number of important respects; sovereignty *per se* is no longer a straightforward guarantee of international legitimacy. Entrenched in certain legal instruments is the view that a legitimate state must be a democratic state that upholds certain common values (Crawford 1994). One significant area in this regard is human rights law and human rights regimes.

5. While all the developments described so far have helped engender a shift away from a purely state-centered international system of "high politics" to new and novel forms of geogovernance, a further interesting example of this process can be drawn from the very heart of the idea of a sovereign state—national security and defense policy. There has been a notable increase in emphasis upon cooperative security. Indeed, even in this realm, any conception of sovereignty and autonomy which assumes that they denote an indivisible, illimitable, exclusive and perpetual form of public power—embodied within an individual state—is increasingly challenged and eroded.

DEMOCRACY AND GLOBALIZATION: IN SUM

At the end of the second millennium, as indicated previously, political communities and civilizations can no longer be characterized simply as "discrete worlds"; they are enmeshed and entrenched in complex structures of overlapping forces, relations and movements. Clearly, these are often structured and hierarchical but even the most powerful among them—including the most powerful nation-states—do not remain unaffected by the changing conditions and processes of regional and global entrenchment. Five central points can be noted to help characterize the changing relationship between globalization and democratic nation-states. All indicate an increase in the extensiveness, intensity and impact of globalization, and all suggest important points about the evolving character of the democratic political community.

First, the locus of effective power can no longer be assumed to be national governments—effective power is shared, bartered and struggled over by diverse forces and agencies at national, regional and international levels. Second, the idea of a political community of fate—of a self-determining collectivity—can no longer meaningfully be located within the boundaries of a single nation-state alone. Some of the most fundamental forces and processes which determine the nature of life-chances within and across political communities are now beyond the reach of nation-states. Third, there is a growing set of disjunctures between the formal authority of the state—that is, the formal domain of political authority that states claim for themselves—and the actual practices and structures of the state and economic system at the regional and global levels.

Fourth, it is not part of my argument that national sovereignty today, even in regions with intensive overlapping and divided political and authority structures, has been wholly subverted—not at all. But, it is part of my argument that there are significant areas and regions marked by criss-crossing loyalties, conflicting interpretations of rights and duties, interconnected legal and authority structures and so on, which displace notions of sovereignty as an illimitable, indivisible and exclusive form of public power.

Fifth, the late twentieth century is marked by a significant series of new types of "boundary problem." If it is accepted that we live in a world of overlapping communities of fate, where the trajectories of each and every country are more tightly entwined than ever before, then new types of boundary problem follow.

RETHINKING DEMOCRACY IN THE CONTEXT OF GLOBALIZATION

In the liberal democracies, consent to government and legitimacy for governmental action are dependent upon electoral politics and the ballot box. Yet the notions that consent legitimates government, and that the ballot box is the appropriate mechanism whereby the citizen body as a whole periodically confers authority on government to enact the law and regulate economic and social life, become problematic as soon as the nature of a "relevant community" is contested. What is the proper constituency, and proper realm of jurisdiction, for developing and implementing policy with respect to health issues such as AIDS or BSE (bovine spongiform encephalopathy), the use of nuclear energy, the management of nuclear waste, the harvesting of rain forests, the use of non-renewable resources, the instability of global financial markets, the reduction of the risks of the chemical and nuclear warfare?

Against this background, the nature and prospects of the democratic polity need re-examination. I have argued elsewhere that an acceptance of liberal democratic politics, in theory and practice, entails an acceptance of each citizen's equal interest in democracy; that is, a recognition of people's equal interest in self-determination (Held 1995a: part III). Each adult has an interest in political autonomy as a result of his or her status as a citizen with an equal entitlement to self-determination. An equal interest in political autonomy requires, I have also argued, that citizens enjoy a common structure of political action. A common structure of political action entails a shared enjoyment of a cluster of rights and obligations. This cluster of rights and obligations has traditionally been thought of as entailing, above all, civil and political rights and obligations. Again, elsewhere, I have argued that this cluster has to bite more deeply than civil and political rights alone; for the latter leave large swathes of power untouched by mechanisms of access, accountability and control. At stake, in short, is a recognition that a common structure of political action requires a cluster of rights and obligations which cut across all key domains of power, where power shapes and affects people's life-chances with determinate effects on and implications for their political agency.

I think of the cluster of rights and obligations that will create the basis of a common structure of political action as constituting the elements of a democratic public law. If power is to be held accountable wherever it is located—in the state, the economy or cultural sphere—then a common structure of political action needs to be entrenched and enforced through a democratic public law. Such a notion, I believe, can coherently link the ideas of democracy and of the modern state. The key to this is the notion of a democratic legal order—an order which is bound by democratic public law in all its affairs. A democratic legal order—a democratic *Rechtstaat*—is an order circumscribed by, and accounted for in relation to, democratic public law.

The idea of such an order, however, can no longer be simply defended as an idea suitable to a particular closed political community or nation-state. We are compelled to recognize that we live in a complex interconnected world where the extent, intensity and impact of issues (economic, political or environmental) raise questions about where those issues are most appropriately addressed. Deliberative and decision-making centers beyond national territories are appropriately situated when those significantly affected by a public matter constitute a cross-border or transnational grouping, when "lower" levels of decision-making cannot manage and discharge satisfactorily transnational or international policy questions, and when the principle of democratic legitimacy can only be properly redeemed in a transnational context (Held 1995a: ch. 10).

In the context of contemporary forms of globalization, for democratic law to be effective it must be internationalized. Thus, the implementation of what I call a cosmopolitan democratic law and the establishment of a community of all democratic communities—a cosmopolitan community—must become an obligation for democrats; an obligation to build a transnational, common structure of political action which alone, ultimately, can support the politics of self-determination.

Thus, sovereignty can be stripped away from the idea of fixed borders and territories. Sovereignty would become an attribute of the basic democratic law but it could be entrenched and drawn upon in diverse self-regulating realms, from regions and states to cities and local associations. Cosmopolitan law would demand the subordination of regional, national and local sovereignties to an overarching legal framework, but in this framework associations would be self-governing at different levels. A new possibility is anticipated: the recovery of an intensive and more participatory democracy at local levels as a complement to the public assemblies of the wider global order; that is, a political order of democratic associations, cities and nations as well as of regions and global networks. I call this elsewhere the cosmopolitan model of democracy—it is a legal basis of a global and divided authority system, a system of diverse and overlapping power centers, shaped and delimited by democratic law (Held 1995a and 1996).

In this system of cosmopolitan governance, people would come to enjoy multiple citizenships—political memberships in the diverse political communities which significantly affect them. They would be citizens of their immediate political communities and of the wider regional and global networks which impacted upon their lives.

It would be easy to be pessimistic about the future of democracy. There are plenty of reasons for pessimism; they include the fact that the essential political units of the world are still based on nation-states while some of the most powerful socio-political forces of the world escape the boundaries of these units. In reaction to this, in part, new forms of fundamentalism have arisen along with new forms of tribalism—all asserting the a priori superiority of a particular religious, cultural or political identity over all others, and all asserting their sectional aims and interests.

But there are other forces at work which create the basis for a more optimistic reading of democratic prospects. [. . .] There are forces and pressures which are engendering a reshaping of political cultures, institutions and structures. First, one must obviously note the emergence, however hesitatingly, of regional and global institutions in the twentieth century. The UN is, of course, weak in many respects but it is a relatively recent creation and it is an innovative structure which can be built upon. Furthermore, there are, of course, new regional and global transnational actors contesting the terms of globalization—not just corporations but new social movements such as the environmental movement, the women's movement and so on. These are the "new" voices of an emergent "transnational civil society" heard, for instance, at the Rio Conference on the environment, the Cairo Conference on Population Control and the Beijing Conference on Women. In short, there are tendencies at work to create new forms of public life and new ways of debating regional and global issues.

REFERENCES

James Crawford. (1994). *Democracy in International Law*, Cambridge: Cambridge University Press.
David Held. (1995). *Democracy and the Global Order*, Cambridge: Polity Press
David Held. (1996). *Models of Democracy* (second edition). Cambridge: Polity Press.
David Held. (1999). Anthony McGraw, David Goldblatt, and Jonathan Parraton, *Global Transformation*, Cambridge: Polity Press.
Paul Hirst and Grahame Thompson (1996). *Globalization in Question*, Cambridge: Polity Press.
Michael Mann. (1986). *The Sources of Social Power*, Cambridge: Cambridge University Press.
Anthony McGraw. (1992). "Conceptualizing Global Politics" in Anthony McGraw and Paul Lewis (eds.), *Global Politics: Globalization and the Nation State*, Cambridge: Polity Press.
Craig Murphy. (1994). *International Organization and International Change*, Cambridge: Polity Press.

Lessons of September 11:
What Should Schools Teach?*

Svi Shapiro

What do we teach?

The events of September 11, 2001 have left a great deal of confusion and bewilderment in their wake. And the continuing upheaval around the world since then has only added to the general air of fear and consternation. I have found this to be especially so among those with whom I work—teachers and educational administrators. I am frequently asked what it is that we should say to our kids about the horrible and catastrophic events that everyone—including children—has witnessed so vividly. Of course there is no simple answer. Sadly, though perhaps of no great surprise to me, I have been shocked to find that many schools and classrooms have continued along with their usual concerns hardly stopping to focus on the events of the past few months—events that have so shattered the taken-for-granted nature of our lives. The lessons and concerns that constitute the usual stuff of school life have been little disturbed by war, turmoil and the death of thousands of innocents, as well as the not so innocent. The brewing worldwide religious schism, our national emergency, and the new global war have impacted very little what it is that young people are addressing or learning about in their classrooms. It is as if educational institutions had enclosed themselves in bubbles that sealed them off from the human storms raging outside of them. Trying to

---

understand why so little of this has made its way into the classroom is certainly difficult and complex. There is, for example, the need to keep "on task" with material that will be on state-mandated tests—a force that resists and undercuts teachers' interest in creating a more flexible and relevant curriculum. There is perhaps the more subtle effects of emotional denial—that anything has really changed in our lives. There is the difficulty that educators have dealing with disturbing and probably conflictful issues in the classroom. Educational critics (such as Jonathan Kozol) have made clear how much of what we teach in schools is politically sanitized and emotionally neutralized, turning deeply felt and contentious issues into a bland mush. But whatever the reasons, and I suspect that it is a complex mixture of all this, there is something very unsettling about the way that so many schools are not facing up to their moral and social responsibility of addressing the most important issues of our time. Many educational critics have noted just how much of what we learn in school seems to be so removed from the realities and issues that face us in the real world. This is surely a moment when we must begin to ask ourselves whether educators have a responsibility to help students make some moral and intellectual sense of the frightening and enormous events that now face us. If schools have responsibilities beyond training people for jobs, or getting students into college, then we must expect that young people find there a place where they can learn about, explore and grapple with the critical social concerns of their world. This is surely what it means to educate for being citizens in a democratic nation. Perhaps the absence of this kind of engagement in our schools is a testimony to just how little those who lead our nation seem to care about educating young people to be aware, thoughtful and engaged members of our polity, and just how deeply this outlook has shaped the process of learning.

B'TSELEM ELOHIM—IN THE IMAGE OF GOD

In trying to answer my own students' questions about making sense of September 11 and its aftermath, I have suggested to them a number of lessons that I believe stand out as important in a moral, social and political sense. The first thing is the way the terrible attacks reminded us of the extraordinary value of human life. The human slaughter with its incalculable consequences in personal loss, pain and suffering confronts us with the irreplaceably precious and unconditional value that inheres in each individual life. The senseless and horrifying murder underlines for us the sacred or infinite worth that belongs to each person. Such an assertion may seem banal until we remember that the firemen who raced up the stairs of the World Trade Center to save lives didn't stop to find out who they were trying to save—whether they were Black or White, Latino or foreign born, US citizen or migrant. Nor did they check on people's religion, sexual orientation or how wealthy or poor they were. Each life was "B'tselem Elohim"—made in the image of God. The lives were equally valuable whether they were those of wealthy stockbrokers or restaurant waiters and kitchen staff. I have pointed out that for educators there was here a powerful moral lesson; the need to help our students recognize the sacred worth of all human lives. Such a lesson, if it is to be more than sentimental cant, must however also confront the ways, in our personal behavior, institutions and culture, we so often fail to embody this truth. It means attending to the ways we diminish the value and dignity of those we designate as "other" in our world. It means confronting the ways that prejudice works to *misrecognize* the intrinsic humanity of others. It also means learning to understand how such misrecognition functions to legitimate an unjust social order. So, for example, we can blame those who are poor for their economic failure because of what we assume is their laziness, indolence or sheer lack of intellectual capability. And for students engaged in such ethical and critical learning, school itself becomes a good laboratory through which to explore and understand how our society is constantly engaged in making invidious human comparisons. Such comparisons (through, for example, the use of high stakes tests) inevitably diminish the worth of some individuals while elevating the worth of others. They legitimate the hierarchies of student recognition and honor that are the moral axis of contemporary schooling. Difficult as it might be, our lessons on the value of human life require us to look critically at the way school functions as a "sorting machine"—one that celebrates and affirms some students while at the same time devaluing and marginalizing many others. And this process is deeply entangled with issues of race and money. Schools continue to be places where the experience, language and appearance of some place them in a downward spiral of low expectations and prejudicial assumptions regarding their abilities and intelligence. Public education provides us with a powerful example of our society's schizophrenic view of human worth—at once a place that affirms everyone's right to dignity and opportunity, and simultaneously works furiously to differentiate and rank human beings. In contrast to our culture's pervasive focus on creating hierarchies of human worth—whether because of our looks, who we associate with, what we own, how we dress, our celebrity or lack of it—September 11 reminded us if only for a brief moment that each and every life must be regarded as of inestimable value.

AN ETHIC OF CARING

A second lesson concerns our society's rediscovery of the value of public service. The past decade or more has been the era of the triumph of Wall Street. We have been inundated with the message that the most admirable and enviable qualities of our culture reside in the values of the marketplace. Simply put, the message says that there is no better goal than getting rich. It has been a time when our popular culture has aggressively promoted wealth, fame and celebrity as the most desirable virtues. The lure of instant wealth made shows such as "Who Wants To Be A Millionaire" the viewers' choice night after night. Everyone was invited to play the stock market casino through electronic trading. University resources and enrollments tipped strongly towards degrees in business and marketing. Those who sought out other fields that involved caring for others, or serving the public good, seemed quaintly out of step with a culture that more and more emphasized getting rich and taking care of oneself. In election after election the efficiency and effectiveness of the private sector were touted over the waste of government and the ineffectiveness of public institutions. Everywhere it seemed that the watchwords of politicians were deregulation and privatization. Yet in the post-September 11 period we have awoken to another view of reality—one in which a good society is about more than making money and getting ahead. We have witnessed the profoundly moving examples of those whose lives are defined by service to others, and by the way that so many people chose to give to others in the most selfless of ways. It is significant that this alternative to selfishness and self-aggrandizement has, according to recent surveys of students and young people, had its effects in intended career choices. *At the very least we have been reminded in dramatic ways that decent societies are held together not by self-seeking ambitions, but by the ways people serve and care for one another*. Whatever the importance of the marketplace where individuals seek their own advantages, a good society needs a vital "commons" where human beings see each other as fellow citizens whose lives are shared, interdependent and mutually supporting. We have been reminded that the moral center of our society is about our sense of solidarity as a community, and the extent to which people risk, care for and concern themselves about the fate of their fellows. And those who work as public servants—whether as emergency workers, caregivers, protectors, teachers and so on—often embody the best and most noble impulses in our culture. There are, I point out, important educational lessons here. Such lessons require us to teach our children to question the materialistic and success-driven nature of our culture with its promise that enduring meaning is to be found in our "shopaholic" culture. It requires us to challenge the "hidden curriculum" of schools with its emphasis on competitive-individualism—*my* success, *my* brilliance and *my* honors. It suggests too that an education concerned with our moral, not just academic, growth is incomplete if it does not insist on some experience of community service. In the post September 11 world there is much to compel us to rethink the underlying values of education today, which offers little to young people other than an increasingly test-driven rat race. Education, we need to remind ourselves, can instead be a powerful vehicle for teaching the enduring wisdom that a purposeful life is about serving others, caring for those in need and seeking to "repair" the world we find ourselves in.

DEMONIZING THE OTHER

Given the brutal and despicable attack on innocent civilians it is not surprising that September 11 and the events that have unfolded since would unleash angry emotional responses. Yet most of us have tried hard to distinguish the real perpetrators of these deeds from others who might be blamed by what appears to be association—being Muslim, coming from the Middle East or simply having critical things to say about U.S. policy in the world. Our government is to be credited for attempting to make clear that this is not a war with Islam. Sadly, not everyone has heard this message. There have been too many cases of individuals taking out their frustrations on innocent people who are misguidedly associated with the attacks, or acting in ways that are blindly prejudicial. For some the threat to our communities is a license to act with racist hostility towards those who constitute religious or ethnic minorities. Of course this is not just an American problem as the surge in anti-Semitic behavior and aggressive acts (such as the fire-bombing of synagogues in France) across Europe demonstrates. And of course our concern for more security—when, for example, we fly—raises the ugly prospect of ethnic profiling. Still as a society we seem to be far from the mentality that produced Japanese internment camps in World War II. This is to be celebrated as a growth in our moral maturity. Still the lessons here for young people are clear. The world presents us with many causes for frustration, resentment and anger. We know how easily human beings respond to these situations with a blind hatred for whole groups of people who can somehow be blamed for one's present unease and fear. Whether in our own country or elsewhere in the world, there is no lack of the way that human concerns become transformed into a misdirected rage acted out against a convenient scapegoat. Indeed it is not hard to think of current examples where our own anxieties turn into hate-filled and vengeful acts of rage. As educators—whether as teachers or parents—we must acknowledge the entirely human capacity for apprehension and anger, while insisting that these must never be harnessed to the misdirected evil of demonizing whole groups of human beings. In a similar vein, the flags that have recently decorated so many homes and automobiles as a response to recent events represent an assertion of national resolve, and an expression of solidarity with the victims of terrorist attacks as well as those who are asked to defend or safeguard our lives. Yet we must also need to ensure that students are taught the difference between this kind of communal identification and an arrogant and chest-thumping chauvinism in which we somehow believe we are superior to other people and where we celebrate our capacity for military or others forms of domination in the world. We are

seeing again how patriotism easily turns from national pride and communal solidarity into a witch-hunt against those who raise the necessary if disturbing questions about why and how we have become the enemy for other people. Our educational task is to educate people to know the difference between the suspicion
and hostility of what Zygmunt Bauman recently called "neo-tribalism" and the
justifiable pride and mutual concern of a healthy national community.

RAGE AND SOCIAL INJUSTICE

Clearly those who perpetrated these terrorist acts must be brought to justice.
However we must also consider the more difficult question of what is the
source of this terrorism—why so much anger in the world that can be harnessed by those preaching violence and destruction. For students this question is of crucial importance as they are educated into becoming citizens who
can engage some of the most crucial questions of our time. Students surely
need to confront and analyze the global conditions that spawn the rage that
has become terrorism. This will certainly mean that they confront the reality
of the wretched circumstances in which so many human beings presently live.
They will need to recognize the terrible inequalities that pervade our world.
As limited as they are to convey suffering and deprivation, I find it crucial
that young people at least know that as a recent United Nations report noted
a half of the world's population now lives on less than 2 dollars a day, and
that 1.3 billion people must get by on less than 1 dollar a day. Or that 4 billion
people do not have enough food to eat and that 40,000 children die each day
from the inability to purchase basic medications or having access to clean water. All of these numbers give them some glimpse into the degree of hopelessness, deprivation and misery in which so many people live today. While we
have, over the past ten years, been subjected to a celebration of global
triumphalism led by the United States, a critically aware citizenship makes it
vital that we now recognize the scale of social injustice in the world. Where so
many grow up without hope or real possibility for living decent lives we must
expect a growing fury directed at those who have, in comparison, so much.
Our students need to understand that social injustice begets anger which in
turn becomes terror. Of course in many schools the most difficult and controversial issue to address is the fact that for many people around the world
there exists a new kind of empire—one that is economic, cultural and sometimes military—whose epicenter is the United States. If we are to understand
the roots of anger towards the United States we will as teachers have to honestly explore American policies and the extent to which they support explicitly or tacitly entrenched undemocratic and repressive regimes. And we will
have to address the way that corporate interests, usually supported by governments of the rich countries, exercise power and influence in ways that

maintain and exacerbate the imbalances in wealth and living standards in the world. Sadly, I know from my conversations with teachers in the state where I live that raising such issues can often be to put one's career on the line.

MODERNITY AND CULTURAL DISINTEGRATION

More than this however we will need to find ways to explore with our students the destructive social and psychological effects on so many lives of modernity itself. So, for example, educated citizens will need to better understand what the political scientist Benjamin Barber has called the phenomenon of "MacWorld"—the way in which the high-consuming values of the west, and especially the United States, drive so many people's expectations and desires. However pitiful are the real life circumstances of so many people almost all are constantly exposed to the "good life" as this is portrayed through the images of television, Hollywood and advertising—images that drive home the huge discrepancies in how people live on this earth. Such images with their emphasis on materialistic, sexual and individualistic desires are also an assault on many people's traditional identities and values. Modernity, in its present form, is hugely disruptive to the everyday world of millions of people. It produces a world that breaks down the bonds of communal support replacing it with highly competitive and individualistic social relationships. In this new world the primary identity is a self insatiably hungry for more things, pleasures and experience. It is a place in which mutually supporting relationships give way to a world full of jostling individuals always pushing themselves forward so as to achieve more success and more recognition. Modernity means for many an increasingly transient and precarious world in which the traditional anchors of people's life-world are disrupted and dislocated by rapid economic and cultural change. The unimpeded flows of global market forces mean for many a world saturated by uncertainty and precariousness. Control of the life of one's community moves to far away and unaccountable centers of power. Jobs are often miserably paid and workers toil in cruel conditions. In these conditions livelihoods are unpredictable and frequently demand that families are uprooted by the need for workers to move far away from their loved ones in order to provide an income for them. And powerful new cultural influences move easily and quickly across national boundaries with the help of instantaneous electronic technologies as well as mass media. They bring a message of change, flux and endless desire—a world of always changing fads, fashions and tastes. In the restless world of capitalist consumption the enemy is any kind of traditional belief system that might constrain the constant "disembedding" of who we are and what we want.

As difficult to grasp as all this might be, we will have to ask our students to explore this complex world in ways that seek to understand how it can produce what we can no longer ignore—the dangerous flows of alienation, dis-satisfaction and anger. But beyond this we may want to examine with them the meaning and possibilities of a more humane and socially just kind of modernity (the Tikkun Community's own founding statement would be a great place to start). Such an examination is more than critique; it also demands from our students an affirmation of those dimensions of modernity, which they hold precious, even where they seem to disrupt communal values. These might include democratic rights and equality including the rights of women and minorities. Or perhaps the scientific spirit—free and uncontrolled inquiry, skepticism and a pragmatic attitude towards truth. However we approach these complex questions, what we must make clear to our students is that whether we like it or not, their lives as well as our fate as a nation are inseparably connected to what is happening even in what seems to be far away places. Over the past few years our culture has become increasingly self-absorbed and focused on aberrations and sleaze. Talk shows and news programs have shown pathetically little concern with the seismic social changes affecting so many millions of people. Yet whether for moral reasons or simply self-interest we can no longer afford to continue to bring up a generation of young people who have not learned to grapple with the most critical questions of the 21st century—our global interdependence, American power and the consequences of profound social change with all of its suffering, turmoil and pain.

EDUCATING FOR HOPE

Of course the goal of all these lessons is certainly not to produce a sense of resignation or despair. Our lessons are aimed to increase students' awareness, concern and sensitivity so that as citizens of this country and as part of the world community they have the knowledge and understanding that can help to bring change. Yet, it is an extraordinary fact that with social, political and cultural storms blowing through the world schools continue as if it were another spring day. My daughter (a high school junior) reports to me that during this past school year there has been no attempt to seriously study the meaning or consequences of September 11! Lessons focus on the same tired if iconic material that is so appallingly divorced from the critical issues that now confront us. The typical American classroom, trapped more than ever by the dead hand of "standards" and "accountability," is a world that is emotionally, intellectually and existentially disconnected from the real and pressing demands of the human condition. Filling young minds with information substitutes for questions about meaning, purpose and possibility in the shared spaces of our nation and our planet. The education I am advocating is about hope—the sense that the world can be improved and problems surmounted by concerned and thinking citizens. To teach students so that they have a greater sense of possibility means to challenge cynicism, conformity or the sense of fatalism that many young people have about their world—the belief that not much can be really changed. Of course this involves teaching a different sense of history than the abstract and anaesthetized version that students typically get which suggests little about their capacity to 'make history' by challenging the injustice and inhumanity that surrounds them. This lesson of hope requires that we nurture not only the critical capabilities of young people but also their sense of emotional involvement in the important issues of peace, social justice, human dignity, issues of power and the quest for lives of meaning. It also requires that we nurture our young people's capacities for imagination and creativity (sadly another casualty of the present school testing mania). In order to remake our world one must first be able to re-envision it—to dream that something different can exist in place of what we now have. It means that we nurture the imagination of the young so that what presently confronts us—violence, oppression, human degradation, war, poverty, materialism and spiritual emptiness—are not seen as the inevitable fate of humankind. In this sense schools exist not simply to prepare young people to fit in with what presently is, but to encourage them to be passionate and active agents of change in our world. In this sense, education needs to be understood as more than simply a mirror that reflects the existing culture; it may also represent a light that directs our way to a more hopeful future.

Author Index

Numbers in parentheses are reference numbers and indicate that an author's work is referred to although the name is not cited in the text; numbers in italics indicate the page on which the complete reference is given.

Subject Index